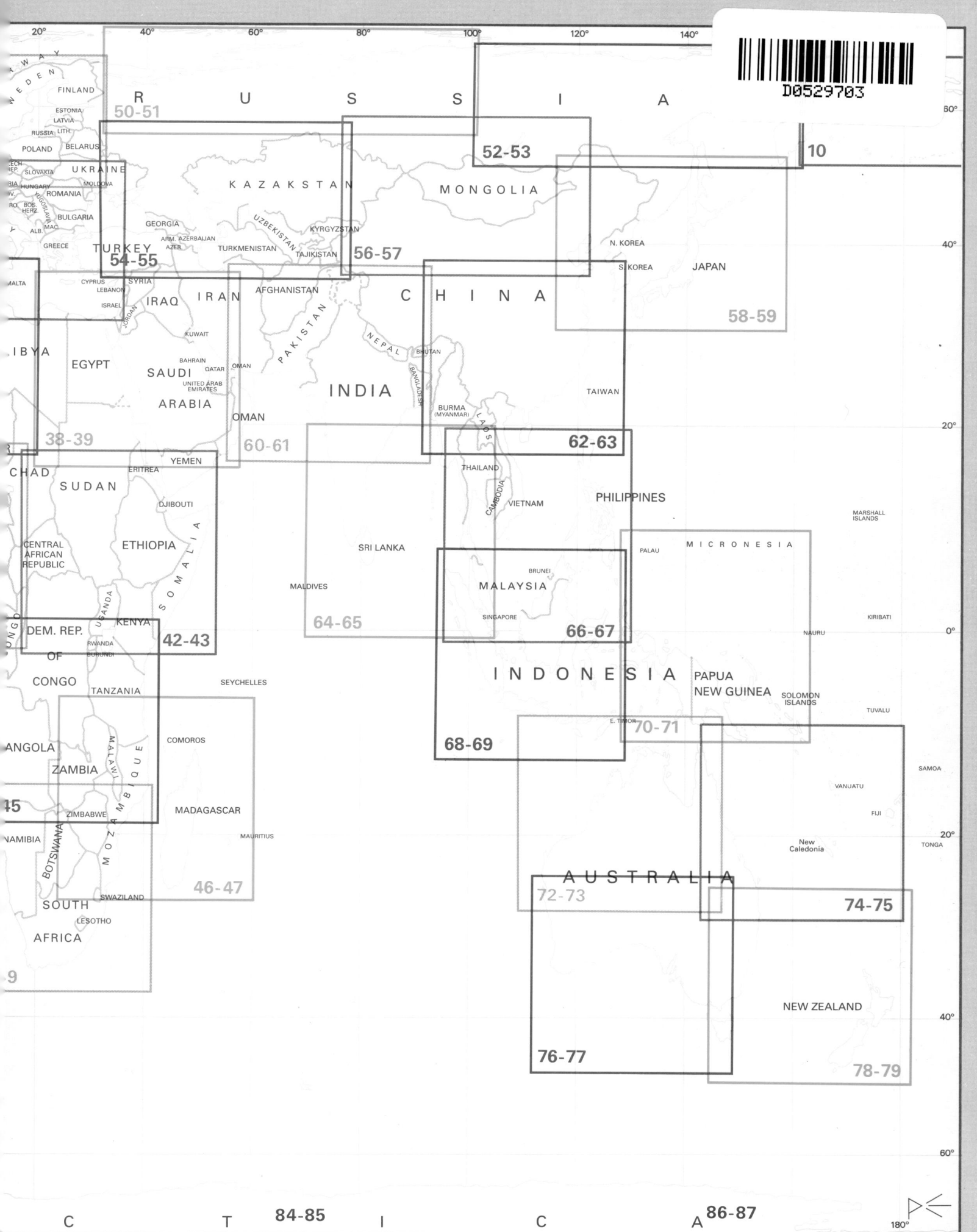

TOPOGRAPHIC MAPS

HAMMOND

Compact
PETERS
WORLD ATLAS

Mapmakers for the 21st Century

Contributors and Consultants

Dr. E.C. Barrett
Professor Ulrich Bleil
Michael Benckert
Wolfgang Behr
Professor Heinz Bosse
Professor Walter Buchholz
Dr. Nicola Bradbear
Carol Claxton
Professor Heinrich Dathe
Mick Dyer
Hellmuth Färber
Jean Fernand-Laurent
Kurt Ficker
Professor Fritz Fischer
Karlheinz Gieseler
Professor Manfred Görlach
Professor Ulrich Grosse
Arnulf Hader
Hazel Hand
Max Hann
Dirk Hansohm
Dr. Günther Heidmann
Professor Wolf Herre
Karl-Heinz Ingenhaag
Jeff Jones
Dr. Andreas Kaiser

Professor Günther Krause
Dr. Manfred Kummer
Daniel Lloyd
Konrad G. Lohse
Wolfgang Mache
Dr. Udo Moll
Georg Möller
Olive Pearson
Dr. Aribert Peters
Birgit Peters
Werner Peters
Thomas Plümer
Detlev Quintern
D.H. Reichstein
Hellmut Schlien
Professor Hermann Schulz
Professor Axel Sell
Eduard Spescha
Piet Summerfield
Jürgen Wendler
Professor Adolf Witte
Professor Karl Wohlmuth
Judith Wood
Siegfried Zademack
Madeleine Zeller

Cartography:

Kümmerly+Frey, Bern (graticules, coastlines, borders, seas, rivers and lakes).
Oxford Cartographers (topographic and thematic maps). www.oxfordcarto.com
Cartographic editor: Terry Hardaker, Oxford Cartographers.
Cover design: Yang Zhao, Hammond World Atlas Corporation.

Library of Congress Cataloging-in-Publication Data

Hammond World Atlas Corporation
   Hammond compact Peters world atlas : the earth in true proportion / Longman Group
UK Limited ; cartography, Kümmerly + Frey, Bern [and] Oxford Cartographers.
      p. cm.
   Copyright 1989 by Akademische Verlagsanstalt, Vaduz. First published in 1989,
updated for 2002.
   Includes index.
   ISBN 0-8437-1832-3
   1. Atlases. I. Title: Compact Peters atlas of the world. II. Longman (Firm) III.
Kümmerly + Frey. IV. Oxford Cartographers. V. Title.

G1021 .H2675 2002
912--dc21

                                                           2002031000

Published in North America
by Hammond World Atlas Corporation
Union, NJ 07083, USA.

Printed in Germany

FOREWORD

In 1493 – one year after Columbus's first voyage to America – the Pope apportioned the non-European world among the most powerful nations of his own continent. By the time Mercator completed his Atlas 100 years later, European domination had spread across the world, and Mercator's Atlas was the embodiment of Europe's geographical conception of the world in an age of colonialism.

Since then thousands of atlases have been published. They differ in many respects from Mercator's, but all have a common feature: they focus on the industrialized countries. The country and continent of origin are represented at a larger scale than other countries and continents. If, together with the age of colonialism, the view of the world that underpinned it is to come to an end, we need a new geography – one that is based on the equal status of all peoples.

This Atlas represents all countries and continents at the same scale. Their actual size and their position in the world can thus be taken directly from the map. This equal presentation is an expression of the consciousness that is gradually replacing our traditional world view.

The use of a single scale for all topographic maps; the principle of fidelity of area; and a new, universally applicable presentation of relief; together, these now make it possible to alter our conception of the world. All 246 thematic maps are also equal-area world maps. The comprehensive presentation in these thematic maps of man, nature, and society is based on the same principle of equality as that underlying the topographic maps.

This Atlas, therefore, offers a way of understanding the history underlying the North-South divide, as well as the tensions between East and West – so often the outcome of the gulf which separates rich and poor.

Arno Peters

CONTENTS

Map Finder for the Topographic Maps . . . . Front Endpaper
Foreword 3
Introduction 6–7
Page Finder for Countries 8
Key to the Topographic Section 9
Sources for Thematic Section 96
Introduction to the Thematic Section 97
Political World Map 112–113
Relief and Vegetation of the World 230–231

THE WORLD IN 43 MAPS AT THE SAME SCALE

THE AMERICAS

Alaska. Canada (North-West) 11
Canada (North) 12–13
Canada (South-West). USA (West) 14–15
Canada (South-East). USA (East) 16–17
USA (South). Mexico. Hawaii 18–19
USA (South-East). Cuba. Caribbean 20–21
Central America. South America (North) . . 22–23
South America (West) 24–25
South America (East) 26–27
South America (Central) 28–29
South America (South) 30–31

EUROPE

Northern Europe 32–33
Southern Europe 34–35
Eastern Europe 50

AFRICA

Africa (North-West) 36–37
Africa (North-East) 38
Africa (West) 40–41
Africa (East) 42–43
Africa (South-West) 44–45
Africa (South-East). Madagascar 46–47
Africa (Southern) 48–49

ASIA

Russia (North-Western Siberia) 51
Russia (Northern Siberia) 52–53
Russia (North-Eastern Siberia) 10

Asia (North-West) 54–55
Russia (South-East). Kazakstan. Mongolia.
     China (North) 56–57
China (North-East). Korea. Japan 58–59
China (South-East). South-East Asia (North) 62–63
Asia Minor 35, 54
Arabian Peninsula 38–39
Asia (South) with India (North) 60–61
India (South). South-East Asia 64–65
South-East Asia. Philippines. Borneo 66–67
Indonesia. Malaysia 68–69
New Guinea. South Pacific 70–71

AUSTRALASIA

Australia (West) 72–73
Australia (North-East). South Pacific 74–75
Australia (South) 76–77
Australia (South-East). New Zealand 78–79

ANTARCTICA

Antarctica (Byrd Land) 80–81
Antarctica (Graham Land) 82–83
Antarctica (Maud Land) 84–85
Antarctica (Wilkes Land) 86–87

THE ARCTIC

Arctic (Canada) 88–89
Arctic (Greenland) 90–91
Arctic (Novaya Zemlya) 92–93
Arctic (Siberia) 94–95

NATURE, MAN AND SOCIETY IN 246 THEMATIC WORLD MAPS

The Continents 98–99
560 Million Years Ago · 280 Million Years Ago ·
180 Million Years Ago · 120 Million Years Ago ·
60 Million Years Ago · Today

Mountains 100–101

Rivers and Seas 102–103

Sun and Climate 104–105
Hours of Sunshine · Incidence of Rays · Evaporation ·
Temperature · Temperature Variation · Precipitation

Natural Dangers 106–107
Volcanoes · Earthquakes · Maritime Earthquakes ·
Hurricanes

Vegetation 108–109
Woodland · Pastureland · Arable Land · Barren Land

People and Cities 110–111

States 112–113

Languages 114–115
French · Spanish · Portuguese · English · German ·
Russian · Italian · Bengali · Malay · Arabic · Chinese ·
Japanese · Hindi · Swahili

Scripts 116–117
Scripts of Chinese Origin · Scripts of Indian Origin ·
Scripts of Greek Origin · Scripts of Latin Origin ·
Scripts of Arabic Origin · The Direction of Writing

Religions 118–119
Natural Religions · Hinduism · Christianity · Islam ·
Buddhism · Confucianism · Shinto · No Religion

Education 120–121
Illiteracy · Primary Education · Secondary Education ·
University · Pupil/Teacher Ratio · Expenditure on Education

The Sciences 122–123
University Teachers · Publication of Scientific Books ·
Researchers and Engineers · Expenditure on the Sciences

Information 124–125
Newspapers · Radio · Television · Books

Communications .126–127
Letters · Telephones · Fax · Internet

Traffic Density 128–129
Railroads · Cars · Air Traffic · Shipping

Population Structure 130–131
Population Density · Population Growth ·
Adults/Children Ratio · Men/Women Ratio

Life Expectancy .132–133

Health 134–135
Medical Attention · Available Hospital Beds ·
Drinking Water Supplies · Infant Mortality

Sport 136–137
Running Events · Jumping Events · Throwing Events ·
Gymnastics · Skiing · Ski Jumping ·
Tobogganing and Bob-Sled Events · Speed Skating ·
Swimming Events · Rowing Events · Sailing Events ·
Figure Skating · Cycling Events · Equestrian Events ·
Single Combat · Ball Games

Nutrition 138–139
Calorie Consumption · Carbohydrates ·
Vegetables and Fruit · Meat · Protein · Fat

Soil Cultivation 140–141

Crop Yield 142–143

Staple Foodstuffs 144–145
Wheat · Barley · Rye · Oats · Millet · Soya · Maize ·
Sorghum · Rice

Animal Husbandry 146–147
Cattle · Horses · Mules · Donkeys · Camels · Buffalo ·
Elephant · Reindeer · Sheep · Pigs · Goats · Bees ·
Chickens · Ducks · Turkeys · Silkworm

Fishing 148–149
Size of Catches · Herring · Cod · Tuna · Flatfish · Squid

Hunting 150–151
Hare, Rabbit · Roe Deer · Red Deer · Elk · Fox · Wolf ·
Bear · Jackal · Antelope · Gazelle · Kangaroo ·
Lynx · Opossum · Beaver · Pheasant · Partridge

Natural Products .152–153
Wood · Rubber · Silk · Cotton · Wool · Skins · Hemp ·
Flax · Honey · Eggs · Grain · Meat · Vegetables · Fruit ·
Sugar · Milk

Mineral Resources 154–155
Iron · Copper · Tin · Lead · Gold · Silver · Platinum ·
Diamonds · Aluminum · Zinc · Manganese · Nickel ·
Chrome · Sulfur · Potassium · Phosphate

Energy 156–157
Oil · Natural Gas · Water Power · Uranium · Coal ·
Total Consumption

Industrial Products 158–159
Metals and Metal Goods · Machines ·
Electrical Appliances · Means of Transport ·
Chemical Products · Glass, Porcelain, Ceramics ·
Oil and Coal Products · Paper, Paper Products ·
Textile Products · Wood Products · Food Products ·
Plastic Products · Rubber · Scientific Instruments ·
Leather and Fur · Shoes

Urbanization 160–161

World Trade 162–163
Natural Products (Import) · Natural Products (Export) ·
Industrial Products (Import) · Industrial Products (Export)

Poor Nations – Rich Nations 164–165

Economic Growth 166–167

Employment Structure 168–169
Agriculture · Transport · Industry · Mining · Building ·
Trade · Energy · Social Professions · Banking

Economic Order .170–171

Unemployment 172–173

Inflation 174–175

Child Labor 176–177

Inequality 178–179

Prostitution 180–181

The Status of Women 182–183
Paid Employment · Housework · Number of Children ·
Monogamy/Polygamy · Participation in Legislation ·
Higher Education

Relative Military Strength 184–185
Armed Forces · Tanks · Fighter Planes ·
Naval Vessels · Nuclear Weapons · Reserve Forces

The Conquest of Space 186–187
Launching Sites for Space Flights · Earth Satellites ·
Manned Space Flights · Interplanetary Space Flights

Instructions for Use of the Index 188
Index 189–228

CARTOGRAPHIC INTRODUCTION

It may come as a shock to realize that all of the atlases we have known until now present a distorted picture of the world. The nature of this distortion, and the reason for it, are now so obvious that it seems hardly possible to have overlooked it for 400 years. The distortion caused by attempting to represent the spherical earth on flat paper is more or less unavoidable, but the distortion caused by the use of inconsistent scales, which has acquired the unquestioned sanction of habit, is not.

We have come to accept as "natural" a representation of the world that devotes disproportionate space to large-scale maps of areas perceived as important, while consigning other areas to small-scale general maps. And it is because our image of the world has become thus conditioned, that we have for so long failed to recognize the distortion for what it is – the equivalent of peering at Europe and North America through a magnifying glass and then surveying the rest of the world through the wrong end of a telescope.

There is nothing "natural" about such a view of the world. It is the remnant of a way of thinking born even before the age of colonialism and fired by that age. Few thinking people today would subscribe to a world-view of this kind. Yet, until now, no atlas has existed that provided a picture of the world undistorted by varying scales.

A single scale
All topographic maps in this atlas are at the same scale: each double-page map shows one-sixtieth of the earth's surface. This means that all the topographic maps can be directly compared with one another. Among the many surprises this unique feature offers may be, for some users, the relative sizes of Great Britain (page 32) and the island of Madagascar (page 47); or, perhaps, the areas respectively covered by Europe (pages 32–33) and North Africa (pages 36–37). For most people it will soon become apparent that their hazy and long-held notions of the sizes of different countries and regions are, in a lot of cases, quite drastically wrong.

But what do we mean by scale? The scale indicator that appears on reference maps only shows distance scale. It enables the user to calculate the factor needed to multiply distances so as to compare them with those on other maps. This is a complex and somewhat tedious exercise that the great majority of users understandably neglects to carry out. Moreover, the number of different scales in conventional atlases is surprisingly high, in general beween twenty and fifty. Thus, the concept of relative scale must become increasingly vague in the user's mind. What is generally not mentioned is that, because it is impossible to transfer the curved surface of the globe correctly to a flat plane, the scale indicator on a map is only valid for a single part of the map, such as a line of latitude.

Distance is only one aspect of scale. Area has also to be considered. Whereas there can be no maps with absolute fidelity of distance, there can be maps with fidelity of area. Fidelity of area (or equal area) means that all countries are shown at the correct size in relation to others. The maps in this atlas preserve fidelity of area, a feature never previously achieved in an atlas. In the Peters Atlas all topographic maps have equal area scale: 1 square centimeter on the maps equals 6,000 square kilometers in reality.

While uniform scale for all parts of the world enables comparisons between all places on an equal footing, the local geography covered at larger scales in other world atlases is omitted from the Peters Atlas. To include enlargements of the more densely populated regions would be to defeat the purpose of this atlas.

A single symbology
This equality of scale offers further advantages besides direct comparability. The basis of any map compilation is the simplification of reality, which cartographers call "generalization." This transfer of the real character of the earth's surface into a system of lines and symbols, which can be graphically represented, has to be adapted to the scale employed. Thus a river or road with all its turns and windings at a scale of 1:100,000 can be drawn nearer to reality (that is, with more detail) than at a scale of 1:1,000,000. Symbols also vary for different scales. Thus the same symbol can mean a town with 50–100,000 inhabitants at one scale, but a city with 1–5 million inhabitants at another. The same elevation may be differently colored on maps of different scales. All such difficulties vanish in this atlas, which by way of its single scale has only one level of generalization and a single set of symbols.

Topographic map colors
The green/brown coloring of most current atlases represents the topographic relief of the region; green stands for low-lying areas, brown for mountainous country, with different shades of the two colors for different elevations. Since, however, both colors (as also the blue of the sea and the white of snow-covered mountains) are borrowed from nature, the user of the atlas may be forgiven for assuming the green parts on the map to represent areas with vegetation and the brown parts to be the barren land. Although this is broadly true in Europe it may not be so elsewhere. For example, in North Africa the lower areas, even those below sea level, are usually deserts, and it is only above a certain height in the mountains that vegetation begins. The green/brown coloring is thus unsuitable for representing relief in an atlas dedicated to an accurate worldview. So in this atlas green represents vegetation, brown barren land, and a mixture of the two colors represents thin or scattered vegetation. Global vegetation data were obtained from 1985–86 satellite photography with the help of the Remote Sensing Unit at the Department of Geography of Bristol University. The resolution of this imagery down to individual units of 20 square kilometers, and its conversion to the Peters base maps by the Remote Sensing Unit, makes this the most up-to-date statement available of the distribution of world vegetation.

Topographic map relief
The tradition of showing relief by colored layers running from green in lowlands, through brown to purple, mauve or white in high mountains, has one further serious disadvantage. The features of the land surface are only

shown along the contours, or lines joining points of equal height. In between, we receive no information about the surface of the land. "Hillshading," or rendering the complete landscape with 3-D shadows to depict the relief, overcomes this. Cartographers have struggled with the best way to create hillshading for hundreds of years. In this atlas the 3-D relief comes from photographing specially made plaster relief models and blending these photos with hand-rendered coloring. In the blending, the relief shading has also been enhanced to eliminate awkward shadows, as for example when the angle of the light from the photo ran directly down a mountain chain thus reducing its impact. The addition of "spot heights" for selected peaks and other points on the map lends precision to the artwork.

The Peters Projection

Anyone who has ever tried to peel an orange and press the peel into a continuous flat piece without tearing will have grasped the fundamental impossibility that lies at the heart of all cartographic endeavour: that fidelity of shape, distance and angle are of necessity lost in flattening the surface of a sphere. On the other hand it is possible to retain three other qualities: fidelity of area, fidelity of axis and fidelity of position. Fidelity of area makes it possible to compare various parts of a map directly with one another, and fidelity of axis and position guarantee correct relationships of north-south and east-west axes by way of a rectangular grid.

In 1973 Arno Peters published his world map, which unites in a single flat map all three achievable qualities – fidelity of area, fidelity of axis and fidelity of position. In this way the real comparative sizes of all countries in the world are clearly visible. For this atlas Arno Peters has generalized the projection principle upon which his World Map was based, so that now each regional map represents the maximum possible freedom from distortion, of area as well as shape. Since map distortions through a projection decrease in proportion to the size of the area depicted – the smaller the area, the smaller the distortion – the forty-three topographical maps in this atlas are considerably closer to reality than is the Peters World Map. In particular these individual maps correct the distortions which are unavoidable on the Peters World Map in the equatorial and polar regions. An indication of how this has been applied can be seen from the shapes of the page areas on the Map Finder (front endpaper). In the north they are horizontal and thin while towards the Equator they are nearly square. The degree of departure from the normal page proportion is a guide to the amount of shape correction applied to the regional maps.

The eight polar maps on pages 80–95 have the same scale as all the other topographical maps. They also have fidelity of area, and represent one-sixtieth of the earth's surface on each double page. Thus the size of the countries and continents shown on them can be directly compared with all the other 35 topographical maps. The fidelity of position and axis which is necessarily lost on polar maps is also absent on these maps.

The thematic maps

The second part of this atlas directs attention to the whole earth. The author has collected data for 246 individual world thematic maps under 45 subject headings. Each of these subject headings is given a double page spread, but if more than one topic is covered under any subject, separate maps are given. Thus under the subject heading "Life Expectancy" only one topic is covered so the double spread comprises a single map, whereas the subject heading "Animal Husbandry" requires sixteen topics and therefore displays sixteen individual maps. The principle of one topic per map also enables all the maps to be represented by simple grades of color, with, usually, a single hue chosen for each topic. Within this hue the range from light to dark color represents low to high values of the topic. In this way all the thematic maps can be understood at a glance, without the necessity for complicated symbols or explanations.

The graticule

The traditional zero meridian running through Greenwich was adopted worldwide in 1884, when Britain was the strongest European colonial power and ruled over a quarter of the world. After the ending of colonialism and with the closure of Greenwich Observatory, there is no reason other than custom for retaining this zero meridian. The international dateline, which is dependent upon the zero meridian, also needs correction, since over its whole length it has been partially diverted where it cuts an inhabited area. The retention of the division into 360 degrees is also, it can be argued, an anomaly in the age of almost worldwide decimalization.

Arno Peters has therefore proposed a new decimal grid in which the zero meridian and the international dateline would become a single line placed in the middle of the Bering Strait, and the earth is divided into 100 decimal degrees east-west and north-south. While for practical reasons the Greenwich system is retained throughout the bulk of the atlas, the new decimal grid is shown on pages 230–231.

The index

Someone consulting an index in search of a district, town or river has until now had to memorize, besides the page number, at least two grid figures, two letters, or a letter and a number. There can be few users of an atlas who have not experienced the irritation of forgetting at least one item in this unwieldy string of digits by the time the relevant map has been located, and the time-consuming exercise of turning back to the index to recall this information. In the Peters Atlas there is, apart from the page number, only a single letter, which can be easily remembered. This innovatory and simple indexing system is explained on page 188.

Digital cartography

The thematic maps in this edition have been revised using the latest available data and completely redrawn digitally, using Apple Mac technology.

The original edition of the atlas used computer techniques to adapt the world map to the 43 individual double spreads in the topographic section, minimizing shape distortion on each spread. This process used Scitex technology with geographic data from the Erdgenössische Technische Hochschule in Berne. The same process is employed in the present edition, which also continues to feature the hand-crafted workmanship of the land surface coloring. The atlas thus reconciles the traditional and digital approaches.

Terry Hardaker

Chief Cartographer
Oxford Cartographers

PAGE FINDER FOR COUNTRIES

Afghanistan 60
Albania 35
Algeria 36–37
Andorra 34
Angola 44
Antigua & Barbuda 21
Argentina 28–29, 30–31
Armenia 54
Australia 72–73, 74, 76–77, 78
Austria 34–35
Azerbaijan 54
Bahamas 21
Bahrain 39
Bangladesh 61
Barbados 23
Belarus 33
Belgium 32–33
Belize 19
Benin 41
Bhutan 61
Bolivia 25, 28
Bosnia-Herzegovina 35
Botswana 48–49
Brazil 23, 24–25, 26–27, 28–29
Brunei 69
Bulgaria 35
Burkina Faso 40–41
Burma (Myanmar) 62, 65
Burundi 45
Cambodia 65, 66
Cameroon 41
Canada 11, 12–13, 14–15
Cape Verde 230
Central African Republic 41, 42
Chad 37, 38, 41, 42
Chile 28, 30
China 56–57, 58, 61, 62–63
Colombia 22–23, 24–25
Comoros 47
Congo 41, 42, 44
Congo, Dem. Rep. of . 42, 44–45, 46
Costa Rica 22
Côte d'Ivoire 40
Croatia 35
Cuba 20–21
Cyprus 35
Czech Republic 33, 34–35
Denmark 33
Djibouti 43
Dominica 23
Dominican Republic 21
Ecuador 24
East Timor 69, 72
Egypt 38
El Salvador 22
Equatorial Guinea 41
Eritrea 38–39, 43
Estonia 33
Ethiopia 43
Fiji 75
Finland 33
France 34
French Guiana 26
Gabon 41, 44
Gambia 40
Georgia 54

Germany 33
Ghana 40
Great Britain & Northern Ireland . . 32
Greece 35
Greenland 90–91
Grenada 23
Guatemala 19, 22
Guinea 40
Guinea-Bissau 40
Guyana 23
Haiti 21
Honduras 19, 22
Hungary 35
Iceland 32
India 60–61, 64
Indonesia 68–69, 70
Iran 39, 54–55, 60
Iraq 39
Ireland 32
Israel 38
Italy 34–35
Jamaica 21
Japan 58–59
Jordan 38
Kazakstan 54–55, 56
Kenya 43, 45
Kiribati 231
Korea, North 58
Korea, South 58
Kuwait 39
Kyrgyzstan 55, 56
Laos 62, 66, 66
Latvia 33
Lebanon 38
Lesotho 49
Liberia 40
Libya 37, 38
Liechtenstein 34
Lithuania 33
Luxembourg 33
Macedonia 35
Madagascar 47
Malawi 45
Malaysia 66–67
Maldives 64
Mali 36–37, 40–41
Malta 35
Marshall Islands 231
Mauritania 36, 40
Mauritius 47
Mexico 18–19
Micronesia 71
Moldova 33, 35
Monaco 34
Mongolia 56–57
Morocco 36
Mozambique 46
Myanmar 62, 65
Namibia 48
Nauru 231
Nepal 61
Netherlands 33
New Zealand 79
Nicaragua 22
Niger 37, 41
Nigeria 41

Norway 33
Oman 39, 60
Pakistan 60
Palau 71
Panama 22
Papua New Guinea 70–71
Paraguay 28–29
Peru 24–25
Philippines 67
Poland 33
Portugal 34
Qatar 39
Romania 35
Russia 10, 33, 50–51, 52–53,
                54–55, 56–57, 58–59
Rwanda 45
St. Kitts Nevis 21
St. Lucia 23
St. Vincent & the Grenadines 23
Samoa 231
San Marino 34
Sao Tomé & Principe 41
Saudi Arabia 38–39
Senegal 40
Seychelles 231
Sierra Leone 40
Singapore 66
Slovakia 33, 35
Slovenia 35
Solomon Islands 71
Somalia 43
South Africa 48–49
Spain 34
Sri Lanka 64
Sudan 38, 42
Suriname 26
Swaziland 49
Sweden 33
Switzerland 34
Syria 38–39
Taiwan 61
Tajikistan 55
Tanzania 45, 46
Thailand 62, 66
Togo 41
Tonga 231
Trinidad and Tobago 23
Tunisia 34, 36–37
Turkey 35, 54
Turkmenistan 54–55, 60
Tuvalu 231
Uganda 42, 45
Ukraine 33, 35, 54
United Arab Emirates 39
Uruguay 28–29
USA . . 11, 14–15, 16–17, 18–19, 20
Uzbekistan 55
Vanuatu 75
Venezuela 23
Vietnam 62, 66
Western Sahara 36
Yemen 39, 43
Yugoslavia 35
Zambia 44–45
Zimbabwe 49

THE WORLD IN 43 MAPS AT THE SAME SCALE
EACH MAP SHOWS ONE-SIXTIETH OF THE EARTH'S SURFACE.

The colors used on the maps simulate those found in nature

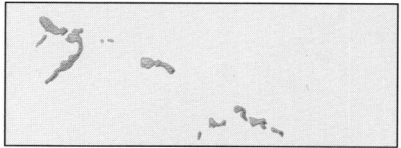

Water (Lakes, Seas, Oceans)

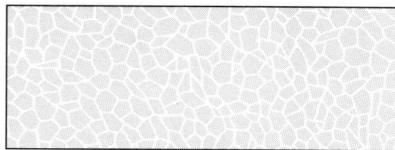

Ice Shelf

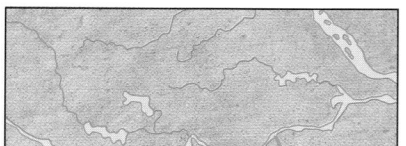

Vegetation (Plains)

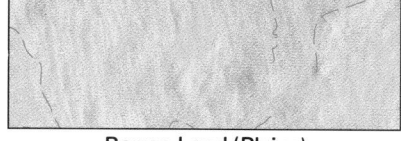

Barren Land (Plains)

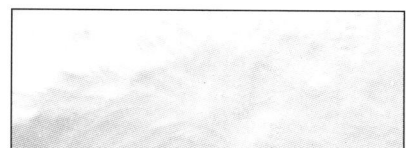

Continental Ice (Plains)

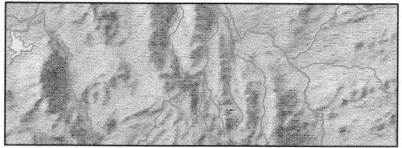

Vegetation (Hills)

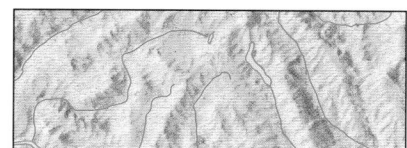

Barren Land (Hills)

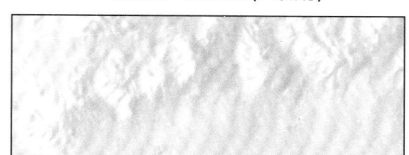

Continental Ice (Hills)

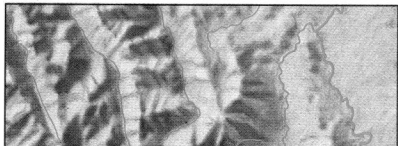

Vegetation (Mountains)

Barren Land (Mountains)

Continental Ice (Mountains)

In order to give more exact information about heights, spots with heights in meters have been given over all maps:

- •1236   1236 Meters above Sea Level
- •-25   25 Meters below Sea Level

Communications are shown in different colors and line thicknesses:

——	Railroad
——	Road
═══	Highway
═ ═ ═	Highway in Tunnel
∿∿∿	River
⊢⊢⊢	Canal

Boundaries are given following information from the United Nations:

- ∙ - ∙	International Boundary
∿∿	International Boundary on River
- ∎ - ∙	Disputed International Boundary
∙∙∙∙∙	State Boundary

On each double page the 1000 largest and most important cities and towns are shown; if the double page shows sea as well as land, there are proportionally fewer:

- ○   fewer than 100,000 inhabitants
- ⦿   100,000 – 1,000,000 inhabitants
- ▪   1,000,000 – 5,000,000 inhabitants
- ⬟   over 5,000,000 inhabitants

In order to make it easier to find the adjoining map, indicators have been given in the grey margins of the maps:

   Map of adjoining area is on page 25.

Finally there are other geographical features:

- ⚓   Waterfall
- ≡≡≡   Swamp, Marsh
- ⬭   Salt Lake
- - - - -   Coral Reef
- ∴   Archaeological Site
- ⊔⊔⊔⊔   Great Wall of China

The new decimal grid (based upon the International Date Line, which has been placed in the middle of the Bering Strait) can be found only on the world map on pages 230–231. The following 43 individual maps still show the old grid (based upon the London suburb of Greenwich).

- 25°E   25 degrees Longitude East
- 50°W   50 degrees Longitude West
- 30°N   30 degrees Latitude North
- 60°S   60 degrees Latitude South
- - - -   Tropics

In order to make the maps easier to read various type styles have been used:

Anatolia	Physical Features
Milan	Cities and towns (capital cities underlined)
CUBA	Countries
TEXAS	States
INDIAN OCEAN	Oceans, Seas

All maps in this Atlas follow the same projection principle:

    Peters Projection (fidelity of area, axis and position)

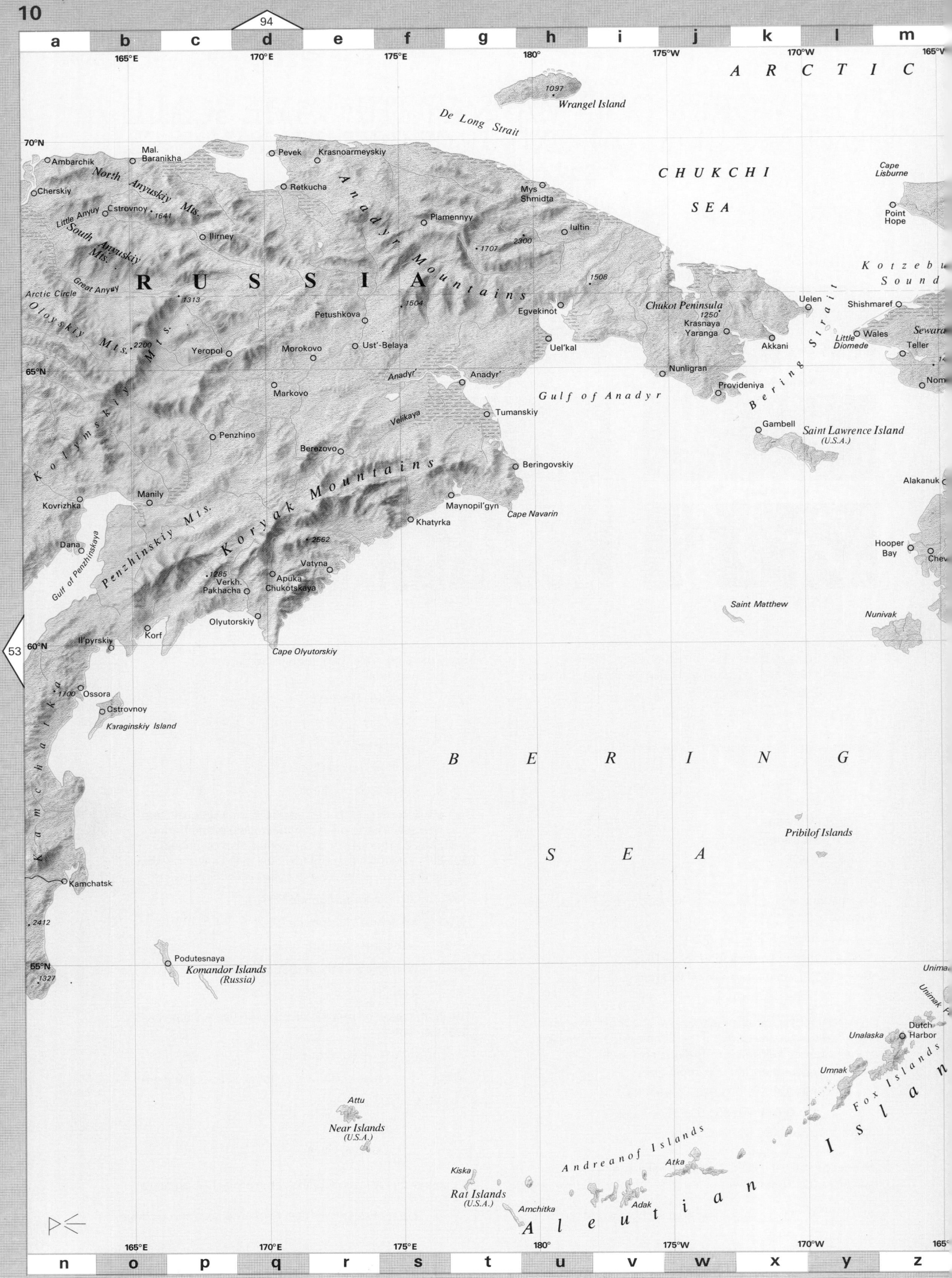

a b c 94 d e f g h i j k l m

A R C T I C

165°E   170°E   175°E   180°   175°W   170°W   165°V

Wrangel Island
·1097

De Long Strait

C H U K C H I

S E A

70°N

Ambarchik
Mal.
Baranikha
Pevek   Krasnoarmeyskiy

Cape
Lisburne

Cherskiy
Retkucha
Mys
Shmidta

Point
Hope

North Anyuskiy Mts.
Little Anyuy
Ostrovnoy ·1641
Plamennyy

K o t z e b u
S o u n d

Ilirney
Iultin

South Anyuskiy
Mts.
·1707 2300

Chukot Peninsula
1250·

Uelen
Shishmaref

Arctic Circle

R U S S I A
·1313

·1504
·1508

Krasnaya
Yaranga

Sewara

Oloyskiy Mts. ·2200
Petushkova

Egvekinot
Akkani
Little
Diomede
Wales
Teller

Great Anyuy

65°N
Yeropol
Morokovo
Ust'-Belaya
Uel'kal

Nunligran
Nom

Markovo
Anadyr'
Anadyr'

Gulf of Anadyr
Provideniya

Velikaya
Tumanskiy

Penzhino
Berezovo

Gambell
Saint Lawrence Island
(U.S.A.)

Koryak Mountains
Beringovskiy

Manily
Maynopil'gyn
Cape Navarin

Alakanuk

Kovrizhka
Khatyrka

·2562

Dana
Vatyna

Hooper
Bay
Chev

·1285
Verkh.
Pakhacha
Apuka
Chukotskaya

Saint Matthew

Nunivak

Olyutorskiy

Il'pyrskiy Korf
Cape Olyutorskiy

60°N

·1700 Ossora

Ostrovnoy

Karaginskiy Island

B E R I N G

53

Kamchatka

Pribilof Islands

S E A

Kamchatsk

·2412

55°N
Podutesnaya
Komandor Islands
(Russia)

Unima

·1327

Uninak P

Dutch
Harbor

Unalaska

Attu
Umnak

Near Islands
(U.S.A.)

Fox Islands

Andreanof Islands
Atka

Aleutian Island

Kiska

Rat Islands
(U.S.A.)
Amchitka
Adak

n o p q r s t u v w x y z

165°E   170°E   175°E   180°   175°W   170°W   165°

This map shows 1/60 of the earth's surface

a   b   c   d   e   f   g   h   i   j   k   l   m

89

125°W   120°W   115°W   110°W   105°W   100°W

A R C T I C

Queen   E *l i z a b e t h*   *I s l a n d*

Meighen Island

O C E A N

80°N

Borden Island

Prince Gustav Adolf

S v e r d r u p

Ellef Ringnes Island

Hassel Sound

Amund Ringne
Island

Magnetic
North Pole (1992)

Corn
Belche

B E A U F O R T

Mackenzie-King Island

•457

Sea

Lougheed Island

Grinr

Prince Patrick Island

P a r r y   I s l a n d s

•320

Bathurst Island

Cornwal

S E A

Mould Bay

•1067

•457

McClure Strait

M e l v i l l e   I s l a n d

75°N

Resolu

Dundas Peninsula

V i s c o u n t   M e l v i l l e   S o u n d

Cornwa

Cape
Prince Alfred

•248

Peel Sound

Stefansson
Island

B a n k s   I s l a n d

Hadley Bay

Storkerson
Peninsula

M c C l i n t o c k   C h a n n e l

Prince of Wales Island

Prince of Wales
Strait

Prince Albert
Peninsula

•640

Franklin
Strait

Sachs Harbour

Minto Inlet

V i c t o r i a

•762

Cape
Bathurst

Holman Island

I s l a n d

Amundsen Gulf

Prince   Albert   Sound

70°N

Cape Parry

Cape Baring

Wollaston
Peninsula

•518

Victoria Strait

King William
Island

Paulatuk

Dolphin and Union Strait

Read Island

Dease Strait

•221

Cambridge Bay

Gjo
Ha

•366

Coronation   Gulf

Queen   Maud   Gulf

Adelaide

•609

Bluenose Lake

Coppermine
(Kugluktuk)

Perry Island

Sherman
Basin

Peninsula

Colville Lake

•518

•244

MacAlpine
Lake

460

Fort Good
Hope

Great Bear Lake

Port Radium
(Echo Bay)

Takijuk Lake

•823

Arctic Circle

Bathurst
Inlet

N U N

•1003

Contwoyto
Lake

Garry Lake

Back

Fort Franklin
(Déline)

Aberdeen Lake

Baker

Norman
Wells

11   65°N

Hottah Lake

Lake

•704

122

Fort Norman
(Tulit'a)

NORTH-WEST

Aylmer Lake

Thelon

Ba

•2164

Rae Lakes

Warburton
Lake

Clinton
Colden
Lake

Dubawnt
Lake

Lac
La Martre

413•

Wrigley

•1577

Snare River

Artillery Lake

Yathkyed
Lake

TERRITORIES

Lac la Martre

221

C

Edzo

Rae

Yellowknife

Reliance

Whitefish
Lake

Mount
Sir James
McBrien
2762

Snowdrift
(Lutselk'e)

•354

A

N

Mount
Hunt
2748

Fort Simpson
•1548

*Great
Slave
Lake*

Nonacho
Lake

Ennadai
Lake

Nahanni Butte

Fort
Providence

Fort Resolution

Mackenzie

Wholdaia
Lake

YUKON

Hay River

Dawson Landing

Kasba Lake

•349

TERRITORY

Enterprise

•594

Nueltin Lake

Watson
Lake

Fort Liard

Tathlina
Lake

Fort Smith

60°N

Thlewie

1763

Nelson Forks

Slave River

Uranium
City

Eldorado

Caribou

R

Caribou

Stony Rapids

•1036

Mountains

•236

Lake
Athabasca

Steamboat

Fort Nelson

Athabasca River

Fort Chipewyan

Rabbit Lake

Churchill Peak
3049

Hay River

Peace River

Wollaston
Lake

3048

High Level

674

Cree Lake

Reindeer
Lake

B R I T I S H

•340

A L B E R T A

859

S A S K A T C H E W A N

Kinoosao

Southern
Indian
Lake

C O L U M B I A

672

Lynn Lake

M A N I T

Mount Pattullo
2729

Manning

•1094

Fort McMurray

Frobisher Lake

Southend

251

Mount Burden
2324

Fort
St. John

Peace River

Peter
Pond
Lake

Churchill
Lake

Island Falls

•390

•2047

Dawson Creek

Rycroft

McLennan

Churchill

Thompson

Lake
Williston

Chetwynd
869

Tupper

High Prairie

Lesser
Slave Lake

Buffalo
Narrows

•553

Lac
La Ronge

Mackenzie

Grande Prairie

Valleyview

Slave Lake

Fort Black

Flin Flon

Wabowden

Hazelton

McLeod Lake

1259

Smith

55°N

n   o   p   q   r   s   t   u   v   w   x   y   z

14   15

125°W   120°W   115°W   110°W   100°W

Mackenzie   Mountains

Franklin   Mountains

This map shows 1/60 of the earth's surface

90

90°W   85°W   80°W   75°W   70°W   65°W

Nansen Sound

Axel Heiberg Island   Eureka

Agassiz Ice Cap

80°N

I s l a n d s

Ellesmere Island

Norwegian Bay

Bjorne Peninsula

Sydney Ice Cap • 1328

Smith Bay

Graham Island

Table Island

North Lincoln Land

Jones Sound

• Grise Fjord

Baffin

75°N

• 290

D e v o n Island   • 1887

Bay

rrow Strait

Cape Clarence

Dundas Harbour

Lancaster Sound

Somerset Island

Prince Regent Inlet

Admiralty Inlet

• 549

• Arctic Bay

Borden Peninsula

• 1189

Bylot Island • 2134

Buchan Gulf

Brodeur Peninsula

244 •

Eclipse Sound

Pond Inlet

Gulf

Bernier Bay

oothia ninsula

• 572

of

518 •

• 1554

Boothia

Fury and Hecla Strait

Baffin

Clyde

70°N

Spence Bay (Taloyoak)

Pelly Bay

• 558

Jens Munk Island

Rowley Island

Foley

Barnes Ice Cap • 1250

Henry Kater Pen.

Davis Strait

s • 229

Simpson Peninsula

Pelly Bay

Committee Bay

Wales Island

Melville Peninsula

• Hall Beach

Prince Charles • 30 Island

Island

Home Bay

• 503

Rae Isthmus

Repulse Bay •

381 •

Foxe Basin

Koukdjuak

Nettiling Lake

Penny Ice Cap • 2591

Kivitoo

Broughton Island

V U T

Wager Bay

Lyon Inlet

Vansittart Island

Nabukjuak

Amadjuak Lake

Nunatak

Pangnirtung

Cumberland Peninsula

• 2134

Cape Dyer

Exeter Sound

65°N

90

Roes Welcome Sound

Southampton Island • 625

Foxe Channel

Foxe Peninsula

• 411

Cape Dorset

Cumberland Sound

Hall • 1148

Hoare Bay

Chesterfield Inlet

Coral Harbour

Bell Peninsula

Salisbury Island

305 •

Amadjuak Lake

Big Island

Lake Harbour

Iqaluit (Frobisher Bay)

Peninsula

Labrador

Chesterfield Inlet (Igluligaarjuk)

Fisher Strait

Evans Strait

Coats Island

Nottingham Island

Hudson Strait

Meta Incognita Peninsula

Frobisher Bay

Loks Land

Rankin Inlet

D

Mansel Island

• 540

• Ivujivik

Salluit

• Purtuniq

• 661

Resolution Island

A

Whale Cove

Kangiqsujuaq

Sea

Eskimo Point (Arviat)

Akulivik

Cape Hopes Advance

Akpatok Island

Port Burwell

Cape Chidley

ATLANTIC OCEAN

Hudson

Ungava Peninsula

Povungnituk

Ungava Bay

60°N

Cape hurchill

Churchill

Ottawa Islands

• 390

• 1621

Ramah

Bay

Inukjuak

Kangiqsualujjuaq

NEWFOUNDLAND

McClintock

aux Feuilles

Kuujjuaq

Koksoak

ort Nelson

York Factory

• 472

Lake Minto

Nutak

• 1076

A

• 196

Shamattawa

Fort Severn

L a b r a d o r

Q U E B E C

• 451

Fraser

Nain

O N T A R I O

Winisk

Belcher Islands

Kuujjuarapik

Lac à l'Eau-Claire

• 241

Caniapiscau

• 876

Hopedale

Severn

Cape Henrietta Maria

Lake Bienville

55°N

90°W   85°W   80°W   75°W   70°W   65°W

16   17

0   100   200   300 miles   Average linear scale   0 100 200 300 400 500 Km

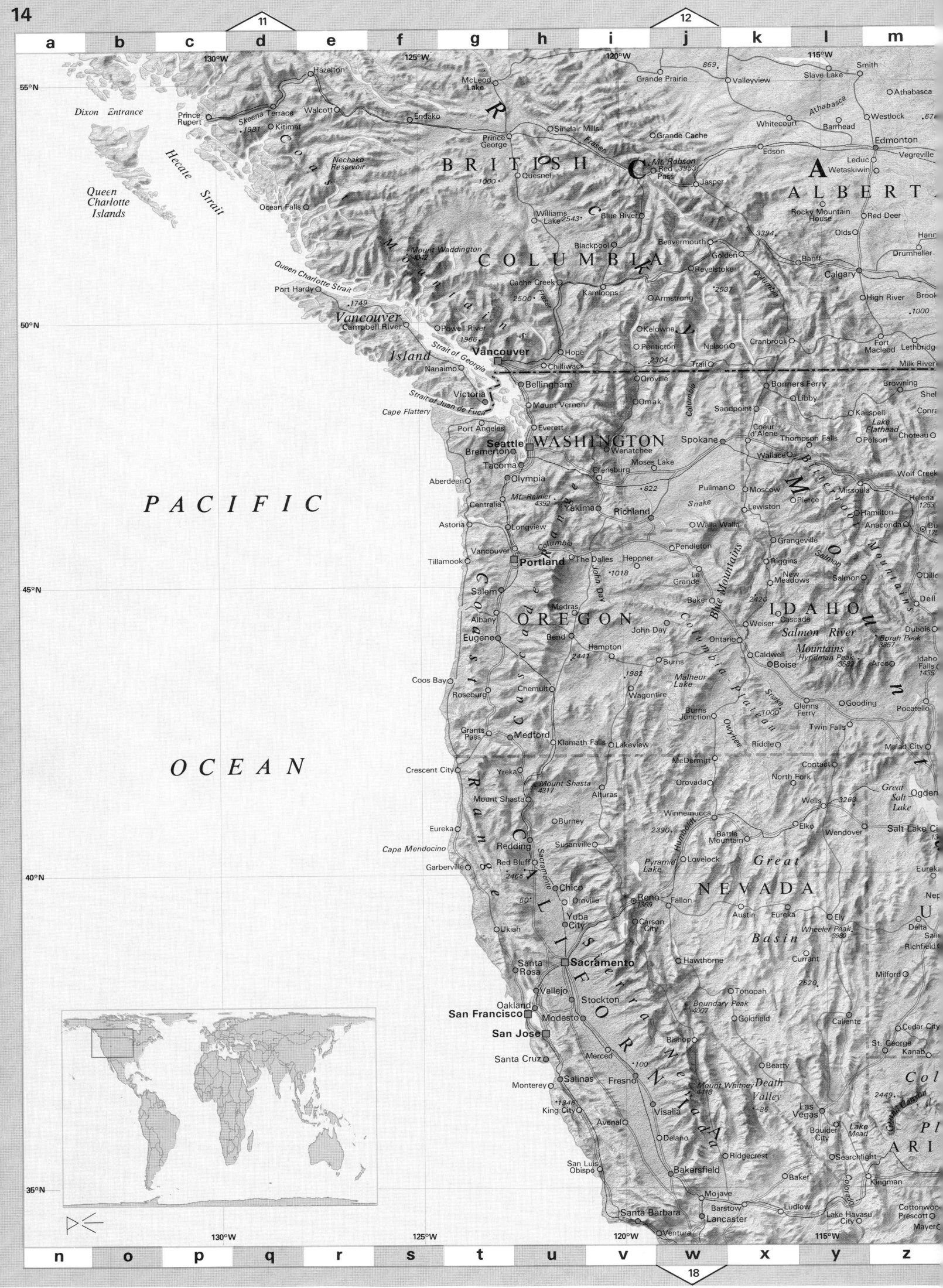

a b c d e f g h i j k l m

55°N

130°W

125°W

120°W

115°W

Dixon Entrance

Queen
Charlotte
Islands

Hecate Strait

PACIFIC

OCEAN

50°N

45°N

40°N

35°N

BRITISH

COLUMBIA

ALBERTA

WASHINGTON

OREGON

IDAHO

NEVADA

CALIFORNIA

130°W

125°W

120°W

115°W

n o p q r s t u v w x y z

18

This map shows 1/60 of the earth's surface

a b c d e f g h i j k l m

110°W   105°W   100°W   95°W   90°W

13

CANADA

SASKATCHEWAN   MANITOBA   ONTARIO

Grand Centre · Beaver · Meadow Lake · Flin Flon · Wabowden · Moose Lake · Gods Lake · Bearskin Lake · Big Trout Lake
Lloydminster · North Saskatchewan · .747 · The Pas · Norway House · Island Lake · North Caribou Lake · Wunnummin Lake
Wainwright · North Battleford · Prince Albert · Melfort · Tisdale · Hudson Bay · .823 · Cedar Lake · Lake Winnipeg · Berens River · .396 · Sandy Lake · .178
.914 · Adanac · Biggar · Saskatoon · Swan River · .217 · Pipangikum Lake · Cat Lake · Albany
Kindersley · North Battleford · 490 · Wynyard · Dauphin · Lake Winnipegosis · .305 · Red Lake · .359 · Lake St. Joseph
.789 · Rosetown · Davidson · Yorkton · Melville · Winnipegosis · Lake Manitoba · Riverton · Sioux Lookout
Central Butte · Indian Head · .710 · Neepawa · Winnipeg Beach · Pinawa · Kenora · Dryder · Trans Canada Highway
Swift Current · Moose Jaw · Regina · Milestone · .678 · Minnedosa · Winnipeg · .500
Medicine Hat · Maple Creek · .1082 · Shaunavon · Assiniboia · Weyburn · Virden · Brandon · Portage la Prairie · Middleboro · Fort Frances · Rainy Lake · English River · Atikokan · Thunder Bay
Deer · South Saskatchewan · Gladmar · Estevan · .1000 · Westhope · Morden · Red River · International Falls · Fort Frances · .500

55°N

50°N

UNITED STATES

MONTANA   NORTH DAKOTA   MINNESOTA   WISCONSIN

Chester · Big Sandy · Malta · Glasgow · Wolf Point · Culbertson · Williston · Kenmare · Stanley · Minot · Rugby · Langdon · Grafton · Devils Lake · .300 · Thief River Falls · Upper Red Lake · Lower Red Lake · Grand Marais · .646
Havre · Milk · Fort Peck Reservoir · Sidney · Lewistown · Great Falls · Stanford · Jordan · Glendive · .1108 · Sakakawea Reservoir · Carrington · Grand Forks · Crookston · Bemidji · Grand Rapids · Hibbing · Virginia · Lake Superior
Townsend · Harlowton · Roundup · Miles City · Baker · Belfield · Dickinson · Bismarck · Jamestown · Valley City · Fargo · Moorhead · Fergus Falls · Brainerd · .381 · Duluth · Superior · Apostle Islands
Livingston · Billings · Forsyth · .1076 · Bowman · Lemmon · Linton · Oakes · Frederick · .500 · Sisseton · Alexandria · Little Falls · Pine City · Ashland · Ironwood · Rhinelander
Bozeman · Granite Peak 3917 · Hardin · Ashland · Broadus · Buffalo · Bison · Mobridge · Selby · Aberdeen · Watertown · Ortonville · Willmar · St. Cloud · Rice Lake · Ladysmith · Merrill
Canyon · Cody · Grey Bull · Sheridan · Cloud Peak 4016 · Buffalo · Sundance · .840 · Lake Oahe · Gettysburg · Montevideo · .619 · Minneapolis St. Paul · River Falls · Chippewa Falls · Wausau · Eau Claire · Marshfield
Snake River · Moran · Worland · Gillette · Spearfish · Pierre · Huron · Brookings · Minnesota · Marshall · New Ulm · Red Wing · Faribault · Tomah · Rochester · La Crosse

WYOMING   SOUTH DAKOTA   IOWA   MISSOURI   ILLINOIS

45°N

40°N

35°N

NEW MEXICO   TEXAS   OKLAHOMA   ARKANSAS

COLORADO   KANSAS   NEBRASKA

Denver · Pikes Peak 4300 · Colorado Springs · Pueblo · Albuquerque · Santa Fe · Amarillo · Oklahoma City · Tulsa · Fort Smith · Little Rock · Memphis

16

19

0   100   200   300 miles
0   100   200   300   400   500 Km
Average linear scale

a b c d e f g h i j k l m

12

95°W 90°W 85°W 80°W 75°W

M A N I T O B A

55°N

Shamattawa

Fort Severn

Winisk

Hudson Bay

Cape Henrietta Maria

Belcher Islands

Great Whale

Kuujjuarapik

Lac l'E Cla

Gods Lake

Bearskin Lake

Big Trout Lake

Winisk Lake

James

Point Louis XIV

.168

Kanaaupscow

Island Lake

Sandy Lake .276

North Caribou Lake

Wunnummin Lake

.88

Attawapiskat

Bay

Akimiki Island

Chisasibi

La Radisson

Sakami

.195

La Gra

Pipangikum Lake

.396

Cat Lake

Attawapiskat Lake

Ogoki

Albany

Moosonee

Fort Albany

Hannah Bay

James Bay

Eastmain

Fort Rupert

Eastmain

.100

Red Lake .359

Lac Seul

Fort Hope 268

Missinaibi

Moosonee

Abitibi

Rupert

La

Lake Mistas

Pinawa .317

Lake St. Joseph

358.

Armstrong

O N T A R I O

Nakina

Longlac

Hearst

Fraserdale

Kapuskasing

Cochrane

Kesagami Lake

Q

Lake Evans .232

U

Chibougamau

.556

Chapais

Kenora

Dryden

Sioux Lookout

Lake Nipigon

Geraldton

C A N A D A

Monts Deloge .533

Lake Abitibi

Matagami

Middleboro

Trans Canada Highway

English River

.500

Nipigon

Longlac

Marathon

390.

Timmins

Noranda

Senneterre

Fort Frances

Atikokan

Schreiber

White River

New Liskeard .693

Kirkland Land

Val-d'Or

.609

International Falls

Rainy Lake

Grand Marais .646

Isle Royale

Wawa

Chapleau .640

Témiscaming

Gouin Reservoi

Thief River Falls

Upper Red Lake

Thunder Bay

Lake Superior

.665

Blind River

Espanola

Sudbury .196

North Bay

Cabonga Reservoir

Ste-Agathe-des-Monts .960

St-Jérô

358.

Lower Red Lake

Hibbing

Virginia

Copper Harbor

Houghton

Sault Ste. Marie

Sturgeon Falls

Pembroke

Maniwaki

Mont Laurier

Bemidji

Grand Rapids .436

Duluth .471

Cloquet

Superior

Apostle Islands

Ironwood .573

.603

Marquette

Seney

322.

Little Current

Manitoulin Island

Parry Sound

Georgian Bay

Huntsville

Bancroft .419

Buckingham

Hull

Cornwall

Montréal

Ottawa

Fergus Falls .381

Mille Lacs

Ashland

Iron Mountain

Mackinaw City

Tobermory

Owen Sound

North Bay

Orillia

L. Simcoe

Perth

Smith's Falls

Brockville

Salaber-De-Valley

Brainerd

Little Falls

.454

Rice Lake

Rhinelander

Escanaba

Petoskey

Lake Huron

Port Elgin

Midland .573

Barrie

Peterborough

Kingston

Glen Falls

.637

M I N N E S O T A

Alexandria

Pine City

St. Cloud

Ladysmith

Merrill

Menomineen

Marinette

Grayling

Goderich

Kitchener-Waterloo

Hamilton .200

Oshawa

Belleville

Watertown

Willmar

Minnesota

Rice Lake

Chippewa Falls

Wausau

Sturgeon Bay

Green Bay

M I C H I G A N

Cadillac

Ludington

Bay City

Saginaw

Sarnia

London

St. Catharines

Rochester

Syracuse

N E W

.190

Mo Marc

Minneapolis St. Paul

Eau Claire

Marshfield

Stevens Point

Appleton

Manitowoc

Sheboygan

Midland

Flint

St. Thomas

Niagara Falls

Buffalo

Seneca Lake

Utica

Albany

Schenectady

45°N

15

Marshall

.510

New Ulm

Faribault

Mankato

Red Wing

W I S C O N S I N

Winona

Oshkosh

Fond du Lac .369

Portage

.223

Muskegon

Grand Rapids

Lansing

Ann Arbor .358

Detroit

Windsor

London

Hamilton .200

Fredonia

Dansville

Jamestown

Ithaca

Elmira

Y O R K

Lake Ontario

Caskill Mountains .1284

Kingston

.1281

Hud

Rochester

Spencer

Albert Lea

Austin

Decorah

La Crosse .494

Madison

Janesville

Racine

Kalamazoo

Battle Creek

Jackson

Toledo

Detroit

Lake Erie

Erie

Meadville .424

Ashtabula

.775

Olean

Binghampton

Kane

Mansfield

Williamsport

Scranton

Newburgh

Danbury

Bridgepo

Storm Lake

Fort Dodge

Webster City

Mason City .300

Dubuque .436

Freeport

Rockford

Beloit

Kenosha

Milwaukee

Chicago

South Bend

Gary

Fort Wayne

Findlay

Napoleon

Sandusky .424

Cleveland

Youngstown

Clearfield

P E N N S Y L V A N I A

.675

Scranton

Paterson

Newark

Elizabeth

Allentown

Ne

Omaha

Council Bluffs

Denison

Ames .290

Newton

I O W A

Iowa City

Cedar Rapids

Rochelle

De Kalb

Elgin

Joliet

Morris

Kankakee

Lafayette

Kokomo

Lima

Kenton

Mansfield

Canton

Wheeling

Johnstown .956

Greensburg

Altoona .706

Harrisburg

Reading

Lancaster

Trenton

Wilmington

Philadelph

Des Moines

Knoxville

Oskaloosa

Ottumwa

Burlington

Galesburg

Peoria .236

Wabash

Danville

Rantoul

Champaign

Muncie

Springfield

Columbus

Newark .424

Cambridge

Cumberland

Bickle Knob .1222

Hagerstown

M A R Y L A N D

N E W J E R S E Y

40°N

St. Joseph

Atchison

Bethany .300

Kirksville

Keokuk

I L L I N O I S

Bloomington

Quincy

Beardstown

Decatur

Springfield

Anderson

Indianapolis

Richmond

Dayton

O H I O

Washington Court House

Marietta

Parkersburg

Clarksburg .1222

Elkins

Arlington

Alexandria

Annapolis

Cambridge

Cape May

Cape May

Leavenworth

Macon

Hannibal .367

Jacksonville

Terre Haute

I N D I A N A

Bloomington

S T A T E S

Richmond

Chillicothe

Athens

Hillsboro

W E S T

.412

Culpeper

Fredericksburg

.23

Salisbury

Kansas City

Independence

Columbia

Sedalia

Jefferson City

Litchfield

Alton

Vandalia

Effingham .322

Cincinnatti

Ohio

Portsmouth

Maysville

V I R G I N I A

Charleston

Richwood

.1476

Spruce Knob

M

Lexington

Park

Washington DC

Vineland

Atlant City

Topeka

Ottawa

Emporia

Clinton

M I S S O U R I

St. Louis

Festus

Mt. Vernon

Jasper

Bedford

Louisville

Evansville

Morehead

Huntington

.1234

Charlottesville

Richmond

Patersburg

Williamsburg

Hampton

Newport News

Fort Scott

Nevada

Lebanon

Bolivar

Lake Ozark

Rolla

Sullivan

Perryville .540

West Frankfort .314

Owensboro

Elizabethtown

Berea

V I R G I N I A

Williamson

Pikeville

Beckley .1274

Roanoke

Bluefield

Lynchburg

Norfolk

Emporia

Portsmouth

35°N

Independence .300

Miami

Bartlesville

Joplin

Aurora

Neosho

Branson

Springfield .510

Cabool

Poplar Bluff

Cape Girardeau

Cairo

Paducah

Central City

K E N T U C K Y

Bowling Green

Glasgow

Lake Cumberland

Somerset .532

Hazard

Wytheville

Marion

Mount Rogers .743

Mount Airy

Martinsville

Danville

Roanoke Rapids

Greensboro

Durham

Raleigh

Elizabeth City

Tulsa

Tahlequah

Vinita

Muskogee

A R K A N S A S

Clarksville

Newport

Blytheville

Dyersburg

Tennessee

Nashville

Murfreesboro

Cumberland .307

Kingsport

Winston Salem

Clingmans Dome .2025

.1916

.1784

High Knob

Rockwood

Knoxville

Asheville

N O R T H

Kannapolis

Hickory

Charlotte

Goldsboro

Rocky Mount

New Bern

Pamlico Sound

Henryetta

Fort Smith

Poteau

Fayetteville

Ozark Plateau

Marshall

Hardy

Jonesboro

Jackson

Columbia

Lawrenceberg

Fayetteville .879

Chattanooga

Cleveland

.2901

Mt Mitchell

Hendersonville

C A R O L I N A

Greensboro

Spartanburg

Greenville

Fayetteville

Rockingham

Cape Hatteras

McAlester

Little Rock

Brinkley

West Memphis

Memphis

Florence

Huntsville

Greenville

.100

.100

95°W 90°W 85°W 80°W 75°W

n o p q r s t u v w x y z

19 20

This map shows 1/60 of the earth's surface

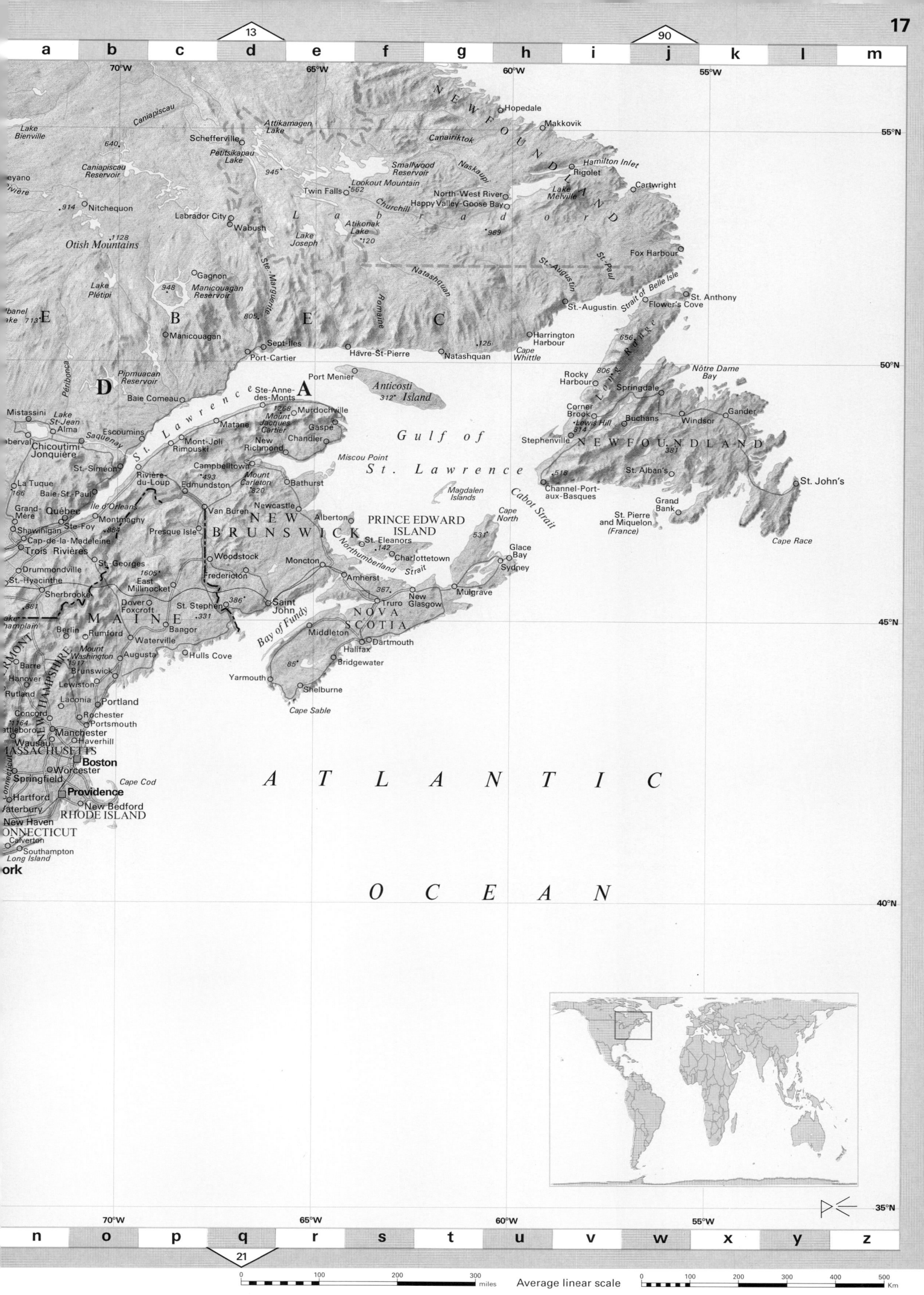

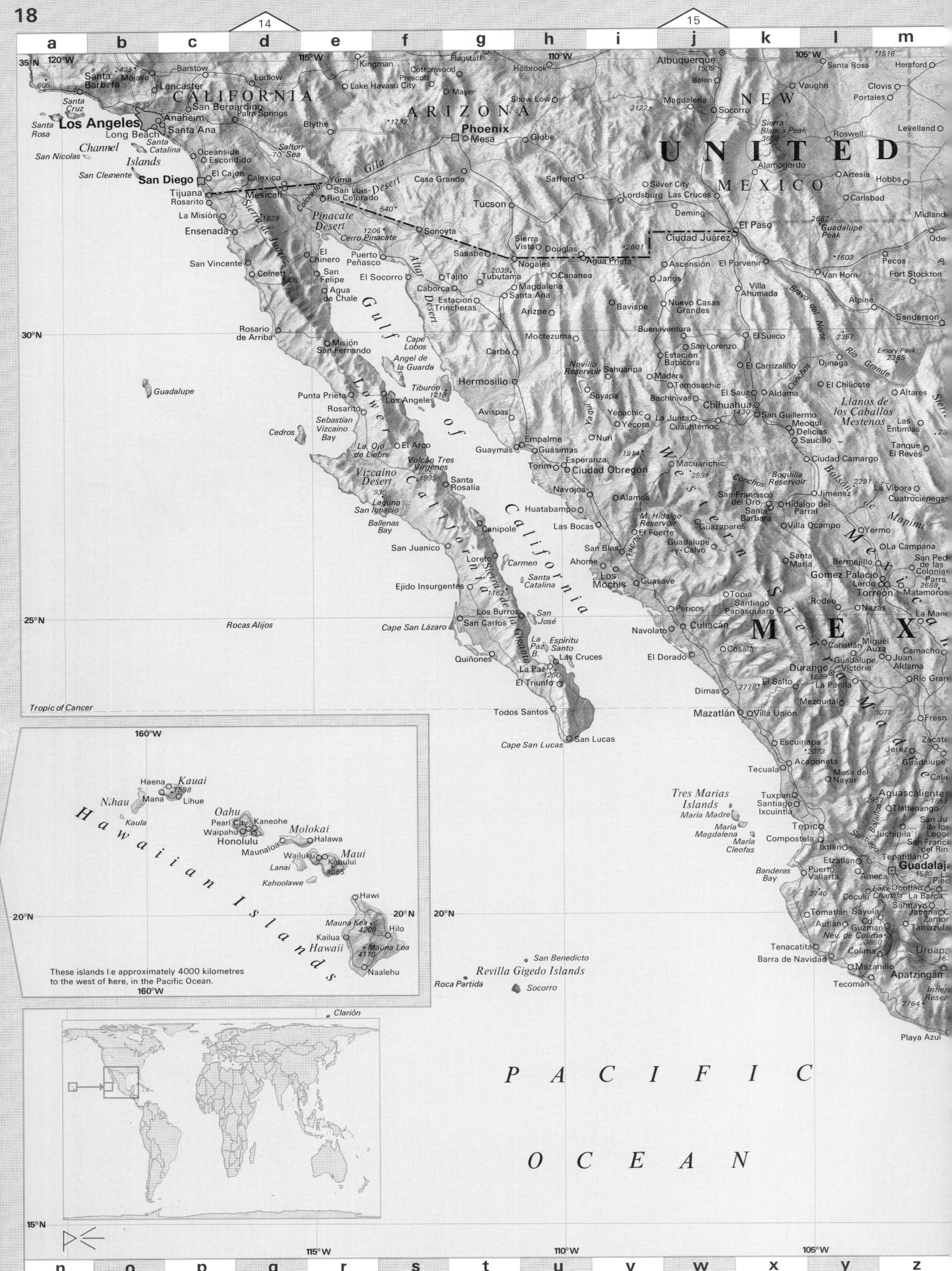

14   15

a b c d e f g h i j k l m

35°N 120°W   105°W *1516
Santa Barbara *2435 Barstow   Ludlow   Kingman Cottonwood Flagstaff* Holbrook   Albuquerque *1509 Santa Rosa   Hereford
605 Santa Mojave Lancaster   Prescott   Magdalena *3122   Belen   Vaughn   Clovis
Cruz Santa Barbara   Lake Havasu City Mayer   Show Low   Socorro   Portales
Santa   CALIFORNIA   San Bernardino   ARIZONA   NEW   Roswell
Rosa Los Angeles Anaheim Palm Springs   Blythe   *1732 Phoenix Globe   UNITED   Sierra
Channel Long Beach Santa Ana   Salton 70   Mesa   Blanca Peak Levelland
Santa Catalina Oceanside Escondido   Sea   Safford   Silver City *3659 MEXICO   Alamogordo Artesia
San Nicolas Islands San Diego El Cajon Calexico Yuma San Luis Gila Desert Casa Grande   Lordsburg Las Cruces   Hobbs
San Clemente   San Diego Tijuana Mexicali Rio Colorado   540*   Tucson   Deming El Paso *2667 Carlsbad   Midland
Rosarito   San Luis-Desert   Ciudad Juárez Guadalupe   Ode
La Misión *1829   Pinacate   1206   Sierra   *2039   Nogales Agua Prieta *2601 Peak *1603   Pecos
Ensenada   Sierra de Juárez Desert Cerro Pinacate Sonoyta Altar Desert Sierra Douglas   Ascensión El Porvenir   Fort Stockton
San Vicente   El Chinero Puerto   Vista Sásabe Tubutama   Janos Villa   Van Horn   Alpine
Colnett *3069 San Peñasco El Socorro Tajito Magdalena Cananea   Bavispe Ahumada   Sanderson
Agua Felipe   Caborca Estación Santa Ana   Nuevo Casas   Llanos de
de Chale   Trincheras Arizpe   Buenaventura San Lorenzo Grandes   los Caballos
30°N   Cape   Hermosillo Moctezuma   Novillo Estación El Sueco   *2357 Mestenos
Rosario   Lobos Carbó   Reservoir Babícora   Rio Emory Peak
de Arriba   Misión   Angel de   Soyapa Sahuaripa Madera   Ojinaga   2385
Guadalupe San Fernando la Guarda   Temósachic El Carrizalillo   El Chilicote   Altares
Punta Prieta Tiburón Los Angeles 1218 Avispas Yepachic La Junta Bachinivas El Sauz Conchos
Rosarito   Nuri Meoqui Chihuahua Aldama
Sebastián Cedros   Empalme Yécora Cuauhtémoc 1430 San Guillermo   Tanque
Vizcaino Bay   Guásimas Esperanza Torim 1914 Delicias El Revés
La Ojo El Arco Volcán Tres Guaymas   Ciudad Obregón   Macuarichic Saucillo Western
de Liebre Vírgenes Santa   Navojoa Alamos *2591
Vizcaino 1995 Rosalia Huatabampo   San Francisco Ciudad Camargo 2291 La Víbora
Desert 935   del Oro Santa Boquilla   Cuatrociénegas
Laguna   Las Bocas El Fuerte Barbara Reservoir Jiménez Mapimí
San Ignacio   Canipole San Blas Guazapares Hidalgo del   2688
Ballenas   Ahome   M. Hidalgo Villa Ocampo Parral   La Campana
Bay   San Juanico Loreto Los Mochis Reservoir   Santa
San   Carmen Santa Guasave   Topia   Bermejillo San Pedro
Juanico   Catalina Guamúchil Santiago Rodeo Gómez Palacio de las Colonias
Ejido Insurgentes   1162   Pericos Papasquiaro   Nazas Lerdo Parra
25°N Rocas Alijos Cape San Lázaro San Carlos San Culiacán Cosalá Canatlán Torreón 2688 Matamoros
Quiñones   La Paz José Navolato El Dorado Durango Miguel Camacho La Manc
La Paz Espíritu Las Cruces   Auza Juan
El Triunfo Santo 1250 Dimas 2778 El Salto Guadalupe Aldama Río Gran
Tropic of Cancer   La Parilla Victoria
Todos Santos   Mezquital   3078 Fresn
Cape San Lucas San Lucas   Mazatlán Villa Unión   Zacate
Escuinapa   Jerez   Guadalupe
Tecuala 2073   Calii
160°W   Acaponeta   Mesa del
Haena Kauai   Tuxpan Nayar   Aguascalientes 1863
Nihau *1598 Oahu Tres Marias Santiago   Tlaltenango San Ju
Mana Lihue Pearl City Kaneohe Islands Ixcuintla   de los
Kaula Waipahu Honolulu Molokai María Madre Tepico   Juchipila Lagos San Franc
Honolulu Halawa   María Compostela Ixtlán del Rin
Maunaloa Maui Magdalena Etzatlán Tepatitlán
Lanai Wailuku Kahului María Puerto   Guadalaj
Kahoolawe 3055 Cleofas Vallarta Ameca 1540 La Pied
Banderas 2740 Cocula Chapala
Hawi Bay Lake La Barca Zamor
20°N 20°N Tomatlán Sahuayo Jacona Tamazula
Mauna Kea Hilo Autlán Cd. Sayula
These islands l e approximately 4000 kilometres *4208 Kailua Guzmán Colima Uruapa
to the west of here, in the Pacific Ocean. Hawaii Mauna Loa   Nev. de Colima 16.
160°W *4170 Naalehu Tenacatita 3860 Mazanillo Apatzingán
Clarión   San Benedicto Barra de Navidad Colima Inflern
Revilla Gigedo Islands Tecomán 2764 Reser
Roca Partida Socorro Playa Azul

PACIFIC

OCEAN

n o p q r s t u v w x y z

115°W 110°W 105°W

This map shows 1/60 of the earth's surface

a b c d e f g h i j k l m

16

100°W 95°W 90°W 85°W 35°N

Altus .751 Ada McAlester Corinth Florence Huntsville Decatur Gainesville

ulia Lawton 722 Little Rock Arkansas Tupelo 246 Cullman Gadsden Marietta

Plainview Wichita Falls OKLAHOMA Arkadelphia Pine Bluff Clarksdale Columbus Birmingham Tuscaloosa Atlanta

bbock Sherman Paris ARKANSAS Greenville Winona Bessemer .734 College Park

Big Fort Worth Irving Garland STATES El Dorado Lake Vicksburg MISSISSIPPI Meridian Opelika .425 Macon GEORGIA

Spring Abilene Arlington Dallas Marshall Minden 67 Providence Jackson 149 Selma Montgomery Phenix City Columbus

.864 Sweetwater Tyler Longview Shreveport Monroe ALABAMA Greenville Eufaula Dawson

San Angelo .832 Brownwood TEXAS Waco .233 Nacogdoches Natchitoches Brookhaven Laurel Jackson Andalusia Albany Tifton

Kerrville New Temple Killeen Lufkin Red River Alexandria McComb Hattiesburg Dothan .105 Marianna Thomasville Valdosta

Edwards Braunfels Austin Jasper Toledo LOUISIANA Mobile Crestview Chattahoochee

Plateau Colorado Huntsville Bend Baton Hammond Biloxi Gulfport Pascagoula Pensacola Fort Panama City Tallahassee

784 Reservoir Lake Charles Rouge Slidell Kenner Walton

Armistad San Antonio Houston Beaumont Lafayette New Orleans Beach 30°N

Del Rio Reservoir New Braunfels Pasadena Baytown New Iberia Houma Cape San Blas Apalachee

Ciudad Gonzales Texas City Mississippi Bay

Acuña Uvalde Lake Galveston Delta

Pearsall Jackson FLORIDA

ra Bra Piedras Victoria .50

Negras Rio Three Corpus Christi

Tule Allende Grande Rivers

Nueva Rosita Kingsville

San Sabinas 277

enaventura Nuevo Laredo Laredo .302

Monclova Falcon Laguna

Sabinas Reservoir Madre

oncepción Hidalgo Ciudad McAllen

del Oro 2648 Mier Harlingen

San Tiburcio Monterrey Reynosa Brownsville

4054 2796 China Matamoros

Matehuala Saltillo CO Gulf of

1599 Montemorelos Laguna

Rayones Madre 25°N

Charcas Linares La Carbonera Mexico 20

1794

Aramberri Jiménez

oncepción San Luis Ciudad Victoria CUBA

Salinas Potosí Pinar del Rio

Cerritos Ciudad Madero Desterrada Guanahacabibes

San Luis Tampico Pérez Peninsula Isla de

.3353 Potosí Ciudad Arenas Dzilam de Rio Lagartos Cape Catoche Pinos

Rio Verde Valles Nuevo Bravo Chiquilá Straits of

Cárdenas Pánuco Progreso Tizimin Puerto Yucatán

León Verde Laguna Triangulos Mérida Motul Espita Juárez

Guanajuato Tamazunchale Tamiahua Izamal Cancún

Silao Tuxpan Arcas Maxcanú Valladolid Puerto Morelos

puato Zacualtipan Bay of Calkini Ticul Tekax Peto Cozumel

Querétaro Poza Rica Campeche Tekax .100

Santiago Celaya Papantla Bolonchén de Rejón Tulum

roleón Salvatierra Pachuca Huauchinango Campeche Yucatán

2850 Acámbaro 2426 Martínez Sihochac Chunhuhub Ascensión Bay

Maravatio Tula de la Torre Champotón Felipe Espiritu Santo

Zinapecuaro Tulancingo Tlapacoyan Peninsula Carrillo Bay

Mexico City Apan Perote Jalapa Puerto

Morelia Texcoco Calpulalpan Veracruz Ciudad 310 Chetumal

Patzcuaro Toluca Puebla Citlaltépetl del Carmen Laguna de Gulf

Zitácuaro Apizaco 5700 Términos Mamantel

Tacambaro Atlixco Orizaba Coscomatepec Frontera of

Jorullo Cuernavaca Izúcar de Córdoba Alvarado Comalcalco Balancán Altamira Honduras

3098 Taxco Matamoros Orizaba Tlacotalpan Chichón BELIZE

Jojutla Acatlán 1879 San Andrés Villahermosa 2224 Belize Swan Island

Baltas Ciudad Tehuacan Tierra Tuxtla Macuspana Belmopan (Hond.)

Cerro de Altamirano M. Alemán Blanca Coatzacoalcos Tenosique Turneffe Islands

Chotla Reservoir Acayucan Isthmus Morelos Palenque Flores

2466 Huajuapan Tuxtepec Minatitlán of Paso Real 1122

Zihuatanejo Chilapa de León Coixtlahuaca Jesús Carranza Comitán

atlán Tecpan Nochixtlán Tehuantepec San Cristóbal Puerto Gulf

Atoyac Tlaxiaco .1546 las Casas Cortés Bay Islands of

Tierra Oaxaca Mitla Tuxtla 2727 Chiapa de Corzo Roatán Guanaja

Colorada Ejutla Paso Real Gutiérrez Utila Honduras

Pinotepa Miahuatlán Matías Mar Tela La Ceiba

Acapulco San Marcos Nacional Juchatengo Romero Muerto Arriaga San Pedro Trujillo

Puerto .3139 Tehuantepec Salina Tonalá Sula HONDURAS

Escondido Juchitán Cruz Angostura Puerto

Puerto Reservoir GUATEMALA Barrios Puerto

Angel Gulf of Huixtla Pijijiapan Lempira

Tehuantepec 4220 Huehuetenango Motagua 15°N

Tapachula Quezaltenango .2865

Guatemala

100°W 95°W 90°W 85°W

n o p q r s t u v w x y z

22

0 100 200 300 miles   Average linear scale   0 100 200 300 400 500 Km

This map shows 1/60 of the earth's surface

35°N

OLINA
Goldsboro
Fayetteville
New
Bern
Jacksonville
Morehead City
Lumberton
Wilmington

Myrtle Beach
orgetown

Hamilton ○ *Bermuda (U.K.)*

A T L A N T I C

30°N

Sargasso Sea

O C E A N

25°N

Grand
Bahama
Island
Great
Abaco
Island

Nicholls
Town **Nassau**
Eleuthera
*New
Providence*
○ *Behring
Point*
*Andros
Islands*
Cat

BAHAMAS

San Salvador

Rum Cay

Tropic of Cancer

*Great
Exuma
Island*
*Long
Island*

reat Bahama Bank

*Crooked
Island*

Acklins

*Mayaguana
Island*

Morón
cetas
Ciego de Avila
cti
ritus
Nuevitas

Camagüey

BA

Victoria de
las Tunas
Banes

Holguín
Grand Caicos
*Turks and Caicos
Islands (U.K.)*

Bayamo
Palma
Soriano
Baracoa
*Great Inagua
Island*
Manzanillo
2005
Niquero
Santiago
de Cuba
Guantánamo

20°N

a
t
e

Port-de-Paix
D O M I N I C A N
Cap-Haïtien
Puerto Plata
Gonaïves
Mao
Santiago
R E P U B L I C
HAÏTI
La Vega
San Francisco
St-Marc
3175
de Macorís

JAMAICA
Anse
d'Hainault
Port-au-Prince
San Juan
Puerto Rico(U.S.A.)
Virgin Islands (U.K.)

Montego
Bay
2680
La Romana
Bayamón
San Juan
Anguilla (U.K.)
Spanish
Town
Les Cayes
Jacmel
Barahona
**Santo
Domingo**
Mayagüez
1338
Carolina
Caguas
*Virgin
Islands
(U.S.A.)*
St. Martin
Philipsburg
Barbuda
May Pen
Kingston
Ponce
*Netherlands
Antilles*
Codrington
St. Croix
(U.S.A.)
Basseterre
**ANTIGUA AND
BARBUDA**

*A
n
t
i
l
l
e
s*
**ST KITTS
NEVIS**
St. John's
Antigua
Montserrat
Plymouth
(U.K.)

B
E
A
N
S
E
A
*Guadeloupe
(France)*
Pointe-
à-Pitre
Basse-Terre

Leeward Islands
D O M I N I C A

Roseau

15°N

0 100 200 300 miles
Average linear scale
0 100 200 300 400 500 Km

MEXICO

Amatenango
Huixtla
Tapachula
Mazatenango
Quezaltenango
Huehuetenango
Lago de Izabal
GUATEMALA
Antigua 3752 ⊡ Guatemala 1502
Escuintla
Santa Ana
Ahuachapan 2386
Sonsonate
San Salvador
Zacatecoluca
EL SALVADOR

Puerto Barrios
Puerto Cortés
San Pedro Sula
Tela
La Ceiba
Trujillo
HONDURAS
Juticalpa
2435
Patuca
Puerto Lempira
Cabo Gracias á Dios
Coco
Cayos Miskitos

Santa Rosa
La Paz
2310
Tegucigalpa
2438
Cordillera Isabella
Nacaome
San Miguel
Estelí
Gulf of Fonseca
1745

Puerto Cabezas
Prinzapolca
Providencia (Col.)
San Andrés (Col.)

Chinandega
León
Managua
Granada
Lake
Rivas
Santa Elena
Cabo
Liberia
2020
NICARAGUA
Matagalpa
Escondido
Rama
Bluefields
Mosquito Coast
1133
Lake Nicaragua
San Carlos
San Juan
San Juan del Norte

COSTA
Puntarenas
Alajuela Heredia
San José
3432
Turrialba
3820 Chirripo
Nicoya Peninsula
Gulf of Nicoya
RICA

Almirante
Puerto Cortés
David
3475
2826
Santiago
Gulf of Chiriqui
Puerto Armuelles
Coiba
Azuero Peninsula
1400
Pedasi
Colón
Panama Canal
Balboa
Panamá
Penonomé
Rey
Perlas Archipelago
PANAMA
2621
Ailigandi
La Palma
El Real
Riosucio
Gulf of Mosquitos
Gulf of Darien
Gulf of Panama
Punta Manzanillo

PACIFIC

OCEAN

Malpelo (Col.)

Darwin
Wolf
Pinta
Marchena
Genovesa
1707
San Salvador
Fernandina
Santa Cruz
Isabela
Puerto Villamil
Santa Maria
San Cristóbal
Galapagos Islands (Ecuador)
Española
Equator

Barranquilla
Baranoa
Cartagena
Calar
Arjona
Plat
Carmen
Lorica
Sincele
Montería
Necoclí
San Jorge
Caucasia
Chigorodó
Zaragoza
3959
Yarumal
Cisneros
Bello
4083
Medellín ⊡ 1541
Quibdó
Aguad
Cabo Corrientes
Honda
2149
Manizales 5399
Cartago 1424
Pereira
Armenia
Ibag
Punta Chirambirá
4250
Tulua
Buenaventura
Palmira
Cali
Santander
Neiva
Nev. de Huila 5750
Gorgona
Guapi
Popayán
4566
Garzón
El Bordo
Patia
Tumaco
Cabo Manglares
San Lorenzo
Túquerres
Pasto
Mocoa
Esmeraldas
Punta Galera
Rosa Zárate
Esmeraldas
4764
Ipiales
Tulcán
San Gabriel
Puerto Asis
4930
Ibarra
Cayambe 4790
4794
Quito ⊡ 2819
Aguarico
La Tagu
Puerto Leguizam
Bahia de Caráquez
Machachi
5698
Baeza
Coca
Cotopaxi 5263
Manta
Tena
Cabo Pantoja
Portoviejo
Ambato
Chimborazo 6272
ECUADOR
Napo
Santa Ma
Africa
Riobamba
La Puntilla
Salinas
Babahoyo
Guayaquil
5230
Alausi
Macas
Pastaza
Montalvo
Azogues
Cuenca
Curaray
Tigre
Florenc
Espir
Chapar
C
P
Marsell
CARI
Daule

Franco Central Cordillera
West Cordillera
Eastern Cordillera
Magdalena
Atrato
San Juan
Sinú
Nechí

PÆ

This map shows 1/60 of the earth's surface

70°W 65°W 60°W

DOMINICA **Roseau**
15°N

Martinique-Passage
B E A N   S E A
Martinique
Fort-de-France (France)

St.-Lucia-Passage
Castries SAINT LUCIA

St.-Vincent-Passage

L e s s e r   A n t i l l e s

BARBADOS
SAINT
VINCENT **Kingstown** **Bridgetown**
AND
GRENADINES

A T L A N T I C

Cabo
Gallinas Aruba Curaçao *Netherlands*
(Neth.) *Antilles* Blanquilla Saint George's GRENADA
Willemstad (Ven.)
Guajira 820 *Bonaire*
Peninsula Paraguaná
Punto Fijo Peninsula Puerto Cumarebo Islas
Los Roques Tobago
Riohacha Maicao Coro (Ven.) Margarita Scarborough
Santa *Gulf of* La Asunción TRINIDAD
Marta Cristóbal Colón *Venezuela* Tortuga AND
5800 San Carúpano Port TOBAGO
énaga Rafael Churuguara *Tocuyo* Maiquetía 2765 of Spain 940
alledupar Maracaibo La Puerto Cabo Codera Cumaná Trinidad
Concepción Cabimas Carora San Cabello **Caracas** Güiria *Gulf of*
1900 Felipe Maracay Puerto La Cruz Caripito Paria
Cesar Ciudad Valencia La Victoria Barcelona San
3750 Ojeda Barquisimeto San Juan 2660 Caripito Fernando
Machiques *Lake* Acarigua do los Morros Pariti Anaco *Serpent's Mouth* 10°N
Maracaibo 3652 El Sombrero Valle de Cantaura Maturín
Catatumbo Bocono la Pascua Zaraza *Guanipa* Tigre *OCEAN*
El Banco Guanare El Tigre Manamo
Casigua Mérida 5007 Calabozo Tucupita
San Carlos Barinas El Baúl Pariaguán Orinoco
del Zulia Guárico Barrancas Delta
Ocaña Valera *Cordillera de Mérida* Grande Amacuro
Cúcuta 3652 San Fernando Boca del Ciudad Delta
Apure de Apure Pao Guayana 792 San José de Amacuro
ucaramanga Pamplona San Cristóbal Mantecal Caicara de Ciudad Upata Boca Grande
4100 Orinoco Bolívar Serrania de Imataca Hossororo
Barrancabermeja Arauca 1863 Maripa El Callao
Málaga **V E N E Z U E L A** 1839 La Paragua Marlborough
Socorro 5493 Arauca La Urbana Las El Dorado Cuyuni Suddie
Capanaparo Trincheras Georgetown
Casanare Cravo Norte Santa María Caura Mayupa La Escalera Peters Bartica New Amsterdam
5°N

22

85°W   80°W   75°W

COLOMB

Tumaco
Patia
El Bordo
Florencia
Calamar
Buenos Aires
Miraflore
Cabo Manglares
Túquerres
Pasto
Mocoa
Cuñare
San Lorenzo
4764
Ipiales
Puerto Asís
Macuje
Esmeraldas
Tulcán
Puerto Huitoto
Punta Galera
4930
San Gabriel
La Tagua
Rosa Zárate
Ibarra
Cayambe
Puerto Leguizamo
Otavalo
5843
Araracuara
Palmero

0°   *Equator*

Quito
2819
4794
Coca
Aguarico
La Chorrera
Bahía de Caráquez
Machachi
Cotopaxi 5896
Baeza
Napo
Manta
Latacunga
Tena
Cabo Pantoja
Chimborazo 6272
Ambato
ECUADOR
Curaray
Santa María
El Encanto
Portoviejo
Riobamba
Arica
Jipijapa
5230
Montalvo
San Cristóbal
Guayaquil
Babahoyo
Marsella
Santa Clotilde
La Puntilla
Alausí
Macas
Pastaza
Salinas
Puná
Morona
Mazán
Gulf of Guayaquil
Cuenca
Azogues
Vargas Guerra
Andoas
Iquitos
Machala
4138
Tigre
Tamshiya
Zarumilla
Santa Isabel
Correntes
Sargento Lores
Santa Lu
Tumbes
Loja
Zamora
Puerto Pardo
Santa C
Zorritos
3810
Cariamanga
Santiago
Nauta
Mancora
Borja
Concordia
Bagazán
Yavari
Talara
Las Lomas
Orellana
Barranca
Marañón
Requena
Elvira
Cabo Pariñas
Sullana
San Ignacio
P
Bretaña
Neuva Alejandria
Santa C
Paita
Chulucanas
3139
Jeberos
Piura
Huancabamba
4153
3779
Yurimaguas
Pacaya
Punta Aguja
Jaén
Bagua
Moyobamba
Dos de Mayo
Rodrigues
Bayóvar
3840
Rioja
Ucayali
Boa Fé
517
Olmos
4193
Chachapoyas
Santa Isabel
Cruzeiro do Sul
Lobos Island
Santa Cruz
Tarapoto
609
Lambayeque
Ferreñafe
Bambamarca
Saposoa
Orellana
Juruá
Chiclayo
Cajamarca
Juanjui
Contamaná
Pacasmayo
4694
E
Tiruntán
San Pedro de Lloc
Bolívar
Tocache Nuevo
Pucallpa
4333
Cajabamba
Taumatu
4487
Masisea
Trujillo
Otuzco
4947
Tayabamba
Aguaytia
Virú
Santiago de Chuco
Huacrachuco
Tingo María
Puerto Inca
5755
W
Llata
6768
Chimbote
Caraz
Huascaran
Puerto Portillo
Casma
Huaraz
La Unión
Huánuco
Bolognesi
4986
Ambo
Puesta o
Huarmey
Chiquián
Varadero
Yerupaja
5748
Oxapampa
Atalaya
Cajatambo
Cerro de Pasco
R
Pativilca
La Merced
U2brbamba
Puerto Rico
Huacho
Huaral
La Oroya
Satipo
Camisea
Chancay
Jauja
Fitzcarra
5334
Callao
Matucana
Huancayo
Pampas
Lima
Yauyos
Apurimac
Huancavelica
Huanta
Quillabamba
San Vicente de Cañete
Huamanrazo 5231
Pumasillo
Ayacucho
6246 Uruban
Chincha Alta
6271
Chincheros
Huancapi
U
Chincha Islands
Pisco
Andahuaylas
Abanca
5350
5652
Ica
Chalhuanca
5211
Palpa
Puquio
5185
Coracora
1725
Nazca
Santo Tomás
San Juan
Lampalla
Cotahu
5522
Coropo 6425
Caraveli
Chuquibam
Chala
Atico
Ocoña
Camaná
Mollend

PACIFIC

OCEAN

0°
5°S
10°S
15°S

This map shows **1/60** of the earth's surface

85°W   80°W   75°W

a b c d e f g h i j k l m

23

VENEZUELA

GUYANA

70°W · 65°W · 60°W · 55°W

Mesa de Yambi

Uainambi · San Carlos · El Mango · Caracarai · Biloku · *Kamoa Mts.* · Serra Acaraí

Jibóia · Vista Alegre · Serra Tapirapecó Curupira · São José do Anauá · Anauá · Paru de Oeste

Mitú · Cucúi · Pico de Neblina 3014 · Demini · Catrimani

Vaupés · Içana · *Negro* · Padauiri · Araça · Catrimani · *Branco* · *Jauperi* · *Mapuera* · *Trombetas*

Iuareté · Uaupés 360 · *Negro* · Tapurucuara · Calanaque · Jaú · *Jauperi* · 0°

Taracuá · Uaupés · São José · Barcelos · Tupanacca · Santa Maria · Nhamunda · Oriximiná · Óbidos

Lérida · *Vaupés* · Marcelino · Maraã · *Unini* · Moura · Airão · Santo Antônio · Uatumã · Faro · Santarém

Apaporis · La Pedrera · Japurá · Foz do Mamoriá · Fonte Boa · *Jaú* · Manacapuru · Urucará · Tupinambarama · Parintins · Belterra

Puerto Miraña · Vila Bittencourt · Santo Antônio de Içá · Alvarães · Tefé · Badajós-See · Codajás · Manaus · Itacoatiara · Amazon · Ilha · Mauês · Brasília Legal

Arica · Santa Clara · Içá · Tontantins · São Paulo de Olivença · Renascença · Piorini-See · Badajós · Anamã · Nova Olinda do Norte · Mucajá

Pebas · Caballococha · Leticia · Benjamin Constant · Boca do Mutúm · Concórdia · Tefé · Coari · Purus · Diamantina · Madeira · Borba · Mauês · Laranjal · Itaituba · San Luis de Tapajós

Caxias · *Jutaí* · .100 · Carauari · *Urucu* · Itaboca · Arumã · Prêto do Igapó Açu · Novo Aripuanã · Terra Preta · Santa Helena · 5°S

S · Jutaí · *Juruá* · Coari · Jaburu · Piranhas · Tapauá · Boca do Acará · Manicoré · Canumã · Lajinha · *Tapajós* · *Jamanxim*

Três Bocas · Liberdade · Tapauá · Boca do Acará · S · Castanhal · Sucunduri · Jacareacanga · .200 · Creporizinho · Posto Curuá

Eirunepé · Soledade · Santos Dumont · Tapauá · Aliança · Pirapetinga · Ipixuna · Saurê · Manuelzinho

Canindé · **B R A Z I L** · Mamoriá · Lábrea · Prainha Nova · Sucurundi · Barra do São Manuel

Tarauacá · Envira · Boca do Moaco · Pauini · Manjuriã · Humaitá · .100 · Jatuarana · Samaumá · Recreio · Arapari · 26

Tarauacá · Feijó · Manuel Urbano · Foz do Pauini · Boca do Curuqueté · Pôrto Velho · Calama · Jiparaná · Jacaretinga · Juruena · Gêlo · Serra do Cachimbo

Santa Rosa · Sena Madureira · 138 · *Purus* · Pôrto Alegre · Bom Jardim · 404 · Jamari · Caratianas · Tabajara · Iracema · Aripuanã · Cachimbo

Esperanza · Iaco · Rio Branco · Abunã · Manoa · Abunã · Taquaras · Jaciparaná · Ariquemes · Jarú · Aarão · Aripuanã · Serra dos Apiacás · 10°S

Balta · Canamaria · Acre · Villa Bella · Antuerpia · 200 · Pôrto do Cajueiro

Alerta · Xapuri · Puerto Rico · Madre de Dios · Riberalta · Guajará Mirim · Serra dos Pacaas Novos · Rondônia · Fontanillas · Serra do Norte · Pôrto dos Gauchos · Pôrto Atlântico · Serra dos Caiabis

a · Las Piedras · 356 · Brasileia · Cobija · Porvenir · Guajará Mirim · 800 · Presidente Hermes · Pimenta Bueno · Acampamento de Indios · Pouso Alegre · Carmem

Providencia · Iñapari · Iberia · Fortaleza · Beni · Yata · Fortaleza · Serra · José Bonifácio · Serra do Tombador · Marape · Serra Formosa

Manú · Madre de Dios · Puerto Maldonado · Puerto Heath · Cavinas · Mamoré · Costa Marques · dos · Vilhena · Juruena · Uriariti · Lucas

intuya · Madidi · 100 · San Joaquin · Baures · Santo Antônio · Parecis · Pimenteiras · Ponta da Pedra

Quince Mil · Astillero · Ixiamas · Lago Rogaguado · Itonamas · Mategua · Puerto Alegre · Santa Isabel · Campo dos Parecis

Cuzco · Auzangate 6394 · Macusani · Lago Rogagua · Magdalena · Lago de San Luis · El Carmen · La Esperanza · 702 · Diamantino · Rosario Oeste · Mato Grosso Plateau

Urcos · Sandia · Santa Ana · Reyes · San Martin · Puerto Alegre · Tapirapua · Várzea Grande · Cuiabá

mayo · Sicuani · 5852 · Carabaya · 5443 · Palomani 5999 · Apolo · San Borja · San Ignacio · Trinidad · Perseverancia · La Esperanza · Blanco · Paragua · 1095 · Mato Grosso · 15°S

Ayaviri · Azángaro · Huancané · Llanos de Mojos · Loreto · La Noria · Salinas · Pôrto Esperidião · Cáceres · Poconé · Jaciara · Mato Grosso Plateau

Yauri · Juliaca · Puerto Acosta · 6388 · Santa Ana · BOLIVIA · Mato Grosso · 1150 · Pôrto Esperidião

5641 · Lake Titicaca · Ancohuma · Ben · Puerto Marquez · Ascensión · Concepción · Serra Aguapei · Descalvados · São Lourenço

Puno · Achacachi · Coroico · Chuluman · Illimani 6402 · Todos Santos · San Javier · San Ignacio · San Matías · Laguna Uberaba · Pôrto Jofre

La Paz 3577 · Guaqui · Viacha · Cochabamba · Puerto Villarroel · Montero · El Cerro · El Carmen · San José de Chiquitos · Laguna Concepción · Itiquira · Pedro Gomes

Moquegua · Calacoto · Corocoro · Sicasica · 5035 · Portachuelo · 614 · Cordillera · Santa Cruz · Serra de Santiago · Amolar

Arica 70°W · Sajama 6542 · Oruro · Uncía · Aiquile · Valle Grande · Comarapa · Santa Cruz · Llanos de Chiquitos · Robore · 60°W · 55°W

n o p q r s t u v w x y z

28

0 · 100 · 200 · 300 miles · Average linear scale · 0 · 100 · 200 · 300 · 400 · 500 Km

VENEZUELA

Caura
2100
Mayupa
2950
1890
La Escalera
Puricama
Cavanayen
Arabelo
Paraguá
Cerro Jaua
Mesa del
Meseta
Santa Elena
de Uairen
Catisimiña
Caron
Gran
Sabana
Roraima
2810
2040
Tumatumari
Rockstone
New
Amsterdam
Linden
Totness
Paramaribo
Mana
Sinnamary
Nieuw
Nickerie
Groningen
Moengo
St. Laurent
Kourou
Cayenne
Paranam
Brokopondo
Apoera
Apatou
Montsinery
Kaw
Régina
Cabo Orange

Serra Parima
Serra Curupira
Serra Tapirapecó
1047

Matturuca
1240
Depósito
Uaricoera
Boa Vista
Lethem
Kanuku Mts.
Dadanawa
Oronoque
Isherton
Biloku
Kamoa Mts.
734
Serra Acaraí

SURINAME
Prof. van
Blommestein
Lake
Aurora
694
Juliana Top
1230
1026
Bakrakondre
Grand
Santi
French
Guiana
Tapanahoni
Patience
710
St. Georges
Oiapoque
Vila Velha
Cunani
Calçoene
Amapá
Maracá
Cabo Norte

Serra do Apiau
Tacutu
Caracaraí
Anauá
New
Papaí
Maloca
Velha
Serra
690
Tumucumaque
882
Pôrto Poet
Meriruma
635
Serra Lombarda
Lorenço
Aporema
Ferreira Gomes

São José
do Anauá
Catrimani
Branco
Trombetas
Maloca
Malaripó
315
Acampamento
Jari
Serra
do Navio
Terezinha
Araguari
Pôrto
Grande
Janaucú

Calanaque
Jauaperi
Mapuera
Arere
Paru de Oeste
Paru
Barraca
da Boca
228
Monte
Dourado
Boca do
Jari
Macapá
Pôrto
Santana
Canal
Queimada
Caviana
Mexiana
Chaves
Afuá
Marajó Bay
Cabo
Maguarinho

Barcelos
Tupanacca
Moura
Unin
Culuni
Santa
Maria
Nhamunda
Oriximiná
Óbidos
Mulata
Ramos
305
Almeirim
Grande de Gurupá
Anajás
Cachoeira
do Arari
Marajó
Souré
Vi
Castanh

Tefé
Lago
Badajós
Airão
Santo Antônio
Urucará
Faro
Alenquer
Prainha
Monte
Alegre
Amazon
Pôrto
de Moz
Breves
Abaetetuba
Moju
Belém
Pará

Piorini
Lago
Piorini
Manacapuru
Manaus
Itacoatiara
100
Tupinambarama
Parintins
Belterra
Santarém
Curua-Uná
Pacoval
Victoria
Belo Monte
Portel
Cametá
Mocajuba
Tomé-Açu
Capim

Coari
Badajós
Anama
Nova Olinda
do Norte
Ilha
Maués
Brasília
Legal
Altamira
Caima
229
Tucuruí
Pindobal
Gurupizinh

Itaboca
Codajós
Purus
Diamantina
Madeira
Borba
Mucajá
Maués
Laranjal
Itaituba
Rurópolis
Iriri
Pôrto
Alegre
Sem-Tripa
Jatobá
Serra dos Carajás
399
Jatobal
São
Félix
Iting

Jaburu
Tapauá
Piranhas
Arumã
Terra Preta
Canumã
San Luis
de Tapajós
Santa
Helena
Paga-
Conta
Forte
Veneza
José
Rodrigues
Marabá
São João
de Araguai

Aliança
Boca do Acará
Manicoré
Novo
Aripuanã
Canumã
Lajinha
Tapajós
Posto
Curuá
Araras
São Sebastião
Carajás
Tocantinóp
Xambioá

Lábrea
Castanhal
Jacareacanga
Sauré
Creporizinho
Cajueiro
Jojoca
Posto
Cocraimore
Xingu
São Félix
do Xingu
Tucumã
Xinguara
Araguaína
Babaçuland

Pirapetinga
Humaitá
100
Prainha Nova
Sucunduri
Barra do
São Manuel
Manuelzinho
Curua
Fresco
Gorotiré
Garimpo
Cumaru
Redenção
Guarai
Araguacema
Pec
Alfon

Jamari
Jatuarana
Samaumã
Recreio
500
Araparí
Gêlo
Serra do Cachimbo
Cachimbo
Campo
Alegre
Conceição
do Araguaia
Santana do Araguaia
Barreira
do Campo
Miracema
do Norte
24

Calama
Pôrto
Velho
Jaciparaná
Caratianas
Tabajara
Iracema
Aarão
Aripuanã
Fontanillas
Plara-Açu
Xingu
São José
do Xingu
Campo de
Diauarum
Santa
Teresinha
Paraíso do Norte
de Goiás
Cristalandia
Fátima
Pôrto
Nacion

Ariquemes
Jaru
Rondônia
Presidente
Hermes
Acampamento
de Indios
Pôrto do
Cajueiro
Serra do Norte
Posto Alto
Manissaua
São Félix
Gurupi
Natividade
Tocanti

Antuerpia
800
242
Pimenta
Bueno
Pôrto
dos Gauchos
Pôrto
Atlântico
Caiabis
Xingu
Pôrto
dos Meinacos
Pôrto dos
Meinacos
Mortes
186
Gurupi
240

Fortaleza
Serra dos Pacaas Novos
Pouso Alegre
Serra do Tombador
José
Bonifácio
Uariri
Marape
Lucas
Carmem
Pôrto Artur
Mato Grosso
Plateau
635
Peixe
Araguaçu
São Miguel
do Araguaia
Bandeirante
Porangatu
Alvorada
Alto Paraíso
de Goiá
156

Costa Marques
Magdalena
San Joaquin
Mategua
Santo Antônio
Vilhena
Juruena
Ponta da Pedra
Campo dos Parecis
Serra dos Parecis
El Carmen
Puerto
Alegre
Santa Isabél
Pimenteiras

BOLIVIA

Lago de
San Luis

BRAZIL

This map shows 1/60 of the earth's surface

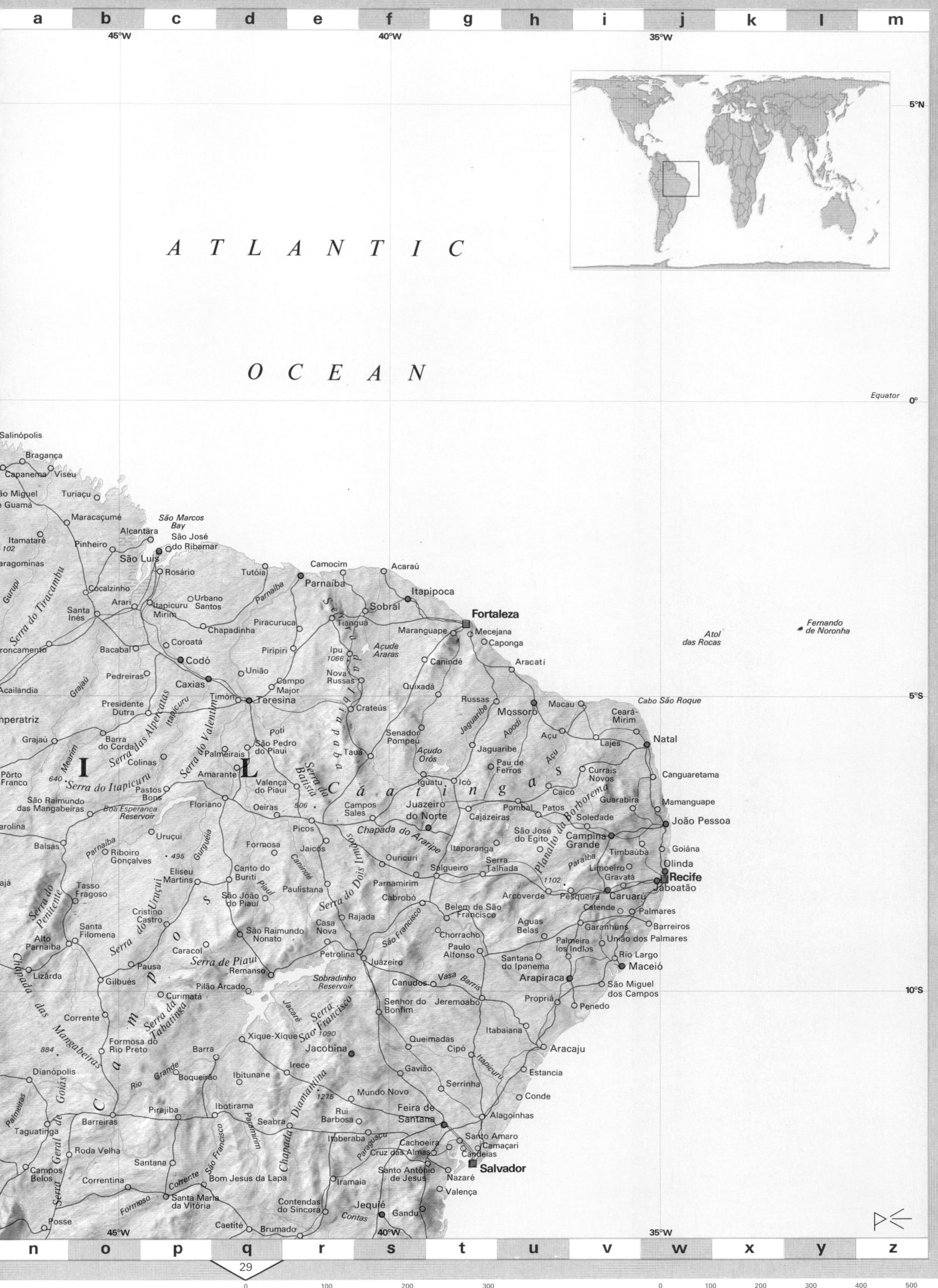

A T L A N T I C

O C E A N

Average linear scale

a b c d e f g h i j k l m

25

PERU

BOLIVIA

ARGENTINA

PARAGUAY

CHILE

URUGUAY

PACIFIC OCEAN

15°S
20°S
25°S
30°S
35°S

70°W   65°W   60°W

Abancay Chalhuanca Urcos Auzangate 6394 Macusani Sicuani Ixiamas Lago Rogagua Santa Ana El Carmen Puerto Alegre Ponta da Pedra
5211 Santo Tomás Sandia 5852 Reyes Rapulo San Ignacio Blanco La Esperanza Serra de Huanchaca Guaporé Campo dos Parecis 702 Diamantino
Yauri Ayaviri 5443 Apolo Santa Ana Apere Trinidad Río Miguel Perseverancia La Noria 1095 Mato Grosso Várzea Grande Rosari Oeste
Cotahuasi Huancané Puerto Acosta San Borja Llanos de Mojos Loreto Ascensión San Martín La Noria Descalvados Tapirapua Cuia
Coropuna 6425 Chivay Juliaca Puno Illampu 6485 Ancohuma 6388 Puerto Marquez San Javier San Ignacio Lagoa Uberaba Pôrto Esperidião Cáceres Poconé Cuiabá
Chuquibamba Ampato 6310 Chacani 6075 5822 Arequipa 2304 5486 La Paz 3577 Viacha Illmani 6402 Coroico Concepción San José de Chiquitos El Cerro Laguna Concepción 1150 Pôrto Jofre
Ocoña Camaná Mollendo Moquegua 5593 5781 Guaqui 5213 Calacoto Todos Santos Puerto Villarroel Montero Portachuelo Santa Cruz Santo Corazón Roboré Grand
Ilo Tarata Tacora 5988 Charana Umala Sicasica Quillacollo Cochabamba Comarapa Llanos de Chiquitos Serra de Santiago Santa Ana Pantanal
Arica Putre Guallatiri 6060 Sajama 6542 Corque Oruro 5383 Totora 3200 Río Valle Grande Banados del Izozog Amolar Taquari
Tacna Cuya Nama Sabaya 5869 Lago de Coipasa Challapata 5023 Sucre 2790 Tarabuco Río Grande Cabezas Yuti Fortín Ravelo 727 Fortín Max Paredes Puerto Suárez Corumbá
Pisagua Huara Sillajuay 5995 Río Mulatos 3976 Potosí Lagunillas Charagua Patapeti Fortín Gral. Eugenio Garay Pôrto Esperança Aquídauana
Iquique 5218 Salar de Uyuni Uyuni Cord. de Chichas Vitichi Azurduy Camiri 998 Timane Bahía Negra Guaicurus Aquidau
Pintados Collahuasi 5320 5739 Cotagaita Pilaya Villa Montes Fortín Gral. Fortín Madrejón Fuerte Olimpo Bonito Jardir
Lagunas 1590 Ollague 5865 Alota San Pablo 5695 Tupiza Tarija Yacuiba Garrapatal Pôrto Murtinho Bella Vista Ponta Pora 700
Tocopilla Quillagua 1825 Conchi Tocorpuri 5833 San Pablo Mojo Villazón La Quiaca 5029 Fortín Hernandarias Mariscal Estigarribia Filadelfia Puerto Piñasco Aquidabán
Maria Elena 2293 Chuquicamata Calama Licancabur 5921 Abra Pampa Rosario Bermejo Dr. Pedro P. Peña Verde Fortín Juan de Zalazar Puerto Sastre San Pedro Ypé J
Mejillones San Pedro de Atacama Carmen Alto 6050 Humahuaca San Ramón de la Nueva Orán Embarcación Juan Sola Los Blancos Fortín General Diaz Pozo Colorado Monte Concepción Lima
Antofagasta Salar de Atacama 5890 Catua Salinas Grandes Libertador Gral. San Martín Ingeniero Guillermo Nueva Juárez Lindo San Pedro Coronel Oviedo
Varillas Augusta Victoria Pular 6225 5594 Chani 6200 San Salvador de Jujuy San Pedro Las Lomitas Pozo del Tigre Benjamín Aceval San Estanisla
Caleta el Cobre Socompa 6031 San Antonio de los Cobres Salar de Pocitos General Güemes Teuco Villa Hayes Asunción
Paposo Los Vientos Llullaillaco 6723 Salar de Arizaro Cachi 6720 Salta Joaquín V. González Palo Santo Clorinda Paraguari
Taltal Salar Punta Negra Antofalla 6440 Mojones 5990 Cachi Metán Rosario de la Frontera Pampa de los Guanacos Castelli Pirané Tres Isletas Villarrica
Santa Catalina 5700 Salar de Antofalla Colorados 6049 Antofagasta de la Sierra Cafayate Monte Quemado Formosa Caazapá
Diego de Almagro El Salvador 5070 Nevada 6400 Santa María San Miguel de Tucumán Chaco Austral Presidencia Roque Sâenz Peña Pilar San Juan Bautista
Chañaral Ojos del Salado 6880 4920 Hondo-Reservoir Termes de Río Hondo Tintina Charata Presidencia de la Plaza Resistencia San Ignacio Encarnac
Caldera Copiapó 6080 Pissis 6858 Fiambalá Belén Concepción Andalgalá Santiago del Estero La Banda Villa Angela Corrientes Posad
Castilla Bonete 6872 Tinogasta Salar de Pipanaco Catamarca Villa San Martín Añatuya Villa Guillermina Empredrado Apóstoles
Huasco 5830 Jagüe Mejicana 6250 Chumbicha Frias Bandera Tostado Reconquista Goya Bella Vista Santo Tomé
Vallenar Cabo Bascuñan Toro 6380 Chilecito Recreo Pinto Vera Chalchaqui Curuzú Cuatiá Mercedes São B
Domeyko Villa Unión La Rioja Villa Ojo de Aqua Salado Esquina Yapeyú Uruguaiana
La Higuera Guandacol Chamical Cruz del Eje Dèan Funes Ceres San Cristóbal Curuzú Cuatiá Bella Unión Quarai
La Serena Rivadavia Tortolas 5332 San José de Jáchal San Agustín de Valle Fértil Laguna Chiquita Morteros San Justo La Paz Chajari Artigas
Coquimbo Olivares 6262 5510 Patquia Chepes Salsacate Alta Gracia 2880 Rafaela Esperanza Santa Fé Concordia Salto
Ovalle Zanjón Córdoba San Francisco Paraná Villaguay Tacuarembó
Maitencillo Combarbalá 5620 San Juan Villa Media Agua Villa Dolores Quines Oliva Río Tercero Villa Maria Diamante Victoria Concepción del Uruguay Paysandú
Illapel Mercedario 6770 Pampa de las Salinas Santa Rosa del Conlara Río Cuarto Cañada de Gómez Gualeguaychu Negro-Reservoir
Salamanca Chincolco Aconcagua 6959 Mendoza San Luis 1599 La Carlota Rosario Gualeguay Mercedes Florida
Valparaíso San Felipe La Calera Tupungato 6800 San Martín La Paz Justo Daract Vicuña Mackenna Vanado Tuerto San Nicolas San Pedro Concordia Canelone
Santiago San Bernardo 5830 Tunuyán Mercedes Rufino Junin Luján Martinez Buenos Aires Carmelo Cardona
San Antonio Rancagua 5290 Buena Esperanza Huinca Renancó General Villegas Lincoln Chacabuco Chivilcoy Lobos Montevide
Rapel 5160 San Rafael Diamante Atuel Salado Unión La Plata Magdalena
Santa Cruz San Fernando 4860 General Alvear Curico Constitución

This map shows 1/60 of the earth's surface

n o p q r s t u v w x y z

30

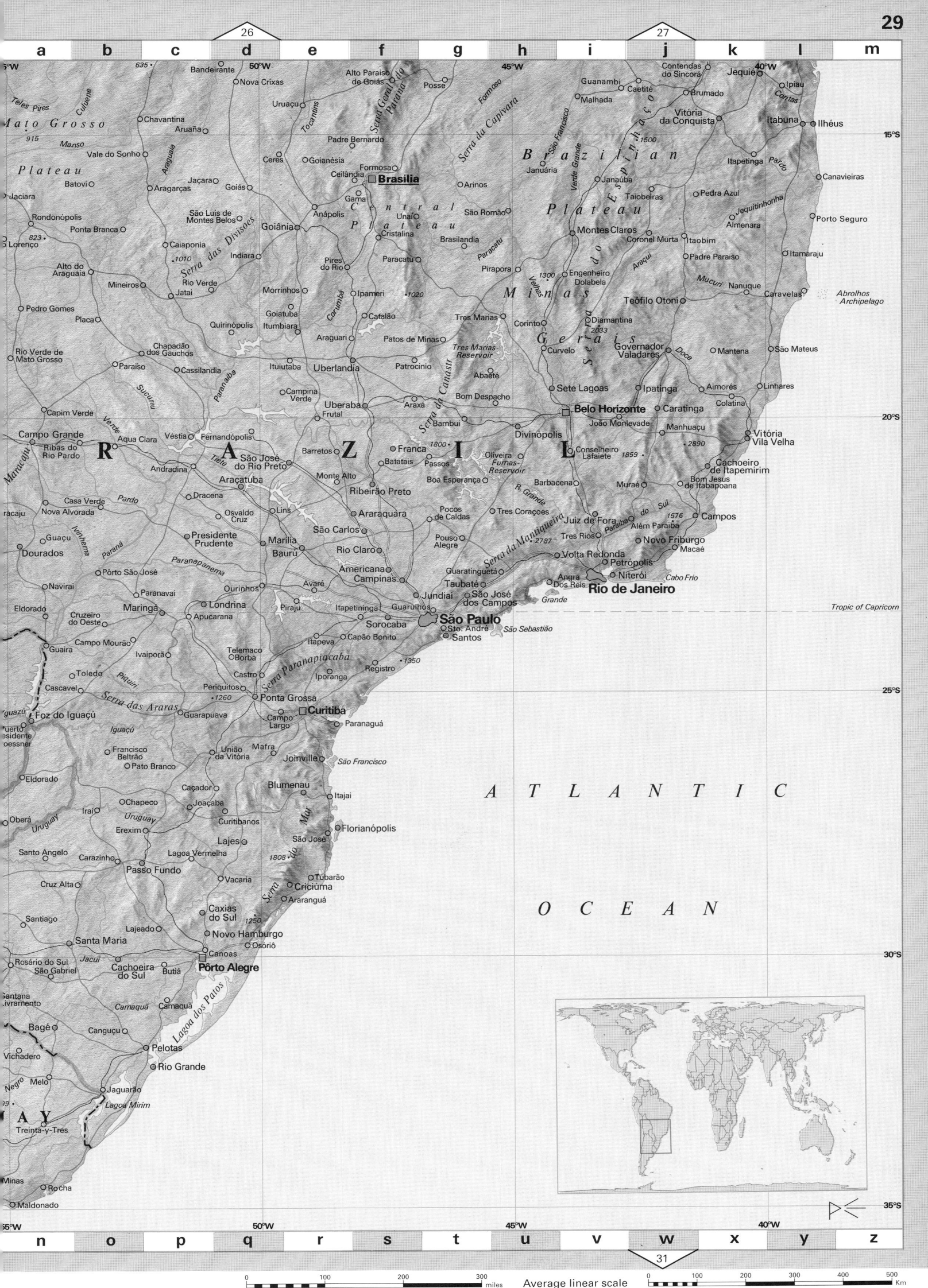

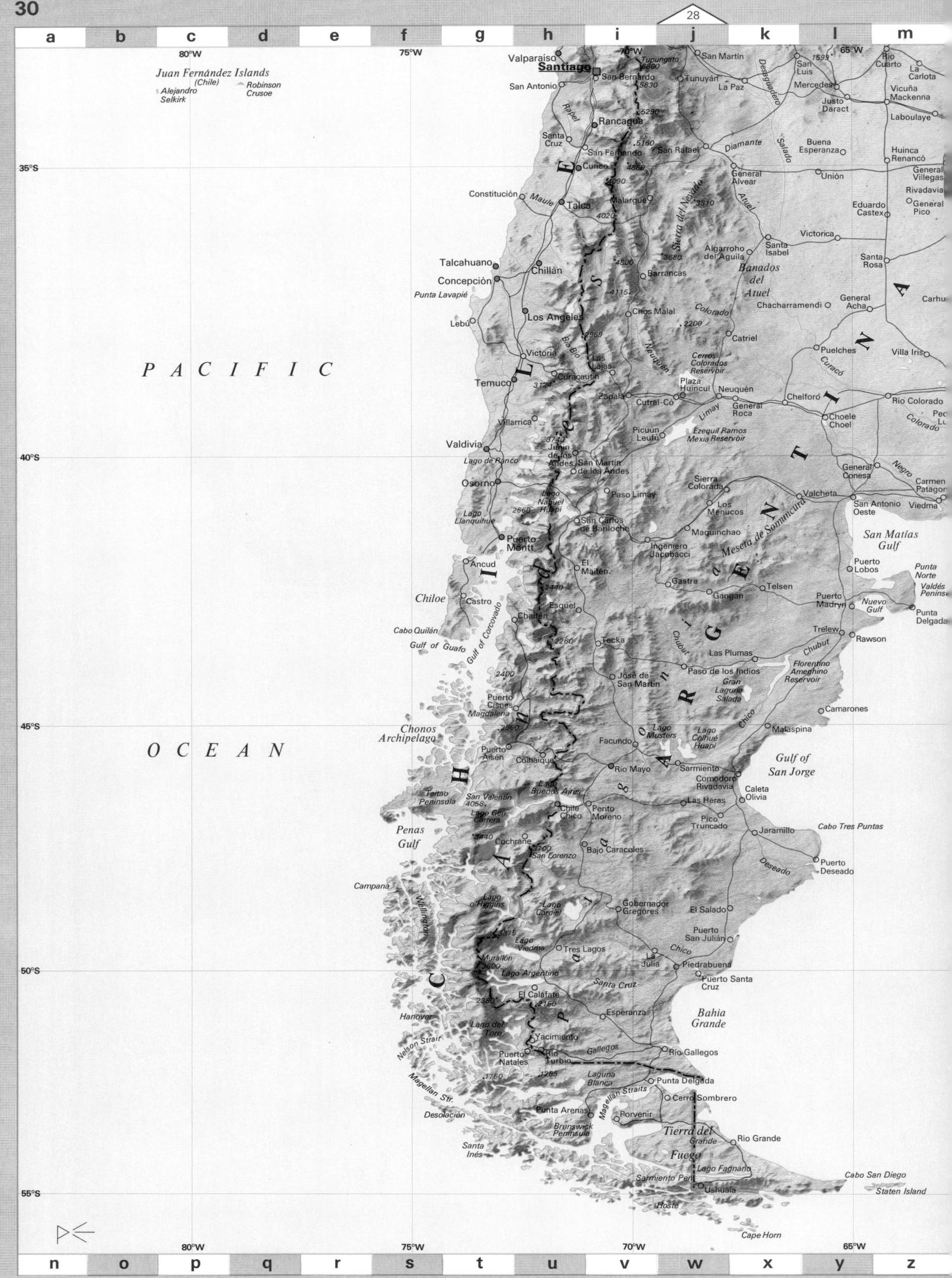

80°W   75°W   70°W   65°W

Juan Fernández Islands
(Chile)
Alejandro   Robinson
Selkirk   Crusoe

Valparaíso
Santiago
San Bernardo
San Antonio
Tupungato
6800
San Martin
Desaguadero
1599
Rio
Cuarto
La
Carlota
Vicuña
Mackenna
San Luis
Tunuyán
La Paz
Mercedes
Justo
Daract
Laboulaye

Rapel
Rancagua
5290
5830
5160
Santa
Cruz
San Fernando
San Rafael
Diamante
Salado
Buena
Esperanza
Huinca
Renancó

35°S
Curicó
4869
4090
General
Alvear
Unión
General
Villegas

Constitución
Maule
Talca
Malargue
4020
Atuel
Eduardo
Castex
General
Pico

3510
Victorica
Rivadavia

Sierra del Nevado
Santa
Isabel
Santa
Rosa

Talcahuano
Chillán
4800
Algarroho
del Aguila
Barrancas
3680
Bañados
del
Atuel
Chacharramendi
General
Acha
Carhu

Concepción
Punta Lavapié
4115
Colorado
2200
Catriel
Puelches
Villa Iris

Lebu
Los Angeles
Chos Malal
Cerros
Colorados
Reservoir

Bío Bío
2969
Victoria
Las
Lajas
Neuquén
Plaza
Huincul
Neuquén
Chelforó
Río Colorado

PACIFIC
Temuco
3124
Curacautín
Zapala
Cutral-Có
General
Roca
Choele
Choel
Colorado

Villarrica
Limay
Picún
Leufú
Ezequil Ramos
Mexia Reservoir

Valdivia
3740
Junín
de los
Andes
San Martín
de los Andes
Paso Limay
Sierra
Colorada
General
Conesa
Negro
Carmen
Patagon

40°S
Lago de Ranco
Los
Menucos
Valcheta
San Antonio
Oeste
Viedma

Osorno
Lago
Nahuel
Huapí
2660
Maquinchao
San Matías
Gulf

Lago
Llanquihue
San Carlos
de Bariloche
Ingeniero
Jacobacci
Gangan
Telsen
Puerto
Lobos
Punta
Norte
Valdés
Penins

Puerto
Montt
Meseta de Somuncurá
Puerto
Madryn
Nuevo
Gulf
Punta
Delgada

Ancud
El
Maitén
3440
Gastre

Chiloe
Castro
Esquel
Chaitén
Paso de los Indios
Gran
Laguna
Salada
Florentino
Ameghino
Reservoir

Cabo Quilán
Gulf of Corcovado
2260
Tecka
Chubut
Chubut
Rawson

Gulf of Guafo
2400
José de
San Martín
Las Plumas
Camarones

45°S
Chonos
Archipelago
Puerto
Cisnes
Magdalena
2960
Lago
Musters
Lago
Colhué
Huapi
Chico
Malaspina
Gulf of
San Jorge

OCEAN
Puerto
Aisén
Colhaique
Facundo
Sarmiento
Comodoro
Rivadavia
Caleta
Olivia

Río Mayo
Las Heras
Pico
Truncado
Cabo Tres Puntas

San Valentín
4058
Lago
Buenos Aires
Chile
Chico
Perito
Moreno
Jaramillo
Deseado
Puerto
Deseado

Taitao
Peninsula
Lago Gen.
Carrera
3410
Cochrane

Penas
Gulf
3700
San Lorenzo
Bajo Caracoles

Campana
Gobernador
Gregores
El Salado
Puerto
San Julián

Wellington
Lago
o'Higgins
Lago
Cardiel
Chico
La
Julia
Piedrabuena

Murallón
3600
5375
Lago
Viedma
Tres Lagos
Santa Cruz
Puerto Santa
Cruz

50°S
Lago Argentino
El Calafate
2150
Esperanza
Bahia
Grande

Hanover
2380
Lago del
Toro
Yacimiento
Gallegos
Río Gallegos

Nelson Strait
Puerto
Natales
Río
Turbio
1285
Punta Delgada

1750
Laguna
Blanca
Cerro Sombrero

Magellan Str.
Punta Arenas
Porvenir
Tierra del
Fuego
Grande
Río Grande

Desolación
Brunswick
Peninsula
Magellan Straits
Lago Fagnano
Cabo San Diego

Santa
Inés
Sarmiento Pen.
Ushuaia
Staten Island

55°S
Hoste
Cape Horn

80°W   75°W   70°W   65°W

This map shows 1/60 of the earth's surface

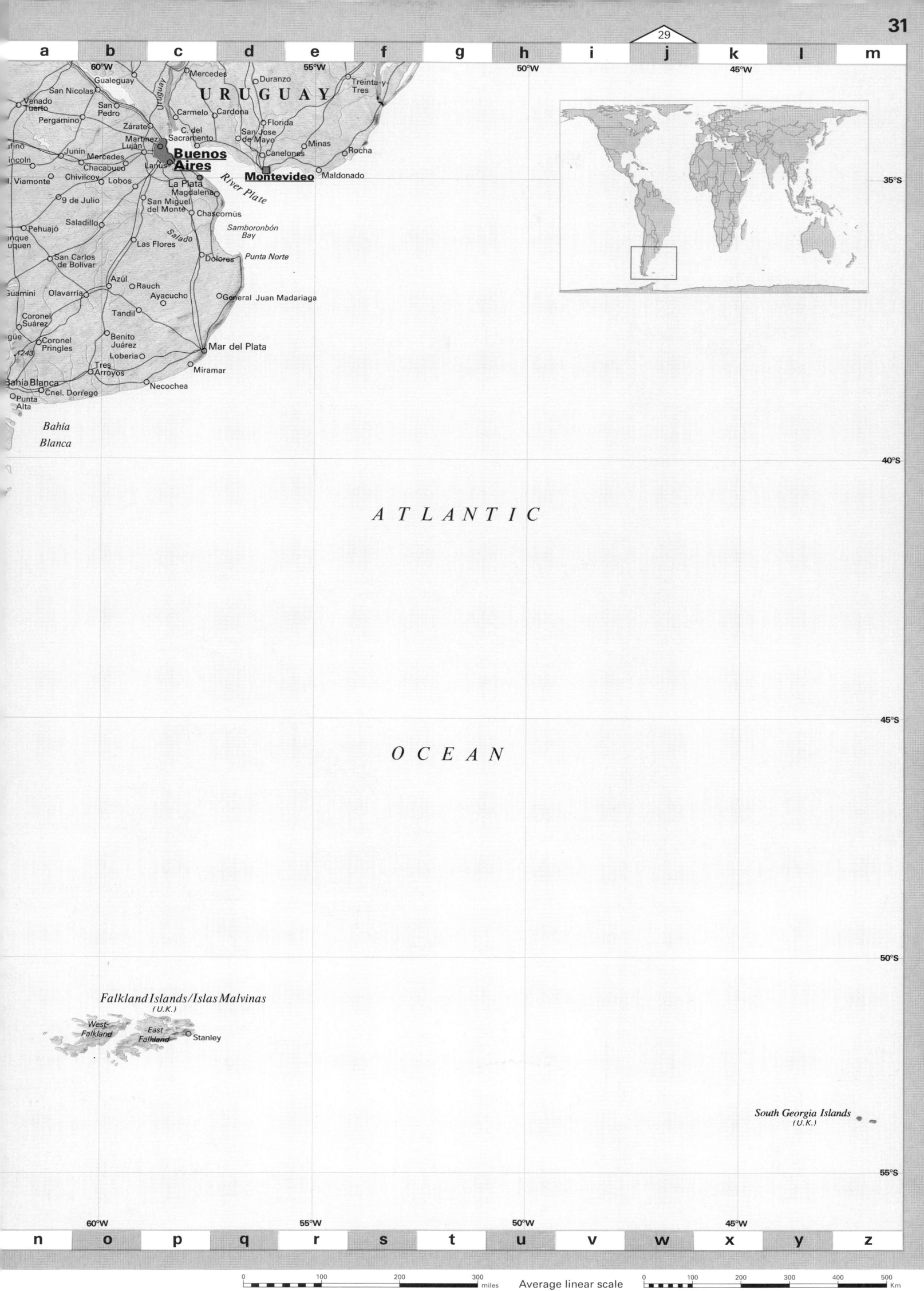

60°W   55°W   50°W   45°W

Mercedes

U R U G U A Y

Gualeguay   Duranzo   Treinta-y-Tres

San Nicolas

Venado Tuerto   San Pedro   Carmelo   Cardona

Pergamino   Zárate   C. del Sacramento   Florida

Martinez   San Jose de Mayo

fino   Junín   Mercedes   Luján   Minas

Lincoln   Chacabueo   **Buenos Aires**   Canelones   Rocha

Lanús

I. Viamonte   Chivilcoy   Lobos   **Montevideo**   Maldonado

9 de Julio   La Plata   Magdalena

35°S

San Miguel del Monte   *River Plate*

Saladillo   Chascomús

Pehuajó   *Samboronbón Bay*

nque   San Carlos de Bolivar   Las Flores   Dolores   *Punta Norte*

uquen

Guamini   Azúl   Rauch   Olavarria   Ayacucho   General Juan Madariaga

Coronel Suárez   Tandil

gue   Coronel Pringles   Benito Juárez   Mar del Plata

1243   Loberia

Tres Arroyos   Miramar

Bahía Blanca   Cnel. Dorrego   Necochea

Punta Alta

Bahía Blanca

40°S

A T L A N T I C

45°S

O C E A N

50°S

Falkland Islands / Islas Malvinas
(U.K.)

West-Falkland   *East Falkland*   Stanley

55°S

South Georgia Islands
(U.K.)

0   100   200   300 miles   Average linear scale   0   100   200   300   400   500 Km

Greenland
(Denmark)

Scoresby Sound

Scoresbysund

Jan Mayen
(Norway)

70°N

20°W   15°W   10°W   5°W   0°

A   R   C   T

Denmark Strait

O   C   E   E

Cape Horn

Arctic Circle

Fontur

Isafjördur

Húna Bay

Akureyri

ICELAND

•1765

65°N

Breidhi Fjord

1400

Vatnajökull

Djúpivogur

Akranes

2119 •

Faxa Bay

Reykjavik

Keflavik

Reykjanes

Faeroe Islands
(Denmark)

60°N

Shetland
Islands

Lerwick

A   T   L   A   N   T   I   C

Orkney
Islands

Cape
Wrath

Pentland Firth

Thurso

Lewis

Minch

Hebrides

Moray Firth

90

Skye

Inverness

Elgin

Loch
Ness

Highlands

•1309

Aberdeen

S C O T L A N D

Fort William •1343

N   O   R

Mull

Perth

Dundee

Stirling

Edinburgh

Islay

Glasgow

Berwick
upon
Tweed

GREAT BRITAIN

Ayr

Newcastle
upon Tyne

55°N

North Channel

AND

Sunderland

S   E

Londonderry

Carlisle

NORTHERN
IRELAND

Belfast

Middlesbrough

NORTHERN IRELAND

Donegal
Bay

Lough Neagh

Portadown

Sligo

Isle of
Man

Douglas

Leeds

York

Kingston upon Hull

Blackpool

Dundalk

Irish

Manchester

Westport

IRISH

Sea

Liverpool

Sheffield

Athlone

Holyhead

Stoke-on-
Trent

Galway

Anglesey

Derby

Nottingham

Dublin

•1085

Norwich

886

Roscrea

Leicester

Shannon

Arklow

Birmingham

Coventry

Cambridge

REPUBLIC

Limerick

Wexford

WALES

Ipswich

926

Aberystwyth

Killarney

Waterford

Fishguard

Oxford

Luton

Cork

Swansea

Thames

Southend-
on-Sea

O   C   E   A   N

Cape Clear

St. George's Channel

Cardiff

Reading

London

Dover

Ostend

Bristol

Bristol Channel

Southampton

Dover

Ghen

Land's End

Penzance

Exeter

Bournemouth

Brighton

Isle of
Wight

Strait of

Calais

Lille

Valenciennes

Plymouth

English Channel

Abbeville

50°N

Cherbourg

Amiens

St. Quen

Guernsey

Le Havre

Rouen

Compiè

Channel Islands
(U.K.)

Jersey

Caen

Seine

Évreux

Gulf of St. Malo

Granville

Paris

Brest

St. Brieuc

Alençon

Chartres

F   R   A   N   C

Rennes

Le Mans

Orleans

Lorient

Loire

Auxerre

20°W   15°W   10°W   5°W   0°

St. Nazaire

Angers

Tours

Nantes

This map shows 1/60 of the earth's surface

5°E 10°E 15°E 20°E 25°E 30°E

North Cape 70°N

I C

N

Söröya Hammerfest Cape Kiberg
Vesterålen Senja Tromsö Skibotn Alta 1139 Lakselv 623 Tana Tana Kirkenes Pečenga
Lofoten Islands Andöya Langöya 1590 Kebnekaise Muonio Lake Inari Ivalo 636 Lotte Paduňskoye More
Vest Fjord Bognes Narvik 2117 Kiruna Kolari Torne Kemijärvi Kuusamo RUSSIA
Bodö 1906 2090 Sarek Gällivare 807 211 Tornio Kemi Lake Pyaozero
Svartisen 1599 Lönsdal Hornavan 697 Lule Luleå Raahe Oulu Kalevala 263
Mo-i-Rana 1915 1609 Arjeplog Pite Skellefteå Kajaani Lake Pielis Reboly 65°N
Mösjöen Lake Udd Skellefte Lycksele 355 Kuopio
Vikna Kvigtind 1703 Storuman Ume Umeå Vaasa 125 Kyyjärvi FINLAND 239 Joensuu 279
Steinkjer Grong 1390 Åre Strömsund Örnsköldsvik Jakobstad Kökkola Lake Oulu Sortavala
Kristiansund Trondheim Trondheimsfjord 1796 Östersund Kramfors 530 Ångermann Jyväskylä Lake Saimaa Imatra Lake Ladoga
Molde Åndalsnes Oppdal Lake Stor 1009 Sveg Ljungan Sundsvall Pori Näsi Lake Päijänne Tampere Lappeenranta
Ålesund Dombås 2183 Tynset Ljusnan 430 Hudiksvall Parkano Hämeenlinna Lahti Vyborg
Målöy 2038 2469 Galdhöpiggen Övre Årdal Särna 774 Söderhamn Vantaa Kotka
Sognefjord Gudvangen 1862 Lillehammer Lake Mjösa Hamar Klar Gävle Turku Helsinki (Helsingfors) Espoo St. Petersburg 179
Bergen 1660 Eidfjord Grungedal Drammen Gol Kongsvinger Borlänge Dal Uppsala Hankö Gulf of Finland Narva Kolpino
Hardangerfjord Hönefoss Oslo Karlstad Örebro Västerås Mariehamn 62 Tallinn Chudovo
Haugesund Evje Larvik Fredrikstad Lake Vänern Lake Mälar Stockholm Åland Islands (Finland) Hiiumaa ESTONIA Luga Novgorod
Stavanger Arendal Uddevalla Lidköping Lake Vättern Linköping Norrtälje Saaremaa Tartu Lake Peipus (L. Chud) Lake Ilmen
Egersund Kristiansand Skagerrak Cape Skagen Göteborg Borås 377 Jönköping Västervik Visby Gulf of Riga Pärnu 145 Valga Pskov Ostrov Staraja Russa Lovat
Frederikshavn Gotland Ventspils Riga 311 Daugav'pils Velíkije Luki
Ålborg Kattegat Halmstad Växjö Kalmar Öland Liepāja LATVIA Jekabpils Dvina Nevel' RUSSIA
Jutland 173 Randers Århus Helsingborg Kristianstad Karlskrona Klaipeda Siauliai 228 Panevėžys Opochka
DENMARK Helsingör Malmö Bornholm (Denmark) Neman LITHUANIA Postavy Polotsk 259 Vitebsk
Holstebro Copenhagen (Kobenhavn) Zealand 207 Ystad Gulf of Danzig Kaliningrad RUSSIA Sovetsk Kaunas Vilnius Molodetschno 342 Orsha Smolensk 55°N
Esbjerg Kolding Odense Fünen The Sound Chernyakhovsk Lida Minsk Borisov
Svendborg Lolland Falster Cape Arkona Rügen Slupsk Gdynia Gdansk Suwalki Grodno Baranovichi Mogilev
Flensburg Kiel Bay Stralsund Pomeranian Bay Koszalin Elblag Olsztyn Lomza Bialystok Slonim BELARUS Krichev
Heligoland Bight Lübeck Bay 56 Greifswald Szczecinek Tczew Vistula Slutsk 192 Dovsk
Wilhelmshaven Bremerhaven Kiel Lübeck Rostock Wismar Neubrandenburg Schwerin Szczecin Stargard Bydgoszcz Grudziadz 312 Pripet Gomel
Frisian Islands Emden Hamburg Elbe 176 Torun Bug Marshes Klintsy
Groningen Leeuwarden Bremen Oshabrück Hannover (Hannover) Wittenberge Neuruppin Gorzow-Wlkp. Wloclawek Poznan Warta Kutno Warsaw (Warszawa) Siedlce Brest Pinsk Mozyr
Emmen HERLANDS Amsterdam Enschede Osnabrück Brunswick (Braunschweig) Potsdam Berlin Frankfurt Oder POLAND Lodz Kalisz 289 Lublin Kovel Chernigov
Utrecht Arnhem Münster Dessau Magdeburg 162 Leszno Piotrków Radom Lutsk Novograd-Volynskiy Nezhin
Rotterdam Eindhoven GERMANY Dortmund Göttingen Halle Leipzig Cottbus Legnica Wroclaw Czestochowa Kielce Zamosc Rovno 252 Zhitomir Kiev (Kyyiv)
Antwerp (Antwerpen) Düsseldorf 840 Kassel Weimar Erfurt Gera Dresden Elbe (Labe) 240 Kiev Reservoir
Brussels (Bruxelles) Essen Aachen Cologne (Köln) Bonn 689 774 983 Chemnitz 1603 Hradec Králové Walbrzych Katowice Krakow Przemysl L'viv UKRAINE
GIUM Liège Charleroi Koblenz Bad Hersfeld Frankfurt Plauen 244 Karlovy Vary Kolin Olomouc Ostrava Bielsko-Biala Rzeszow Ternopol 383 Vinnitsa
LUXEMBOURG Trier 816 Wiesbaden Würzburg Bamberg Prague (Praha) Plzen Ceske Budejovice 1457 CZECH REPUBLIC Uihlava Brno Znojmo 1490 Zilina 2663 Gerlachovsky 346 Ivano-Frankovsk Kolomyya Mogilev-Podol'skiy Cherkassy
Luxembourg Thionville Mannheim Nuremberg (Nürnberg) Olomouc 1725 Zakopane SLOVAKIA 2043 Presov Košice Uzgorod Dniester Kamenets-Podol'skiy 50°N
Metz Saarbrücken Karlsruhe Regensburg Danube Passau 1592 Zvolen Mukachevo Chernovtsy Belaya Tserkov
Nancy Stuttgart Augsburg Memmingen Munich (München) Linz Danube Vác Györ HUNGARY Miskolc Nyiregyhaza Baia Mare 2305 Pietrosu Botosani Suceava Pervomaysk
Reims Chaumont Mulhouse Freiburg Lake Constance 1493 Zugspitze 2963 Salzburg 2075 AUSTRIA Dachstein 2996 Vienna (Wien) Bratislava Budapest Satu Mare Debrecen ROMANIA Balti MOLDOVA
Troyes Dijon Besançon Basle Zürich SWITZERLAND Inn 2713 Innsbruck Leoben Danube Orgejev South Bug 30°E
5°E 10°E 15°E 20°E 25°E

0 100 200 300 miles
Average linear scale
0 100 200 300 400 500 Km

BALTIC SEA Gulf of Bothnia Gulf of Riga Lappland NORWAY SWEDEN

This map shows 1/60 of the earth's surface

a b c d e f g h i j k l m

Dresden 15°E · Wałbrzych · Wrocław · 20°E · Kielce · Zamość · Lutsk · Rovno · Korosten · *Kiev Reservoir* · Nezhin · Sumy · 35°E
Elbe · Hradec · Częstochowa · Vistula · L'viv · Novograd · Zhitomir · **Kiev** · Priluki · Akhtyrka
Prague · Králové · P O L A N D · Rzeszow · Przemyśl · Volynskiy · (Kyyiv) · Lubny · **Khar'kov**
(Praha) · 1603 · Katowice · Krakow · 20°E · U K R A I N E · Poltava · Valki
CZECH REPUBLIC · Ostrava · Bielsko-Biala · ·1490 · Stryy · Ternopol · Belaya · Tserkov · Cherkassy · Kremenchugskoye · Pereshchepino
Izen · Olomouc · 1725 · Zakopane · Khmel'nitskiy · Vinnitsa · Reservoir · Kremenchug
Jihlava · Žilina · Gerlachovsky · 1349a · Ivano · Podol'skiy · Uman' · Znamenka · Novomoskovsk
Česke · Znojmo · Brno · 1592 · Prešov · Frankovsk · Kolomyya · Mogilev · Kirovograd · Dneprodzerzhinsk
dějovice · Danube · 2043 · Košice · Uzgorod · Mukachevo · Chernovtsy · Podol'skiy · Pervomaysk · **Dnepropetrovsk**
 zburg · **Vienna** · **Bratislava** · S L O V A K I A · Miskolc · Nyíregyháza · Krivoy Rog · Nikopol · Zaporozh'ye
ssau · Linz · (Wien) · 2075 · Győr · Satu · Baia Mare · Suceava · Botoşani · Bălţi · Nikolayev
U S T R I A · Danube · Vác · Debrecen · Mare · Pietrosu · **MOLDOVA** · Orgejeŭ · *Kakhovskoye*
2996 · Leoben · **Budapest** · H U N G A R Y · Oradea · 2305 · Iaşi · **Chisinău** · Tiraspol · Kherson · *Reservoir*
gastein · Graz · Veszprém · Cluj Napoca · ·2103 · Bacău · Odessa · Novaya · Melitopol
Klagenfurt · Balaton · Nagykanizsa · Szeged · Tirgu · Siret · Bolgrad · Belgorod · Kakhovka
2863 · Maribor · Varazdin · Lake · Pecs · Arad · Mureş · Braşov · Tiraspol · 18. · Sea of
Ljubljana · **Zagreb** · Drava · Subotica · Timişoara · Sibiu · Galati · Azov
SLOVENIA · CROATIA · Osijek · Zrenjanin · Vršac · R O M A N I A · Karkinitskiy · Dzhankoy
asle · Rijeka · Karlovac · Sava · Brod · Novisad · Deva · Negoiu · Bolgrad · Bay · Crimea · 45°N
Pula · Krk · Bihać · Banja · Mitrovica · 2509 · 2548 · Tulcea · Simferopol'
Cres · Luka · BOSNIA- · Danube · Turnu- · Pitești · *Mouths of* · Sevastopol' · 1259 · Jalda
Zadar · HERZEGOVINA · Zenica · **Belgrade** · Smederevo · Severin · Ploiești · *the Danube* · Feodosiya
Pag · Šibenik · 2107 · Tuzla · (Beograd) · Morava · Craiova · **Bucharest** · Constanța
A D R I A T I C · Split · **Sarajevo** · YUGO- · Svetozarevo · (București)
Ancona · Brac · Hvar · Jablanica · SLAVIA · Vidin · Danube · Ruse · B L A C K
Korčula · 2387 · Niš · Rosiori
Ascoli · Peljesac · Dubrovnik · Dinaric Alps · Leskovac · Pirot · Kolarovgrad · S E A
onte Corno · Pescara · Podgorica · Ivangrad · Priština · Vraca · Pleven · Varna
2914 · 2693 · Tŭrnovo · Burgas
Avezzano · 2793 · Prizren · Balkan · Sliven
Campobasso · Shkodër · Kumanovo · **Sofia** · B U L G A R I A
2747 · (Sofiya) · Stara Zagora · Cape
Foggia · A L B A N I A · **Skopje** · Velés · Musala · 2925 · Ince
ples · Benevento · Bari · MACEDONIA (F.Y.R.) · Blagoevgrad · Plovdiv · Sinop
(poli) · Potenza · **Tirana** · Ohrid · Bitola · Rhodone · Kŭrdžali · Edirne · Karabük · Kastamonu · Samsun
Salerno · Brindisi · (Tiranë) · Lake · 2191 · Lüleburgaz · Ereğli · 2565
Taranto · Lecce · Durrës · Prespa · Edessa · Sérra · Komotini · **Istanbul** · 2068
Sapri · 2248 · Vlorë · Lake · G · Kavalla · Tekirdağ · Üsküdar · Adapazari · Corum · Turhal
Gulf of · Korça · R · Thessaloniki · Thasos · *Sea of Marmara* · İzmit · Bolu · Gerede · Turhal
Taranto · Capo Santa Maria · Kozáni · Chalkidike · Bandirma · Bursa · Bilecik · 40°N · 54
Corigliano · di Leuca · 2633 · 2911 · Imbros · Canakkale · 2543 · Kirikkale · 2346
Corfu · Jánina · Lemnos · ·Troy · Eskişehir · **Ankara** · Yozgat · A n a t o l i a
Cosenza · Corfu · Pindus · Trikala · Lárisa · A E G E A N · Ayvalik · Kütahya · Lake Tuz
Catanzaro · Cephalonia · Vólos · S E A · Lesbos · Manisa · Afyon · Kayseri
I O N I A N · Levkas · Northern · Akhisar · 2446 · Aksaray · 3916
Lipari · Agrinion · Sporades · Chíos · İzmir · Alaşehir · Konya · Niğde
Islands · 1965 · Delphi · Euboea · Cyclades · Sámos · Aydin · Lake · Ereğli
lermo · Messina · S E A · Chalkis · Menderes · Denizli · Beyşehir · Kozan · 3488
Etna · Reggio · Gulf of Corinth · **Athens** · Southern · Muğla · Antalya · Karaman · Adana
Riposto · 3340 · Patras · (Athinai) · Sporades · Taurus · Geyhan
ltanissetta · Catania · 2224 · (Pátrai) · Piraeus · Ándros · Tínos · Mersin · Iskenderun
Agrigento · Syracuse · Korinth · Zante · Náxos · (Içel) · 3097 · Antakya
cata · Gela · (Siracusa) · Pyrgos · Tripolis · Mílos · Alanya · Antalya
Noto · Kalamai · Gulf of · Fethiye · 1795
Ragusa · Cape Akrítas · Antalya · Finike · Cape Anamur
Cape Matapan · Cape Maléa · Rhodes · Anamur · Cape
mel · Kithira · 1215 · Andreas
Gozo · **Valletta** · R A N E A N · Sea of Crete · Rhodes · Latakia
MALTA · Kánea · Iráklion · **CYPRUS** · Famagusta
Melambes · **Nicosia** · 1385
2456 · Cape Arnauti · Olympus · Tartus
Crete · ·1951 · Larnaca
Paphos · Tripoli
Limassol · 3097
LEBANON
Beirut · Zahle
Damascus
ipoli · Khoms · Al Bayda · Darnah · Sur · Qunaitra
Al Marj · 882 · Golan
Tarhuna · Misurata · Al Jabal al Akhdar · Heights · Dar'a
·81 · Beni · Benghazi · Al Abyar · Tobruk · Hadera · Irbid
Walid · ·1247
ISRAEL · WEST
Qaminis · Tel-Aviv-Jaffa · BANK · Zarqa
Gulf of · ·159 · Al Adam · Al Burdi · Haifa · **Amman**
Beni · Sirte · Al Adam · Sidi Barrâni · *Nile Delta* · GAZA · Dead
Walid · **Jerusalem** · Sea
Buerát el Hsun · L I B Y A · Sallûm · Mersa · Rosetta · Gaza · Al Karak
·1 · Sirte · Matruh · Baltim · Al · Port Said · Beer
15°E · 20°E · 25°E · Fuka · Damanhur · Mansura · Suez · Sheba
Y A · E G Y P T · **Alexandria** · 30°E · Dumyat · Canal · 35°E
35°N

n o p q r s t u v w x y z

0 · 100 · 200 · 300 · miles
Average linear scale
0 · 100 · 200 · 300 · 400 · 500 · Km

a   b   c   d   e   f   g   h   i   j   k   l   m

15°W   10°W   5°W   0°

Sines
Odemira   Ourique   Aljustrel   Aracena
PORTUGAL   Mértola   Sevilla   SPAIN   Córdoba   Jaén   2036   Lorca   Murcia
Portimão   Tavira   Huelva   Marchena   Lucena   Granada   Baza   Guadix   Águilas
Sagres   Lagos   Faro   Jerez de la   1654   Antequera   Sa. Nevada   Almería   Cartagena
Gulf of   Frontera   Ronda   Málaga   Motril
Cádiz   Cádiz   Ubrique
Algeciras   Gibraltar (U.K.)   Ténes
Str. of Gibraltar   Ceuta (Sp.)   Mostaganem   Chelif
Tangier   Tetuan   Oran   Relizane   Mass
Asilah   Chechaouen   Al Hoceima   Melilla (Sp.)   Mohammadia   Mascara
El Arisch   Nador   Beni Saf   Sidi   Tia
Ksar el Kebir   Midar   Ghazaouët   bel-Abbes
Ouezzane   Ouerrha   Aknoul   Tlemcen   M
Sidi   Taza   Guercif   Oujda   Marhoum
Mehdia   Kacem   Fes   Ras-al-Ma
Salé   Kenitra   Sefrou   Taourirt   El Aricha   Hauts   pla
Rabat   Meknes   3190   Ain   Bougtob
Khemisset   Azrou   Outat-el-Hadj   Debdou   Benimathar   El Bayadh
Casablanca   Rommani   Missour   Tendrara   Méchéria   Sahar
Azemmour   Berrechid   Ksabi   Bou Arfa   Ain Sefra   2236   Bréz
El Jadida   Khouribga   Oued   Midelt   Talsinnt   Mengoub   Figuig
Zem   3741   Rich   2670
Oualidia   Settat   Beni Mellal   Ksar es Souk   Beni Cunif
Sidi   Oum   Demnate   Goulmina   Kenadsa   Colomb   834
Safi   Bennour   Benguerir   Marrakech   4071   Ighil   Tinerhir   Erfoud   Béchar   Taghit
Tensift   Chichaoua   Demnate   Rissani   Abadla   Igli
Essaouira   Amizmiz   Jebel Igdet   High Atlas   Agdz   Tazzarine   Taouz   Beni Abbès
3616   Toubkal   Tazenakht   Great Western
Agadir   Taroudannt   4165   Zagora   757   Kerzaz
Inezgane   Tagounite   Tabelbala   Ksabi   Timimoun
Anti Atlas   Charouine
Tiznit   2359   Tata   Hamada of Dra   Gourara   Taa
Sidi Ifni   1250   Bani   Tinfouchy   890   Sbaa
Bou Izakarene   Djebel   Foum   Bou Akba   Adrar   Tamentit
Tantan   Dj. Ouarkziz   El Aassane   Ouahila   El Mansour   Titaf
Tindouf   Sali
Tarfaya   A   Aoulef
C. Yubi   Al Farcia   437   Mcherrah   Reggane   el Arab
Daora   Hagunia   Iguidi Erg   Bordj Flye   L   G   E
El Aaiún   Aftout   Sainte Marie
Lemsid   Smara   El Eglab   680
C. Bojador   Chenachane
Bojador   Tifariti   S   Chech   Erg   a
Amasin   Ain   Yetti
701   ben Tili   Chegga
Guelta   Bir   Chech   Tanezrouft   Tanezro
Zemmour   Oum Greine   Rhallamane   Aioun Abd
Zemmour   Bir el Khzaim   el Malek
Dakhla   WESTERN   370   Kreb en Naga   305   Erg el Ahmar   315
Aargub   Bir   Karet   El Hank   A Er Oukar   273
Rio de Oro   Enzarah   Zedness   El Mreïti   Hamada   Safia   361
Imilili   500   Agueraktem
G. de Cintra   639   Aguelt el Melah   Hamada el Haricha
Zouerate   250   Taoudenit   El Maia
Cap   Agailas   Fdérik   Hammami   296   El Khenachich   321
Barbas   Maktei   330   322   Bordj-Moktar
Bir   Tichla   Zug   647   Ouarane   Er Mreyer   450
Gandus   Choûm   Guelb er   El Djouf   Jafene   Douaouir   Tessalit
Nouâdhibou   Richat   284   Timétrine
Güera   Azefal   Ouadane   MAURITANIA   Mabrouk   Timétrine   Adr
Cape   Akchar   Ksar   Aguelock   750
Nouâdhibou   Atar   Torchane   Chinguetti   Azaouad   MALI   Ifo
20°N   Oujeft   Adafer
Tidra   501
C Timiris   Akjoujt   Adrar   Meraia   Anéfis
Nouamrhar   Faye   Aouker   Aougar
88   Dabar Tichitt   In Alay   Anou Meller
23°   Tamassoumit   Tidjikja   Tichitt   Dahar Oualata   Oudeïka   Agamor
Nouakchott   Tagant   Akreijit   334   Bamba   Niger   Bourem
554   Moudjeria   318
Trarza   Boutilimit   Tamchaket   Oualata
15°W   Aleg   Mal   10°W   5°W

Madeira (Portugal)
Funchal   Desertas

ATLANTIC

OCEAN

Canary
Islands
(Spain) Tenerife
Pico   Santa
de Teide   Cruz
3718
Gomera   Guia   1949   Las
Palmas
Lanzarote
Arrecife
Puerto del Rosario
Fuerteventura

30°N

25°N

SAHARA

MOROCCO

Middle Atlas

Hamada du Guir

Gulf

Atlas

Erg er Raoui

Kahal Tabelbala

ALGE

Sahara

Maktei

El Djouf

Hamami

This map shows 1/60 of the earth's surface

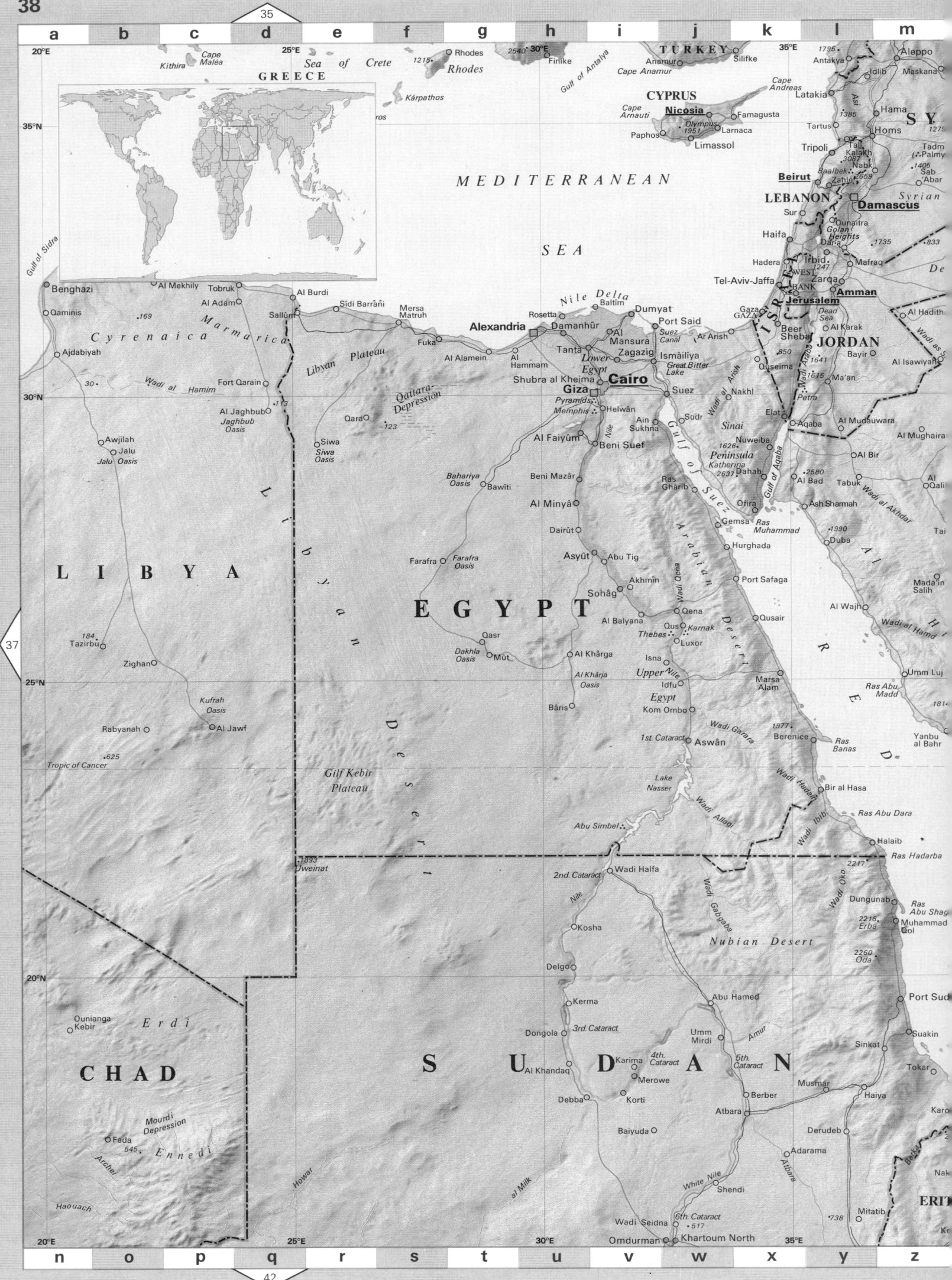

20°E   25°E   30°E   35°E

Kithira   Cape Maléa   Sea of Crete   Rhodes   .1215   Finike   Gulf of Antalya   Cape Anamur   Anamur   TURKEY   Silifke   35°E   .1795   Aleppo

GREECE   Rhodes   2540   30°E   Cape Andreas   Antakya   Idlib   Maskana

35°N   Kárpathos   CYPRUS   Latakia   .1385   Hama   S Y.
ros   Cape Arnauti   Nicosia   Famagusta   Tartus   Tadm   .1279
Paphos   Olympus .1951   Larnaca   Tripoli   Tall Kalakh   (* Palm
Limassol   Baalbek .3087   .659   .1405   Sab Abar

M E D I T E R R A N E A N   Beirut   LEBANON   Zahlé   Syrian   .1735   .833
Sur   Golan Heights   Damascus   De
Haifa   Qunaitra   Dara   .1735

S E A   Hadera   Irbid   .1247   Mafraq   .833
Nile Delta   Baltim   Tel-Aviv-Jaffa   WEST   Zarqa   Amman
Rosetta   Dumyat   BANK   Jerusalem
Alexandria   Damanhûr   Port Said   Gaza   GAZA   Dead Sea   Al Hadith
Benghazi   Al Mekhily   Tobruk   Al Burdi   Sidi Barrâni   Al Mansura   Suez Canal   Beer Sheba   Al Karak   Wadi as S
Qaminis   Al Adám   Sallûm   Mersa Matruh   Tanta   Zagazig   Ar Arish   JORDAN   Bayir   Al Isawiyah
Ajdabiyah   .169   Marmarica   Fuka   Al Alamein   Al Hammam   Lower   Ismâiliya   .850   Quseima   .1641   Ma'an
Cyrenaica   Libyan Plateau   Egypt   Cairo   Great Bitter Lake   Nakhl   .1615   Petra
30°N   .30   Wadi al Hamim   Fort Qarain   Shubra al Kheima   Suez   Sudr   Elat   Aqaba   Al Mudauwara
Al Jaghbub   .113   Qattara-Depression   Giza   Pyramids,   Helwân   Sinai   .1626   Nuweiba   Al Bir   Al Mughaira
Jaghbub Oasis   Qara   .123   Memphis   Ain Sukhna   Peninsula Katherina   Dahab   Al Bad   .2580   Tabuk   Al Qali
Awjilah   Siwa   Al Faiyûm   Beni Suef   .2637   Ofira   Ash Sharma   Wadi al Akhdar
Jalu   Siwa Oasis   Ras Ghârib   Gemsa   Ras Muhammad   Duba   .1990   Tai
Jalu Oasis   Bahariya Oasis   Beni Mazâr   Hurghada   Mada in Salih
Al Minyâ   Al Wajh   Wadi al Hamd
L I B Y A   Libyan   Bawiti   Dairût   Port Safaga   Al Qali
E G Y P T   Asyût   Abu Tig   Qena   Quseir
37   Farafra   Farafra Oasis   Sohâg   Akhmîn   Karnak   Marsa   Umm Luj
.184   Tazirbú   Qasr   Al Balyana   Thebes   Alam   Ras Abu   .181
Zighan   Dakhla Oasis   Mût   Al Khârga   Luxor   Madd
25°N   Upper   Isna   Nile   Yanbu al Bahr
Kufrah Oasis   Al Khârja Oasis   Idfu   Egypt   1977
Rabyanah   Al Jawf   Bâris   Kom Ombo   Berenice   Ras Banas
Tropic of Cancer   .625   1st. Cataract   Aswân   Wadi Gârara   Bir al Hasa   Ras Abu Dara
Gilf Kebir Plateau   Lake Nasser   Wadi Allaqi   Wadi Hadaib   Halaib   Ras Hadarba
.1893   Abu Simbel   Wadi Oko   .2217
Uweinat   2nd. Cataract   Wadi Halfa   Wadi Gabgaba   Dungunab   Ras Abu Shag
Nile   Nubian Desert   .2218 Erba   Muhammad Col
Kosha   .2260 Oda
20°N   Delgo   Port Sud
Ouninga Kebir   Erdi   Kerma   Abu Hamed   Suakin
Dongola   3rd. Cataract   Umm Mirdi   Amur   Sinkat
C H A D   S U D A N   Al Khandaq   Karima   4th. Cataract   5th. Cataract   Musmar   Haiya
Debba   Merowe   Berber   Karo
Mourdi Depression   Korti   Atbara   Derudeb
Fada .545   Baiyuda   Adarama
Ennedi   White Nile   Nak
Archei   Shendi   Mitatib   ERIT
Howar   .738
Haouach   Wadi Seidna   6th. Cataract   .517
20°E   25°E   Omdurman   Khartoum North   30°E   35°E

This map shows 1/60 of the earth's surface

a b c d e f g h i j k l m

40°E 45°E 50°E 55°E

Raqqah
Dayr az Zawr
851
al Hayl
708
Jabal at Tinef
866
Abu Kamal
Suwar
Al Hasakah
1463
Sinjar
Tall 'Afar
Mosul
Arbil
Zab
Sharqat
Kirkuk
lesser
Saqqez
Baneh
Sulaimaniyah
Qojur
Takestan
Qazvin
Amol
Ghaem Shahr
Mayamey
Damghan
Elburz Mts.
Damavand 5671
Damavand
Semnan
Torud
Tabas

IRAQ
Anah
Wadi ath Tharthar
Tigris
Ar Rutbah
Al Hadithah
Tikrit
Lake Tharthar
Bahr al Milh
Ar Ramadi
Baghdad
Ba'qubah
Diyala
Jalula
Karand
Tuz Khurmatu
1097
Ravansar
Bakhtaran
1322
Eslamabad-e-Gharb
2656
Ilam
2041
Karkheh
Kangavar
3393
Hamadan
3572
Malayer
Arak
1775
Qareh Su
Saveh
Qom
Daryacheh-ye-Namak
Kashan
3565
Natanz
3899
Ardestan
Anarak
Khor
35°N
Dasht-e-Kavir
Garmsar
Tehran
Karaj
Zarand
Razan
Borujerd
3075
Khorramabad
Azna
Mahallat
Daran
3432 Oshtoran
Dez
4549
Zard 4294
Shahr-e-Kord
Najafabad
1590
Isfahan
Nain
3197
Ardakan
Yazd
Darband
Aliabad

IRAN
Dasht-e-Lut

Al Aziziyah
Al Hillah
Al Kut
Mehran
Dehloran
Dezful
Shush
4298
Qomsheh
Izadkhast
Abadeh
3746
Dinar 4432
Dehbid
Saadatabad
Abarqu
3965
3472
Rafsanjan
Baghin
Kerman
3143
Zarand
Karbala
An Najaf
Ad Diwaniyah
Ar Rifa'i
Al Amarah
Ahwaz
Masjed-e-Soleiman
Karun
Ramhormoz
Ramshir
Behbahan
Mehriz
Bafq
Ravor
30°N
Shir Kuh 4074

Ash Shubaiyai
An Nasiriyah
As Samawah
Al Qurnah
Hawr al Hammar
Bandar-e-Khomeini
Hendijan
Nurabad
3218
Shiraz
Persepolis
Daryacheh-ye-Tashk
Hoseinabad
Daryacheh-ye-Bakhtegan
Sirjan
Laleh Zar 4374
Bafi
Turaif
321
Ar'ar
Wadi Ar'ar
1070
Al Jalamid
Ad Duwaid
Sakakah
Al Jawf
Rafha
Ansab
Linah
908

KUWAIT
Basra
Umm Qasr
Al Faw
Bubiyan
Jahra
Kuwait
Ahmadi
299 Wadi al Batin
Al Wafra
Mina Saud
Bandar-e-Rig
Bushehr
Ras Halileh
Khormuj
Borazjan
Firuzabad
1960
Kazerun
1539
Zeydan
Kangan
2804
Gavbandi
Bastak
Bandar-e-Margam
Dezhgan
Qeys
Bandar-e-Lengeh
Qeshm
Bandar Abbas
Minab
Qeshm
Str. of Hormuz

An Nafud
Jubbah
Al Maiyah
Ha'il 1500
Bir Shari
Tabah
Samirah
Buraidah
Al Qaisumah
Ad Dibdibah
Safaniyah
Qaryat al 'Ulya
Sarar
Abu Hadriyah
Al Jubayl
Ras Tannurah
Dhahran
Dammam
Manama
Ar Ruwais
Al Hasa

ARABIAN GULF

BAHRAIN
G. of Bahrain
QATAR
Dukhan
Doha
Karana
Umm Sa'id
Ash Sha'am
2081 Musandam Pen.
OMAN
Dibba
Ras al Khaimah
Sharjah
Dubai
Jebel Ali
Fujairah
25°N
Gulf of Oman
Shinas
Sohar

SAUDI
Khayber
Hulaifah
Uqlat al Suqur
Az Zilfi
Unaizah
Al Majm'ah
Ushairah
Shaqra
Ad Dahna
Ash Shumlul
Khurais
Al Udailiyah
Abqaiq
Al Hufuf
Salwa
Jabal adh Dhanna
As Sila
Marawah
Abu al Abyad
Abu Dhabi
Al Khaznah
Tarif
Al Khabura
Al Ain
Hajar Mts.
Al Bitinah
Ghadi
Ibri
3018 Bahla

ARABIA
Buwatah
Al Hanakiyah
Medina
Badr Hunain
As Sidr
Mahd adh Dhahab
Al Qurain
Khuff
Durma
Riyadh
Ad Dawadimi
Sulaimaniyah
Harad
Muhairiqah
Halaban
Al Hillah
Khamis Mushait
Masturah
Zalim
Afif
Al Quwarah

UNITED ARAB EMIRATES
Bu Hasa
Habshan
Taraq
An Nashash
Liwa Oasis
Umm al Samim
Wadi Aswad
Al Khaburah

Khulais
Madrakah
As Suq
Mecca
1630
Taif
Arafat 2386
Turabah
Ar Rauda
As Sawadah
Layla
1012
Jabal Tuwayq
Ad Dahna
Al Uruq al Mu'aridah
Sabkhat Matti

Al Lith
Bani Sar
Qal'at Bishah
Wadi Bishah
Al Khamasin
As Sulaiyil
Wadi Tathlith

Ar Rub' al Khali
20°N

Al Ulaya
Tathlith
An Nimas
Al Qunfudhah
Khay
3133
Abha
Ad Darb
Zahran
Najran
Sa'dah
Hima'
Thamud
Sanaw

OMAN
Dhofar
Wadi Shihan
Wadi Qitbit
Thamarit
Salalah
Raisut
Mirbat
Kuria Muria Islands
Sahil al Jazir
Sauqira Bay
Sharbithat
Ras Sharbithat

Mersa Teklay
817
Farasan Is.
Jizan
Midi
Huth
Al Hazm
Hajjah
3360
Dahlak Islands

YEMEN
Jabal al Qamar
Jabal al Qara
Al Ghaydah
Qamar Bay
Al Jiz
Wadi Masilah
Sayun
Haynan
Ras Fartak

ARABIAN SEA

43

miles 0 100 200 300
Average linear scale
0 100 200 300 400 500 Km

15°W

Moudjéria

Boûmdeïd

Tamchaket

Aoukâr

In Alay

Oudeika

Bamba

Bour

Boutilimit

Mederdra

Aleg

Mâl

Kiffa

Montagnes de l'Affolé •600

Ayoûn el Atroûs

Oualâta

Néma

I r î g u i

Tombouctou

Doro

Rosso

Dagana

Bogué

Senegal

Kaédi

Mbout

Kankossa

Kobenni

Timbedgha

Amourj

Bassikounou

Lake Faguibine

Goundam

Niafounké

Tuar

St. Louis

Louga

Matam

Maghama

Hamoud

Nioro du Sahel

Ballé

Nara

S a h e l

Nampala

Lac Débo

Hombori •1155

Douentza

MAURITANIA

15°N

Dakar

Cape Verde

Thiès

Mbour

Diourbel

Mbaké

Ferlo

Linguère

Fourdou

Sélibabi

Birou

Sokolo

Macina

Mopti

Bandiagara

Djibo

Kaolack

Malème-Hodar

Kidira

Kayes

Koniakari

Diéma

M A L I

Ségou

San

Ouahigouya

Dédougou

B U R K

SENEGAL

Koumpentoûm

Tambacounda

Bamba

Diamou

Bafoulabé

Didiéni

Banamba

Niger

Bani

Djenne

Nouna

Yako

Kaya

Boulsa

Banjul

Karang

Georgetown

Gambia

Dialakoto

Dialafara

Toukoto

Kolokani

Koulikoro

Bla

Koutiala

Koudougou

Houndé

Bobo-Dioulasso

Léo

Po

Zabré

Baw

GAMBIA

Sere Kunda

Brikama

Basse Santa Su

Niokolo Koba

Saraya

Kita

Kati

Fana

Mpessoba

Sikasso 820•

Toéssé

Tenkod

Bignona

Kolda

Casamance

Farim

Kédougou

Satadougou

Bamako

Baguinéda

Garalo

505

Banfora

Gaoua

Lawra

Navrongo

Bolgatanga

Gambac

Ziguinchor

GUINEA-BISSAU

Mansêa

Bafatá

Koundara

•1538

Ouéléssébougou

Bougouni

Koundougou

Tumu

Wa

Yala

Walev

Bissau

Corubal

Kogon

Gaoual

Tougué

Siguiri

Manankoro

Pogo

Gaoua

Ga

White

Black Volta

Pig

Bissagos Islands

Catió

Fouta Djalon

Labé 1264•

Pita

Dinguiraye

Garalo

Samatiguila

Ouangolodougou

Bouna

Sawla

Tama

Boké

Fatala

Konkouré

Dabola 1028

Kouroussa

Odienné

Boundiali

Ferkéssédougou

Bole

Maluwe

GUINEA

Boffa

Fria

Kindia

Kavendou 1421•

Mamou 1094•

•1015

Sanouyah

Kankan

Korhogo

Kong 430•

Koutouba

Sala

10°N

Conakry

Forécariah

Little Scarcies

Kabala

Faranah

Bohodoyou

Samatiguila

Morondo

Kanawolo

Bondoukou

Goumeré

Bamboi

Kintampo

Kambia

Rokel

Makeni

Koidu

Loma Mts. 1948

Kissidougou

Kérouané

Bako

Koro

Kani

Katiola

Techiman

Atebub

Freetown

SIERRA LEONE

Guéckédou

Macenta 1656•

Tibé 1504

Beyla 1257•

Touba

Séguéla

Kossou Reservoir

Bouaké 700•

GHANA

Bo

Pendembu

Kenema

Zorzor

Nzérékoré 1752•

Biankouma

Man 1189•

Bouaflé

Berekum

Sunyani

Mampong

Pujehun

Sewa

Moa

Loffa

Sanniquellie

Danané

Duékoué

Yamoussoukro

Dimbokro

Abengourou

Konongo

Kumasi

Nkawkaw

Sherbro Island

Mano River

Bomi Hills

St. Paul

Gbarnga

Ganta

Guiglo

Daloa

Toumodi

Akoupé

Awaso

Obuasi

Koforidu

Dunkwa

Oda

Monrovia

Bong

Mani

Tapeta

Toulepleu

Tchien

CÔTE D'IVOIRE

Gagnoa

Lakota

Agboville

Prestea

Accr

Tarkwa

Cape Co

LIBERIA

Buchanan

Cess

Tai

Soubré

Dabou

Grand-Lahou

Abidjan

Grand-Bassam

Sekondi-Takoradi

Gold Coas

5°N

Juarzon

•396 *Niénokoué*

Greenville

Grabo

Sassandra

San Pédro

Ivory Coast

Grain Coast

Cavally

Plibo

Tabou

Harper

A T L A N T I C

O C E A

Equator

0°

15°W

10°W

5°W

This map shows 1/60 of the earth's surface

5°E   10°E   15°E

Anou Mellene · .500
Agamor
Dibella

Tegguida-n-Tessoum
Aouderas
Akrereb
Agadez
Agadem
Ouyu
Bezze
Denga
Homodji
Toro
Doum

Tillia
Tchin-Tabaradene
.500
Mazalet
Termit N. Massif de Termit .710

Vallée de l'Azaouak
Azaouak

In Talak
Abala
Tahoua
Tanout
Task
Idaye
Ngourti · .280

Ménaka
Tilemsès
Aderbissinat
.403
Ngourti
Moul

15°N
Ansongo

Abala
Illéla
Madaoua
Tessaoua
Zinder
Goudoumaria
Maïné-Soroa
Nguigmi
Rig-Rig
Nokou
Kanem

N   I   G   E   R

.550
Niger
Tillabéri
Ouallam
Filingué
Burni-Nkonni
.302
Matankari
Dogondoutchi
Illela
Katsina
Nguru
Gashua
Geidam
Bosso
Komadugu
Lake Chad
Mao
Mondo
Am Raya
Moussoro

Niamey
Torodi
Say
Dosso
Sokoto
Maradi
Dungas
Hadejia
Dapchi
Damakar
Mainé-
Baga
Massaguet
N'Gouri
Ngoura

A
Kantchari
Argungu
Kaura Namoda
Nguru
Munguno
Dikwa
.296
Massakori

Fada-Ngourma
Diapaga
Koulou
Sokoto
Birnin-Kebbi
Gusau
Kano
Wudil
Hadejia
Potiskum
Damaturu
Maiduguri
Bama
Fort-Foureau
N'Djamena
.442
CHAD

Kamba
Gaya
Talata Mafara
Anka
Faskari
Funtua
Foggo
Kari
Buni
Biu
Mubi
Mokolo
1141
Guélengdeng
Massenya
Chari

Kandi
Tanguiéta
.550
Béroubouay
Bembéréké
Zuru
Yelwa
Zaria
Zalanga
Gongola
Gombe
Wuyo
Maroua
Bongor
Bousso

BENIN
Natitingou
Boukombé
Djougou
Wawa
Kontagora
Birnin Gwari
Kaduna
1594
Goura
Bauchi
Bara
Moutouroua
Ham

NIGERIA
10°N

Lama-Kara
Bassari
.772
Sokodé
Bassila
Parakou
Yashikera
Kaiama
Tegina
Minna
Kafanchan
1625
Kagora
1518
Pankshin
Jos
Numan
Yola
Garoua
Pala
Kelo
Lai

TOGO
Blitta
Kilibo
Igbetti
Jebba
Bida
Abuja
Akwanga
Wamba
Zamko
Jalingo
Guidjiba
Moundou
Koumra
Doba

Kpessi
.845
Savé
Agoaré
Ilorin
Niger
Baro
Lafia
Ibi
Wukari
Beli
Poli
Tcholliré
Touboro
Baïbokoum
Gore
Bébour

Atakpamé
Savalou
Ogbomosho
Iseyin
Oyo
Ede
Oshogbo
Ilesha
Ado Ekiti
Lokoja
Benue
Makurdi
Takum
Mbé
Béka
Ngaoundéré
Bélel
Bocaranga

Nuatja
Abomey
Iwo
Ife
Ibadan
Ikerré
Kabba
Okene
Ayangba
Oturkpo
Adamaoua Highlands
Doualayel
Banyo
Béla-Oya
Meiganga
Bozoum
Bossangoa

Kpalimé
Tsévié
Abeokuta
Akure
Owo
Ondo
Ijebu Ode
Ogun
Ogoja
1890
Nkambé
3008
Tibati
CENTRAL

Lomé
Ouidah
Cotonou
Porto Novo
Lagos
Lekki
Ilaro
Benin City
Enugu
Ikom
Bamenda
2335
Foumban
Yoko
Garoua Boulaï
Babouà
Bouar
Bombale
AFRICAN

Slave Coast
Sapele
Onitsha
Afikpo
Cross
Mamfe
2740
Bafoussam
Dschang
Bafang
Nkongsamba
Bafia
Nanga Eboko
Bertoua
Batouri
Kenzou
Berberati
Bania
REPUBLIC

Warri
Aba
Port Harcourt
Calabar
2050
Yabassi
Ndjolé
Sanaga
Goyoum
Carnot
Bossembélé

Ughelli
Brass
Bonny
Mt. Cameroon 4100
Buea
Douala
Edéa
Eséka
Yaoundé
Abong Mbang
Boumba
Berberati
Nola
5°N

Limbe
Malabo
1890
Luba
2662
Bioko Island
Nyong
Mbalmayo
Dja
Yokadouma
Bayanga

N
Gulf
of
Guinea
Ebolowa
Sangmélima
Lokomo
Bomassa

Principe
Ambam
Moloundou
Bomassa

SÃO TOMÉ
AND PRINCIPE
EQUATORIAL
GUINEA
Bata
Ebebiyin
Niefang
Bitam
Oyem
1200
Tembo
Ntam
Souanké
Sembé
Ouesso
Liouesso

Mbini
1200
Mbini
937
Nkolabona
Mékambo
CONGO

São Tomé
São Tomé
2024
Evinayong
Cocobeach
Mitzic
Makokou
Pikounda

Libreville
Kougouleu
Lalara
.980
Booué
Likouala
Makoua

GABON
Ndjolé
Kellé
.500
Okondja
Ewo
Boundji

Port-Gentil
Lambaréné
Ogooué
875
Lastoursville
Mossaka

Annobón (Equa.Guinea)
Mimongo
Moanda
Okoyo
Congo

Ombouè
Koulamoutou
Mouila
Franceville

15°E

0   100   200   300 miles   Average linear scale   0   100   200   300   400   500 Km

42

38

a   b   c   d   e   f   g   h   i   j   k   l   m

20°E

15°N

CHAD

Bodélé

Koro Toro

Fada

Archei

Ennedi

Haouach

Ouagat

Kapka
1220

The

Umm Saggat

Sindi

Magrur

Wadi Howar

Wadi al Milk

Haraza 1127

Omdurman

Khartoum North

Khartoum

Umm Inderaba

Nile

Shendi

6th Cataract

Wadi
Seidna

•517

Karma

Maba

Azum

Kordofan

White Nile

Blue Nile

Salal

Sahel

Biltine

Haddad

Hamrat al Shaikh

Sodiri

Umm
Saiyala

El Hasaheisa

El Gezira

Wad Medani

Rime

Abéché

al Junayna

Kebkabiya

El Fasher

Umm Keddada

al Dueim

Sennar

al Ouaday

Ati

Oum Hadjer

Adré

Dam Gamad

Bara

Tendelti

Kosti

Rabak

Singa

Batha

Zalingei

•3071
Jebel
Marra

Menawashei

Wad Banda

El Obeid

Er Rahad

Umm Ruwaba

El Jebelein

Guedi
•1506

Mongo

Mangalmé

Goz Beida

Kass

Kirim 640

al Nahûd

Abu Zabad

Dilling

Abu Habi

Renk

Ed Damazin

Lake
Roseires

1613•

Bitkine

Batha

Azoum

Nyala

al Udaiya

al Fûla

Nuba
Mountains

Turum
•1122

Abou Deïa

Idd al Ghanam

Gandi

al Da'ain

Babanusa

al Muglad

•842

Kadugli

•1325

Mélfi

Zakouma

Am Timan

Rahad al Berdi

Ibra

Talodi

•1093

Kurmuk

SUDAN

Eiguig

Kendégué

Haraze

Oulou

Birao

Dango
790•

Bahr al Arab

Sumaih

Tungaru

Paloich

Bambesi
•2185

10°N

Charï

Soudan

Salamat

Kéita ou Doka

Aouk

Ouandja

Tiroungoulou

Toussoro
1330•

Yata

Bora

Raga

Nasir

Dembi

Gambela

Koumra

Sarh

Bangoran

Ndélé

Massif
des Bongos

•850

Ouadda

1050•

Sopo

Wau

Aweil

Bahr al Ghazel

Akobo

Maro

Ouham

Gribingui

Kotto

Ndji

Pongo

Toni

Kongor

41

Kabo

Bamingui

Haute
Kotto

Busseri

Rumbek

White Nile

Pibor Post

Batangafo

Ouandago

Kaga
Bandoro

Mbrès

Boungo

Yalinga

Maridi

Mvolo

Bor

Bossangoa

Bouca

Dékoa

Bria

CENTRAL AFRICAN

Vovodo

Ibba

Angeleri
•838

Kenamuke
Swamp

Sibut

Bambari

REPUBLIC

Chinka

Ouara

Obo

Tambura

Li Yuba

Mundri

Medi

Mongalla

5°N

Bogangolo

Tomi

Ouaka

Kotto

Mbari

Dembia
Rafaï

Zémio

Sue

Doruma

Maridi

Juba

Ele
Tria

Damara

Kouango

Alindao

Bangassou

Gambo

M'bomou

Yambio
1067

Garmabe

Ngangala

•1940

Kapoeta

Bossembélé

Kongbo

Mobaye

Monga

Matundu

Bili

Ese

1065•

Abo

Yei

Lalyo

Torit

Kinyeti
3187

Lokich

Bangui

Bimbo

Zongo

Gbadolite

Mobayi-
Mbongo

Yakoma

Uele

Bili

Api

Ango

Bambili

Niangara

Dungu

Faradje

Kajo-Kaji

Nimule

Kakur

Mbaïki

Zinga

Bosobolo

Lua Dekere

Bondo

Api

Bambesa

Baranga

Rungu

Watsa

Aba

Laropi

Kaabong

•2381

Loyoro

Boyabo

Libenge

Businga

Abumonbazi

Angu

Titule

Poko

Isiro

Gombari

Arua
1310

Aru

Gulu

Pajule

Kitgum

Kotido

Moroto

Lobaye

Gemena

Dua

Bodala

Likati

Dulia

Buta

Medje

Nepoko

Wamba

Watsa

Mahagi
•2448

Anaka

Lira

Amuc

Soroti

CONGO

Enyélé

Kungu

Budjala

Mongola

Modjamboli

Ibembo

Telé

Zambeke

Kole

Ituri

Bomili

Nia Nia

Mambasa

Komanda

Bunie

Fataki
Lake
Albert

UGANDA

Masindi

Lake
Kyoga

Mbale

Dongou

Mobeka

Lisala

Busu-Djanoa

Lindi

Hoima

Nakasongola

Kamuli

Impfondo

Makanza

Bongandanga

Basoko

Aruwimi

Banalia

Bafwabalinga

Batama

Hoyo
•1450

Ntoroko

Fort
Portal

Kyanjojo

Kayunga

Kaliro

Iganga

Tororo

Lulonga

Basankusu

Lopori

Yahuma

Yambuya

Bengamisa

Beni

Mubende

Jinja

Giri

Ubangui

Waka

Maringa

Djolu

Lingomo

Yekana

Isangi

Yangambi

Kisangani

Madula
Boyoma Falls

Opienge

Butembo

Margherita Peak
•5109

Kasese

Kampala

Likouala-aux-Herbes

Mbandaka

Ruki

Ingende

Befale

Samba

Befori

Yatolema

Maiko

Lubero

Lake
Edward

•2197

Masaka

Entebbe

Sese
Islands

Kisumu

DEMOCRATIC

REPUBLIC

OF

CONGO

Yali

Boende

Wema

Watsi

Ekoli

Pene-
Tungu

Ubundu

•956

Kirundu

Lubutu

Mitumba
Mountains

•2341

Ishasha
River

Rutshuru

Lake
Edward

Bushenyi

Mbarara

Kikagati

Bukoba

Lake

Victoria

Kisii

Kilkoris

0°

Bikoro

Kalamba

Lake
Tumba

Busira

Lomela

Watsi-Kengo

Tshuapa

Busanga

Ikela

Likoto

Opala

Lomani

Congo

Walikale

Masisi

Karisimbi
4507•

Goma
Gisenyi

Lake
Kivu

Kayonza

Kyaka

Ukerewe
Island

Nansio

Banagi

Yandja

Bolia

Inongo

Kiri

Lake
Mai-Ndombe

Yalifafu

Yolombo

Monkoto

Lowa

Punia

Kabunga

Kabale

Kyaka

Kavumu

Kigali

RWANDA

Ruhengeri

Kabunga

TANZANIA

Ntadembele

20°E

25°E

30°E

n   o   p   q   r   s   t   u   v   w   x   y   z

44

This map shows 1/60 of the earth's surface

a b c d e f g h i j k l m

Red Sea · **Gulf of Aden** · **INDIAN OCEAN**

YEMEN

Thamud · Al Ghaydah · Wadi al Jiz · Makrah · Qamar Bay · Ras Fartak · Sayhut · al Shihr · Riyan 2185 · al Mukalla · Hadramaut · Sayun · Haynan · Sirwa · al Baida · Lawdar · Ahwar · Ghadir · Aden · Lahej · 850 · Turbah · Ta'izz · Hays · Zabad · Ibb · Manar 3350 · al Baida · al Rawda · Dhamar · Bait al Faqih · Isbil 3190 · Hodeida · San'a 2242 · al Mahdad 3360 · Az Zaydiyah · Hajjah · al Hazm · Huth · Sa'dah · Midi · Jizan · Farasan Islands · Dahlak Islands · Az Zuqar

ERITREA

Derudeb · 2585 · Mersa Teklay · Nakfa · Barka · Keren · 2617 · Massawa · Mitatib · .738 · Kasala · Akordat · Asmara 2374 · Dekemhare · shm irba · Showak · Adi Quala · Adi Keyih · Asimba 3248 · Humera · Keren · Adigrat · Gedaref 699 · Aksum · Adwa · Adigrat · Lake Assale · Mekele · Kwiha · Maychew · Ramlu 2130 · Danakil · Adi Arkay · Mesfinto · Ras Dashen 4550 · Musa Ali 2063 · Metema · Gonder 2223 · Kobbo · Assab · Atbara · Gorgora · Abune Yosef 4190 · Weldiya · Bab al Mandab · Lake Tana · Addis Zemen · Debre Tabor · Asayta · Randa 1783 · Tadjourah · Bahir Dar · Guna 4135 · Betehor · Dese · Awash · Tendaho · Arta · **Djibouti** · Tisisat Falls · Kembolcha · Lake Abbe · Ali-Sabieh · uba · Beleya 3131 · Abay (Blue Nile) · Bati · Dikhil

DJIBOUTI

ETHIOPIA

Danglia · Choke Mtn · Motan 4052 · Karakore · Gewane · 1789 · Berbera · Mait · al Mado 1826 · Las Koreh · Bosaso 2200 · El Gal · Hodda 1400 · Bereda · Cape Guardafui (Raas Caseyr) · 2960 · Bure · Ethiopian Mountains · Abuye Meda 4305 · Dejen · Erigavo · Abd al Kuri · Debre Markos · Fiche · Debre Birhan · Dire Dawa · Buramo · Hargeisa · Burao · Carcar Mountains · Las Dave · Ras Hafun · Dideso · ETHIOPIA Highlands · Amara 3146 · Sheno · Awash · 3292 · Babile · Harer · Jijiga · Arde 1858 · Wadi Grahel · Gimbi · 2408 · Hagere Hiywot · **Addis Ababa** · Asbe Tafari · 1856 · 2064 · El Dab · Bur Anod 1097 · Gardo · Bender Beila · Nekempt · Arjo · Debre Zeit · Nazret · Gugu 3060 · Ahmar Mountains · Kirit · Sinugif · Bedele · Ghion · 3719 · Welkite · Lake Ziway · Fik · Degeh Bur · El Dab · Las Anod · Garoe · Eil · Metu · Agaro · Jima · Lake Langano · Asela · Kaka 4190 · Hamarro Hadad · Rabableh · Gore · Lakes Abiyata · Lake Shale · Shibeli · Warder · Baduen · Berdale · El Hamurre · Maigudo 2386 · Shashemene · 2119 Awetu · Godinlave · Galcaio · Bonga · 2743 · Awasa · Goba · Imi · Kebri Dehar · Ghelinsor · Mirsale · Shishinda · Sodo · Dila · Megalo · Gode · Shilabo · Dusa Mareb · Obbia · Mizan Teferi · Wendo · Mendebo Mountains · El Kere · Kelafo · Sinadogo · Maji · Jinka · Arba Minch · Lake Abaya · Kibre Mengist · Hargele · Mustahil · Ferfer · El Bur · Omo · Lake Chamo · Negele · 1441 · Filtu · Lema Shilindi · Belet Huen · Maas · Key Afer · Gidole · Konso · Yet · El Dere · Kelem · Yabelo · Dawa · Dolo · Hoddur · Tigieglo · Bulo Burti

KENYA

kwol · Banya Fort · Mega · Chelago · Ramu · Mandera · Lugh Ganana · Calie Corar 566 · ertang · itaung · Lake Turkana · Moyale 1280 · Sololo · Baidoba · .600 · Mahaddei Uen · Adale · ekol · North Horr · Buna · El Wak · El Uach · Bur Acaba · Uanle Uen · Giohar · Lodwar · rukumu · Chalbi Desert · Loiyangalani · Marsabit · Tarbaj · Dinsor · Afgoi · **Mogadishu** (Muqdisho) · Lokichar · Nyiru 2752 · South Horr · Wajir · Bardera · Coriolei · Merca · Lokori · Baragoi · Kapedo · Laisamis · Archer's Post · Mado Gashi · Habaswein · Belesc Cogani · Saco Uen · Duguima · Shibeli · Brava · Maralal · 2375 · Kisima · Garba Tula · Liboi · Afmadu · Gelib · Eldoret · Isiolo · Meru · Saka · Hagadera · Giamama · Araara · Baringo Lodge · Nyahururu 2360 · Nanyuki · Kenya (Kirinyaga) 5200 · Garissa · Kisimaio · Equator · sabet · Nakuru · Kericho · Gilgil · 3994 · Embu · Tana · Kolbio · Naivasha · Kijabe · Thika · Kitui · Hola · Narok · **Nairobi** · Machakos · Mokowe · Patta Island · Lake Natron · Magadi · Kajiado · Mutomo

SOMALIA

Benadir · Juba · Ogaden · Fafen · Shibeli

n o p q r s t u v w x y z

0 100 200 300 miles · Average linear scale · 0 100 200 300 400 500 Km

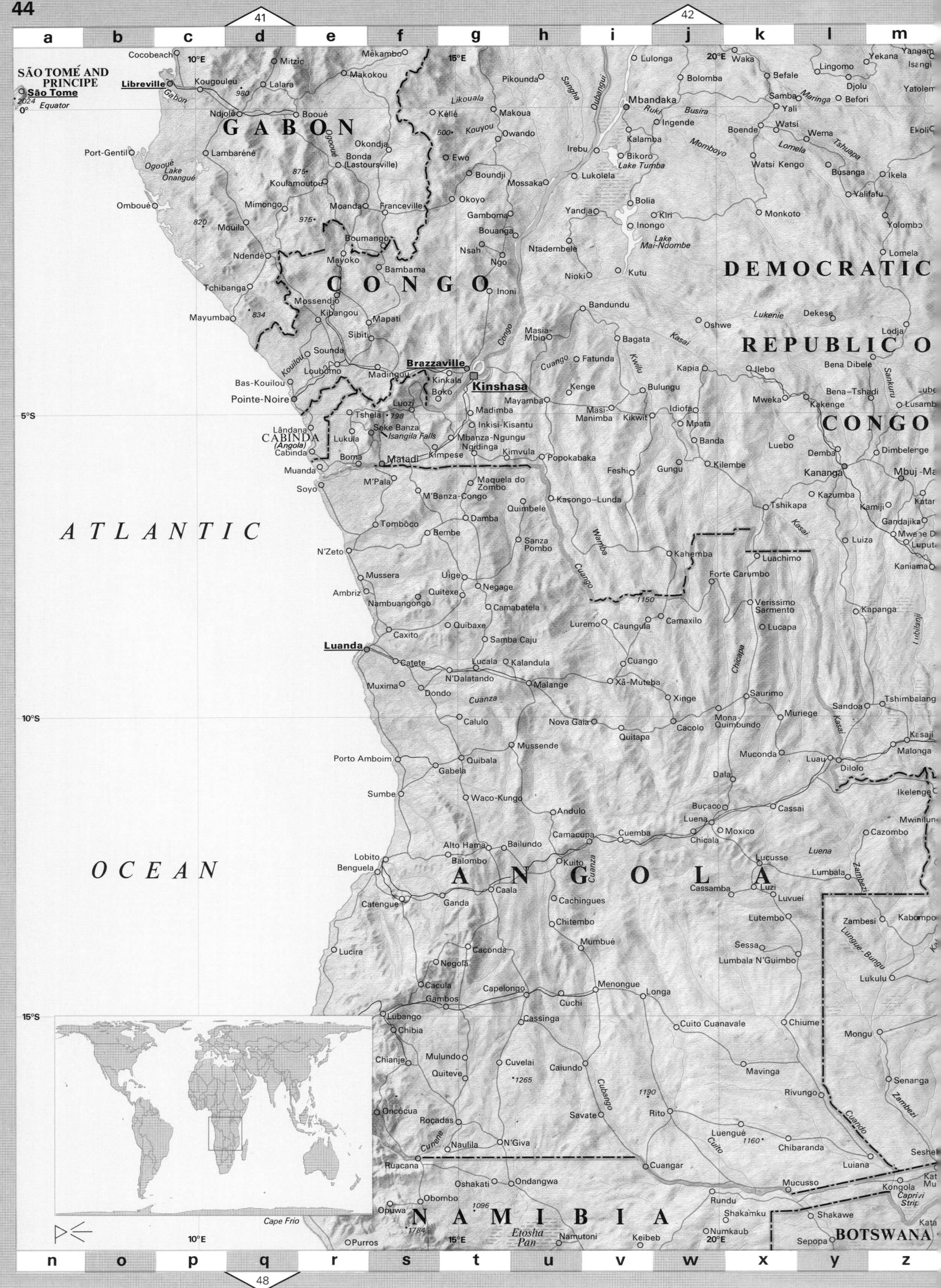

a   b   c   41   d   e   f   g   h   i   j   42   k   l   m

SÃO TOMÉ AND PRINCIPE
São Tome
2024
0° Equator

Cocobeach
Libreville
Kougouleu
Lalara
Mitzic
Mékambo
Makokou
980
Pikounda
Lulonga
Waka
20°E
Yekana
Isangi
Lingomo
Djolu
Yangam
Ndjolé
Booué
Okondja
Bonda
(Lastoursville)
Kéllé
Kouyou
500·
Makoua
Owando
Mbandaka
Ingende
Boende
Watsi
Wema
Samba
Maringa
Befori
Yatolem
Yali
Port-Gentil
Lambaréné
Koulamoutou
875·
Moanda
Franceville
Ewo
Boundji
Mossaka
Irebu
Kalamba
Bikoro
Lake Tumba
Watsi Kengo
Busanga
Ikela
Yalifafu
Ekoli

G A B O N
Lake Onangué
Ombouё
Mimongo
975·
Boumango
Mayoko
Bambama
Okoyo
Gamboma
Bouanga
Yandja
Bolia
Kiri
Inongo
Monkoto
Yolombo
Mouila
820
Nsah
Ngo
Lake Mai-Ndombe
Lomela

Mayumba
834
Tchibanga
Mossendjo
Kibangou
Mapati
Sibiti
C O N G O
Ndendé
Mavoko
Inoni
Nioki
Kutu
Bandundu
Masia-Mbio
Oshwe
Lukenie
Dekese
Lodja
Bagata
D E M O C R A T I C

Sounda
Loubomo
Madingou
Brazzaville
Kinkala
Boko
Kinshasa
Mayamba
Cuango
Fatunda
Kwilu
Kapia
Ilebo
Bena Dibele
R E P U B L I C O
Mweka
Bena–Tshadi
Kakenge
Lusamb

Bas-Kouilou
Kouilou
Loubomo
Luozi
Tshela
798·
Madimba
Inkisi-Kisantu
Kenge
Masi-Manimba
Kikwit
Idiofa
Mpata
Banda
Luebo
Demba
Dimbelerge
C O N G O
Pointe-Noire
Lândana
CABINDA
(Angola)
Cabinda
Lukula
Séke Banza
Isangila Falls
Mbanza-Ngungu
Ngidinga
Kimpese
Kimvula
Popokabaka
Feshi
Gungu
Kilembe
Kazumba
Tshikapa
Kananga
Kamiji
Mbuj–Ma
Katar
5°S
Boma
Matadi
Muanda
M'Pala
Maquela do Zombo
Kasongo–Lunda
Mwene D
Luputa
Soyo
M'Banza-Congo
Luiza
Kaniama

A T L A N T I C
Tombôco
Bembe
Damba
Quimbele
Sanza Pombo
Wamba
Kahemba
Luachimo
Kapanga
N'Zeto
Forte Carumbo
Verissimo Sarmento
Lucapa
Mussera
Uîge
Negage
Cuango
1150
Camaxilo
Ambriz
Quitexe
Camabatela
Luremo
Caungula
Lubilanji
Nambuangongo
Caxito
Quibaxe
Samba Caju
Cuango
Xá-Muteba
Saurimo
Tshimbalang
Luanda
Lucala
Kalandula
Quitapa
Xinge
Cacolo
Mona-Quimbundo
Muriege
Sandoa
Catete
N'Dalatando
Malange
Nova Gaia
Muconda
Luau
Dala
Dilolo
Kasaji
Malonga
Muxima
Dondo
Cuanza
Kesaji
10°S
Calulo
Quibala
Mussende
Quitapa

Porto Amboim
Gabela
Waco-Kungo
Andulo
Buçaco
Luena
Moxico
Cazombo
Mwinilun
Sumbe
Camacupa
Cuemba
Chicala
Lucusse
Ikelenge
Alto Hama
Bailundo
Camacupa
Cassai
Lumbala
Luena
Lobito
Balombo
Kuito
A N G O L A
Cuanza
Cassamba
Luzi
Luvuei
Zambezi
Benguela
Caala
Cachingues
Lutembo
Zambesi
Kabompo
Catengue
Ganda
Chitembo
Mumbué
Sessa
Lumbala N'Guimbo
Lukulu
Lucira
Caconda
Lungué-Bungo
Kal
Negola
Capelongo
Menongue
Longa
Chiume
Cacula
Gambos
Cuchi
Mongu
Cassinga
Cuito Cuanavale
15°S
Lubango
Chíbia
Mavinga
Senanga
Chianje
Mulundo
Cuvelai
Caiundo
Cubango
1190
Rivungo
Quiteve
1265·
Cuito
1160·
Chibaranda
Luengue
Seshe
Oncócua
Roçadas
Savate
Rito
Cuangar
Luiana
Mucusso
Kongola
Caprivi Strip
Kat
Mu
Naulila
N'Giva
Luena
Ruacana
N A M I B I A
Oshakati
Ondangwa
Rundu
Shakámku
Keibeb
Numkaub
Shakawe
Sepopa
BOTSWANA
Opuwa
Purros
Obombo
1096·
1784·
Cape Frio
Etosha Pan
Namutoni

10°E   15°E   20°E

n   o   p   q   48   r   s   t   u   v   w   x   y   z

43

a b c d e f g h i j k l m

Kisangani
Madula
Opienge
yoma
Falls
Maiko
Pene-Tungu
undu
Kirundu
956
Lubutu
koto
Lomami
Punia
1040
Mitumba Mountains
Lowa
Kindu
Kalima
Walikale
Masisi
Goma
Lake Kivu
Kabunga
3044
Gisenyi
Kibuye
Karisimbi 4507
Lubero
Butembo
Kasindi
Lake Edward 2341
Ishasha River
Rutshuru
Kahale
Ruhengeri
RWANDA
Kigali
Gitarama
Kayonza

Beni
Margherita Peak 5109
Fort Portal
Kasese
Lake George 2197
Bushenyi
Mbarara
Kikagati
Kyaka

30°E
Kyenjojo
Mubende
Masaka

UGANDA

Kaliro
Iganga
Jinja
Kampala
Entebbe
Sese Islands
Lake Victoria
Bukoba
Ukerewe Islands

35°E
Kayunga
Tororo
Eldoret
Kakamega
Kisumu
Kericho
Kisii
Kilkoris
Narok

Loruk
Baringo Lodge
Kapsabet
Nyahururu
2277
Nakuru
Gilgil
Naivasha
3100
2775
Kijabe
Nairobi 1662

Archer's Post
Isiolo
Meru
Nanyuki
Mt Kenya (Kirinyaga) 5200
Embu
Thika
Mwingi
Kitui

Garba Tula
Mado Gashi
Saka
Garissa
Hola
Mokowe

40°E
Afmadu
Belesc Cogani
Liboi
SOMALIA
Kisimaio
Kolbio
Equator 0°
Patta Island

Kirundu
Kabondo
Kalima
Mwenga
Ktutu
Nyunzu
Niemba
Ulindi
Kabalo
Katompi
Kaloko
bongo
1060
Pidi
Kikondja
Malemba Nkulu
Luena
Congo
Busanga
lwezi
Kambove
Luambo
Likasi
Minga
Mununga

KENYA

Kisii
Banagi
Tarime
Musoma
Mara
Mwanza
Nansio

Masaka
Nyakanazi
Geita
Ngudu
Shinyanga
Nzega
Manonga
Kahama
Ibologero
Igombe

Oldeani
3188
Arusha
Makuyuni
Mbulu
Ndareda 3420
Katesh
Singida
Kondoa Irangi
2193
Dodoma

Narok
Kajiado
Magadi
Lake Natron
Namanga
2942
Meru 5895 4556
Oloitokitok
Kilimanjaro
Moshi
Same
2124
Manyami
Korogwe
Handeni

Masai Steppe
Kongwa
Gairo
Mpwapwa
Msata
Chalinze
Morogoro
Kilosa 2287
2646
Mikumi
Kisarawe

Tsavo
Mtito Andei National Park
Teavo
Mwatate
Kwale
Lushoto
Segera
Tanga
Zanzibar
Zanzibar Island
Bagamoyo
Dar-es-Salaam

Malindi
Kilifi
Mombasa
Pemba Island
INDIAN
5°S

TANZANIA

Kasulu
Kigoma
Uvinza
Tabora
Sikonge
Itigi
Manyoni
Kitunda
Rungwa
Rungwa
Iringa
2576
Ifakara
2072
Sao Hill

Mahenge
Luhombero
Mbuyuni
Mkomazi

OCEAN
Mafia Island
Kilindoni
Mohoro
Nangurukuru

46

Lake Tanganyika
Mpanda
Malagarasi
Ugalla
Lake Rukwa
Namanyere
Sumbawanga
2418
Kasanga
Chunya
Makongolosi
Mbeya
Uyole 1286
Rungwe
Njombe
Kipembawe

10°S
Lindi
Mingoyo
Mtwara
Nachingwea
Masasi
Nangomba
Newala
Cape Delgado

Pweto
Sumbu
Mpulungu
Mbala
Nakonde
Tunduma
Itungu
Karonga
Chilumba
Livingstonia
2606
Rumphi

Marungu Mountains
Chiengi
Mpulungu
Mbala
Chambeshi
Nchelenge
Mporokoso
Kawambwa
Kapatu
Kasama
Mbesuma
Isoka
Chinsali
1475
Chisoso
Chama
Mzuzu
Mzimba
Chikwa
Lundazi

Lake Mweru
Mitwaba
Lake Upemba
Kabondo Dianda
Mukana
Kasembe
Luwingu
Mansa
Samfya
Lake Bangweulu
Mpika
Chilonga

1139
Kamina
Kabongo
Kabondo

Kasenga
Bunkeya
Muchinga Mountains
Luangwa
Gumbiro
Songea
Lukumburu

Lake Malawi (Lake Nyasa)
Nkhata Bay
Chamba

Tunduru
Masuguru
Diaca
Mueda
Mocimboa da Praia
Macomia

Solwezi
Kipushi
Lubumbashi
Mokambo
Chililabombwe
Chingola
Mufulira
Kitwe 1350
Ndola 1261
Luanshya

Kapalala
Mukuku
Chibembe
Nkhotakota
Kasungu
Maniamba 1836
Litunde
Lichinga
Malanga

Montepuez
Nantulo
Metoro
Pemba

Kasempa
Chembe
Kanona
Serenje

ZAMBIA
Kabwe
Kapiri Mposhi
Chifwefwe
Liangua
Luangwa
Chipata
Mchinji
Petauke
Katete
Nyimba
Lilongwe
Salima

Massangulo
Maúa
Messalo
Marrupa
Nungo
Namapa

Landless Corner
Mumbwa
Rufunsa
Fingoè
Lúrio
Mandimba
Cuamba
Ribauè
Mutuali
Namialo

Kachalola
Nyimba
Dedza 2035
Mangochi
Balaka
Gurué
2419
200
Alto Molócuè
Nampula
Monapo
Lumbo
Moçambique

MALAWI

Namwala
Mazabuka
Lusaka 1279
Zumbo
Kariba Reservoir
Songo
Chiúta
Zomba
Lake Chilwa
Limbe 3000
2133
Blantyre

Liupo
Nametil

15°S

1220
Namwala
Lubungu
Kariba
Kaoma
Zambezi
Mhangura
Mount Darwin
Nyamapanda
Tete
Changara
Tambara
Caia
Mopeia
Quelimane
Pebane
Namacurra
Moma
Mocuba
Mucubela
Angoche
Nacala
Nacaroa
2064

Kalomo
Livingstone
Victoria Falls
Binga
Choma
1204
Karoi
Banket
Kadoma
Chegutu
Gokwe
ZIMBABWE
Harare 1472
Mvurwi
Bindura
Mutoko
Rusape
Inyanga
596
1868
Inhaminga
Gorongosa
105
Chinde
40°E

andamatenga
Hwange
Gwai River
Dete
Kariba
Binga
Sanyati
Kafue
Nyamapanda
Guro
Catandica
Sena
Nsanje
Mocuba

MOZAMBIQUE

30°E
35°E

n o p q r s t u v w x y z

49

0 100 200 300 miles
Average linear scale
0 100 200 300 400 500 Km

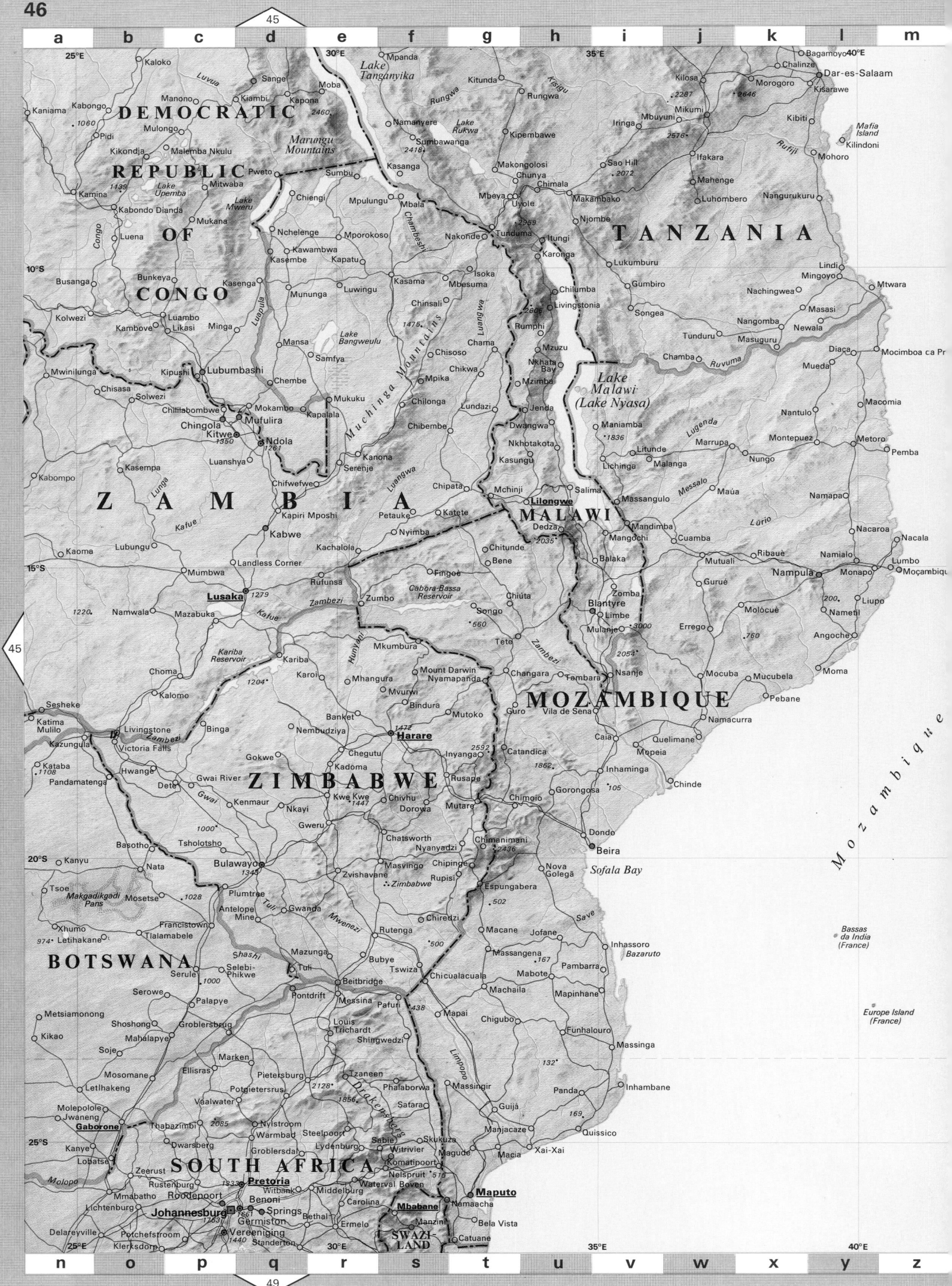

| a | b | c | d | e | f | g | h | i | j | k | l | m |

25°E
30°E
35°E
40°E

Kaloko
Mpanda
Bagamoyo

DEMOCRATIC
Luvua
Sange
Moba
Lake
Tanganyika
Kitunda
Chalinze
Dar-es-Salaam
Kilosa
Morogoro

Manono
Kiambi
Kapona
.2287
.2646
Kisarawe

Kabongo
Mulongo
.2460
Rungwa
Rungwa
Mbuyuni
Mikumi
Mafia
Island

Kaniama
.1060
Kikondja
Malemba Nkulu
Marungu
Mountains
Namanyere
Lake
Rukwa
Sumbawanga
.2418
Kipembawe
Iringa
.2578
Ifakara
Mahenge
Kilindoni
Mohoro

Pidi
Lake
Upemba
Mitwaba
Pweto
Sumbu
Kasanga
Makongolosi
Chunya
Sao Hill
.2072
Luhombero
Nangurukuru

REPUBLIC
.1139
Lake
Mweru
Chiengi
Mpulungu
Mbala
Uyole
Tunduma
.2959
Itungi
Makambako
Njombe

Kamina
Kabondo Dianda
Nchelenge
Mporokoso
Nakonde
Karonga
Lukumburu
Luena

Luena
Mukana
Kawambwa
Kapatu
Isoka
Chilumba
Lindi

Busanga
OF
Kasembe
Mbesuma
Livingstonia
Gumbiro
Songea
Nachingwea
Mingoyo
Mtwara

Bunkeya
Kasenga
Mununga
Luwingu
Kasama
Chinsali
Rumphi
Mzuzu
Chamba
Ruvuma
Masasi
Newala
Mueda
Mocimboa ca Pr

Kolwezi
Kambove
Luambo
Likasi
Minga
Mansa
Samfya
Lake
Bangweulu
.1475
Chisoso
Chama
Nkhata
Bay
.2606
Nangomba
Masuguru
Diaca

Mwinilunga
CONGO
Kipushi
Lubumbashi
Chembe
Mukuku
Mpika
Chikwa
Mzimba
Chilonga
Litunde
Marrupa
Nungo
Namapa
Macomia

Chisasa
Solwezi
Chililabombwe
Mokambo
Kapalala
Chilonga
Lundazi
Jenda
Maniamba
.1836
Lichinga
Malanga
Montepuez
Metoro
Pemba

Chingola
Mufulira
Kitwe
.1350
Ndola
.1261
Kanona
Serenje
Chibembe
Dwangwa
Nkhotakota
Kasungu
Lake
Malawi
(Lake Nyasa)
Lugenda
Maúa
Nantulo

Luanshya
Chifwefwe
ZAMBIA
Kapiri Mposhi
Kabwe
Chipata
Katete
Mchinji
Lilongwe
Dedza
Salima
Massangulo
Messalo
Lúrio
Nacaroa
Nacala

Kaoma
Lubungu
Landless Corner
Petauke
Nyimba
Chitunde
Bene
Mangochi
Balaka
Cuamba
Mutuali
Gurué
Ribauè
Namialo
Lumbo
Moçambique

15°S

Kabompo
.1220
Namwala
Mumbwa
Rufunsa
Fingoé
Cabora-Bassa
Reservoir
Songo
Ghiúta
Zomba
Blantyre
Limbe
Molócuè
Errego
Nampula
Monapo

Lusaka
.1279
Zumbo
Zambezi
.560
Tete
Mulanje
.3000
.2054
.760
Angoche

Namwala
Mazabuka
Kafue
Mkumbura
Zambezi
Changara
Tambara
Nsanje
Mocuba
Mucubela
Moma

Kaoma
Kariba
Reservoir
Karoi
Mhangura
Mount Darwin
Nyamapanda
Guro
Vila de Sena
MOZAMBIQUE
Pebane

Sesheke
Katima
Mulilo
Kazungula
Livingstone
Victoria Falls
Binga
.1204
Kariba
Mvurwi
Bindura
Mutoko
Caia
Quelimane
Mopeia

Kataba
.1108
Pandamatenga
Hwange
Dete
Gwai River
Banket
Nembudziya
.1472
Harare
Inyanga
.2592
Catandica
.1862
Gorongosa
.105
Inhaminga
Chinde

20°S

Basotho
.1000
Gokwe
Kadoma
Chegutu
ZIMBABWE
Rusape
Chimoio
Mutare
Dondo
Beira

Tsholotsho
Kwe Kwe
.1447
Chivhu
Dorowa
Chimanimani
.2436
Sofala Bay

Kanyu
Nata
Bulawayo
.1345
Zvishavane
Masvingo
.Zimbabwe
Nyanyadzi
Chipinge
Rupisi
Nova
Golegã
Espungabera

Tsoe
Mosetse
.1028
Plumtree
Antelope
Mine
Gwanda
Chiredzi
Macane
Jofane
.502
Bassas
da India
(France)

Xhumo
.974
Letlhakane
Tlalamabele
Rutenga
.500
Massangena
.767
Mabote
Pambarra
Bazaruto

BOTSWANA
Serule
Mazunga
Bubye
Tswiza
Chicualacuala
Machaila
Mapinhane

Metsiamonong
Selebi-Phikwe
.1000
Tuli
Beitbridge
Messina
Pafuri
.438
Mapai
Chigubo
Funhalouro
Massinga

Serowe
Palapye
Pontdrift
Louis
Trichardt
Shingwedzi
.132
Inhambane

Kikao
Shoshong
Mahalapye
Soje
Marken
Pietersburg
Tzaneen
Phalaborwa
Massingir
Panda

25°S

Letlhakeng
Mosomane
Ellisras
Potgietersrus
.2128
Phalaborwa
Safara
Guijá
Manjacaze
Quissico

Molepolole
Jwaneng
Gaborone
Thabazimbi
.2085
Nylstroom
Warmbad
Steelpoort
Lydenburg
Sabie
.1856
Witrivier
Skukuza
Magude
Macia
Xai-Xai

Kanye
Lobatse
Zeerust
Rustenburg
Dwarsberg
Groblersdal
Sabie
Nelspruit
.575
Komatipoort
Magude
Namaacha
Maputo

SOUTH AFRICA
.1933
Pretoria
Witbank
Middelburg
Carolina
Waterval Boven
Mbabane
SWAZI
LAND
Manzini
Bela Vista

Lichtenburg
Mmabatho
Roodepoort
Johannesburg
.1667
Benoni
Springs
Bethal
Ermelo
Mbabane
Catuane

Delareyville
Potchefstroom
Klerksdorp
Vereeniging
Germiston
.1440
Standerton

Molopo
Vaalwater

25°E
30°E
35°E
40°E

| n | o | p | q | r | s | t | u | v | w | x | y | z |

This map shows 1/60 of the earth's surface

a b c d e f g h i j k l m

45°E 50°E 55°E 60°E

Aldabra Island

I N D I A N   O C E A N

10°S

Moroni
COMOROS

Comoros Islands
Moheli
Anjouan

Dzaoudzi
Mayotte (France)

Antsiranana

Ambilobe

Nosy-Bé
Hell-Ville

Iharaña

Tsaratanana
2876
Mountains

Sambava

Andapa

Antsohihy

Antalaha

Befandriana Av.
1218

Ambohitralanana

Mahalevona
Maroantsetra

15°S

Mahajanga

Port-Bergé-Vaovao

Mandritsara

Marovoay

Mampikony

Mananara

Betsiboka

1301

Mahavavy

Miarinarivo

Nosy Boraha

Juan de Nova

1325

Maevatanana

Andriamena

M A D A G A S C A R

1545

Morafenobe

Vohidiala
Toamasina

Antsalova

Ankazobe

Tsiroanomandidy

Antananarivo
1351

Manambolo

2643

Mandoto

Betafo

Mahanoro

Tsimafana

Antsirabe

Tsiribihina

Morondava

Mahabo

2140

Fandriana

Ambositra

20°S

Port Louis
MAURITIUS

Mandabe

Mananjary

Fianarantsoa

Irondro

Saint-Denis
3069
Réunion (France)

Mangoky

Ambalavao
Manakara

Isalo Mountains

2658

Ankazoabo
1348

Ihosy

Ivohibe

Manombo

Farafangana

Toliara

Andranovory

Mangoro

Betroka
1824

Vangaindrano

Tropic of Capricorn

Betioky

Ampanihy

1957

Antanimora

Taolañaro

25°S

Tsihombe

Ambovombe

C h a n n e l

45°E 50°E 55°E 60°E

n o p q r s t u v w x y z

0 100 200 300 miles

Average linear scale

0 100 200 300 400 500 Km

44

10°E 15°E 20°E

ANGOLA

Namibe
Chibia
Cassinga
Chiume
Mongu

Tômbua
(Porto Alexandre)
Chianje
Mulundo
Cuvelai
Caiundo
Cuito Cuanavale
Senanga

Tambor
·900
Quiteve
·1265
Savate
·1190
Rito
Luengué
Rivungo

Oncócua
Roçadas
Cubango
Xamavera
Chibaranda
Luiana

Iona
N'Giva
Cuangar
Mucusso
Kong

Foz do Cunene
·2195
Cunene
Naulila
Rundu
Shakamku
Shakawe

Ruacana
Obombo
Oshakati
Ondangwa
Okavango
Sepopa

Orupembe
Opuwa
Ovamboland
·1096
Keibeb
Numkaub
·950
Gumare
*Okavengo
Delta*

Cape Frio
·1784
Namutoni
*Etosha
Pan*
·1093
Tsumeb
Tsumkwe
Mount Aha
·1070

Purros
Kowares
Okaukuejo
Otavi
·2149
Grootfontein
Tsau
To

Terrace Bay
·869
Kamanjab
Goreis
Outjo
Otjiwarongo
·1932
Okakarara
Dekar
Ghanzi

Khorixas
Kalkfeld
NAMIBIA
Hochfeld
Kalkfontein
Takatshwaane

*Brandberg
2579*
Uis Mine
Omaruru
2350
Steinhausen
·1537 Buitepos
Kule
BOT

Cape Kruis
Usakos
Okahandja
Witvlei
Gobabis
Kalahar

Henties Bay
Anschluss
Windhoek
1654
Dordabis
Leonardville
·1000
Kang

Swakopmund
·160
Rehoboth
Derm
Aranos
Ukwi
Tshane

Walvis Bay
·2334
Abbabis
Kalkrand
Stampriet
Mariental
Mpaathutlwa
Pan
Makopong

Tropic of Capricorn
Sesriem
Maltahöhe
Gochas
·1046
Nossob
Terr
Firm

A T L A N T I C
Naribis
Zaris
Asab
Asanib
Twee
Rivier
Koës
Tshabong

Helmeringhausen
·1185
Twee Rivieren
Molopo
Frylincksp

*Great Tiraz
1867*
Béthanie
Gemsbok
·1000

Lüderitz
Aus
Keetmanshoop
Aroab
Kurumar
Sishen
1832

Goageb
Narubis
*Gr. Karasberge
2202*
Dariël

Pomona
Witpütz
Grünau
·1107
Karasburg
Kurumar

O C E A N
Alexander Bay
Orange
1341
Ariamsvlei
·903
Upington
Orange
Postmasburg

Viooldsdrif
Augrabies
Falls
Keimoes
Griekwasta

Port Nolloth
Steinkopf
Onseepkans
Kakamas
S

Nababeep
Pofadder
Kenhardt
Groblershoop

Springbok
Namies
Marydale
Prie

·30°S
Platbakkies
Van Wyksvlei
Copperton

Garies
Brandvlei
Vosburg
Brits

Loeriesfontein
Carnarvon
Victo
West

Bitterfontein
Nieuwoudtville
Williston
Loxton

Vanrhynsdorp
Calvinia
Fraserburg
Sak

Clanwilliam
Sutherland
Fish
Beaufort
West
Kiewie

Slippers Bay
Citrusdal
*Komsberg
1721*
Prince Albert Road
Great Karo

Vredenburg
·1040
Laingsburg
*Little Swartberge
2325*
Willowm

Saldanha
*Gr. Winterhoek
2078*
Touws River
Oudtshoorn
Haarlem

Malmesbury
Wellington
Worcester
Little Karoo
George
Kny

Cape Town
Strand
Swellendam
Mosselbaai

*Cape of
Good Hope*
Caledon
Witsand
Stilbaai

Cape Agulhas
Agulhas

10°E 15°E 20°E

This map shows 1/60 of the earth's surface

a b c d e f g h i j k l m

25°E 30°E 35°E 40°E

Mumbwa Rufunsa Fingoè Chiúta Zomba Gurué Nampula Moçambique
Lusaka 1279 Zumbo Cabora Bassa - Reservoir Songo MALAWI Liupo Nametil
1220 Namwala Lake Kafue Kafue Zambezi Tete Blantyre Mulanje Molócuè Nametil Angoche
Kariba Reservoir Kariba Mkumbura 3000 Errego 760
A M B I A Kalomo Choma Karoi Mhangura Mount Darwin Changara Tambara Nsanje Mocuba Mucubela Moma
Sesheke Livingstone Binga Mvurwi Bindura Nyamapanda Guro Vila de Sena Namacurra Pebane
Katima Mulilo Zambezi Victoria Falls Hwange Gokwe Banket 1472 Mutoko Guru 2592 Catandica Caia Mopeia Quelimane
Kazungula Dete Gwai River ZIMBABWE Harare Chegutu Rusape Inyanga Catandica Inhaminga Chinde
Kataba 1108 Pandamatenga Kenmaur Kadoma Chivhu Mutare Chimoio Gorongosa 1862 105
Tsoe Nata Basotho Nkayi Kwe Kwe 1447 Dorowa Chimanimani Nova Golegã Sofala Bay
Kanyu Tsholotsho Bulawayo 1343 Gweru Chatsworth Nyanyadzi Chipinge Beira Mozambique Channel
Xhumo 974 Tlalamabele Plumtree 1028 Chiredzi Rupisi Espungabera Dondo Bassas da India (France)
Letlhakane Mosetse Antelope Mine Zvishavane Masvingo Save 20°S
Francistown Mwenezi Rutenga Macane Jofane Inhassoro
W A N A Serule 1000 Tuli Mazunga 500 Massangena Mabote Bazaruto Europe Island (France)
Metsiamonong Sercwe Selebi-Phikwe Bubye 502 Machaila Pambarra Mapinhane
Kalamare Palapye Pontdrif Beitbridge Tswiza Chicualacuala Chigubo Massinga
Kikao Soje Messina Pafuri 438 Mapai Funhalouro 132
Dutlwe Mosomane Mahalapye Louis Trichardt Shingwedzi Panda Inhambane
Letlhakeng Molepolole Ellisras Marken Phalaborwa Massingir Guijá 169
Gaborone Vaalwater Pietersburg Tzaneen Satara Magude Manjacaze Quissico
Kanye 1479 Thabazimbi 2128 Potgietersrus 1856 Steelpoort Skukuza Macia Xai-Xai 25°S
Lobatse Dwarsberg Nylstroom Sable Witrivier Komatipoort
Zeerust Warmbad Groblersdal Lydenburg Nelspruit 515 Maputo
Molopo Rustenburg Pretoria 1333 Middelburg Waterval Boven Mbabane Namaacha
orokweng Mmabatho Lichtenburg Roodepoort 1753 Benoni Witbank Carolina Manzini SWAZI LAND Bela Vista
Delareyville Potchefstroom Johannesburg Germiston Ermelo Catuane
Vryburg Klerksdorp 1661 Vereeniging Bethal Standerton Piet Retief Lavumisa
Schweizer-Reneke Wolmaransstad Parys Vaal Reservoir 1440 Vaal Frankfort Volksrust 2277 Pongola Mkuze
Reivilo Christiana Heilbron Utrecht Vryheid Lake St. Lucia
Warrenton Bloemhof Kroonstad Reitz Newcastle 1532 Mtubatuba
Barkly West Bultfontein Welkom Bethlehem Harrismith Dundee Ulundi
Kimberley Winburg Senekal Ficksburg Ladysmith Eshowe Richards Bay
1426 Bloemfontein Clocolan Mont aux Sources 3266 Estcourt Tugela Greytown
TH Luckhoff Faursmith Maseru 3096 3482 Himeville Pietermaritzburg
Wepener Mafeteng LESOTHO Durban 30°S
Trompsburg Smithfield Zastron Moyeni Mount Fletcher Kokstad Ixopo 1000 Umzinto
P.K. le Roux Reservoir Hendrik Verwoerd Reservoir Orange Lady Grey Harding Port Shepstone
Colesberg Aliwal North Mount Frere Port Edward
Middelburg Steynsburg 2052 Barkly East Maclear 1677 Elliot Umtata Port St. Johns
ICA Lady Frere Idutywa Coffee Bay
Graaff-Reinet Cradock Queenstown Stutterheim King William's Town
Somerset East Fort Beaufort 500 Grahamstown East London
Kirkwood Bell
Steytlerville 1627 Port Alfred
Uitenhage Port Elizabeth
mansdorp Jeffreys Bay

I N D I A N

O C E A N

35°S

25°E 30°E 35°E 40°E

n o p q r s t u v w x y z

0 100 200 300 miles   Average linear scale   0 100 200 300 400 500 Km

85°N

35°E 40°E 45°E 50°E 55°E 60°E 65°E

A R C

A R C

80°N

Alexandra Land   George Land   Salisbury I.   Jackson I.   Rudolf I.   Karla-   La Rons'yer   Yeva-Liv
Luidzhi   Aleksandra   Graham Bell
Hooker I.   Hall I.   Wilczek Land   Island
McClintock I.   Sal'm

F r a n z   J o s e f   L a n d   Zem

75°N

Russkaya Gavan   •102.2

Smidovich

N o v a y a   Z e m l y a

K A R A   S E A

Sedova
1115
Stolbovoy

70°N

B A R E N T S   S E A

Litke

•260

Cape Uanga

Krasino

•162
Vaigač   *B a i d a r*

Proliv Karskiye Vorota

Amderma

Pay-Khoy   •467   Ust'-Kara

Kolgujev   Chernaya   Yangarey   *T u n d r a*
166   Dresvyanka   •201

Murmansk   Cape Kanin Nos   Khal'mer-Yu   •1218

Makarikha   Koreyver   Vorkuta   Yeletskiy

Mončegorsk   •242   •106   Nar'yan   *B o l' s h e z e m e l' s k a y a*   Kolva
•1191   Mar
Kirovsk   *K a n i n*   Velikovisochnoye   Pay-yer   •   Labytnangi
397   *P e n i n s u l a*   Volonga   Makarikha   Abez'   1499   Salekar
Kandalakša   *Č e š a*   •463   Trosh   Narodnaya
K o l a   *B a y*   Mezen'   Nonburg   Usa   Inta   1894
Arctic Circle   Stafonovo   Ust'Tsil'ma   •155   Saranpaul'
Mezen'   Izhma   Kosyu   Vanzevat
Kandalaksa Gulf   *Gulf*   Azopol'ye   Pechora   Patrasuy   Kash
White   Kadzherom   Berezovo   Feculki
Sea   Pinega   Politovo   Kedva   •164   Kyrta   1617   North Sasva
Dvina Bay   Shomvukva   Voyvozh   *N o r t h e r n*   Muligort
Severodvinsk   Vendenga   •324   Ukhta
65°N   Archangel   Loptyuga   Vey Vozh   •1108   Nyaksimvol   Sergina
Belomorsk   Onega Bay   Pinega   Zheleznodorozhnyy   Troitsko-Pechorsk   Khangokurt
Onega   Mikun   Puzla   Porog   Suyevatpaul   Po'yan
Segeža   Irta   *R U S*   Kur'ya   Sovetskiy
•417   Verkhnyaya   Syktyvkar   Ust'Kulom   303   Ivdel'   Komsomol'skiy
Medvežjegors   Toyma   Vizinga   •1027   Polunochnoye   Pionerskiy
Kizema   Kotlas   •213   Cherdyn   1493   Mt lym'
Petrozavodsk   Konoša   239   Kazhim   *U v a l y*   Denezkin
Kargopol   Velikiy   Noshul'   Kama   Kamen
60°N   Podporoze   Vel   Ustyug   Pyatigory   Krasnotur'insk   162   •78
Totma   Kirs   Solikamsk
Tichvin   Nikol'sk   Murashi   Kudymkar   Berezniki   Lobva   Sos'va
Lake   Nizhniy   *N o r t h e r n*   Gubakha   •883
Onega   Yenangsk   Kamskoje   Verkhniy Tura   100
Čerepovec   •292   Vetluga   Kirov   Reservoir   Krasnokamsk   Nizhniy Tagil
Vologda   Bui   Vetluzhskiy   Novo-Vyatsk   Glazov   Perm'   •321   Turinsk
Rybinsk   Kotel'nich   Kez   Kungur   Artemovskiy
Reservoir   Pizhma   Igra   Tavda
Rybinsk   Kostroma   Nolinsk   Votkinsk   Pervoural'sk   Yekaterinburg   Tyum
•343   Jaroslavl   Uren   Yaransk   Krasnoufimsk   Degtyarsk   Bogdanovich   Talitsa
Ostashkov   Kinesma   Kil'mez   Izhevsk   Sysert'   Yalutorovsk
Torzhok   Tver   Iwanovo   Krasnyye-Baki   217   Agryz   Kamensk-
Nelidovo   Staritsa   Klin Dmitrov   Kovrov   Yoshkar   Malmyzh   Sarapul   Ural'skiy   Shadrinsk
Ržev   Volokolamsk   Sergiyev Posad   Vladimir   Ola   Arsk   Neftekamsk   Nyazepetrovsk   Kasli
Dubna   Balashikha   Dzerzhinsk   •115   Cheboksary   Naberezhnyje   Kamensk
Moscow   Noginsk   Nizhniy   Yadrin   Celny
(Moskva)   Orechovo   Novgorod   Kazan'   Mamadysh
Odintsovo   Zujevo   Murom   235   50°E   55°E   65°E
35°E   Elektrostal   45°E

This map shows 1/60 of the earth's surface

70°E   75°E   80°E   85°E   90°E   95°E   100°E   85°N

T I C   *O C E A N*

S e v e r n a y a   Z e m l y a

Schmidta

Ushakova

Komsomolets   Cape Berga
Pioner   80°N
262 Oktyabr'skoy Revolyutsii
Vize   800
Shokal'skogo Str.
West Siberian Sea   Bolshevik

Nordenshel'da
Mys Zelaniya   Isačenko   Russkiy
Arch. Taimyr   Cape Oskara

Troynoy   Niž Taimyra 75°N
Arkticheskogo   512
Instituta   Mikhaylova   *T a i m y r   P e n i n s u l a*
171   *B y r r a n g a   M o u n t a i n s*

Pyasina Bay   Pjasina   223   Tareya   Verkh. Taimyra   Lake
Taimyr
Belyy   Sokalsky   Vilkicky   Dikson   Makarova   Novay
Drovyanaya   Sibirjakov   Zyryanka   279 Pura   Lake
47   Oleni   415   Dudypta   Labaz Isayevskiy Kheta
Tambey   Taran   *Gyda Bay*   Gol'chikha   Agapa   Ust'-Avam   Payturma Boganida   Kargo
Yuribey   *Yenisey Bay* Oshmarino   Kresty   Volochanka   Boyarka
Yamal   Lake   Napalkovo   Gyda   Yakovlevka   Yangoda   Chernaya   Dolgany   Kochikha
Neyto   *Gyda Peninsula* Karaul   Ust'-Port Chernaya   Maimeca
Peninsula 75   Khokiley   Dudinka   Ayan 1403 70°N
Yaptiksale   160   Antipayuta   Lake   Lake Lama 1612   *P u t o r a n a*
66   Taz Bay   Yamburg   202   Noril'sk Pjasina   1274   2036 Kamen *M o u n t a i n s*
82   Lake   Nakhodka   Potapovo Lake Keta Ambar
Yarongo   Yarroto   Yepoko   Tazovskiy   Khantayka Lake   Kureyka   Lake
Novyy Port   Nyamboyoto   65   Khantayskoye   Khantayskoye   Anama
Shchuch'ye Yada   Sidorovoko   Yermakovo Reservoir   814   Agata Lake
Gornyy Kazymsk Shuga   Yanov Stan Karasino Igarka   Vivi
Nyda   Taz   Ust'-Kureyka   Severnaja
Pangody   Urengoy   Krasnosel'kup   Farkovo Turukhan   Chirinda
Staryy Nadym   Chasel'ka   Kostino Turukhansk   *T u n g u s k o y e*
112   42   Tolka   22   Bugarikta   Tembenchi
168   Vyngapur   Tolka   698 Noginskiy Niznaja Tunguska Tutonchany Chiskovo Vivi Tura
Kazymskaya Kazym   Kikiakki   Nizhneimbatskoye *M o u n t a i n s* 552 Uchami Nidym
Numto   *U v a l y*   Noyabr'sk   Khalesavoy   Ratta   Matyl'ka   Verkhneimbatskoye   970
Siberian Pokacheva   Taz   Yeloguy   Kuzmov'ka
Nazym   Yermakovo Agan   Kolik'yegan   Sabun   Bakhta Poligus
Kedrovyy Ljamin   Pim   77 Korliki   Yeloguy Sumarokovo Podkamennaya Tunguska Baykit
Khanty-Mansiysk Ob' Surgut   Ust'Kolik'yegan   Kellog   Osinovo   Korda Ounja
Irtysh   Nizhnevartovsk   Vach 55 Lar'yak Velmo1-oye Vayvida Mutoray
Strezhevoy   Vanzhil'kynak   Sym   Yartsevo Teya Ust'Kamo
Kintus   Aleksandrovskoye Nazina   Sym   Sym Polkan Kamo Taimba 60°N
99 Demyanskoye   Negotka Kadzhi   951   Novoyerudinskiy
Ust'Tym   Tym   Nazimovo   695 Yarkino
Cherpiya Gerasmikova Katyl'ga Vasjugan Kargasok Lugovatka Ust'Pit Bryanka Cadobec Panovo
Demyanka   Onegva Yar   Ket   Ust'Ozernoye Kamenka Bedopa
Tobol'sk   Bystryy Staritsa Alipxa Vorozheyka Yeniseysk Angara Boguchany Kova
Baykalovo   Kolpashevo Belyy Yar   Lesosibirsk Strelka Rodina Chuna Karamysheva 636
Irtysh   Tevriz 142 L'vovka Mogochin Baturino 211 Galanino Oktyabr'sk Asansk
Tara Parbig   Komsomol'sk Altat Predivinsk Aban Shelayevo
122   Biaza Bakchar Moryakovskiy Tegul'det Meletsk Birilyussy 530 Vydrind
Golyshmanovo 124 Zaton 258 Achinsk Shivera Chunskiy Nevanka
Ishim   Panovo Bol'sherech'ye Pikhtovka Yurga Tomsk Mariinsk Bogotol Pamyat Uyar Borodino Bratsk
Chumakovo   Anzhero Nazarovo 818 Krasnojarsk Taishet
Nazyvayevsk Tyukalinsk Pokrovka Sudzhensk   Kansk
70°E   75°E   80°E   85°E   90°E   95°E   100°E

S I A

0   100   200   300 miles   0   100   200   300   400   500 Km
Average linear scale

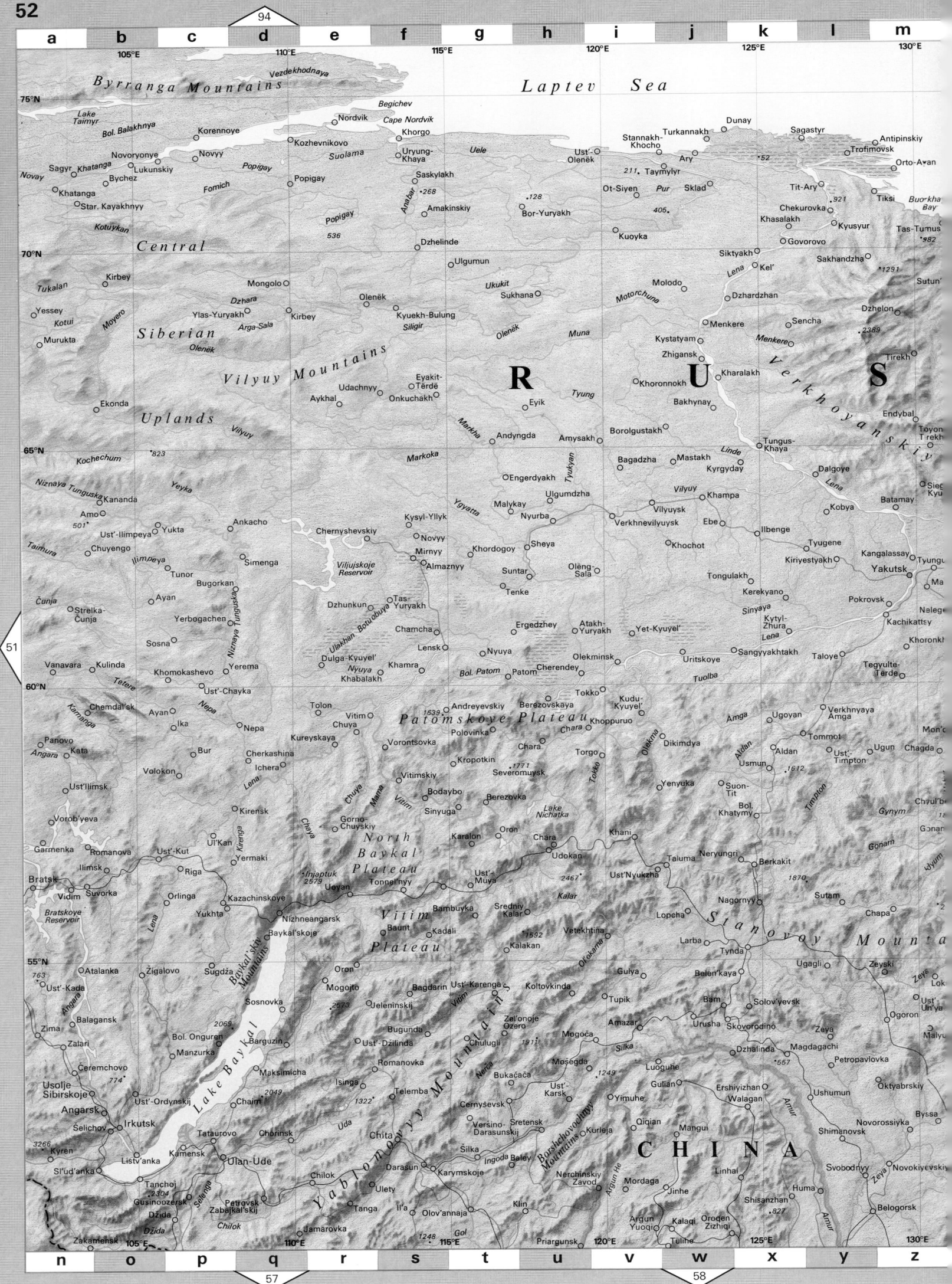

Byrranga Mountains   Vezdekhodnaya   **Laptev   Sea**

Lake Taimyr   Bol. Balakhnya   Korennoye   Begichev   Cape Nordvik   Dunay   Sagastyr   Antipinskiy

Novay   Sagyr   Khatanga   Novoryonye   Lukunskiy   Novyy   Kozhevnikovo   Khorgo   Uele   Ust'-Olenëk   Stannakh-Khocho   Turkannakh   Ary   ·52   Trofimovsk   Orto-Ayan

Khatanga   Bychez   Popigay   Suolama   Uryung-Khaya   Pur   Sklad   Tit-Ary   ·921   Kyusyur   Tas-Tumus

Star. Kayakhnyy   Fomich   Popigay   Saskylakh   211·   Taymylyr   405·   Chekurovka   Khasalakh   Tiksi   Buorkha Bay

Kotuykan   Popigay   536   ·268   Amakinskiy   ·128   Bor-Yuryakh   Ot-Siyen   Kuoyka   Govorovo   ·982

Central   Dzhelinde   Ulgumun   Siktyakh   Sakhandzha   ·1291

Tukalan   Kirbey   Mongolo   Ukukit   Molodo   Lena   Kel'   Dzhardzhan   Sutun'

Yessey   Dzhara   Olenëk   Sukhana   Motorchuna   Menkere   Sencha   Dzhelon

Kotui   *Moyero*   Ylas-Yuryakh   Kirbey   Kyueykh-Bulung   Kystatyam   ·2389

Murukta   **Siberian**   *Arga-Sala*   *Siligir*   Olenëk   Zhigansk   Menkere   Tirekh

Olenëk   *Muna*   Khoronnokh   Kharalakh   Endybal

Ekonda   **Vilyuy Mountains**   Eyakit-Tërdë   **R**   **U**   Bakhynay   **S**   Toyon Trekh

Uplands   Udachnyy   Onkuchakh   Eyik   Tyung   Linde   Tungus-Khaya

Vilyuy   Aykhal   Markha   Andyngda   Borolgustakh   Bagadzha   Mastakh   Kyrgyday   Dalgoye   Sieg Kyu

Kochechum   ·823   Yeyka   Markoka   Engerdyakh   Tyukyan   Ulgumdzha   Vilyuy   Khampa   Kobya   Batamay

Nizhnaya Tunguska   Kananda   Malykay   Nyurba   Vilyuysk   Verkhnevilyuysk   Ebe   Kiriyestyakh   Kangalassay   Tyungu

Amo   Yukta   Ankacho   Kysyl-Yllyk   Ygyatta   Khordogoy   Sheya   Olëng-Sala   Khochot   Ilbenge   Tyugene   Yakutsk

501·   Ust'-Ilimpeya   Chernyshevskiy   Novyy   Ma

Taimura   Chuyengo   Simenga   Mirnyy   Almaznyy   Suntar   Tenke   Tongulakh   Kerekyano   Pokrovsk   Nelege

Ilimpeya   Tunor   Bugorkan   *Viljujskoje Reservoir*   Tas-Yuryakh   Dzhunkun   Chamcha   Ergedzhey   Atakh-Yuryakh   Yet-Kyuyel'   Sinyaya   Kytyl-Zhura   Kachikatts

Čunja   Ayan   Yerbogachen   *Ulakhan Botuobuya*   Ergedzhey   Lena   Khoronk

Strelka-Čunja   Sosna   Dulga-Kyuyel'   Lensk   Nyuya   Olekminsk   Uritskoye   Sangyyakhtakh   Taloye   Tegyulte-Tërde

Vanavara   Kulinda   Khomokashevo   Yerema   *Nyuya Khabalakh*   Khamra   *Bol. Patom*   Patom   Cherendey   *Tuolba*

Kamanga   *Tetere*   Ust'-Chayka   Tokko   Kudu-Kyuyel'   Amga   Ugoyan   Verkhnyaya Amga

Chemdal'sk   Ayan   Nepa   Tolon   Vitim   1639·   Andreyevskiy   Berëzovskaya   Khoppuruo   Mon'o

Panovo   Kata   Ika   Chuya   **Patomskove Plateau**   Chara   Olëkma   Dikimdya   Tommot

Angara   Bur   Kureyskaya   Polovinka   Chara   Torgo   Usmun   Aldan   Ust'-Timpton   Ugun   Chagda

Ust'-Ilimsk   Cherkashina   Vorontsovka   Kropotkin   1771·   Severomuysk   Tokko   Yenyuka   ·1612   Suon-Tit   *Timpton*   Chyul'b

Vorob'yeva   Ichera   Vitimskiy   Bodaybo   Berëzovka   *Lake Nichatka*   Bol. Khatymy   Gynym   Gonan

Garmenka   Romanova   *Lena*   Sinyuga   Karalon   Oron   Chara   Khani   *Gonam*

Bratsk   Vidim   Ilimsk   Ust'-Kut   Ul'kan   Yermaki   **North Baykal Plateau**   Ust'-Muya   Udokan   Taluma   Neryungri   Berkakit   ·2

Bratskoye Reservoir   Riga   Orlinga   Kirensk   *Kirenga*   Injaptuk 2579   Ueyan   Tonnel'nyy   2467·   Ust'Nyukzha   Nagornyy   Lopcha   1870·   Sutam   Chapa

Lena   Kazachinskoye   **Vitim Plateau**   Bambuyka   Sredniy Kalar   Kalar   *Stanovoy   Mounta*   Larba   Tynda

Atalanka   Žigalovo   Sugdža   *Baykal'skij Mountains*   Nízhneangarsk   Baykal'skoje   Baunt   Kadali   1592·   Vetekhtina   *Okokan*   Ugagli   Zeyski   Zeya

763·   Ust'-Kada   Oron   Mogojto   Ust'-Karenga   Koltovkinda   Gulya   Belen'kaya   Bam   Solov'yevsk   Ust' Un'ya

Zima   Balagansk   Bol. Onguren   Barguzin   2069·   Bagdarin   2573   Jeleninskij   *Vitim*   Zel'onoje Ozero   Tupik   Amazar   Urusha   Skovorodino   Zeya   Loki

Zalari   Manzurka   Sosnovka   Bugunda   Ust'-Dzilinda   *Chulugli*   1911·   Mogoča   Silka   Dzhalinda   Magdagachi   Ogoron   Malyu

Lake Baykal   Romanovka   Nerča   Bukačača   ·1249   Luoguhe   ·557   Petropavlovka   Byssa

Usolje Sibirskoje   Angarsk   Ust'-Ordynskij   Chaim   2049   Isinga   Telemba   Ust'-Karsk   Yimuhe   Gulian   Ershiyizhan   Walagan   Ushumun   Oktyabrskiy

3266·   Kyren   Selichov   Irkutsk   Listv'anka   Chorinsk   1322   Uda   Versino-Darasunskij   Sretensk   Cernyšev   Qiqian   Mangui   Amur   Novorossiyka

Sl'ud'anka   Kamensk   Ulan-Ude   Chilok   Chita   Šilka   Ingoda   Beley   Nerohinskiy Zavod   Okurleja   Yimuhe   **CHINA**   Svobodnyy   Novokiyevskiy

Tatarovo   Darasun   Karymskoje   Nerohinskiy   Mordaga   Jinhe   Linhai   Huma   Belogorsk

Tanchoj   2304   Petrovsk Zabajkal'skij   Tanga   Il'a   Olov'annaja   Klin   Argun Yuoqi   Kalaqi   Oroqen Zizhiqi   Shisanzhan   ·827   *Amur*   Zeya

Gusinoozersk   Džida   *Chilok*   Jamarovka   1248   Gol   Priargunsk   Tulihe

Zakamensk   **Yablonovyy Mountains**   *Basshchovochnyy Mountains*

This map shows 1/60 of the earth's surface

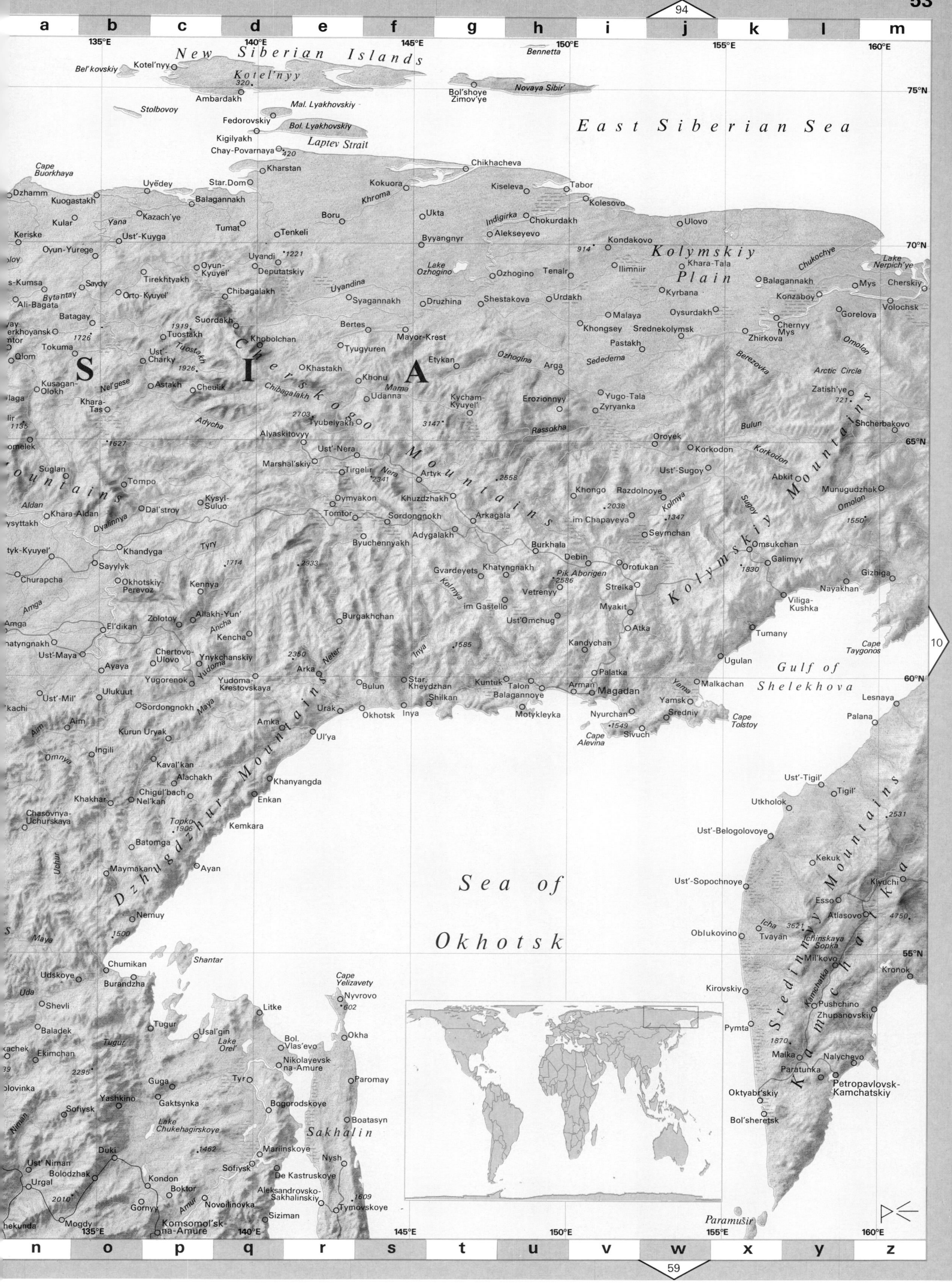

a b c d e f g h i j k l m

135°E 140°E 145°E 150°E 155°E 160°E

New Siberian Islands

Bennetta

Bel'kovskiy Kotel'nyy
Kotel'nyy
320.

Ambardakh

Bol'shoye
Zimov'ye *Novaya Sibir'*

75°N

East Siberian Sea

Stolbovoy

Mal. Lyakhovskiy

Fedorovskiy

Bol. Lyakhovskiy

Kigilyakh

Chay-Povarnaya 420. *Laptev Strait*

Cape
Buorkhaya

Kharstan

Chikhacheva

Dzhamm

Star.Dom

Kokuora

Kiseleva Tabor

Kuogastakh Uyёdey

Balagannakh Khroma

Ukta Indigirka Chokurdakh Kolesovo

Kular Yana Kazach'ye

Tumat

Boru

Byyangnyr Alekseyevo Ulovo

Kondakovo

*Kolymskiy
Plain*

70°N

Keriske

Oyun-Yurege

Tenkeli

Ust'-Kuyga

Saydy Oyun-
Kuyel' Uyandi .1221 Deputatskiy

Tirekhtyakh

Lake
Ozhogino Ozhogino Tenalr

914. Khara-Tala

Ilimniir Kyrbana

Chukochye

Lake
Nerpich'ye

Bytantay Orto-Kuyel' Chibagalakh Uyandina Syagannakh Druzhina Shestakova Urdakh Malaya Khongsey Srednekolymsk Balagannakh Mys Cherskiy

Ali-Bagata Suordakh Bertes Mayor-Krest Ozhogina Arga Sededema Pastakh Zhirkova Konzaboy Gorelova Volochsk

Batagay 1919. Tuostakh Khobolchan Tyugyuren Etykan Chernyy
Mys Omolon

65°N

S I A

This map shows 1/60 of the earth's surface

a b c d e f g h i j k l m

51

60°E 65°E 70°E 75°E

Kungur · Talitsa · Tevriz · Irtysh · .142
Krasnoufimsk · Pervoural'sk · Yekaterinburg · Ishim · Tara · Tara · Biaza
Ufa · Nyazepetrovsk · Degtyarsk · Bogdanovich · Yalutorovsk · .122 · Panovo · Bol'sherech'ye · .124
Kasli · Kamensk-Ural'skiy · Golyshmanovo · Tyukalinsk · Pokrovka
SIBERIA · Shadrinsk · Ishim · Nazyyayevsk · Lyubinskiy · Tatarsk
Asha · Min'yar · Suleya · Zlatoust · Chelyabinsk · Kurgan · Makushino · Petropavlovsk · Isil'kul · Omsk · Kalachinsk · Chistoozernoye · Barabinsk
Ufa · Ust'-Kata · Shumikha · Petukhovo · Presnovka · Lake Chany · 55°N · Kupino
Chudinovo · Kurtamysh · Presnogor'kovka · Petrovka · Krasnoarmeyesk · Lake Ul'kenkaroy · Cherlak
Chernikovsk · Plast · Troitsk · Ust'-Uyskoye · Dem'yanovka · Mar'yevka · Kzyltu · Zhelezinka · Lake Azhbulat · Kachiry
Beloretsk · Verkhneural'sk · Komsomolets · Borovskoye · Uritskiy · Peski · Volodarskoye · Kokchetav · Lake Selety-Tengiz · Shuga
Krasnousol'skiy · Magnitogorsk · Varna · Kustanay · Stavropolka · Ruzayevka · Aydabul' · Makinsk · Aksu · Bestobe · Pavlodar · Jamyševo
Sterlitamak · Kaga · Kartaly · .447 · Dzhambul · Naurzum · Yesil · Dzhaksy · Atbasar · Zhaltyr · Zholymbet · Yermentau · Ekibastuz · Yermak · Maykain
Baymak · Bredy · Tobol' · Tobol' · Kushmurun · Novoishimskiy · Astana · Novodolinka · Karashoky
Troitskoye · Orsk · Terensay · Akkarga · Derzhavinsk · .391 · Sabyndy · Karashoky · Ajryk
Saraktash · Krasnoyarskiy · Dznetygara · Arkalyk · Lake Tengiz · Kurgal'dzhino · Aktau · Korobovskiy · Kiikkaškan
Mednogorsk · Martuk · Dombarovskiy · Tolybaya · Aksuat · Sonaly · Temirtau · Saran · Ul'yanovskoye · .621 · 50°N · Kajnar
Aktyubinsk · Khrom-Tau · Karabutak · Turgay · Shenber · .633 · Abay · Karaganda · Karagayly
Alga · Temir · Emba · Saga · Brali · Ulutau · Dar'inskiy · Atasu · Uspenskiy · Nuru · Myylybulak · Zhamshi
Uil · .316 · Irgiz · Kyzyluy · Baykonur · Dzhezkazgan · Ayshirak · Kiik · Agadyr' · Uplands
Karaulkeldy · Shakhty · Nikol'skiy · Kyzyl-Dzhar · Mointy · Dagandely
Zharkamys · Chelkar · Togyz · KAZAKSTAN · Balkhash · Sajak
Chushakyl' · .343 · Akespe · Aral'sk · Beleutty · Karazhingil · Lake Balkhash
Sokyrbulak · Kokaral · Bugun · Kazalinsk · Leninsk · 59. · Bet-Pak-Dala · Tomar · Karabas · .603
Kulanov · Barsa-Kel'mes · Zhanay · Dzhusaly · Betpak-Dala Steppe · Kashkanteniz · Kuuygan · Uštobe
Kyushe · Aral Sea · Vozrozhdeniya · Kyzyl-Orda · Kamkaly · Mynaral · Burylbaytal · 45°N · Taldy-Kurgan
Urt · Uzynkair · Erimbet · Syrdarja · Aksumbe · Algatart · Khantau · Aktogaj · Saryozek
Šatlyk · Urga · Chilli · Yany-Kurgan · .2176 · Furmanovka · Čemolgan · Kapčagajskoje Reservoir
Muinak · Kazakdarya · .146 · Kentau · Uyuk · Tatty · Almaty · Kapčagaj · Čilik
Lake Sudočje · Chimbay · Turkestan · Kara Tau · Džambul · Bishkek · Kaskelen · Ala-Tau · Ananjevo
Kungrad · .335 · Kyzyl Kum · Lugovoi · Kara-Balta · .3817 · Issyk-Kul' · Prževal'sk
Lake Sarykamyškoje · Bol'ševik · Chodzeili · Mynbulak · Uchkuduk · Arys' · Cimkent · Toktogul Res. · Toktogul · Čajek · Ottuk · Shan
Kun'a-Urgenč · .473 · Zarafshan · .4503 · Pik Dankowa · Karasaj · .5982
Tašauz · Turtkul' · Cardara · Tashkent · Namangan · Taš-Kumyr · KYRGYZSTAN · Naryn · Tarägay · .4929
Urgenč · .81 · UZBEKISTAN · Jangijul' · Andižan · Kok-Jangak · Lake Catyrk'ol · Sari Bulak
Lebap · Cardarinskoje Reservoir · Angren · Kokand · Margilan · Oš · Gul'ča · .4641 · Čatyrtāš · Akqi
Gorel'de · .2165 · Gulistan · Syrdarja · Fergana · Kašgar · Yopurga
Darvaza · Gizhduvan · Navoi · Džizak · Khujand · Bekabad · Kajrakkumskoje Reservoir · Sugun · Sanchakou
TURKMENISTAN · Buchara · Kagan · Kattakurgan · Ura J'ube · .5509 · Daraut-Kurgan · Irkeštam · Kashgar
Kara Kum · Kabakly · Alat · Samarkand · Mubarek · Ajni · Ala · Lenina · .7134 · Yopurga
Kizyl-Arvat · .224 · Čardžou · Šachrisabz · Dzirgatal · .7495 · Lake Karakul' · CHINA
Bachardok · Karši · .4643 · TAJIKISTAN · Mt. Communism · Opal
Arčman · Tezejet · Repetek · Novabad · Viščary · Arkbajtal · Kungur · Shache
Ashgabat · .2243 · Dernau · Dushanbe · Kul'ab · Murgab · .6083 · Mamazair · .2215
Tedžen · Mary · Bajram Ali · Nička · Keriči · Kurgan-T'ube · Chorog · Pamir · Yecheng
Artyk · Dušak · Karakumskiy Canal · .293 · Dusti · Faidzabad · Mazar
Quchan · .3147 · Murgab · Termez · Andkhoy · Aqcha · Kunduz · Zebak · Qala Panja · Misgar · Muji
Dašt · Bojnurd · Khurasan · Sheberghan · Khulm · Taliqan · Hindu Kush · .6625 · .7228 · K2 · .8611
Mayamey · Sabzevar · .8416 · Mashhad · Sarakhs · Sar-i-Pul · Mazar-i-Sharif · Baghlan · Doshi · Tirich Mir · Rakaposhi · Yasin · .7690 · .7788 · Gilgit
N · Neishabur · Takhta Bazar · Maimana · Aibak · Doab-i Mikhe Zarin · AFGHANISTAN · PAKISTAN · Chitral · .5715 · Karakoram Range
Qaisar · Bala Murghab · Sabz · Drosh · Indus · Chilas · Ronda

60°E 65°E 70°E 75°E

n o p q r s t u v w x y z

60

0 100 200 300 miles · Average linear scale · 0 100 200 300 400 500 Km

a b c d e f g h i j k l m

51

n o p q r s t u v w x y z

Onega Yar
Vasyuganye
L'vovka
80°E
Staritsa
Kolpashevo
Ket
85°E
Belyy Yar
parabel
Mogochin
Baturino
Komsomol'sk
Čulym
90°E
Vorozheyka
Yeniseysk
Lesosibirsk
Strelka
Galanino
95°E
Angara
Rodina
Čuna
Oktyabr'sk
Boguchany

142
parbig
Parbig
Bakchar
Asino
Tegul'det
Meletsk
211
Altat
Predivinsk
Asansk
Shelayevo
Vydrin
530

Tara
Biaza
Pikhtovka
166
258
Moryakovskiy Zaton
Mariinsk
Bogotol
Achinsk
Pamyat
698
Kan
Aban
Nevanka

Pokrovka
Chumakovo
Tomsk
Yurga
Anzhero-Sudzhensk
Nazarovo
Krasnojarsk
Uyar
Borodino
Kansk
Taysh
Zamzor

55°N
Chistoozernoye
Lake Chany
Kupino
Ob'
Chulym
Ob'
Novosibirsk
R U S
Kemerovo
Tsentral'nyy
818
Uzhur
Mana
Krasnoyarskoye Reservoir
Bujedzul'
Mina
Nizneucinsk
Gutara

Barabinsk
Ordynskoye
Cherepanovo
T'agun
Krasnobrodskiy
Kiseľ'ovsk
Tom'
Čulym
Sira
Sorsk
Bellyk
1778
Art'omosk
vostochny Mot
Gavrika
Pokrovsk

Lake Azhbulat
Karasuk
Kamenna-Obi
Suzun
Tal'menka
Prokopjevsk
Novokuzneck
2178
Černogorsk
Abakan
Minusinsk
Kuragino
Burgon
Kazyr
Pik Grandioznyj 2922
Uda Alyguzer

Kachiry
Khabary
Len'ki
Pavlovsk
Barnaul
Troickoje
621
Mundybas
Meždurečensk
Birikul
2456
Bujba
Sevi
Toora-Chem
Bol Yenisey

Pavlodar
Kulunda
Rodino
Alejsk
286
Bijsk
Bil
Tastagol
Taštyp
Sajanogorsk
Šušenskoje
Idzim
2682
Balgazya
2584
Samagaltaj
2658

Yermak
Jamyševo
Pospelicha
Alel
Altejskij
Turočak
Abakan Mts
Abakan
Sajan Mountains
Mountains
Cadan
2972
Yenisey
Kyzyl
Saryg-Sop
Kyzyl-Chem
Us'-Bel'dir

Kulundinskaya
Ščerbakty
Rubcovsk
1206
Čaryšskoje
Altai
Lake Telekoje
Cel'us
2930
3487
Čodro
Ak-Dovurak
Tannu Mountains
Malčin
Baruun Turuun
Naryn
Čagan-Uul

Ajryk
Molgary
Irtyš
Dolon
Gorn'ak
Bel'agaš
Semonaicha
Tuekta
2820
Katun'
Inja
Kuraj
Kyzyl-Chaja
Oróg Nuur
Uvs Nuur
Turgen
Chirgis Nuur
Ofgii
2928
Ojgon Nuur
Teimen Nuur
Sang Dale Nuu

50°N
Semipalatinsk
Sugan
606
Ust'-Kamengorsk
2776
4506
Argut
Koš-Agač
4029
Čagaan Nuur
Ulgij
Chovd Gol
Erdene Büren
2896
Jaruu
Hang

Kiikkaškan
Kajnar
Čarsk
Serebr'ansk
Georgilevka
1608
Bol'šenarymskoje
Lake Markakol'
264.5
Kurčum
Buran
Korti Linchang
Čagaan Gol
Altaj
Tolbo Nuur
Kobdo
Char Us Nuur
Manchan
Dzeteg
Dzavchan Gol
Aldar
Uliastaj
3906
Bujant

KAZAKSTAN
Madenijet
Ajaguz
1305
Belaja Škola
Buran
Ertix He
Burqin
Beitun
Altay
3243
Manchan
Mönch 4362
Chajrchan
Ovoot
Tamč
3578
Čagaan-Olom

Sajak
Taskesken
Tarbagataj Mts
2992
Zajsan
Muz Tau
3816
Ulungur Hu
Beitun
Fuyun
Sarbulak
MO
Türgen
Bugat
Beger

Karabas
Aktogaj
Lake Sasykkol'
Urdžar
Tacheng
Zajsan
Utubulak
Jili Hu
Ulungur
Bulgan
3479
Altaj
Dzachuj
Bajan-Ondo

Lake Balkhash
Lepsy
756
Žarsuat
Lake Alakol'
Toli
Karamay
Manas Hu
Junggar Pendi
Gov'Chonin
3802
Bajan-Ondo

Uštobe
Matai
Sarkand
2923
Tachakou
Kangxiwar
Santanghu
Altay

Taldy-Kurgan
Aktogaj
4442
Wenquan
Ebinur Hu
Bole
Jinhe
Jiangjumiao
Nom

Servozek
Panfilov
Sayram Hu
Borohoro Shan
Usu
Shihezi
Qitai
Barkol Hu
Yiwu
Karlik Shan
4925
Cag Bogd

Kapčagaj
Kapčagayskoye Reservoir
Ili He
Qapqal
Ining
Nilka
Changji
Ganhezi
Manas
Urumchi
Bogda Feng 5445
3951
Qijiaojing
Barkol Kazak
Liaodun
Hami
Mergol

Čilik
Cundža
3638
Tekes
Xinyuan
Narat
Tien Shan
Houxia
Baiyanghe
Qiquanhu
Liushuquan
Yandun
Mingshui
Gongpoquan

Čemolgan
Almaty
4876
Kegen
Zhaosu
Tekes
4553
Kaidu
Bulguntay
Ewirgol
Turpan
154
Shanshan
2584
Weiya
Xingxingxia
Jiangjuntai

Kaskelen
Ananjevo
Lake Issyk-Kul
Narynkol
Pik Pobedy 7439
Keyi
Yengisar
Yanqi Huizu Zizhixian
Bosten Hu
1524
Daquan
Hongliuyuan
Jiangquanzi

Rubacje
Převal'sk
Yakrik
Qarqi
Korla
Yuli
Bei Shan
1762
Zhangjiaquan
Anxi
Qiaowan
Choushui

KYRGYZSTAN
Naryn Taragay
Karasaj
Pik Dankova 5982
Kuqa
Xinhe
Tarim
Konqi
1238
Lop Nur
Shule
Kumkuduk
Dunhuang
Dongbatu
Jiayuguan

Čatyrtaš
4929
Toxkan
Yakrik
Aksu
Tarim
Tarim Liuchang
Shazaoyuan
Changma
Jiuquan

San Bulak
Sanchakou
Liuchang
Awat
Aral
Yengisu
1099
C
Aksay
5298
Qilian Shan 5547
Tsin

40°N
Sugun
Yopurga
Yarkant
1066
Ikanbujmal
Luobuzhuang
Donglúk
Miran
Ruoqiang
Waxxari
Xorkol
Obo Liang
Niubiziliang
Lénghu
Da Qaidam
5030

Markit
Tarim Basin
1082
Takla Makan Desert
Aktaz
Qarqan
Suhai Hu
Huahaizi
Qarhan
5827

East
Shache
1570
Tongguzbasti
Qiemo
Hadilik
Altun Shan
5810
Gas Hu
Youshashan
2774
Tsaidam Basin
Iqe
Har Hu

Hasalbag
Yecheng
Koxlax
Turkestan
Andirlangár
Tura
6140
Ayakkum Hu
Mangnai
Shaliangzi
Da Qaidam

Muji
Zawa
Hotan
Qira
Minfeng
Bostan
Aqqikkol Hu
Hoit Taria
Delingha

Mazar Yarkant
Zangguy
K Karakax
Tekliktag 5466
Yutian
6748 Aktag
Karasay
S Muztag 7723
7720
Nur Turu
Dabsan Hu
Xitieshan
Ulan

Kangxiwar
1228
Pulu
n Iun
Boluntay
De Juh
Gölmud
Nan Hulsan Hu
Nomhon
Xiangch
5026

This map shows 1/60 of the earth's surface

52

58

S I A

M O N G O L I A

G O B I

I n n e r   M o n g o l i a

C H I N A

Lake Baykal

North Baykal Plateau

Vitim Plateau

Yablonovy Mountains

Borshchovochny Mts.

Great Khingan Mts.

Ordos

Alashan Desert

Shan

Shantung

Po Hai

Liaotung Bay

Laichow Bay

100°E · 105°E · 110°E · 115°E · 120°E

55°N · 50°N · 45°N · 40°N

Kova, Karamysheva, Vorob'yeva, Garmenka, Ust'Ilimsk, Volokon, Lena, Kirensk, Ui'kan, Gorno-Chuyskiy, Chaya, Chuya, Mama, Vitimskiy, Bodaybo, Sinyuga, Berezovka, Lake Nichatka, Tokko, Taluma, Yenyuka, Ust'Nyukzha, Ilir, Ija, Bratsk, Chunskiyo, Suvorka, Vidim, Ilimsk, Ust'-Kut, Riga, Orlinga, Kirenga, Yermaki, Kazachinskoye, Yukhta, Injaptuk, Uoyan, Tonnel'nyy, L'okma

Irkutsk, Ulan-Ude, Ulan Bator (Ulaanbaatar), Chita, Manchouli, Hailar, Huhehot, Paotow, Peking (Beijing), Tangshan, Tientsin, Dalian, Taiyuan, Shihkiachwang, Tsinan, Tzepo, Tsingtao

Lanchow, Sining, Yinchuan, Wuwei, Datong

100   200   300 miles · Average linear scale · 100 200 300 400 500 Km

52

Ingoda
Baley
Klin
RUSSIA
Borzya
Nerchinsky Zavod
Priargunsk
Manchouli
Hulun Nur
Hailar
Qagan
Xin Barag Youqi
Xin Barag Zuoqi
Buyr Nur
Tamsagbulag
MONGOLIA
Gobi
Dong Ujimqin Qi
Inner
Bulag Sum
Nungnain Sum
Xi Ujimqin Qi
Qagan Qulut
Jirin Gol
Holt Sum
Xilin Hot
Hexigten Qi
Ongniud Qi
Zhenglan Qi
Chifeng
Weichang
Luan He
Fengning
Longhua
Chengteh
Kuancheng
Miyun
Great Wall
Lulong
Peking (Beijing)
Tangshan
Ba Xian
Tientsin
Ziya He
Cangchow
Yanshan
Tehchow
Boxing
Tzepo
Tsinan
Weifang
Jiao Xian
Tai'an
Yanzhou
Tsining
Tsaochuang
Suchow
Lienyunkang
Suhsien
Huaibei
Lake Hungtze
Huaiyin
Hongze
Pengpu
Lake Kaoyu
Hwainan
Yangchow
Hefei
Lujiang
Taichow
Nantung
Chu Xian
Nanking
Changshu
Wuhsi
Wuhu
Suchow
Xuancheng
Lake Tai
Tonkling
Anking
Kashing
Hangchow
Shanghai

Argun He
Nerchinsky Zavod
Mordaga
Jinhe
Linhai
Huma
Shimanovsk
Svobodnyy
Zeya
Novokiyevskiy Uval
Ust'Niman
Urgal
Chegdomyn
Duki
Bolodzhak
Kondon
Bok
Argun Zuoqi
Tulihe
Kalaqi
Shisanzhan
Belogorsk
Chekunda
Mogdy
Komsomol'sk-na-Amure
Argun Youqi
Yuanlin
Oroqen Zizhiqi
Huolongmen
Blagoveshchensk
Bureya
Ust'Tyrma
Tyrma
Amursk
Chen Barag Qi
Yakeshi
Xiao'ergou
Dayangshu
Heihe
Zavitinsk
Bureya
Talandzha
Bolon
Hailar
Morin Dawa
Nenjiang
Sunwu
Raychikhinsk
Arkhara
Khabarovsk
Yirshi
Goukou
Arun Qi
Nehe
Bei'an
Jiayin
Wuyiling
Kruglikovo
Longjiang
Fuyu
Yi'an
Baiquan
Suiling
Nancha
Wuying
Yichun
Khor
Tsitsihar (Qiqihar)
Jalaid Qi
Dorbod
Lanxi
Qing'an
Hokang
Luobei
Tongjiang
Chuker
Xikou
Dashizhai
Daqing
Anda
Suihua
Fujin
Baicheng
Tailai
Zhaoyuan
Shuangcheng
Fangzheng
Kiamusze
Schwangyashan
Sinn
Velikaya Kem
Horqin Youyi Qianqi
Tao'an
Qian Gorlos
Harbin
Dongfanghong
Bikin
Luchegorsk
Svetlovodnaya
Tuquan
Lalin He
Shangzhi
Qitaihe
Hulin
Yasnaya Polyana
Jarud Qi
Dehui
Yushu
Manchuria
Linkou
Dal'nerechensk
Lesozavodsk
Terne
Yolin Mod
Xinkai He
Horqin Zuoyi Zhongqi
Mutankiang
Xiachengzi
Ning'an
Dongjingcheng
Kisi
Lake Khanka
Kirovskiy
Bairin Zuoqi
Kailu He
Changchun
Kirin (Jilin)
Jiaohe
Emu
Suifenhe
Spassk Dal'niy
Arsen'yev
Kavalerovo
Linxi
Bairin Youqi
Xar Moron
Tongliao
Shwangliao
Szeping
Liaoyuan
Huinan
Dunhua
Wangqing
Hunchun
Ussuriysk
Artem
Vangou
Margaritovo
Naiman Qi
Baixingt
Kaiyuan
Qingyuan
Huadian
Jingyu
Liuhe
Linkiang
Tunghwa
Yenki
Hoeryong
Najin
Vladivostok
Nakhodka
Fusin
Xinmin
Fushun
Mukden (Shenyang)
Huanren
Changpai Shan
Paektu-san
Ch'ongjin
Chuuronjang
Yi Xian
Xi He
Liao He
Penki
Liaoyang
Anshan
Kuandian
Manp'ojin
Kapsan
Hyesanjin
Harqin
Chinchow
Yingkow
Gai Xian
Antung (Dandong)
Sinuiju
Gushan
Anju
Huich'on
Hamhung
Kimchaek
Pukch'ong
Qinhuangdao
Wudao
Fu Xian
Liaotung Bay
Yalu
NORTH KOREA
Wonsan
Dalian
Chinnamp'o
Hwangju
Ich'on
Haeju
Kaesong
Ch'unch'on
Sokch'o
Kangnung
Penglai
Yantai
Pyongyang
Ongjin
Wonju
Tonghae
Laichow Bay
Cape Chengshan
Inch'on
Seoul
Ch'ungju
Laiyang
Ch'ongju
Andong
Liangcheng
Tsingtao
Taejon
SOUTH KOREA
Junan
Kunsan
Chonju
Taegu
Ulsan
Kwangju
Masan
Pusan
Chinju
Mokp'o
Yosu
Cheju
Quelpart Island (Cheju)

RUSS
Duki
Naykh
Litovka
Sarapulskoye
Birobidzhan
Fuyuan
Kotikova
Glubinnoye
Sidatun
Rudnaya Pristan
Vladivostok
Nakhodka
Terne

SEA OF JAPAN

Oki
Toyan
Kanazawa
Fukui
Tsuruga
Matsue
Tottori
Gifu
Lake Biwa
Kyoto
Nago
Nishinomiya
Osaka
Masuda
Yamaguchi
Fukuyama
Okayama
Himeji
Kobe
Sakai
Matsuzaka
Wakayama
Hiroshima
Takamatsu
Sea
Inland
Tokushima
Shimonoseki
Kita-Kyushu
Ube
Matsuyama
Kochi
Shikoku
Fukuoka
Oita
Bungo Channel
Kii Strait
Tanabe
Sasebo
Kumamoto
Kyushu
Yatsushiro
Nagasaki
Miyazaki
Kagoshima
Osumi Channel
Tanega
Yaku

Korea Strait
Tsushima (Japan)

East China Sea

Yellow Sea

Po Hai

Miaodao Islands

Korea Bay

Grand Canal
Hwang (Huang He)
Shantung

63

This map shows 1/60 of the earth's surface

a b c d e f g h i j k l m

53

140°E · 145°E · 150°E · 155°E

50°N

Kamchatka

Sofiysk
Mariinskoye
De Kastruskoye
Nysh
Amur
Novoilinovka
Aleksandrovsk-Sakhalinskiy
·1509
Siziman
Tymovskoye
Gurskoye
·1628
Sakhalin
Koto
(Russia)
1324
Paramušir

A l i n

·078
Gavan
Poronaysk

S E A   O F

Adzhima
Makarov

O K H O T S K

Onekotan

556
Gulf of Tartary
Samarga
Kholmsk
Yuzhno-Sakhalinsk
Svetlaya
Korsakov

Maksimovka

Simušir

K u r i l   I s l a n d s

La Pérouse Strait

45°N

Wakkanai
Urup

·1129

Iturup

Asahikawa
Kitami

Kunašir

2290
Asahi-dake
Otaru
H o k k a i d o
Nemuro
□ **Sapporo**
2052
Kushiro
Obihiro
Muroran
Uchiura
Bay
Erimo
Hakodate
Ōma
Tsugaru Channel
Aomori
1625

P A C I F I C

40°N

Akita
Marioka
1914
Sakata
Kesen
Ishinomaki
Yamagata
Sendai
Niigata
Fukushima
·2105
Kashiwazaki
Kōriyama
·1977
Iwaki

O C E A N

H o n s h ū
Nagano
Utsunomiya
90
Maebashi
Mito
Matsumoto
Hachioji
□ **Tōkyō** Chiba

J A P A N

35°N

Shirane-san
3192
Kawasaki
3776
□ **Yokohama**
ujiyama
Yokosuka
Shizuoka
·amamatsu

n o p q r s t u v w x y z

140°E · 145°E · 150°E · 155°E

0   100   200   300 miles   Average linear scale   0   100   200   300   400   500 Km

a b c d e f g h i j k l m

55

60°E   65°E   70°E

TURKMENISTAN

Quchan

Mayamey   Sabzevar   3416   Neishabur   Mashhad   Sarakhs   Murgab   Takhta Bazar   Andkhoy   Aqcha   Mazar-i Sharif   Khulm   Kunduz   Faidzabad   Qala Panja
3147
Bardeskan   Kashmar   Torbat-e-Heidariye   Torbat-e-Jam   Kuska   Quala-i Nau   Bala Murghab   Sari-i-Pul   Aibak   Baghlan   Doshi   Zebak   Mastuj   7690
Sheberghan   Maimana   Doab-i Mikhe Zarin   Charikar   Bamian   Chitral   Drosh   5715
35°N   Torbat-e   Tayebad   Herat   Chaghcharan   Daulat Yar   Kuh-e-Baba   Sorabi   Asadabad   Besham Qila
Dasht-e-Kavir   2578   Bidokht   Ghorian   Hari Rud   Farsi   Sangan   Khurd   Kora-i Ashro   1799   Kabul   Jalalabad   Khyber Pass Kabul   Mardan   Abbotabad
Ferdows   Yazdan   Shindand   Farah Rud   Qarah Tarai   3704   Behsud   Ghazni   Gardez   Peshawar   Islamabad
Tabas   Qaen   3650   3823   Matun   Kalabagh   Rawalpindi   Gujarkhan
Deihuk   Farahrod   Qaisar   Uruzgan   Zarghunshar   Bannu   Mianwali   Chakwal
Aliabad   Khusf   Birjand   4182   Tarin Kot   Shahjui   Lakki   Guj
2992   Naiband   Sarbisheh   2560   Nauzad   Qalat-i Chilzai   Razmak   Sargodha   Gujranw
Darband   2729   Nehbandan   Farah   Dilaram   Girishk   Kandahar   Tarnak   Dera Ismail Khan   3377   Jhang   Faisalabad
Zarand   2433   Ravor   2488   Lasho Joayin   Khash Rud   Arghandab   Sakir   Toba & Kakar Ranges   Fort Sandeman   Sulaiman   Maghiana
716   Zabol   Registan   1314   3095   Muslimbagh   Leiah   Okara   Sahiw
Bafq   Darband   Ravor   Zaranj   Safar   Chaman Kand   2641   Qila   Kingri   Multan
Kerman   Siraj   2062   Mirabad   1371   3223   Zargun   Saifullah   Dera   Faz
30°N   Baghin   Helmand   Rudbar   Zargun   3578   Loralai   Ghazi Khan   Ganganaq
Rafsanjan   Nosratabad   Ribat   1643   2208   Quetta   Dera Bugti   Sutlej
Hoseinabad   Laleh Zar   Tahrud   Zahedan   2462   Chagai Hills   Chagai   Mach   1262   Rajanpur   Bahawalpur   Surate
Sirjan   4374   2333   Saltan   2101   Ras Koh   Nushki   Kala   Sibi   Kahan   Pugal   Mahajar   Bikane
Baft   Darzin   Mirjaveh   Nok Kundi   Dalbandin   3003   Kharan   Surab   Jacobabad   Rahimyar-Khan   Rajasthan Canal
Aliabad   Bam   Dehak   Taftan   Ras   Besima   Khuzdar   Shikarpur   Tanot   Bap   Nagaur
Dowlatabad   8941   Khash   Qila Ladgasht   Saravan   Patandar   Jebri   Wad   Larkana   Sukkur   Sri Mohangarh   Pokaran
Hajiabad   3279   Sabzevaran   2548   Bazman   Khash   Central Makran   2283   Awaran   Moro   Khairpur   Shahgarh   Jaisalmer
Qotbabad   Kahnuj   3503   Bampur   Iranshahr   Kuhak   Panjgur   Bela   Sehwan   Sanghar   Myajlar   Jodhp
1564   Hamun-e Jaz Murian   Bampur   Saravan   Hoshab   Myajlar   Phalsund
Bander Abbas   Minab   Jaghin   1950   Remeshk   2110   Sarbaz   Turbat   1454   Moro   Balotra   Pali
Qeshm   Nikshahr   Pishin   Dasht   Kikki   Hab   Mirpur Khas   Barmer
39   Straits of Hormuz   Ras Musandam   2081   Jask   Bahu Kalat   Chabahar   Pasni   Ormara   Chauki   Kotri   Gurha   Arayalli Range
Al Sha'am   2100   Jiwani   Ras Kuh Lab   Ras Nuh   Hyderabad   Luni   1722   Sirohi
OMAN   Ras al Khaimah   Dibba   Hab   Guru Sikhar   Kankrol
25°N   Shinas   Badin   Thatta   Karachi   Virawah   Tharad   Udaipur
Dubai   Fujairah   Virawah
Sharjah   Sohar   Rann of Kutch   Palanpur
Al Ain   As Suwaiq   Radhanpur   Himatna
Al Khaburah   Lakhpat   Mahesana
Ibri   As Sib   Muscat   Rampur   I
3017   Sumail   Quraiyat   Tropic of Cancer   Bhuj   Ahmedabad
Nazwa   Izki   New Kandla
Adam   Sur   Ras al Hadd   Mandvi   Morvi   Nadiad   Vadod
Al Kamil   ARABIAN   Gulf of Kutch   Jamnagar   Dhandhuka   Khambhat
Umm as Samim   Al Ashkhirah   Dwarka   Rajkot   Kathiawar   Bharuch
Ramlat al Wahiba   Porbandar   Bhavnagar   Surat   Tap
SEA   Junagadh   Gulf of Cambay   Navsari
Masirah   Veraval   Diu   (Gulf of Khambhat)   Valsad   156
Daman
20°N   Jawhar   Nas
Duqm   Thane
Ras Madrakah   Bombay (Mumbai)   Wester
Pune
Sharbithat   Ras Sharbithat   Janjira   Bho
Kuria Muria Islands   Koyna Reservoir   Sat
Chiplun
Ratnagiri

60°E   65°E   70°E

This map shows 1/60 of the earth's surface

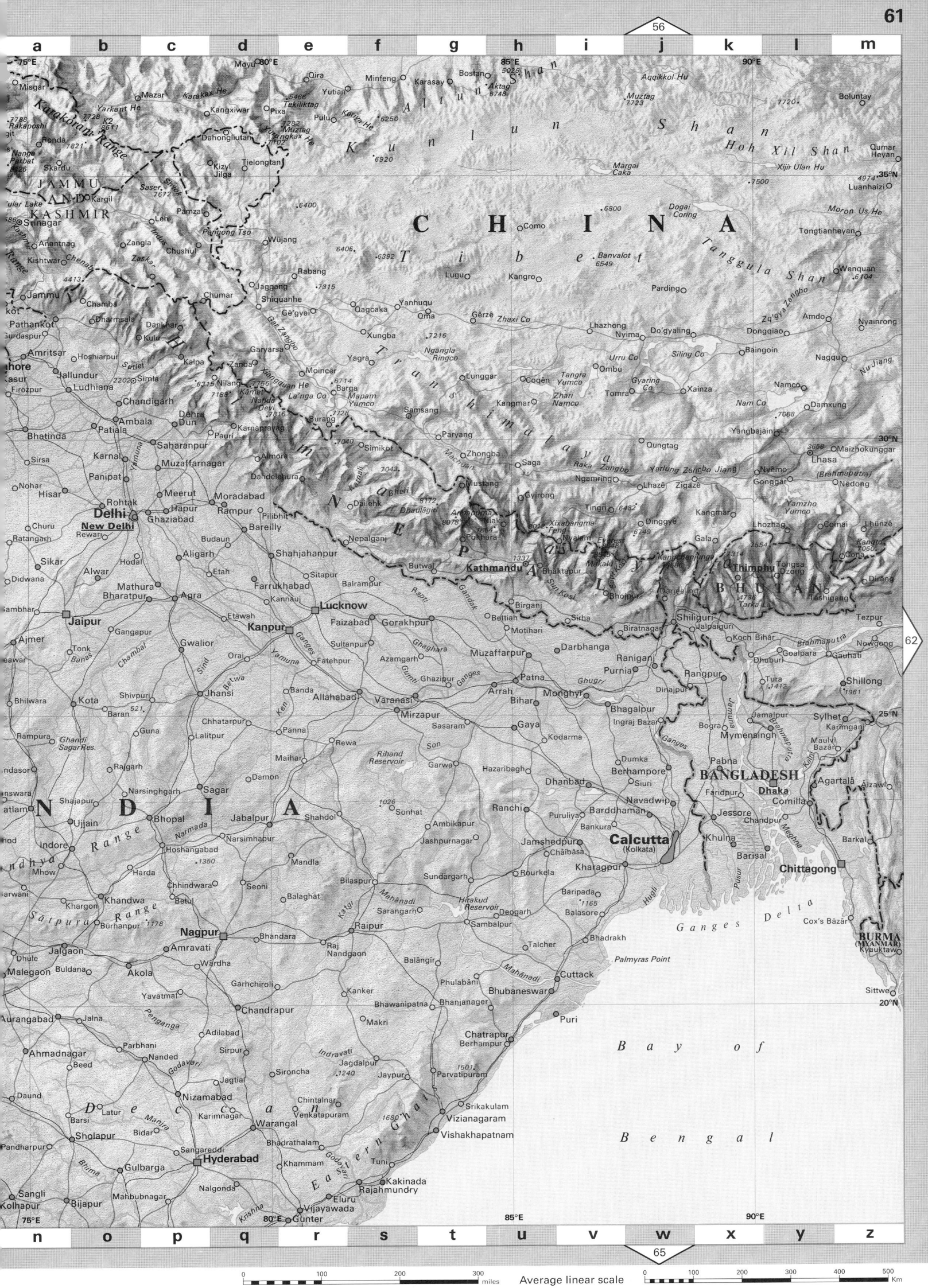

62

Average linear scale

miles

Km

Mangnai
Ganq
Shaliangzi
Suli Hu
Nur Turu
Boluntay
Da Qaidam
Holt Taria
Xitieshan
Qarhan
•3099
Dabsan Hu
•6030
Delingha
Nan Hulsan Hu
Nomhon
Ulan
Tianjun
Gangca
Qinghai Hu
Haiyan
Gangca
Menyuan
Datong
Great Wall
•4070
Wuwei
Yongdeng
Zhongwei
Tongxin
Dingbian
Wuqi
Zichang
Yan'an
•5972
Kun
Lun
Shan
35°N
4974
Luanhaizi
Tongtianheyan
Qumar Heyan
Najl Tal
Golmud
Da Juh
5026
Xiangride
Dulan
Daheba
Gonghe
Nangdoi
Minhe
•1508
Lanchow
Linxia
Dingxi
Guyuan
Jingyuan
•4832
2143
Qingyang
Luochuan
Qing Zang
Wenquan
•6104
Amdo
Nyainrong
Nagqu
Biru
Gaoyuan
Maizhokunggar
Damxung
Zhidoi
Bagan
Zadoi
Dêngqên
Yushu
Nangqên
Domba
Baqên
5189
Ningjing Shan
Kego
Qumarlêb
5816
Chindu
Dainkog
Sêrxu
Tongtian He
Ngoring
Madoi
Cowargarzê
Gyaring Hu
Chalaxung
Maqên Gangri
•6282
Hwang (Huang He)
Bayan Hax Shan
4396
Darlag
Sogruma
Jigzhi
Huashixia
Zêkog
Tongren
Aba
Hongyuan
Maqên
Xingsagoinba
4063
Luqu
Têwo
Zhugqu
Min Xian
Zoigê
Longxi
Tienshui
Wei He
Changwu
Qian Xian
Sanyuan
Xianyang
Sian
Shang Xi
Wei
Tsinling Shan
Ningshan
C H I
Qichuan
•1950
Wanyuan
•2708
Ankang
30°N
Comai
Nêdong
Yarlung Zangbo Jiang
Mainling
Nyingchi
Nehjagbarwa-Feng
7756
Nyainqêntangla Shan
Gongbo'gyamda
6692
Lhari
Banbar
Lhorong
Zhag'yab
Baxoi
Zogang
Dêgê
4750
Jomda
Qamdo
Riwoqê
Dêngqên
4820
Garzê
Yidin
Litang
Batang
Markam
Dêrong
6040
Dêqên
Hengduan
5040
Shan
Dawu
Qianning
Danba
Guan Xian
Jinchuan
Barkam
Kangding
Ya'an
Jiuding Shan
•4984
Mianyang
Nanbu
Daxian
Fengjie
Wanhsien
2370
Hanzhong
Xixiang
Lüeyang
Guangyuan
Santai
Nanchung
Dazhu
Lichuan
Enshi
•1682
Sichuan
Qionglai
Meishan
Chengtu
Jianyang
Hochwan
Suining
Pendi
3002
INDIA
Shillong
•1961
Lumding
Kohima
Tezpur
Nowgong
Guwahati
Silchar
Sylhet
Karimganj
Maulvi
Bazâr
BHUTAN
Tàshigang
61
Cona
Lhünzê
Diràng
Itanagar
Takpa Shiri
6566
Kangto
7060
Ziro
Pangin
Dibrügarh
Brahmaputra
Jorhât
Tinsukia
Saikhoa Ghat
4578
Tagap Ga
Makaw
Mazunzut
Putào
Man Kabat
Zayu
•4353
6740
Shan
Gongshan
Zhongdian
Bijiang
Caojian
4122
Yulongxue Shan
•5686
Lijiang
Jianchuan
Yongren
Jinsha Jiang
Dechang
Dukou
Huili
Zhaotong
Weining
Bijie
Xuanwei
Pan Xian
Anshun
Tungchwan
Zhenning
•2159
Dushan
Tuyun
Kaili
Jing Xiar
Shibing
Tongzi
Tsunyi
Jinsha
Wu Jiang
•2942
Tongren
Xinhuang
Youyang
Qianjiang
Ba Xian
Chungking
2251
Qijiang
Luchou
Xuyong
Julian
Meigu
Xide
Minya Konka
5445
3099
Wutungbiao
Tzekung
Yongchuan
Neikiang
Qianwei
Ipin
Dalou Shan
Rongjiang
•2081
Rong'an
Kweiyang
I
Laibin
Liuch
25°N
Sylhet
Maulvi
Bazâr
Agartala
Comilla
Aizawl
Barkal
BANGLA-
Chittagong
DESH
Cox's Bâzâr
Kyaukpyu
Sittwe
Lonkin
Lawa
2569
Parkai
Mts
3824
Chindwin
Imphal
Tamu
998
Tonzang
Kennedy
•2704
Kalemyo
Kawlin
1672
Naba
Mansi
Bhamo
Myitkyina
Hopin
Tengchong
Baoshan
Luxi
Wandingzhen
Shuangjiang
Lincang
Mogok
Lashio
2168
Monywa
Shwebo
Kyaukme
Mòng Yai
Gangaw
Môngkung
Ta-Kaw
Loi-lem
Taunggyi
Mandalay
Myingyan
Pakokku
Kanbetlet
Victoria
3053
Chauk
1518
Meiktila
Salween
Langhko
Môngton
1907
Siakwan
1560
Qiansuo
Yipinglang
Kunming
•1893
Chuxiong
Anning
Dian Chi
Fengqing
Jingdong
Zhenyuan
Yuanjiang
Jianshui
Kaiyuan
Kokiu
(Gejiu)
1740
Wenshan
Mile
Tonghai
Shiping
Nanpang Jiang
Guangnan
Funing
Anlong
Wangmo
•1424
Xingyi
Tianlin
Bose
1760
Pingguo
Yu Jiang
Pingguo
Hechi
Yishan
Hungshui
Litang
Nanning
Lingshan
Qinzhou
BURMA
(MYANMAR)
Pyinmana
Prome
Henzada
Pegu
Kyaikto
Thaton
Rangoon
(Yangon)
Insein
Thingangyun
95°E
Sandoway
Myanaung
Gwa
Kyaukkyu
Arakan
Mountains
Irrawaddy
Sittang
Pyu
Toungoo
Phrae
Lampang
Chiang
Mai
Doi Inthanon
2590
1854
Phayao
1056
Phu Soai Dao
2102
Nan
Vang Vieng
Sayaboury
Louangphrabang
Pak Sane
Xieng
Khouang
2820
Bia
2286
Rao Go
Nape
Kham
Keut
Thakhek
Dong Hoi
Vinh
Ha Tinh
Thanh Hoa
Vientiane
Nong Khai
Udon Thani
Sakon
Nakhon
1816
Milang
Wang
Saphung
Nam Dinh
Hoa Binh
Hanoi
Haiphong
Gulf
of
Tongking
Dongfang
1879
Yaxian
SOUT
SE
THAILAND
100°E
105°E
Phitsanulok
Chiang Rài
Muang Khoa
Xam Nua
LAOS
20°N
Mekong
Mekong
VIETNAM
Hanoi
Hoa Binh
Haiphong
Ha Coi
Pakhoi
(Beihai)
Bac Ninh
1507
Lang Son
•1193
Pingxiang
Ningming
Tonkin
Tuyen
Quang
Cao Bang
Ha Giang
3076
Lùchun
Jinping
Phongsali
3142
Fan si Pan
Lai Chau
Tuan Giao
1842
Muang Khoa
Jinghong
Jiangcheng
Lancang
Simao
Pu'er
Daluo
2320
Môngkung
Naung
INDIAN
OCEAN

This map shows 1/60 of the earth's surface

Taiyuan
Yutze
Taigu
Yangchuan
2069
Tehchow
Penglai
Yantai
Ongjin
Inch'ŏn
Seoul
Kangnŭng
Wŏnju
Ch'ŏngju

Cape Chengshan

Singtai
Linqing
Boxing
Laiyang
Weifang
Jiao Xian
Taejŏn
Andong

SOUTH

Huo Xian
Fengfeng
Hantan
Anyang
Tzepo
Weifang
Tai'an
Kunsan
Chŏnju
Taegu

Changchih
1619
Hohpi
Tsinan
950
Yanzhou
Tsingtao
Taejŏn

Yellow

Houma
2322
Jiaozuo
Heze
Tsining
Junan
Liangcheng
Kwangju
Chinju
Masan

Hancheng
Sanmenhsia
Loyang
Chengchow
Kaifeng
1440
Qi Xian
Shangkiu
Tsaochuang
Lienyunkang
Sea
Mokp'o
Yŏsu
35°N

37
Lingbao

KOREA

Shangnan
Pingtingshan
Nanzhao
Luohe
Hsuchang
Zhecheng
Huaibei
Suhsien
Binhai
Cheju

Shangnan
Zhenping
Nanyang
Xincai
Fuyang
366
Huaiyin
Huaiyin
Hongze
Quelpart Island
(Cheju)

1612
Tanghe
1140
Luoshan
Pengpu
Lake Hungtze

iyan

Siangfan
Sui Xian
Xinyang
Hwainan
Yangchow
Lake Kaoyu
Taichow
Nantung

EAST CHINA

ng Xian
Nanzhang
Huangchuan
Chu Xian
Nanking
Changshu
Wuhsi

Ichang
Yidu
Macheng
Hefei
Lujiang
Wuhu
Xuancheng
Suchow
Shanghai
SEA

Shasi
Mianyang
Hwangshih
Anking
1860
Tonkling
Lake Tai
Kashing

N **A**

Plain
Wuhan
Tongshan
Chang Jiang
Yangtze
1187
Hangchow

feng
1841
Shaohing
Ningpo
Guoju
Zhoushan Islands
30°N

Han Shu
Changteh
Lake Tungting
Yueyang
1596
Xiushui
Lake Poyang
Kingtehchen
Tunxi
Xin'anjiang
Kinhwa
Quzhou
Linhai

Yiyang
Gao'an
Nanchang
Shangjao
Lishui

Changsha
Siangtan
Xinyu
Fuzhou
Cuixi
2158
Pucheng
Yunhe
Wenchow

anyang
Chuchow
Pingsiang
1290
Gongxi
Nanfeng
Shaowu
Zhenghe
Fuding

Shaoyang
Hengyang
Gan Jiang
Ji'an
Ningdu
1199
1871
Nanping
Ningde

Xiang Jiang
Leiyang
Wuyi Shan
Min Jiang
Sanming
1494
Minqing
Yong'an

Quanzhou
Ningyuan
Chen Xian
Kanchow
Ruijin
Foochow

Dongnan
Qiuling
1902
Shaokwan
1560
Longyan
Putian

Kweilin
Pingle
Yingde
Mei Xian
Changchow
Amoy
(Xiamen)
Taiwan Strait
Taoyŭan
Chilung
Miyako

Lian Xian
Huaiji
Bei Jiang
Longchuan
Zhangpu
Hsinchu
Taipei
Ilan

Ryūkyū Islands
(Japan)
Okinawa
Naha

Luoding
1282
Zhao'an
Jieyang
Swatow
Chaoyang
Taichung
Changhua
3884 Xueweng
Hualien
25°N

Si / Xi Jiang
Canton *(Guangzhou)*
Huizhou
Lufeng
Chiai
3997
TAIWAN
Tropic of Cancer

Foshan
Shun-te
Tainan

1704
Kongmoon
(Jiangmen)
Chuhoi
Kowloon
Hong Kong
Macao
Pingtung
Kaohsiung
Fangshan

Mowming
Yangjiang
Hengchun

PACIFIC

anjiang
Chanchiang
Bashi Channel

Luzon
Strait
Batan Islands

OCEAN

Kuwen
nan Strait
Haikow

20°N

Hainan
Wanning

Babuyan Islands

Cape Bojeador
Laoag
Aparri
Cape Engaño

CHINA

Luzon
Vigan
Bangued
Cordillera Central
Tuguegarao

Sierra Madre

PHILIPPINES

Ilagan
Pulag 2934

0 100 200 300 *miles* Average linear scale 0 100 200 300 400 500 *Km*

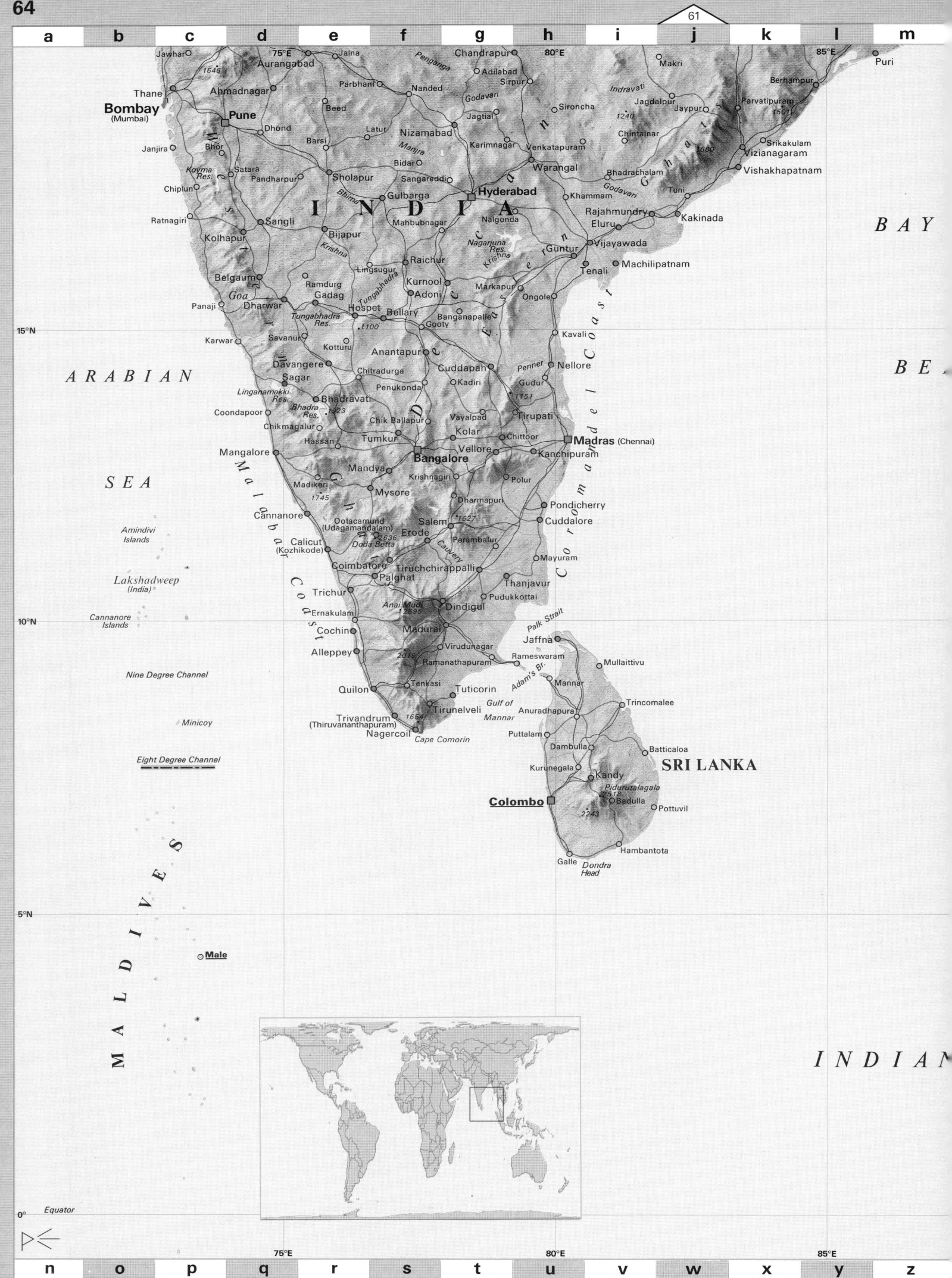

This map shows 1/60 of the earth's surface

a b c d e f g h i j k l m

62

66

n o p q r s t u v w x y z

90°E 95°E 100°E

15°N

10°N

5°N

0°

BURMA (MYANMAR)

THAILAND

LAOS

CAMBODIA

MALAYSIA (WESTERN)

INDONESIA

MALAYA

O F

A L

OCEAN

Andaman Sea

Andaman Islands (India)

North Andaman

Middle Andaman

South Andaman

Little Andaman

Nicobar Islands (India)

Car Nicobar

Katchall

Little Nicobar

Great Nicobar

Ten Degree Channel

Ramree

Cheduba

Preparis

Cocos Islands (Burma)

St. Matthew's

Mergui Archipelago

Kadan

Letsok-Aw

Lanbi

Gulf of Martaban

Mouths of the Irrawaddy

Tenasserim

Gulf of Thailand

Isthmus of Kra

Phu Quoc

Cape Mau

Tonle Sap

Angkor

Phangan

Samui

Khao Luang 1835

Thale Luang

Lake Toba

Simeulue

Nias

Pini

Tanahbala

Tuangku

Riau Islands

Tioman

Lingga Islands

Singkep

Indragiri

Kampar

Strait of Malacca

Malay Peninsula

Kelantan

Perak

Pyinmana

Loikaw

Thayetmyo

Pyinmana

Prome

Toungoo

Myanaung

Pyu

Pyu

Henzada

Pegu

Insein

Kanbe

Basseín

Rangoon (Yangon)

Thingangyun

Kyaikto

Thaton

Pyapon

Moulmein

Ye

Tavoy

Mergui

Chumphon

Ranong

Ban Takua Pa

Thap Put

Phuket

Krabi

Trang

Surat Thani

Ban Na San

Nakhon Si Thammarat

Phatthalung

Songkhla

Hat Yai

Pattani

Sai Buri

Yala

Narathiwat

Terutao

Satun

Langkawi

Alor Setar

Sungai Ko-lok

Kota Baharu

Kuala Terengganu

Sungai Petani

Pinang (George Town)

Butterworth

Dungun

Taiping

Sungai Siput Utara

Ipoh

Kampar

Kuala Kubu Baharu

Raub

Kuala Lipis

Tapis 1512

Kuantan

Bentong

Kuala Lumpur

Petaling Jaya

Kelang

Putrajaya

Seremban

Segamat

Muar

Malacca

Keluang

Blumut 1010

Johor Baharu

SINGAPORE

Kulai

Banda Aceh

Sigli

Lhokseumawe

Bireuen

Lhoksukon

Idi

Peureulak

Geureudong 2855

Calang

Langsa

Meulaboh

Pangkalanbrandan

Tanjungpura

Medan

Kutacane

Tebingtinggi

Leuser 3404

Tapaktuan

Kabanjahe

Pematangsiantar

Tanjungbalai

Singkilbaru

Sihabuhabu 2300

Tarutung

Rantauprapat

Sibolga

Barumun

Dumai

Duri

Balaipungut

Padangsidimpuan

Panyabungan

Pakanbaru

Hutanopan

Lubuksikaping

Payakumbuh

Ophir 2912

Bukittinggi

Padangpanjang

Rengat

Pinmana

Muang Chiang Rai

Chiang Mai 1854

Phayao

Nan

Inthanon •2590

Lampang

Phrae

Mae Sot

Tak

Chiang Mai

Salween 1056

Salween 1854

Mekong

Luang Prabang

Ban Ban

Sayaboury

Vang Vieng

Xieng Khouang 2820 Bia

Pak Sane

Vientiane

Nong Khai

Kham Keut

Thakhek

Wang Saphung

Udon Thani

Sakon Nakhon

Miang 2316

Phitsanulok

Chum Phae

Khon Kaen

Kalasin

Maha Sarakham

Roi Et

Yasothon

Nakhon Sawan

Chaiyaphum

Nakhon Ratchasima

Buriram

Si Sa Ket

Surin

Ubon Ratchathani

Sing Buri

Lop Buri

Suphan Buri

Kanchanaburi

Nakhon Pathom

Chai Si

Chao Phraya

Khiaw 1282

Prachin Buri 849

Samrong

Ban Pong

Bangkok (Krung Thep)

Thon Buri

Chon Buri

Siracha

Sisophon

Battambang

Phetchaburi

Klaeng 1633

Rayong

Chantaburi

Laem Ngop

Chang

Kut

Pursat

Kompong Chhnang 1813

Hua Hin

Hat Lek

CAMBODIA

Phnom Penh

Kompong Som

Prachuap Khiri Khan 1251

758

Soai Dao 2102

Average linear scale

0 100 200 300 miles

0 100 200 300 400 500 Km

62

100°E

105°E

110°E

Gulf of Tongking

Dongfang

Hainan

Yaxian

Par

Quynh Luu

Vinh

Ha Tinh

Dong Hoi

Toungoo

Prome

Myanaung

Pyu

Sittang

BURMA
(MYANMAR)

Henzada

Pegu

Kyaikto

Insein

Thingangyun

Rangoon
(Yangon)

Kanbe

Thaton

Gulf of Martaban

Pyapon

Moulmein

Mae Sot

Tak

1056

1854

Inthanon *2590*

Chiang Mai

Lampang

Phrae

Nan

Phayao

Soai Dao *2102*

Salween

Ye

Tenasserim

Kanchanaburi

Nakhon Pathom

Ban Pong

Thon Buri

Bangkok
(Krung Thep)

Chon Buri

Siracha

Klaeng

Rayong

Chang

Chantaburi

1633

Phetchaburi

Hua Hin

1251

Khiri Khan Prachuap

758

Chumphon

Ranong

Isthmus of Kra

St Matthew's

Phangan

Samui

Ban Takua Pa

Surat Thani

Bari Na San

Luang *1835*

Nakhon Si Thammarat

Mergui Archipelago

Kadan

Mergui

Letsok-Aw

Lanbi

Andaman

Sea

Thap Put

Krabi

Phuket

Trang

Phatthalung

Thale Luang

Hat Yai

Songkhla

Pattani

Sai Buri

Yala

Narathiwat

Terutao

Satun

Langkawi

Alor Setar

Sungai Ko-lok

Kota Baharu

Sungai Petani

Pinang
(George Town)

Butterworth

Pinang

Kelantan

Kuala Terengganu

Sayabury

Vang Vieng

Bia 2820

Xieng Khouang

Pak Sane

Kham Keut

Napa

Rao Go 2286

Vientiane

Nong Khai

Wang Saphung

Udon Thani

Miang 2316

Phitsanulok

Chum Phae

Phetchabun

Nakhon Sawan

Chaiyaphum

Lop Buri

Sing Buri

Suphan Buri

THAILAND

Nakhon Ratchasima

Khon Kaen

Kalasin

Sakon Nakhon

Thakhek

Savannakhet

Sepone

2500 Atouat

Hue

Da Nang

V I E T N A M

L A O S

Roi Et

Maha Sarakham

Buriram

Surin

Si Sa Ket

Warin Chamrap

Ubon Ratchathani

Yasothon

Khemarat

B. Thateng

2009

Pakse

Phiafay

Attopeu

Khong

Kontum

Pleiku

1570

An Tuc

Qui Nhon

Stung Treng

Ban Pu Kroy

Mdrak

Khiaw 1282

Prachin Buri

849

Samrong

Sisophon

Angkor

Battambang

Tonle Sap

C A M B O D I A

Pursat

Kompong Chhnang

Kompong Cham

Kratie

1544

Ban Me Thuot

Nha Trang

Da Lat

1532

Cam Ranh

Bao Loc

Di Linh

Phu Chong

Phnom Penh

Basac

Mekong

Laem Ngop

1813

Kut

Hat Lek

Gulf of Thailand

Kompong Som

Kompong Cham

Chau Phu

My Tho

Saigon (Ho Chi Minh)

Bien Hoa

Vung Tau

Long Xuyen

Rach Gia

Can-Tho

Phu Quoc

Khanh Hung

Mekong Delta

Nam Can

Cape Mau

Nans

Spratly Islands

S O U T H

C

S

15°N

10°N

5°N

0°
Equator

Indragiri

65

Sea

M a l a y

MALAYA

Taiping

Sungai Siput Utara

Ipoh

Kampar

2131

Raub

Kuala Kubu Baharu

Perak

Kuala Lipis

Tapis 1512

Kuantan

Dungun

2171 Chamah

Banda Aceh

Sigli

Lhokseumawe

Bireuen

Choksukon

Idi

Peureulak

Langsa

Pangkalanbrandan

Tanjungpura

Medan

Geureudong 2855

S u m a t

Calang

Meulaboh

Leuser 3404

Kutacane

Kabanjahe

Tebingtinggi

Pematangsiantar

Tanjungbalai

Lake Toba

Sihabuhabu 2300

Singkilbaru

Tapaktuan

Tarutung

Rantauprapat

Simeulue

Barumun

Sibolga

Padangsidimpuan

Nias

Hutanopan

Panyabungan

Pini

Bukittinggi

2912

Lubuksikaping

Payakumbuh

Tanahbala

Padangpanjang

Solok

Siberut

Padang

I N D I A N

O C E A N

Strait of Malacca

Bentong

Kuala Lumpur

Petaling Jaya

Kelang

Putrajaya

Seremban

Malacca

Muar

Segamat

Keluang

Blumut 1010

Johor

Johor

Kuala

Johor Baharu

◼ **SINGAPORE**

Dumai

Rupat

Duri

Balaipungut

Pakanbaru

Rengat

Kampar

Singkep

Berhala Strait

Cape Jabung

Bengkolan Bay

Riau Islands

Lingga Islands

Singkep

MALAYSIA
(WESTERN)

Tioman

Anambas Islands

Anambas Islands (Indonesia)

North Natuna

Natuna

Natuna Islands (Indonesia)

South Natuna Islands

Tambelan Islands

Cape Datu

Datuk Bay

Binatang

Sibu

Sarikei

Kuching

Bandar Sri Aman

Sambas

Pamangkat

Singkawang

Lupar

Pinang

Ngabang

Sanggau

Sintang

Pontianak

Kapuas

Nanga Sokan

Nanga Pinoh

Maya

B

M

S

N

D

O

K

100°E

105°E

110°E

This map shows 1/60 of the earth's surface

115°E

120°E

125°E

Babuyan Islands

Cape Bojeador
Laoag
Cape Engaño
Aparri

Bangued
Tuguegarao
Vigan

Luzon

Cordillera Central

Sierra Madre

Bayombong
Pulog 2934
Ilagan

San Ildefenso Peninsula

Lingayen Gulf
Baguio
Lingayen
Dagupan
San Carlos
San Jose
Cabanatuan

Masinloc
Iba
Tarlac
Angeles
San Fernando
Caloocan

P A C I F I C

15°N

Olongapo
Manila
Quezon
Pasig
Lamon Bay

Manila Bay
Laguna de Bay
San Pablo
Polillo Islands

Lubang
Lipa
Lucena
Lopez
Daet
Catanduanes

Batangas
Naga
Mayon 2452
Virac

Calapan
Boac
Legazpi
Sorsogon

Halcon 2582
Marinduque

Baco 2363
Burias
Bulan
Laoang

Mindoro
Sibuyan
Catarman
Calbayog

San Jose
Tablas
Masbate
Catbalogan

Mindoro Strait

Calamian Group

P H I L I P P I N E S

Masbate
Samar

Panay
Nangtud 2117
Biliran
Tacloban

Roxas
Bogo
Ormoc

Zhongye Islands

San Jose de Buenavista
Iloilo
Silay
Cadiz
Abuyog
Leyte

Cleopatra Needle 1602

Bago
Bacolod
San Carlos
Mandaue
Dinagat

Palawan

Honda Bay
Puerto Princesa

465
Toledo
Cebu

Binalbagan
Guimaras
Cebu
Maasin

10°N

Negros
Bais
Bohol
Surigao
Siargao

Mantalingajan 2085
Bayawan
Tagbilaran
Camiguin

Dumaguete
Dipolog
Dapitan
Siquijor
Butuan

Bugsuk
Oroquieta
Gingoog

Balabac
Ozamiz
Cagayan de Oro

Sulu Sea
Tangub
Iligan
Malaybalay
Bislig

Malayan
Balabac Strait
Pagadian
Marawi

Banggi
Cagayan Sulu

Sea
Jambogan

Davao
Tagum

Kota Kinabalu
Kinabalu 4175
Labuk Bay
Apo 2954

Sandakan

Cotabato
Davao Gulf
Mindanao

O C E A N

70

Moro Gulf
Zamboanga
Digos

Basilan
Koronadal

Beaufort
SABAH

Basilan

General Santos

Bandar Seri Begawan
Brunei Bay

Lahad Datu

Tawitawi
Sulu Archipelago

Kuala Belait
Darvel Bay

Miri
BRUNEI
Sarangani Islands

Tawitawi Group
5°N

LAYSIA (EASTERN)
Mulu 2371
Tawau

Kawio Islands

Sebuku Bay

Celébes Sea
Talaud Islands

ARAWAK
Tarakan
Sangihe

2550
Kayan

Morotai

Guguang 2467
Tanjungredeb
Tobelo
Akelamo

Sangihe Islands
Jailolo

2240 Liangpran
Menyapa 2000
Manado
2292
Ternate
Halmahera

Rapak
Tondano
Weda
Weda Bay

278 aya
Sulawesi (Celebes)
Kotamobagu
Molucca

Muarabadak
2910
Buol
Paleleh
Kuandang
Gorontalo
Gebe

Samarinda
Dondo Bay
2217
Sea
0°

Makassar Strait
Moutong
Tilamuta
Labuha

Mahakam
Mapaga
Gulf of Tomini
Malik
Bacan

Donggala
Palu
Uebonti
Togian Is.
2400
Teku

115°E
120°E
125°E

0 | 100 | 200 | 300 miles

Average linear scale

0 | 100 | 200 | 300 | 400 | 500 Km

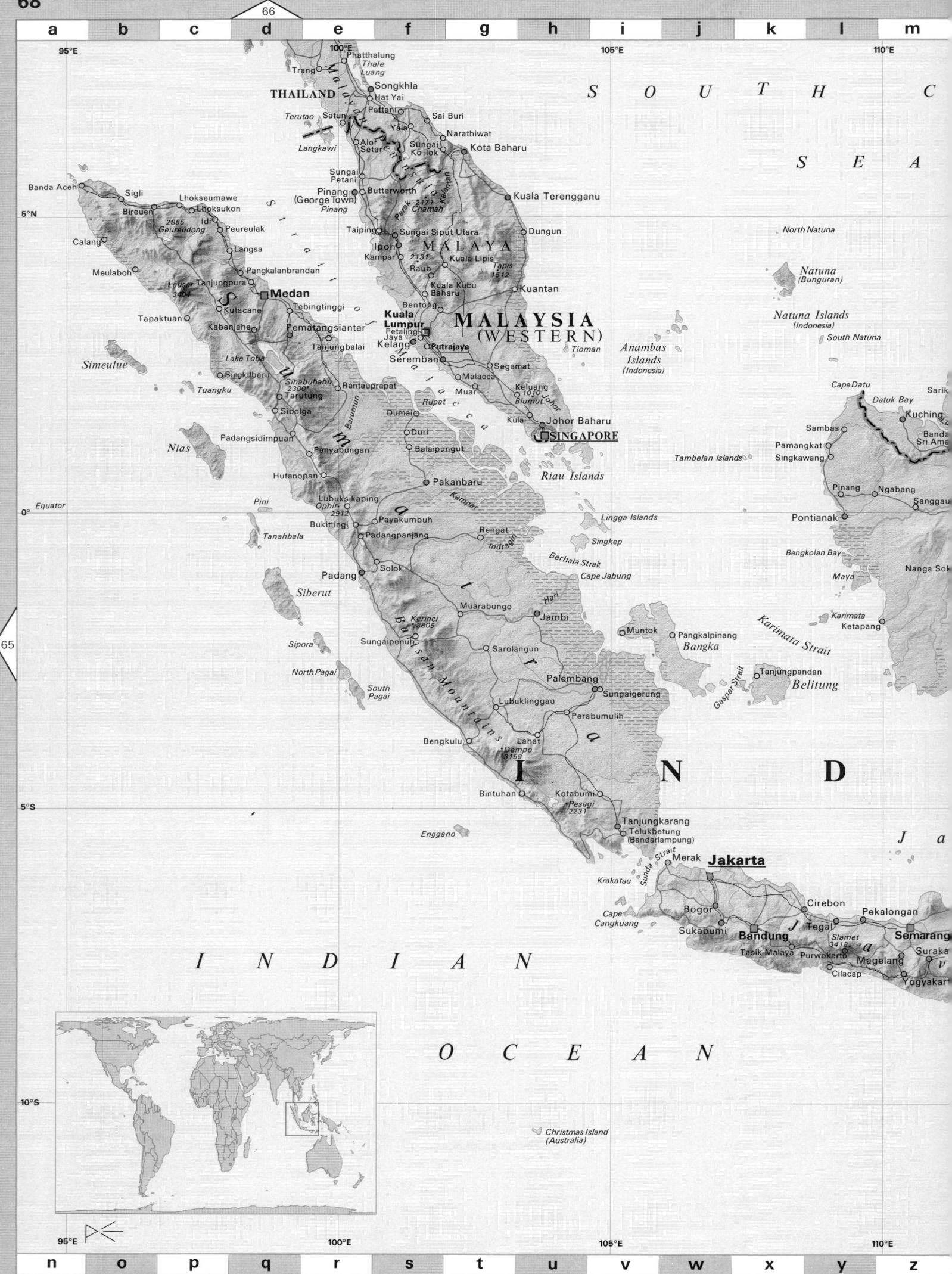

95°E · 100°E · 105°E · 110°E

S O U T H

S O U T H   C

S E A

THAILAND

Phatthalung
Thale Luang
Trang
Songkhla
Hat Yai
Terutao Satun
Pattani
Sai Buri
Yala
Narathiwat
Langkawi
Alor Setar
Sungai Ko-lok
Kota Baharu
Sungai Petani
Butterworth
Pinang (George Town)
Pinang
Kuala Terengganu

5°N

Banda Aceh
Sigli
Bireuen
Lhokseumawe
Lhoksukon
2855 Geureudong
Idi
Peureulak
Calang
Langsa
Meulaboh
Pangkalanbrandan
Taiping
Sungai Siput Utara
2171 Chamah
Dungun
Ipoh
Kampar
2131
Kuala Lipis
North Natuna
Tanjungpura
Leuser 3404
Medan
Tebingtinggi
Kuala Kubu Baharu
Tapis 1512
Kuantan
Natuna (Bunguran)
Kutacane
Kabanjahe
Pematangsiantar
Bentong
Kuala Lumpur
Petaling Jaya
MALAYSIA (WESTERN)
Tianman
Natuna Islands (Indonesia)
Tapaktuan
Tanjungbalai
Lake Toba
Kelang
Putrajaya
South Natuna
Simeulue
Sihabuhabu 2300
Singkilbaru
Seremban
Segamat
Anambas Islands (Indonesia)
Tuangku
Tarutung
Rantauprapat
Malacca
Muar
Keluang 1010
Blumut
Sibolga
Rupat
Dumai
Johor
Nias
Padangsidimpuan
Duri
Kulai
Cape Datu
Sambas
Sarik
Datuk Bay
Kuching
Hutanopan
Bataipungut
Johor Baharu
SINGAPORE
Tambelan Islands
Pamangkat
Banda Sri Ama
Pini
Pakanbaru
Riau Islands
Singkawang
Equator

0°

Lubuksikaping
Ophir 2912
Kampar
Lingga Islands
Pinang
Ngabang
Tanahbala
Payakumbuh
Rengat
Singkep
Pontianak
Bukittingi
Padangpanjang
Indragiri
Berhala Strait
Sanggau
Siberut
Solok
Cape Jabung
Bengkolan Bay
Padang
Muarabungo
Hari
Maya
Nanga Sok
Sipora
Kerinci 3805
Jambi
Karimata
Ketapang
Sungaipenuh
Muntok
Pangkalpinang
Karimata Strait

65

North Pagai
Sarolangun
Palembang
Bangka
Gaspar Strait
Tanjungpandan
Belitung
South Pagai
Lubuklinggau
Sungaigerung
Perabumulih
Bengkulu
Lahat
Dempo 3159

5°S

Bintuhan
Kotabumi
Pesagi 2231
I   N   D
Tanjungkarang
Telukbetung (Bandarlampung)
Enggano
J a
Merak
Jakarta
Krakatau
Sunda Strait
Cirebon
Cape Cangkuang
Bogor
Pekalongan
Sukabumi
Bandung
J
Tegal
Slamet 3418
Semarang
Tasik Malaya
Purwokerto
a
Suraka
Magelang
v
Cilacap
Yogyakart

I N D I A N

O C E A N

Christmas Island (Australia)

10°S

95°E · 100°E · 105°E · 110°E

This map shows 1/60 of the earth's surface

I N A

Balabac Strait

Sulu Sea

PHILIPPINES

Pagadian

115°E

Banggi

Cagayan Sulu

Zamboanga

Moro Gulf

Cotabato

Davao   Tagum

Apo 2954

Mindanao

Jambongan

Basilan

Basilan

Digos   Davao Gulf

Malayan Sea

Kota Kinabalu

Kiñabalu 4175

Labuk Bay

Sandakan

SABAH

Pangutaran Group

Jolo

Koronadal

General Santos

Beaufort

Sulu Archipelago

Sarangani

Brunei Bay

Lahad Datu

5°N

Bandar Seri Begawan

Darvel Bay

Tawitawi

Tawitawi Group

Kawio

Kuala Belait

BRUNEI

Mulu 2371

Tawau

Talaud Islands

Miri

Baram

Sebuku Bay

MALAYSIA (EASTERN)

Sesayap

Celebes Sea

Bintulu

SARAWAK

2550

Kayan

Tarakan

Sangihe

Sangihe Islands

Morotai

Kapuas

2467 *Guguang*

Tanjungredeb

Rajang

atang

B o r n e o

Manado   Klabat 2022

Tobelo

Jailolo

Akelamo

Liangpran 2240

Menyapa 2000

Rapak

Tondano

Halmahera

Ternate   *Saolat 1508*

ang

Buol   Paleleh

Kuandang

Kotamobagu

Weda

Weda Bay

Dondo Bay

2217

M o l u c c a

K A L I M A N T A N

Ogoamas 2913

Moutong   Tilamuta   Gorontalo

Sea

0°

anga Pinoh

Raya 2278

Mahakam

Muarabadak

Dongkalang

Togian Islands

Malik

Bacan Islands

Labuha

Obi

Samarinda

Mapaga

Gulf of Tomini

Teku

Tumbangsamba

Barito

Balikpapan

Donggala

Palu

2400

Peleng

Mo l u

C e r a m Sea

70

Buntok

Sarempaka 1380

Pasangkayu

Poso

Uebonti   Batui

Banggai Islands

Taliabu

Mangole

Sula Islands M

Palangkaraya

Tanjung

Muratus Mountains

Lumu

Sulawesi (Celebes)

Wotu

Gulf of Tolo

c u s

Sampit

Kandangan

Besar 1892

Gandadiwata 3074 Masamba

Palopo

Gulf of Bone

Mekongga 2799

Namlea   *Buru*

Strait of Manipa

Ceram

kalanbuun

Banjarmasin

Kotabaru

Rantekombala 3455

Kendari

Ambon

Batakan

Majene

Kolaka

Cape Selatan

Laut

Parepare

Kolono

O   **N**   **E**   Watampone   **S**   **I**   **A**

Jatisiri

Raha

Muna

Ujung Pandang   Sinjai

Butung

5°S

2871

Kabaena

a   S e a

Masalembo

Baubau

Tukangbesi Islands

B a n d a   S e a

Bawean

Salajar

Madura

Kangean

Bangkalan

Tanahjampea Kalao

Barat Daya Islands

Surabaya

Madura Strait

B a l i   S e a   *L e s s e r   S u n d a   I s l a n d s*

F l o r e s   S e a

Wetar

diun

Semeru 3676

Probolinggo

Banyuwangi

Alor

Malang

Jember

2276 *Bali*

3726

Dili

Leti Islands

adiri a

Denpasar

Lombok

Sumbawa Besar

Raba

Ruteng   2400

Maumere   *Solor Islands*

Atambua   2960

EAST TIMOR

Mataram

Sumbawa

Flores

Ende

Timor

Waikabubak   Waingapu

Sawu Sea

Besikama

10°S

Sumba

Kupang

Sawu

Roti

T i m o r   S e a

115°E   120°E   125°E

0   100   200   300   miles   0   100   200   300   400   500   Km

Average linear scale

130°E 135°E 140°E 145°E

Yap Islands

Faraulep Atoll

Ngulu Atoll

Sorol Atoll

M I C

PALAU ○ Babel Thuap
○ Koror

Woleai Atoll
Ifalik Atoll

Eauripik Atoll

C a r o l i n e

Sonsorol

5°N

P A C I F

Pulo Anna

Merir

P A C I F

Tobi

Helen Reef

O C E A

Morotai

Mapia Islands

○ Akelamo
Halmahera

Ayu Islands

Waigeo

0°

69

Dampier Strait

Kwoko
3000

○ Manokwari
Biak

○ Sorong

Cenderawasih
•Peg Ariak
2939

Yapen

Misool

990•

● Sarmi

C

Steenkool ○

I N D O N E S I A

Van Rees Mountains

○ Jayapura
Vanimo ○

Ceram

Babo ○

*Gulf of
Cenderawasih*

W E S T

Memberamo

○ Aitape

3019•

● Bula

Fakfak ○

Bomberai

Lumi ○
Dreikikir ○ ● Wewak

Ceram

Tobo ○

Kaimana ○

Maoke

Wamena ●

Sepik

Ramu

● Ambon

Java•
5029

P A P U A

Mountains

Mandala•
4702

N e w

e a

Bismarck Range

Kokonau ○

*Kai
Islands*

G u i n e a

Telefomin ●

Kopiago ●
Wabag ●
Mount
Hagen ○

Strickland

Banda Sea

*Aru
Islands*

Tanahmerah ●

Mendi ●
Kubor
4359

2895•

● Go

Damar

*Tanimbar
Islands*

Digul

Mappi ○

Lake
Murray

N E W

● Kikori

Babar

Fly

Selaru

*Dolak
Island*

Sermata

Cape Vals

Merauke ○

*Gulf o
Papu*

● Daru

A R A F U R A   S E A

Torres Strait

10°S

Badu● ●Moa

130°E 135°E 140°E 145°E

*Prince of Wales
Island*   ● Cape York

This map shows 1/60 of the earth's surface

150°E   155°E   160°E

Namonuito Atoll

Murillo Atoll

Fayu   *Hall Islands*

West Fayu   *Pikelot*   *Minto Atoll*

R   O   N   E   S   I   A

Lamotrek Atoll   *Truk Islands*   *Oroluk Atoll*

Elato Atoll   *Satawal*   *Ponape*   *Mokil Atoll*

Losap Atoll   *Senjavin Group*

Namolok   *Pingelap Atoll*

I s l a n d s   *Ngatik Atoll*

Satawan Atoll   *Mortlock Islands*   *Kosrae*

5°N

I   C

N

Kapingamarangi Atoll

Equator   0°

Admiralty Islands

B i s m a r c k   A r c h i p e l a g o   *Kavieng*

Bismarck Sea   *New Ireland*

Rabaul

P A P U A   *Sinewit 2438*

Madang   5°S

ino   *Balbi 2743*

Bangeta 4107   *Walinga*   *New Britain*   *Bougainville*   *Kieta*
                              Kandrian   *(Papua New Guinea)*

Lae   *Nukiki*   *Choiseul*   S O L O M O N
                                                                          Fauro   I S L A N D S
G U I N E A   *Alu*   *Santa Isabel*
                                                            Mono
Morobe   *Vella Lavella*   *Buala*
Kerema   *New Georgia*
                              Owen Stanley Range   *Trobriand or*   *New Georgia Islands*   *Vangunu*   *Malaita*
Victoria 4013   *Popondetta*   *Kiriwina Island*   S o l o m o n
                                                Woodlark   S e a
Port Moresby   *Sogeri*   *D'Entrecasteaux Islands*   **Honiara**
                        Kwikila   *Guadalcanal*   *Popomanaseu 2331*

Alotau   10°S

                                                                                                        San Cristóbal

150°E   155°E   160°E

0   100   200   300   miles   Average linear scale   0   100   200   300   400   500   Km

a · b · c · d · e · f · g · h · i · j · k · l · m

110°E   115°E   120°E   125°E

J a v a   *Bali*
                                    Denpasar
                                          Mataram   *Lombok*   *Sumbawa Besar*   Raba   Ruteng   Maumere   *Solor*   *Alor*   Dili   EAST TIMOR
                                                        .3726   .2400   Ende   Atambua   .2960
                                                        .1400   *Sumbawa*   *Flores*   .2421   *Timor*
                                     I N D O N E S I A   *Sawu*   Besikama

10°S   *Sea*
                                         Waikabubak   Waingapu
                                              Sumba   .1175   Kupang
                                                        .Sawu
                                                        Roti

                                                                                                            T i m o
                                                                                                            Se

                                         .Cartier   Cap Londono

                                                                                          Cape Bougainville   Kalumb...
                                                                                    Bonaparte Archipelago
                                                                                                            Theda

15°S   Kuri Bay   *Kimberl*   *Plate*
I N D I A N   Mount Hann .776   Karunjie
                                                                            Collier Bay   Panter Downs   Gibb River
                                                                    Cape Lévêque   Beverley Springs
                                                            Lombardina   Oobagooma   Mount House
                                                        Beagle Bay   Derby   .927   Tableland
O C E A N   *Dampier Land*   Kimberley Downs   Mt. Broome .936   Glenroy
                                            Coulomb Point   Camballin   *King Leopold Ranges*   *Dur*
                                            Broome   Roebuck Plains   *Fitzroy*   Fitzroy Crossing
                                                        Myroodah   Mount Huxley .522   Margaret River
                                            Dampier Downs   Nerrima   Bohemia Downs
                                            Lagrange   .247   Christmas Creek
                                            Frazier Downs
                                                        Anna Plains   *Eighty Mile Beach*

20°S   Wallal Downs   *Great Sandy Desert*   Lake Greg...
                                        Port Hedland   Goldsworthy   Mount .418 Elliott
                            Barrow Island   Dampier   Roebourne   Shay Gap   Yarrie
                                    Whim Creek   Kangan   Warrawagine
                                Cooya Pooya   *Yule*   Marble Bar   Bamboo Creek   *Percival Lakes*
                    North West Cape   Yarraloola   Millstream   *W E*   *S T E R N*   Lake Auld
                    Exmouth   Onslow   Pannawonica   Mount Florance   Nullagine   Lake Dora   Tabletop .427
                                Mount Minnie   Wittenoom   Lake Blanche
                    Learmonth   Yanrey   *Hamersley Range*   *Fortescue*   *A*   *U*   *S*
                                    Tom Price   Talawana   Lake Disappointment
                            Uaroo   Wyloo   .1073   Mount Tom Price   *Gibson Desert*
                                            Mount .1251   Mount Meharry   Mount Newman .1053   Newman
                    Tropic of Capricorn   Mount Palgrave .704   Ashburton Downs   Paraburdoo
                                Ullawarra   *Ashburton*   Turee Creek   Bulloo Downs
                            Winning   Lyndon   Minnie Creek   Kumarina
                    Cape Cuvier   *Lake McLeod*   Mount Augustus .1105   Augustus   Mount Vernon   *A U S T R A L I A*
                                        Waldburg Range   Three Rivers   Mount Essendon .906   *Carnarvon Range*
25°S   Carnarvon   Gascoyne Junction   Dairy Creek   *Gascoyne*   Milgun   Neds Creek   .738   Glenayle
            Cape Inscription   *Shark Bay*   Denham   Mount Seabrook   Peak Hill   *Lake Nabberu*   Granite Peak   Carnegie
                                .552   *Lake Carnegie*   Warburton .623
                        Byro   .732 *Mount Hale*   Karalundi   Yelma   Mount Talbot
            Useless Loop   Hamelin Pool   Mileura   Wiluna   Wonganoo
                    Tamala   Curbur   Kalli   Meekatharra
                            Murchison   .530   Tuckanarra   Gidgee
                    Wannoo   Yallalong   Big Bell   Cue   Booylgoo Springs
                    Kalbarri   Billabalon   Murgoo   Sandstone   Agnew   .594   *Great*

110°E   115°E   120°E   125°E

n · o · p · q · r · s · t · u · v · w · x · y · z

This map shows 1/60 of the earth's surface

130°E 135°E 140°E 145°E

Ceti Islands

Cape Vals

Merauke

PAPUA NEW GUINEA

Daru

Gulf of Papua

Torres Strait

Coral

A r a f u r a   S e a

10°S

Sea

Badu Moa

Prince of Wales Island

Cape York
Bamaga

Great Barrier Reef

Cape Van Diemen

Cape Croker

Wessel Islands

Melville Island

Bathurst Island

Van Diemen Gulf

Beagle Gulf

Murgenella

Maningrida Milingimbi Galiwinku

Nhulunbuy
Yirrkala Cape Arnhem

Camburinga

183

Andoom Weipa Iron Range
555
Lockhart River
Aurukun Wenlock

Belyuen Darwin
Darwin River Noonamah
Batchelor Mudginbarry
Adelaide River
Oenpelli
Mount Howship 385
213

Arnhem Land

Anson Bay

Daly River Tipperary Burrundie Pine Creek El Sherana
366

Port Keats

Katherine Bamyili Mainoru

Angurugu Rose River
Umbakumba
Groote Eylandt

Gulf of Carpentaria

Coen
506
Princess Charlotte Bay
640

Joseph Bonaparte Gulf

Cape York

Edward River Strathmay 213 Breeza Plains Cape Flattery

15°S

Forrest Ninbing

Wyndham

Victoria Willeroo
Timber Creek Larrimah
Delamere
227

Mataranka Elsey Roper Bar Roper Ngukurr
Limmen Bight

Nathan River Bing Bong
Borroloola

Sir Edward Pellew Group

Peninsula
Mitchell River 366

Cooktown Laura
Strathleven Rossville
Dunbar Daintree Mossman
Inkerman Galbraith Gamboola Mareeba Cairns
1375

Kununurra
Lake Argyle

Victoria River Downs Daly Waters
Hidden Valley
Top Springs O.T. Downs McArthur
103 Robinson River

Mornington 152
Mornington
Wellesley Islands
Bentinck

Wollogorang Karumba
Westmoreland

Vanrook Walsh
Miranda Downs Chillagoe Almaden Atherton 1611
Delta Downs
Maggieville Abingdon Downs
Bartle Frere
Innisfail
Silkwood

Turkey Creek
Ord River
Halls Creek

Inverway Wave Hill
288
Hooker Creek

Newcastle Waters 251 Elliott
Lake Woods
Renner Springs Brunette Downs
Creswell Downs Benmara
Anthonys Lagoon
Barkly Tableland
347
291
Alexandria Alroy Downs

Corinda Burketown Normanton Croydon Georgetown Einasleigh
Doomadgee Floraville Blackbull Gilbert River Conjuboy Ingham
Augustus Downs Wondoola 742
Lawn Hill Gregory Downs Donors Hill Claraville 194 Forsayth
Riversleigh 200 Iffley Esmeralda Robinhood Greenvale
Herbert Vale Kamileroi Canobie Savannah Downs Lyndhurst
Thorntonia
Gunpowder Maryvale

Nicholson
Gordon Downs
Sturt Creek
Baluna
Balgo

N O R T H E R N
Tanami

Tennant Creek Frewena
436
240 Wonarah
Camooweal
Avon Downs
Yelvertoft Dalgonally Mount Sturgeon 732 Lolworth
Kajabbi Boonderoo Mount Stewart 1067

20°S

Lake White
Lake Wills

T E R R I T O R Y
Desert
464
Mount Davidson
Wauchope Kurundi Hatches Creek Austral Downs
Warrabri Elkedra Lake Nash
Annitowa
Davenport Range

Mount Isa Cloncurry Julia Creek Maxwelton Richmond Hughenden Pentland Torrens Creek
Mary Kathleen McKinlay Kynuna Whitewood
Duchess
Lake Buchanan

Lake Mackay

Willowra Barrow Creek
Willowra
Tea Tree Woodgreen Utopia Ooratippra Argadargada 339
Yuendumu
808

Urandangi 380 Dajarra Corfield Aberfoyle
Carandotta Chatsworth Middleton Lerida Corinda
Tobermorey Linda Downs Toolebuc Winton Eastmere
Lucy Creek Roxborough Downs 392 Chorregon Muttaburra
Marqua Boulia Morella Aramac
Lake Galilee
Tangorin

R A L I A
1067 Mount Wedge
Aileron

Mount Liebig
1524 Haast Bluff
Hamilton Downs
Glen Helen
Macdonnell Ranges Alice Springs Ringwood
Areyonga Santa Teresa
901
Harts Range
1167 Indiana

L
Glenormiston 236 Marion Downs
Vergemont Arrilalah Barcaldine
Coorabulka Diamantina Lakes Longreach
Breadalbane Davenport Downs Connemara Isisford Yalleroi
Bedourie Stonehenge Blackall
Glengyle Lake Machattie Monkira Palparara Emmet
Jundah Yaraka 594

A

Lake Macdonald
Lake Hopkins
Lake Neale Lake Amadeus

Henbury
Angas Downs Deep Well
Engoordina
Finke

Simpson

Georgina
Diamantina
Thomson
Barcoo

25°S

Giles Meteorological Station
Docker River
Petermann Range
Curtin Springs 867 Ayers Rock Erldunda
Mulga Park Kulgera
New Crown Finke

Mount Cockburn 1138
1058 Mount Davies
Amata 1439
Musgrave Ranges Ernabella Fregon
De Rose Hill Pedirka
Tieyon Abminga

Durrie Betoota Windorah Retreat Listowel Downs Adavale 329
Birdsville Tonbar Lynwood
Alton Downs Cadelga Keeroongooloo Thylungra Quilpie
Pandie Pandie Cordillo Downs 120 300 Eromanga Cheepie Westgate
Goyder Lagoon Clifton Hills 304 Galway Downs Lake Yamma Yamma 316 Charleville
Innamincka Tobermory Toompine Wyandra
Cowarie Cooper Creek Nockatunga Thargomindah Coongoola

Victoria Desert

S O U T H   A U S T R A L I A
917 Everard Park Granite Downs
Welbourn Hill Alberga Oodnadatta Mount Dutton Warburton Lake Eyre

130°E 135°E 140°E 145°E

74

0 100 200 300 miles | 0 100 200 300 400 500 Km

Average linear scale

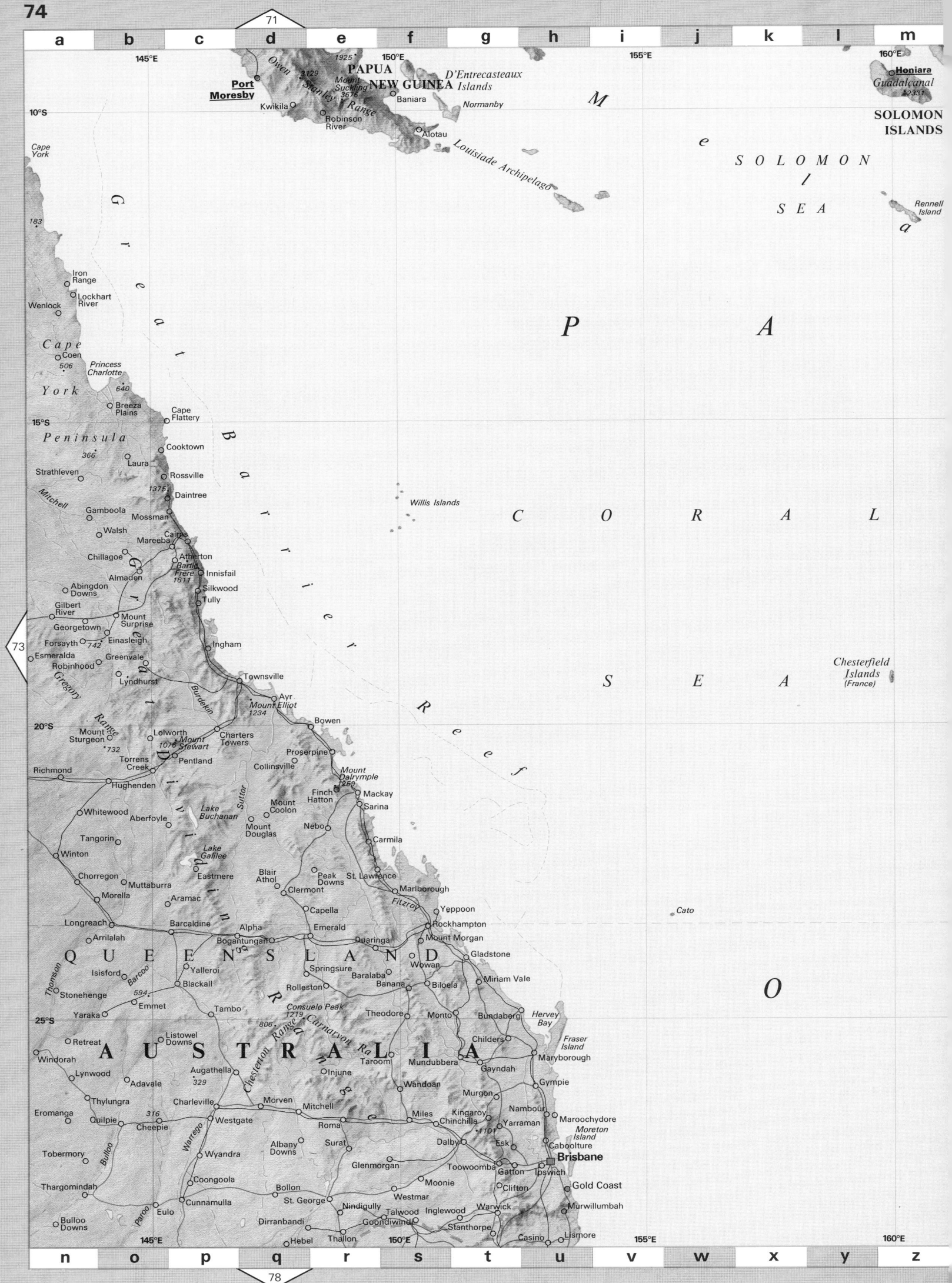

71

a b c d e f g h i j k l m

145°E 150°E 155°E 160°E

Honiara
Guadalcanal
2331

Owen

Stanley Range
3129
Mount
Suckling
3676

**PAPUA
NEW GUINEA**

*D'Entrecasteaux
Islands*

**Port
Moresby**

Kwikila

10°S

Robinson
River

Baniara

Normanby

M

**SOLOMON
ISLANDS**

Alotau

Louisiade Archipelago

e

S O L O M O N

S E A

i

Cape
York

183

*Rennell
Island*

a

Iron
Range

Lockhart
River

Wenlock

C o r a l

Cape

Coen
506

*Princess
Charlotte*

640

York

15°S

Breeza
Plains

Cape
Flattery

Willis Islands

C O R A L

Strathleven

P e n i n s u l a

366

Laura

Cooktown

Mitchell

Gamboola

Walsh

Rossville

1375

Daintree

Mossman

Chillagoe

Almaden

Cairns

Mareeba

Atherton
*Bartle
Frere*
1611

Innisfail

G r e a t

Abingdon
Downs

Silkwood

Tully

Gilbert
River

Georgetown

Mount
Surprise

Forsayth 742

Einasleigh

Ingham

73

Esmeralda

Robinhood

Greenvale

Lyndhurst

*Chesterfield
Islands
(France)*

Townsville

20°S

Gregory

Mount
Sturgeon

732

Lolworth
1076

Burdekin

Ayr

Mount Elliot
1234

Charters
Towers

Bowen

Range

Torrens
Creek

Mount
Stewart

Pentland

Collinsville

Proserpine

Richmond

Hughenden

D

Mount
Dalrymple
1259

Whitewood

Aberfoyle

*Lake
Buchanan*

Mount
Coolon

Finch
Hatton

Mackay

Sarina

Suttor

Tangorin

Mount
Douglas

Nebo

*Lake
Galilee*

Carmila

Winton

Chorregon

Muttaburra

Eastmere

Blair
Athol

Peak
Downs

St. Lawrence

Morella

Aramac

Clermont

Fitzroy

Marlborough

Capella

Yeppoon

Longreach

Barcaldine

Alpha

Emerald

Duaringa

Rockhampton

Arrilalah

Bogantungan

Mount Morgan

Q U E E N S L A N D

Gladstone

Thomson

Isisford

Barcoo

Yalleroi

Springsure

Baralaba

Wowan

Stonehenge

594

Blackall

Rolleston

Banana

Biloela

Miriam Vale

Yaraka

Emmet

Tambo

Consuelo Peak
1219

Theodore

Monto

Bundaberg

*Hervey
Bay*

806

Retreat

Listowel
Downs

Range

Childers

*Fraser
Island*

25°S

Windorah

Lynwood

Augathella

329

Carnarvon Range

Chesterton Range

Injune

Taroom

Mundubbera

Gayndah

Maryborough

Adavale

Wandoan

Murgon

Gympie

Thylungra

Charleville

Morven

Mitchell

Miles

Kingaroy

Nambour

Maroochydore

Eromanga

Quilpie

316

Westgate

Roma

Chinchilla

Yarraman

*Moreton
Island*

Cheepie

Surat

Dalby

Esk

Caboolture

Tobermory

Wyandra

Albany
Downs

1101

Gatton

Brisbane

Thargomindah

A U S T R A L I A

Glenmorgan

Moonie

Toowoomba

Ipswich

Clifton

Gold Coast

Coongoola

Bollon

Westmar

Bulloo
Downs

Eulo

Cunnamulla

St. George

Nindigully

Goondiwindi

Talwood

Inglewood

Warwick

Murwillumbah

Dirranbandi

Hebel

Thallon

Stanthorpe

Casino

Lismore

145°E 150°E 155°E 160°E

78

n o p q r s t u v w x y z

This map shows 1/60 of the earth's surface

165°E

170°E

175°E

180°

n

Kirakira
San Cristobal

*Santa Cruz
Island*

e   *I*   *F*   *I*   *C*

s

*Banks
Islands*

15°S

*Espíritu
Santo*   *1879*

*Vanua
Levu*   Lambasa
(Labasa)

1032

Malekula

*New
Hebrides*   *a*

*Koro
Sea*

VANUATU

FIJI

Efate
Vila

Nandi
(Nadi)   Tavua
Mount Victoria
1324

Viti Levu

Singatoka
(Sigatoka)   **Suva**

Erromango

20°S

1650.

*Loyalty
Islands
(France)*

*New
Caledonia
(France)*   Houailu

Bourail

Nouméa

Tropic of Capricorn

E   *A*   *N*

25°S

165°E

170°E

175°E

180°

0   100   200   300
miles
Average linear scale

0   100   200   300   400   500
Km

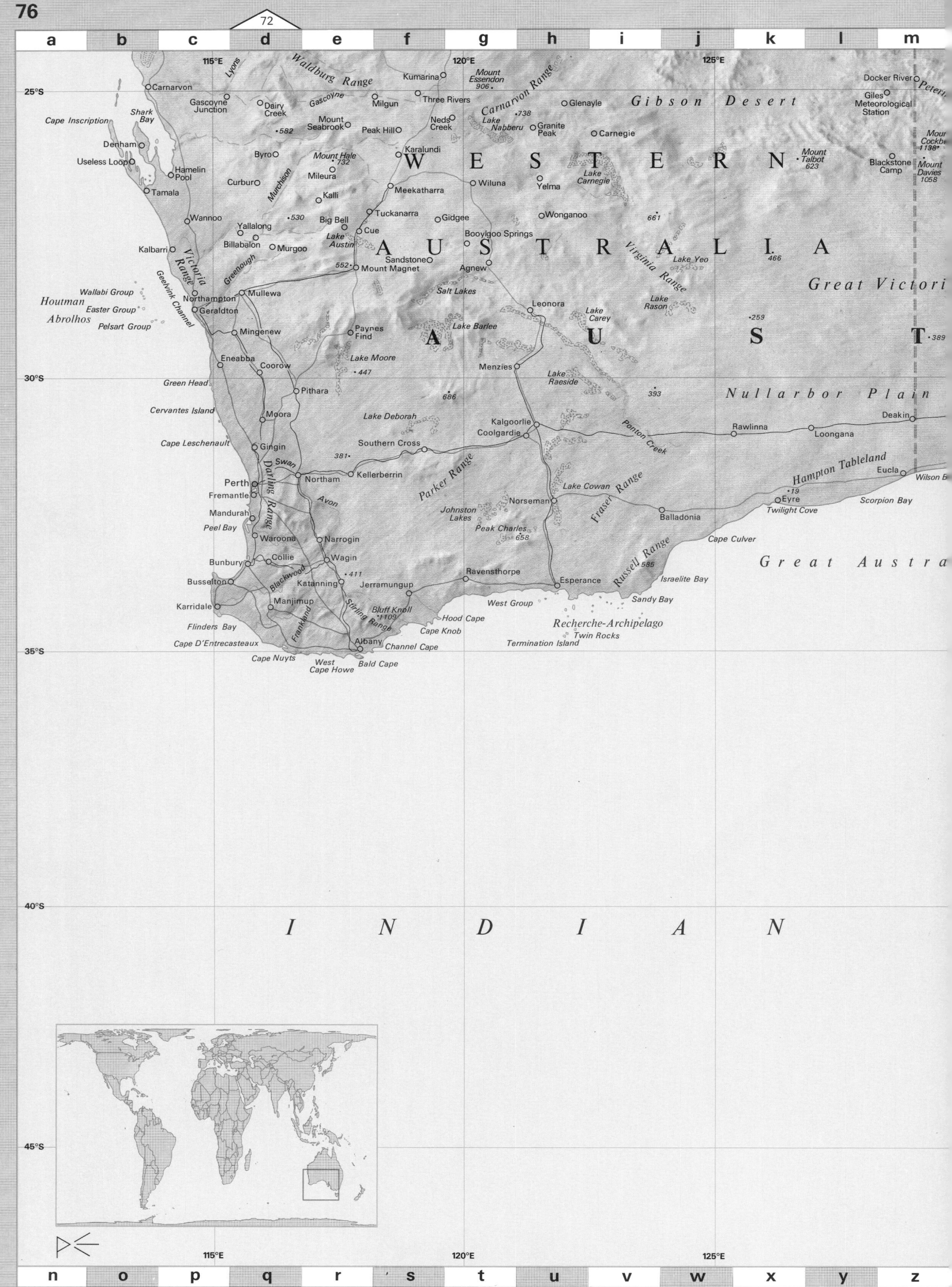

a   b   c   d   e   f   g   h   i   j   k   l   m

115°E · Lyons · Waldburg Range · Kumarina · 120°E · Mount Essendon 906 · Carnarvon Range · Gibson Desert · 125°E · Docker River · Peterm

25°S · Carnarvon · Gascoyne Junction · Dairy Creek · Gascoyne · Milgun · Three Rivers · Glenayle · Giles Meteorological Station · Mour Cockb 1138

Cape Inscription · Shark Bay · Mount Seabrook · ·582 · Peak Hill · Neds Creek · Lake Nabberu · ·738 · Granite Peak · Carnegie · Mour Davies 1058

Denham · Byro · Mount Hale ·732 · Karalundi · Blackstone Camp

Useless Loop · Hamelin Pool · Curburo · Mileura · WESTERN · Mount Talbot 623

Tamala · Wannoo · Kalli · Meekatharra · Wiluna · Yelma · Lake Carnegie

Yallalong · ·530 · Big Bell · Tuckanarra · Gidgee · Wonganoo · ·661

Kalbarri · Billabalon · Murgoo · Cue · AUSTRALIA · Lake Yeo · ·466

Lake Austin · Sandstone · Booylgoo Springs

Northampton · Mullewa · 552· · Mount Magnet · Agnew · Virginia Range · Great Victori

Houtman · Wallabi Group · Geraldton · Greenough · Salt Lakes · Leonora · Lake Rason

Abrolhos · Easter Group · Mingenew · Paynes Find · Lake Barlee · Lake Carey · ·259

Pelsart Group · A · U · S · T · ·389

Eneabba · Coorow · Lake Moore · Menzies · Nullarbor Plain

Green Head · ·447 · Lake Raeside · ·393

Cervantes Island · Pithara · Lake Deborah · ·686 · Kalgoorlie · Rawlinna · Loongana · Deakin

Moora · Coolgardie · Ponton Creek

Cape Leschenault · Gingin · Southern Cross · ·381

Swan · Northam · Kellerberrin · Parker Range · Lake Cowan · Fraser Range · Hampton Tableland · Eucla

Perth · Avon · Norseman · Eyre · Scorpion Bay · Wilson B

Fremantle · ·19 · Twilight Cove

Mandurah · Johnston Lakes · Balladonia

Peel Bay · Narrogin · Peak Charles 658 · Cape Culver

Waroona · Wagin · Russell Range · Great Austra

Bunbury · Collie · ·411 · Ravensthorpe · Esperance · ·585 · Israelite Bay

Busselton · Katanning · Jerramungup · West Group · Sandy Bay

Karridale · Manjimup · Hood Cape · Recherche-Archipelago · Twin Rocks

Flinders Bay · Bluff Knoll ·1109 · Cape Knob · Termination Island

Cape D'Entrecasteaux · Stirling Range · Albany · Channel Cape

Cape Nuyts · West Cape Howe · Bald Cape

35°S

30°S

40°S

I   N   D   I   A   N

45°S

n   o   p   q   r   s   t   u   v   w   x   y   z

115°E · 120°E · 125°E

This map shows 1/60 of the earth's surface

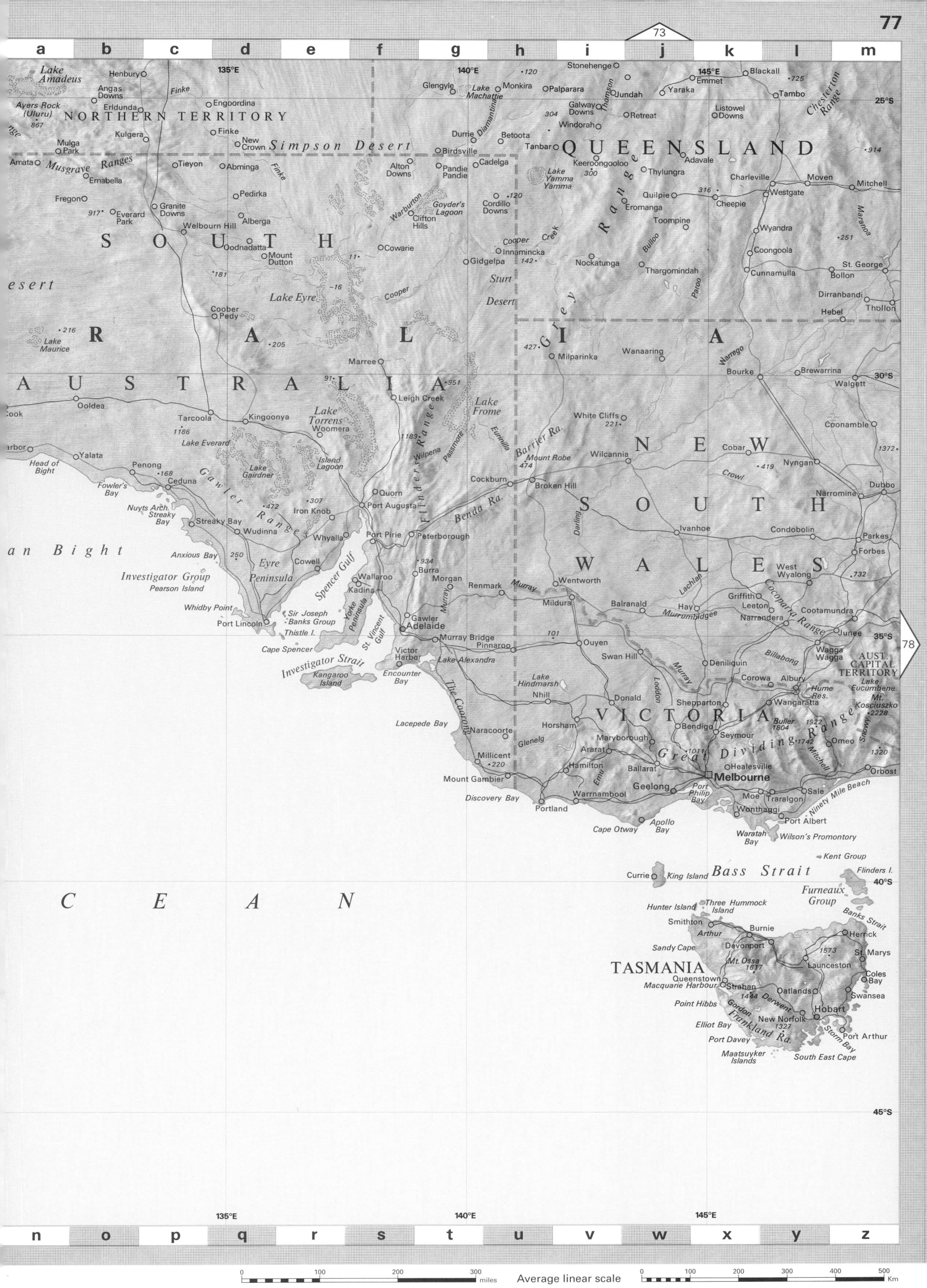

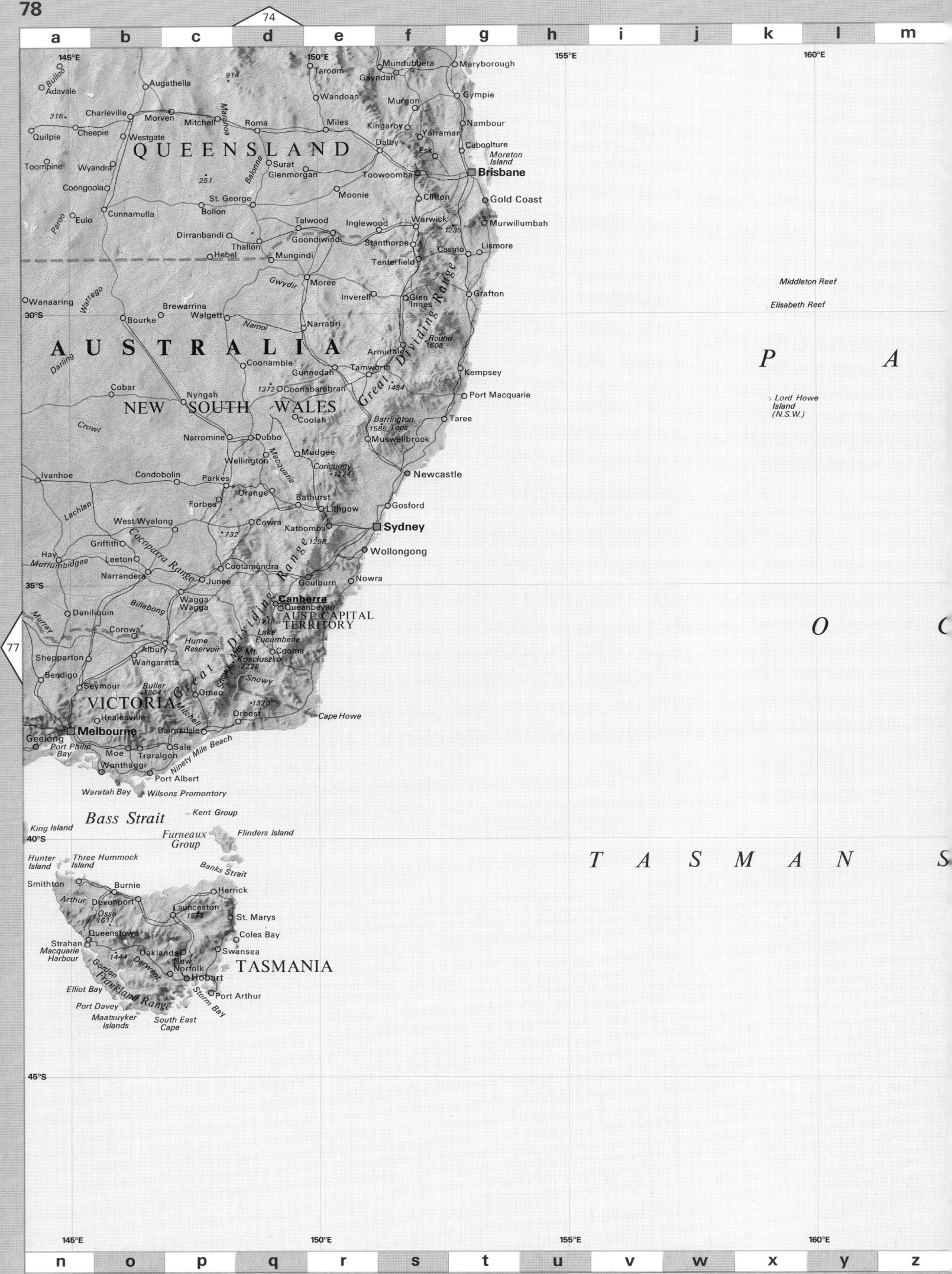

145°E 150°E 155°E 160°E

74

77

QUEENSLAND

Bulloo
Adavale
Augathella
Taroom
Mundubbera
Maryborough
914
Charleville
Morven
Mitchell
Roma
Miles
Wandoan
Murgon
Gympie
316
Quilpie
Cheepie
Westgate
Gayndah
Nambour
Kingaroy
Yarraman
Caboolture
Dalby
Toompine
Wyandra
Surat
Glenmorgan
251
Toowoomba
Moonie
Clifton
Brisbane
Coongoola
St. George
Bollon
Gold Coast
Cunnamulla
Talwood
Inglewood
Warwick
Moreton Island
Eulo
Dirranbandi
Thallon
Goondiwindi
Stanthorpe
Murwillumbah
1239
Hebel
Mungindi
Tenterfield
Casino
Lismore

AUSTRALIA

Wanaaring
Brewarrina
Gwydir
Moree
Inverell
Glen Innes
Grafton
Middleton Reef
30°S
Bourke
Walgett
Narrabri
Elisabeth Reef
Namoi
Coonamble
Armidale
Round 1608
P
A
Cobar
Nyngan
1372
Coonabarabran
Tamworth
Kempsey
NEW SOUTH WALES
Coolah
1494
Port Macquarie
Lord Howe Island (N.S.W.)
Narromine
Dubbo
Barrington Tops 1585
Muswellbrook
Taree
Crowl
Mudgee
Wellington
Macquarie
Coricudgy 1224
Ivanhoe
Condobolin
Parkes
Newcastle
Orange
Bathurst
Forbes
Lithgow
Gosford
732
Cowra
Katoomba
Sydney
West Wyalong
1298
Griffith
Cootamundra
Wollongong
Hay
Leeton
Junee
Goulburn
Nowra
Murrumbidgee
Narrandera
35°S
Wagga Wagga
Canberra
Deniliquin
Billabong
Queanbeyan
1919
AUST. CAPITAL TERRITORY
Corowa
Lake Eucumbene
Murray
Albury
Hume Reservoir
Cooma
77
Shepparton
Wangaratta
Mt. Kosciuszko 2228
Snowy
Bendigo
Seymour
Buller 1804
Omeo
1320
VICTORIA
Healesville
Mitchell
Orbost
Cape Howe
Geelong
Melbourne
Bairnsdale
Port Phillip Bay
Moe
Sale
Traralgon
Ninety Mile Beach
Wonthaggi
Port Albert
Waratah Bay
Wilsons Promontory
Kent Group

Bass Strait

King Island
Furneaux Group
Flinders Island
40°S
Hunter Island
Three Hummock Island
Banks Strait
T A S M A N   S
Smithton
Burnie
Herrick
Arthur
Devonport
Launceston
Ossa 1617
1573
St. Marys
Queenstown
Coles Bay
Strahan
Oaklands
Swansea
Macquarie Harbour
1444
Derwent
New Norfolk
TASMANIA
Gordon
Frankland Range
Hobart
Elliot Bay
Port Arthur
Port Davey
Storm Bay
Maatsuyker Islands
South East Cape

45°S

145°E 150°E 155°E 160°E

This map shows 1/60 of the earth's surface

165°E   170°E   175°E   180°E

Norfolk
Island
(Australia)

75

C I F I C

30°S

Macauley
Island
Kermadec Islands   Curtis
(N.Z.)   Island

E   A   N

Three Kings
Island

North Cape

35°S

Ninety
Mile Beach

Kaitaia
Bay of Islands

774

Whangarei

Dargaville   Great Barrier
Island

Hauraki
Gulf

Auckland

Waikato   Bay of Plenty   Te Araroa

Tauranga   East Cape

Hamilton   Whakatane

NORTH ISLAND   1478

Tokoroa   Rotorua

Taumarunui   Taupo   Gisborne

Lake Taupo   Wairoa

New Plymouth   Ngauruhoe
Egmont   1291   Hawke Bay

2518   Ruapehu   Napier

Hawera   2797   Hastings

NEW ZEALAND   Wanganui   40°S

E A   Palmerston
North

Collingwood   Paraparaumu Tararua Range

Karamea   Tasman   1571 Masterton
Bight   Bay   Picton   Lower Hutt

Nelson   Blenheim   Wellington
Richmond Range   Cape Palliser

Westport   Cook Strait

Travers
2337

Greymouth   Kaikoura

Hokitika

SOUTH ISLAND   Arthurs
Pass

Waipara

Mt. Cook   Arrowsmith
(Aoraki)   2795   Canterbury Plains   Christchurch
3764
Haast   Ashburton   Banks
Lake   Peninsula
Pukaki
Aspiring   Twizel   Canterbury
3027   Bight
Milford Sound   Waitaki
Queenstown   Timaru
Lake
Wakatipu   Oamaru   45°S
Te Anau   2035
Jane Peak   Clutha
Alexandra

West Cape   Lumsden

Gore   Dunedin
Foveaux Strait   Invercargill

Stewart
Island   Bounty
Islands
Southwest Cape   (N.Z.)

Snares
Islands

165°E   170°E   175°E   180°E

n o p q r s t u v w x y z

0   100   200   300
miles   Average linear scale   0   100   200   300   400   500
Km

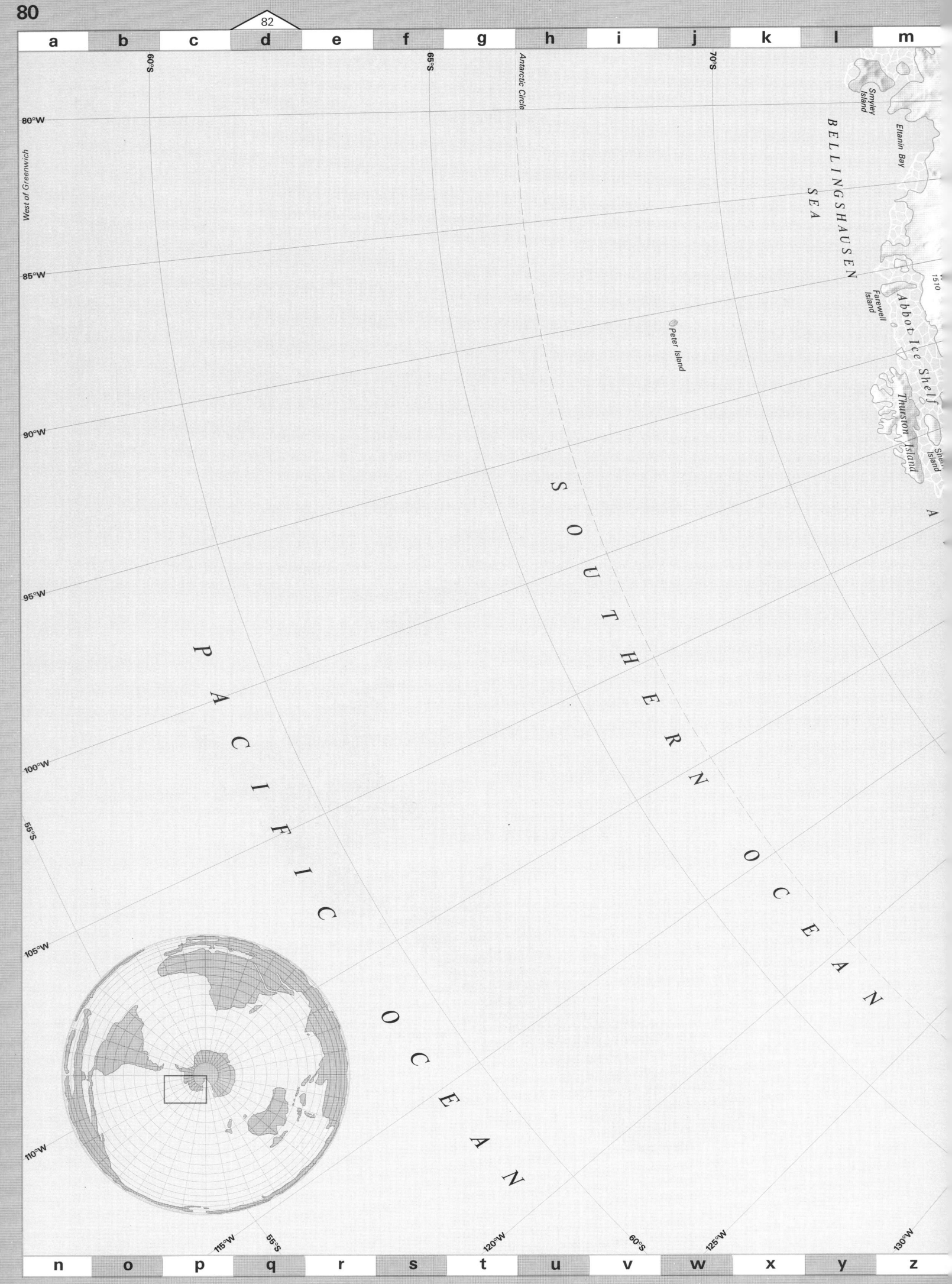

80°W

85°W

90°W

95°W

100°W

105°W

110°W

60°S

65°S

70°S

Antarctic Circle

West of Greenwich

Smyley Island

Ettanin Bay

B E L L I N G S H A U S E N   S E A

1510

Farewell Island

Abbot Ice Shelf

Thurston Island

Sherm Island

A

Peter Island

S O U T H E R N   O C E A N

P A C I F I C   O C E A N

115°W

55°S

120°W

60°S

125°W

130°W

This map shows 1/60 of the earth's surface

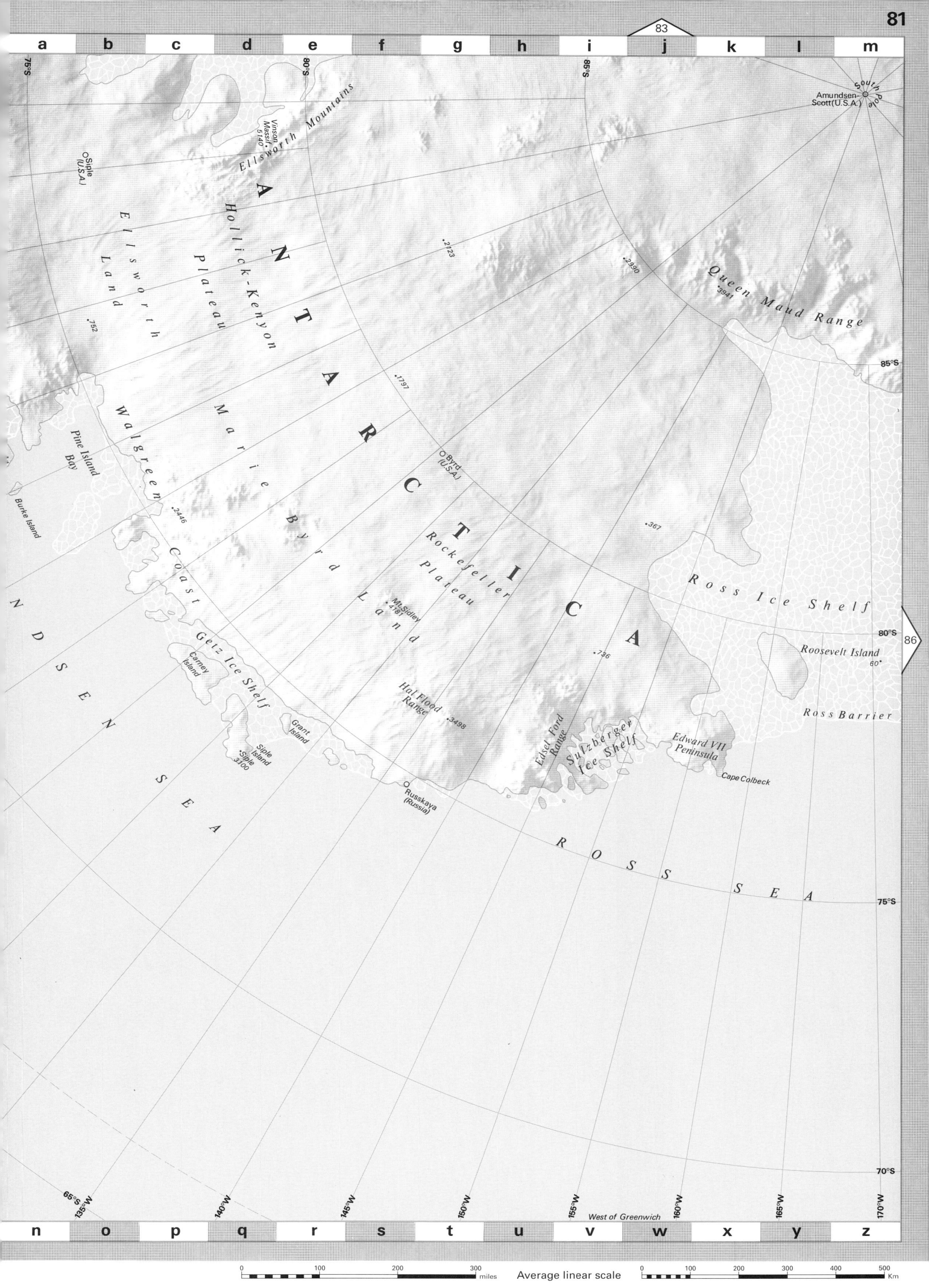

75°S

Siple
(U.S.A.)

Vinson
Massif
5140·

Ellsworth Mountains

80°S

·2123

·2990

Queen Maud Range
·3941

A

N

Hollick-Kenyon
Plateau

Ellsworth
Land

·752

85°S

T

·1797

85°S

A

Walgreen
Coast

Marie

Byrd

Land

Byrd
(U.S.A.)

R

C

·367

Ross Ice Shelf

Pine Island
Bay

Burke Island

·2446

Rockefeller
Plateau

T

I

C

80°S

86

Roosevelt Island
60·

Getz Ice Shelf

Carney
Island

Mt.Sidley
4181·

A

·736

Ross Barrier

N

D

S

E

N

Grant
Island

Siple
Island
3110·

Hal Flood
Range
·3498

Edsel Ford
Range

Sulzberger
Ice Shelf

Edward VII
Peninsula

Cape Colbeck

Russkaya
(Russia)

R

O

S

S

S

E

A

75°S

S

E

A

70°S

65°S
155°W

140°W

145°W

150°W

155°W
West of Greenwich

160°W

165°W

170°W

0   100   200   300   miles

Average linear scale

0 100 200 300 400 500 Km

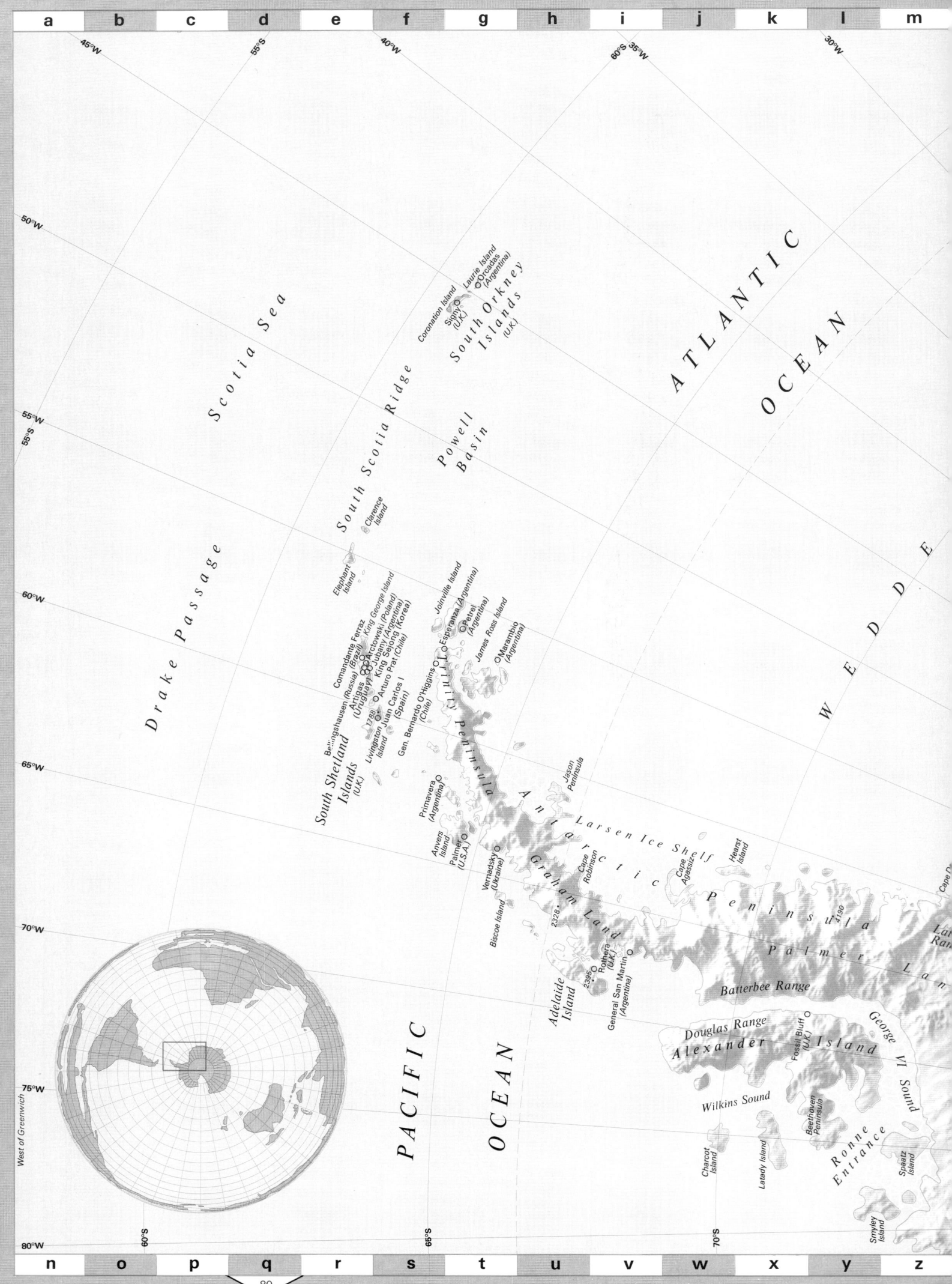

a b c d e f g h i j k l m

45°W   55°S   40°W   60°S 35°W   30°W

50°W

ATLANTIC

Scotia Sea

OCEAN

55°W

55°S

Coronation Island
Laurie Island
Signy (U.K.)
Orcadas (Argentina)

South Orkney
Islands
(U.K.)

South Scotia Ridge

Powell
Basin

Drake Passage

Clarence
Island

60°W

W
E
D
D
E

Elephant
Island

Joinville Island
Esperanza (Argentina)
Petrel
(Argentina)

Comandante Ferraz (Brazil)
Bellingshausen (Russia)
Artigas (Uruguay)
Arctowski (Poland)
1788 Jubany (Argentina)
King George Island
Livingston King Sejong (Korea)
Island Arturo Prat (Chile)
Juan Carlos 1
(Spain)
Gen. Bernardo O'Higgins
(Chile)

James Ross Island
Marambio
(Argentina)

Trinity Peninsula

65°W

South Shetland
Islands
(U.K.)

Primavera (Argentina)

Anvers
Island
Palmer
(U.S.A.)

Vernadsky
(Ukraine)

Antarctic

Graham Land

Jason
Peninsula

Larsen Ice Shelf

Cape
Robinson

Cape
Agassiz

Hearst
Island

Peninsula

Palmer Lan

Cape D

Biscoe Island

2328

70°W

2390
Rothera
(U.K.)

Batterbee Range

Larsen
Ran

Adelaide
Island

General San Martin
(Argentina)

Douglas Range

George VI Sound

Alexander   Island

Fossil Bluff (U.K.)

PACIFIC

Wilkins Sound

Beethoven
Peninsula

Ronne
Entrance

75°W

OCEAN

Charcot
Island

Latady Island

Spaatz
Island

West of Greenwich

60°S   65°S   70°S

80°W

Smiley
Island

n o p q r s t u v w x y z

This map shows 1/60 of the earth's surface

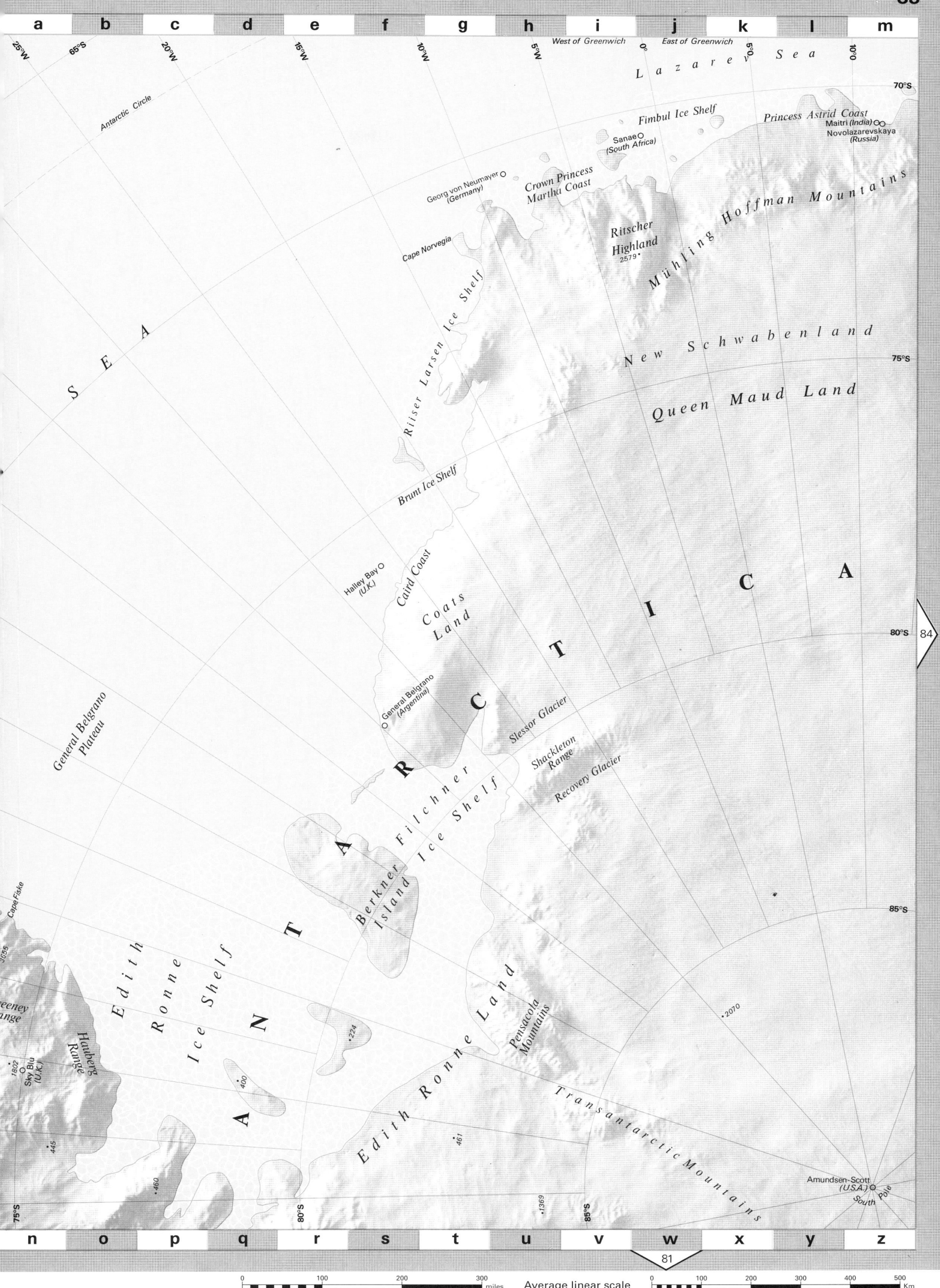

a b c d e f g h i j k l m

25°W

65°S

20°W

15°W

10°W

5°W

West of Greenwich 0° East of Greenwich

5°E

10°E

70°S

L a z a r e v   S e a

Antarctic Circle

Fimbul Ice Shelf

Princess Astrid Coast

Sanae ○
(South Africa)

Maitri (India) ○○
Novolazarevskaya
(Russia)

Georg von Neumayer ○
(Germany)

Crown Princess
Martha Coast

Mühling Hoffman Mountains

Cape Norvegia

Ritscher
Highland
2579 •

S   E   A

R i s e r   L a r s e n   I c e   S h e l f

N e w   S c h w a b e n l a n d

75°S

Q u e e n   M a u d   L a n d

Brunt Ice Shelf

C   A

Halley Bay ○
(U.K.)

C a i r d   C o a s t

*Coats
Land*

80°S

84

T

R

General Belgrano
Plateau

C

General Belgrano ○
(Argentina)

Slessor Glacier

I

Shackleton
Range

Recovery Glacier

A

Cape Fiske

Filchner

85°S

3655 •

Berkner
Island

Ice Shelf

Sweeney
Range

*E
d
i
t
h*

*R
o
n
n
e*

*I
c
e*

*S
h
e
l
f*

N

• 224

T

Hauberg
Range

1802 •
Sky Blu
(U.K.)

• 2070

*Pensacola
Mountains*

A

• 460

• 400

E d i t h   R o n n e   L a n d

445 •

Transantarctic Mountains

461 •

Amundsen-Scott
(U.S.A.)

75°S

80°S

85°S

• 1369

South
Pole

n o p q r s t u v w x y z

0   100   200   300
miles   Average linear scale

0   100   200   300   400   500
Km

East of Greenwich

10°E   15°E   20°E   25°E   30°E   35°E   40°E   65°S

70°S

Lazarev Sea

Riiser Larsen Sea

Cosmonaut Sea

Antarctic Circle

Princess Astrid Coast

Maitri (India)

Novolazarevskaya (Russia)

Princess Ragnhild Coast

Riiser Larsen Peninsula

Lützow Holm Bight

Syowa (Japan)

Crown Prince Olaf Coast

Molodezhnaya (Russia)

Casey Bay

Amundsen Bay

Tula

Asuka (Japan)

Prince Harald Coast

Christensen Mountains

Princess Ragnhild Land

•2470

•2588

Enderby Land

75°S

Queen Maud Land

•2900

•3602

•3955

Dome Fuji (Japan)

A N T A R C T I C A

Prince

Lambert Glacier

83

80°S

Amery Highlands

•3732

85°S

•3106

Sovetskaya (Russia)

Amundsen-Scott (U.S.A.)

South Pole

85°S   80°S   75°S

This map shows 1/60 of the earth's surface

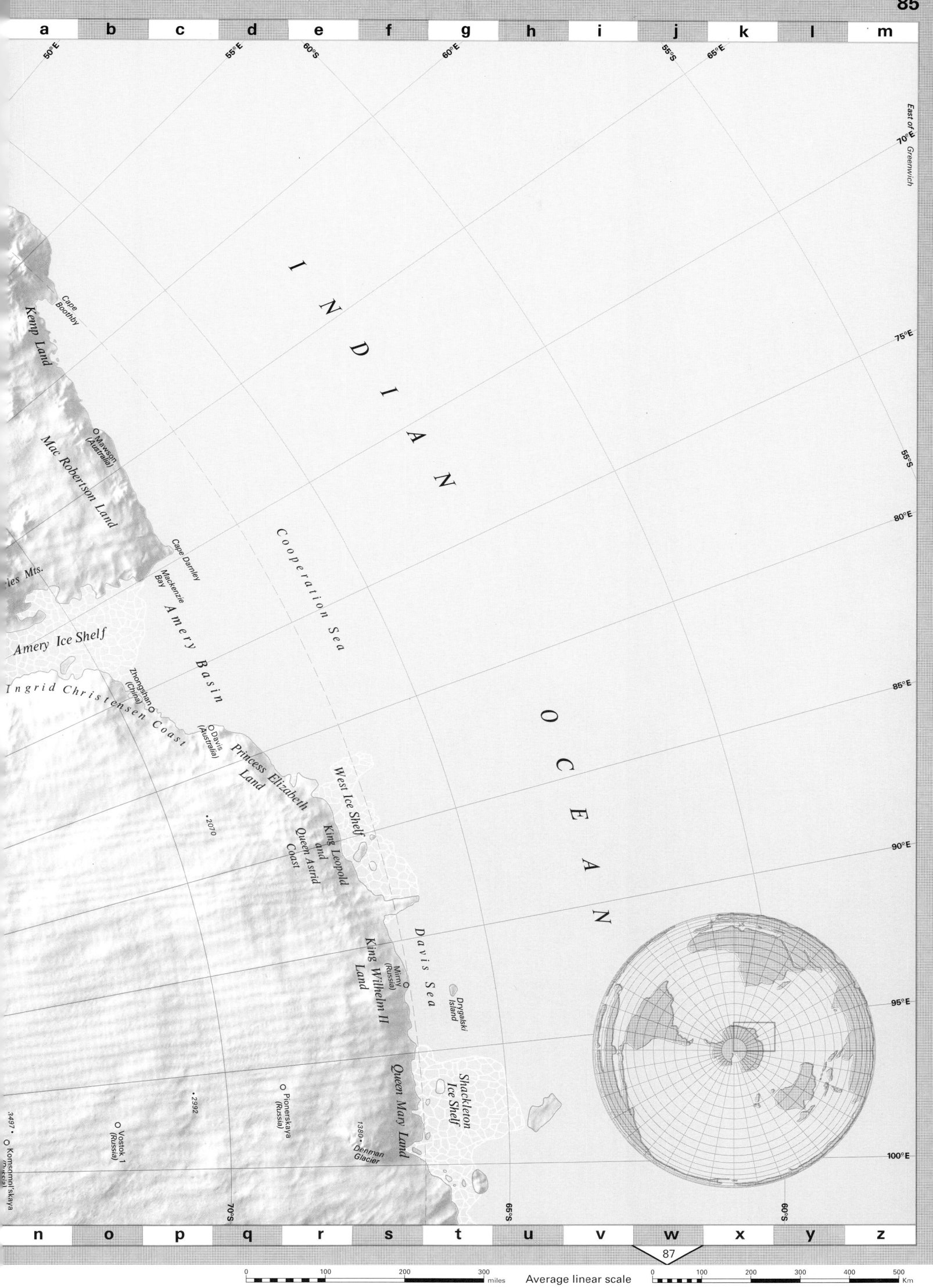

50°E   55°E   60°S   60°E   55°S   65°E

East of Greenwich

70°E

75°E

55°S

80°E

85°E

90°E

95°E

100°E

Cape
Boothby

Kemp Land

Mawson
(Australia)

Mac Robertson Land

…les Mts.

Cape Darnley

Mackenzie
Bay

Amery Ice Shelf

Amery Basin

Ingrid Christensen Coast

Zhongshan
(China)

Davis
(Australia)

I N D I A N

C o o p e r a t i o n   S e a

Princess Elizabeth
Land

West Ice Shelf

King Leopold
and
Queen Astrid
Coast

O C E A N

Davis Sea

King Wilhelm II
Land

Mirny
(Russia)

Drygalski
Island

. 2070

. 2992

Pionerskaya
(Russia)

Queen Mary Land

Shackleton
Ice Shelf

Denman
Glacier

Vostok 1
(Russia)

3497 .

Komsomol'skaya
(Russia)

70°S   65°S   60°S

87

0   100   200   300   miles   Average linear scale   0   100   200   300   400   500   Km

Amundsen-Scott
(U.S.A.)
South Pole

•3094

•3297

•3488

•2827

•3702

Beardmore Glacier

Mt. Kirkpatrick
4528

•4282

T r a n s a n t a r c t i c

A N T A R C T I C A

•3716

Ross Ice Shelf

M o u n t a i n s

•4025

Ross Barrier

Scott Base O O McMurdo
(U.S.A.)
Terror • • Erebus
3262   3743
Ross
Island

•2675

R O S S   S E A

•2468

Cape
Washington

George V
Land

•2828

*Victoria
Land*

Rennick Glacier

*Oates
Land*

Ninnis Glacier

Coulman
Island

Hallett O
(New Zealand/U.S.A.)

Leningradskaya
(Russia)
O

Cape Hudson

Cape Adare

Cape Hooker

Cape
Cheetham

International Dateline

Sturge
Island

*Balleny
Islands*

West of Greenwich   East of Greenwich

This map shows 1/60 of the earth's surface

85

70°S

65°S

60°S

Antarctic Circle

100°E

East of Greenwich

Knox Coast

105°E

Budd Coast

Casey O
(Australia)

Cape Poinsett

110°E

Sabrina Coast

W
i
l
k
e
s
L
a
n
d

.2868

Banzare Coast

115°E

Voyeykov
Ice Shelf

120°E

.2400

Porpoise
Bay

S O U T H E R N   O C E A N

Adélie
Land

55°S

Dumont-d'Urville
(France)

125°E

Mertz

Cape
Gray

Dumont d'Urville Sea

South Magnetic Pole
(1995)

130°E

150°E

145°E

60°S

140°E

55°S

135°E

0   100   200   300 miles   Average linear scale   0   100   200   300   400   500 Km

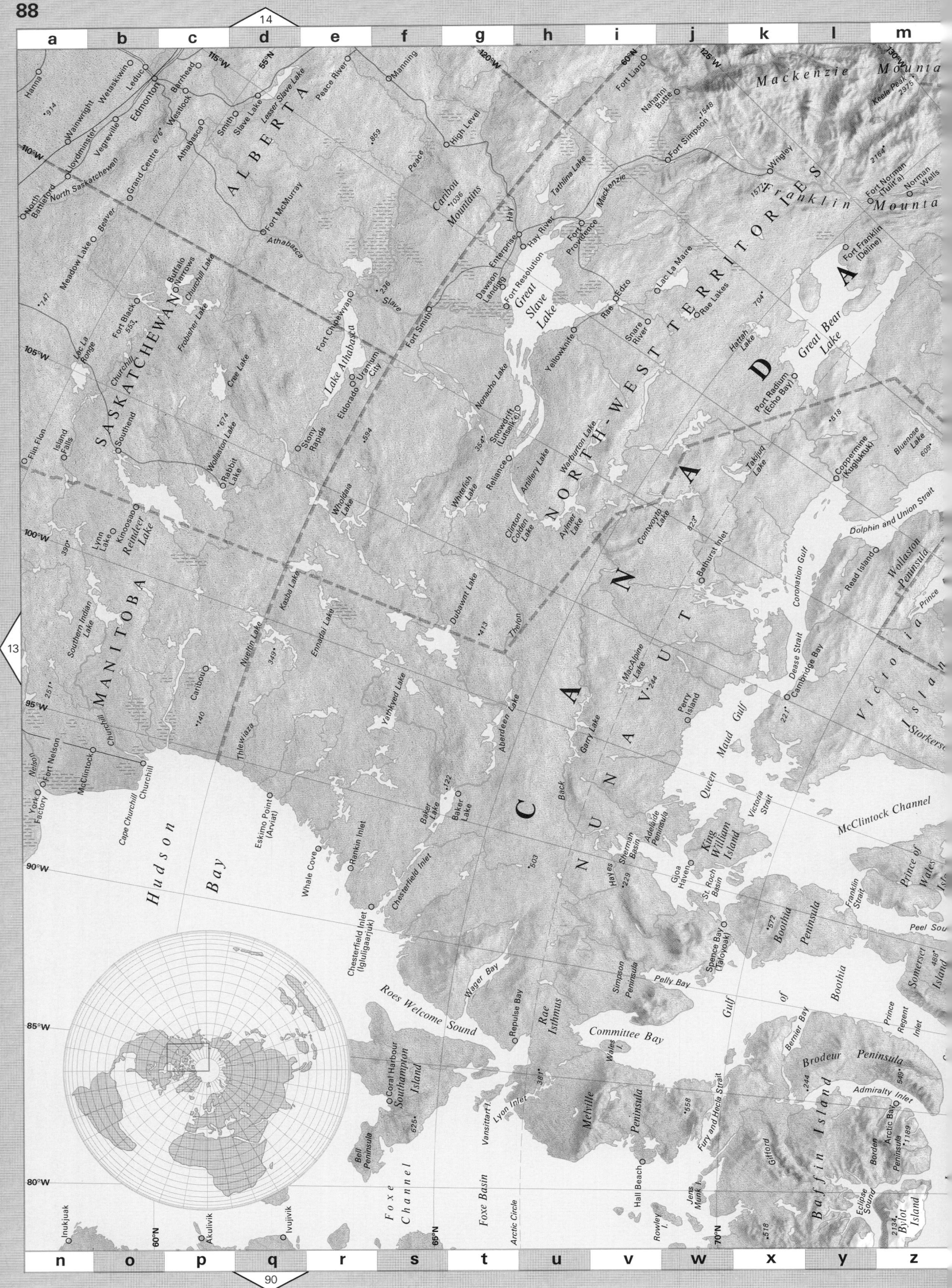

55°N

115°W

110°W

105°W

100°W

95°W

90°W

85°W

80°W

60°W

120°W

125°W

130°W

Hanna
•914
Wainwright
Vegreville
Lloydminster
North
Battleford
North Saskatchewan
Meadow Lake
•747
Island Falls
Flin Flon
Nelson
York Factory
McClintock
Fort Nelson
Churchill
Cape Churchill
Lynn Lake
390°
Kinoosao
Southend
Lac La Ronge
Fort Black
553°
Reindeer Lake
Southern Indian Lake
251°
Churchill
Caribou
•140
Thlewiaza
Nueltin Lake
349°
Ennadai Lake
Wollaston Lake
Rabbit Lake
•674
Cree Lake
Stony Rapids
Eldorado Uranium City
•564
Kasba Lake
Yathkyed Lake
Dubawnt Lake
•413
Thelon
Frobisher Lake
Churchill Lake
Lake Athabasca
Fort Chipewyan
Fort Black
Otter
Buffalo Narrows
Grand Centre
676°
Athabasca
Smith
Slave Lake
Fort McMurray
Athabasca
Lesser Slave Lake
Barrhead
Westlock
Leduc
Wetaskiwin
Edmonton
Peace River
Manning
High Level
Peace
•869
Hay
Caribou Mountains
•7036
Slave
•236
Fort Smith
Fort Resolution
Dawson Landing
Enterprise
Hay River
Fort Providence
Great Slave Lake
Snowdrift (Lutselk'e)
354°
Reliance
Artillery Lake
Clinton Colden Lake
Aylmer Lake
Whitefish Lake
Nonacho Lake
Yellowknife
Rae
Edzo
Snare River
Lac La Martre
Tathlina Lake
Fort Simpson
Fort Liard
Nahanni Butte
•1548
Wrigley
1572°
Mackenzie
Rae Lakes
704°
Warburton Lake
Contwoyto Lake
823°
Takijuq Lake
•818
Coppermine (Kugluktuk)
Port Radium (Echo Bay)
Great Bear Lake
Fort Franklin (Deline)
Hattah Lake
Franklin Mounta
Fort Norman (Tulit'a)
Norman Wells
2164°
Keele Peak
2975
Mackenzie Mounta
Bluenose Lake
605°
Read Island
Wollaston Peninsula
Prince
Dolphin and Union Strait
Dease Strait
Cambridge Bay
221°
Coronation Gulf
Bathurst Inlet
Perry Island
MacAlpine Lake
•244
Garry Lake
Back
Aberdeen Lake
Beverly Lake
•503
Baker Lake
•122
Chesterfield Inlet
Franklin Inlet
Whale Cove
Eskimo Point (Arviat)
Chesterfield Inlet (Igluligaarjuk)
Wager Bay
Repulse Bay
Rae Isthmus
Roes Welcome Sound
Coral Harbour
Southampton Island
625°
Bell Peninsula
Foxe Channel
Foxe Basin
Arctic Circle
Rowley
Jens Munk I.
Hall Beach
Wales I.
Lyon Inlet
381°
Vansittart I.
Melville Peninsula
Committee Bay
Pelly Bay
Simpson Peninsula
Boothia Peninsula
572°
Gulf of Boothia
Spence Bay (Taloyoak)
Gjoa Haven
St. Roch Basin
229°
Hayes
Sherman Basin
King William Island
Adelaide Peninsula
Victoria Strait
Queen Maud Gulf
McClintock Channel
Storkerso
Victoria Island
Prince of Wales Isl
Franklin Strait
Peel Sou
Somerset Island
485°
Bernier Bay
Prince Regent Inlet
Brodeur Peninsula
244°
Admiralty Inlet
Gifford
Borden Peninsula
1189°
•518
Eclipse Sound
2134°
Bylot Island
Baffin Island
Arctic Ba
549°
ALBERTA
SASKATCHEWAN
MANITOBA
NORTH-WEST TERRITORIES
NUNAVUT
CANADA
Hudson Bay
Inukjuak
Akulivik
Ivujivik

60°N

65°N

70°N

This map shows 1/60 of the earth's surface

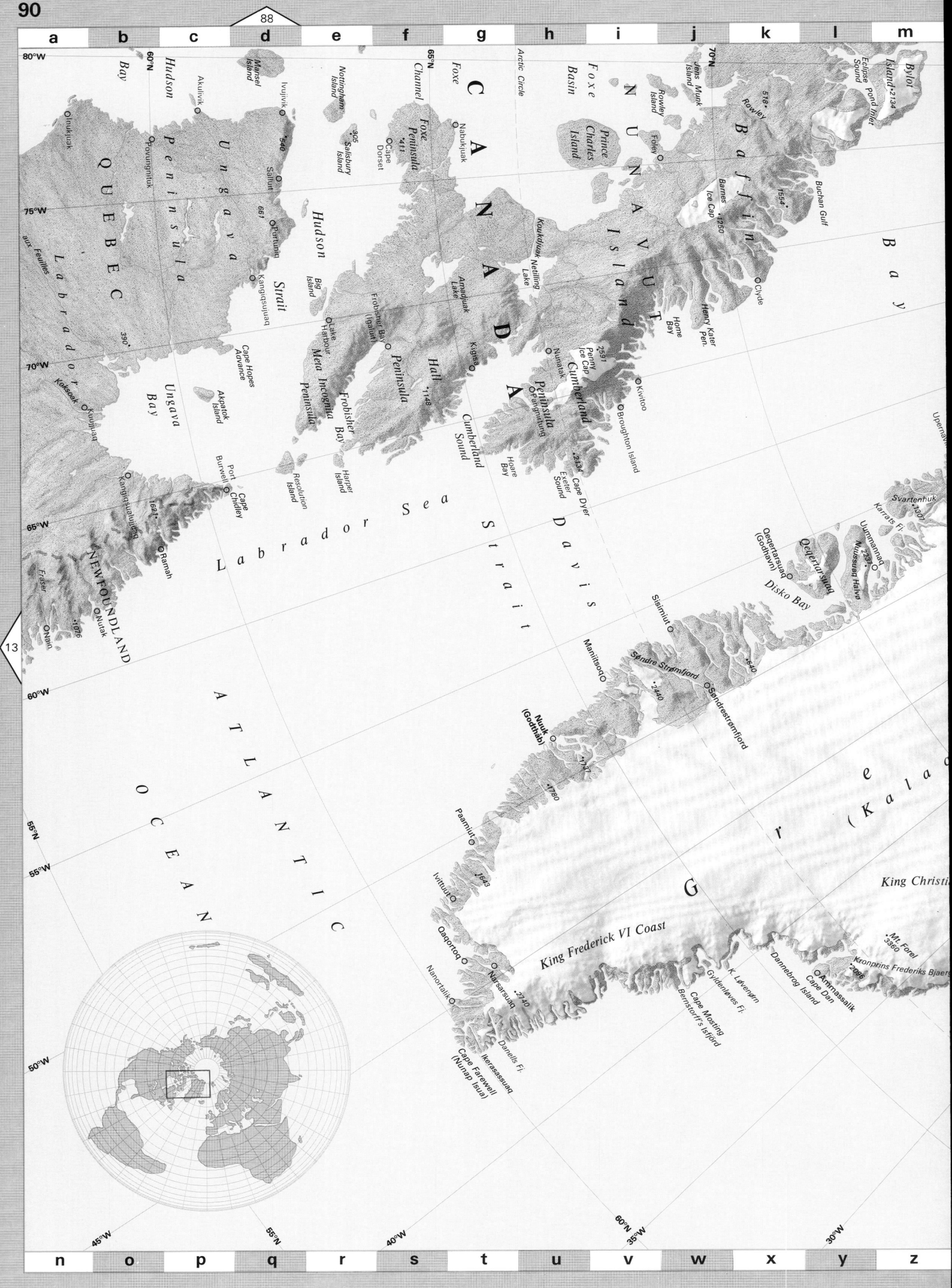

a b c d e f g h i j k l m

n o p q r s t u v w x y z

80°W

Oinukjuak

Hudson Bay

60°N

Akulivik

Povungnituk

QUEBEC

Mansel Island

Ungava Peninsula

Ivujivik

540

Salluit

75°W

661°

Purtunu

Kangiqsujuaq

39°

Labrador

70°W

Koksoak

Kuujjuaq

Nottingham Island

Salisbury Island

Foxe Channel

305

Cape Dorset

65°N

Foxe Peninsula

411°

Nabukjuak

CANADA

Foxe

Arctic Circle

Foxe Basin

NUNAVUT

Prince Charles Island

70°N

Rowley Island

Jens Munk Island

Foley

518°

Rowley

Ice Cap

Barnes Ice Cap 1250

1554°

Baffin

Bylot Island 2134

Eclipse Sound

Pond Inlet

Buchan Gulf

Bay

Koukdjuak

Netting Lake

Home Bay

Henry Kater Pen.

Clyde

Hudson Strait

Big Island

Lake Harbour

Frobisher Bay (Iqaluit)

Meta Incognita Peninsula

Amadjuak Lake

Hall Peninsula

1148°

Kingnait

Cumberland Sound

2591°

Penny Ice Cap

Nunatak

Pangnirtung

Cumberland Peninsula

2134°

Cape Dyer

Broughton Island

Kivitoo

Ungava Bay

Cape Hopes Advance

Akpatok Island

Frobisher Bay

Resolution Island

Harper Island

Hoare Bay

Exeter Sound

Davis

Upernav

Kangiqsualujjuaq

Port Burwell

Cape Chidley

1621°

Labrador Sea

Strait

Svartenhuk 1130°

Karrats Fj.

65°N

Fraser

NEWFOUNDLAND

Ramah

1076°

Nutak

Nain

Qeqertarsuaq (Godhavn)

Sisimiut

Disko Bay

Uummannaq 2735°

Nuussuaq Halvø

Qeqertarsuaq

640°

ATLANTIC

Søndre Strømfjord

Maniitsoq

2440°

Søndrestrømfjord

60°W

OCEAN

Nuuk (Godthåb)

1747°

1780°

G (Kala

King Christi

55°W

Paamiut

Ivittuut

1663°

55°N

King Frederick VI Coast

r

King Frederick VI Coast

Qaqortoq

Mt. Forel 3360°

Kronprins Frederiks Bjaer

50°W

Narsarsuaq

2740°

Nanortalik

Danells Fj.

Ikerasassuaq

Cape Farewell (Nunap Isua)

K. Løvenørn

Gyldenløves Fj.

Cape Mosting

Bernstorff's Isfjord

Dannebrog Island

Cape Dan

Ammassalik

2000°

45°W

55°N

40°W

35°W

60°N

30°W

13

This map shows 1/60 of the earth's surface

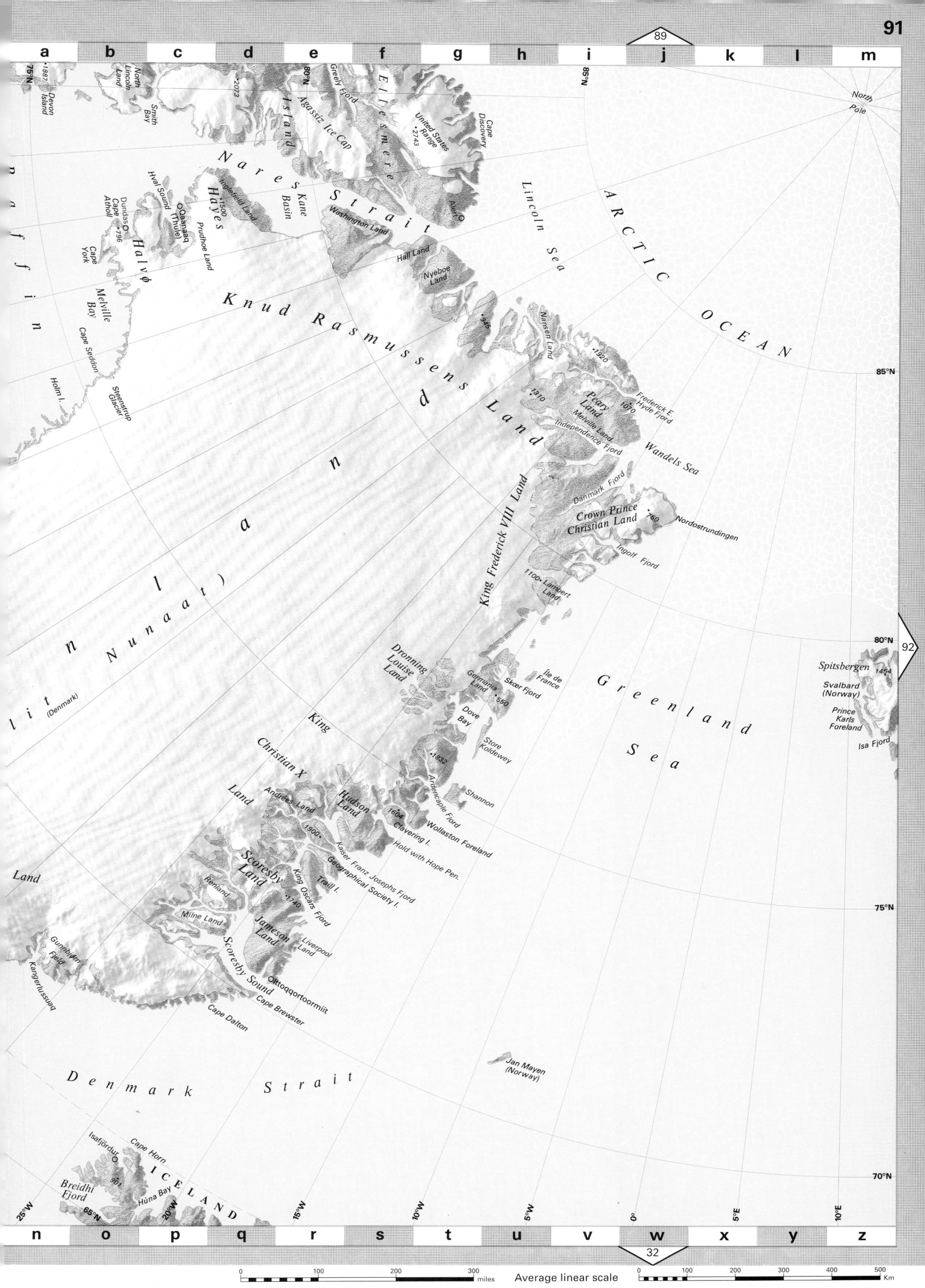

a b c d e f g h i j k l m

North Pole

A R C T I C   O C E A N

85°N

85°N

80°N

Shmidta

Komsomolets

Severnaya
Zemlya

Pioner

Ushakova

Vize

West Siberian Sea

Cape berga

Cape
Peschanyy

Shokal'skoy

Oktyabr'skoy
Revolyutsii

Cape
Mednyy

Bolshevik

Vilkitskogo
Strait

Vilkitskiy
Strait

Arch.

Russkiy
Nordenshel'da
Arch. Cape
Oskara

Taimyr

Byrranga Mts.

Taimyr Peninsula

Isačenko

Troynoy

Arktičeskogo
Instituta

Mikhaylova

Pya

Di

Yeva-Liv

La Ronc'yer

Graham
Bell
Island

Rudolf I.

Karla-Aleksandra
Jackson I.
Salisbury I.
Luidzhi

Wilczek
Land

Hall

Sal'm

Franz   Josef   Land

Alexandra
Land

George
Land

Hooker I.
McClintock I.

White
Island

North East Land

Hinlopenstr.

Spitsbergen

1454

Isa Fjord

Barentsburg

Longyearbyen

Barents Island

Edge Island

933

Svalbard
(Norway)

B A R E N T S

S E A

80°N

K A R A   S E A

Mys Zelaniya

Russkaya Gavan

Smidovich

Sedova

Stolbovoy

Litke

Krasino

Vilkicky

Sokalsky

Belyy

Drovyan

Proliv
Karskiye Vorota

Vaigat

162

Pechora Sea

75°N

Bear Island
(Norway)

Kolguyev
156

Maločemel'skaya Tundra

Narya
Mar

Cherne

Dresyan

Ti

75°N

North Cape

Sörőy

Hammerfest

Senja

Tromsö

NORWEGIAN SEA

Skibotn

Tana

Lakselv

Alta

1135

Tana

Kirkenes

Ivalo

636

FINLAND

Lake
Inari

623

Lotta

Petsenga

Murmansk

Padunskoye
More

Monçegorsk

Kirovsk

397

Kola

Arctic Circle

Cape
Kanin Nos

Kanin

Češa
Bay

Volonga

Mezer'
Gulf

Stafanovo

Mezen

Azopol'ye

Mezen

Velikovisochnoye

242

Velikovisochnoye

10°E

15°E

20°E

25°E

30°E

35°E

40°E

45°E

65°N

70°N

n o p q r s t u v w x y z

33

This map shows 1/60 of the earth's surface

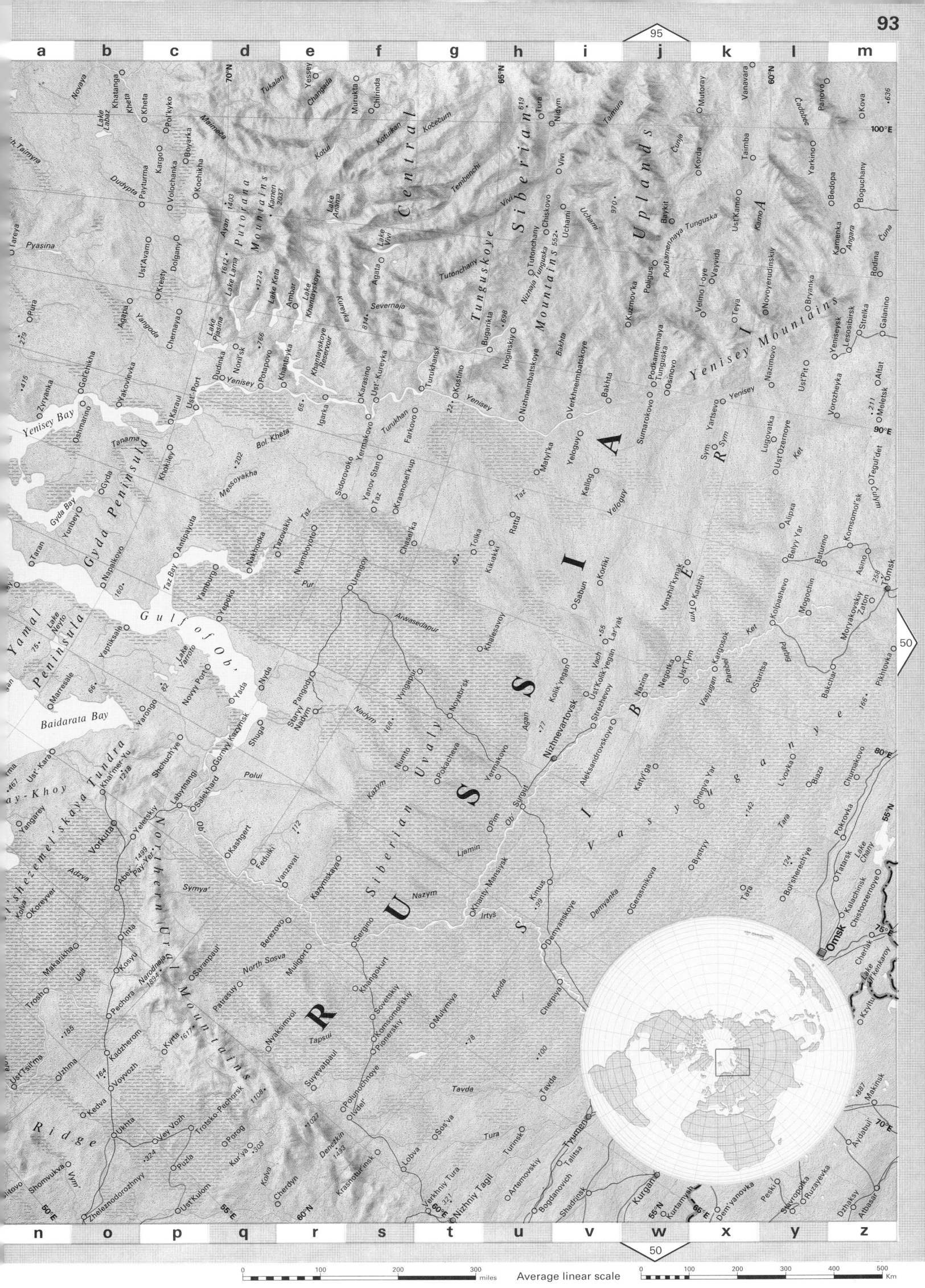

70°N

Chukchi

Sea

Mys Shmidta

180°

Long

i

Strait

·1097

Wrangel Island

Ilirney

Retkucha

Krasnoarmeyskiy

Pevek

Northern Anyuskiy Mountains

Southern Anyuskiy Mountains

·1641

Bol. Anyuy

Kolymskiy Mountains

Korkodon

Korkodon

Su

Oro

Zyr

Bulun

Onon

Zatishye

Yugo-Tala C

Oscrovnoy

Mal. Anyuy

Cherskiy

Mal. Ambarchik

Mal. Baranikha

Gorelova

Volochsk

Konzabov

Mys

Lake Nerpich'ye

Chukochye

Zhirkova

Chernyy

Mys

Oysurdakh

Konzabov

Berezovka

Srednekolymsk

Khongseyo

Balagannakh

Khara-Tala

Kyrbana

Malaya

Sededema

Pastakh

Shestakova

Urdakh

Kolymskiy

Plain

Iliimniir

Kondakovo
·974

Ulovo

Bryangnyt

Tenair

Oznogino

Lake Ozhigino

Uv

East Siberian

Sea

75°N

Tabor

Kolesovo

Indigirka

Chokurdakh

Alekseyevo

Ukta

Tenkeli

Kiseleva

Chikhacheva

Khroma

Boru

Kokuora

Balagannakh

Khastan

Kuoga

Uyadey

Star. Dom

Ka

New Siberian Islands

Bennetta

Novaya Sibir

Bol'shoye

Laptev Str.

Bol. Lyakhovskiy

Chay-Povarnaya

Kigilyakh

Cape Buzkhaya

Orto

Trofimove

Antipinskiy C

Sagas-Tyrkan

Dunay

Zimovye

Fedorovskiy

Mal. Lyakhnovskiy

Stolbovoy

·320

Ambardakh

Kotel'nyy

Kotel'nyy

Bel'kovskiy

80°N

89

85°N

A R C T I C

O C E A N

North Pole

Komsomolets

Konsomolets

96°N

92

Mal. Taimyr

Oktyabr'skoy Revolyutsii

Cape Berga

Shokal'skogo Str.

·800

Cape Peschanny

Bolshevik

Vilkicki Str.

·313

Laptev Sea

Begichev

Verzdekhodnaya

Byrranga Mountains

Lake Taimyr 572

Cape Oskara

Niž Taimyra

75°N

This map shows 1/60 of the earth's surface

Average linear scale

Principal sources for the thematic maps: Amnesty International Report 2001. * www.ancientscripts.com 2001. * Buch und Buchhandel in Zahlen. Frankfurt 1987. * British Geological Survey, Natural Environment Research Council: World Mineral Statistics 1979-1983. 1995-1999. * Brown, Louise: Sex Slaves: The Trafficking of Women in Asia. London 2000. * CIA World Factbook 2000. * Dathe, Heinrich und Paul Schöps (eds.): Pelztieratlas. Jena 1986. * Deutsche Gesellschaft für Luft und Raumfahrt: Astronautische Start-Verzeichnisse und Raumflugkörper-Statistiken 1957-1987. * Diercke Länderlexikon. Braunschweig 1983. * Durrell, Lee: State of the Ark. London 1986. * www.eia.doe.gov 2001. * Encyclopedia Britannica. 15th ed. 32 vls. 1985. * Encyclopedia Britannica Book of the Year 1986. 1987. 1988. * www.ethnologue.com 2001. * Fischer Weltalmanach 1986. 1987. 1988. 2001. 2002. * Food and Agricultural Organization of the United Nations (FAO) Rome: FAO Production Yearbook 1985. 1986. FAO Food Balance Sheets 1975-1977. 1979-1981. FAO Yearbook of Fishery Statistics 1983. FAO Trade Yearbook 1986. www.fao.org 2001. * Haack. Atlas zur Zeitgeschichte. Gotha 1985. * Herre. Wolf und Manfred Röhrs: Haustiere - zoologisch gesehen. Stuttgart 1973. * www.infoplease.com 2001. * Institut für Seeverkehrwirtschaft und Logistik, Bremen: Shipping Statistics Yearbook 2000. * The International Institute of Strategic Studies (ILSS): The Military Balance 1986-1987. 1995/1996. 2000. * International Labour Organization (ILO) Geneva: Yearbook of Labour Statistics 1978. 1979. 1980. 1981. 1982. 1983. 1984. 1985. 1986. 1987. Income Distribution and Economic Development. An Analytical Survey. Geneva 1984. Sixth African Regional Conference. Application of the Declaration of Principles and Programme of Action of the World Employment Conference. Geneva 1983. STAT Working papers, Bureau of Statistics 1950-2010. Geneva 1997. www.ilo.org 2001. * International Road Transport Union: World Transport Data. Geneva 1985. * International Telecommunication Union: Table of International Telex Relations and Traffic. Geneva 1987. * Inter-Parliamentary Union (IPU): Women in Parliament 1988. Participation of Women in Political Life and in Decision-Making Process. Geneva 1988. Distribution of Seats Between Men and Women in National Assemblies. Geneva 1987. www.ipu.org 2001. * Jain, Shail: Size Distribution of Income. Compilation of Data. World Bank Staff Working Paper No.190. Nov. 1974. Washington 1975. * Kidron, Michael and Ronald Segal: The State of the World Atlas. London 1981. The New State of the World Atlas (revised ed.). London 1987. * Kurian, George Thomas: The New Book of World Rankings. New York 1984. * Länder der Erde. Berlin 1985. * McDowell, Jonathan: Harvard-Smithsonian Center for Astrophysics. * Meyers Enzyklopädie der Erde (8 vls.). Mannheim 1982. * Moroney, John R.: Income Inequality. Trends and International Comparisons. Toronto 1979. * Myers, Norman (ed.): GAIA - Der Öko-Atlas unserer Erde. Frankfurt 1985. * www.nasa.gov 2001. * Nohlen, Dieter and Franz Nuscheler (eds.): Handbuch der Dritten Welt. 8 vls. Hamburg 1981-1983. * Ökumene Lexikon. Edited by Hanfried Krüger, Werner Löser et al. Frankfurt 1983. * Peters, Arno: Synchronoptische Weltgeschichte. 2 vls. Munchen 1980. * Saeger, Joni and Ann Olson: Der Frauenatlas. Frankfurt 1986. * Serryn, Pierre: Le Monde d'aujourd'hui. Atlas économique. social, politique, stratégique. Paris 1981. * South: South Diary 1987. 1988. * Statistisches Bundesamt, Wiesbaden: Statistisches Jahrbuch 1999. Statistik des Auslandes. Vierteljahreshefte zur Auslandsstatistik. 1985-1987. Statistik des Auslandes. Länderberichte. * Stockholm International Peace Research Institute (SIPRI): SIPRI Yearbook 1987. World Armaments and Disarmament. New York 1987. * Taylor, Charles Lewis and David A. Jodice: World Handbook of Political and Social Indicators. New Haven. London 1983. * UNESCO: Statistical Yearbook 1974. 1975. 1976. 1977. 1978. 1979. 1980. 1981. 1982. 1983. 1984. 1985. 1986. 1987. * UNICEF: The State of the World's Children 1987. * The United Nations (UN): UN Statistical Yearbook 1983/84. 1999. UN Demographic Yearbook 1972. 1979. 1984. 1985. 1986. National Accounts Statistics. Compendium of Income Distribution Statistics. New York 1985. UN Energy Statistics Yearbook 1984. UN Yearbook of International Trade Statistics 1982. 1983. 1984. 1986. 1998. Selected Indicators of the Situation of Women 1985. UN Industrial Statistics Yearbook 1983. 1984. World Conference of the United Nations Decade for Women: Equality, Development and Peace. Copenhagen 1980. World Culture Report 2000. World Education Report 2000. World Health Report 2000. The World's Women 2000. Activities for the Advancement of Women: Equality, Development and Peace. Report of Jean Fernand-Laurent. 1983. UNCTAD Handbook of Statistics 2000. UNIDO International Yearbook of Industrial Statistics 1995. 1996. 1997. 1998. 1999. 2000. 2001. www.un.org 2001. * University of Stellenbosch, Department of Development Administration and the Institute for Cartographic Analysis: The Third World in Maps. 1985. * Westermann Lexikon der Geographic. Edited by Wolf Tietze. Braunschweig 1968. * World Almanac & Book of Facts 1985. 1986. 1987. * The World Bank: World Development Report 1980. 1981. 1982. 1983. 1984. 1985. 1986. 1987. 1999/2000. 2000/2001. World Labour Report 1984. World Tables 1984. World Atlas of the Child 1979. Social Indicators of Development 1987. The World Bank Atlas 1987. World Economic and Social Indicators. Document of the World Bank. 1980. World Development Indicators 2001. www.worldbank.org 2001 * World Energy Resources 1985-2020, Renewable Energy Resources. The Full Reports to the Conservation Commission of the World Energy Conference. Published for the WEC by IPC Science and Technology Press 1978. * The World in Figures. Editorial information compiled by the Economist. London 1987. * World Health Organization (WHO), Geneva: World Health Statistics. Annual. * Völker der Erde. Bern 1982. * Voous, K.H.: Atlas of European Birds. New York 1960.

NATURE, MAN AND SOCIETY
IN 246 THEMATIC MAPS

Each map presents a single subject. As a result, it is possible to dispense with symbols and allow the information to be expressed entirely in terms of color: dark colors for high values, light for low ones. This makes it easy to see and assimilate the content of the maps - an important feature, since up to 16 maps can be dedicated to a single subject.

The individual subject should not be considered in isolation. The mutual interaction between all spheres of life, the intricacies of nature and culture, of economics, nations and society, mean that each of the subjects can be understood only in connection with the other 45 double-page spreads.

This richness and multiplicity of facts and insights is however the minimum which someone of our time must have in mind if he wishes to form his own opinion on the current situation in the world and in his own country. Without this effort, his own view of the world can never be clear and reliable.

Over 40,000 individual pieces of factual information have been compiled for these 246 thematic world maps. They were obtained almost exclusively from published materials of the United Nations and other international organisations. There reliability is presumed, and an average of annual data available from 1980 onwards has been calculated. Where official figures were not available, estimates were made in consultation with the leading experts in the various fields concerned. No indication is given of these estimates, since their reliability is no less than that of the official figures.

The names of countries appear also on the small world maps. These can be read with the aid of a magnifying glass or by reference to the large whole-page maps such as that of "States" on pages 112-113.

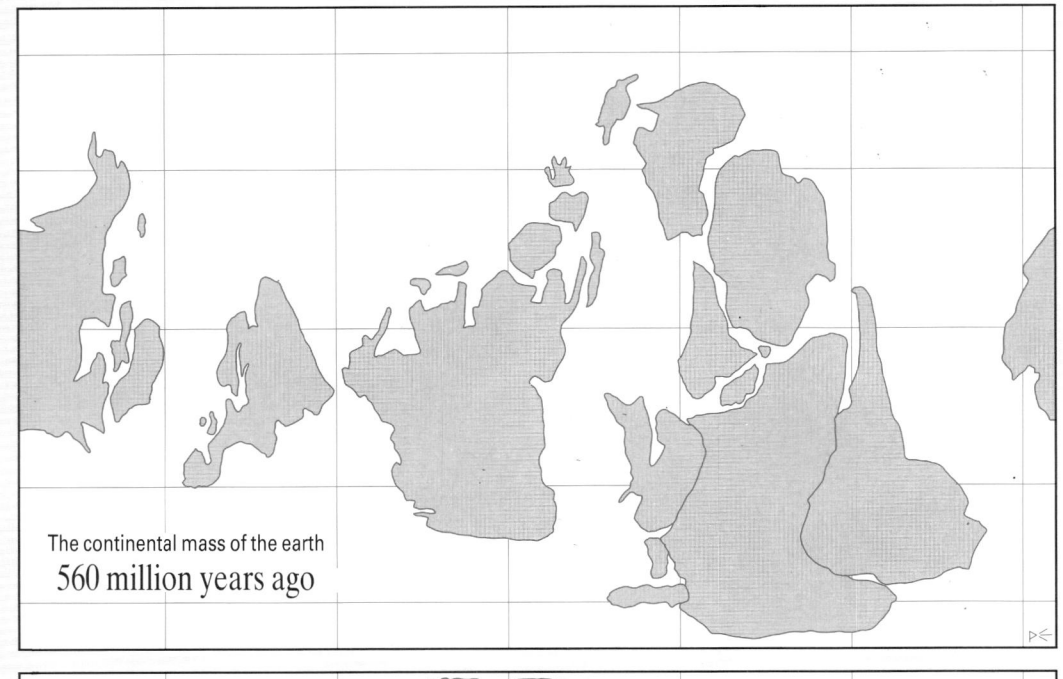

The continental mass of the earth
560 million years ago

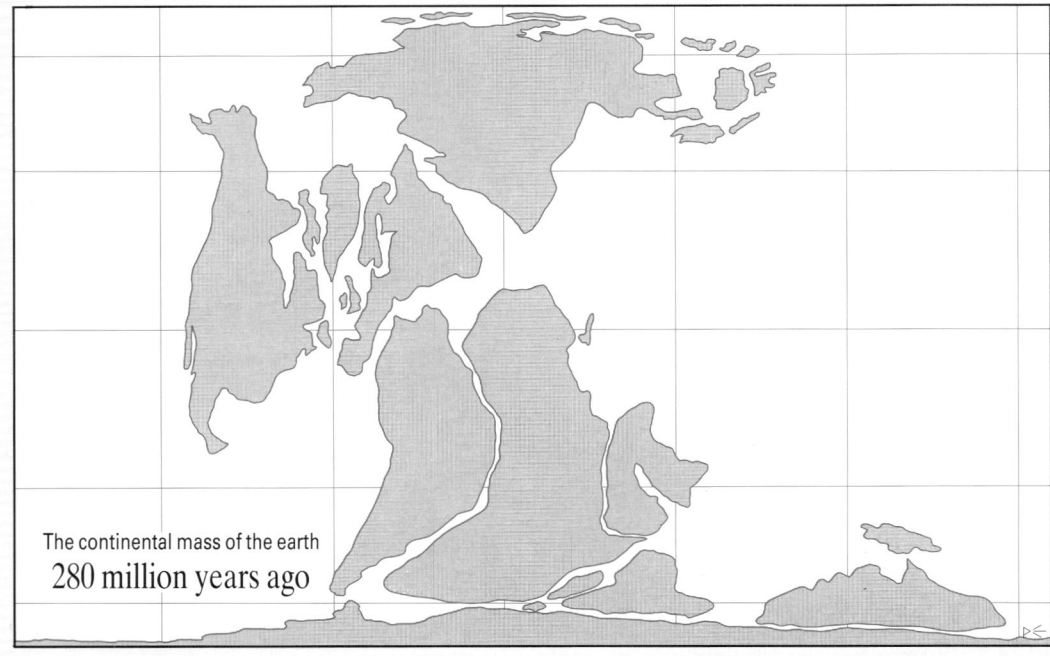

The continental mass of the earth
280 million years ago

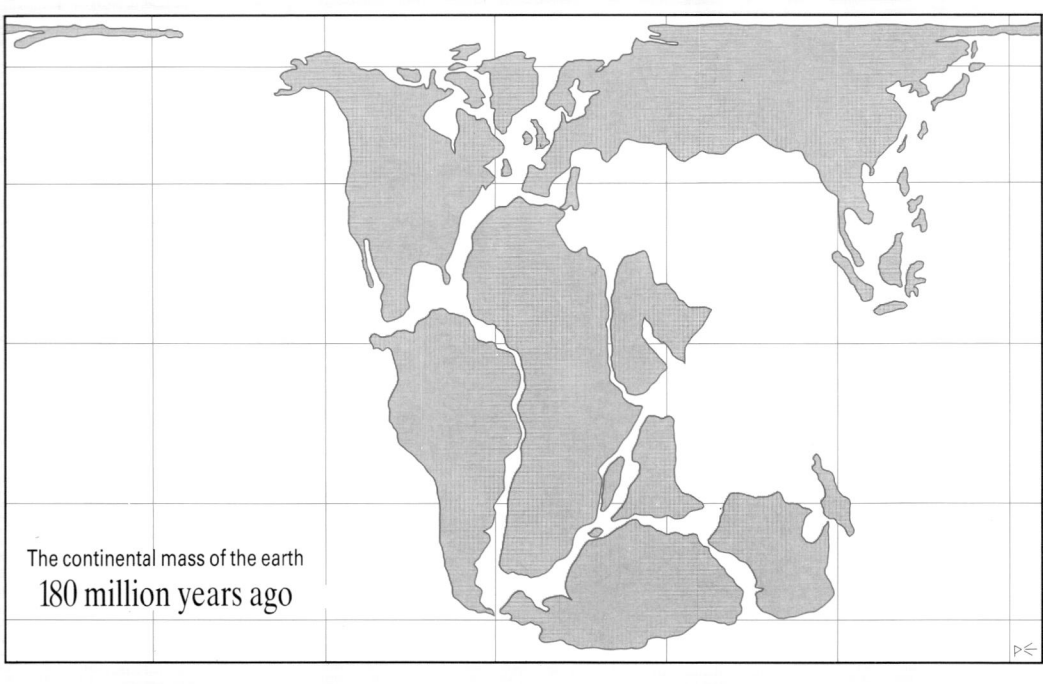

The continental mass of the earth
180 million years ago

The continental mass of the earth

TODAY

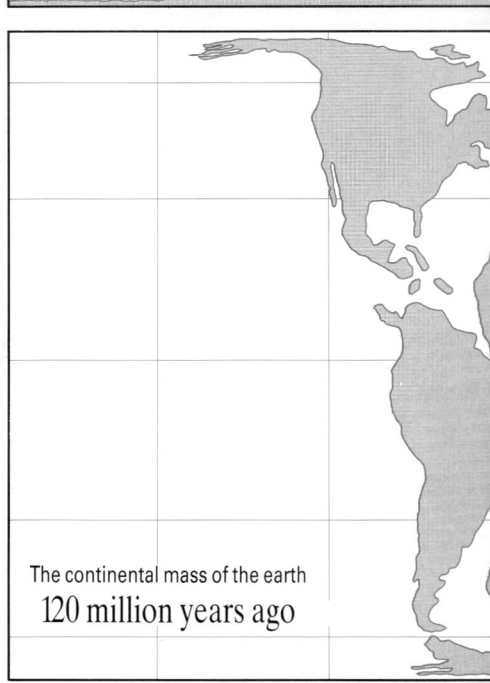

The continental mass of the earth
120 million years ago

THE CON

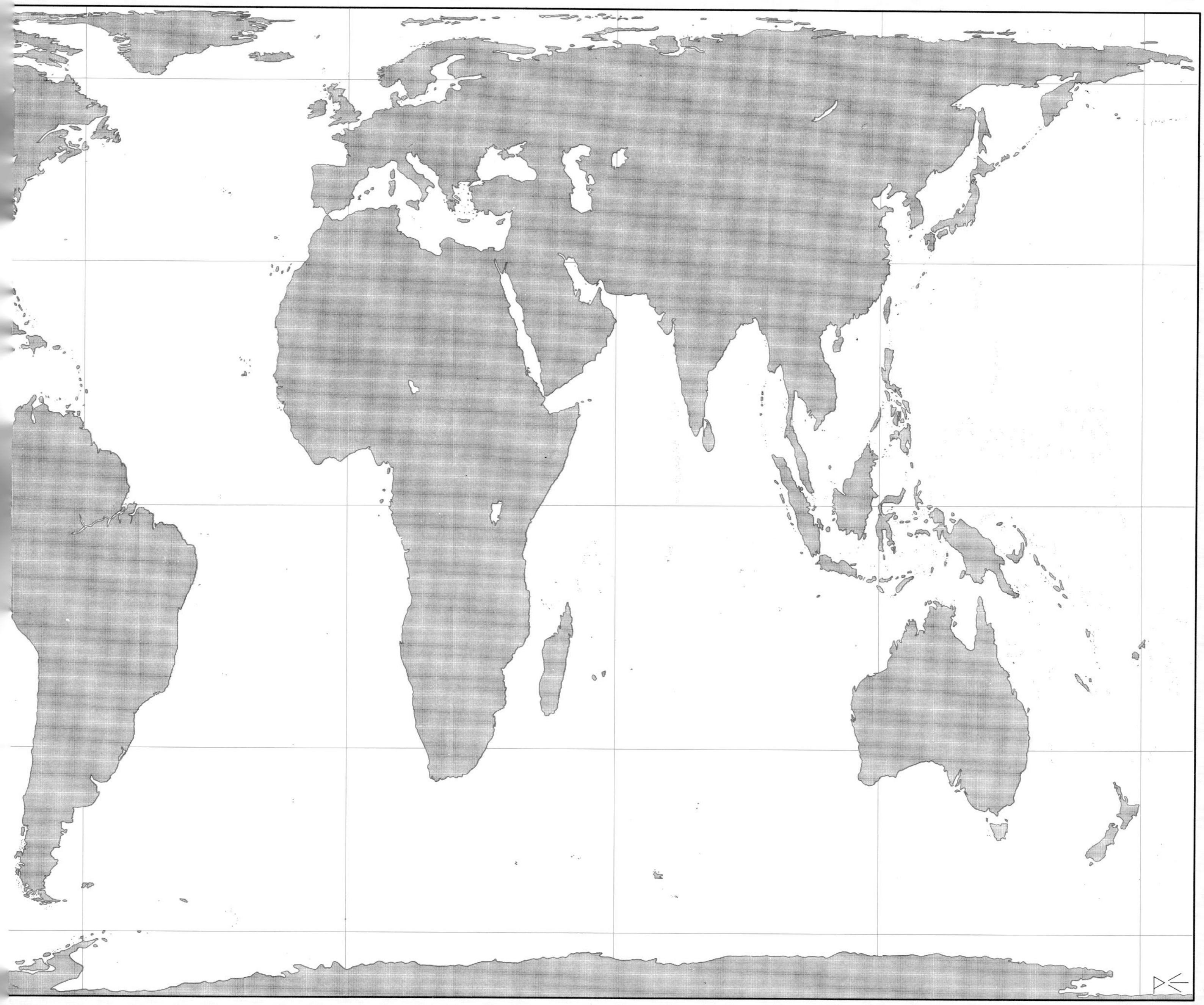

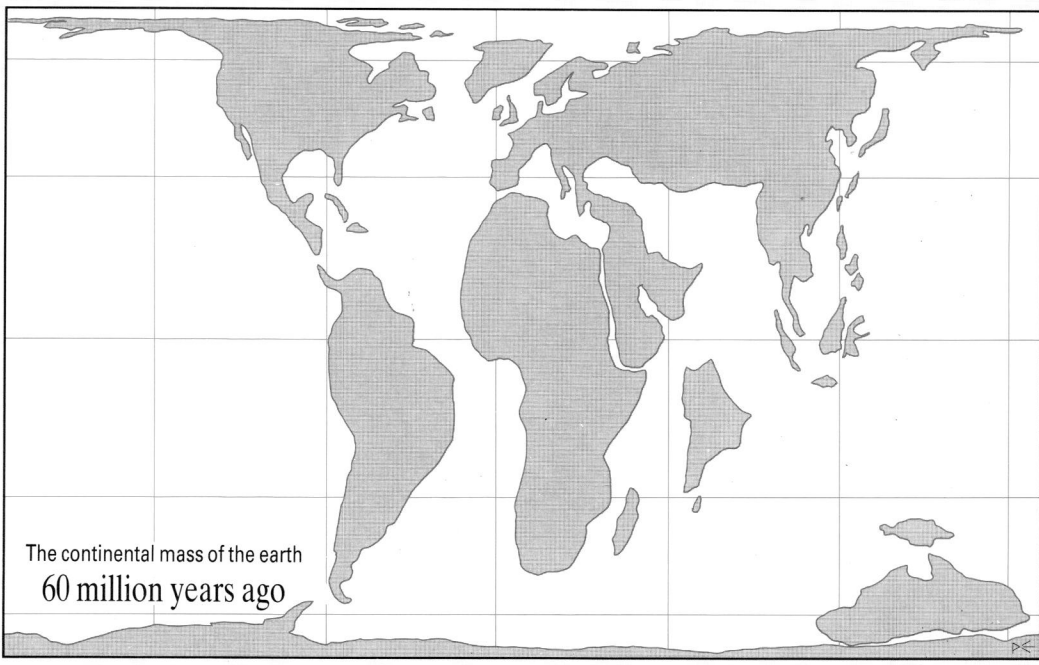

The continental mass of the earth
60 million years ago

TINENTS

MOUN

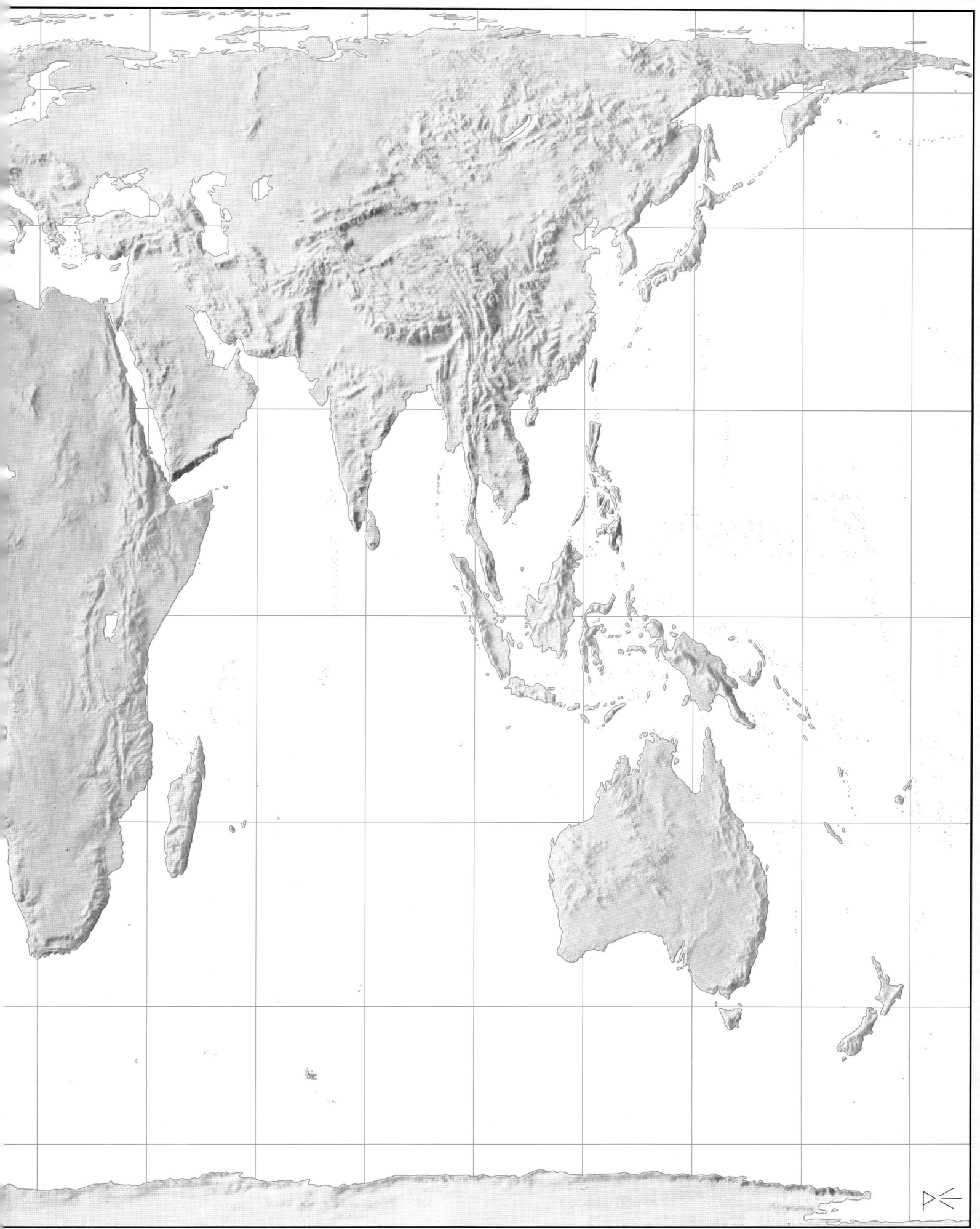

TAINS

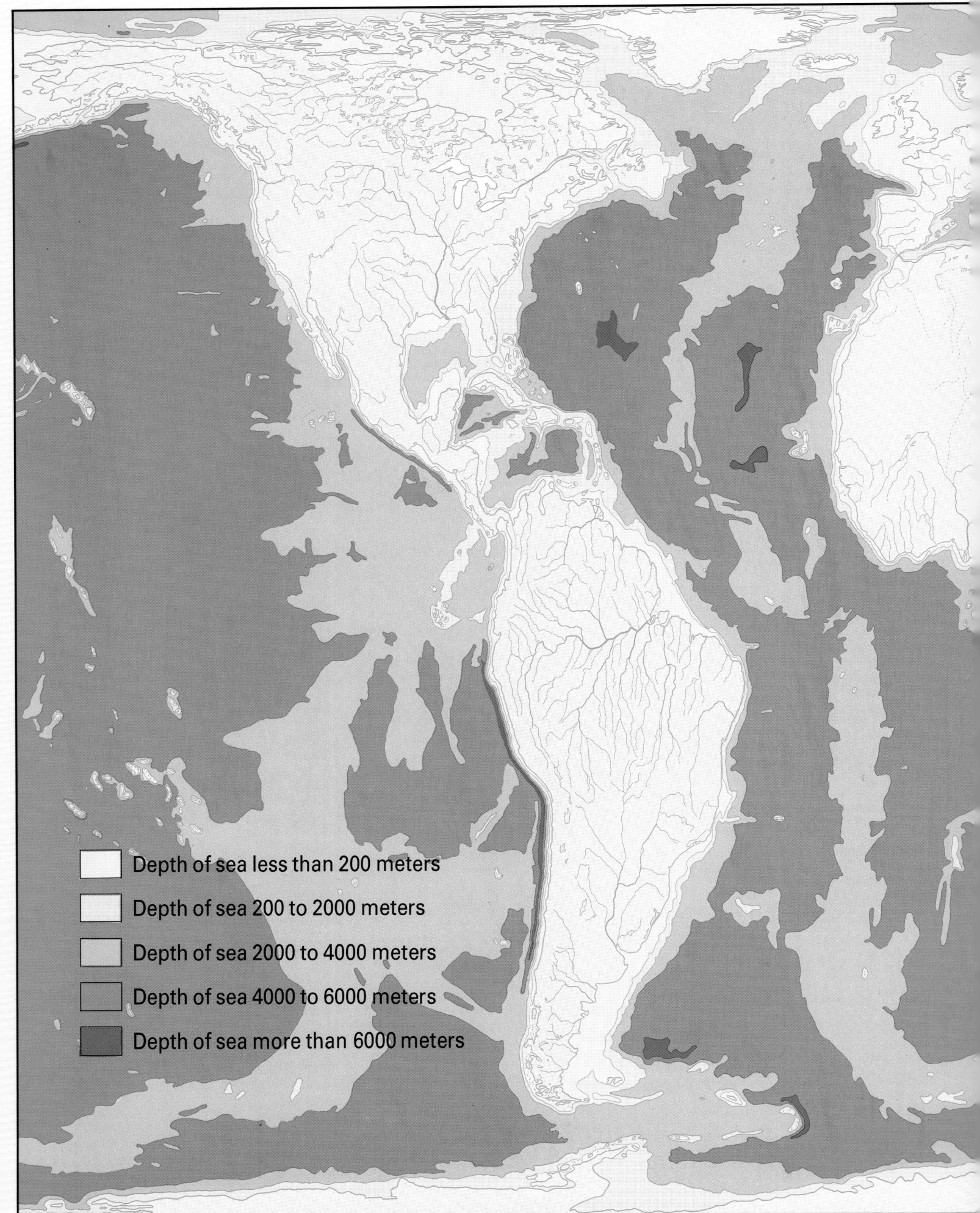

Depth of sea less than 200 meters

Depth of sea 200 to 2000 meters

Depth of sea 2000 to 4000 meters

Depth of sea 4000 to 6000 meters

Depth of sea more than 6000 meters

RIVERS A

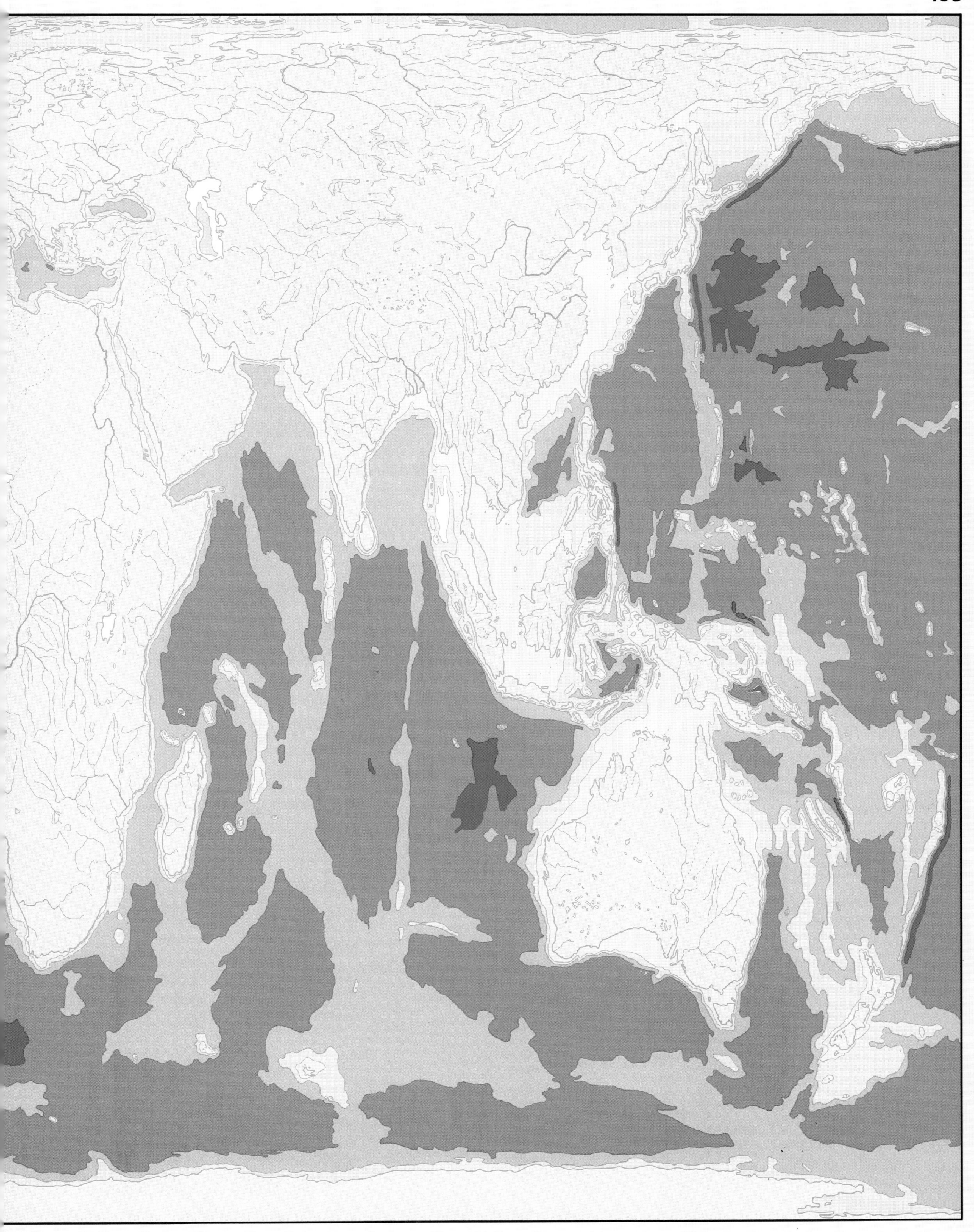

ND SEAS

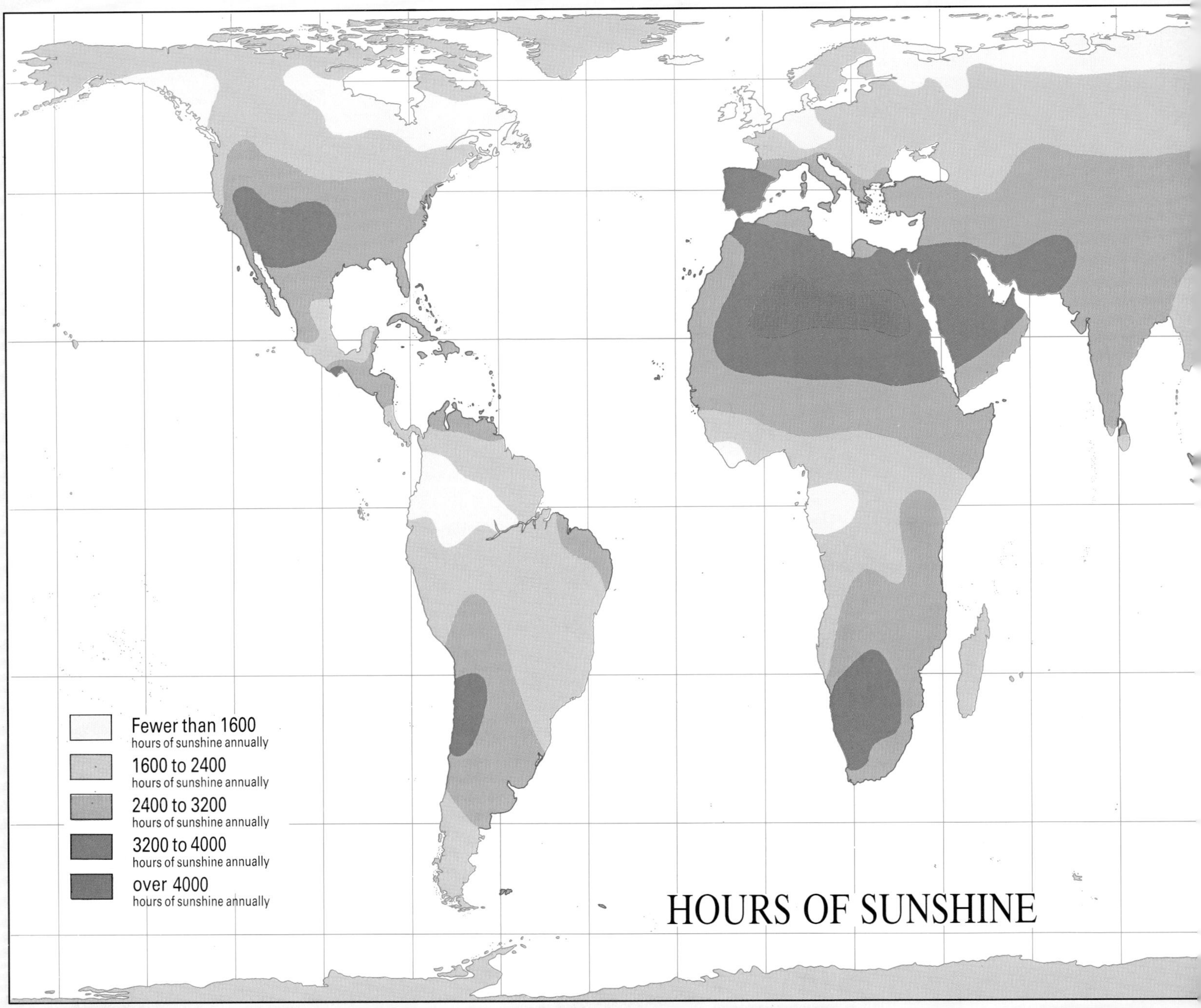

Fewer than 1600
hours of sunshine annually

1600 to 2400
hours of sunshine annually

2400 to 3200
hours of sunshine annually

3200 to 4000
hours of sunshine annually

over 4000
hours of sunshine annually

HOURS OF SUNSHINE

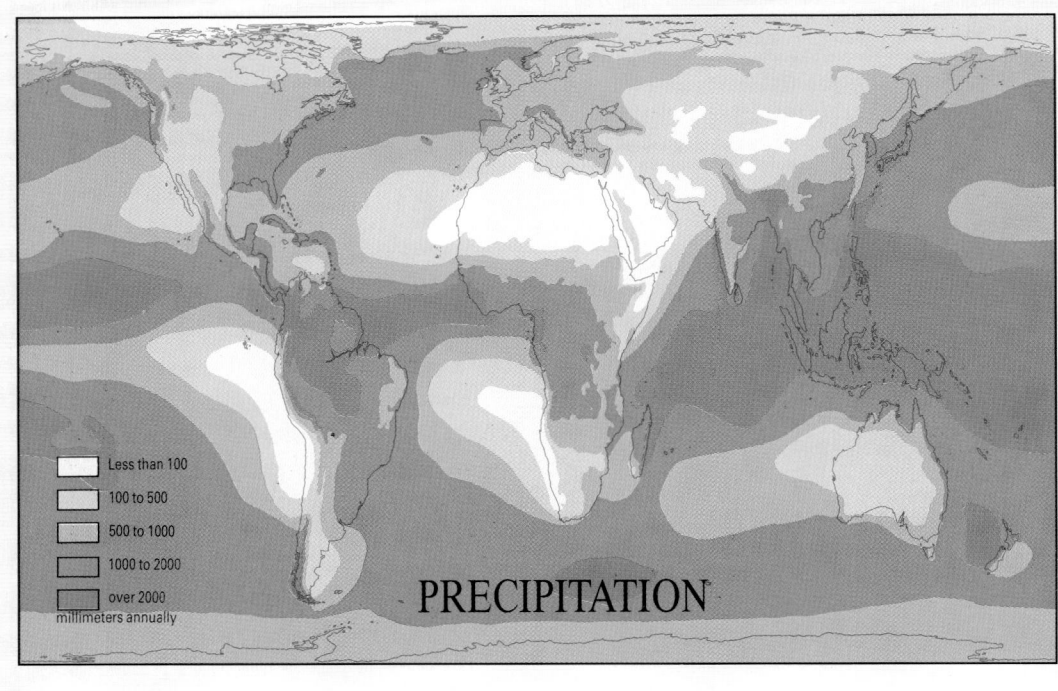

Less than 100

100 to 500

500 to 1000

1000 to 2000

over 2000
millimeters annually

PRECIPITATION

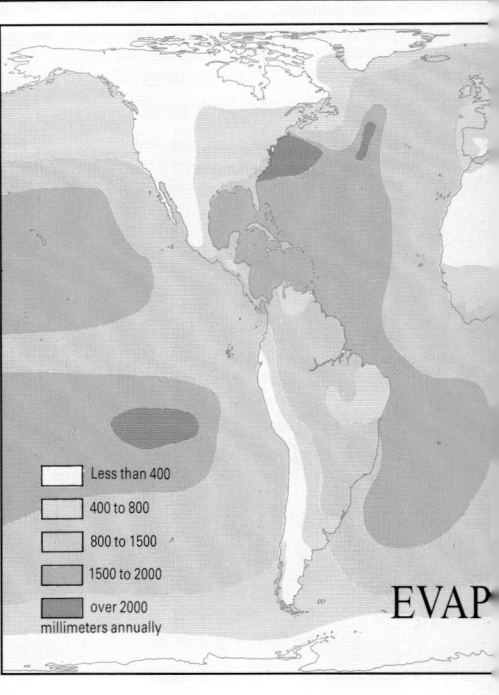

Less than 400

400 to 800

800 to 1500

1500 to 2000

over 2000
millimeters annually

EVAP

SUN AND

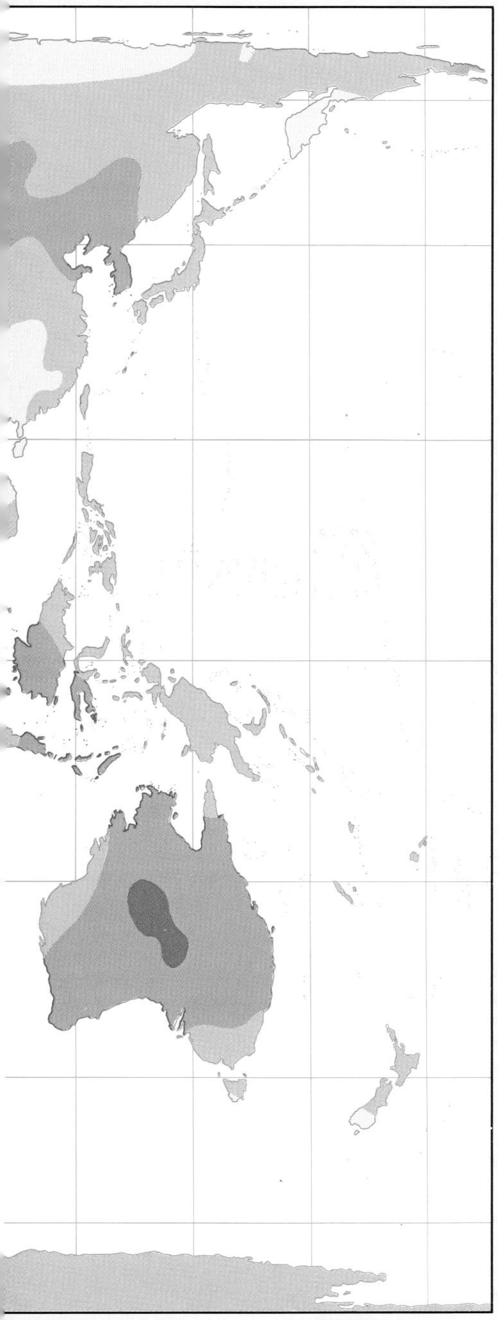

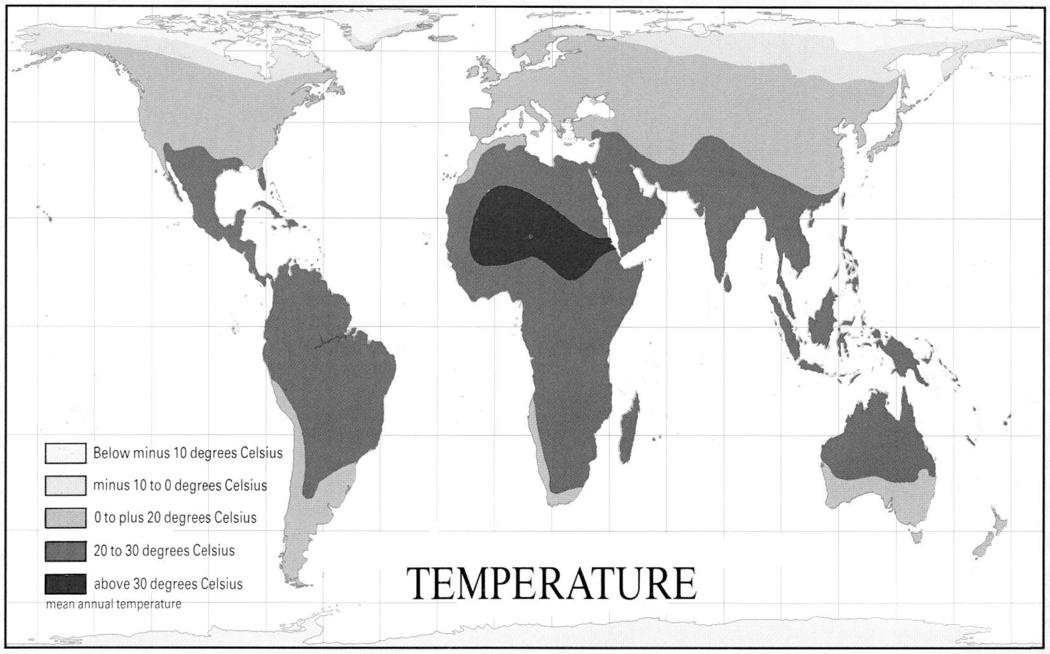

TEMPERATURE

	Below minus 10 degrees Celsius
	minus 10 to 0 degrees Celsius
	0 to plus 20 degrees Celsius
	20 to 30 degrees Celsius
	above 30 degrees Celsius

mean annual temperature

TEMPERATURE VARIATION

	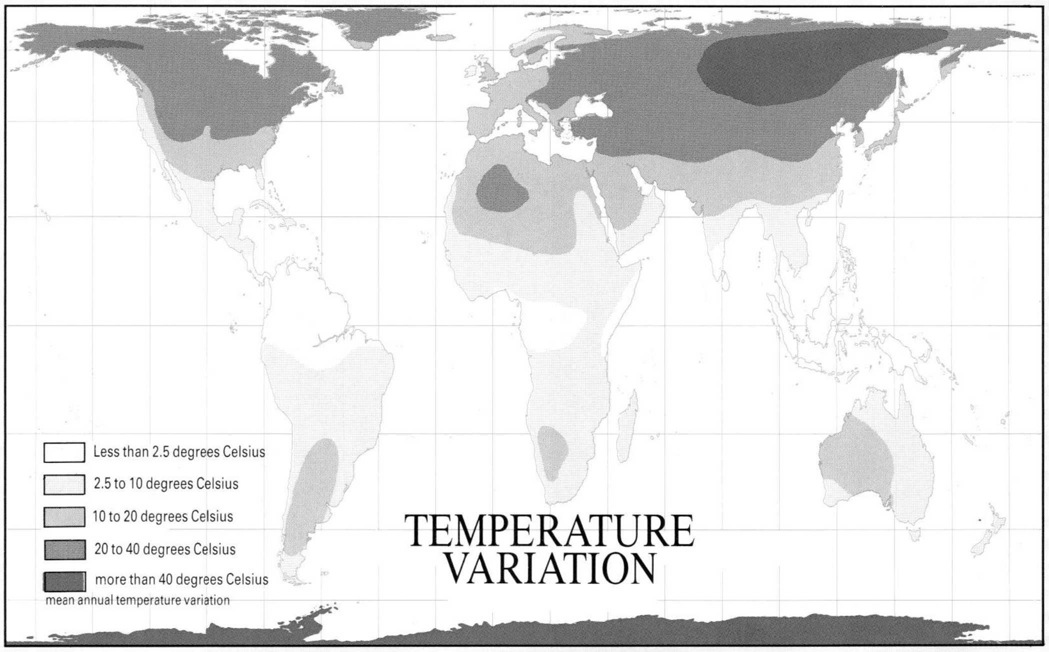 Less than 2.5 degrees Celsius
	2.5 to 10 degrees Celsius
	10 to 20 degrees Celsius
	20 to 40 degrees Celsius
	more than 40 degrees Celsius

mean annual temperature variation

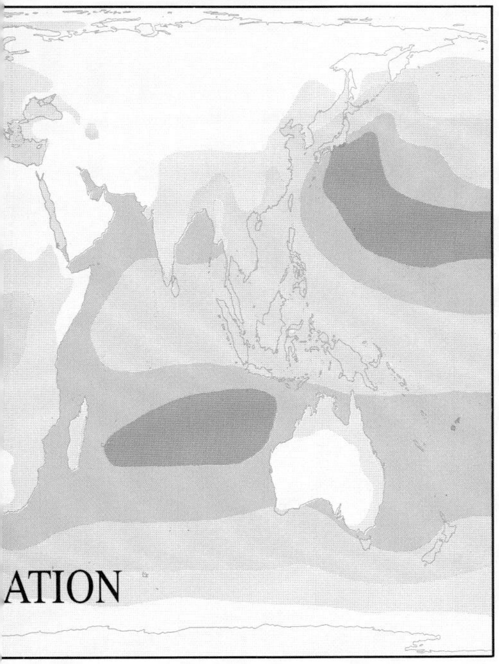

INCIDENCE OF RAYS

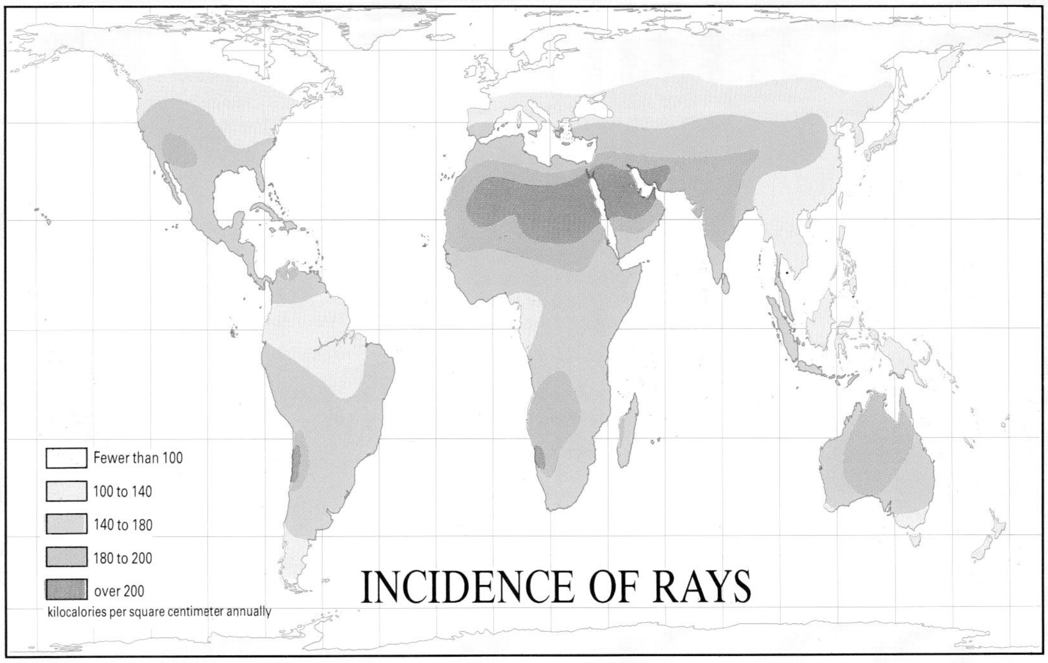

	Fewer than 100
	100 to 140
	140 to 180
	180 to 200
	over 200

kilocalories per square centimeter annually

ATION

CLIMATE

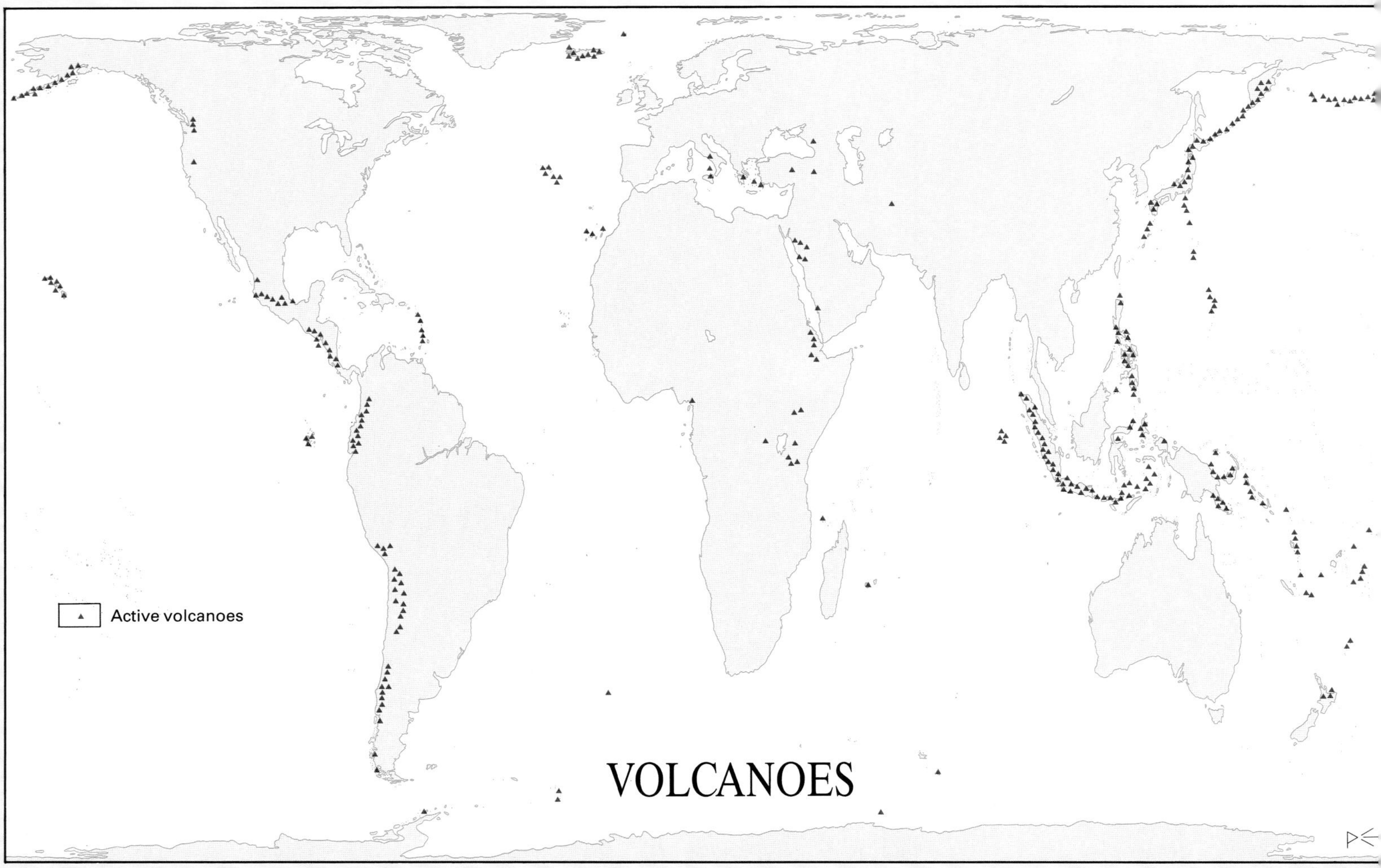

VOLCANOES

Active volcanoes

MARITIME EARTHQUAKES

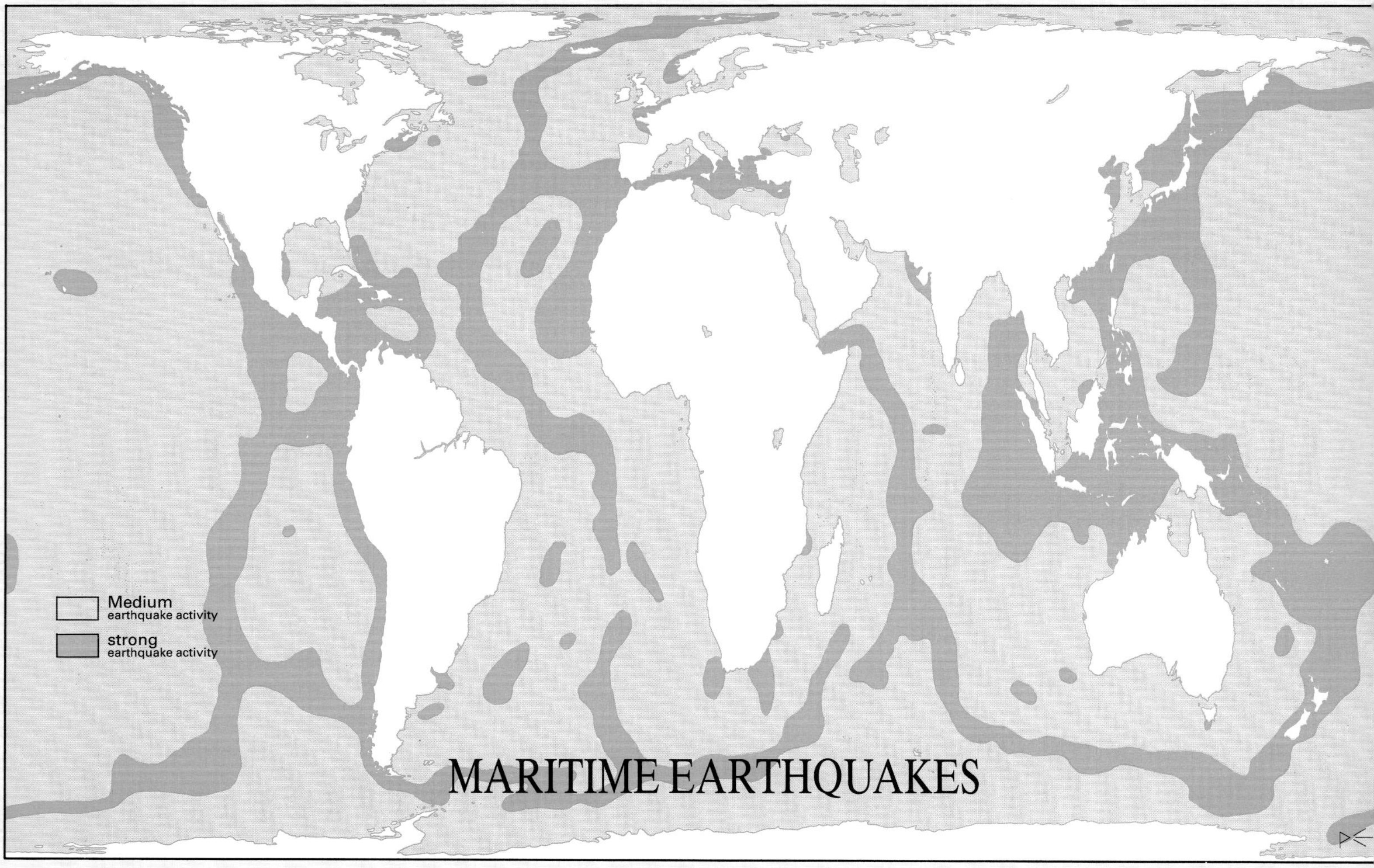

Medium
earthquake activity

strong
earthquake activity

NATURAL

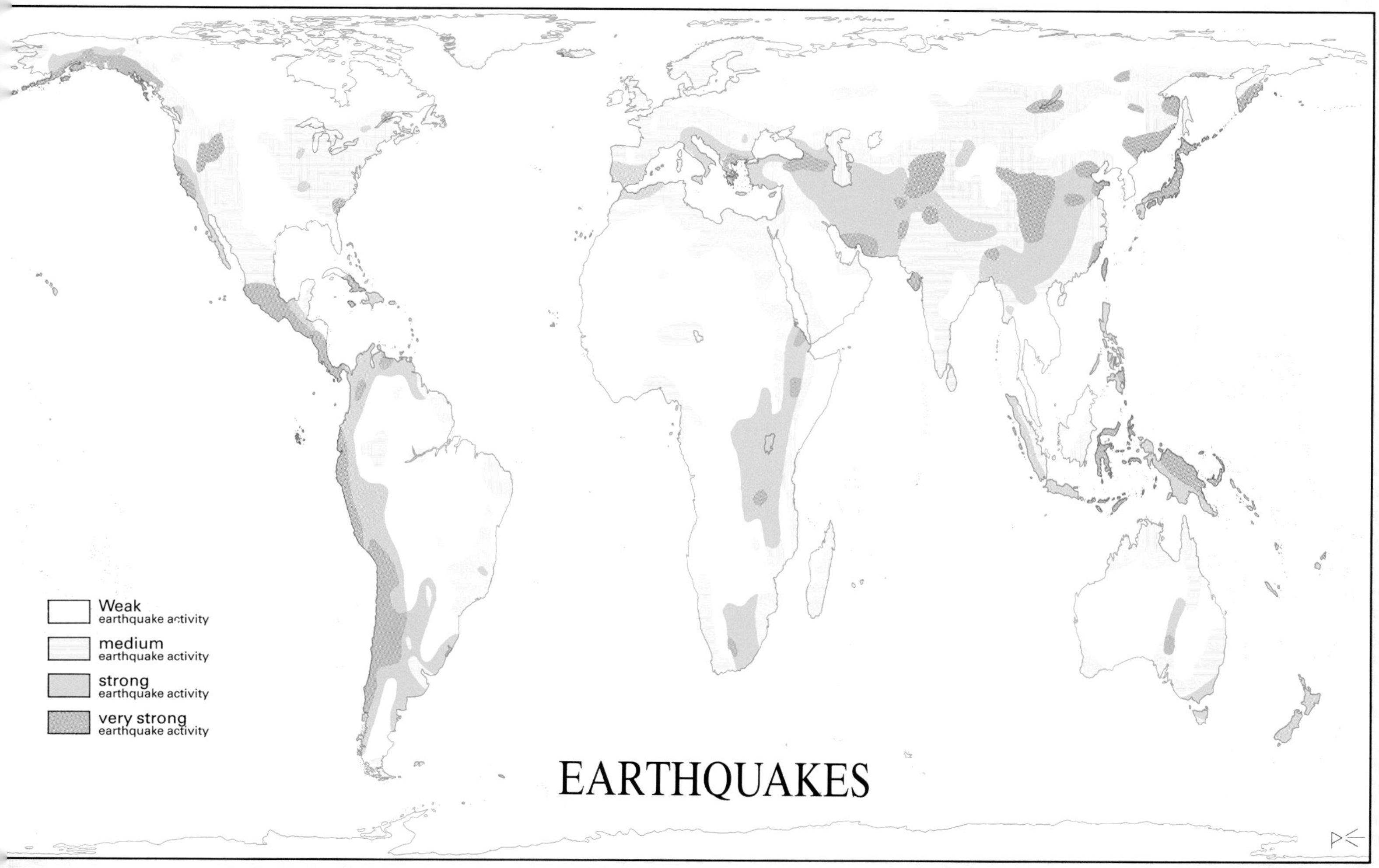

Earthquakes legend

- **Weak** earthquake activity
- **medium** earthquake activity
- **strong** earthquake activity
- **very strong** earthquake activity

EARTHQUAKES

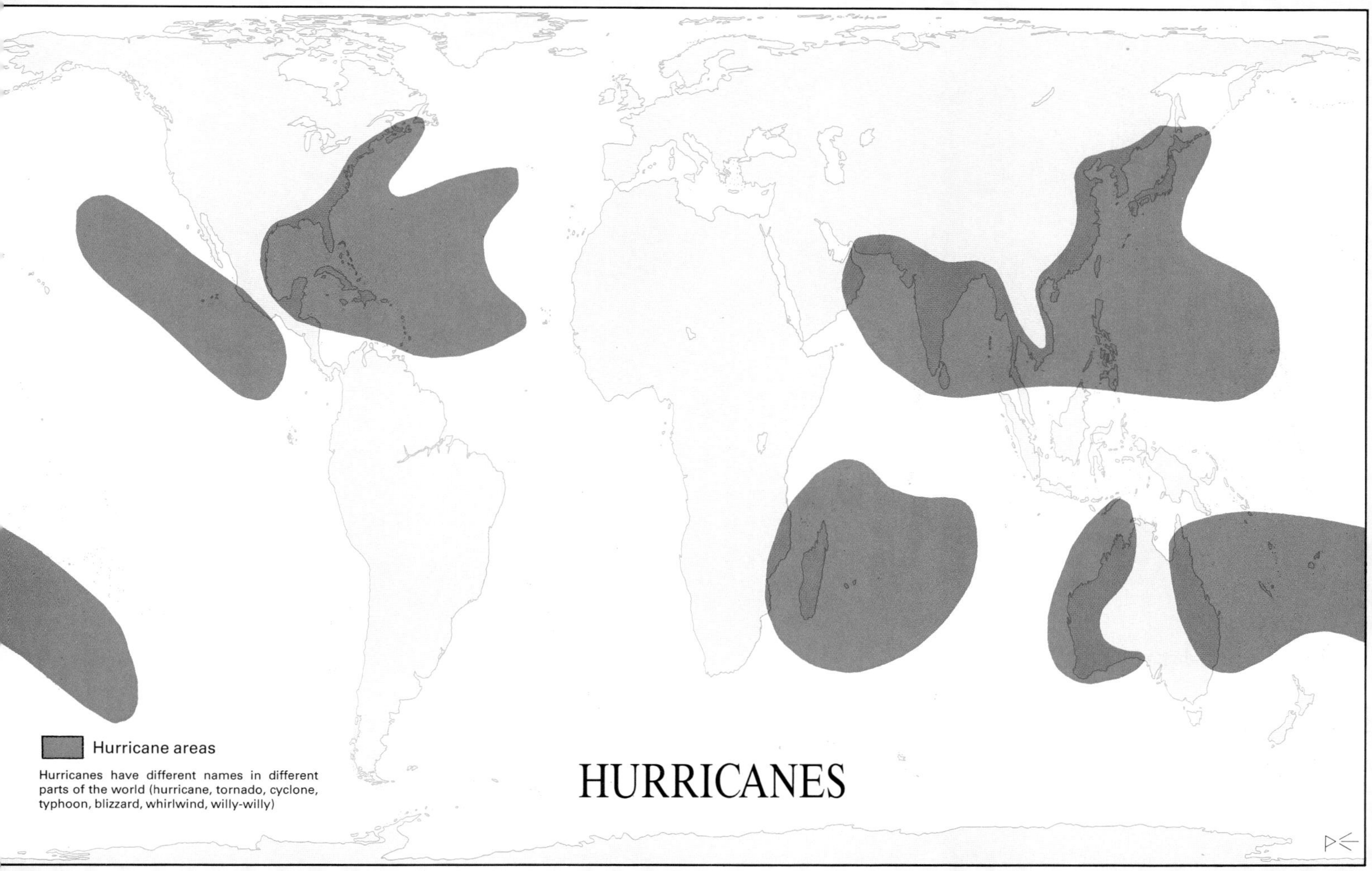

- **Hurricane areas**

Hurricanes have different names in different parts of the world (hurricane, tornado, cyclone, typhoon, blizzard, whirlwind, willy-willy)

HURRICANES

DANGERS

less than half

more than half

of this region is covered by trees

WOODLAND

less than half

more than half

of this region is pastureland

PASTURELAND

VEGE

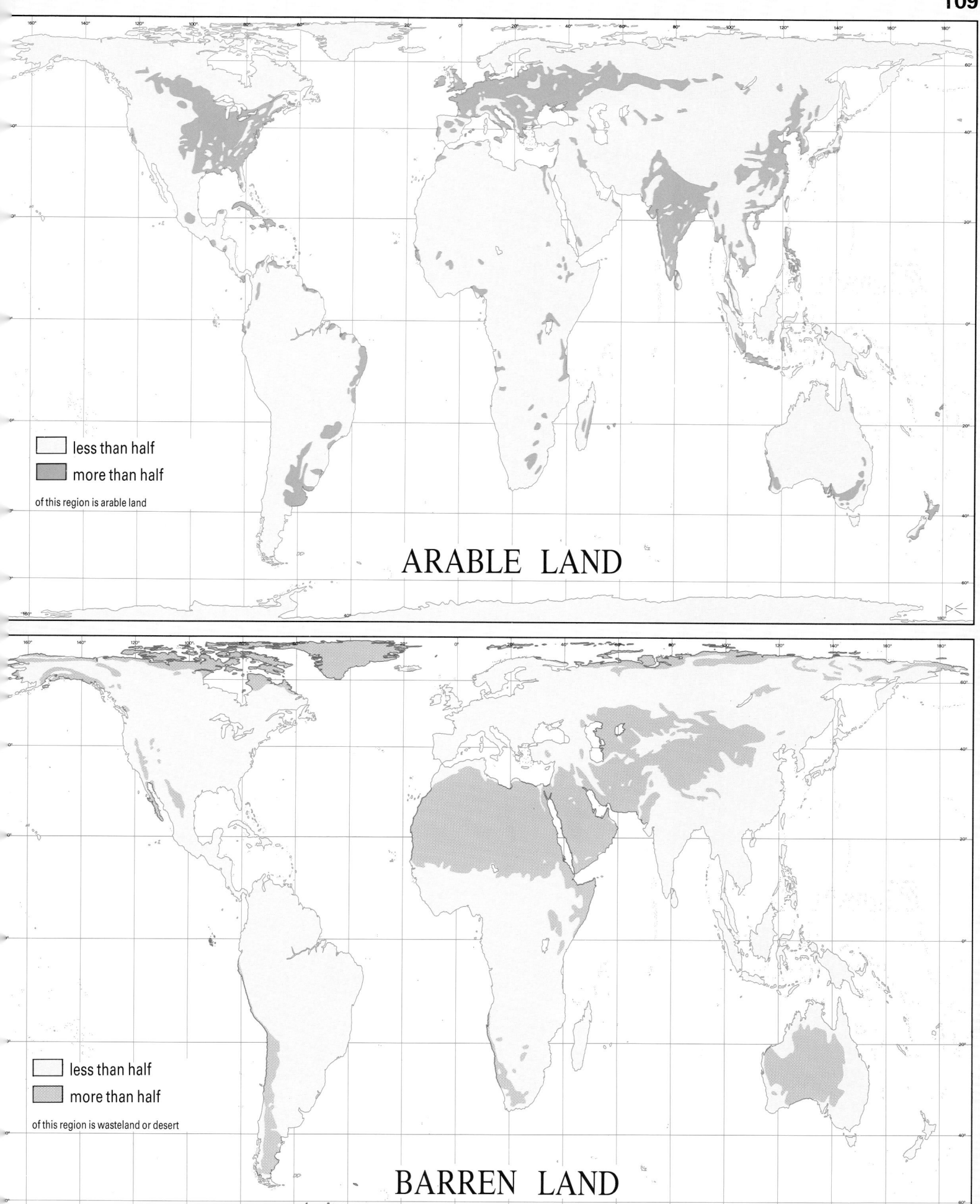

less than half

more than half

of this region is arable land

ARABLE LAND

less than half

more than half

of this region is wasteland or desert

BARREN LAND

TATION

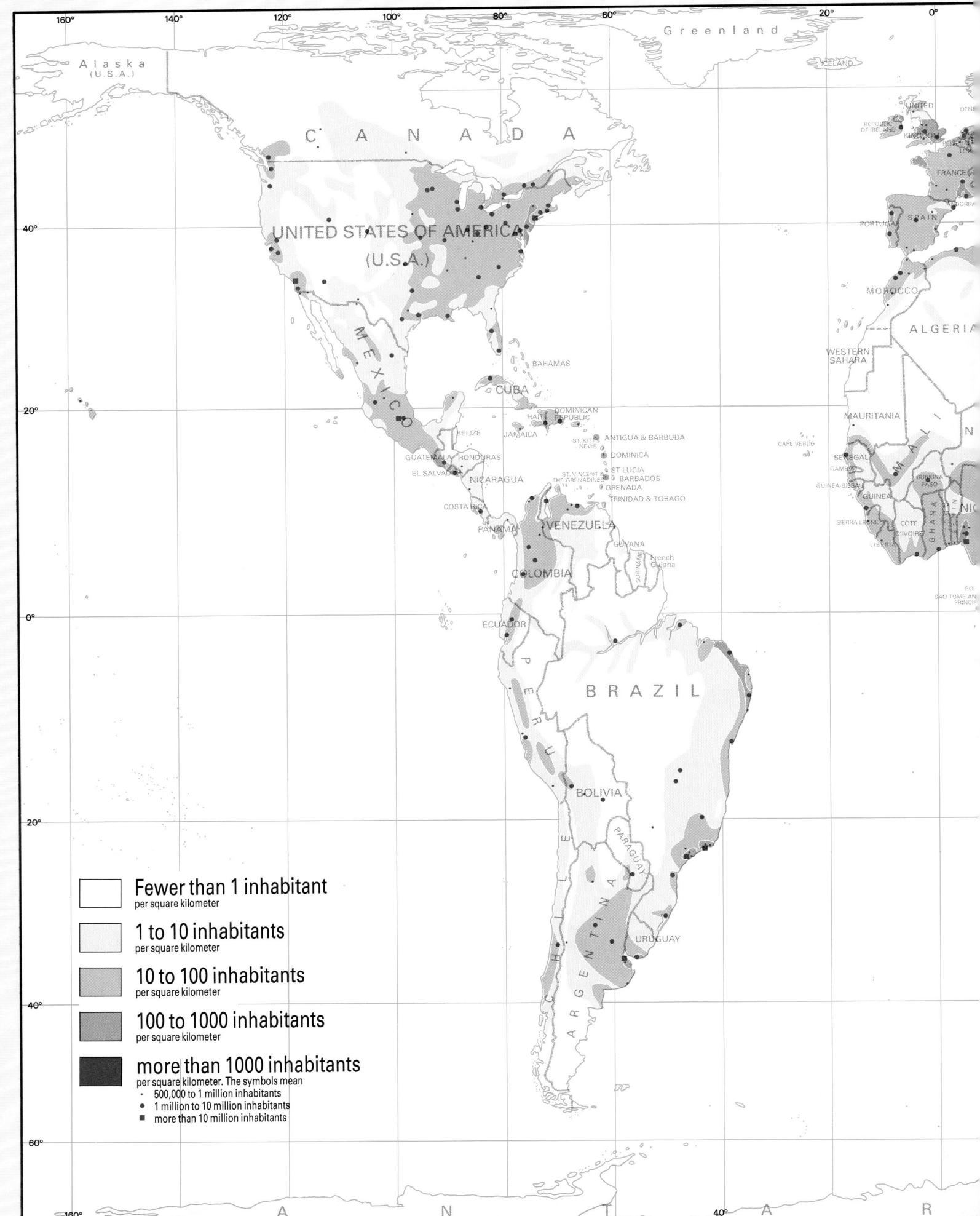

Fewer than 1 inhabitant
per square kilometer

1 to 10 inhabitants
per square kilometer

10 to 100 inhabitants
per square kilometer

100 to 1000 inhabitants
per square kilometer

more than 1000 inhabitants
per square kilometer. The symbols mean
· 500,000 to 1 million inhabitants
● 1 million to 10 million inhabitants
■ more than 10 million inhabitants

PEOPLE A

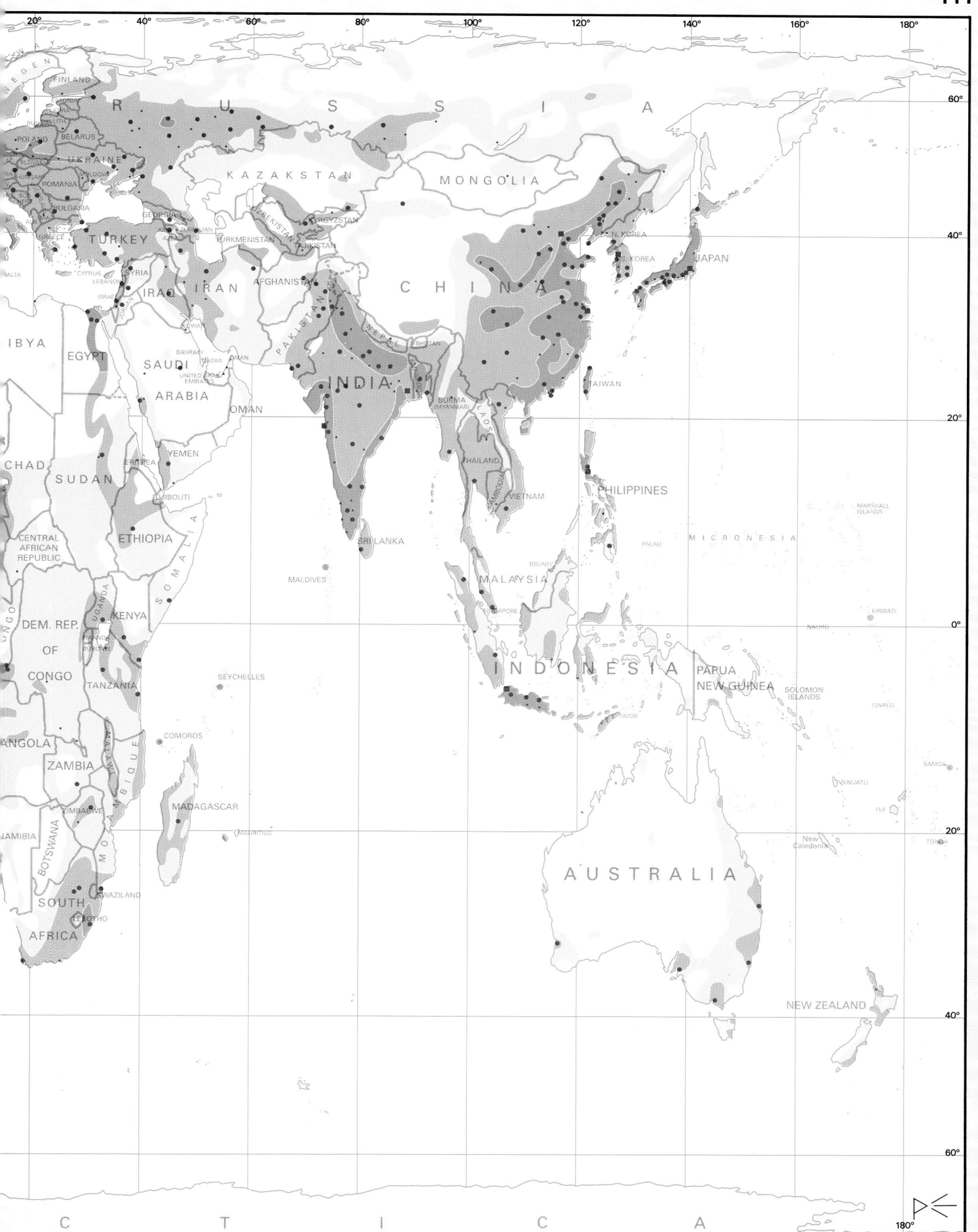

ND CITIES

160° 140° 120° 100° 80° 60° 40° 20° 0°

Alaska
(U.S.A.)

Greenland

ICELAND

UNITED

C A N A D A

REPUBLIC
OF IRELAND

DENM

KINGDOM

NL
BELGIUM
LUX.

40°

UNITED STATES OF AMERICA

(U.S.A.)

FRANCE

ANDORRA

PORTUGAL

SPAIN

M
E
X
I
C
O

MOROCCO

A L G E R I A

BAHAMAS

WESTERN
SAHARA

20°

CUBA

DOMINICAN
REPUBLIC

HAITI

MAURITANIA

M
A
L
I

N

JAMAICA

BELIZE

ST. KITTS
-NEVIS

ANTIGUA & BARBUDA

CAPE VERDE

GUATEMALA HONDURAS

DOMINICA

SENEGAL

EL SALVADOR

NICARAGUA

ST. VINCENT &
THE GRENADINES

ST LUCIA
BARBADOS

GAMBIA

BURKINA
FASO

GUINEA-BISSAU

COSTA RICA

GRENADA

GUINEA

G
H
A
N
A

T
O
G
O

B
E
N
I
N

NI

TRINIDAD & TOBAGO

PANAMA

SIERRA LEONE

CÔTE
D'IVOIRE

VENEZUELA

LIBERIA

GUYANA

0°

COLOMBIA

S
U
R
I
N
A
M
E

French
Guiana

EQ.
SAO TOME AND
PRINCIPE

ECUADOR

P
E
R
U

B R A Z I L

20°

BOLIVIA

C
H
I
L
E

P
A
R
A
G
U
A
Y

A
R
G
E
N
T
I
N
A

URUGUAY

40°

60°

160°

A N T A R

160°

STA

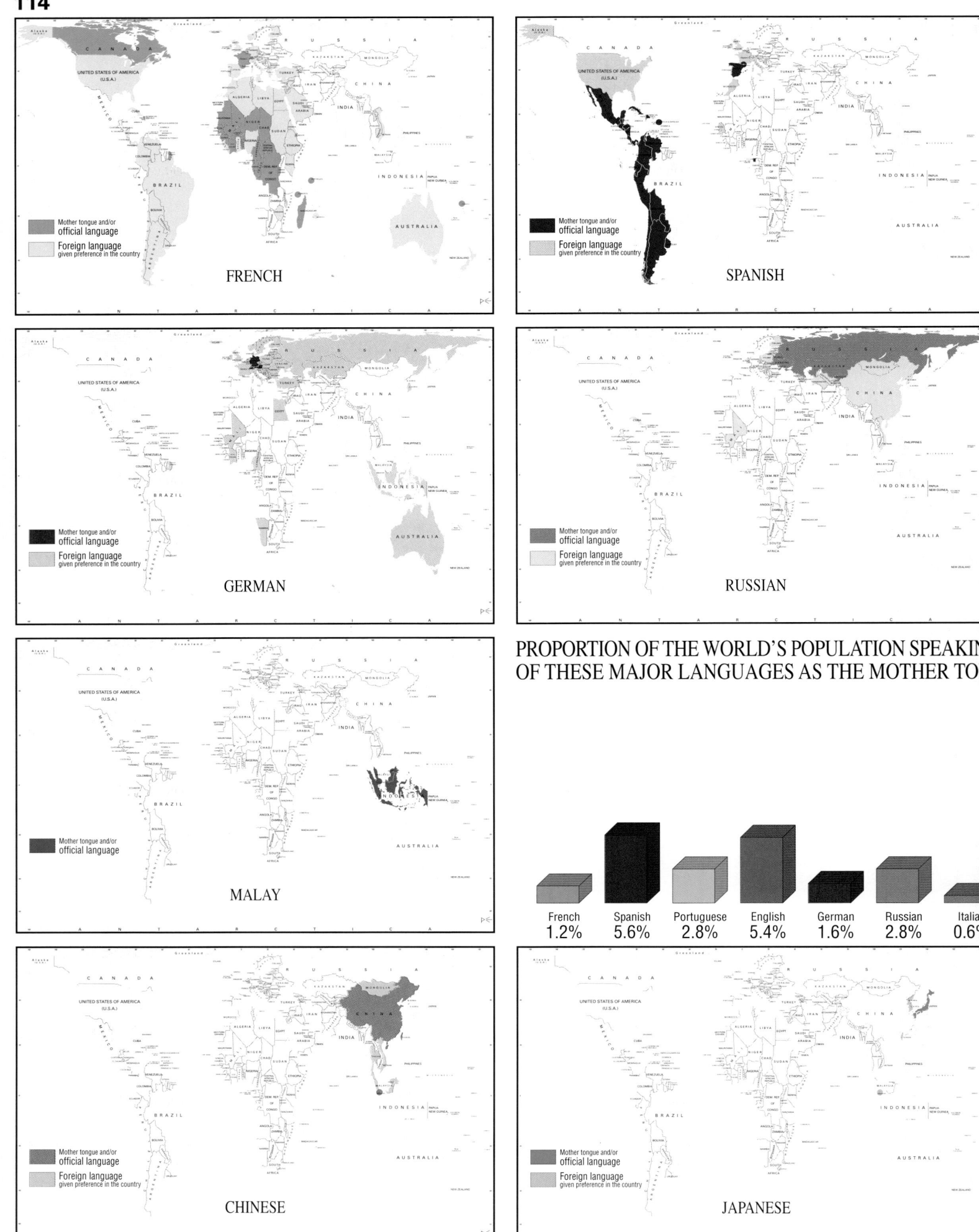

FRENCH

SPANISH

Legend (French): Mother tongue and/or official language / Foreign language given preference in the country

Legend (Spanish): Mother tongue and/or official language / Foreign language given preference in the country

GERMAN

RUSSIAN

Legend (German): Mother tongue and/or official language / Foreign language given preference in the country

Legend (Russian): Mother tongue and/or official language / Foreign language given preference in the country

MALAY

Legend (Malay): Mother tongue and/or official language

PROPORTION OF THE WORLD'S POPULATION SPEAKIN
OF THESE MAJOR LANGUAGES AS THE MOTHER TON

French	Spanish	Portuguese	English	German	Russian	Italian
1.2%	5.6%	2.8%	5.4%	1.6%	2.8%	0.6%

CHINESE

JAPANESE

Legend (Chinese): Mother tongue and/or official language / Foreign language given preference in the country

Legend (Japanese): Mother tongue and/or official language / Foreign language given preference in the country

LANGU

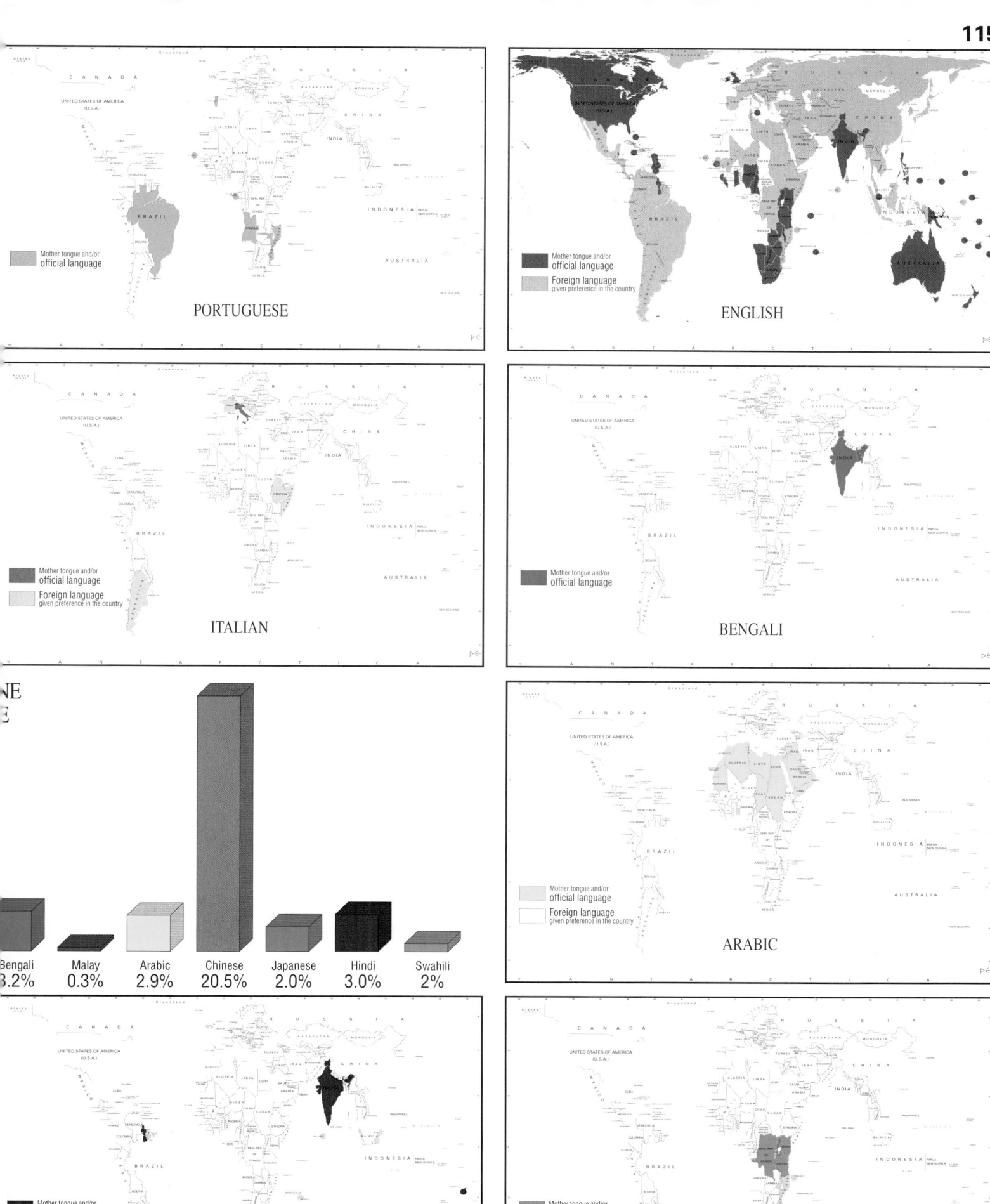

PORTUGUESE

ENGLISH
- Mother tongue and/or official language
- Foreign language given preference in the country

ITALIAN
- Mother tongue and/or official language
- Foreign language given preference in the country

BENGALI
- Mother tongue and/or official language

Bengali	Malay	Arabic	Chinese	Japanese	Hindi	Swahili
3.2%	0.3%	2.9%	20.5%	2.0%	3.0%	2%

ARABIC
- Mother tongue and/or official language
- Foreign language given preference in the country

HINDI
- Mother tongue and/or official language
- Foreign language given preference in the country

SWAHILI
- Mother tongue and/or official language
- Foreign language given preference in the country

UAGES

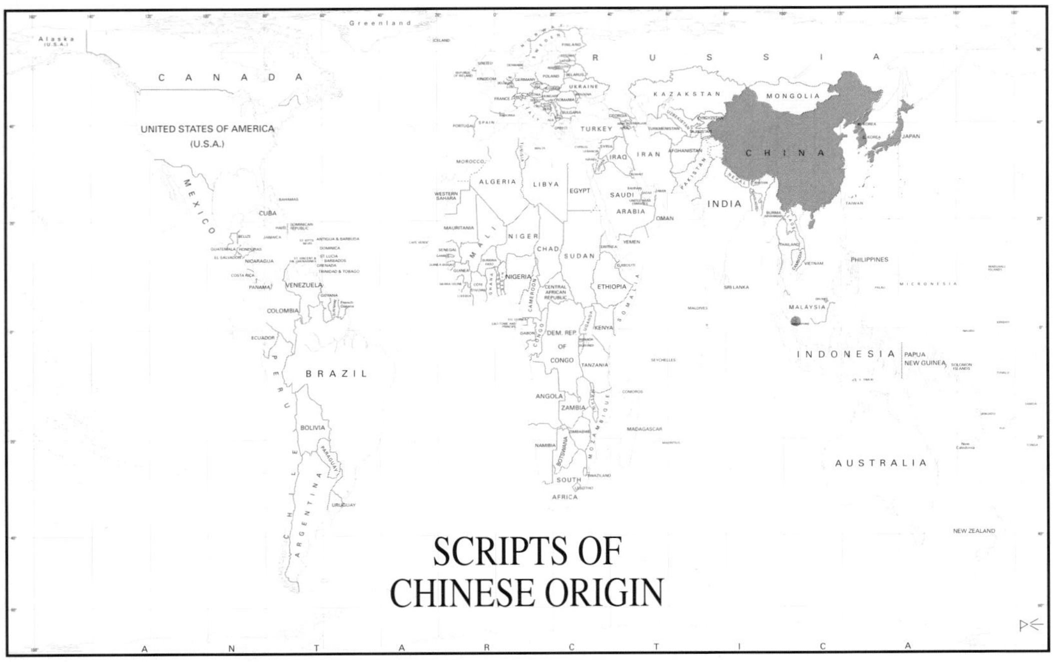
CANADA
UNITED STATES OF AMERICA (U.S.A.)
RUSSIA
CHINA
INDIA
BRAZIL
AUSTRALIA
ANTARCTICA
SCRIPTS OF CHINESE ORIGIN

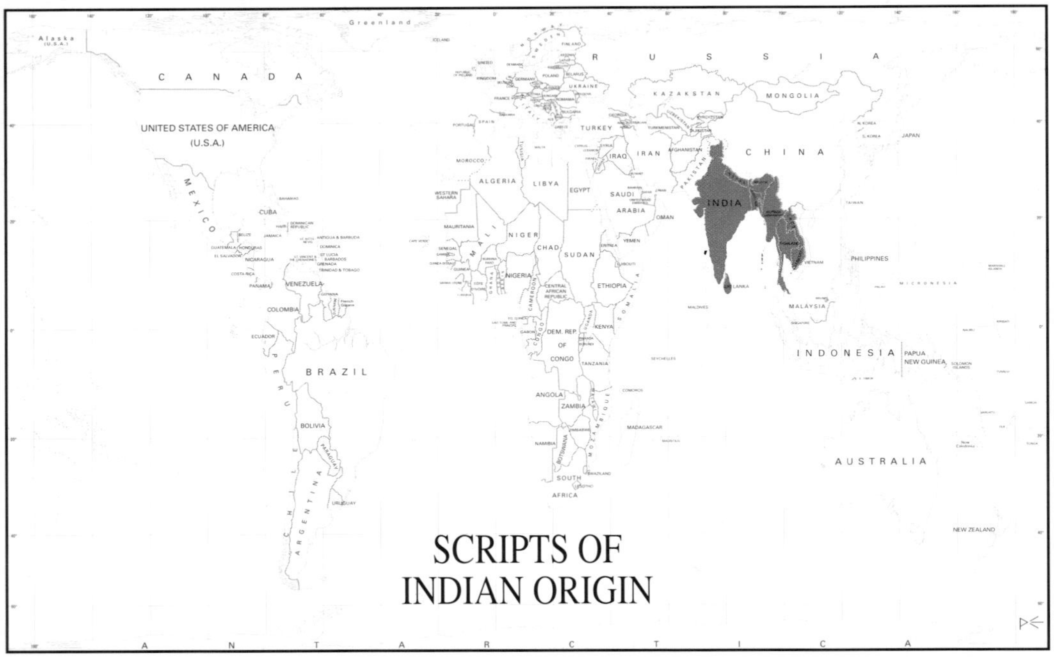
CANADA
UNITED STATES OF AMERICA (U.S.A.)
RUSSIA
CHINA
INDIA
BRAZIL
AUSTRALIA
ANTARCTICA
SCRIPTS OF INDIAN ORIGIN

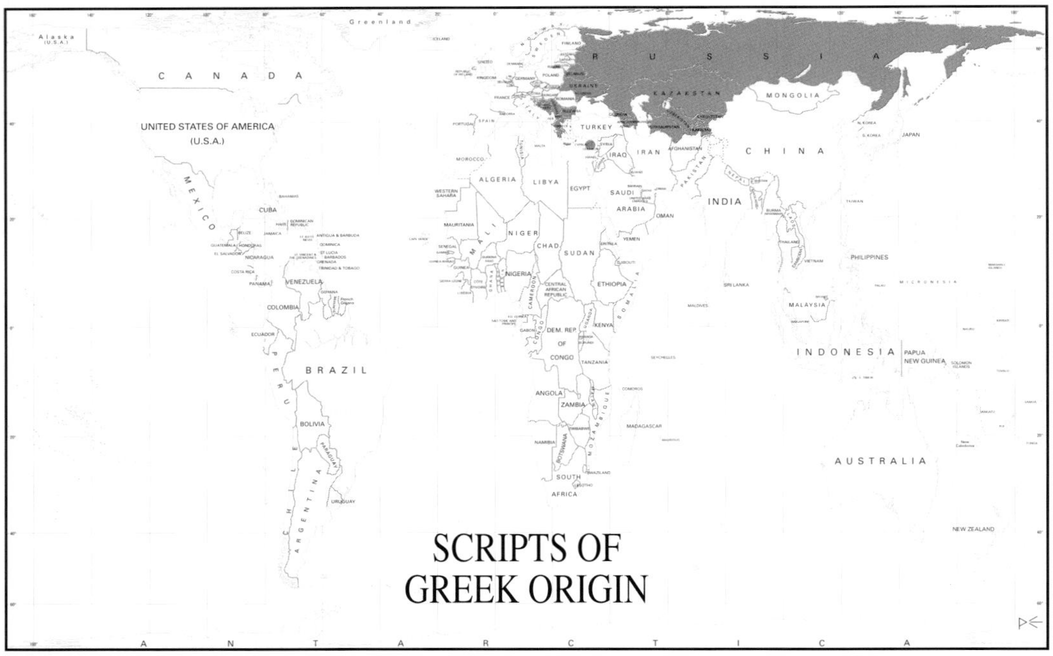
CANADA
UNITED STATES OF AMERICA (U.S.A.)
RUSSIA
CHINA
INDIA
BRAZIL
AUSTRALIA
ANTARCTICA
SCRIPTS OF GREEK ORIGIN

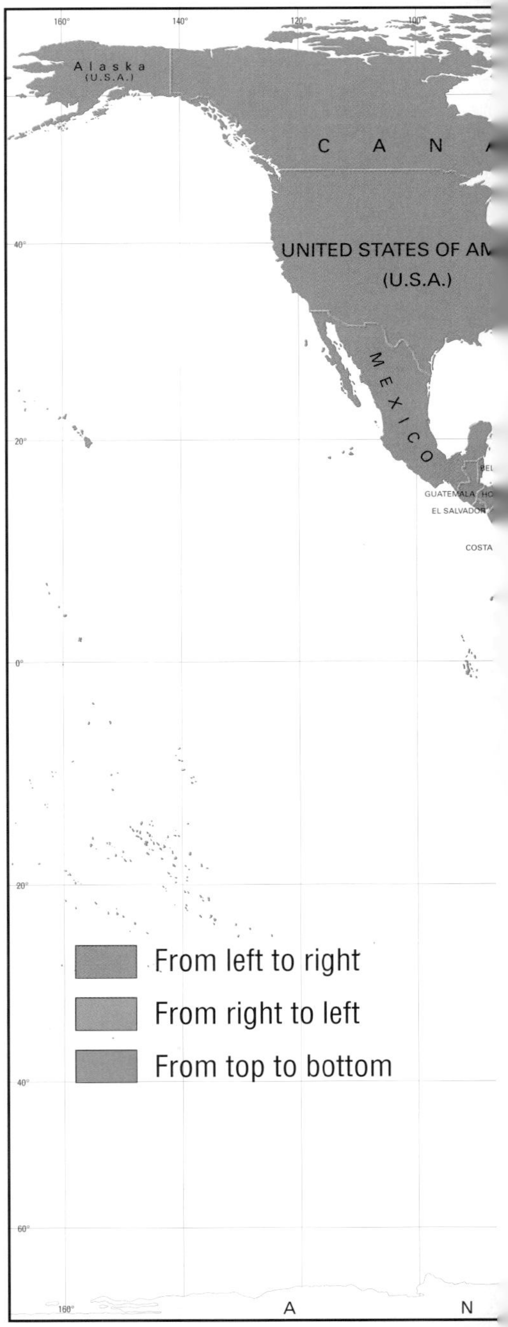
Alaska (U.S.A.)
CAN
UNITED STATES OF AM
(U.S.A.)
MEXICO
From left to right
From right to left
From top to bottom

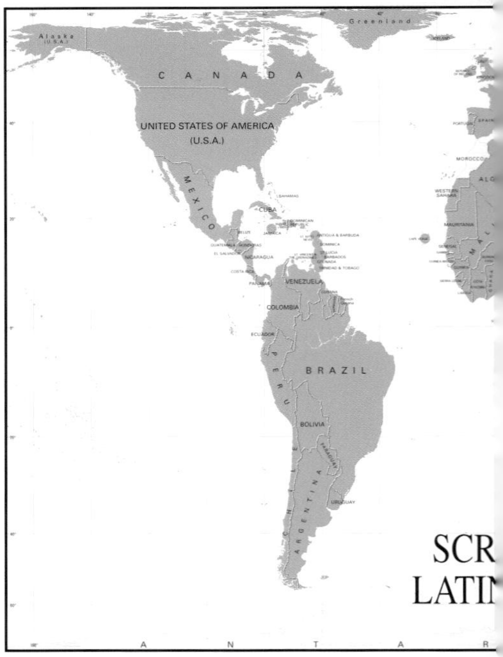
CANADA
UNITED STATES OF AMERICA (U.S.A.)
BRAZIL
SCR
LATI

SCR

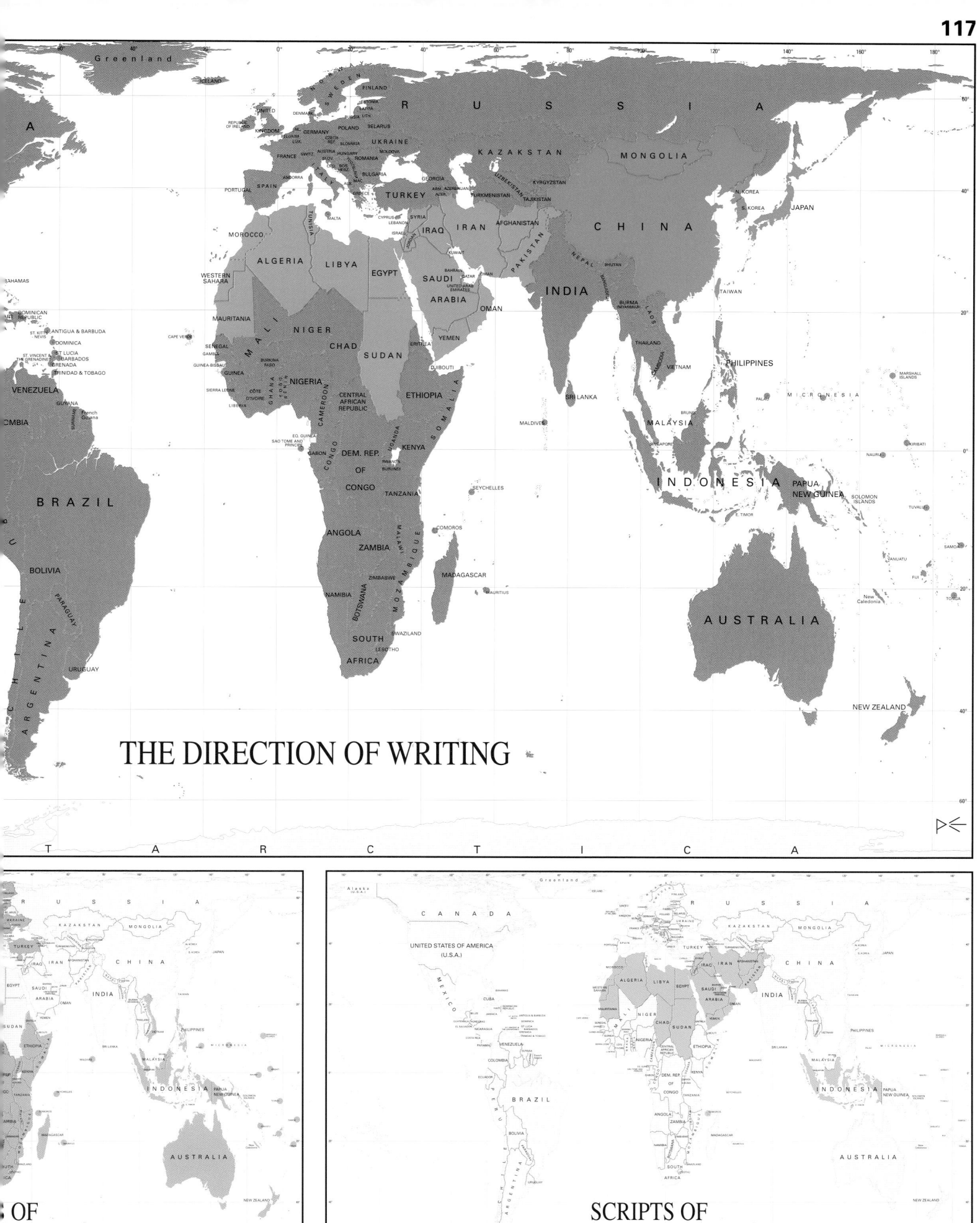

THE DIRECTION OF WRITING

SCRIPTS OF
ARABIC ORIGIN

OF
IGIN

PTS

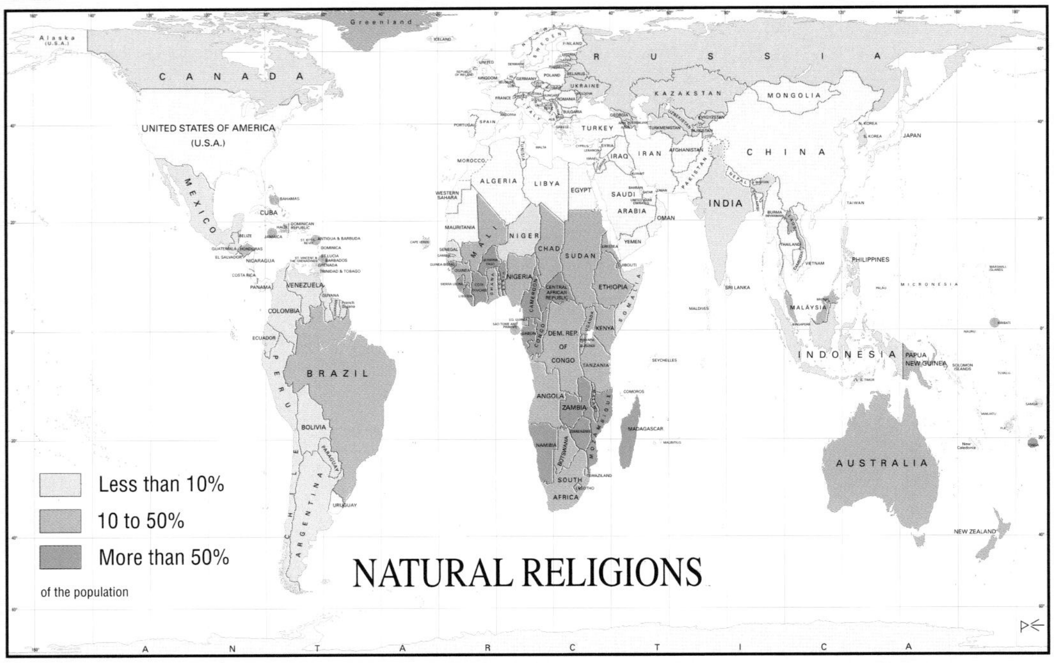

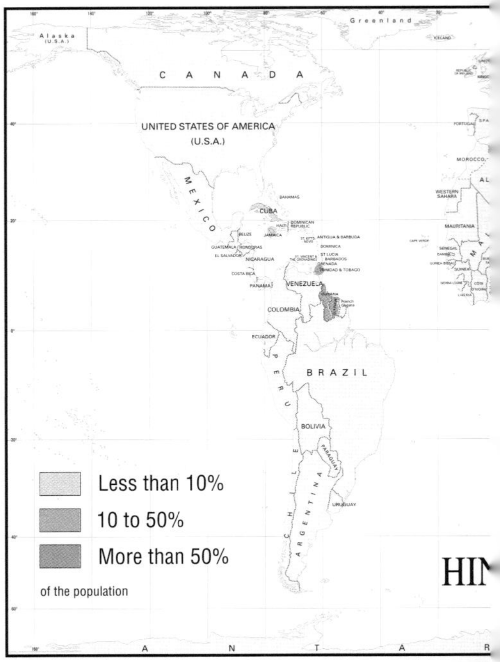

NATURAL RELIGIONS

Less than 10%
10 to 50%
More than 50%
of the population

ISLAM

Less than 10%
10 to 50%
More than 50%
of the population

BUDDHISM

Less than 10%
10 to 50%
More than 50%
of the population

Less than 10%
10 to 50%
More than 50%
of the population

HIN

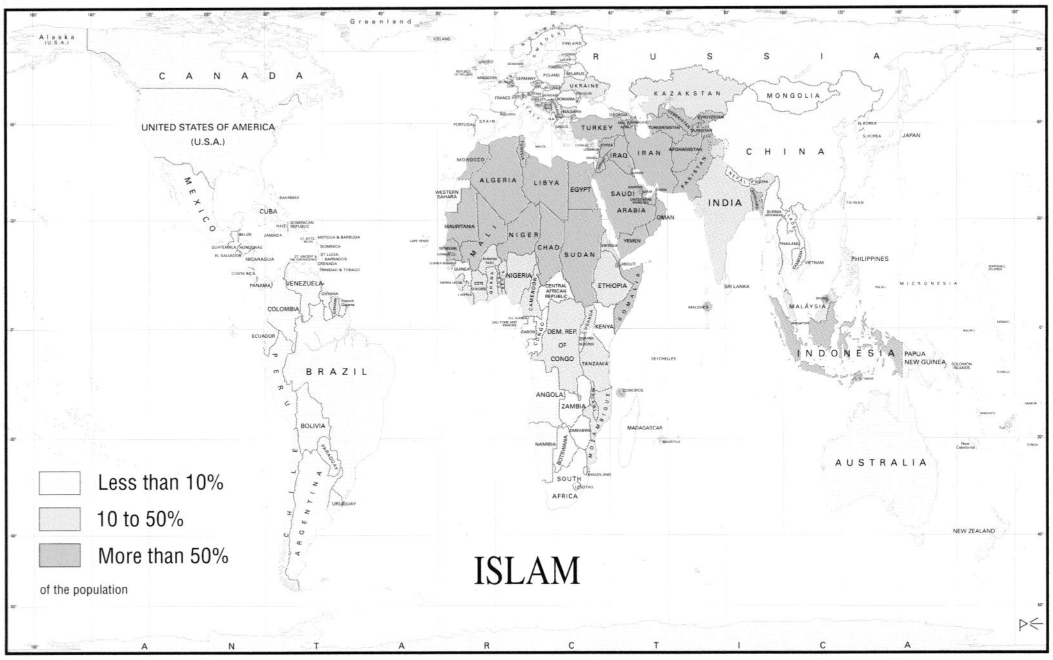

ONLY RELIGIONS WHOSE ADHE
OVER 1% OF THE WORLD'S POP
INCLUDED ON THESE TWO PAG

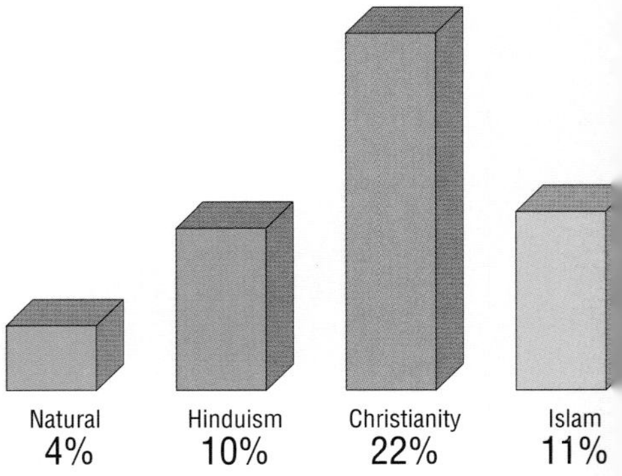

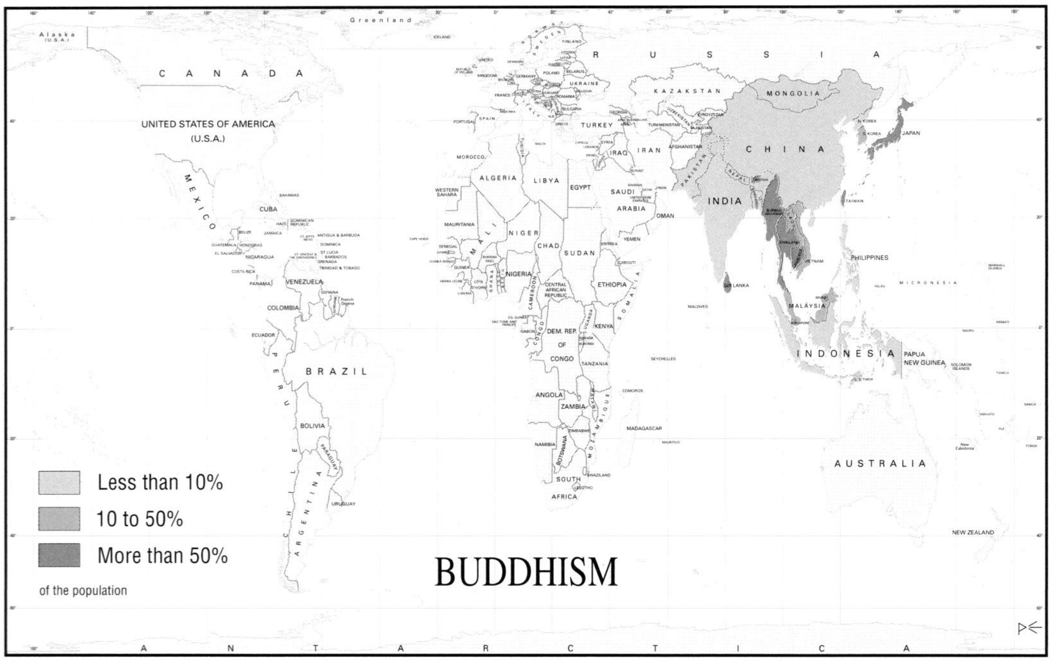

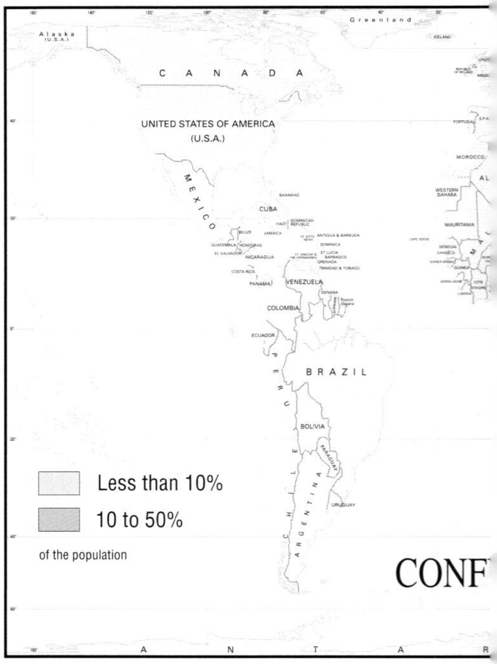

Natural	Hinduism	Christianity	Islam
4%	10%	22%	11%

Less than 10%
10 to 50%
of the population

CONF

RELIG

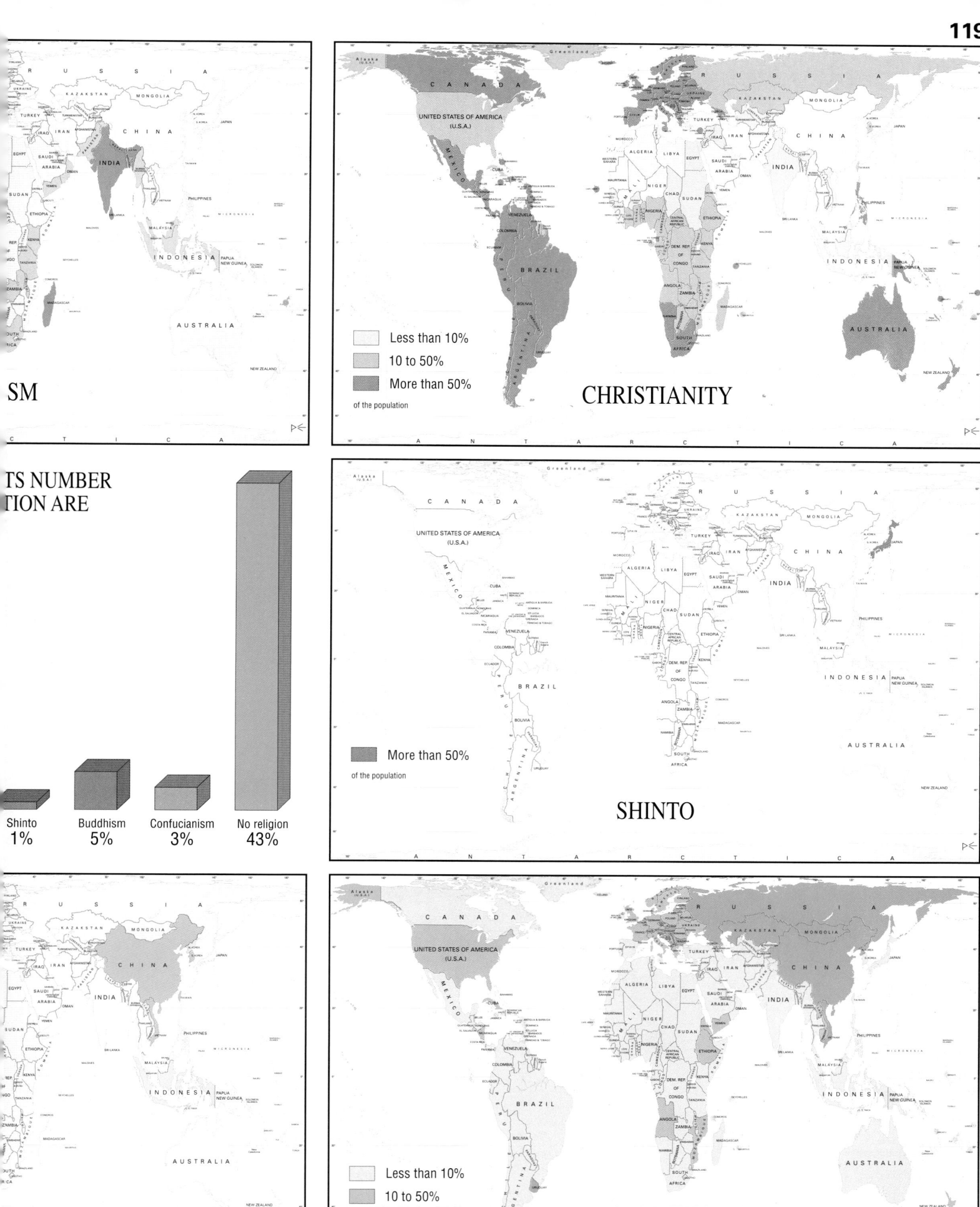

SM

CHRISTIANITY

Less than 10%

10 to 50%

More than 50%

of the population

TS NUMBER
TION ARE

Shinto
1%

Buddhism
5%

Confucianism
3%

No religion
43%

More than 50%

of the population

SHINTO

ANISM

NO RELIGION

Less than 10%

10 to 50%

More than 50%

of the population

IONS

Greenland

Alaska
(U.S.A.)

C A N A D A

UNITED STATES OF AMERICA
(U.S.A.)

MEXICO

CUBA
BAHAMAS
BELIZE
GUATEMALA HONDURAS
EL SALVADOR NICARAGUA
COSTA RICA
PANAMA

HAITI
DOMINICAN
REPUBLIC
JAMAICA

ST KITTS
NEVIS
DOMINICA
ST LUCIA
ST VINCENT & BARBADOS
THE GRENADINES GRENADA
TRINIDAD & TOBAGO

ANTIGUA & BARBUDA

VENEZUELA
GUYANA
SURINAM
French
Guiana
COLOMBIA
ECUADOR

P
E
R
U

B R A Z I L

BOLIVIA

PARAGUAY

C
H
I
L
E

A
R
G
E
N
T
I
N
A

URUGUAY

NORWAY
SWEDEN
FINLAND
ESTONIA
DENMARK LATVIA
LITHUANIA
UNITED
KINGDOM
REPUBLIC
OF IRELAND
BELGIUM GERMANY POLAND BELARUS
FRANCE SWITZ. AUSTRIA HUNGARY
ANDORRA ITALY ROMANIA
PORTUGAL SPAIN BULGARIA
GREECE

R U S S I A

UKRAINE

MOLDOVA

GEORGIA
AZERBAIJAN
ARM.

KAZAKSTAN

UZBEKISTAN
TURKMENISTAN
TAJIKISTAN
KYRGYZSTAN

TURKEY
CYPRUS
LEBANON SYRIA
ISRAEL IRAQ
JORDAN
MALTA

IRAN

MOROCCO
WESTERN
SAHARA
ALGERIA LIBYA EGYPT
SAUDI
ARABIA

QATAR
UNITED ARAB
EMIRATES
OMAN

BAHRAIN
KUWAIT

CH

INDIA

SRI LANKA

MALDIVES

MAURITANIA
CAPE VERDE
SENEGAL
GUINEA-BISSAU
GUINEA
SIERRA LEONE
LIBERIA
GHANA
NIGER
NIGERIA
CHAD
SUDAN
CENTRAL
AFRICAN
REPUBLIC
CAMEROON
EQ. GUINEA
SAO TOME AND
PRINCIPE
GABON
CONGO
DEM. REP.
OF
CONGO
ANGOLA
ZAMBIA
NAMIBIA
BOTSWANA
SOUTH
AFRICA
LESOTHO
SWAZILAND
ZIMBABWE
TANZANIA
KENYA
UGANDA
ETHIOPIA
SOMALIA
DJIBOUTI
COMOROS
MADAGASCAR
MAURITIUS
SEYCHELLES

	Less than 1%
	1 to 5%
	5 to 20%
	20 to 50%
	50 to 80%
	More than 80%

of the total population

ILLITERACY

A N T A R C T I

C A N A D A

UNITED STATES OF AMERICA
(U.S.A.)

MEXICO

Alaska

Greenland

R U S S I A

KAZAKSTAN

MONGOLIA

CHINA

JAPAN

TURKEY

IRAQ IRAN
AFGHANISTAN

INDIA

MOROCCO
WESTERN
SAHARA
ALGERIA LIBYA EGYPT
SAUDI
ARABIA
OMAN
YEMEN
NIGER
CHAD SUDAN
NIGERIA
CENTRAL
AFRICAN
REP.
CAMEROON
DEM. REP.
OF
CONGO
KENYA
TANZANIA
ANGOLA
ZAMBIA
SOUTH
AFRICA

PHILIPPINES

MALAYSIA

I N D O N E S I A

PAPUA
NEW GUINEA

MICRONESIA

AUSTRALIA

NEW ZEALAND

VENEZUELA
COLOMBIA
ECUADOR
PERU
BRAZIL
BOLIVIA
ARGENTINA

	Less than 40%
	40 to 60%
	60 to 80%
	More than 80%

of the appropriate age group

PRIMARY EDUCATION

A N T A R C T I C A

C A N A D A

UNITED STATES OF AMERICA
(U.S.A.)

MEXICO

Alaska

Greenland

MOROCCO
WESTERN
SAHARA
MAURITANIA

CUBA

VENEZUELA
COLOMBIA
ECUADOR
BRAZIL
BOLIVIA
ARGENTINA

	Less than 40%
	40 to 60%
	60 to 80%
	More than 80%

of the appropriate age group

SECONDA

A N T A R

EDUC

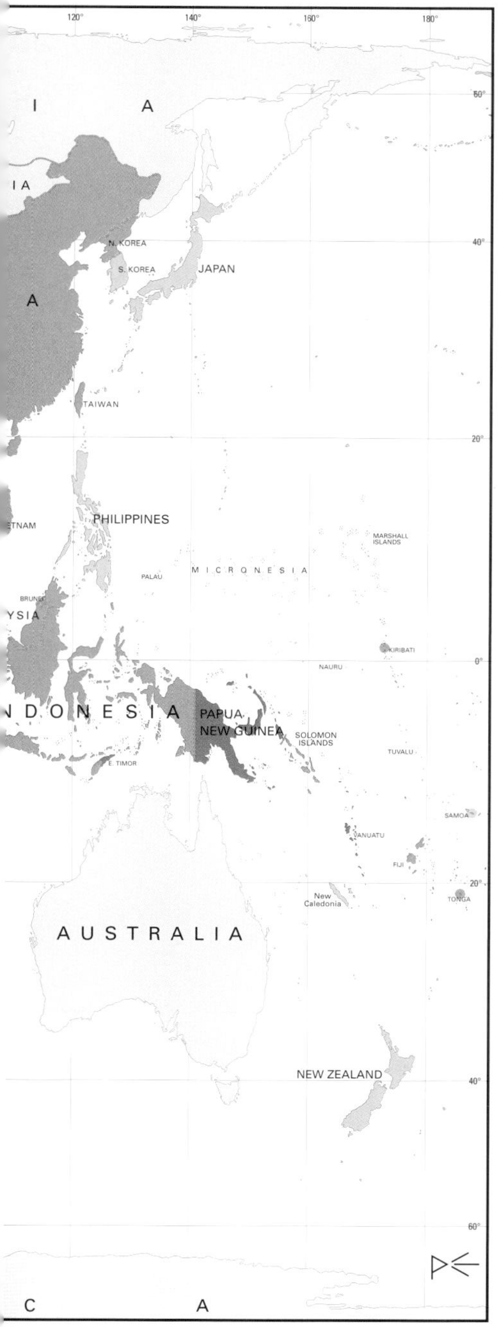

PUPIL / TEACHER RATIO

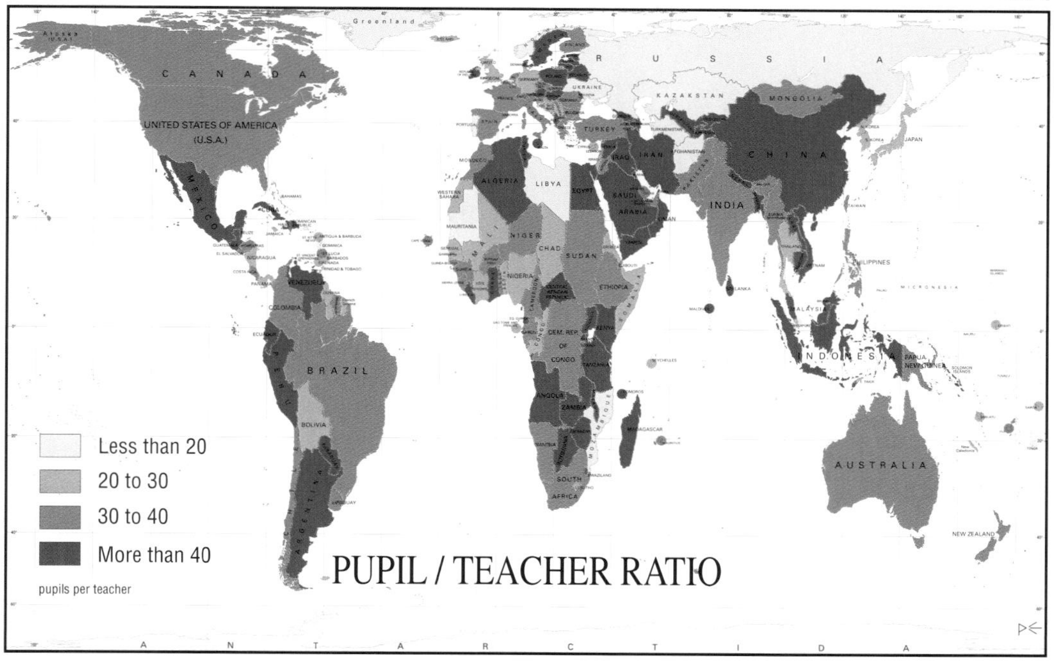

Less than 20
20 to 30
30 to 40
More than 40

pupils per teacher

UNIVERSITY

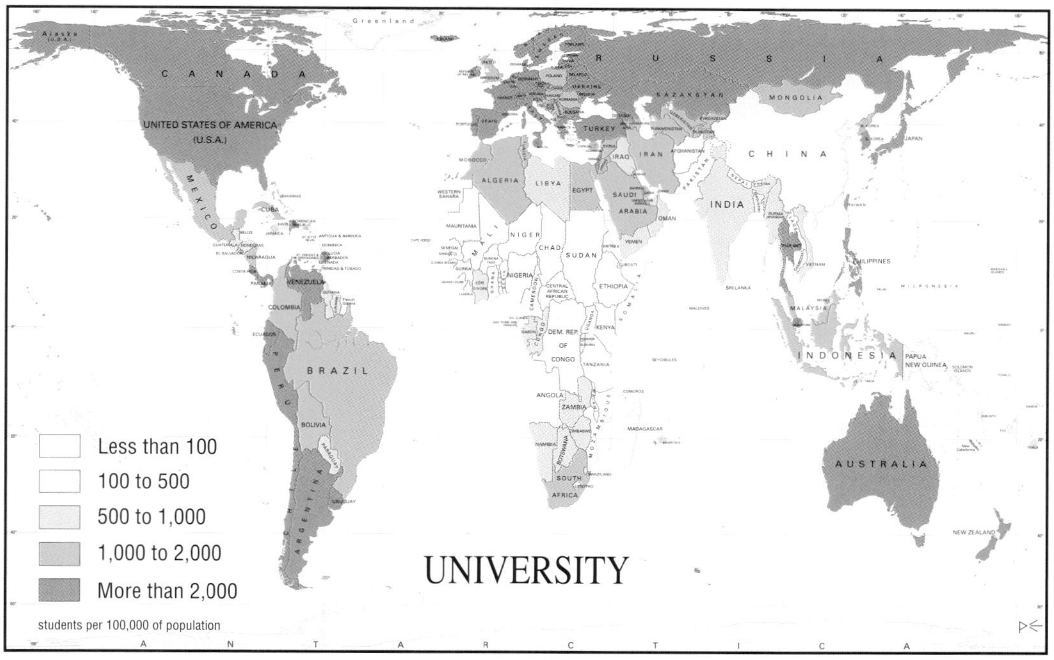

Less than 100
100 to 500
500 to 1,000
1,000 to 2,000
More than 2,000

students per 100,000 of population

EXPENDITURE ON EDUCATION

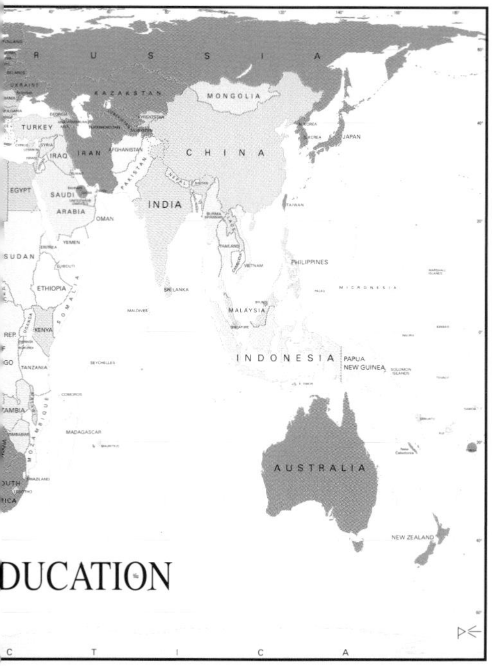

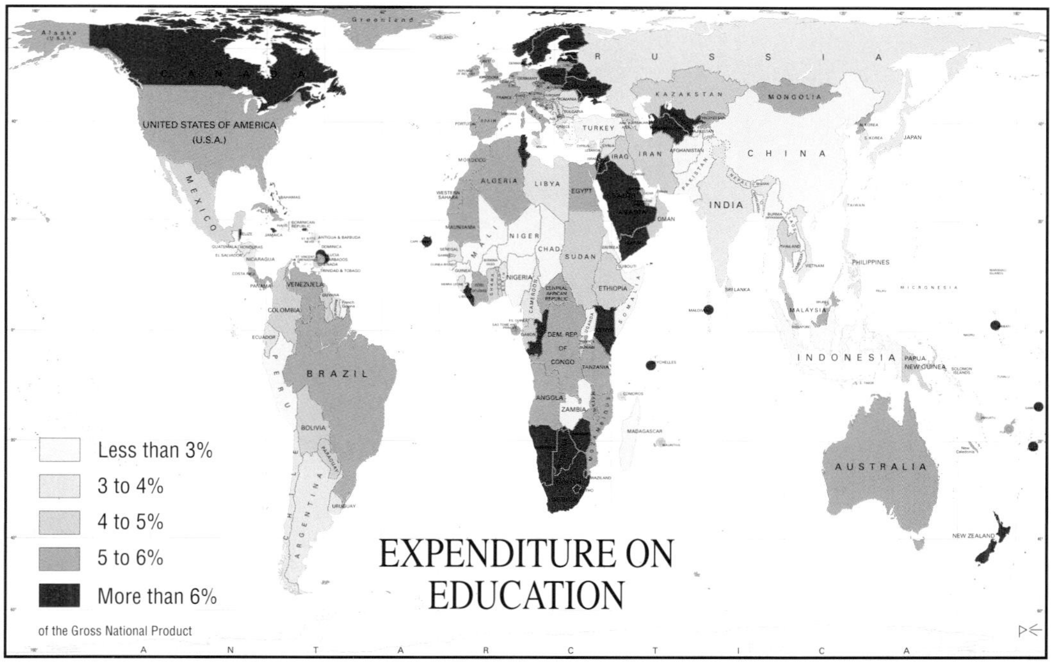

Less than 3%
3 to 4%
4 to 5%
5 to 6%
More than 6%

of the Gross National Product

DUCATION

ATION

UNIVERSITY TEACHERS

Legend:

Very few
less than 50 per million of population

Few
50 to 100 per million of population

Average
100 to 500 per million of population

Many
500 to 1,000 per million of population

Very many
more than 1,000 per million of population

Map labels: Alaska (U.S.A.), CANADA, UNITED STATES OF AMERICA (U.S.A.), MEXICO, Greenland, RUSSIA, KAZAKSTAN, MONGOLIA, CHINA, JAPAN, N. KOREA, S. KOREA, INDIA, TURKEY, IRAN, IRAQ, SAUDI ARABIA, OMAN, PAKISTAN, AFGHANISTAN, NEPAL, TAIWAN, BURMA (MYANMAR), THAILAND, VIETNAM, LAOS, PHILIPPINES, MALAYSIA, INDONESIA, PAPUA NEW GUINEA, AUSTRALIA, NEW ZEALAND, BRAZIL, PERU, BOLIVIA, CHILE, ARGENTINA, PARAGUAY, URUGUAY, VENEZUELA, COLOMBIA, ECUADOR, GUYANA, French Guiana, PORTUGAL, SPAIN, FRANCE, POLAND, UKRAINE, BELARUS, UNITED KINGDOM, FINLAND, SWEDEN, ICELAND, MOROCCO, ALGERIA, LIBYA, EGYPT, WESTERN SAHARA, MAURITANIA, MALI, NIGER, CHAD, SUDAN, NIGERIA, ETHIOPIA, KENYA, TANZANIA, DEM. REP. OF CONGO, ANGOLA, ZAMBIA, ZIMBABWE, NAMIBIA, BOTSWANA, SOUTH AFRICA, MADAGASCAR, MOZAMBIQUE, SOMALIA, YEMEN, CAMEROON, CENTRAL AFRICAN REPUBLIC, CUBA, BAHAMAS, JAMAICA, HAITI, DOMINICAN REPUBLIC, GUATEMALA, HONDURAS, EL SALVADOR, NICARAGUA, COSTA RICA, PANAMA, BELIZE, TRINIDAD & TOBAGO, SRI LANKA, MALDIVES, SEYCHELLES, COMOROS, MAURITIUS, MICRONESIA, MARSHALL ISLANDS, PALAU, NAURU, KIRIBATI, TUVALU, VANUATU, FIJI, SAMOA, SOLOMON ISLANDS, New Caledonia, ANTARCTICA

RESEARCHERS AND ENGINEERS

Legend:

Very few
less than 100 per million of population

Few
100 to 500 per million of population

Average
500 to 1,000 per million of population

Many
1,000 to 5,000 per million of population

Very many
more than 5,000 per million of population

Map labels: Alaska (U.S.A.), CANADA, UNITED STATES OF AMERICA (U.S.A.), MEXICO, Greenland, ICELAND, RUSSIA, KAZAKSTAN, MONGOLIA, CHINA, JAPAN, N. KOREA, S. KOREA, INDIA, TURKEY, IRAN, IRAQ, SAUDI ARABIA, OMAN, PAKISTAN, AFGHANISTAN, NEPAL, TAIWAN, BURMA (MYANMAR), THAILAND, VIETNAM, PHILIPPINES, MALAYSIA, INDONESIA, PAPUA NEW GUINEA, AUSTRALIA, NEW ZEALAND, BRAZIL, PERU, BOLIVIA, CHILE, ARGENTINA, PARAGUAY, URUGUAY, VENEZUELA, COLOMBIA, ECUADOR, GUYANA, French Guiana, PORTUGAL, SPAIN, FRANCE, POLAND, UKRAINE, BELARUS, UNITED KINGDOM, FINLAND, SWEDEN, REPUBLIC OF IRELAND, MOROCCO, ALGERIA, LIBYA, EGYPT, WESTERN SAHARA, MAURITANIA, MALI, NIGER, CHAD, SUDAN, NIGERIA, ETHIOPIA, KENYA, TANZANIA, DEM. REP. OF CONGO, ANGOLA, ZAMBIA, ZIMBABWE, NAMIBIA, BOTSWANA, SOUTH AFRICA, MADAGASCAR, MOZAMBIQUE, SOMALIA, YEMEN, CAMEROON, CENTRAL AFRICAN REPUBLIC, CUBA, BAHAMAS, JAMAICA, HAITI, DOMINICAN REPUBLIC, GUATEMALA, HONDURAS, EL SALVADOR, NICARAGUA, COSTA RICA, PANAMA, BELIZE, TRINIDAD & TOBAGO, SRI LANKA, MALDIVES, SEYCHELLES, COMOROS, MAURITIUS, MICRONESIA, MARSHALL ISLANDS, PALAU, NAURU, KIRIBATI, TUVALU, VANUATU, FIJI, SAMOA, SOLOMON ISLANDS, New Caledonia, KYRGYZSTAN, TURKMENISTAN, ANTARCTICA

THE SC

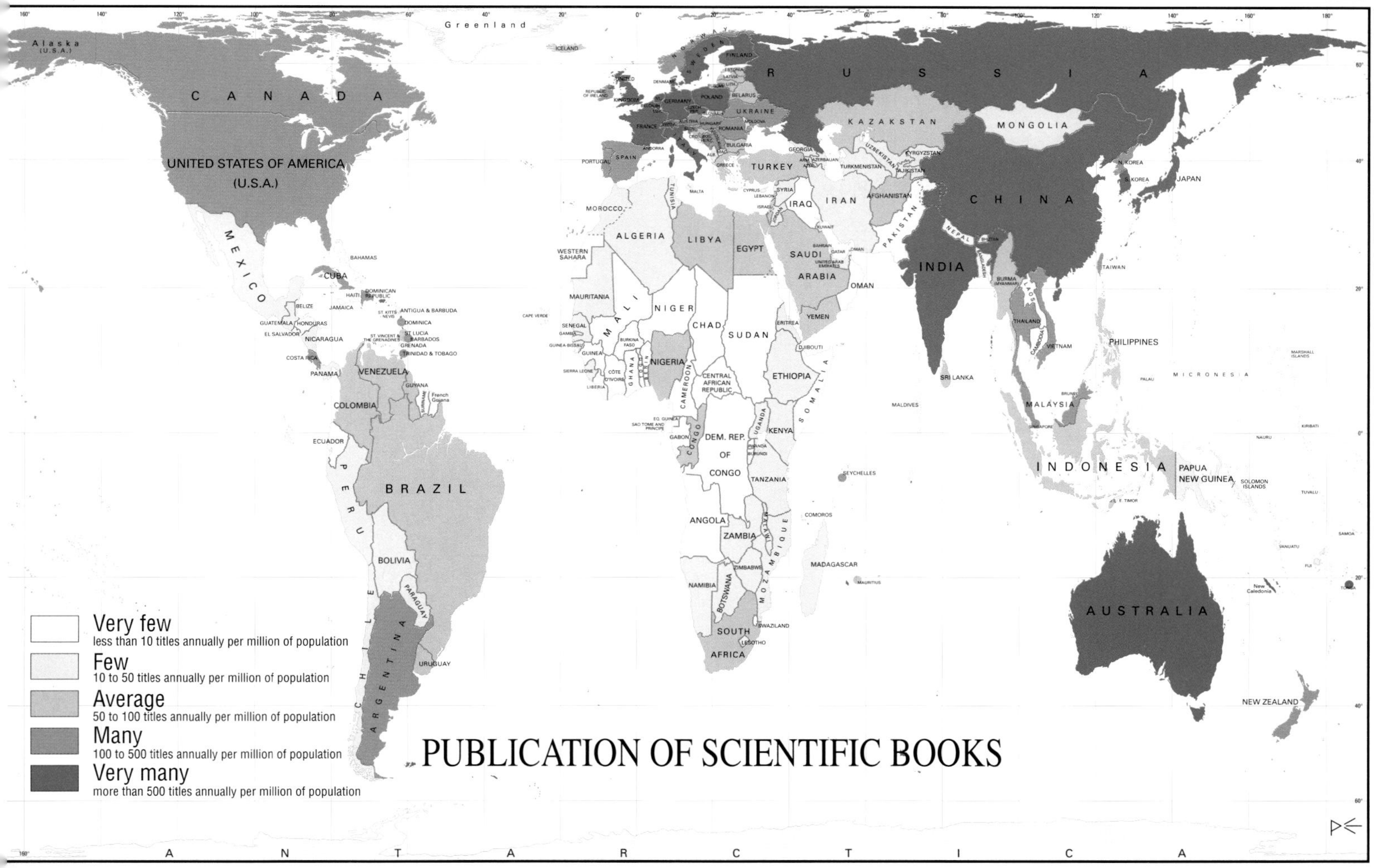

PUBLICATION OF SCIENTIFIC BOOKS

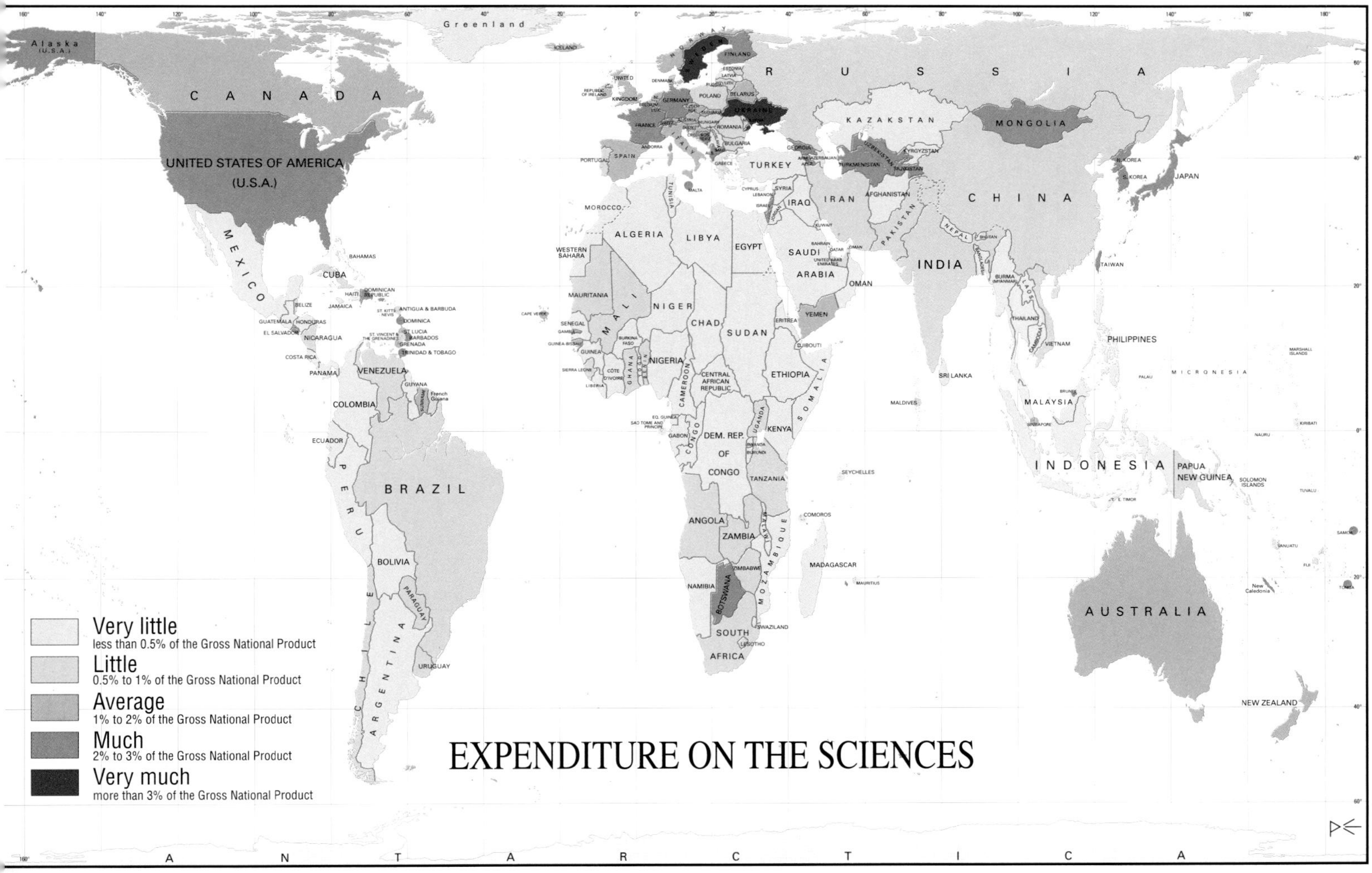

Very few
less than 10 titles annually per million of population

Few
10 to 50 titles annually per million of population

Average
50 to 100 titles annually per million of population

Many
100 to 500 titles annually per million of population

Very many
more than 500 titles annually per million of population

EXPENDITURE ON THE SCIENCES

Very little
less than 0.5% of the Gross National Product

Little
0.5% to 1% of the Gross National Product

Average
1% to 2% of the Gross National Product

Much
2% to 3% of the Gross National Product

Very much
more than 3% of the Gross National Product

ENCES

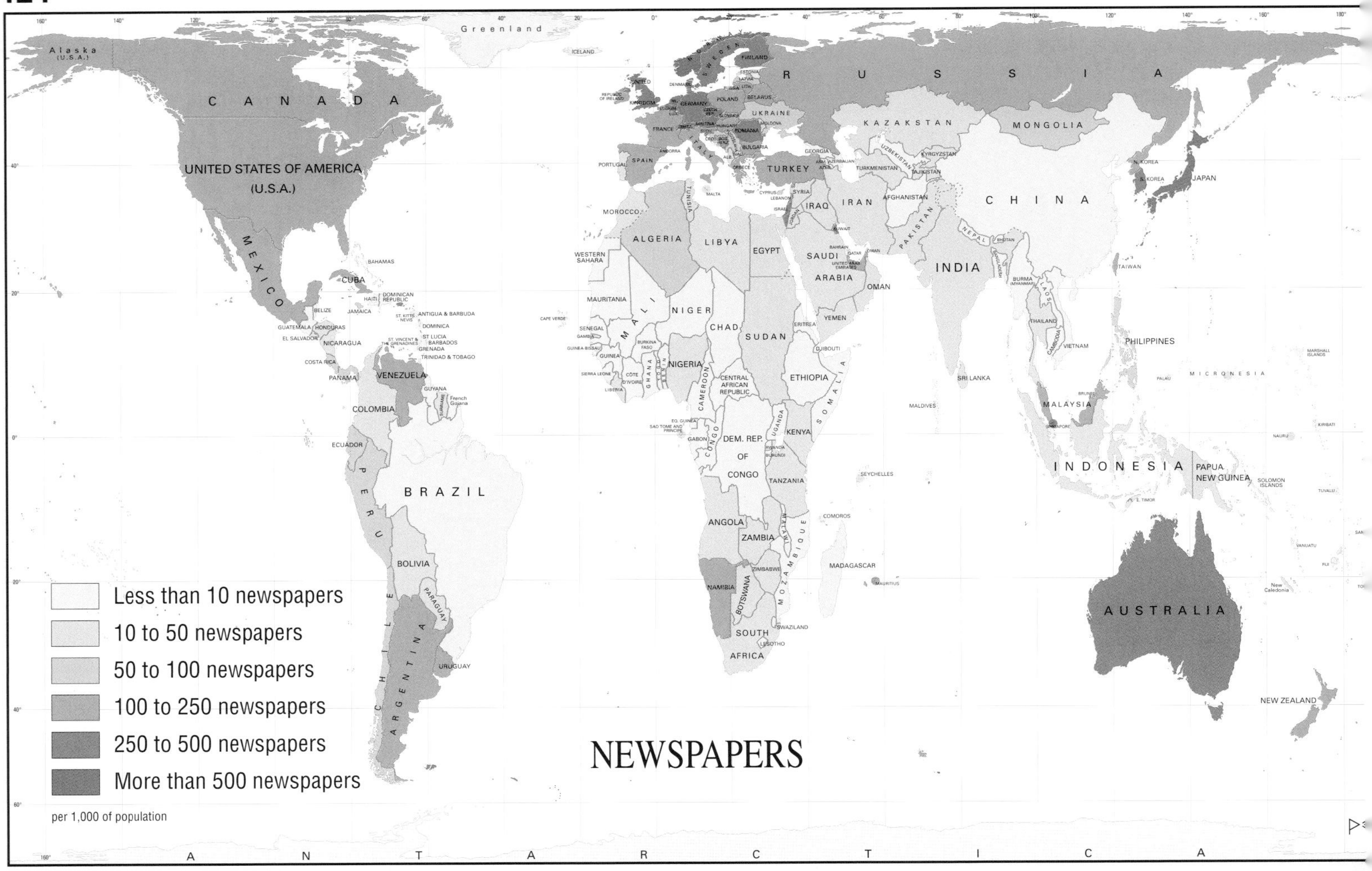

Greenland

NEWSPAPERS

Less than 10 newspapers
10 to 50 newspapers
50 to 100 newspapers
100 to 250 newspapers
250 to 500 newspapers
More than 500 newspapers

per 1,000 of population

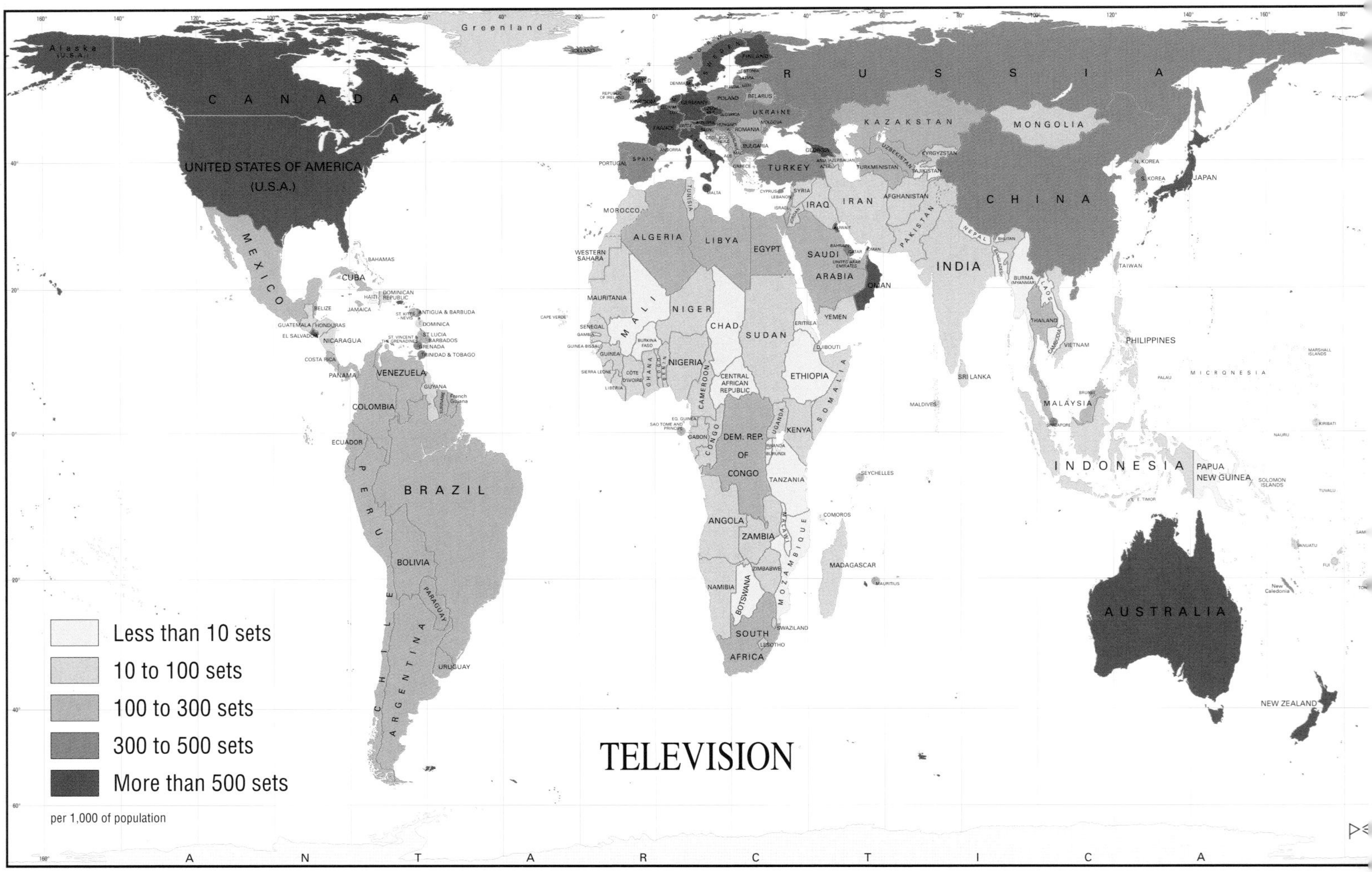

TELEVISION

Less than 10 sets
10 to 100 sets
100 to 300 sets
300 to 500 sets
More than 500 sets

per 1,000 of population

INFOR

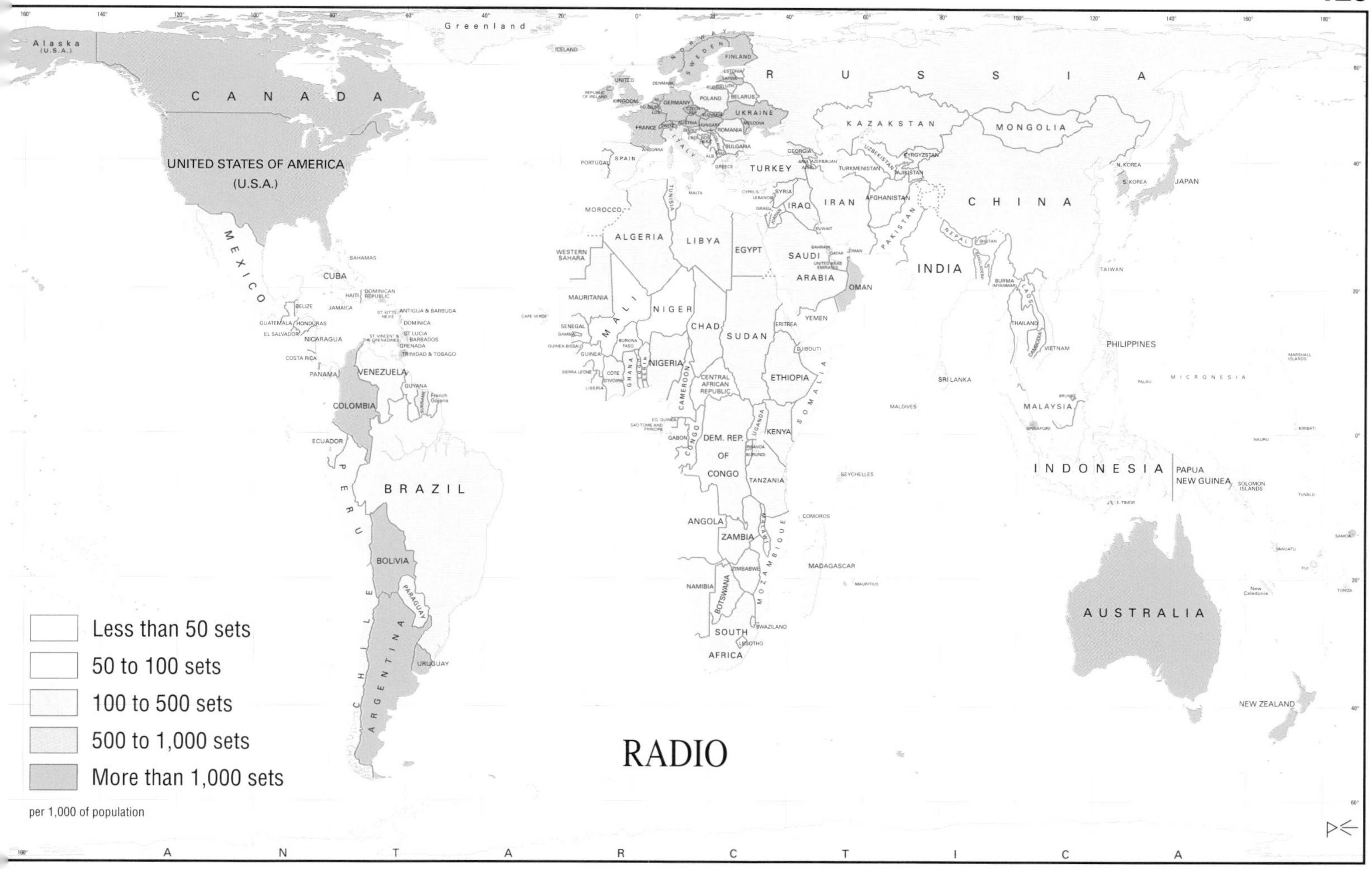

RADIO Map

Greenland
ICELAND
Alaska (U.S.A.)
C A N A D A
UNITED STATES OF AMERICA (U.S.A.)
MEXICO
CUBA
BAHAMAS
BELIZE
HAITI
DOMINICAN REPUBLIC
JAMAICA
GUATEMALA / HONDURAS
EL SALVADOR
NICARAGUA
COSTA RICA
PANAMA
ANTIGUA & BARBUDA
ST KITTS & NEVIS
DOMINICA
ST LUCIA
BARBADOS
GRENADA
ST VINCENT & THE GRENADINES
TRINIDAD & TOBAGO
VENEZUELA
GUYANA
French Guiana
COLOMBIA
ECUADOR
PERU
BRAZIL
BOLIVIA
PARAGUAY
CHILE
ARGENTINA
URUGUAY

SWEDEN
FINLAND
UNITED KINGDOM
IRELAND
GERMANY
POLAND
BELARUS
FRANCE
UKRAINE
RUSSIA
KAZAKSTAN
MONGOLIA
PORTUGAL
SPAIN
ITALY
GREECE
TURKEY
GEORGIA
UZBEKISTAN
KYRGYZSTAN
TURKMENISTAN
N. KOREA
S. KOREA
JAPAN
MOROCCO
ALGERIA
LIBYA
EGYPT
SYRIA
IRAQ
IRAN
AFGHANISTAN
PAKISTAN
CHINA
NEPAL
INDIA
TAIWAN
WESTERN SAHARA
MAURITANIA
MALI
NIGER
CHAD
SUDAN
SAUDI ARABIA
OMAN
YEMEN
ERITREA
BURMA (MYANMAR)
THAILAND
VIETNAM
PHILIPPINES
CAPE VERDE
SENEGAL
GAMBIA
GUINEA-BISSAU
GUINEA
SIERRA LEONE
LIBERIA
COTE
GHANA
NIGERIA
CAMEROON
CENTRAL AFRICAN REPUBLIC
ETHIOPIA
SOMALIA
SRI LANKA
MALDIVES
MALAYSIA
SINGAPORE
BRUNEI
PALAU
MICRONESIA
MARSHALL ISLANDS
SAO TOME AND PRINCIPE
EQ. GUINEA
GABON
CONGO
DEM. REP. OF CONGO
KENYA
TANZANIA
SEYCHELLES
INDONESIA
PAPUA NEW GUINEA
SOLOMON ISLANDS
NAURU
KIRIBATI
TUVALU
ANGOLA
ZAMBIA
MOZAMBIQUE
MALAWI
COMOROS
NAMIBIA
BOTSWANA
ZIMBABWE
MADAGASCAR
MAURITIUS
SOUTH AFRICA
SWAZILAND
LESOTHO
AUSTRALIA
NEW Caledonia
VANUATU
FIJI
SAMOA
TONGA
NEW ZEALAND

A N T A R C T I C A

Less than 50 sets
50 to 100 sets
100 to 500 sets
500 to 1,000 sets
More than 1,000 sets

per 1,000 of population

RADIO

BOOKS Map

Greenland
ICELAND
Alaska (U.S.A.)
C A N A D A
UNITED STATES OF AMERICA (U.S.A.)
MEXICO
CUBA
BAHAMAS
BELIZE
HAITI
DOMINICAN REPUBLIC
JAMAICA
GUATEMALA / HONDURAS
EL SALVADOR
NICARAGUA
COSTA RICA
PANAMA
ANTIGUA & BARBUDA
ST KITTS & NEVIS
DOMINICA
ST LUCIA
BARBADOS
GRENADA
ST VINCENT & THE GRENADINES
TRINIDAD & TOBAGO
VENEZUELA
GUYANA
French Guiana
COLOMBIA
ECUADOR
PERU
BRAZIL
BOLIVIA
PARAGUAY
CHILE
ARGENTINA
URUGUAY

SWEDEN
FINLAND
UNITED KINGDOM
IRELAND
DENMARK
GERMANY
POLAND
BELARUS
FRANCE
UKRAINE
RUSSIA
KAZAKSTAN
MONGOLIA
PORTUGAL
SPAIN
ITALY
BULGARIA
GREECE
TURKEY
GEORGIA
UZBEKISTAN
KYRGYZSTAN
TURKMENISTAN
N. KOREA
S. KOREA
JAPAN
MOROCCO
ALGERIA
LIBYA
EGYPT
IRAQ
IRAN
AFGHANISTAN
PAKISTAN
CHINA
NEPAL
INDIA
TAIWAN
WESTERN SAHARA
MAURITANIA
MALI
NIGER
CHAD
SUDAN
SAUDI ARABIA
OMAN
YEMEN
ERITREA
BURMA
THAILAND
VIETNAM
PHILIPPINES
CAPE VERDE
SENEGAL
GAMBIA
GUINEA-BISSAU
GUINEA
SIERRA LEONE
LIBERIA
COTE
GHANA
NIGERIA
CAMEROON
CENTRAL AFRICAN REPUBLIC
ETHIOPIA
SOMALIA
SRI LANKA
MALDIVES
MALAYSIA
PALAU
MICRONESIA
MARSHALL ISLANDS
SAO TOME AND PRINCIPE
EQ. GUINEA
GABON
CONGO
DEM. REP. OF CONGO
KENYA
TANZANIA
SEYCHELLES
INDONESIA
PAPUA NEW GUINEA
SOLOMON ISLANDS
NAURU
KIRIBATI
TUVALU
ANGOLA
ZAMBIA
MOZAMBIQUE
MALAWI
COMOROS
NAMIBIA
BOTSWANA
ZIMBABWE
MADAGASCAR
MAURITIUS
SOUTH AFRICA
SWAZILAND
LESOTHO
AUSTRALIA
New Caledonia
VANUATU
FIJI
SAMOA
TONGA
NEW ZEALAND

A N T A R C T I C A

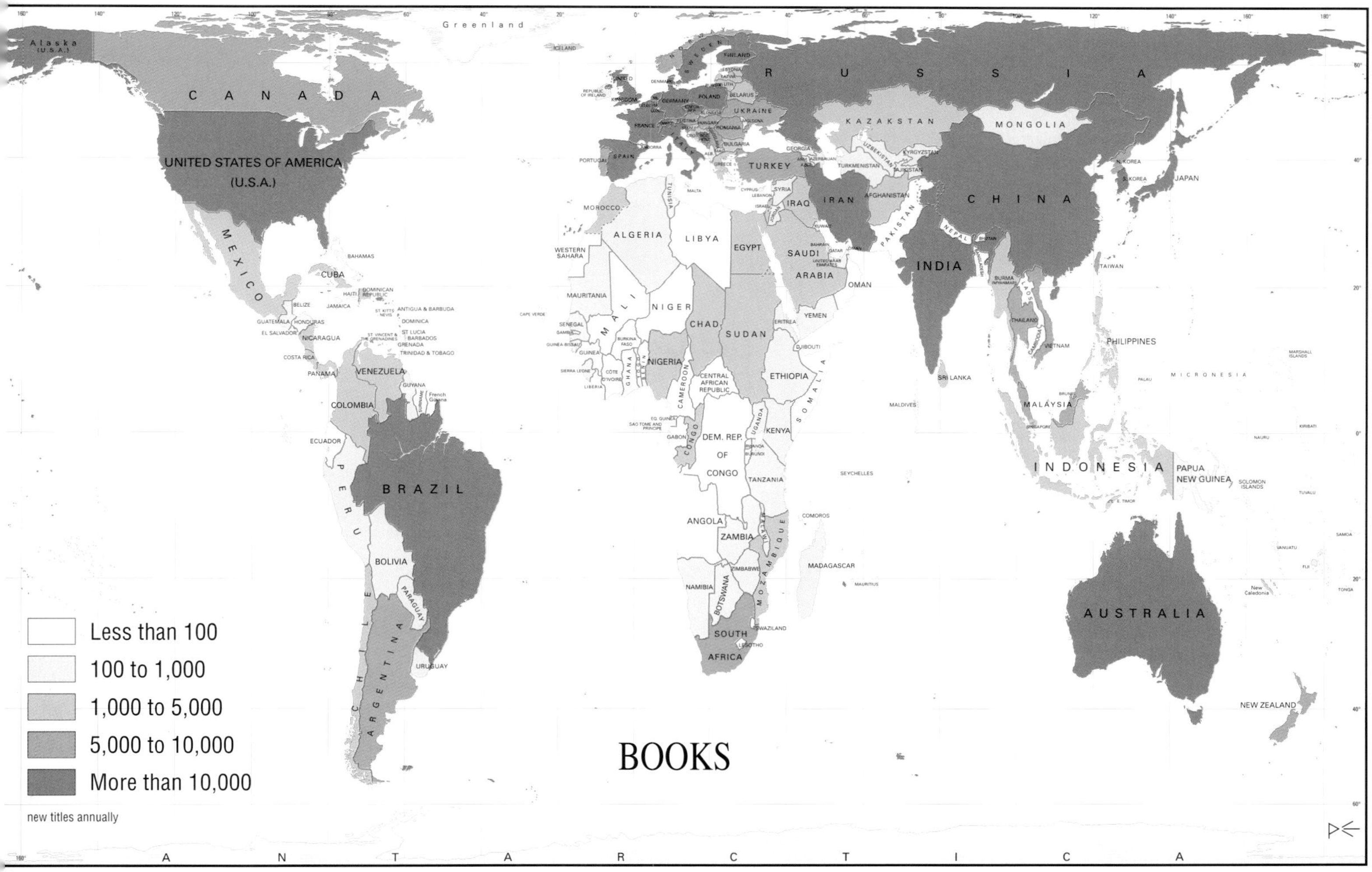

Less than 100
100 to 1,000
1,000 to 5,000
5,000 to 10,000
More than 10,000

new titles annually

BOOKS

ATION

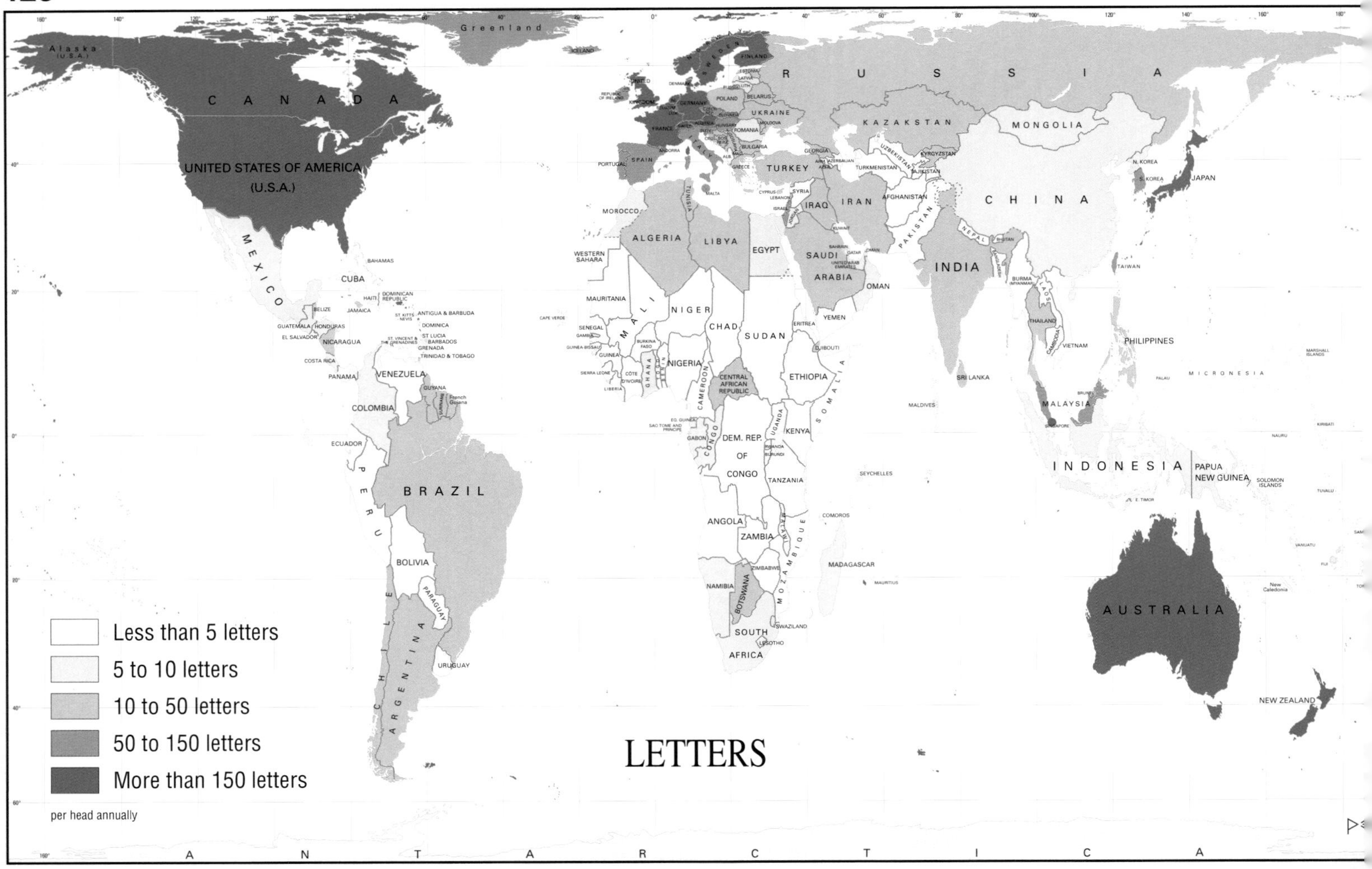
LETTERS
Less than 5 letters
5 to 10 letters
10 to 50 letters
50 to 150 letters
More than 150 letters
per head annually
Alaska
Greenland
CANADA
UNITED STATES OF AMERICA (U.S.A.)
MEXICO
CUBA
VENEZUELA
COLOMBIA
BRAZIL
PERU
BOLIVIA
PARAGUAY
ARGENTINA
CHILE
URUGUAY
RUSSIA
KAZAKSTAN
MONGOLIA
CHINA
JAPAN
UKRAINE
TURKEY
IRAN
IRAQ
SAUDI ARABIA
INDIA
ALGERIA
LIBYA
EGYPT
MOROCCO
MALI
NIGER
CHAD
SUDAN
NIGERIA
ETHIOPIA
DEM. REP. OF CONGO
TANZANIA
ANGOLA
ZAMBIA
MOZAMBIQUE
SOUTH AFRICA
MADAGASCAR
INDONESIA
PAPUA NEW GUINEA
PHILIPPINES
MALAYSIA
AUSTRALIA
NEW ZEALAND
ANTARCTICA

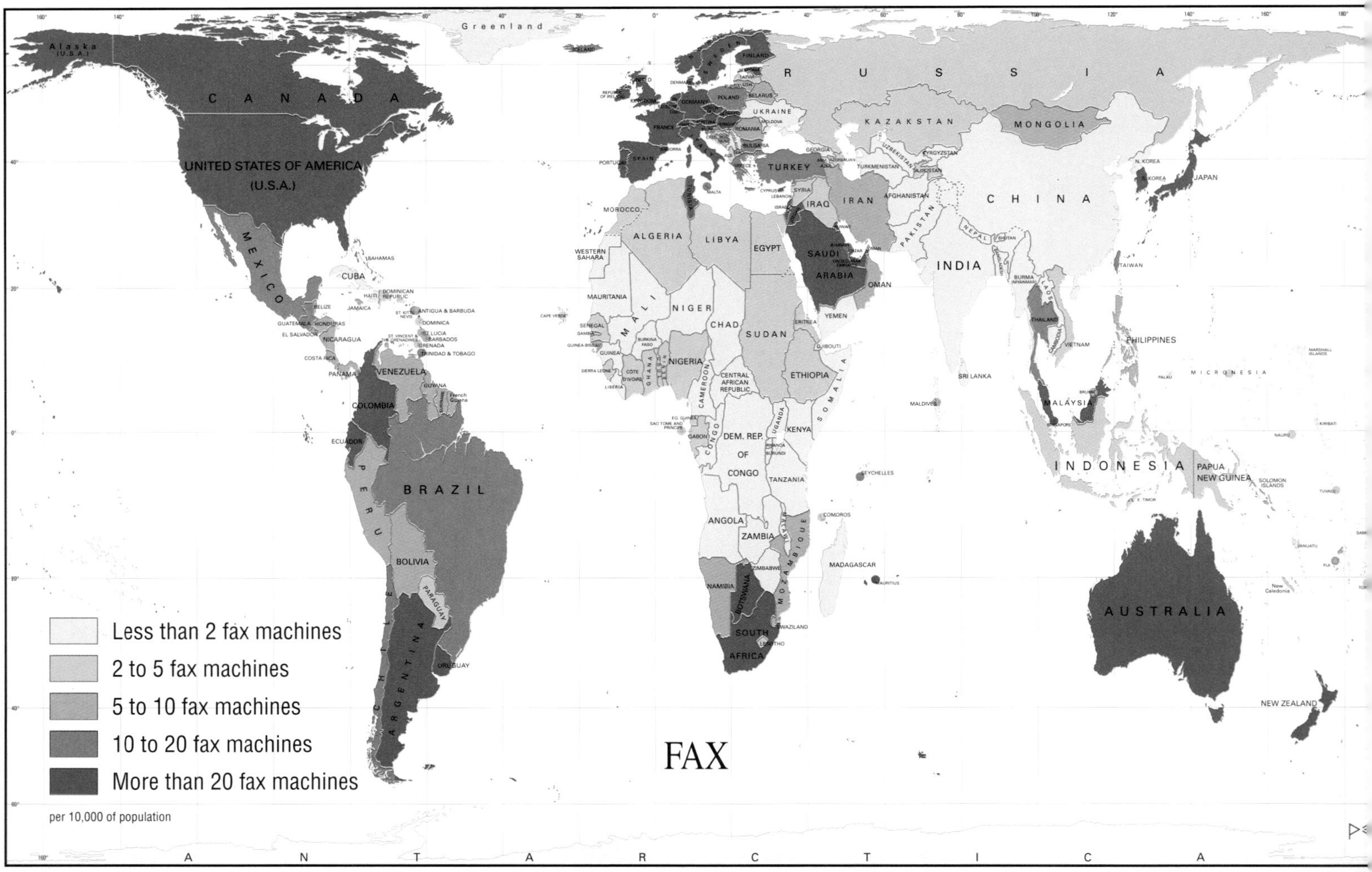
FAX
Less than 2 fax machines
2 to 5 fax machines
5 to 10 fax machines
10 to 20 fax machines
More than 20 fax machines
per 10,000 of population
Alaska
Greenland
CANADA
UNITED STATES OF AMERICA (U.S.A.)
MEXICO
CUBA
VENEZUELA
COLOMBIA
BRAZIL
PERU
BOLIVIA
PARAGUAY
ARGENTINA
CHILE
URUGUAY
RUSSIA
KAZAKSTAN
MONGOLIA
CHINA
JAPAN
UKRAINE
TURKEY
IRAN
IRAQ
SAUDI ARABIA
INDIA
ALGERIA
LIBYA
EGYPT
MOROCCO
MALI
NIGER
CHAD
SUDAN
NIGERIA
ETHIOPIA
DEM. REP. OF CONGO
TANZANIA
ANGOLA
ZAMBIA
MOZAMBIQUE
SOUTH AFRICA
MADAGASCAR
INDONESIA
PAPUA NEW GUINEA
PHILIPPINES
MALAYSIA
AUSTRALIA
NEW ZEALAND
ANTARCTICA

COMMUN

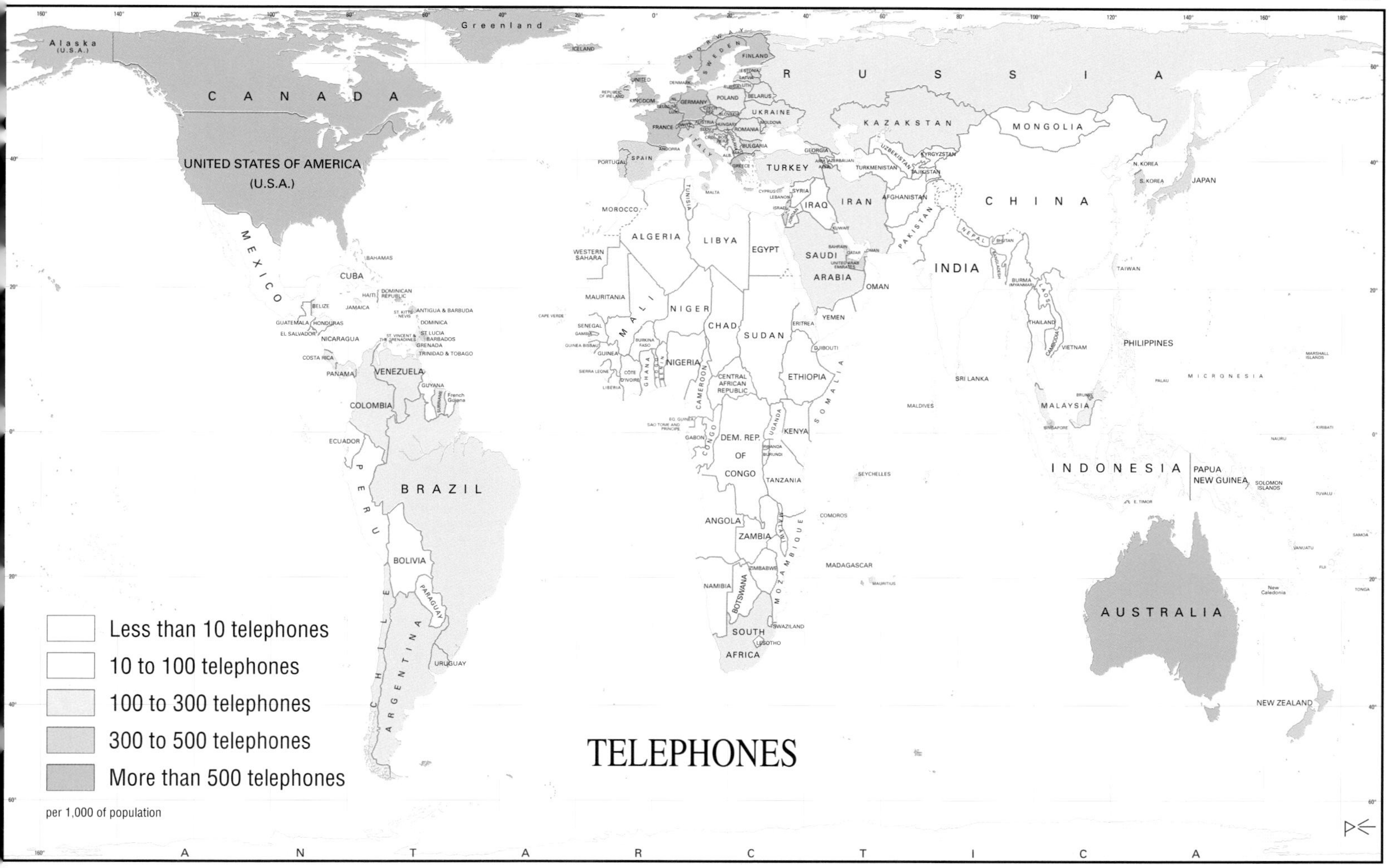

TELEPHONES

- Less than 10 telephones
- 10 to 100 telephones
- 100 to 300 telephones
- 300 to 500 telephones
- More than 500 telephones

per 1,000 of population

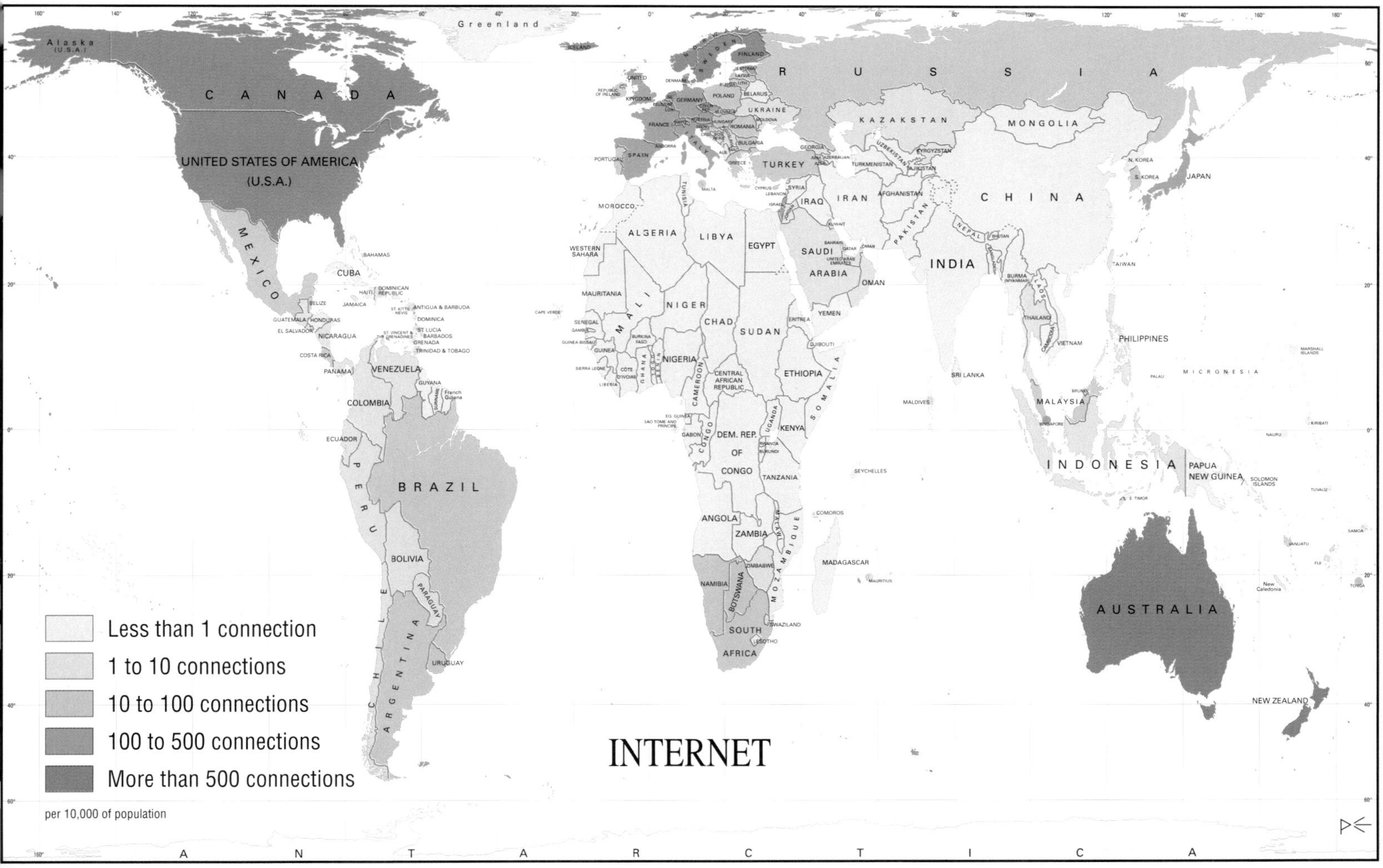

INTERNET

- Less than 1 connection
- 1 to 10 connections
- 10 to 100 connections
- 100 to 500 connections
- More than 500 connections

per 10,000 of population

ICATIONS

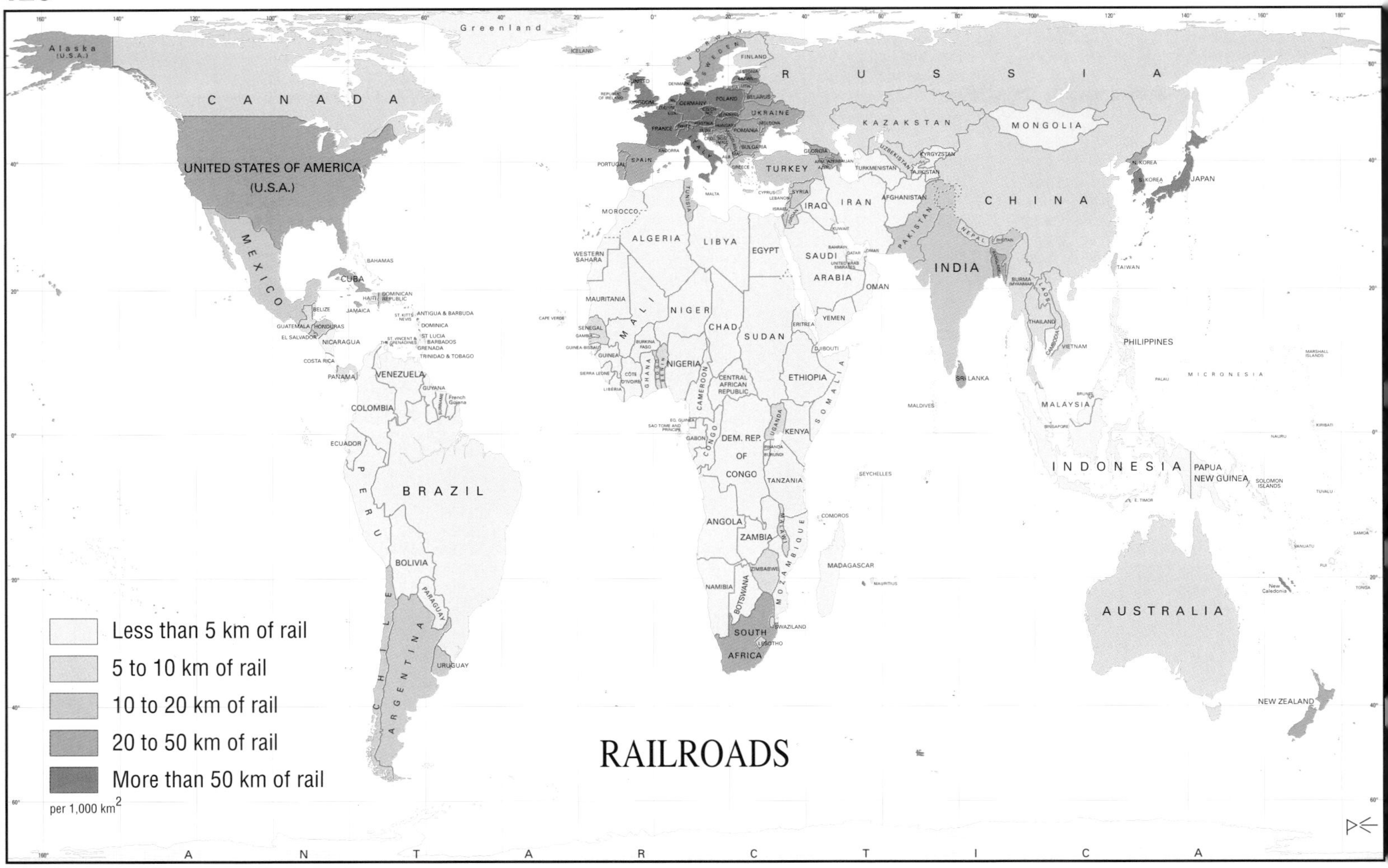
RAILROADS
Less than 5 km of rail
5 to 10 km of rail
10 to 20 km of rail
20 to 50 km of rail
More than 50 km of rail
per 1,000 km²
Greenland
Alaska (U.S.A.)
CANADA
UNITED STATES OF AMERICA (U.S.A.)
MEXICO
CUBA
VENEZUELA
COLOMBIA
ECUADOR
PERU
BRAZIL
BOLIVIA
PARAGUAY
CHILE
ARGENTINA
URUGUAY
RUSSIA
KAZAKSTAN
MONGOLIA
CHINA
INDIA
TURKEY
IRAN
IRAQ
SAUDI ARABIA
EGYPT
LIBYA
ALGERIA
MOROCCO
NIGER
CHAD
SUDAN
ETHIOPIA
NIGERIA
DEM. REP. OF CONGO
KENYA
TANZANIA
ANGOLA
ZAMBIA
NAMIBIA
SOUTH AFRICA
MADAGASCAR
INDONESIA
PAPUA NEW GUINEA
PHILIPPINES
JAPAN
AUSTRALIA
NEW ZEALAND
ANTARCTICA

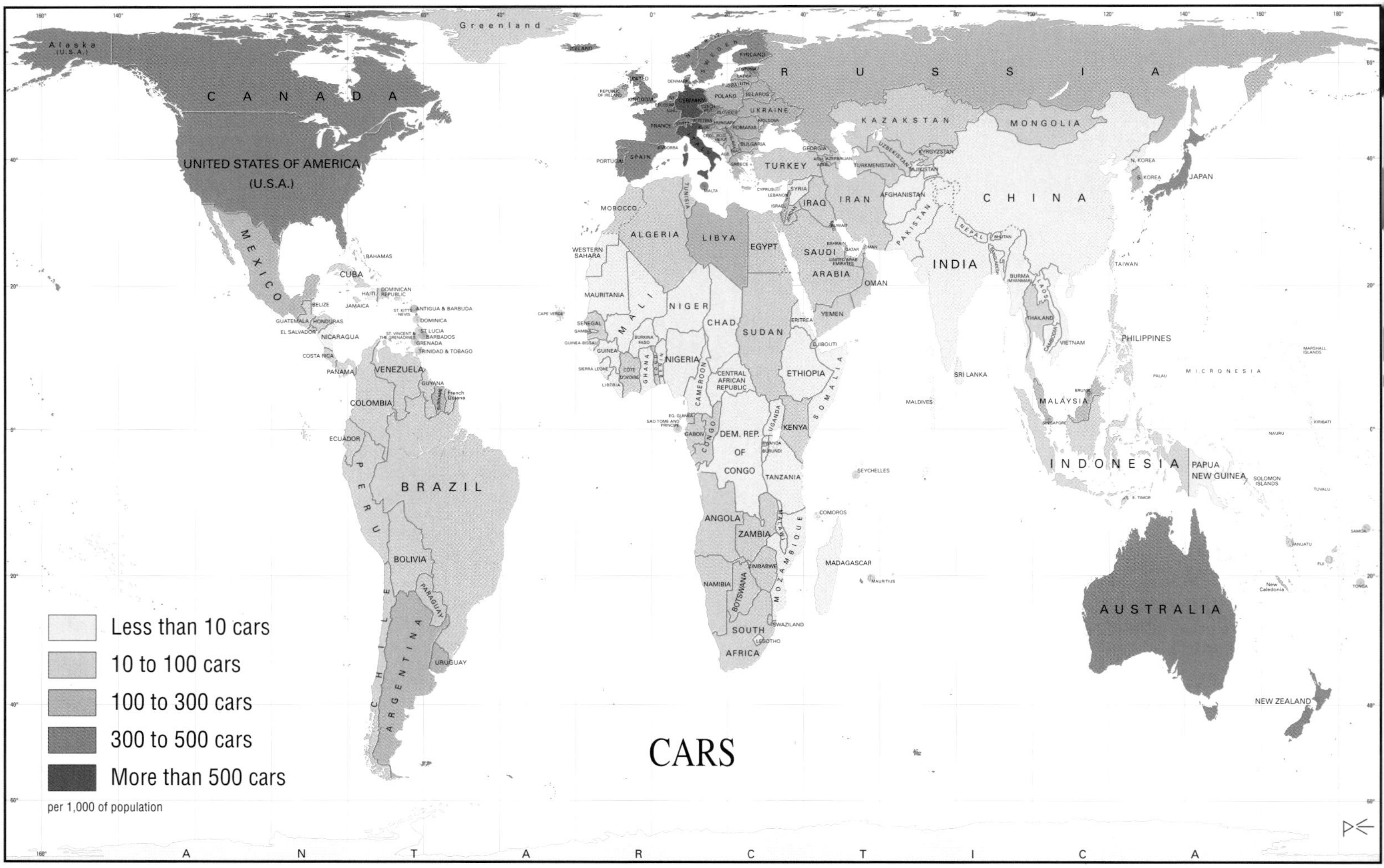
CARS
Less than 10 cars
10 to 100 cars
100 to 300 cars
300 to 500 cars
More than 500 cars
per 1,000 of population
Greenland
Alaska (U.S.A.)
CANADA
UNITED STATES OF AMERICA (U.S.A.)
MEXICO
CUBA
VENEZUELA
COLOMBIA
ECUADOR
PERU
BRAZIL
BOLIVIA
PARAGUAY
CHILE
ARGENTINA
URUGUAY
RUSSIA
KAZAKSTAN
MONGOLIA
CHINA
INDIA
TURKEY
IRAN
IRAQ
SAUDI ARABIA
EGYPT
LIBYA
ALGERIA
MOROCCO
NIGER
CHAD
SUDAN
ETHIOPIA
NIGERIA
DEM. REP. OF CONGO
KENYA
TANZANIA
ANGOLA
ZAMBIA
NAMIBIA
SOUTH AFRICA
MADAGASCAR
INDONESIA
PAPUA NEW GUINEA
PHILIPPINES
JAPAN
AUSTRALIA
NEW ZEALAND
ANTARCTICA

TRAFFIC

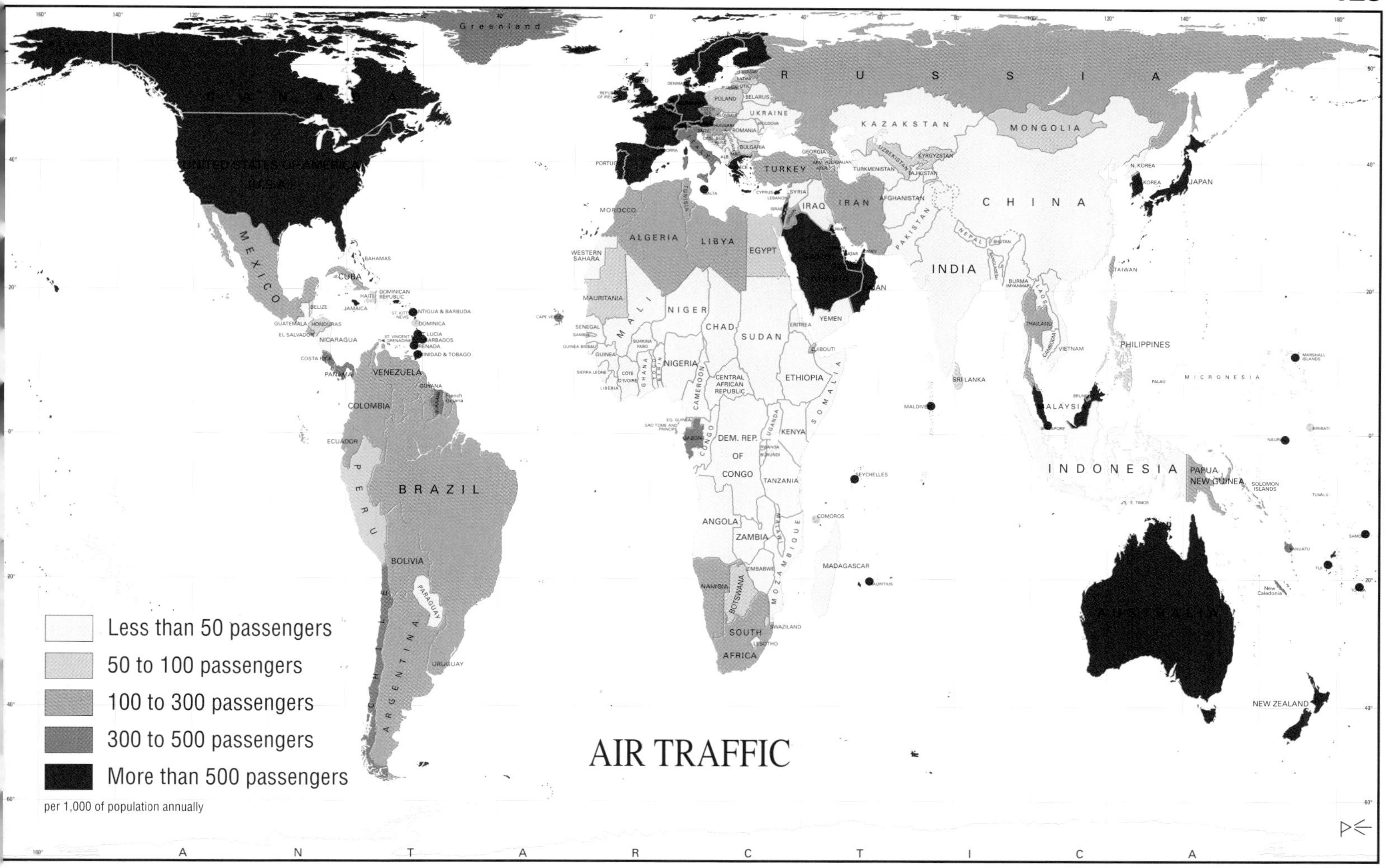

AIR TRAFFIC

	Less than 50 passengers
	50 to 100 passengers
	100 to 300 passengers
	300 to 500 passengers
	More than 500 passengers

per 1,000 of population annually

SHIPPING

	Less than 1 million tonnes
	1 to 10 million tonnes
	10 to 100 million tonnes
	100 to 500 million tonnes
	More than 500 million tonnes

cargo turnover annually

DENSITY

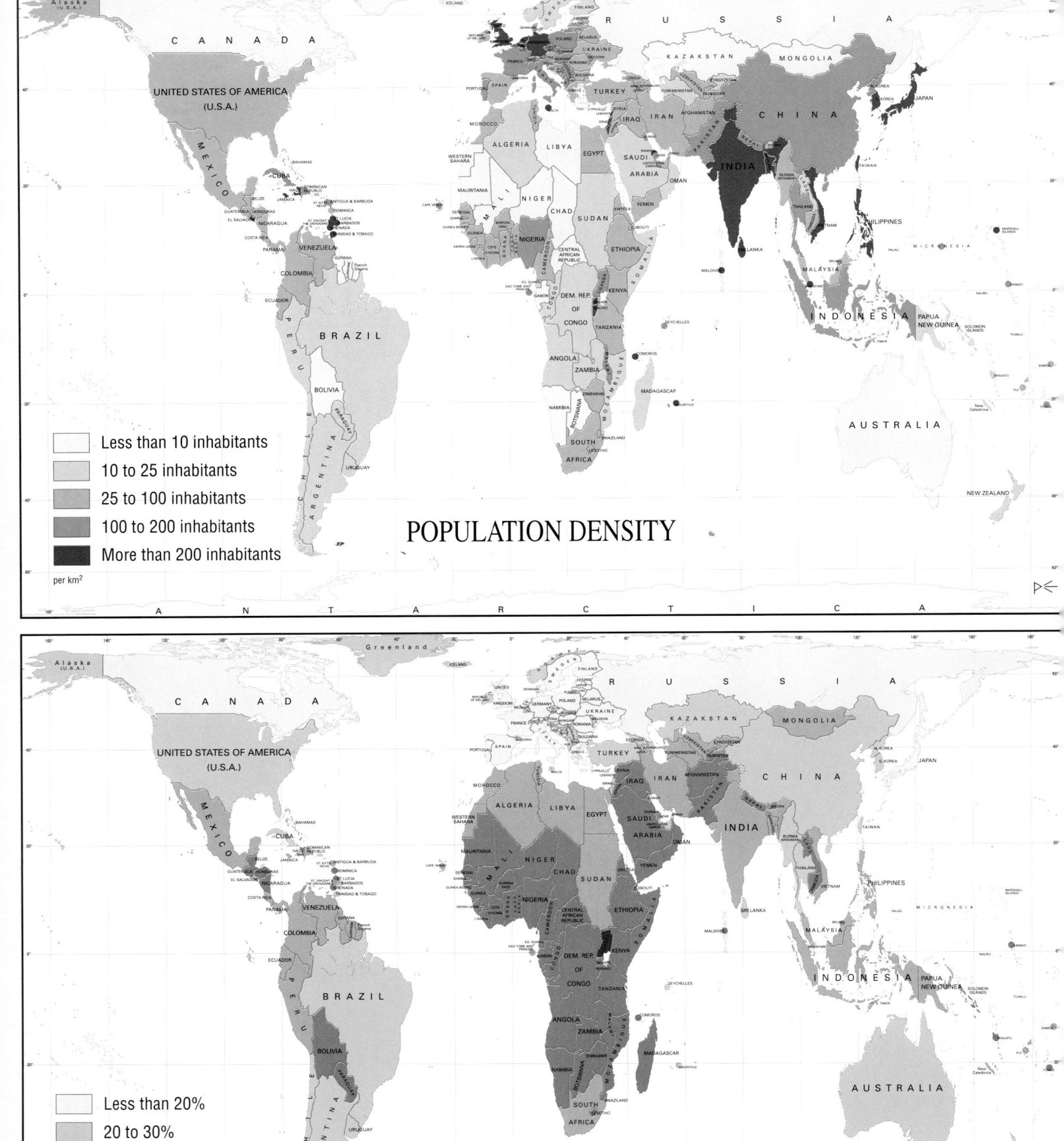

POPULATION DENSITY

Less than 10 inhabitants
10 to 25 inhabitants
25 to 100 inhabitants
100 to 200 inhabitants
More than 200 inhabitants

per km²

ADULTS / CHILDREN RATIO

Less than 20%
20 to 30%
30 to 40%
40 to 50%
More than 50%

of population is less than 15 years old

POPULATION

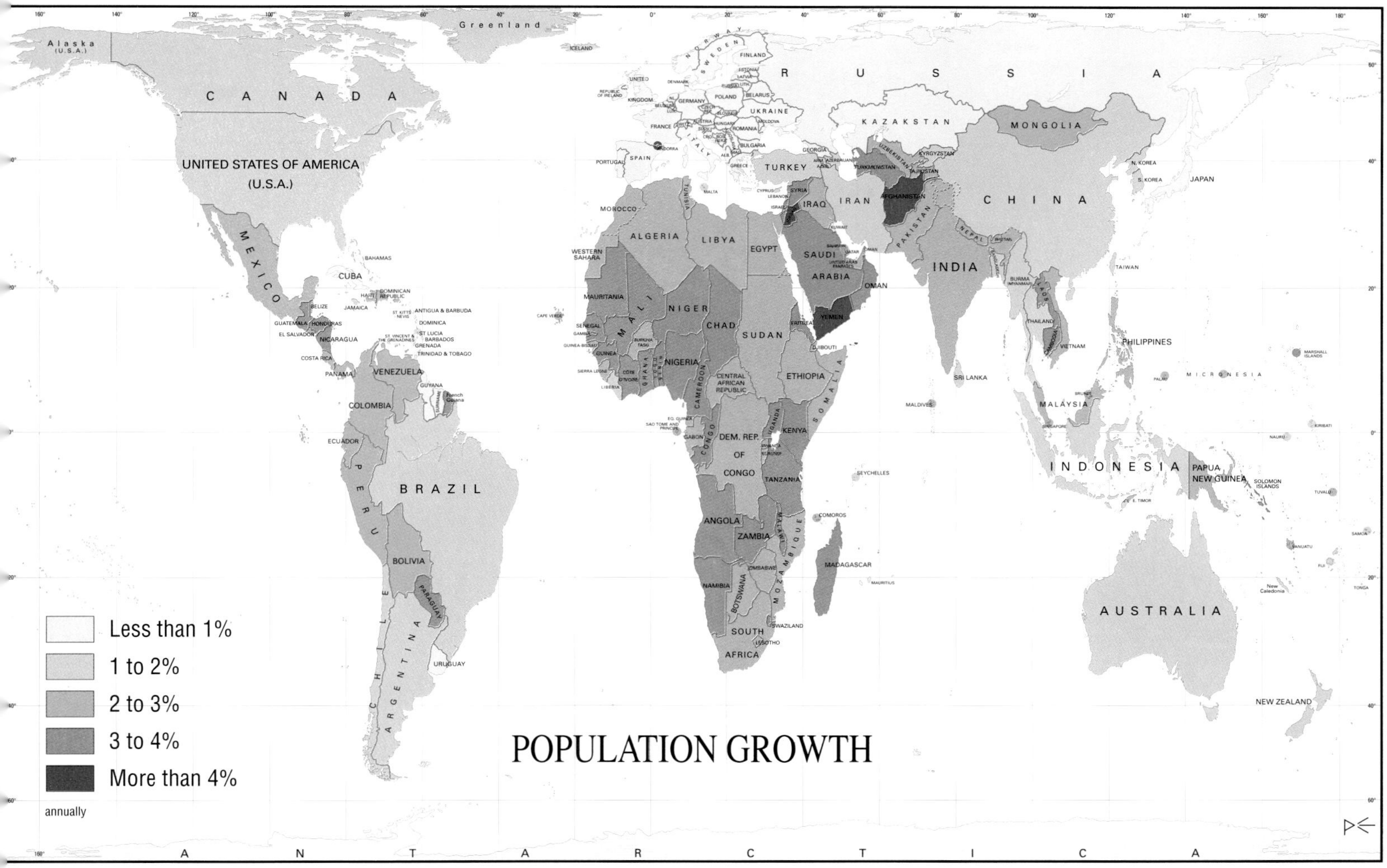
POPULATION GROWTH
Less than 1%
1 to 2%
2 to 3%
3 to 4%
More than 4%
annually
C A N A D A
UNITED STATES OF AMERICA (U.S.A.)
M E X I C O
B R A Z I L
R U S S I A
C H I N A
INDIA
A U S T R A L I A
A N T A R C T I C A

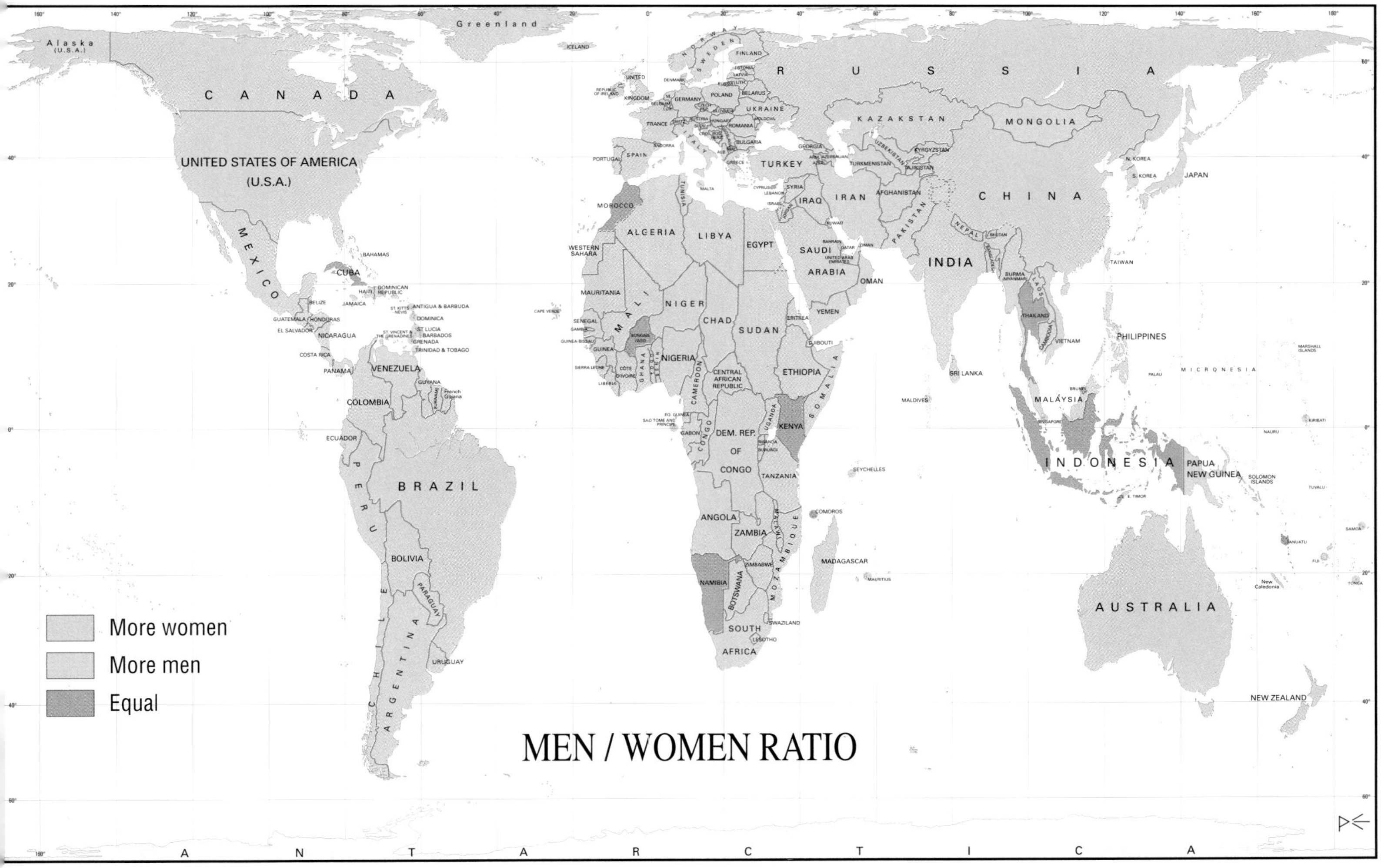
MEN / WOMEN RATIO
More women
More men
Equal
C A N A D A
UNITED STATES OF AMERICA (U.S.A.)
M E X I C O
B R A Z I L
R U S S I A
C H I N A
INDIA
A U S T R A L I A
A N T A R C T I C A

STRUCTURE

Less than 45 years

45 to 55 years

55 to 65 years

65 to 75 years

More than 75 years

LIFE EXP

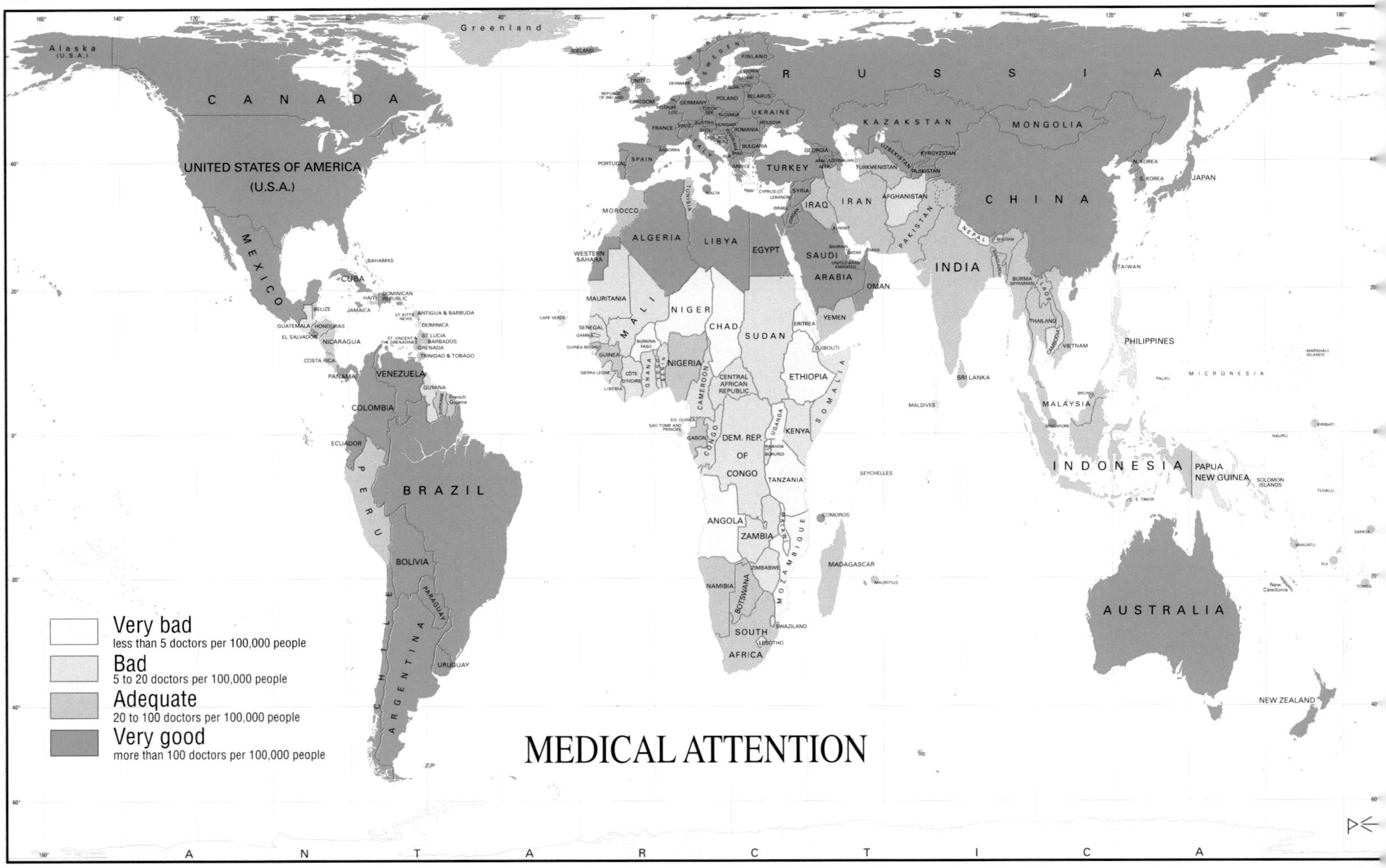

MEDICAL ATTENTION

Very bad
less than 5 doctors per 100,000 people

Bad
5 to 20 doctors per 100,000 people

Adequate
20 to 100 doctors per 100,000 people

Very good
more than 100 doctors per 100,000 people

DRINKING WATER SUPPLIES

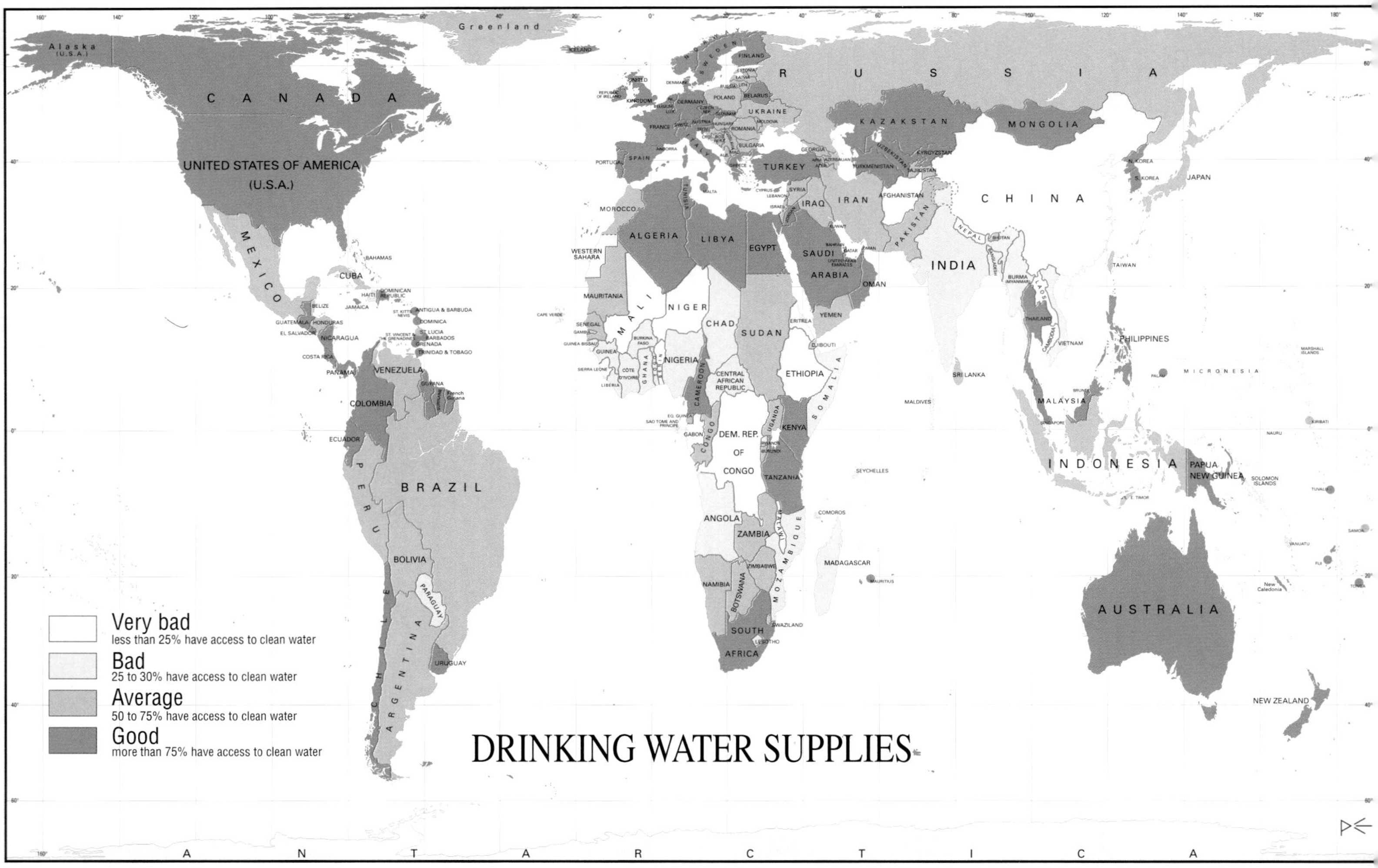

Very bad
less than 25% have access to clean water

Bad
25 to 30% have access to clean water

Average
50 to 75% have access to clean water

Good
more than 75% have access to clean water

HEA

AVAILABLE HOSPITAL BEDS

Far too few
less than 1 bed per 1,000 people

Inadequate
1 to 2 beds per 1,000 people

Almost adequate
2 to 5 beds per 1,000 people

Adequate
more than 5 beds per 1,000 people

INFANT MORTALITY

Low
less than 25 deaths per 1,000 live births

Average
25 to 50 deaths per 1,000 live births

High
50 to 100 deaths per 1,000 live births

Very high
more than 100 deaths per 1,000 live births

LTH

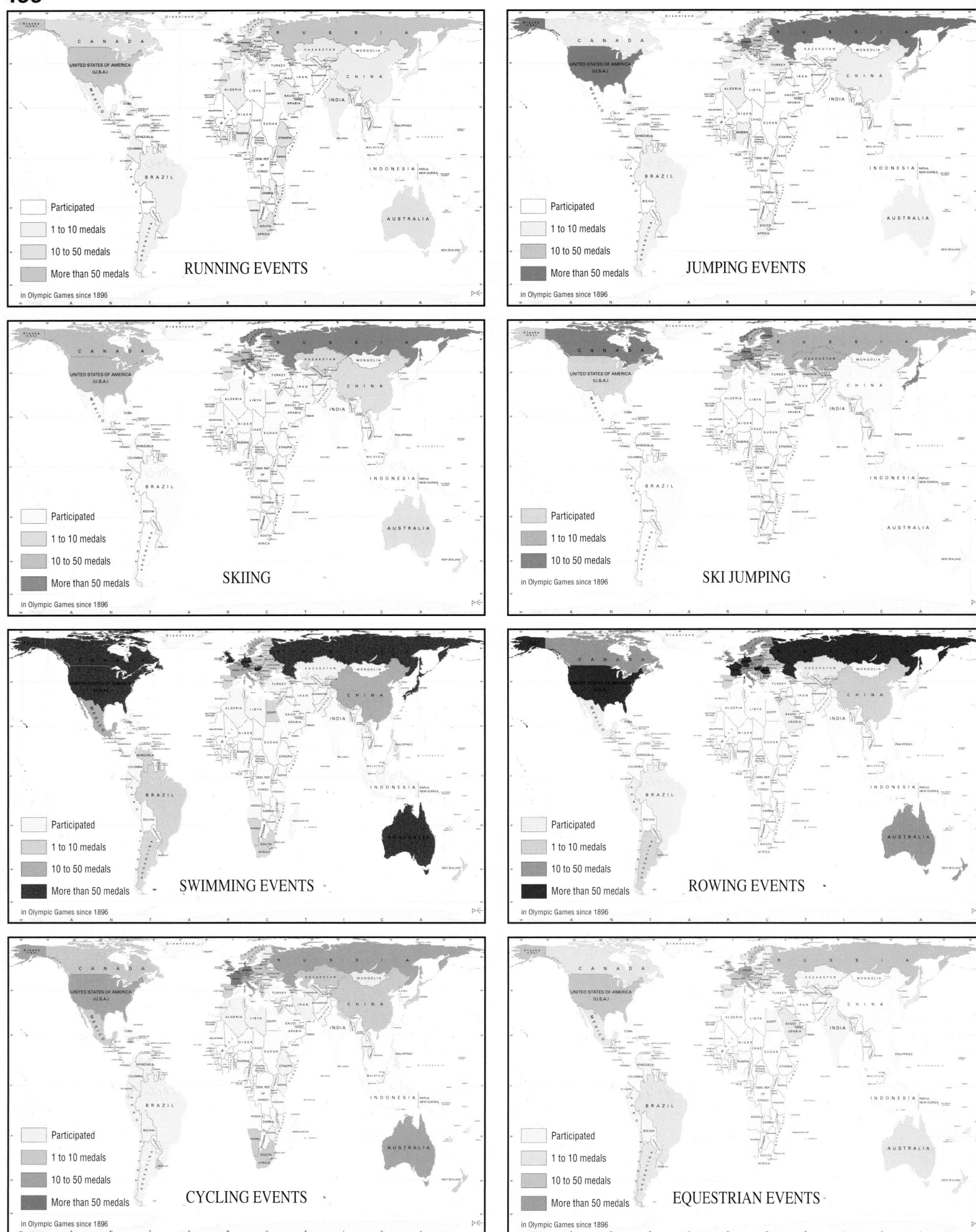

RUNNING EVENTS

Participated
1 to 10 medals
10 to 50 medals
More than 50 medals

in Olympic Games since 1896

JUMPING EVENTS

Participated
1 to 10 medals
10 to 50 medals
More than 50 medals

in Olympic Games since 1896

SKIING

Participated
1 to 10 medals
10 to 50 medals
More than 50 medals

in Olympic Games since 1896

SKI JUMPING

Participated
1 to 10 medals
10 to 50 medals

in Olympic Games since 1896

SWIMMING EVENTS

Participated
1 to 10 medals
10 to 50 medals
More than 50 medals

in Olympic Games since 1896

ROWING EVENTS

Participated
1 to 10 medals
10 to 50 medals
More than 50 medals

in Olympic Games since 1896

CYCLING EVENTS

Participated
1 to 10 medals
10 to 50 medals
More than 50 medals

in Olympic Games since 1896

EQUESTRIAN EVENTS

Participated
1 to 10 medals
10 to 50 medals
More than 50 medals

in Olympic Games since 1896

SPC

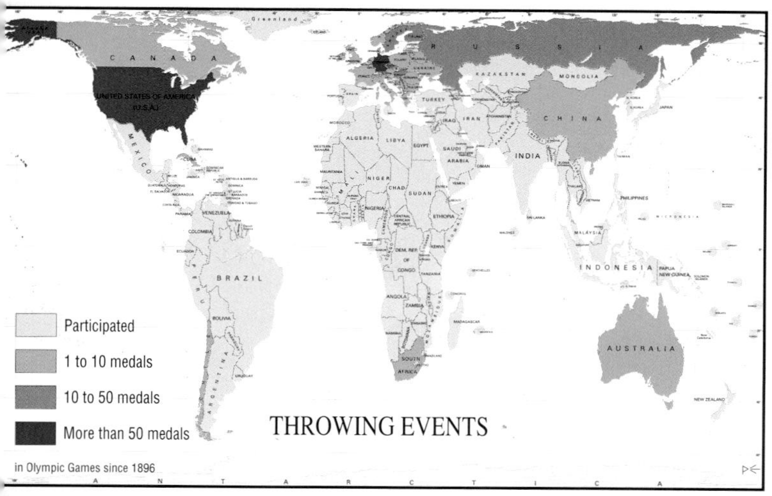

THROWING EVENTS

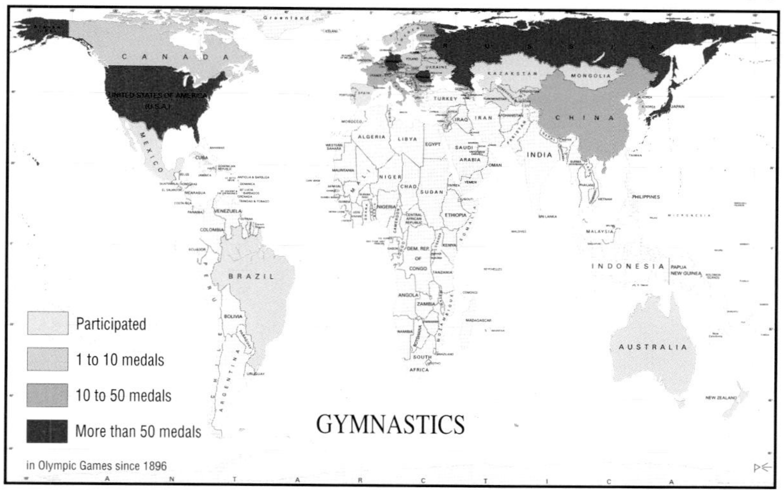

Participated
1 to 10 medals
10 to 50 medals
More than 50 medals

in Olympic Games since 1896

GYMNASTICS

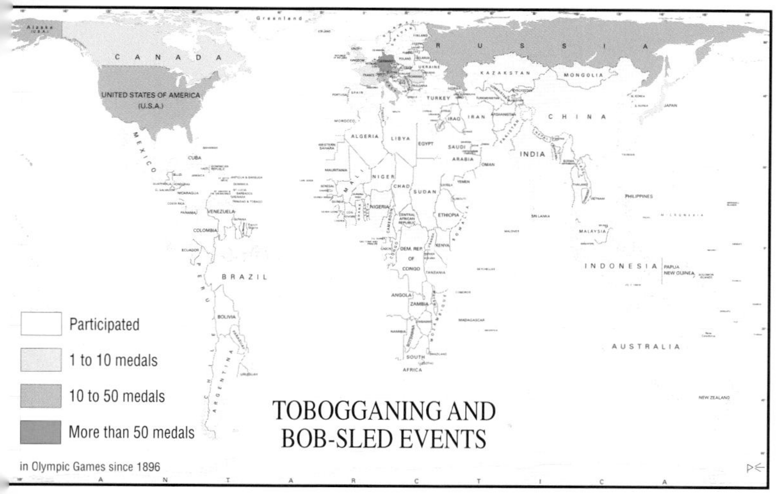

Participated
1 to 10 medals
10 to 50 medals
More than 50 medals

in Olympic Games since 1896

TOBOGGANING AND BOB-SLED EVENTS

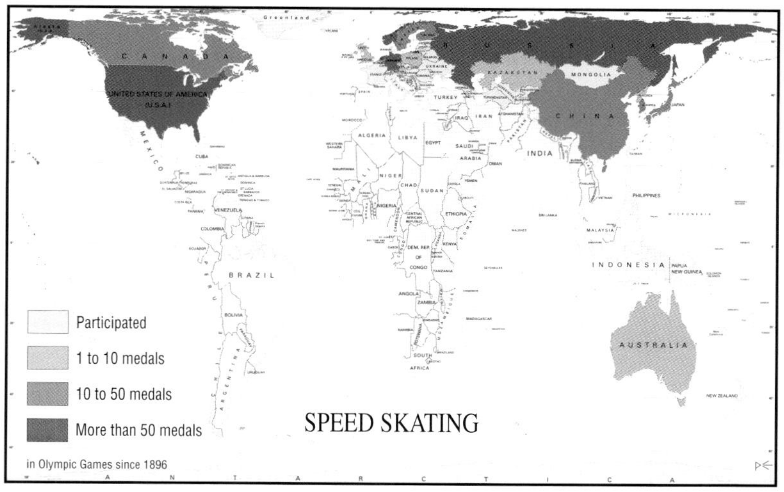

Participated
1 to 10 medals
10 to 50 medals
More than 50 medals

in Olympic Games since 1896

SPEED SKATING

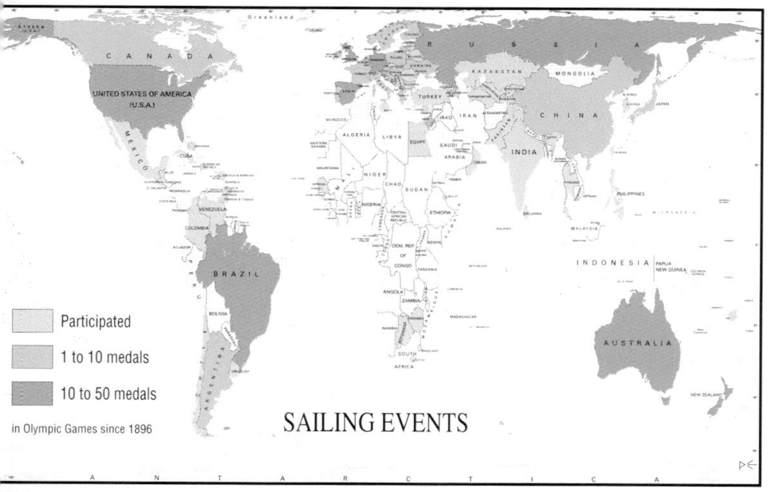

Participated
1 to 10 medals
10 to 50 medals
More than 50 medals

in Olympic Games since 1896

SAILING EVENTS

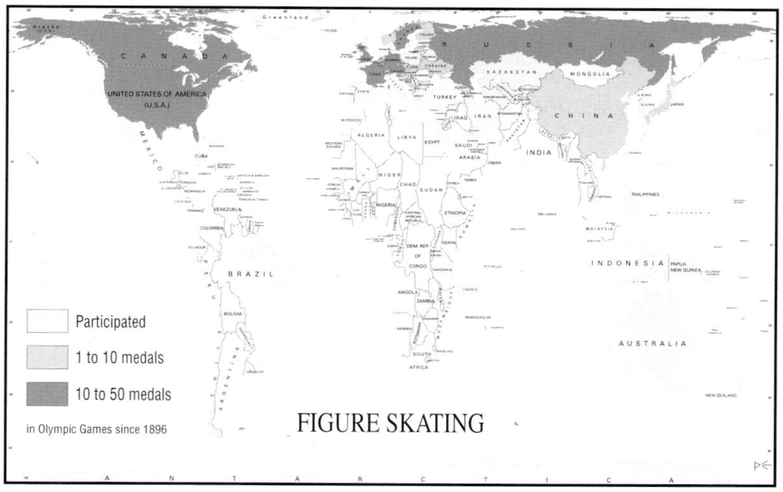

Participated
1 to 10 medals
10 to 50 medals

in Olympic Games since 1896

FIGURE SKATING

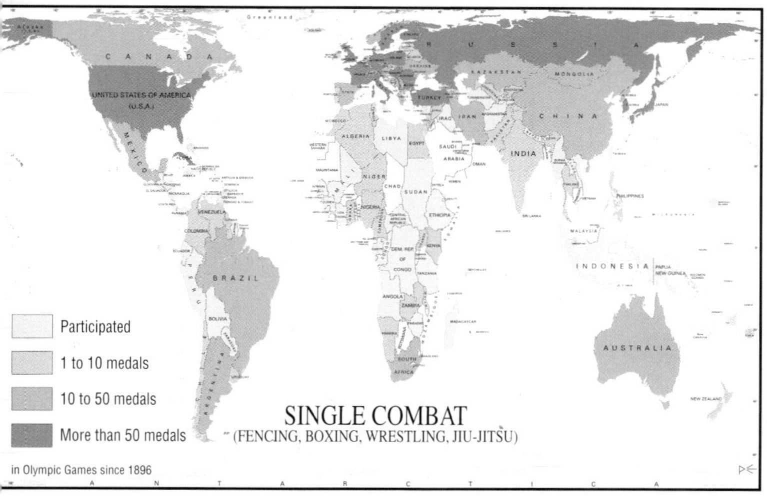

Participated
1 to 10 medals
10 to 50 medals

in Olympic Games since 1896

SINGLE COMBAT
(FENCING, BOXING, WRESTLING, JIU-JITSU)

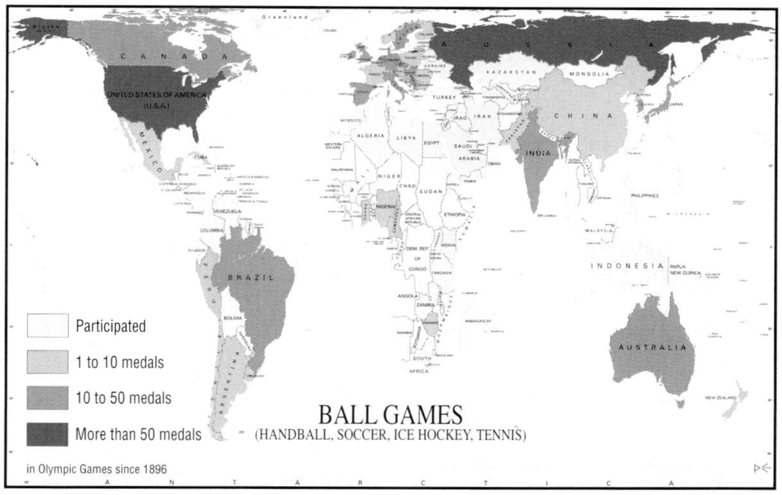

Participated
1 to 10 medals
10 to 50 medals
More than 50 medals

in Olympic Games since 1896

BALL GAMES
(HANDBALL, SOCCER, ICE HOCKEY, TENNIS)

Participated
1 to 10 medals
10 to 50 medals
More than 50 medals

in Olympic Games since 1896

RT

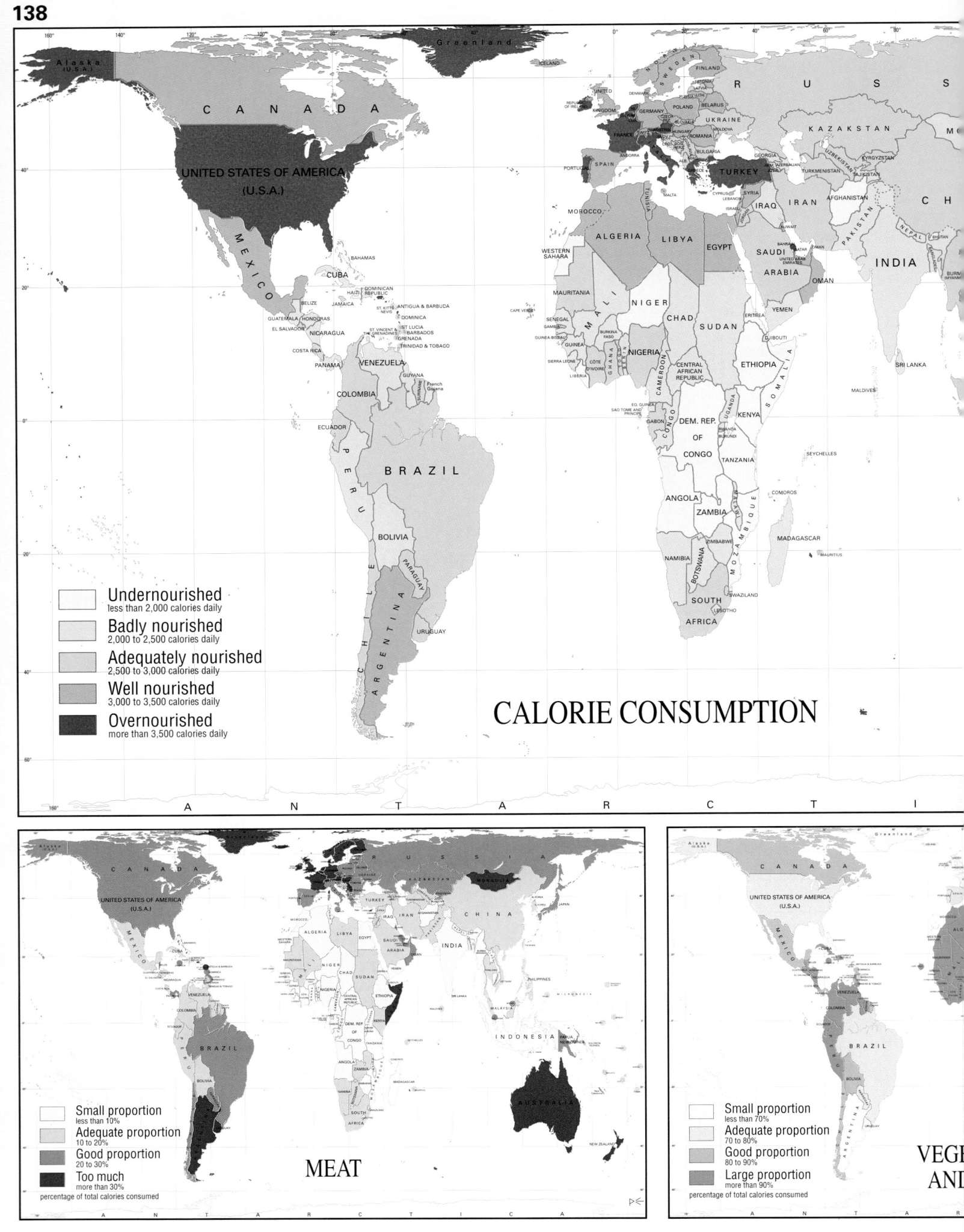

CALORIE CONSUMPTION

Undernourished
less than 2,000 calories daily

Badly nourished
2,000 to 2,500 calories daily

Adequately nourished
2,500 to 3,000 calories daily

Well nourished
3,000 to 3,500 calories daily

Overnourished
more than 3,500 calories daily

MEAT

Small proportion
less than 10%

Adequate proportion
10 to 20%

Good proportion
20 to 30%

Too much
more than 30%
percentage of total calories consumed

VEGE
AND

Small proportion
less than 70%

Adequate proportion
70 to 80%

Good proportion
80 to 90%

Large proportion
more than 90%
percentage of total calories consumed

NUTR

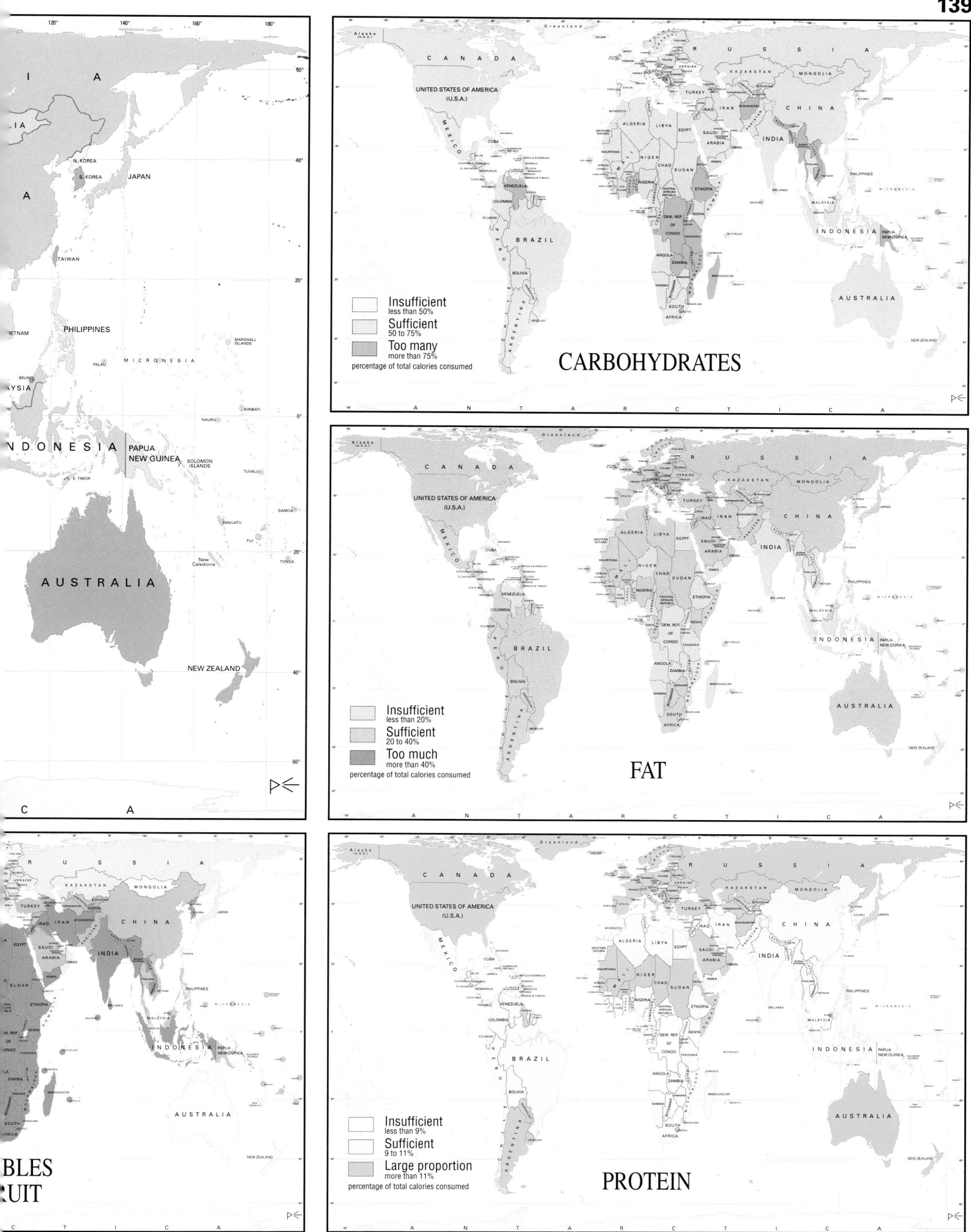

CARBOHYDRATES

Insufficient
less than 50%

Sufficient
50 to 75%

Too many
more than 75%

percentage of total calories consumed

FAT

Insufficient
less than 20%

Sufficient
20 to 40%

Too much
more than 40%

percentage of total calories consumed

PROTEIN

Insufficient
less than 9%

Sufficient
9 to 11%

Large proportion
more than 11%

percentage of total calories consumed

BLES
RUIT

TION

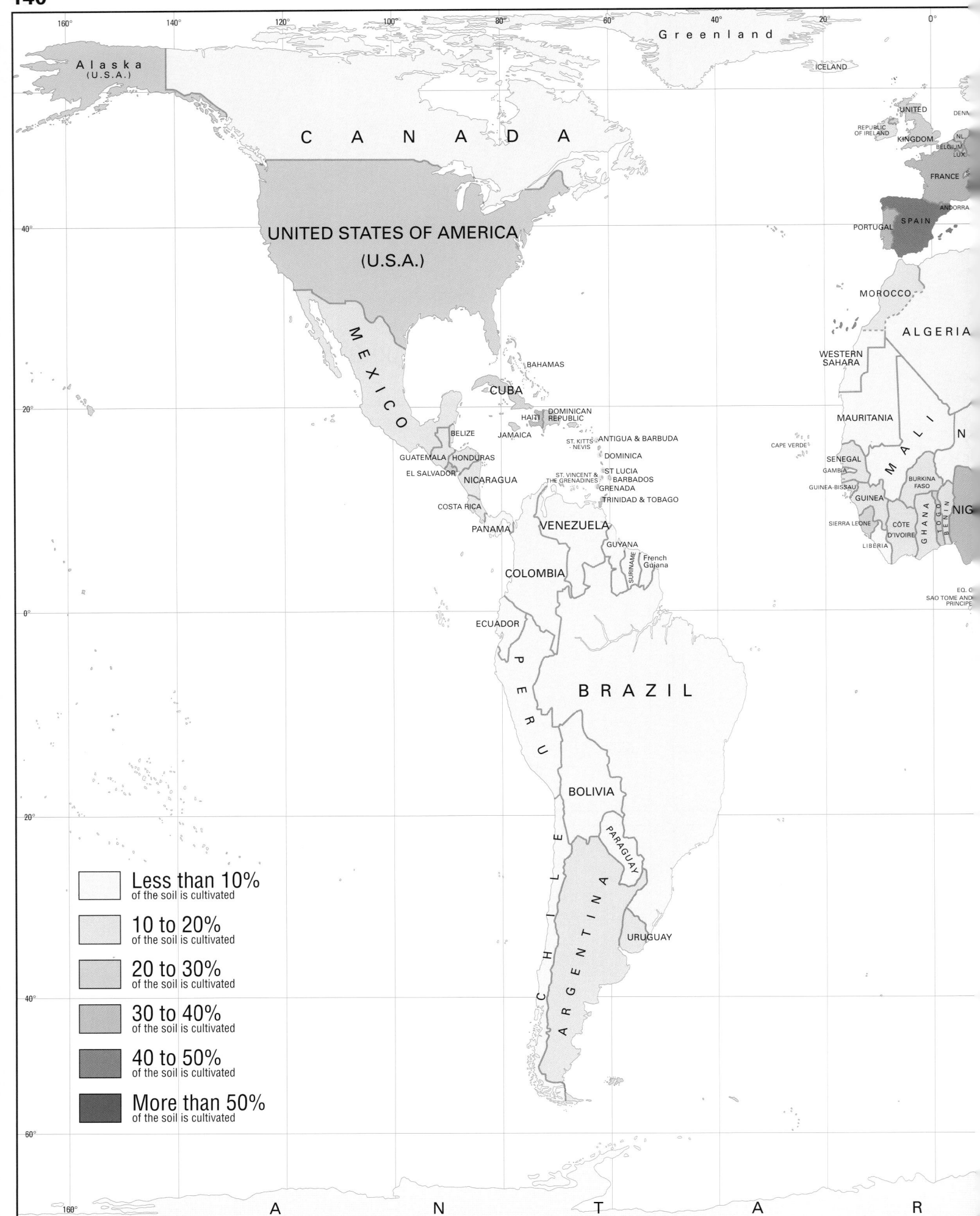

Greenland

Alaska
(U.S.A.)

C A N A D A

ICELAND

UNITED STATES OF AMERICA
(U.S.A.)

REPUBLIC
OF IRELAND

UNITED
KINGDOM

DENM

NL
BELGIUM
LUX

FRANCE

PORTUGAL

SPAIN

ANDORRA

M E X I C O

MOROCCO

ALGERIA

WESTERN
SAHARA

BAHAMAS

CUBA

MAURITANIA

M A L I

N

CAPE VERDE

BELIZE

HAITI

DOMINICAN
REPUBLIC

JAMAICA

GUATEMALA   HONDURAS

EL SALVADOR

NICARAGUA

COSTA RICA

PANAMA

ST. KITTS-
NEVIS

ANTIGUA & BARBUDA

DOMINICA

ST LUCIA

ST. VINCENT &
THE GRENADINES

BARBADOS

GRENADA

TRINIDAD & TOBAGO

VENEZUELA

GUYANA

SURINAME

French
Guiana

COLOMBIA

ECUADOR

P E R U

B R A Z I L

BOLIVIA

P
A
R
A
G
U
A
Y

C
H
I
L
E

A
R
G
E
N
T
I
N
A

URUGUAY

SENEGAL

GAMBIA

GUINEA-BISSAU

SIERRA LEONE

LIBERIA

GUINEA

BURKINA
FASO

CÔTE
D'IVOIRE

GHANA

TOGO

BENIN

NIG

EQ. G

SAO TOME AND
PRINCIPE

	Less than 10% of the soil is cultivated
	10 to 20% of the soil is cultivated
	20 to 30% of the soil is cultivated
	30 to 40% of the soil is cultivated
	40 to 50% of the soil is cultivated
	More than 50% of the soil is cultivated

A N T A R

SOIL CUL

TIVATION

160° 140° 120° 100° 80° 60° 40° 20° 0°

Greenland

ICELAND

Alaska
(U.S.A.)

UNITED

DENM

C A N A D A

REPUBLIC
OF IRELAND

KINGDOM

NL
BELGIUM
LUX.

40°

UNITED STATES OF AMERICA
(U.S.A.)

FRANCE

ANDORRA

PORTUGAL

SPAIN

MOROCCO

M
E
X
I
C
O

BAHAMAS

ALGERIA

WESTERN
SAHARA

CUBA

20°

HAITI

DOMINICAN
REPUBLIC

MAURITANIA

M
A
L
I

N

BELIZE

JAMAICA

CAPE VERDE

GUATEMALA HONDURAS

ST. KITTS-
NEVIS

ANTIGUA & BARBUDA

SENEGAL

BURKINA
FASO

EL SALVADOR

DOMINICA

GAMBIA

NICARAGUA

ST. LUCIA
BARBADOS

GUINEA-BISSAU

GUINEA

C
Ô
T
E

G
H
A
N
A

B
E
N
I
N

NIG

COSTA RICA

ST. VINCENT &
THE GRENADINES

GRENADA

SIERRA LEONE

D'IVOIRE

PANAMA

TRINIDAD & TOBAGO

LIBERIA

VENEZUELA

EQ. G

COLOMBIA

GUYANA

SAO TOME AND
PRINCIPE

SURINAME

French
Guiana

0°

ECUADOR

P
E
R
U

B R A Z I L

BOLIVIA

20°

P
A
R
A
G
U
A
Y

C
H
I
L
E

A
R
G
E
N
T
I
N
A

Less than 100 tonnes
per km² of cultivated land

URUGUAY

100 to 200 tonnes
per km² of cultivated land

200 to 300 tonnes
per km² of cultivated land

40°

300 to 400 tonnes
per km² of cultivated land

More than 400 tonnes
per km² of cultivated land

60°

160° A N T A R

CROP

20° 40° 60° 80° 100° 120° 140° 160° 180°

50°

R U S S I A

SWEDEN FINLAND
ESTONIA
LATVIA
RUSSIA LITH.
POLAND BELARUS
UKRAINE
SLOVAKIA MOLDOVA
HUNGARY ROMANIA
BOS. HERZ.
YUGOSLAV. BULGARIA
ALB. MAC.
GREECE

KAZAKSTAN

MONGOLIA

40°

TURKEY
GEORGIA
ARM. AZERBAIJAN
AZER.
CYPRUS
LEBANON SYRIA
ISRAEL JORDAN IRAQ
IRAN
TURKMENISTAN
UZBEKISTAN KYRGYZSTAN
TAJIKISTAN
AFGHANISTAN

N. KOREA
S. KOREA
JAPAN

C H I N A

LIBYA
EGYPT
SAUDI
ARABIA
KUWAIT
BAHRAIN
QATAR
OMAN
UNITED ARAB
EMIRATES
YEMEN
OMAN

PAKISTAN
NEPAL BHUTAN
BANGLADESH
I N D I A
BURMA
(MYANMAR)

TAIWAN

20°

CHAD
SUDAN
ERITREA
DJIBOUTI

LAOS
THAILAND
CAMBODIA VIETNAM

PHILIPPINES

MARSHALL
ISLANDS

CENTRAL
AFRICAN
REPUBLIC
ETHIOPIA
SOMALIA

SRI LANKA

PALAU

M I C R O N E S I A

UGANDA
CONGO
DEM. REP.
OF
CONGO
RWANDA
BURUNDI
KENYA
TANZANIA

MALDIVES

SEYCHELLES

MALAYSIA

SINGAPORE
BRUNEI

I N D O N E S I A
PAPUA
NEW GUINEA

SOLOMON
ISLANDS

KIRIBATI
NAURU

0°

TUVALU

ANGOLA
ZAMBIA
MALAWI
MOZAMBIQUE
ZIMBABWE
COMOROS

MADAGASCAR

E. TIMOR

SAMOA
VANUATU

FIJI

NAMIBIA
BOTSWANA
SWAZILAND
MAURITIUS

20°

New
Caledonia

TONGA

A U S T R A L I A

SOUTH
AFRICA
LESOTHO

NEW ZEALAND

40°

60°

C T I C A

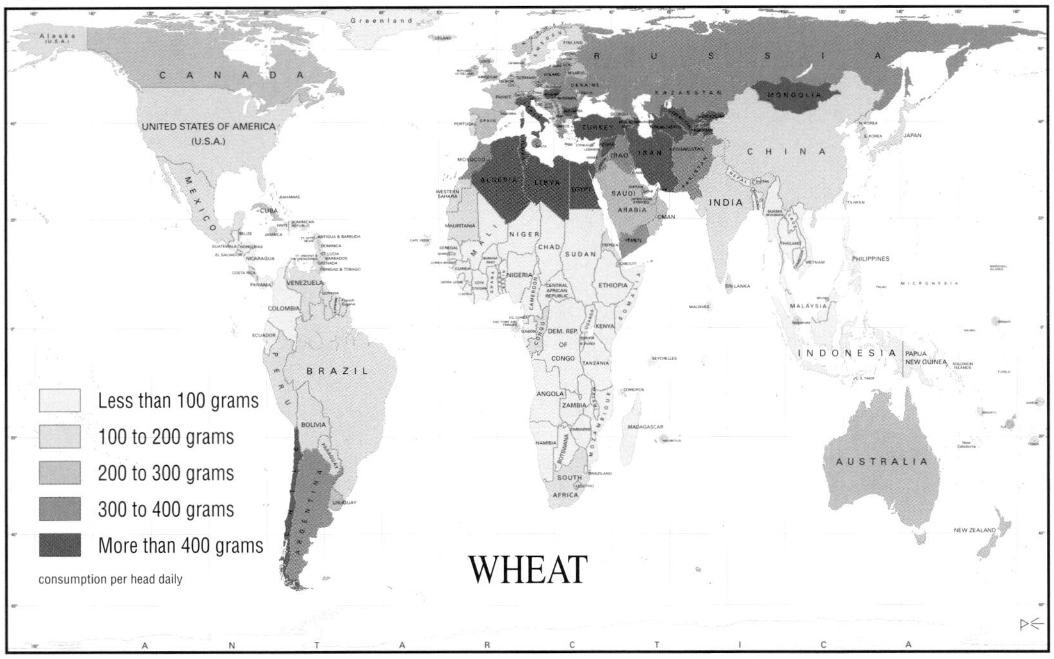

WHEAT

consumption per head daily

- Less than 100 grams
- 100 to 200 grams
- 200 to 300 grams
- 300 to 400 grams
- More than 400 grams

BA

consumption per head daily

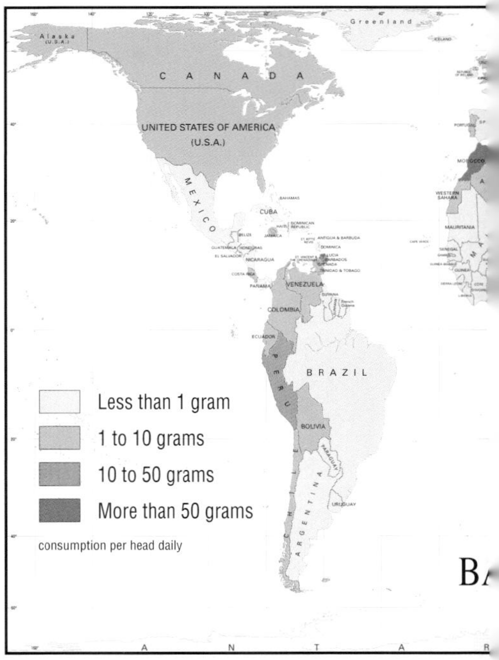

- Less than 1 gram
- 1 to 10 grams
- 10 to 50 grams
- More than 50 grams

OATS

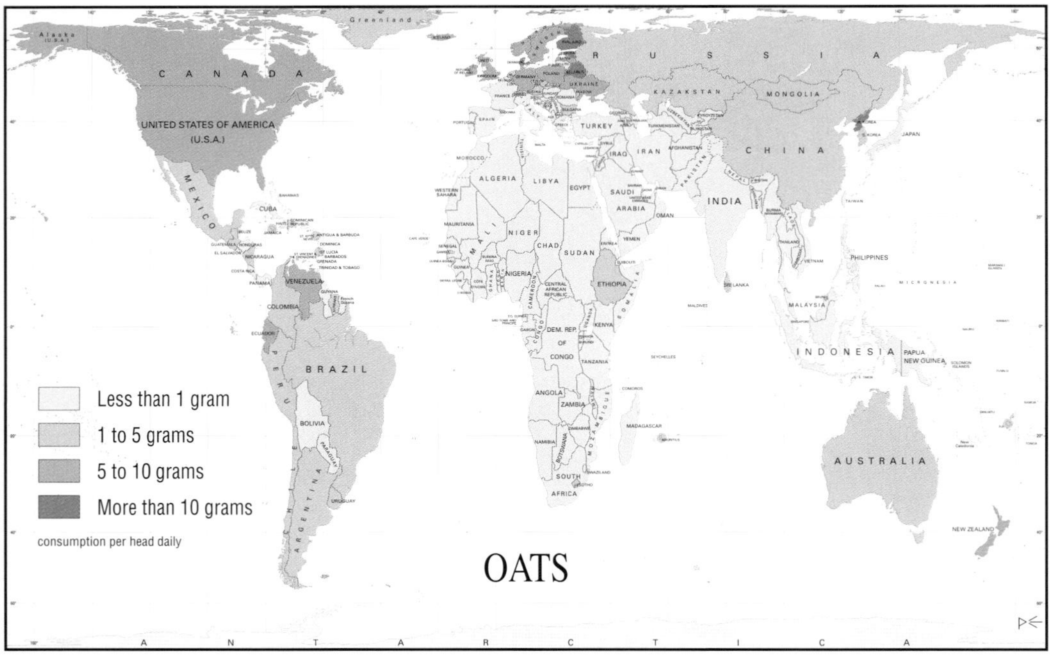

consumption per head daily

- Less than 1 gram
- 1 to 5 grams
- 5 to 10 grams
- More than 10 grams

M

consumption per head daily

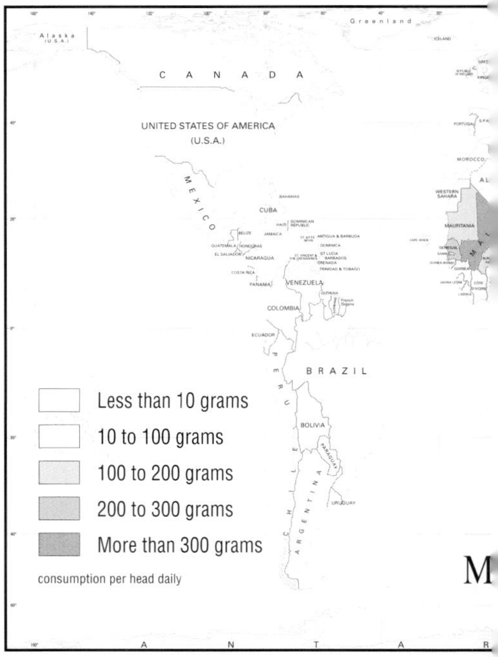

- Less than 10 grams
- 10 to 100 grams
- 100 to 200 grams
- 200 to 300 grams
- More than 300 grams

MAIZE

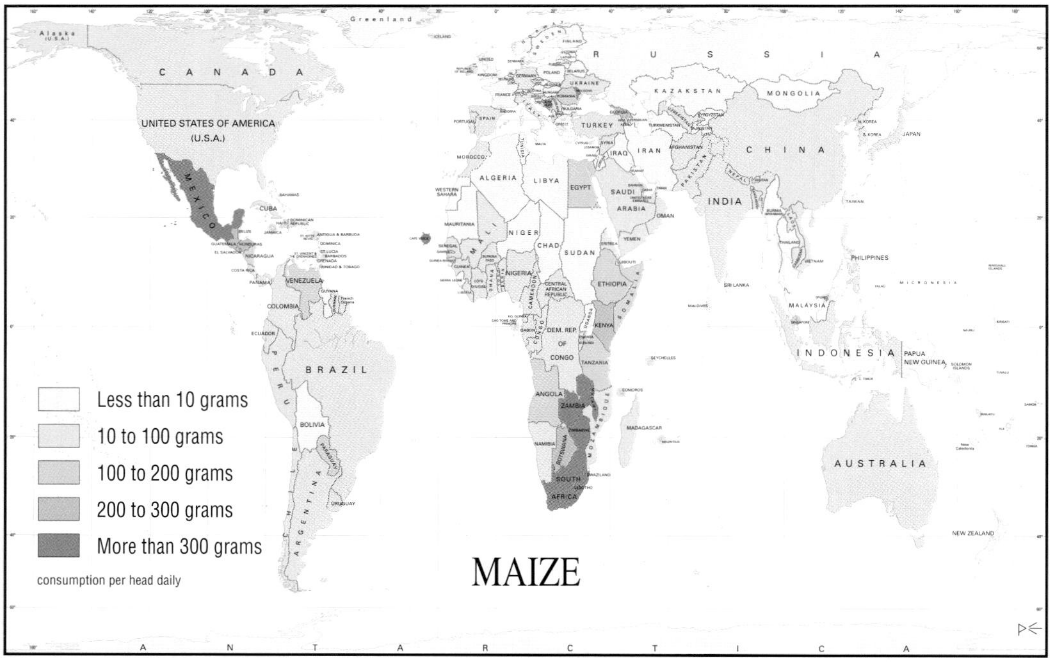

consumption per head daily

- Less than 10 grams
- 10 to 100 grams
- 100 to 200 grams
- 200 to 300 grams
- More than 300 grams

SO

consumption per head daily

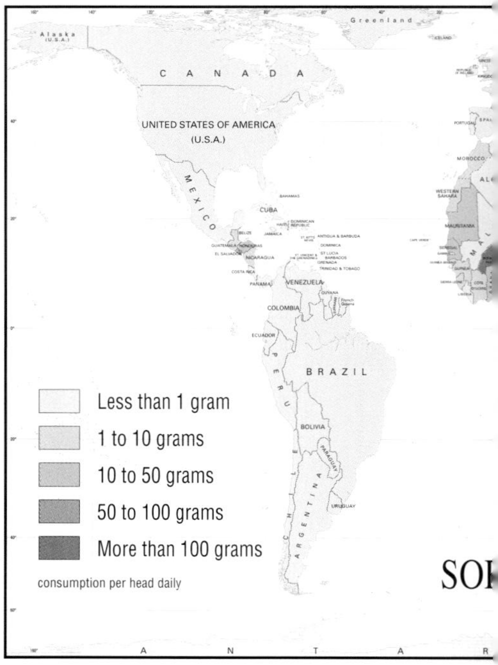

- Less than 1 gram
- 1 to 10 grams
- 10 to 50 grams
- 50 to 100 grams
- More than 100 grams

STAPLE FO

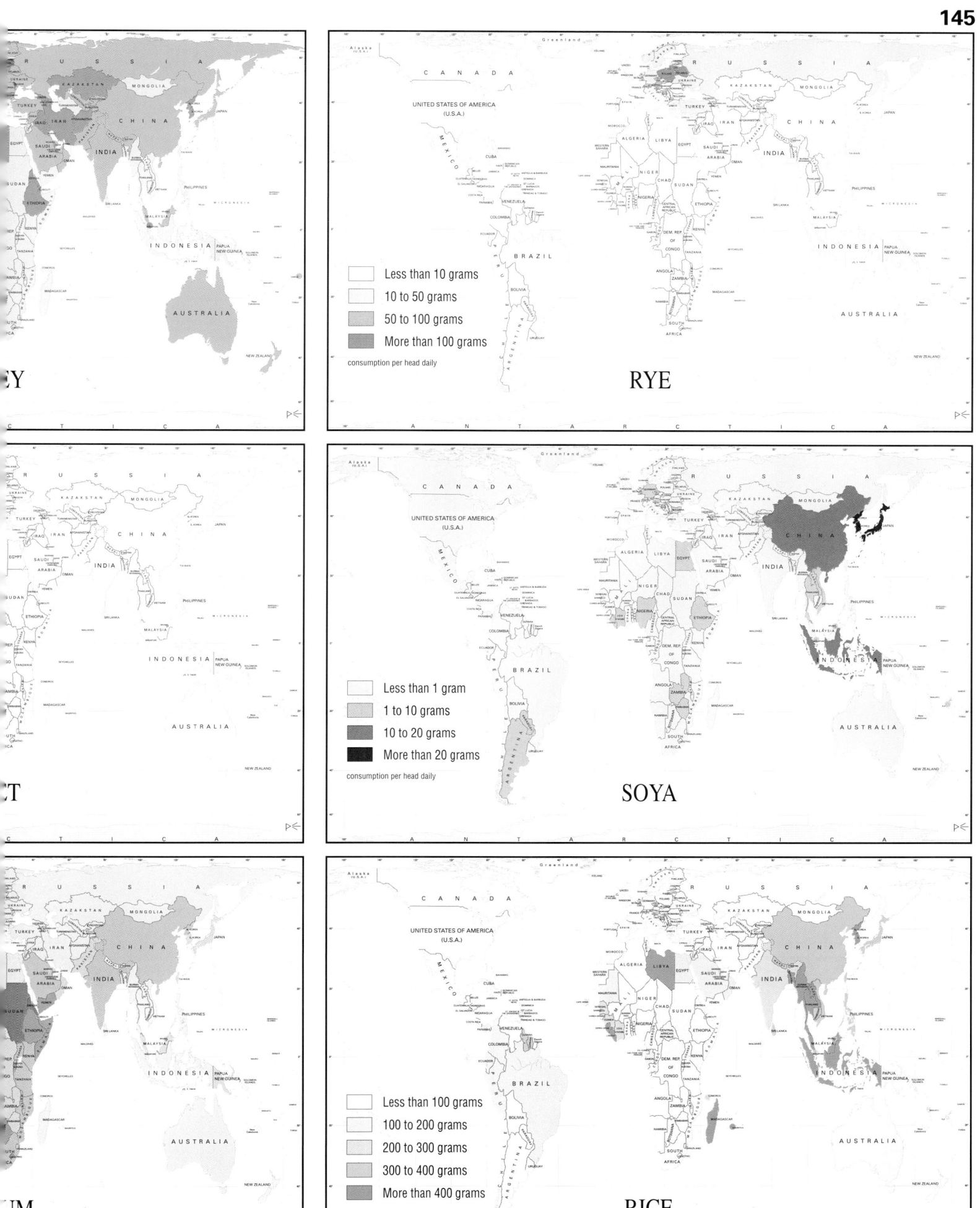

RYE

SOYA

RICE

Less than 10 grams
10 to 50 grams
50 to 100 grams
More than 100 grams
consumption per head daily

Less than 1 gram
1 to 10 grams
10 to 20 grams
More than 20 grams
consumption per head daily

Less than 100 grams
100 to 200 grams
200 to 300 grams
300 to 400 grams
More than 400 grams
consumption per head daily

ODSTUFFS

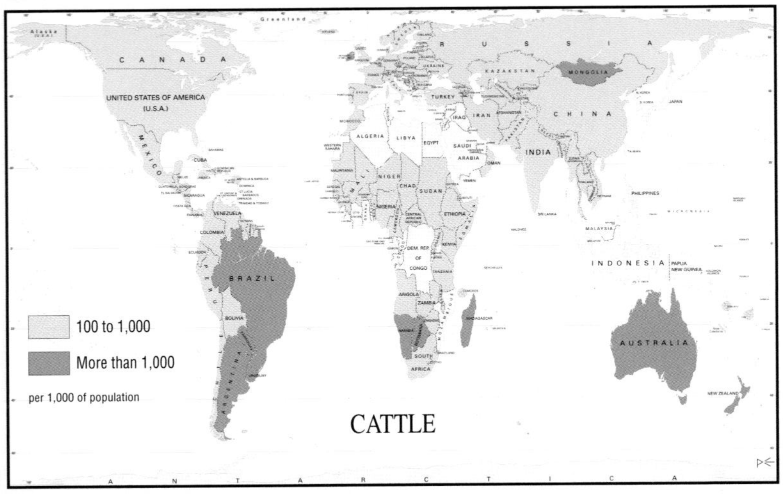

CATTLE

100 to 1,000

More than 1,000

per 1,000 of population

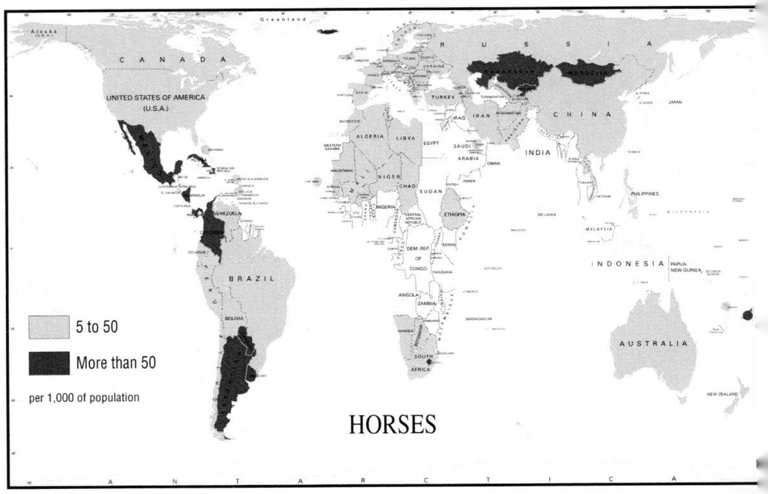

HORSES

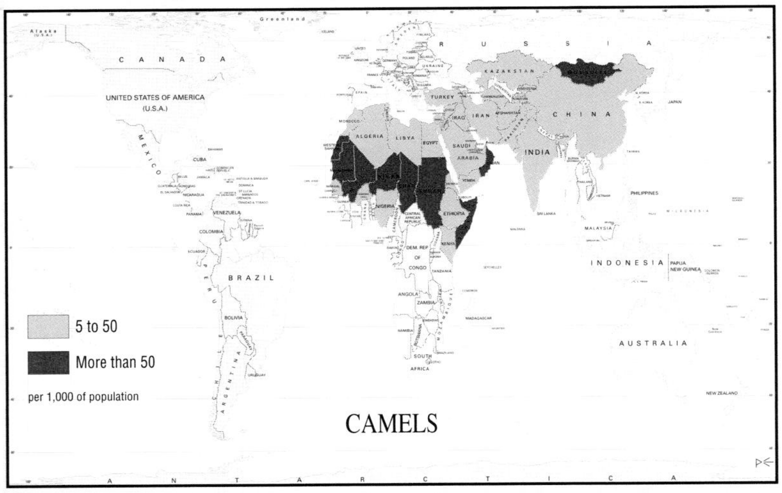

5 to 50

More than 50

per 1,000 of population

CAMELS

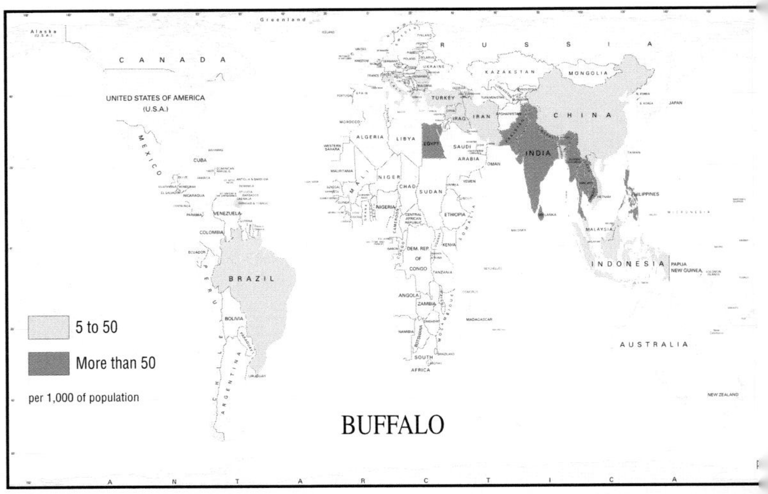

5 to 50

More than 50

per 1,000 of population

BUFFALO

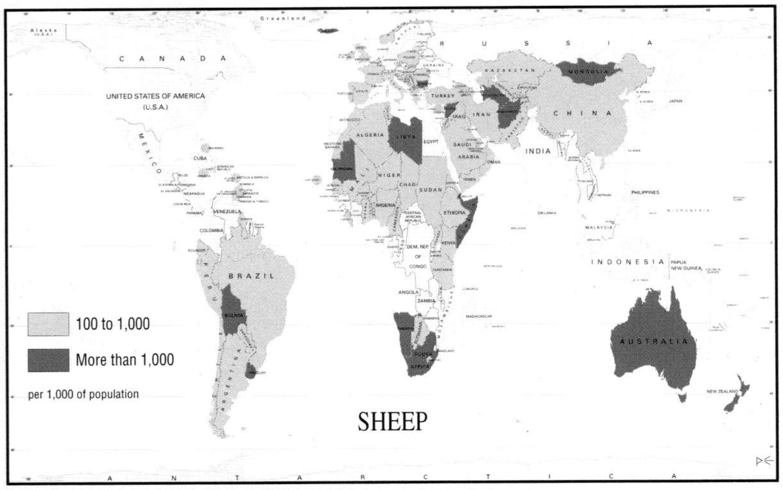

5 to 50

More than 50

per 1,000 of population

SHEEP

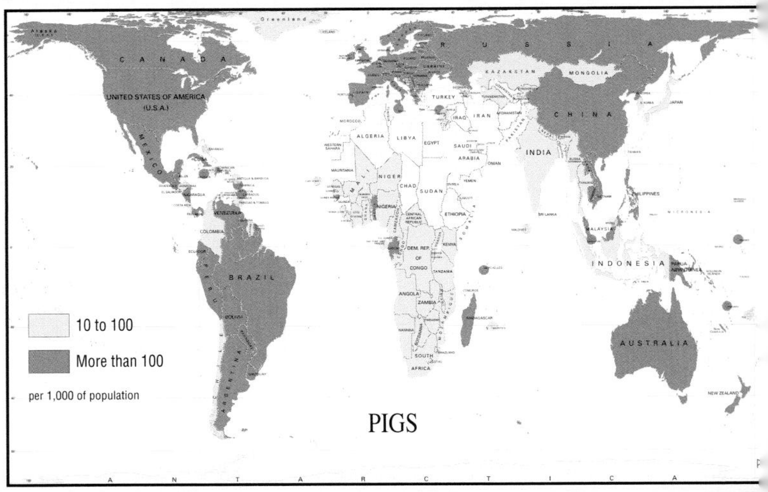

100 to 1,000

More than 1,000

per 1,000 of population

PIGS

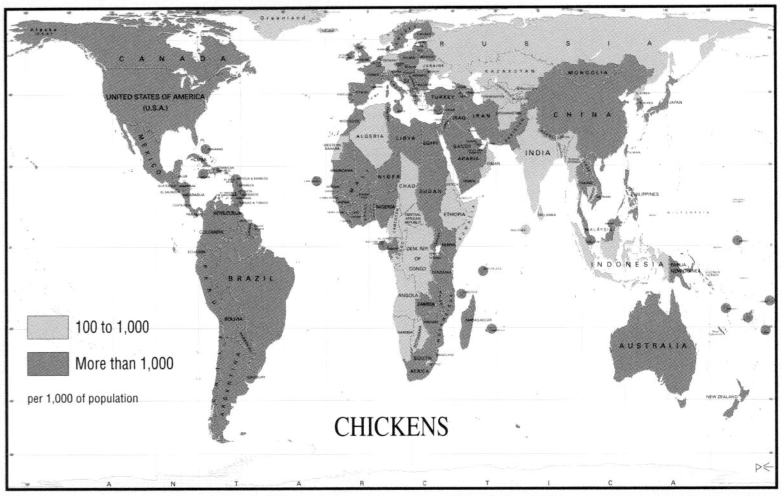

10 to 100

More than 100

per 1,000 of population

CHICKENS

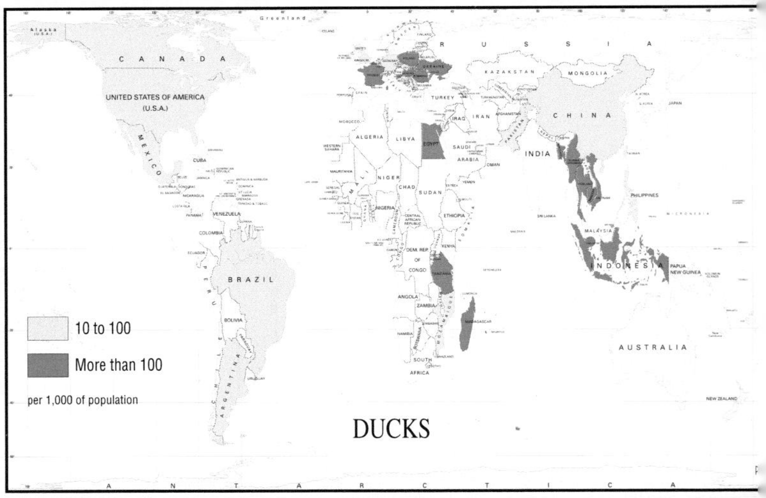

100 to 1,000

More than 1,000

per 1,000 of population

DUCKS

10 to 100

More than 100

per 1,000 of population

ANIMAL H

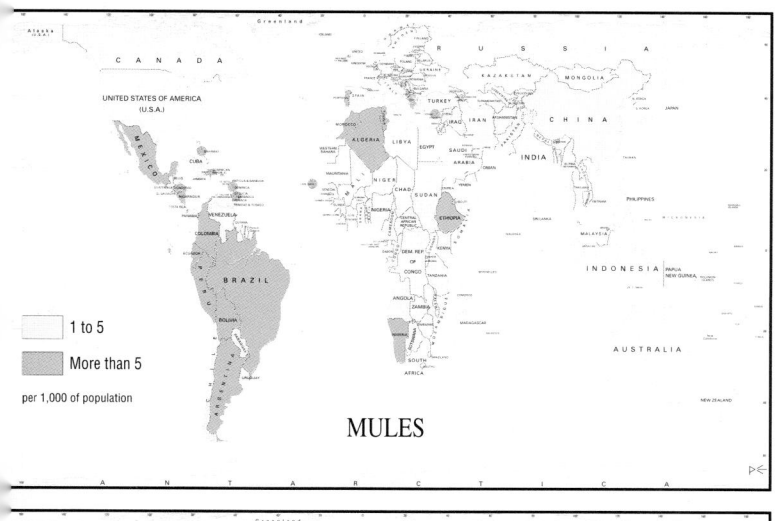

MULES

1 to 5
More than 5

per 1,000 of population

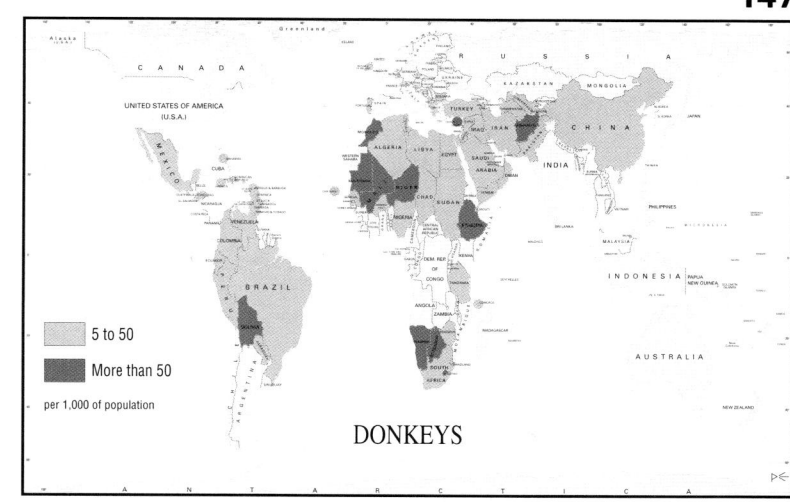

DONKEYS

5 to 50
More than 50

per 1,000 of population

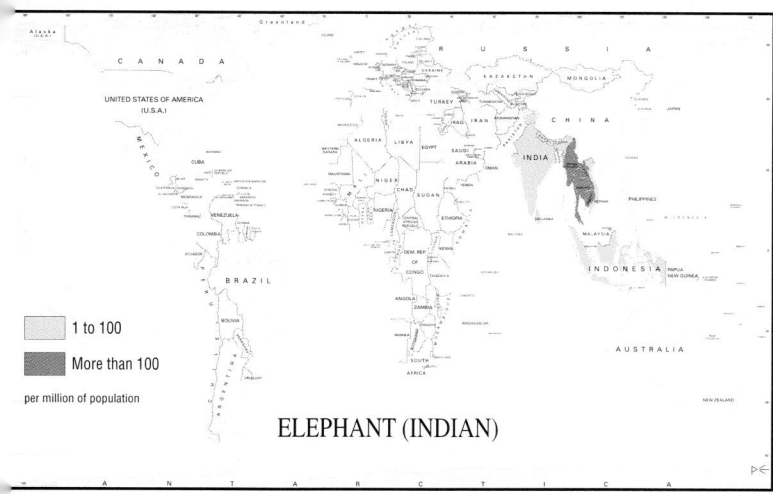

ELEPHANT (INDIAN)

1 to 100
More than 100

per million of population

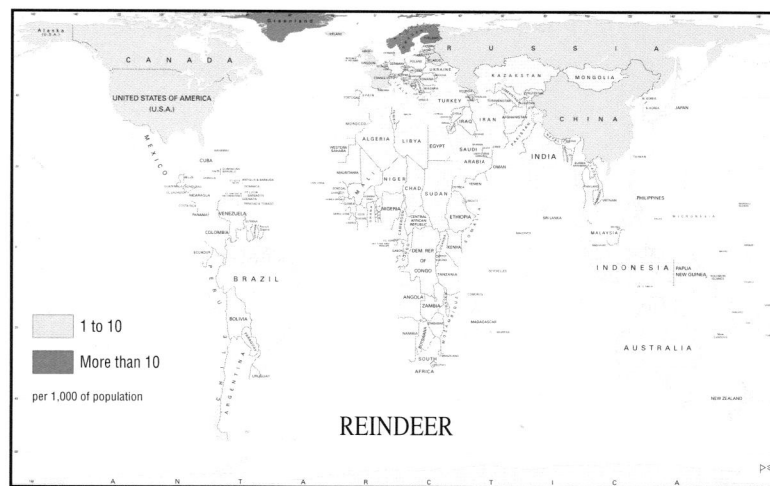

REINDEER

1 to 10
More than 10

per 1,000 of population

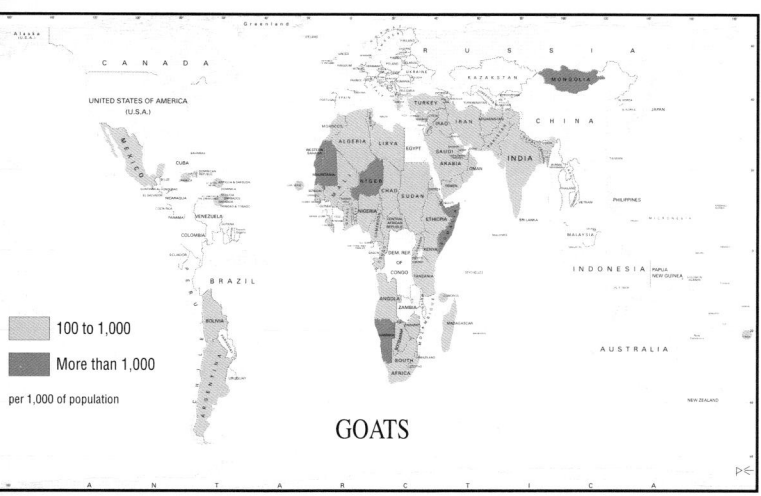

GOATS

100 to 1,000
More than 1,000

per 1,000 of population

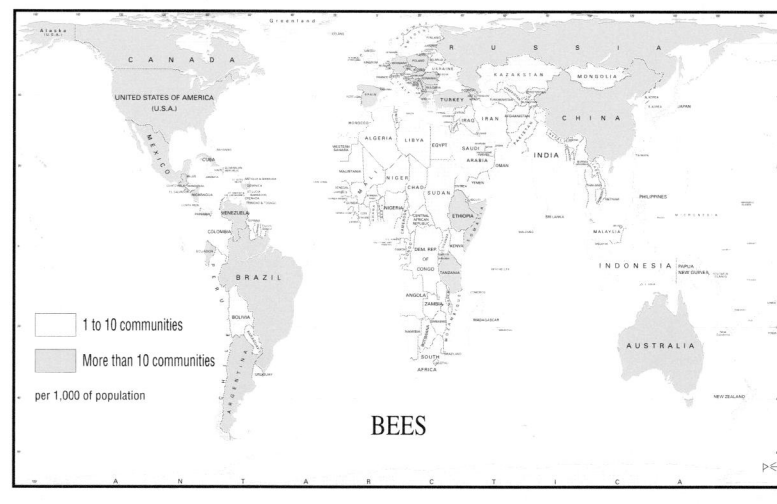

BEES

1 to 10 communities
More than 10 communities

per 1,000 of population

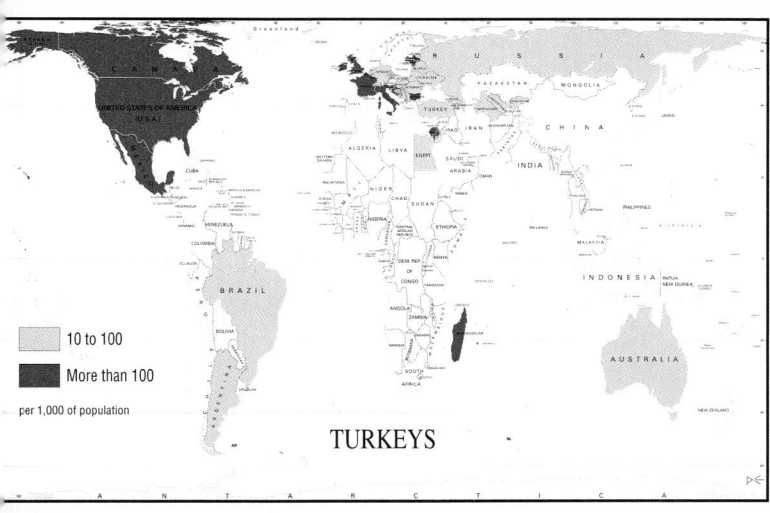

TURKEYS

10 to 100
More than 100

per 1,000 of population

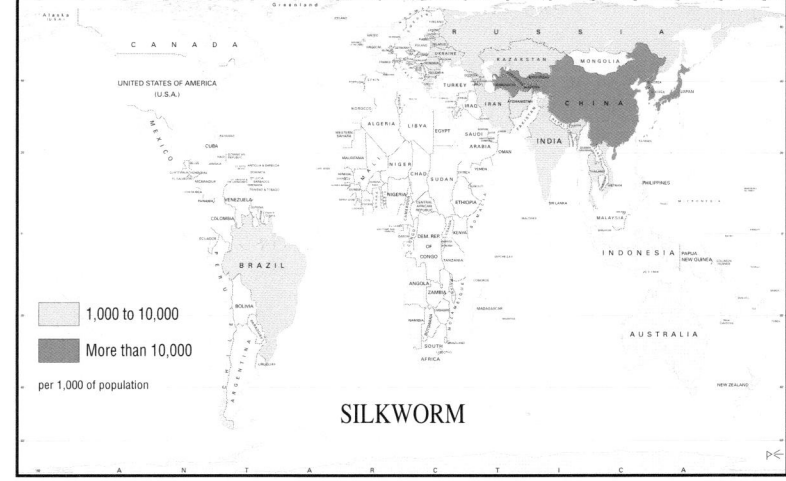

SILKWORM

1,000 to 10,000
More than 10,000

per 1,000 of population

JSBANDRY

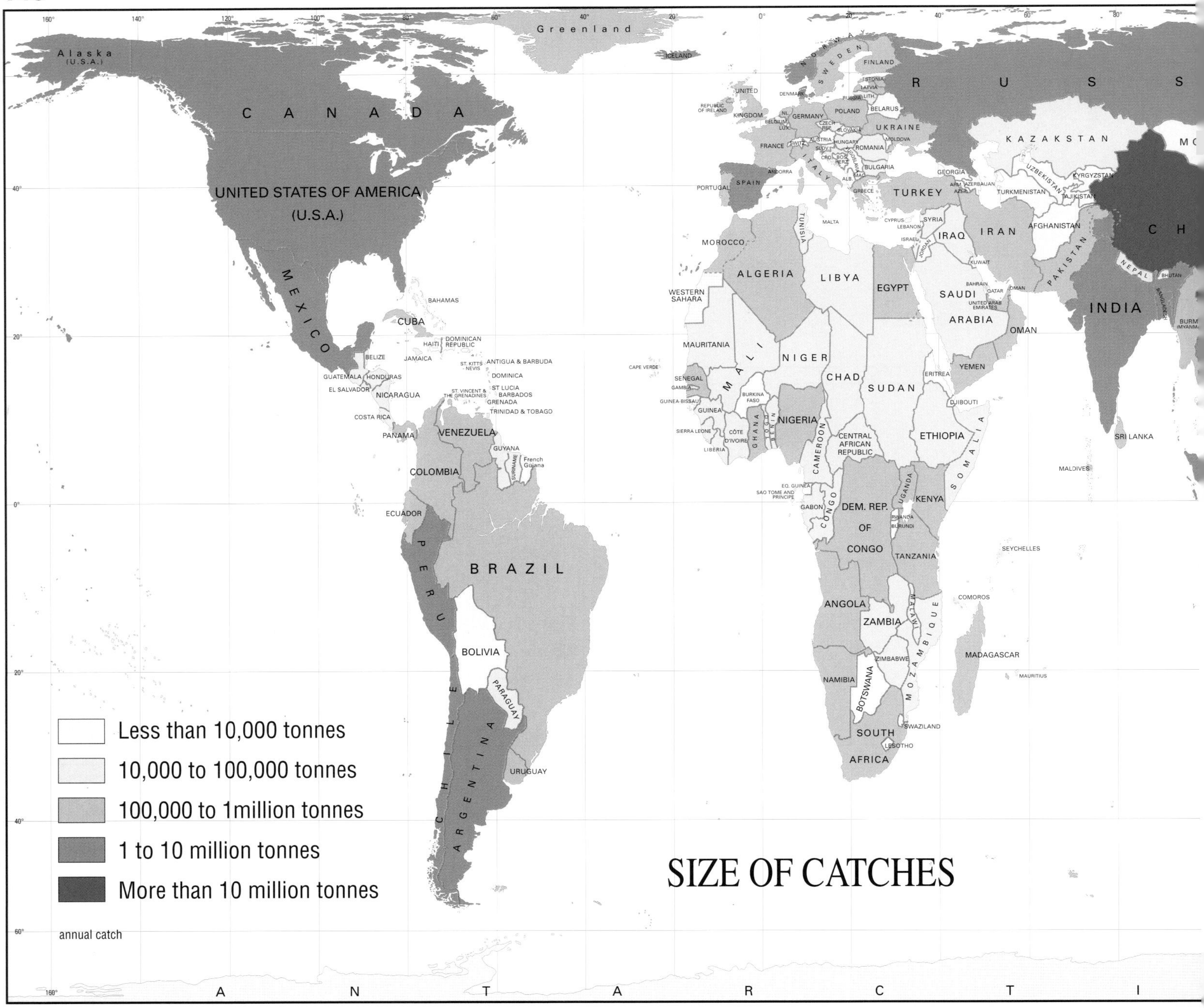

Alaska
(U.S.A.)

Greenland

ICELAND

NORWAY SWEDEN FINLAND

R U S S
R U S S

C A N A D A

ESTONIA
LATVIA
DENMARK LITH.
REPUBLIC
OF IRELAND
UNITED
KINGDOM
NETH.
BELGIUM
GERMANY POLAND BELARUS
LUX. CZECH
FRANCE SWITZ. AUSTRIA HUNGARY UKRAINE
SLOVENIA CRO. ROMANIA MOLDOVA

KAZAKSTAN

MO

UNITED STATES OF AMERICA
(U.S.A.)

PORTUGAL SPAIN
ANDORRA

ITALY BOS. SERBIA
MON. BULGARIA
ALB. GREECE
MALTA

GEORGIA
ARM AZERBAIJAN
TURKEY SYRIA
CYPRUS
LEBANON
ISRAEL IRAQ

UZBEKISTAN
KYRGYZSTAN
TURKMENISTAN TAJIKISTAN

IRAN AFGHANISTAN

C H

M
E
X
I
C
O

MOROCCO

WESTERN
SAHARA

ALGERIA LIBYA

TUNISIA

EGYPT

SAUDI
ARABIA

JORDAN
KUWAIT
BAHRAIN
QATAR
UNITED ARAB
EMIRATES
OMAN

PAKISTAN

NEPAL BHUTAN

INDIA

BURMA
(MYANMAR)

BAHAMAS

CUBA
HAITI
DOMINICAN
REPUBLIC
JAMAICA
BELIZE
GUATEMALA HONDURAS
EL SALVADOR
NICARAGUA
COSTA RICA
PANAMA

ST KITTS &
NEVIS
ANTIGUA & BARBUDA
DOMINICA
ST LUCIA
ST VINCENT & BARBADOS
THE GRENADINES GRENADA
TRINIDAD & TOBAGO

CAPE VERDE

MAURITANIA

M
A
L
I

SENEGAL
GAMBIA
GUINEA BISSAU
GUINEA
SIERRA LEONE
LIBERIA

NIGER

BURKINA
FASO

CÔTE
D'IVOIRE
GHANA
TOGO
BENIN

NIGERIA

CHAD

CAMEROON

CENTRAL
AFRICAN
REPUBLIC

SUDAN

ERITREA

DJIBOUTI

YEMEN

OMAN

ETHIOPIA

SRI LANKA

MALDIVES

SEYCHELLES

VENEZUELA

COLOMBIA

GUYANA
SURINAME
French
Guiana

ECUADOR

P
E
R
U

BRAZIL

BOLIVIA

PARAGUAY

C
H
I
L
E

A
R
G
E
N
T
I
N
A

URUGUAY

EQ. GUINEA
SAO TOME AND
PRINCIPE
GABON
CONGO
DEM. REP.
OF
CONGO
RWANDA
BURUNDI
UGANDA
KENYA

TANZANIA

S
O
M
A
L
I
A

COMOROS

ANGOLA
ZAMBIA

MALAWI

MOZAMBIQUE

MADAGASCAR

MAURITIUS

NAMIBIA
ZIMBABWE
BOTSWANA

SWAZILAND

SOUTH
AFRICA

LESOTHO

	Less than 10,000 tonnes
	10,000 to 100,000 tonnes
	100,000 to 1 million tonnes
	1 to 10 million tonnes
	More than 10 million tonnes

SIZE OF CATCHES

annual catch

A N T A R C T I

	Less than 3 tonnes
	3 to 10 tonnes
	10 to 30 tonnes
	30 to 100 tonnes
	More than 100 tonnes

per 1,000 km² annually

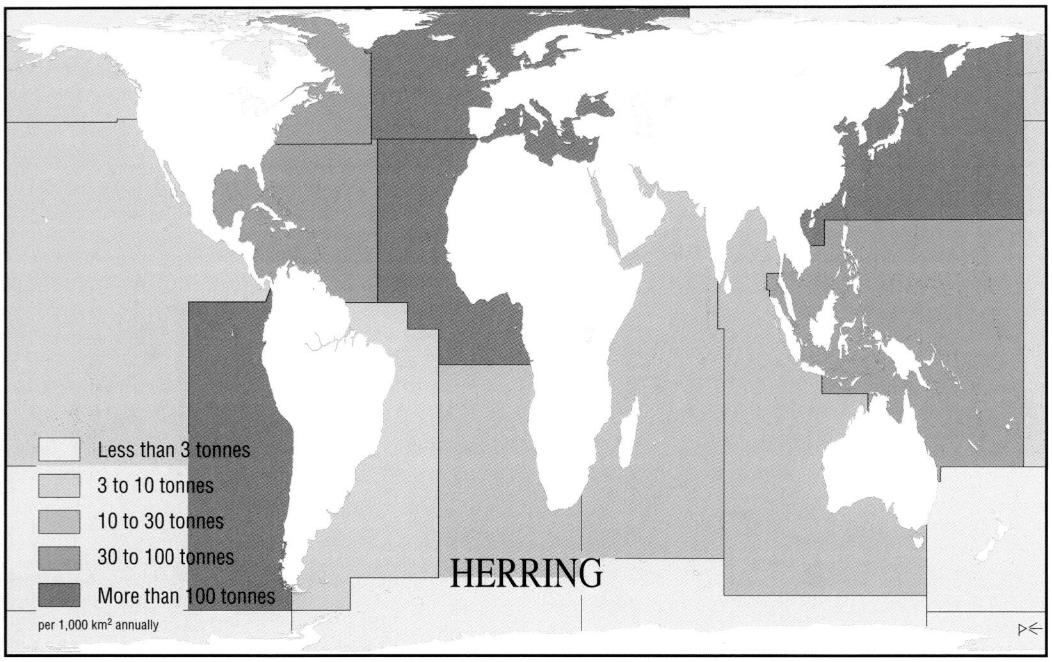

HERRING

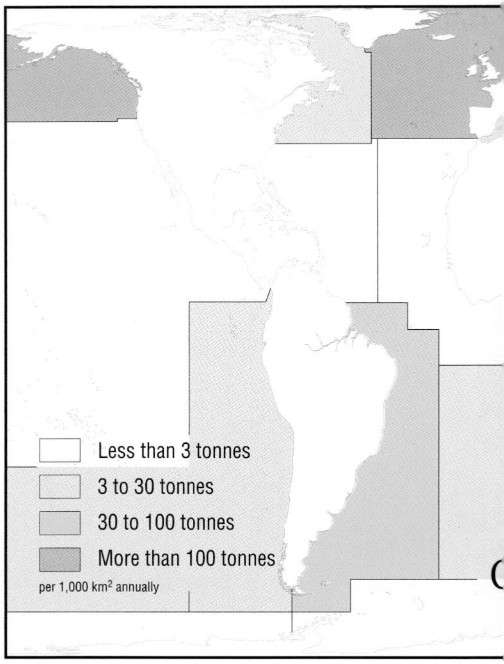

	Less than 3 tonnes
	3 to 30 tonnes
	30 to 100 tonnes
	More than 100 tonnes

per 1,000 km² annually

C

FISH

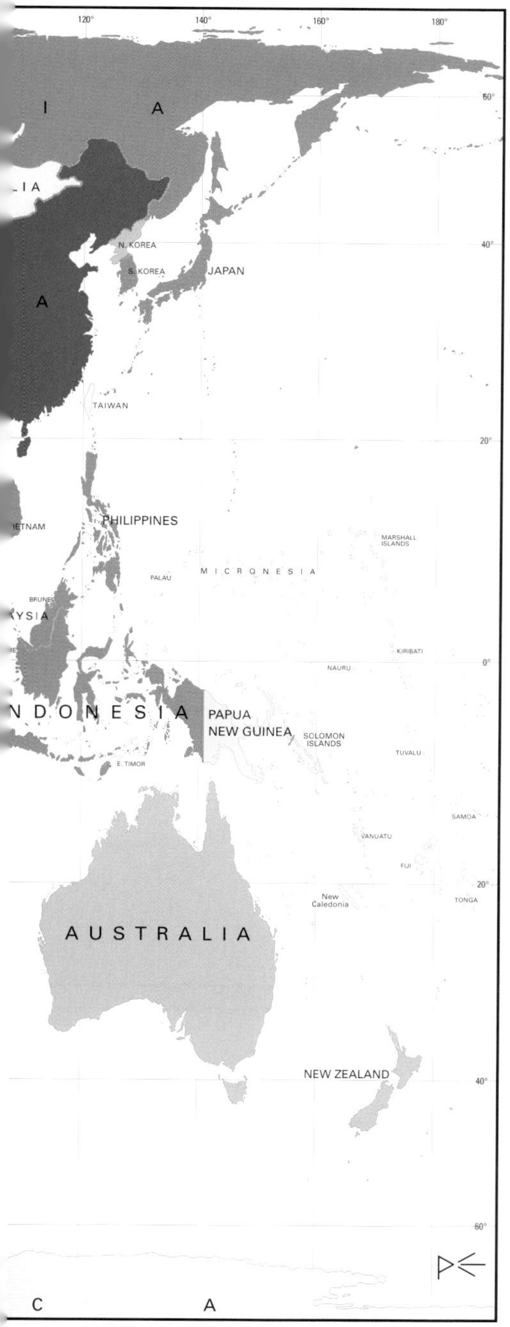

TUNA

	Less than 3 tonnes
	3 to 10 tonnes
	10 to 30 tonnes
	More than 30 tonnes

per 1,000 km² annually

FLATFISH

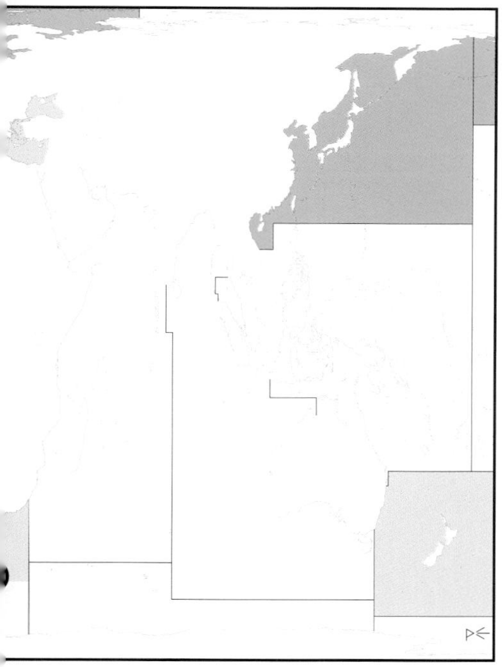

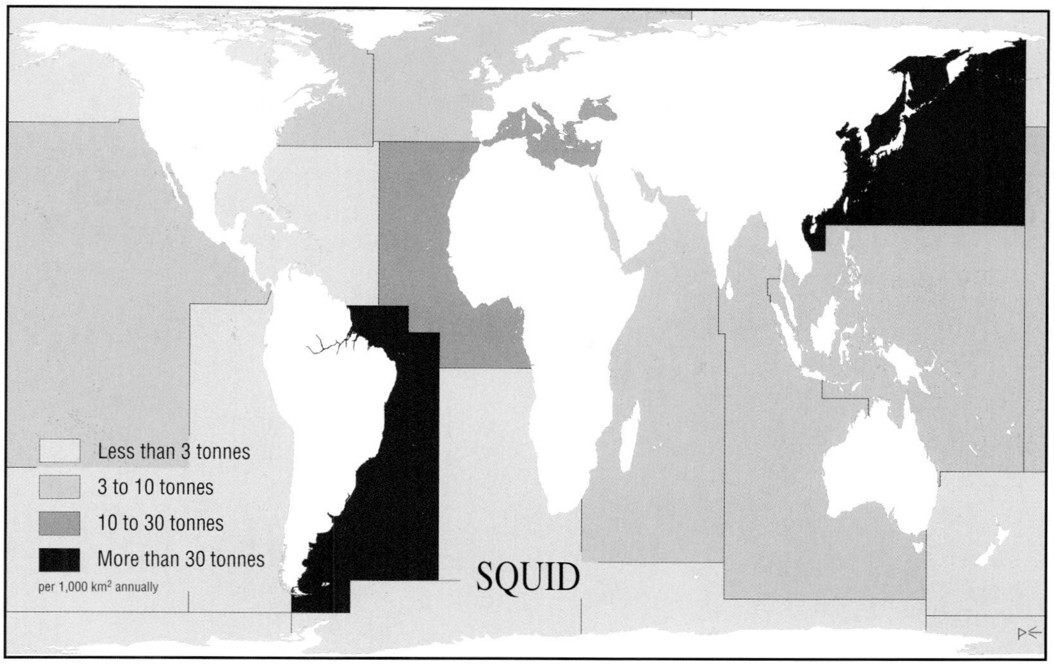

	Less than 3 tonnes
	3 to 10 tonnes
	More than 10 tonnes

per 1,000 km² annually

SQUID

	Less than 3 tonnes
	3 to 10 tonnes
	10 to 30 tonnes
	More than 30 tonnes

per 1,000 km² annually

N. KOREA
S. KOREA
JAPAN
TAIWAN
VIETNAM
PHILIPPINES
PALAU
MICRONESIA
BRUNEI
MALAYSIA
INDONESIA
PAPUA NEW GUINEA
SOLOMON ISLANDS
NAURU
KIRIBATI
MARSHALL ISLANDS
TUVALU
SAMOA
VANUATU
FIJI
New Caledonia
TONGA
AUSTRALIA
NEW ZEALAND

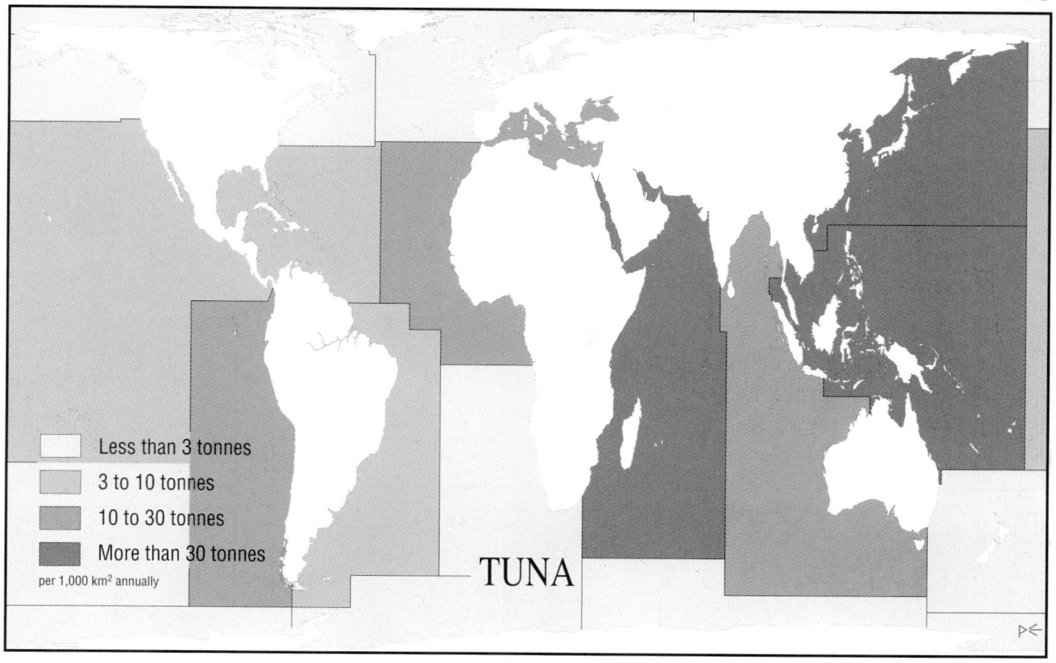

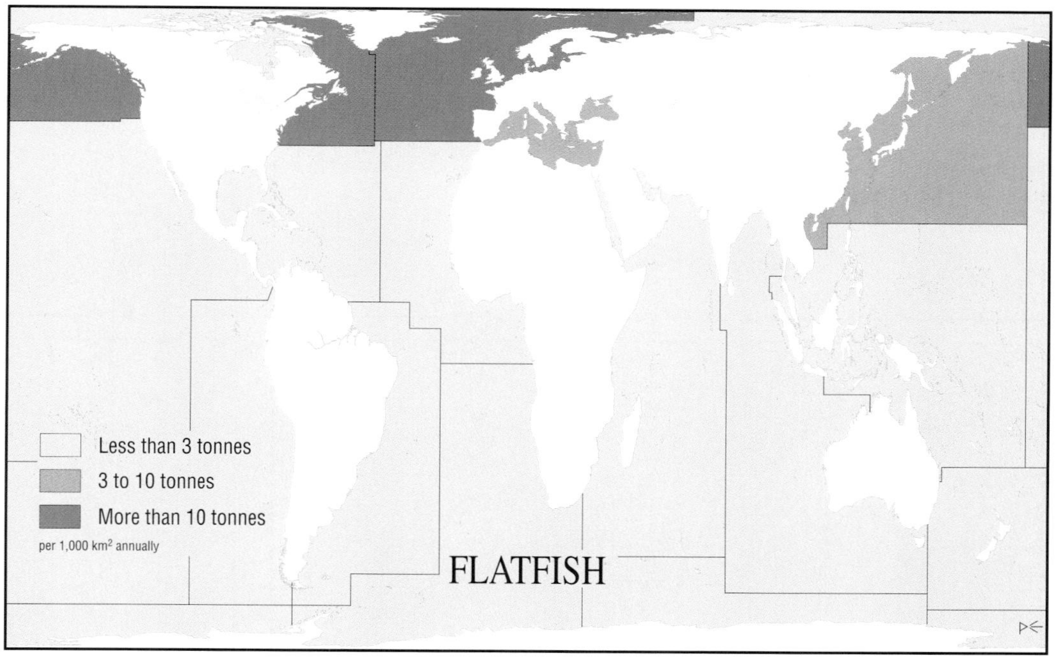

ING

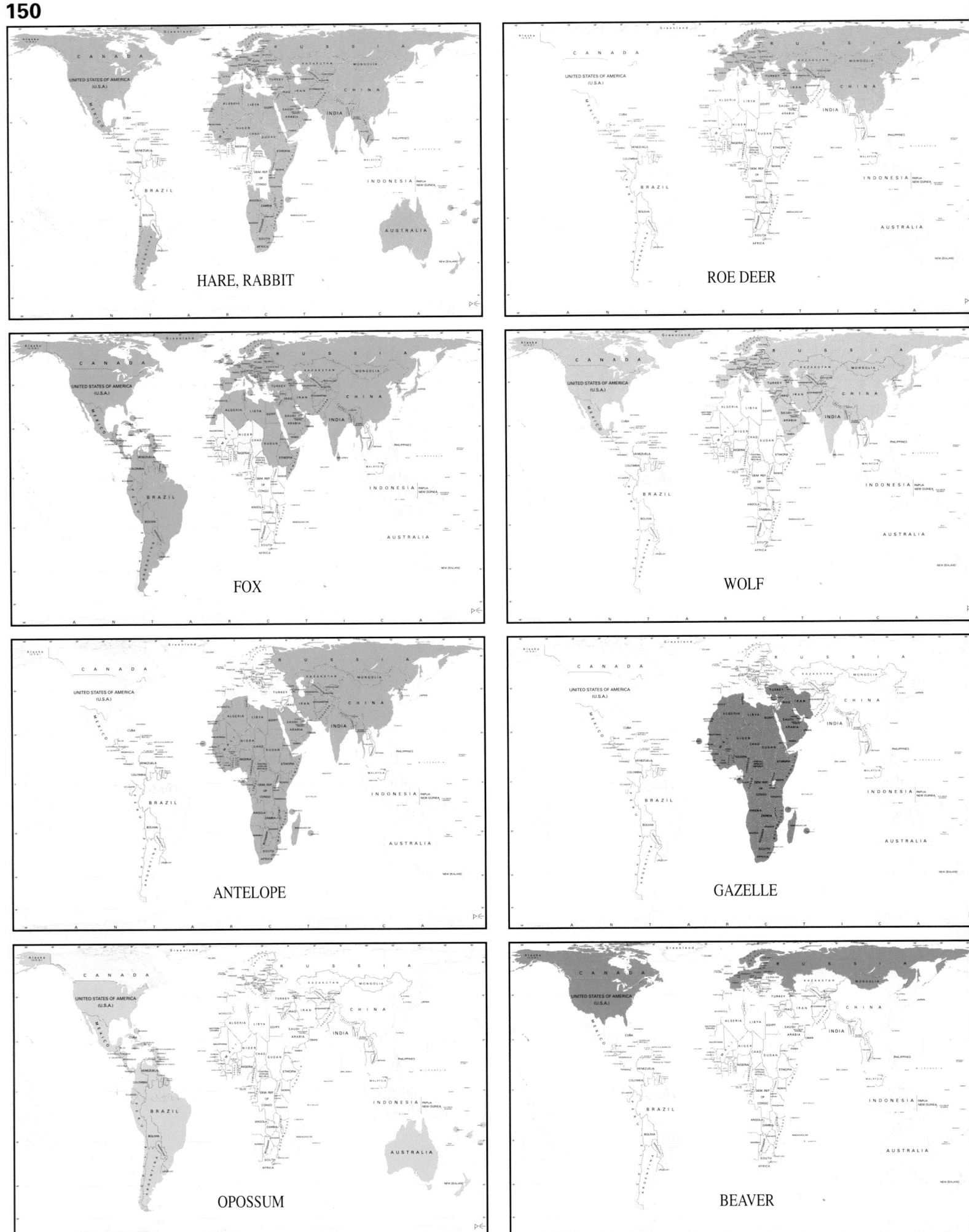

HARE, RABBIT

ROE DEER

FOX

WOLF

ANTELOPE

GAZELLE

OPOSSUM

BEAVER

HUN

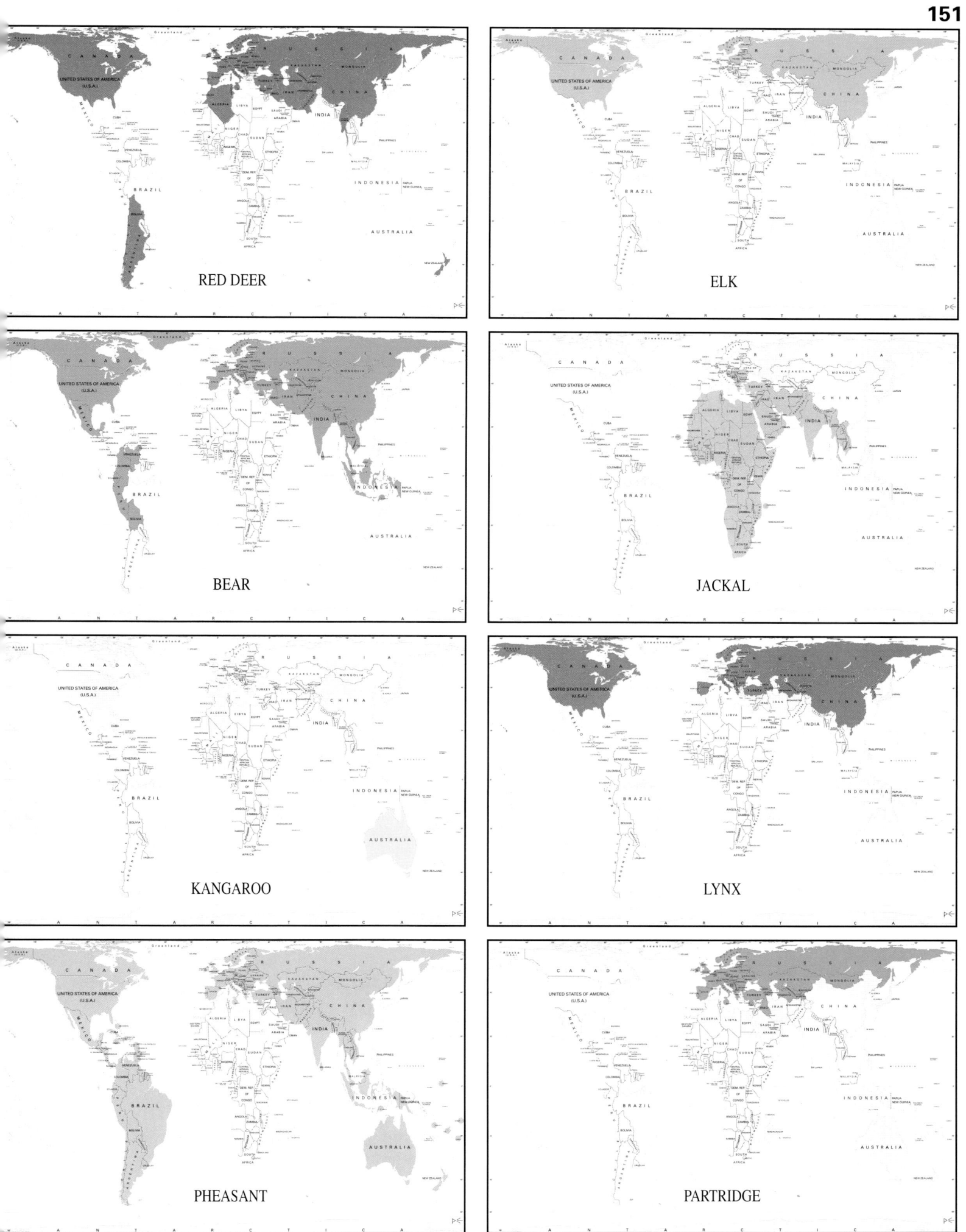

RED DEER

ELK

BEAR

JACKAL

KANGAROO

LYNX

PHEASANT

PARTRIDGE

TING

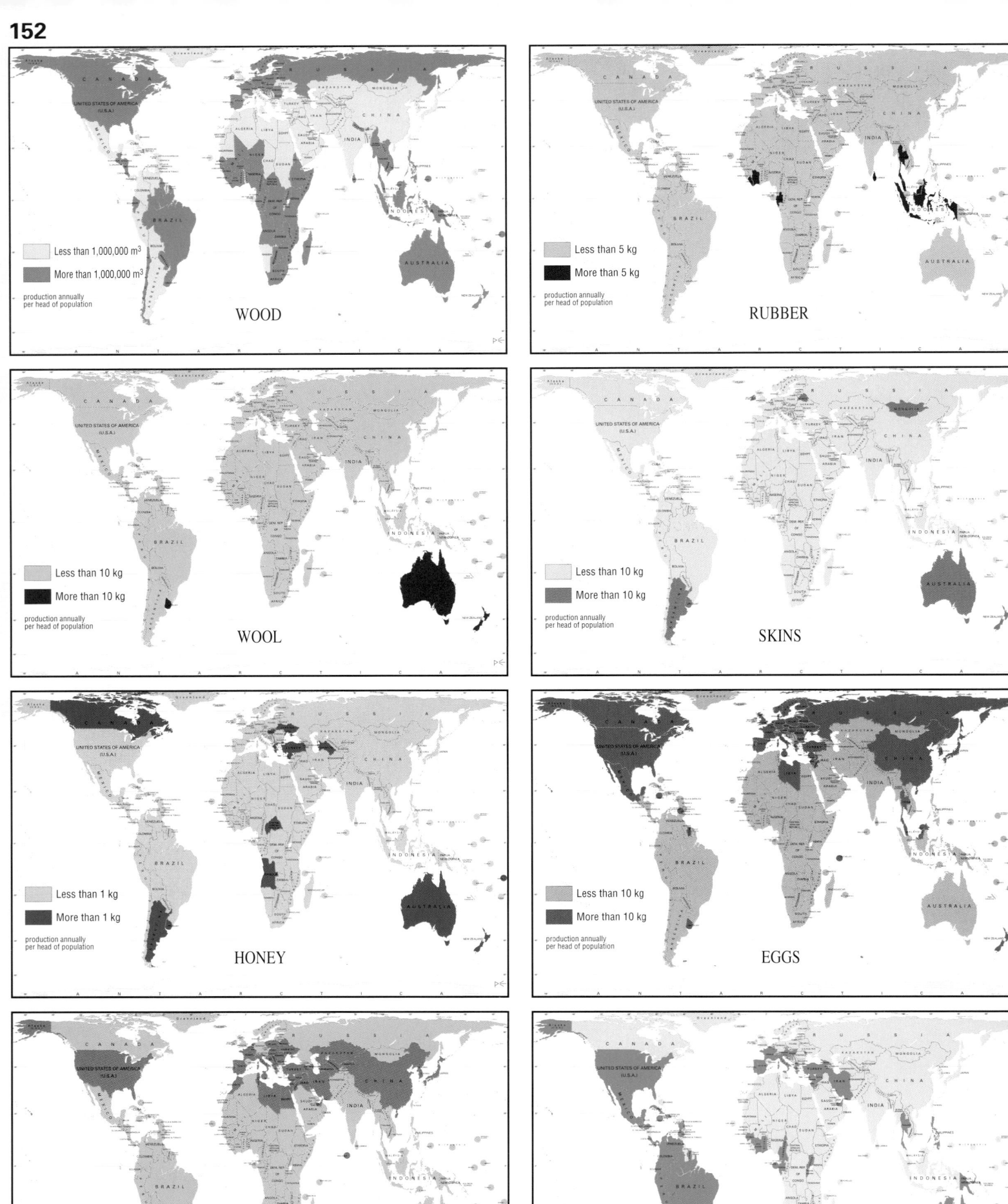

WOOD

RUBBER

Less than 1,000,000 m³
More than 1,000,000 m³

production annually
per head of population

Less than 5 kg
More than 5 kg

production annually
per head of population

WOOL

SKINS

Less than 10 kg
More than 10 kg

production annually
per head of population

Less than 10 kg
More than 10 kg

production annually
per head of population

HONEY

EGGS

Less than 1 kg
More than 1 kg

production annually
per head of population

Less than 10 kg
More than 10 kg

production annually
per head of population

VEGETABLES

FRUIT

Less than 100 kg
More than 100 kg

production annually
per head of population

Less than 100 kg
More than 100 kg

production annually
per head of population

NATURAL

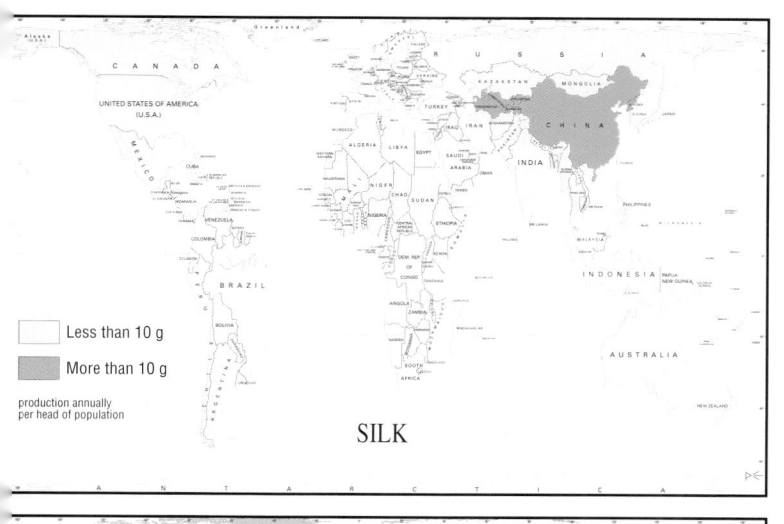

Less than 10 g

More than 10 g

production annually
per head of population

SILK

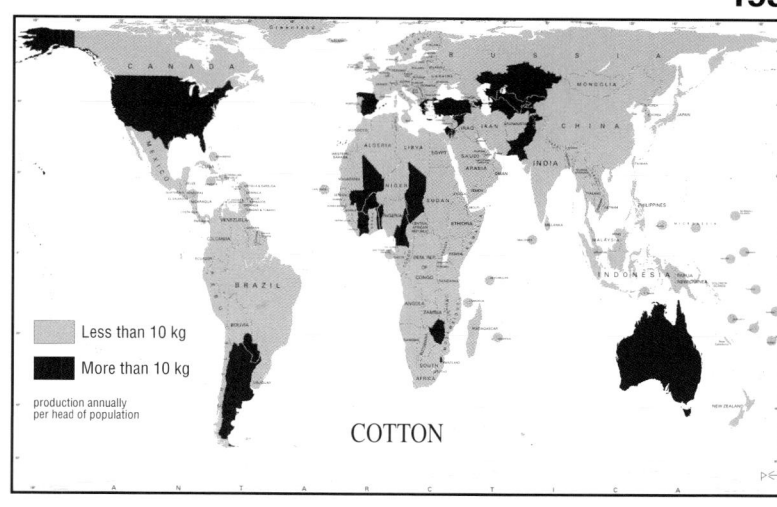

Less than 10 kg

More than 10 kg

production annually
per head of population

COTTON

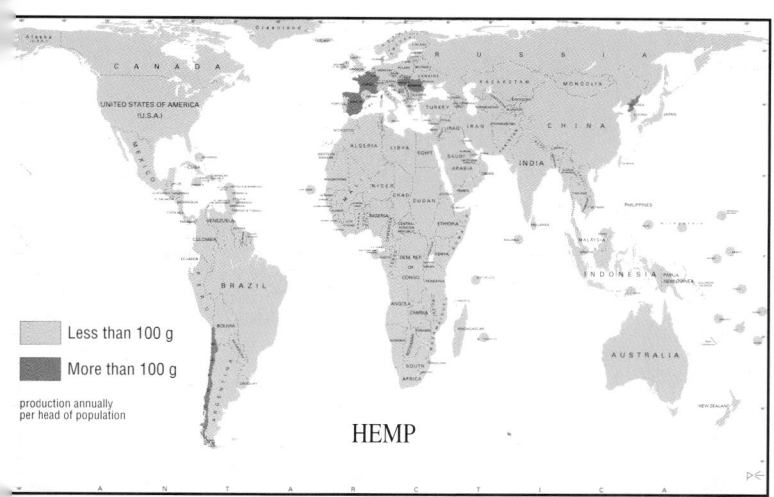

Less than 100 g

More than 100 g

production annually
per head of population

HEMP

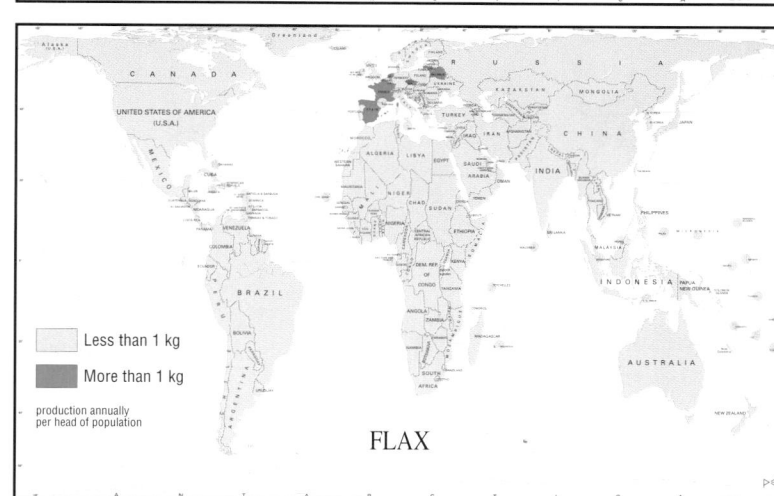

Less than 1 kg

More than 1 kg

production annually
per head of population

FLAX

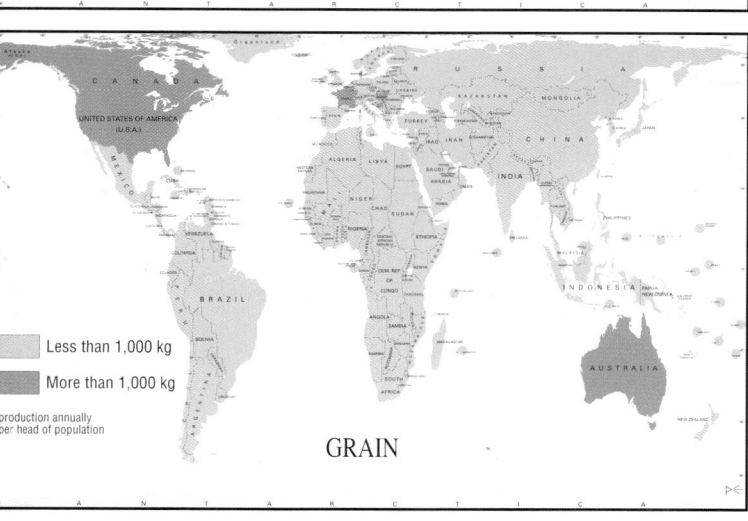

Less than 1,000 kg

More than 1,000 kg

production annually
per head of population

GRAIN

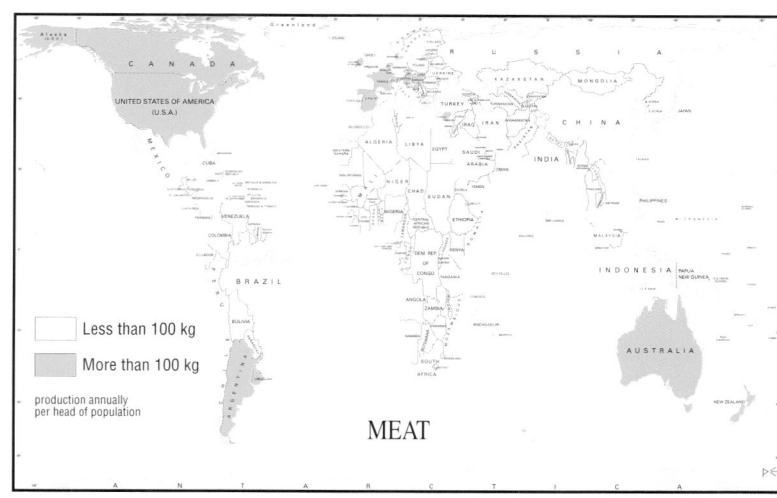

Less than 100 kg

More than 100 kg

production annually
per head of population

MEAT

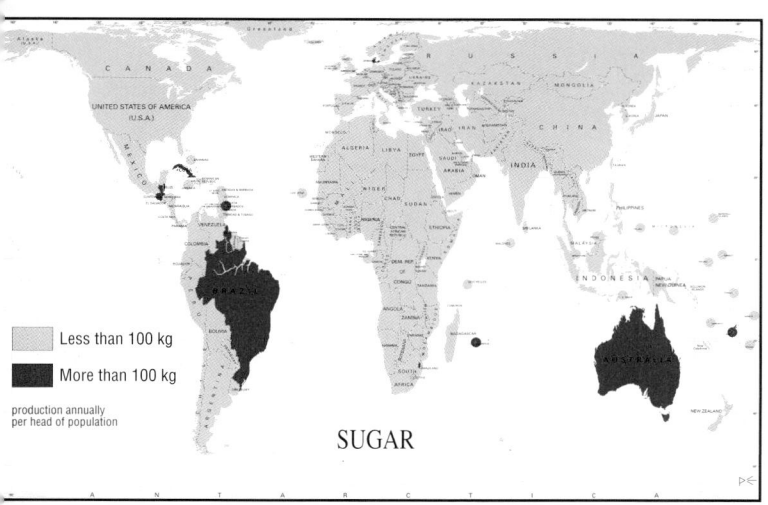

Less than 100 kg

More than 100 kg

production annually
per head of population

SUGAR

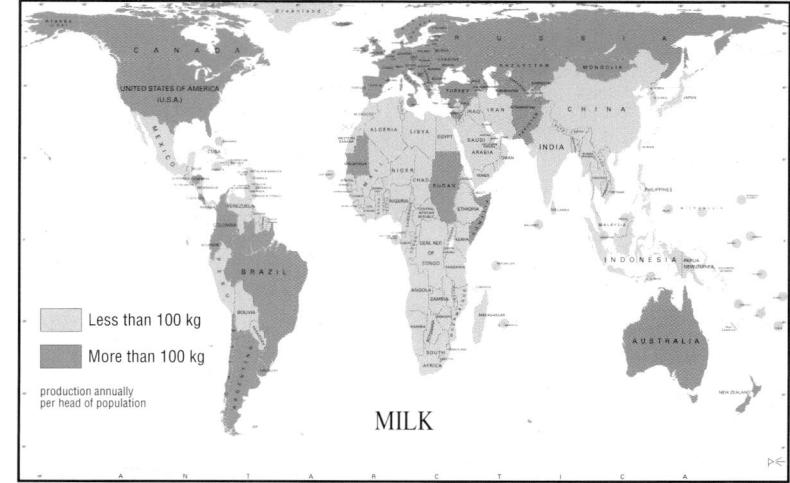

Less than 100 kg

More than 100 kg

production annually
per head of population

MILK

PRODUCTS

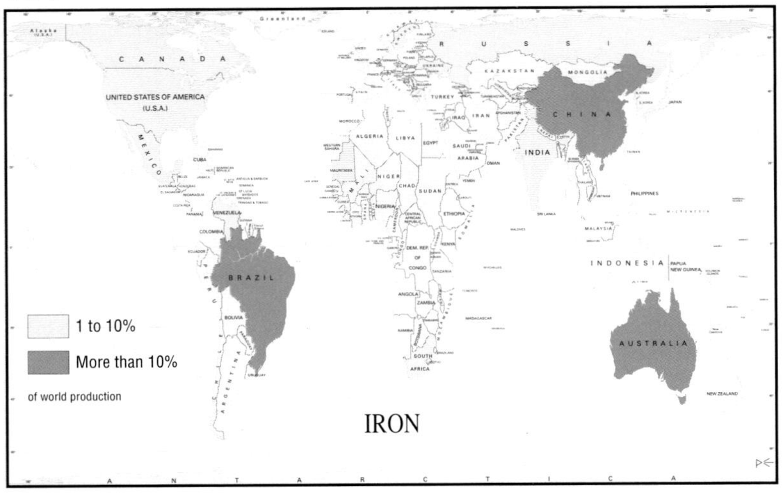

IRON

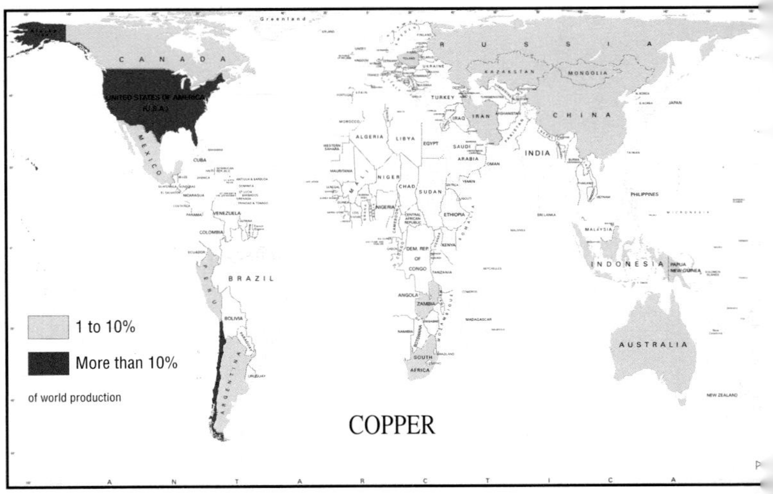

COPPER

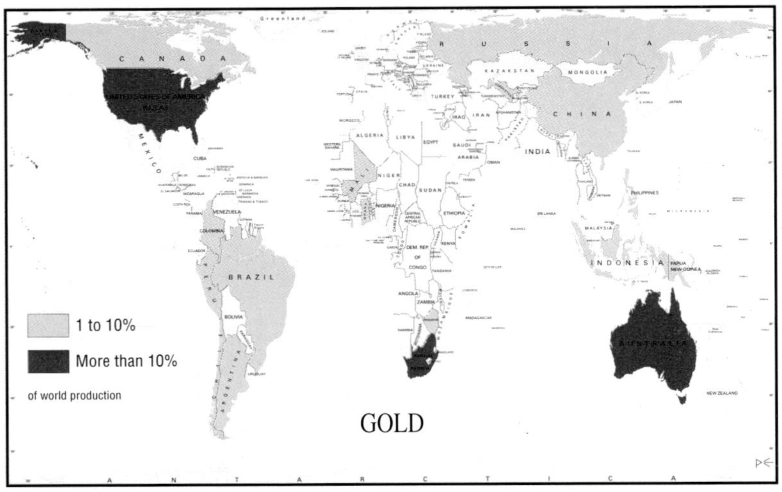

1 to 10%

More than 10%

of world production

GOLD

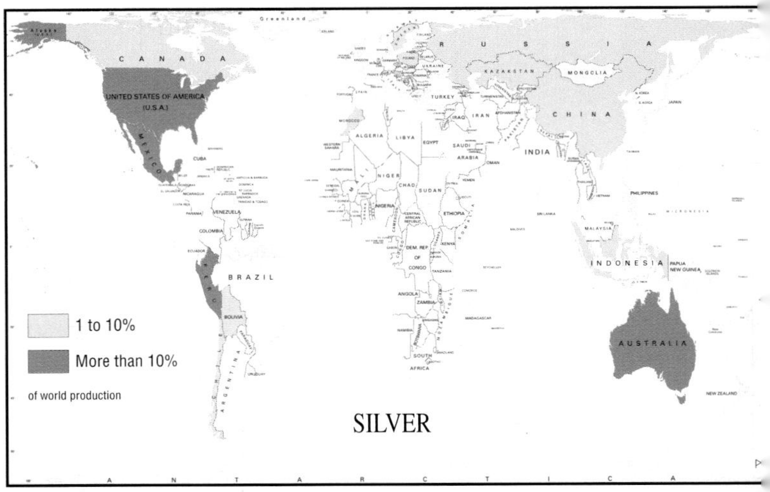

SILVER

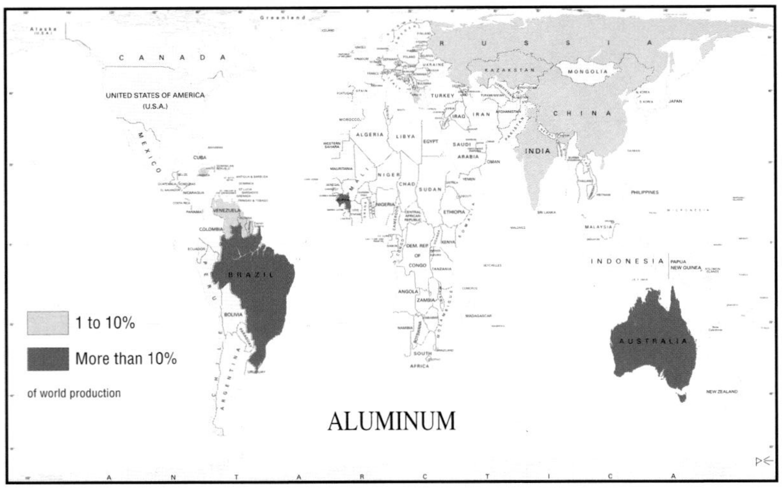

1 to 10%

More than 10%

of world production

ALUMINUM

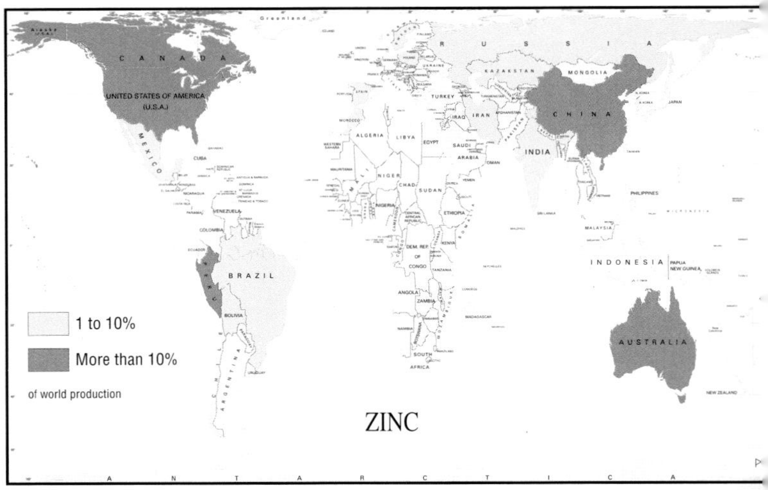

ZINC

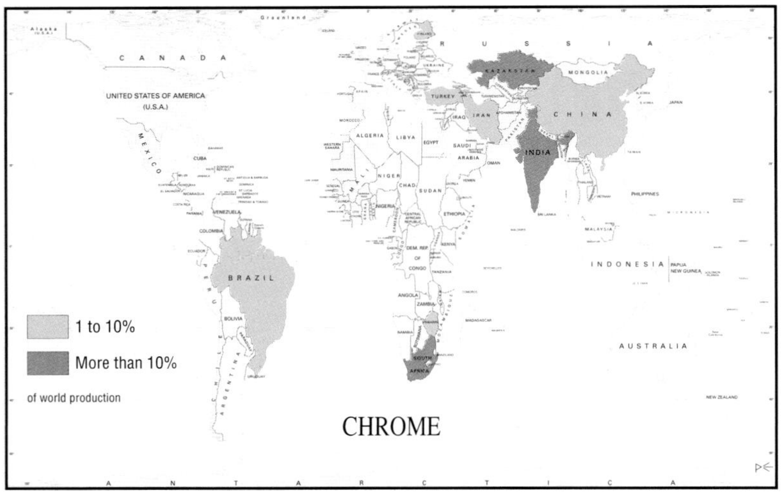

1 to 10%

More than 10%

of world production

CHROME

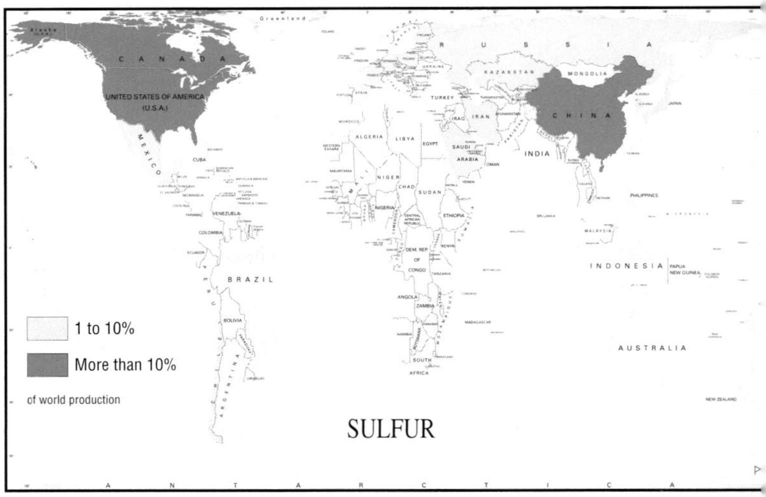

SULFUR

1 to 10%

More than 10%

of world production

MINERAL F

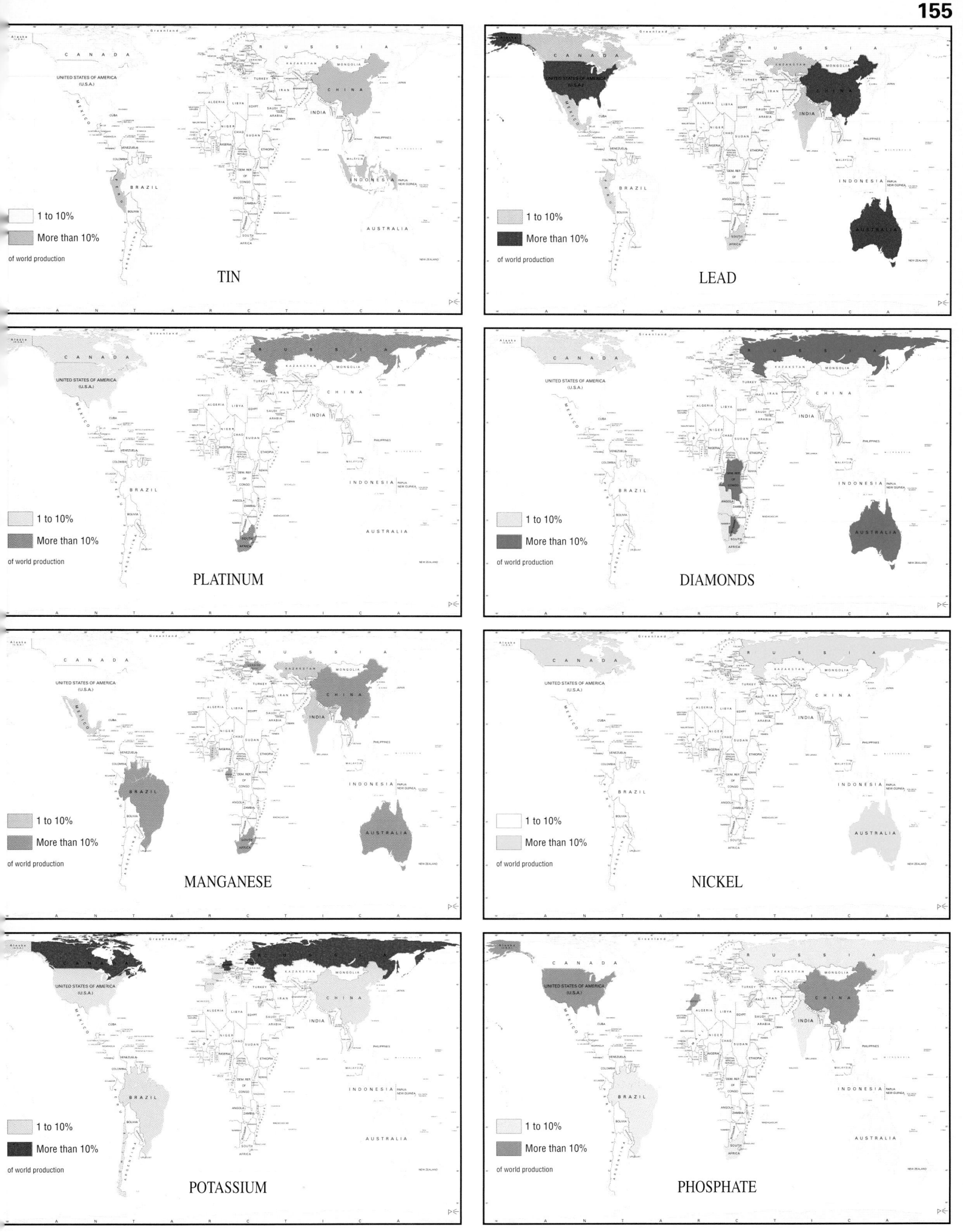

TIN

LEAD

1 to 10%
More than 10%
of world production

PLATINUM

DIAMONDS

1 to 10%
More than 10%
of world production

MANGANESE

NICKEL

1 to 10%
More than 10%
of world production

POTASSIUM

PHOSPHATE

1 to 10%
More than 10%
of world production

ESOURCES

Alaska
(U.S.A.)

Greenland

ICELAND

C A N A D A

UNITED STATES OF AMERICA
(U.S.A.)

MEXICO

BAHAMAS

CUBA
HAITI
JAMAICA
BELIZE
GUATEMALA HONDURAS
EL SALVADOR
NICARAGUA
COSTA RICA
PANAMA

DOMINICAN
REPUBLIC
ANTIGUA & BARBUDA
ST KITTS &
NEVIS
DOMINICA
ST LUCIA
ST VINCENT &
THE GRENADINES BARBADOS
GRENADA
TRINIDAD & TOBAGO

VENEZUELA

COLOMBIA

GUYANA

French
Guiana

ECUADOR

PERU

B R A Z I L

BOLIVIA

PARAGUAY

CHILE

ARGENTINA

URUGUAY

NORWAY
SWEDEN
FINLAND

REPUBLIC
OF IRELAND
UNITED
KINGDOM
DENMARK
ESTONIA
LATVIA
LITH.
POLAND
BELARUS

R U S S I A

NETH.
BELGIUM
LUX.
GERMANY
CZECH
REP.
SLOVAKIA
UKRAINE

K A Z A K S T A N

FRANCE SWITZ.
AUSTRIA
HUNGARY
MOLDOVA
ROMANIA

ANDORRA
SLO.
CRO.
BOS.
SER.
BULGARIA

PORTUGAL
SPAIN
ITALY
ALB. MAC.
GREECE

GEORGIA
UZBEKISTAN
KYRGYZSTAN

AZERBAIJAN
ARM.
TURKMENISTAN
TAJIKISTAN

TURKEY
CYPRUS
SYRIA
LEBANON
ISRAEL
IRAQ
IRAN
AFGHANISTAN

MALTA

MOROCCO

TUNISIA

ALGERIA

LIBYA

EGYPT

SAUDI
ARABIA

KUWAIT
BAHRAIN
QATAR
UNITED ARAB
EMIRATES
OMAN

PAKISTAN

NEPAL

INDIA

WESTERN
SAHARA

MAURITANIA

MALI

NIGER

CHAD

SUDAN

ERITREA

YEMEN

OMAN

CAPE VERDE

SENEGAL

GAMBIA
GUINEA BISSAU
GUINEA
SIERRA LEONE
LIBERIA
CÔTE
D'IVOIRE
GHANA
BURKINA
FASO
BENIN
TOGO
NIGERIA

CAMEROON

CENTRAL
AFRICAN
REPUBLIC

ETHIOPIA

DJIBOUTI

SOMALIA

SRI LANKA

SAO TOME AND
PRINCIPE
EQ. GUINEA
GABON
CONGO
DEM. REP.
OF
CONGO

UGANDA
RWANDA
BURUNDI

KENYA

MALDIVES

ANGOLA

ZAMBIA

TANZANIA

SEYCHELLES

COMOROS

MOZAMBIQUE

MADAGASCAR

MAURITIUS

NAMIBIA

BOTSWANA

ZIMBABWE

SWAZILAND

SOUTH
AFRICA

LESOTHO

Legend

- **Very low:**
  less than 100 kWh per person annually
- **Low:**
  100 to 1,000 kWh per person annually
- **Average:**
  1,000 to 5,000 kWh per person annually
- **High:**
  5,000 to 10,000 kWh per person annually
- **Very high:**
  More than 10,000 kWh per person annually

TOTAL CONSUMPTION

A N T A R C T I

Alaska
(U.S.A.)

Greenland

ICELAND

C A N A D A

R U S S I A

UNITED STATES OF AMERICA
(U.S.A.)

MEXICO

UKRAINE

KAZAKSTAN

MONGOLIA

CUBA

TURKEY

IRAQ IRAN
AFGHANISTAN

C H I N A

JAPAN

BAHAMAS

MOROCCO

ALGERIA
LIBYA
EGYPT

SAUDI
ARABIA
OMAN

INDIA

WESTERN
SAHARA

MAURITANIA

NIGER
CHAD
SUDAN

THAILAND

PHILIPPINES

GUATEMALA
EL SALVADOR
NICARAGUA
COSTA RICA
PANAMA

ANTIGUA & BARBUDA

VENEZUELA

NIGERIA

CENTRAL
AFRICAN
REPUBLIC

ETHIOPIA

SRI LANKA

MALAYSIA

M I C R O N E S I A

COLOMBIA

DEM. REP
OF
CONGO

KENYA

SEYCHELLES

I N D O N E S I A

PAPUA
NEW GUINEA

ECUADOR

PERU

B R A Z I L

ANGOLA

ZAMBIA

TANZANIA

COMOROS

MADAGASCAR

BOLIVIA

NAMIBIA

AUSTRALIA

Legend (OIL)

- Less than 10,000
- 10,000 to 100,000
- More than 100,000

units of 1,000 t annually

SOUTH
AFRICA

ARGENTINA

URUGUAY

NEW ZEALAND

OIL

A N T A R C T I C A

Alaska
(U.S.A.)

Greenland

ICELAND

C A N A D A

UNITED STATES OF AMERICA
(U.S.A.)

MEXICO

BAHAMAS

CUBA

MOROCCO

WESTERN
SAHARA

MAURITANIA

AL

VENEZUELA

COLOMBIA

ECUADOR

PERU

B R A Z I L

BOLIVIA

ARGENTINA

URUGUAY

Legend (NATURAL GAS)

- Less than 10,000
- 10,000 to 100,000
- 100,000 to 500,000
- More than 500,000

units of 1 million m³ annually

NATU

A N T A R

ENE

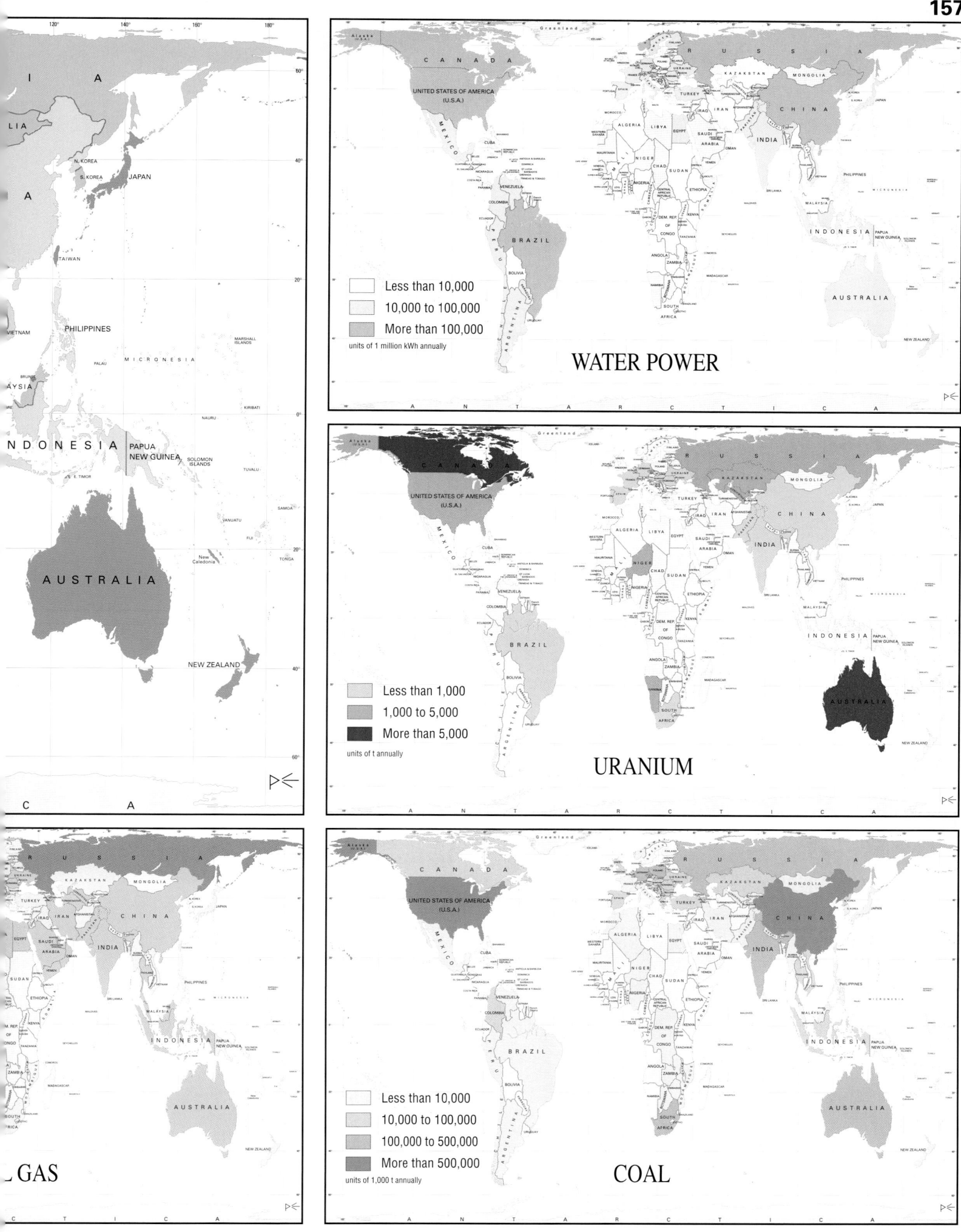

WATER POWER

Less than 10,000
10,000 to 100,000
More than 100,000

units of 1 million kWh annually

URANIUM

Less than 1,000
1,000 to 5,000
More than 5,000

units of t annually

COAL

Less than 10,000
10,000 to 100,000
100,000 to 500,000
More than 500,000

units of 1,000 t annually

GAS

RGY

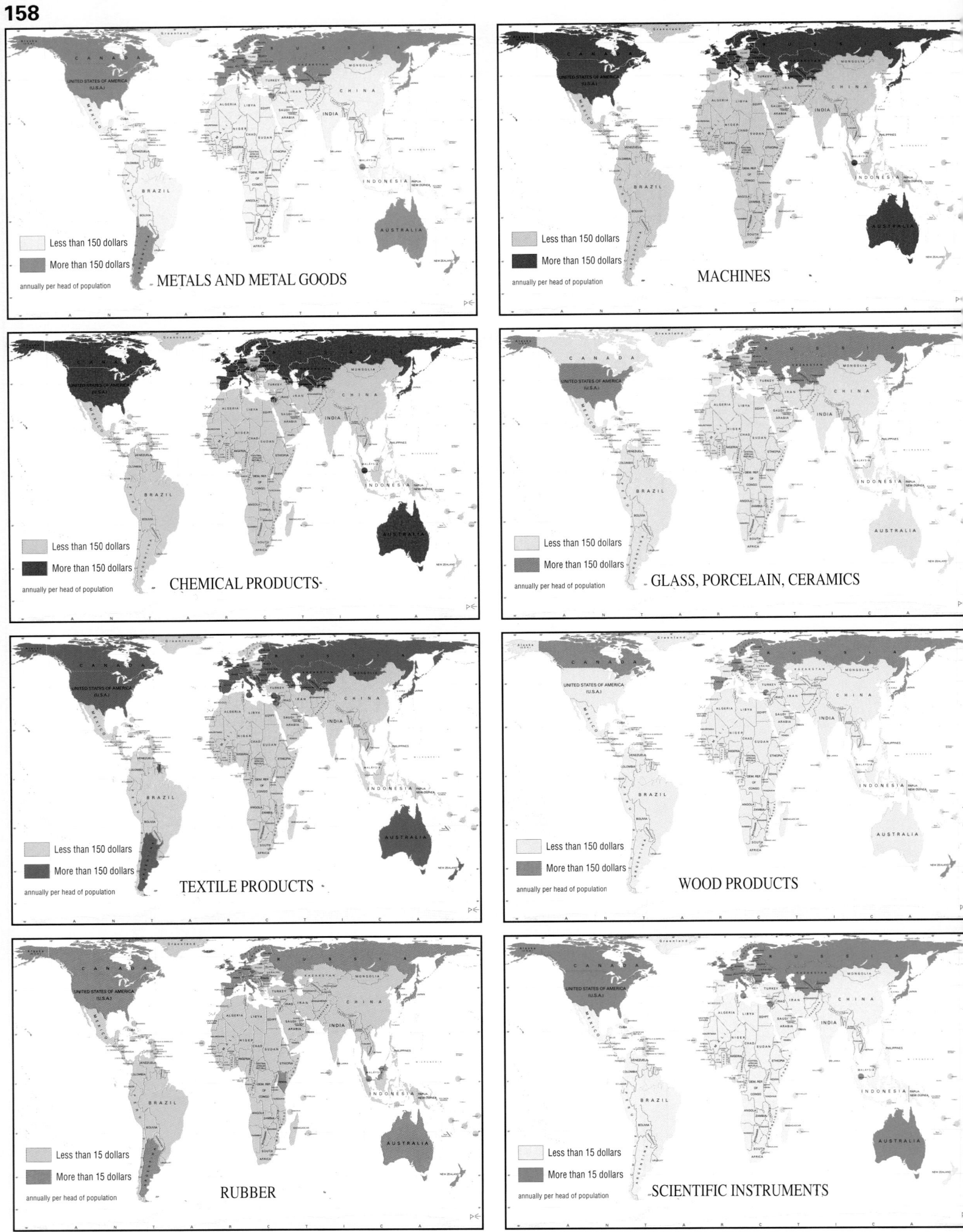

METALS AND METAL GOODS

Less than 150 dollars
More than 150 dollars
annually per head of population

MACHINES

Less than 150 dollars
More than 150 dollars
annually per head of population

CHEMICAL PRODUCTS·

Less than 150 dollars
More than 150 dollars
annually per head of population

GLASS, PORCELAIN, CERAMICS

Less than 150 dollars
More than 150 dollars
annually per head of population

TEXTILE PRODUCTS·

Less than 150 dollars
More than 150 dollars
annually per head of population

WOOD PRODUCTS

Less than 150 dollars
More than 150 dollars
annually per head of population

RUBBER

Less than 15 dollars
More than 15 dollars
annually per head of population

SCIENTIFIC INSTRUMENTS

Less than 15 dollars
More than 15 dollars
annually per head of population

INDUSTRIAL

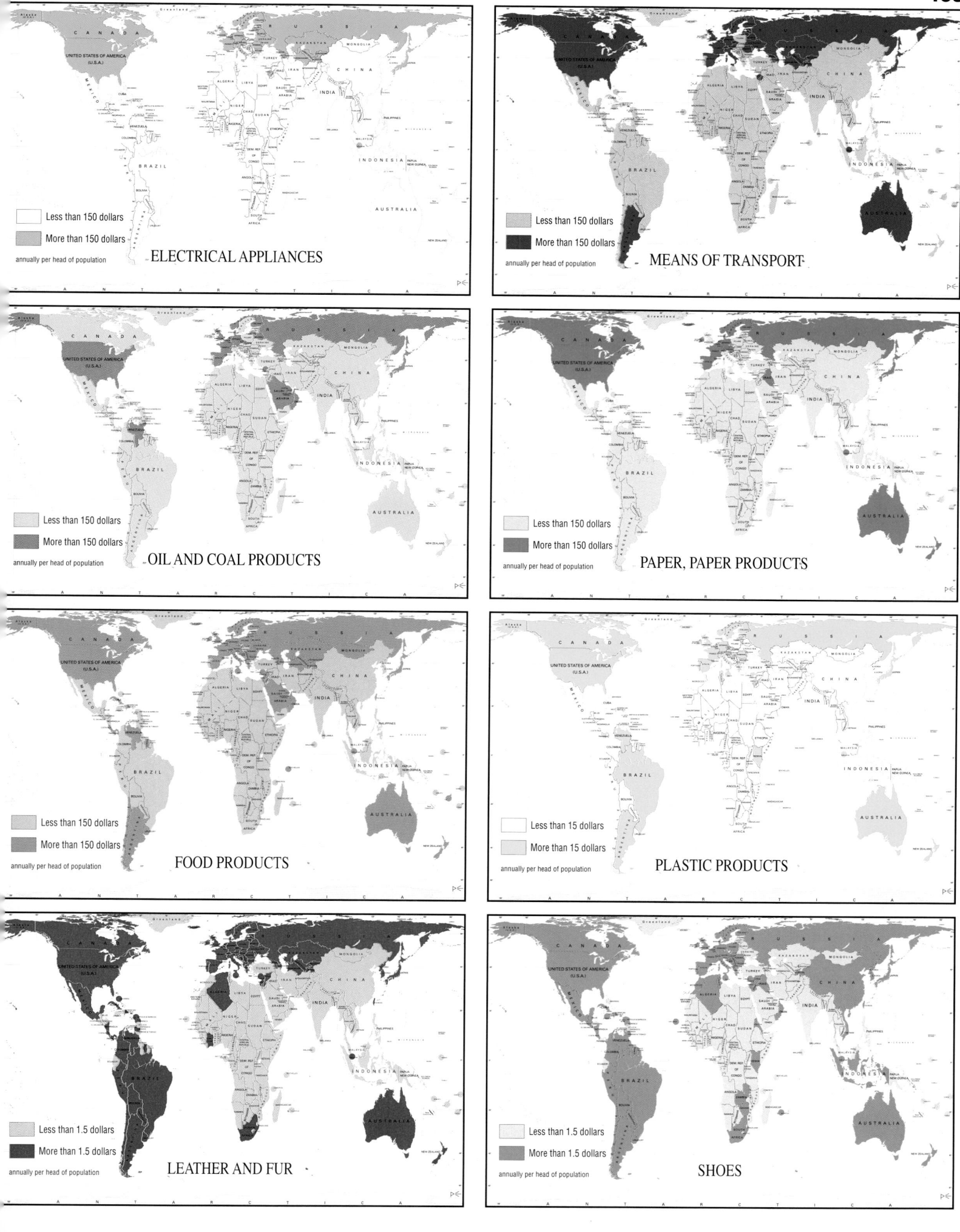

ELECTRICAL APPLIANCES

Less than 150 dollars
More than 150 dollars
annually per head of population

MEANS OF TRANSPORT

Less than 150 dollars
More than 150 dollars
annually per head of population

OIL AND COAL PRODUCTS

Less than 150 dollars
More than 150 dollars
annually per head of population

PAPER, PAPER PRODUCTS

Less than 150 dollars
More than 150 dollars
annually per head of population

FOOD PRODUCTS

Less than 150 dollars
More than 150 dollars
annually per head of population

PLASTIC PRODUCTS

Less than 15 dollars
More than 15 dollars
annually per head of population

LEATHER AND FUR

Less than 1.5 dollars
More than 1.5 dollars
annually per head of population

SHOES

Less than 1.5 dollars
More than 1.5 dollars
annually per head of population

PRODUCTS

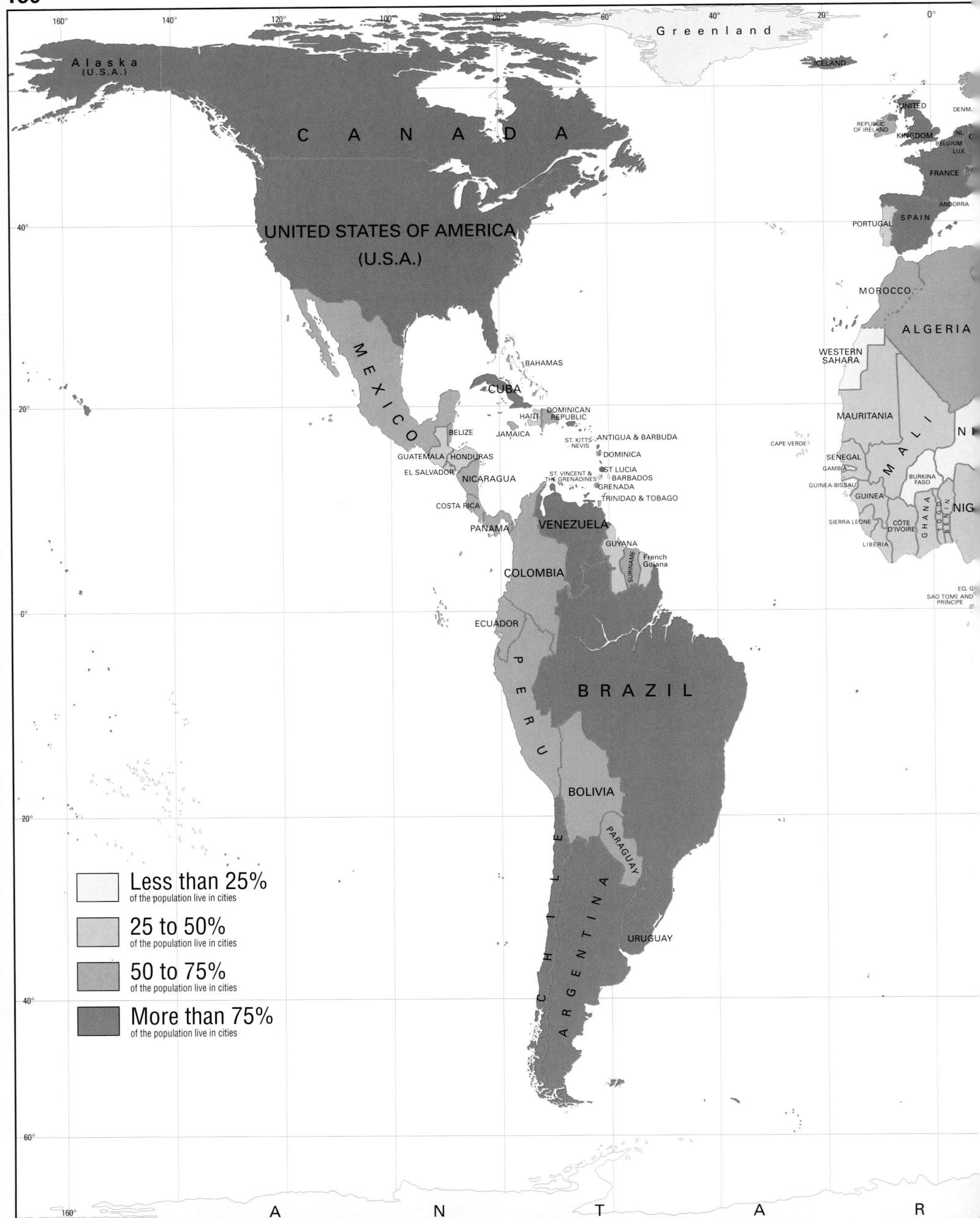

Less than 25%
of the population live in cities

25 to 50%
of the population live in cities

50 to 75%
of the population live in cities

More than 75%
of the population live in cities

URBAN

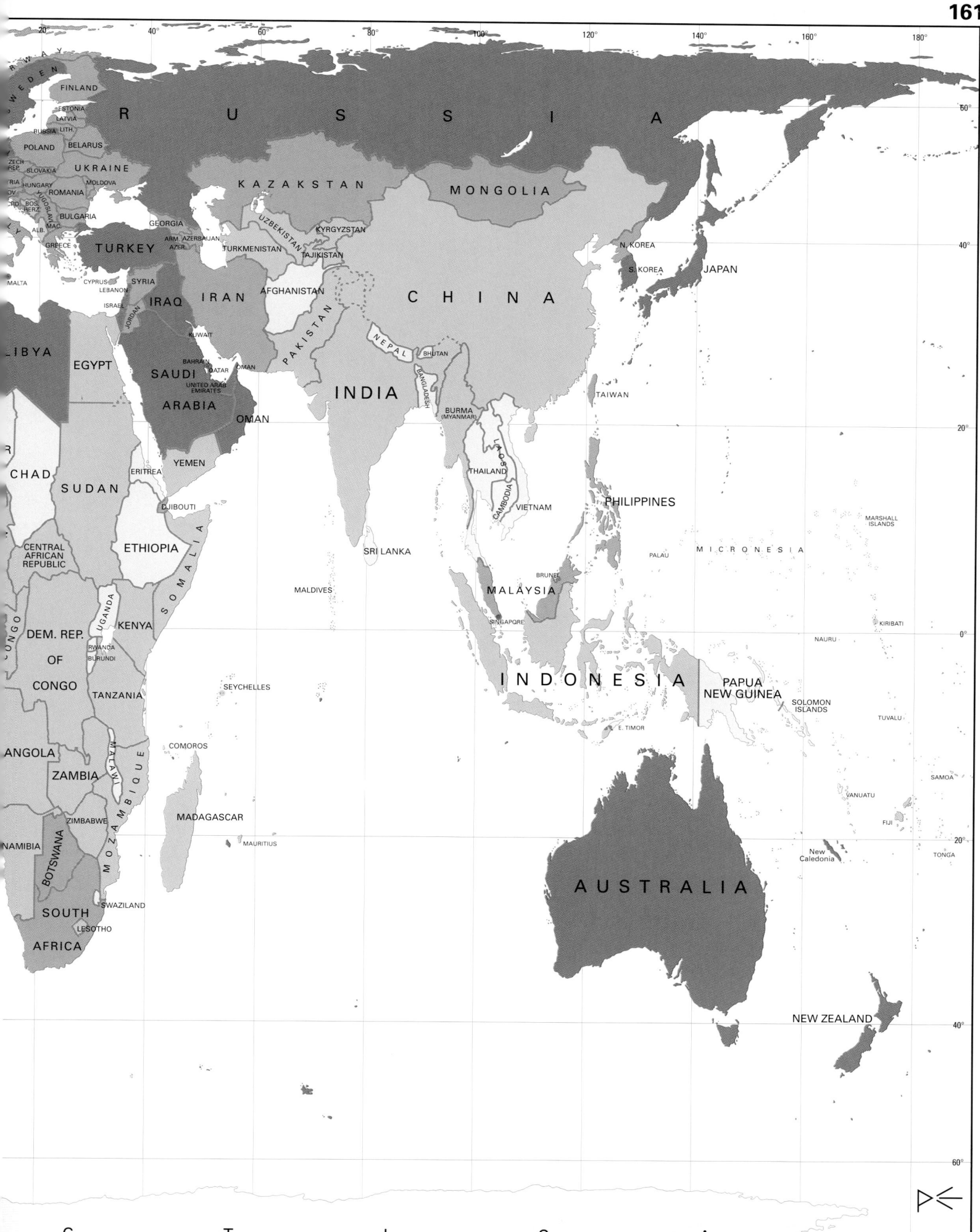

ZATION

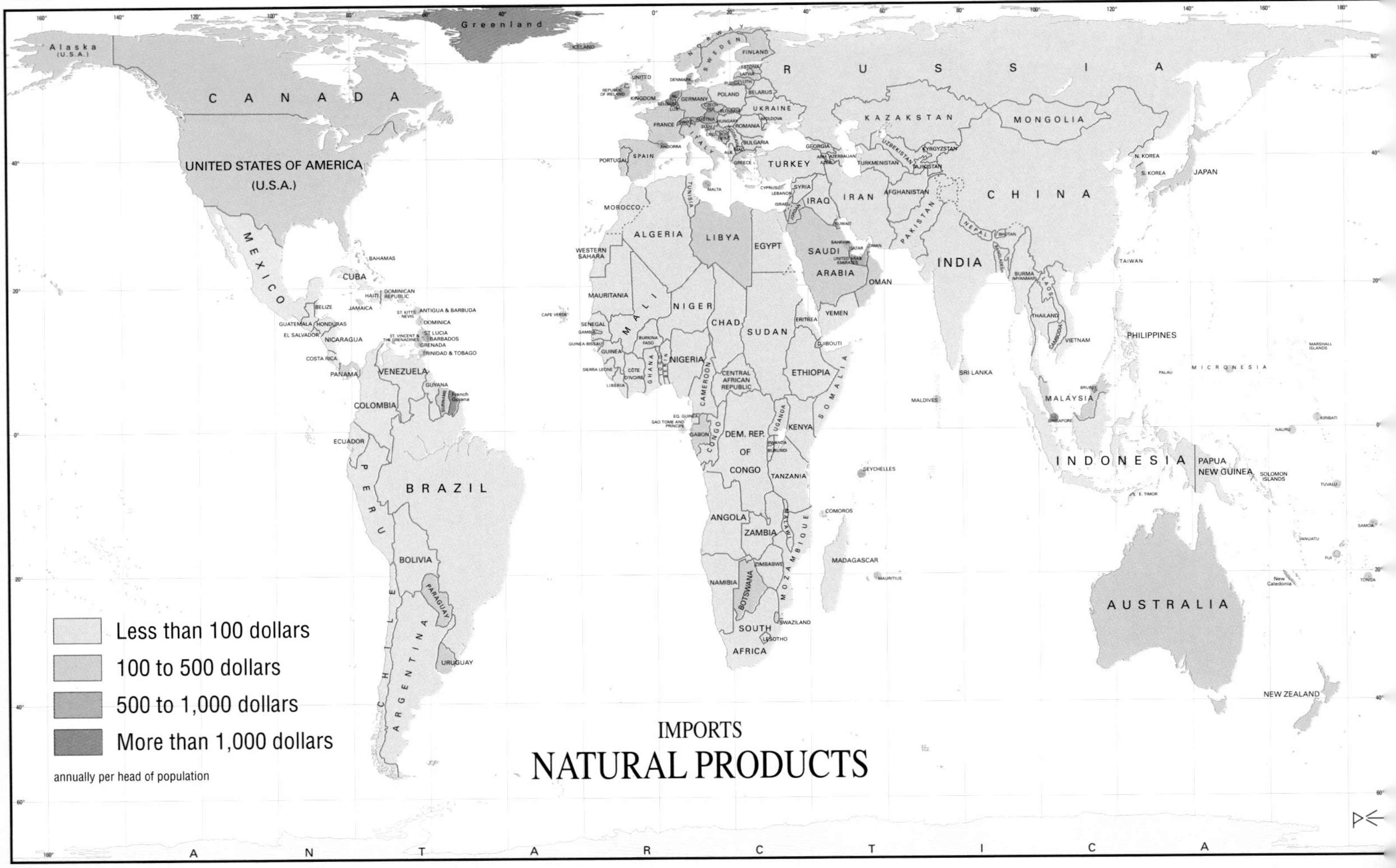
IMPORTS
NATURAL PRODUCTS
Less than 100 dollars
100 to 500 dollars
500 to 1,000 dollars
More than 1,000 dollars
annually per head of population
Greenland
Alaska (U.S.A.)
CANADA
UNITED STATES OF AMERICA (U.S.A.)
MEXICO
CUBA
BAHAMAS
HAITI
DOMINICAN REPUBLIC
BELIZE
JAMAICA
GUATEMALA
HONDURAS
EL SALVADOR
NICARAGUA
COSTA RICA
PANAMA
VENEZUELA
GUYANA
French Guyana
COLOMBIA
ECUADOR
PERU
BRAZIL
BOLIVIA
PARAGUAY
CHILE
ARGENTINA
URUGUAY
ICELAND
NORWAY
SWEDEN
FINLAND
RUSSIA
UNITED KINGDOM
REPUBLIC OF IRELAND
DENMARK
GERMANY
POLAND
BELARUS
UKRAINE
FRANCE
ROMANIA
BULGARIA
SPAIN
PORTUGAL
ITALY
GREECE
TURKEY
GEORGIA
KAZAKSTAN
MONGOLIA
CHINA
N. KOREA
S. KOREA
JAPAN
TAIWAN
PHILIPPINES
MOROCCO
ALGERIA
TUNISIA
LIBYA
EGYPT
WESTERN SAHARA
MAURITANIA
MALI
NIGER
CHAD
SUDAN
ERITREA
ETHIOPIA
SOMALIA
DJIBOUTI
SENEGAL
GUINEA
SIERRA LEONE
LIBERIA
CÔTE D'IVOIRE
GHANA
BURKINA FASO
NIGERIA
CAMEROON
CENTRAL AFRICAN REPUBLIC
GABON
CONGO
DEM. REP. OF CONGO
UGANDA
KENYA
RWANDA
BURUNDI
TANZANIA
ANGOLA
ZAMBIA
ZIMBABWE
MOZAMBIQUE
MALAWI
NAMIBIA
BOTSWANA
SOUTH AFRICA
SWAZILAND
LESOTHO
MADAGASCAR
COMOROS
SEYCHELLES
MAURITIUS
CAPE VERDE
SYRIA
IRAQ
IRAN
AFGHANISTAN
PAKISTAN
SAUDI ARABIA
YEMEN
OMAN
INDIA
NEPAL
BHUTAN
SRI LANKA
MALDIVES
BURMA
THAILAND
VIETNAM
MALAYSIA
INDONESIA
PAPUA NEW GUINEA
AUSTRALIA
NEW ZEALAND
SOLOMON ISLANDS
MICRONESIA
ANTARCTICA

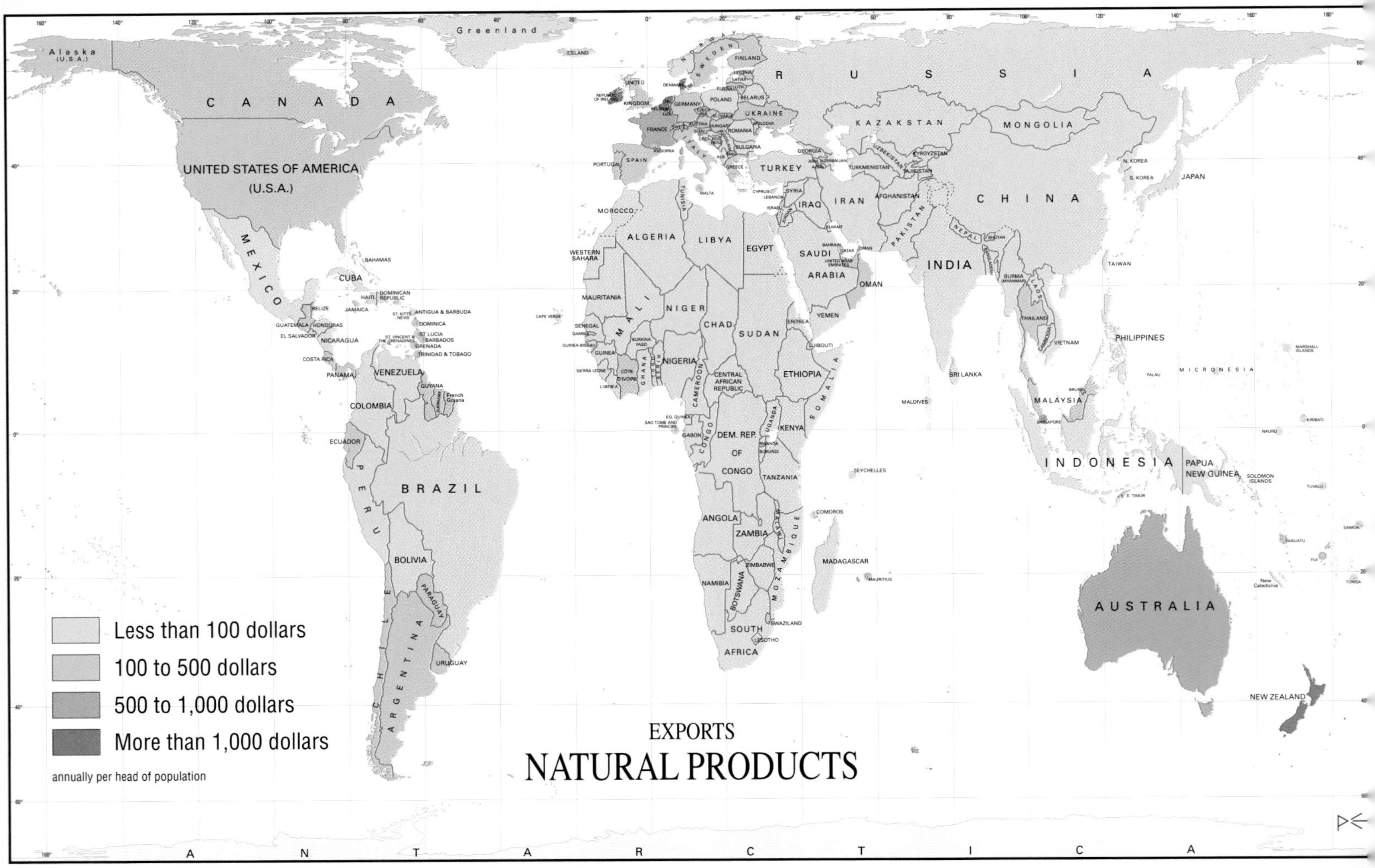
EXPORTS
NATURAL PRODUCTS
Less than 100 dollars
100 to 500 dollars
500 to 1,000 dollars
More than 1,000 dollars
annually per head of population
Greenland
Alaska (U.S.A.)
CANADA
UNITED STATES OF AMERICA (U.S.A.)
MEXICO
CUBA
BRAZIL
PERU
BOLIVIA
PARAGUAY
CHILE
ARGENTINA
URUGUAY
VENEZUELA
COLOMBIA
ECUADOR
RUSSIA
KAZAKSTAN
MONGOLIA
CHINA
JAPAN
INDIA
IRAN
IRAQ
SAUDI ARABIA
OMAN
TURKEY
ALGERIA
LIBYA
EGYPT
MALI
NIGER
CHAD
SUDAN
ETHIOPIA
NIGERIA
DEM. REP. OF CONGO
TANZANIA
ANGOLA
ZAMBIA
MADAGASCAR
SOUTH AFRICA
INDONESIA
PAPUA NEW GUINEA
PHILIPPINES
MALAYSIA
AUSTRALIA
NEW ZEALAND
ANTARCTICA

WORLD

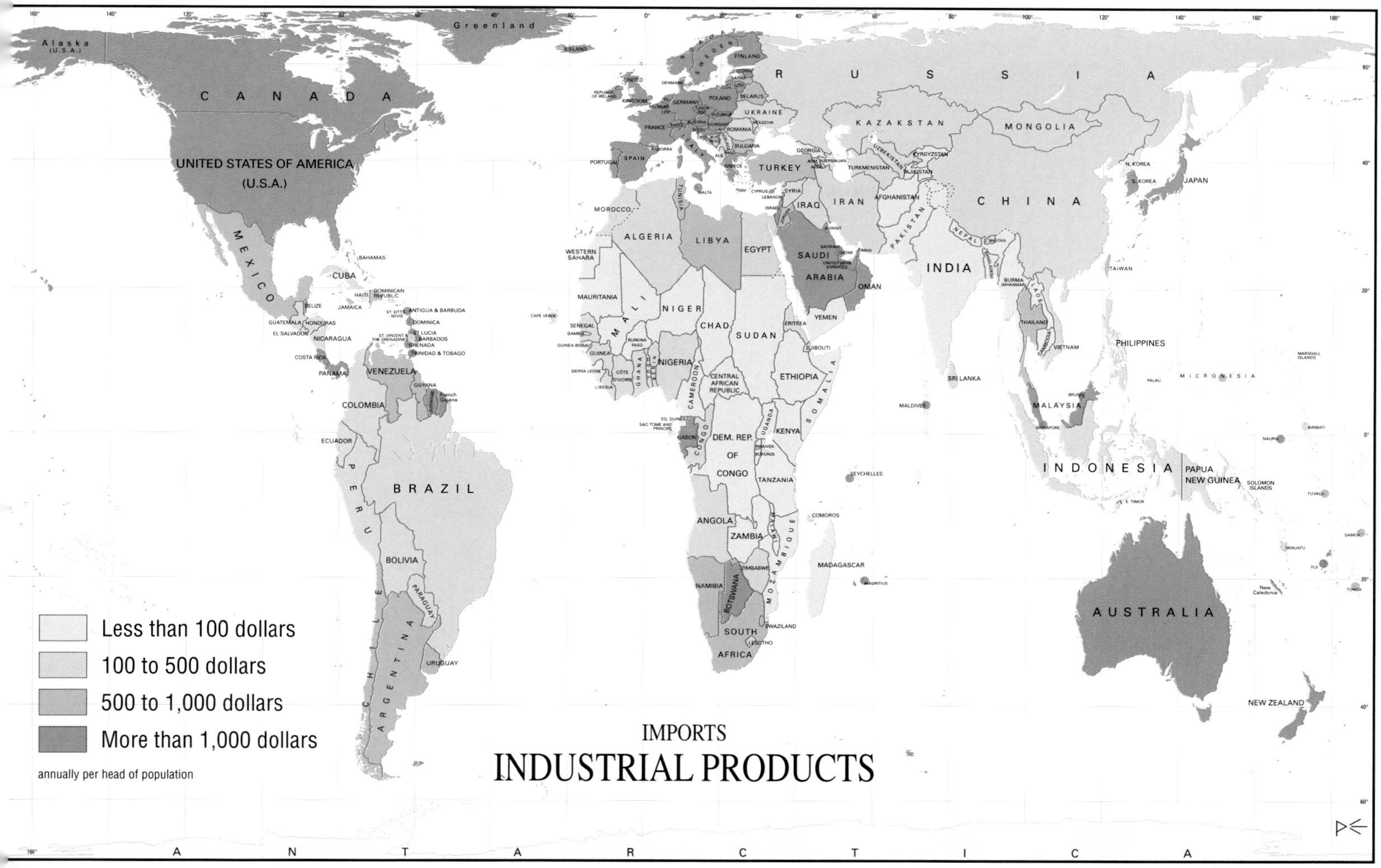

IMPORTS
INDUSTRIAL PRODUCTS

Less than 100 dollars
100 to 500 dollars
500 to 1,000 dollars
More than 1,000 dollars

annually per head of population

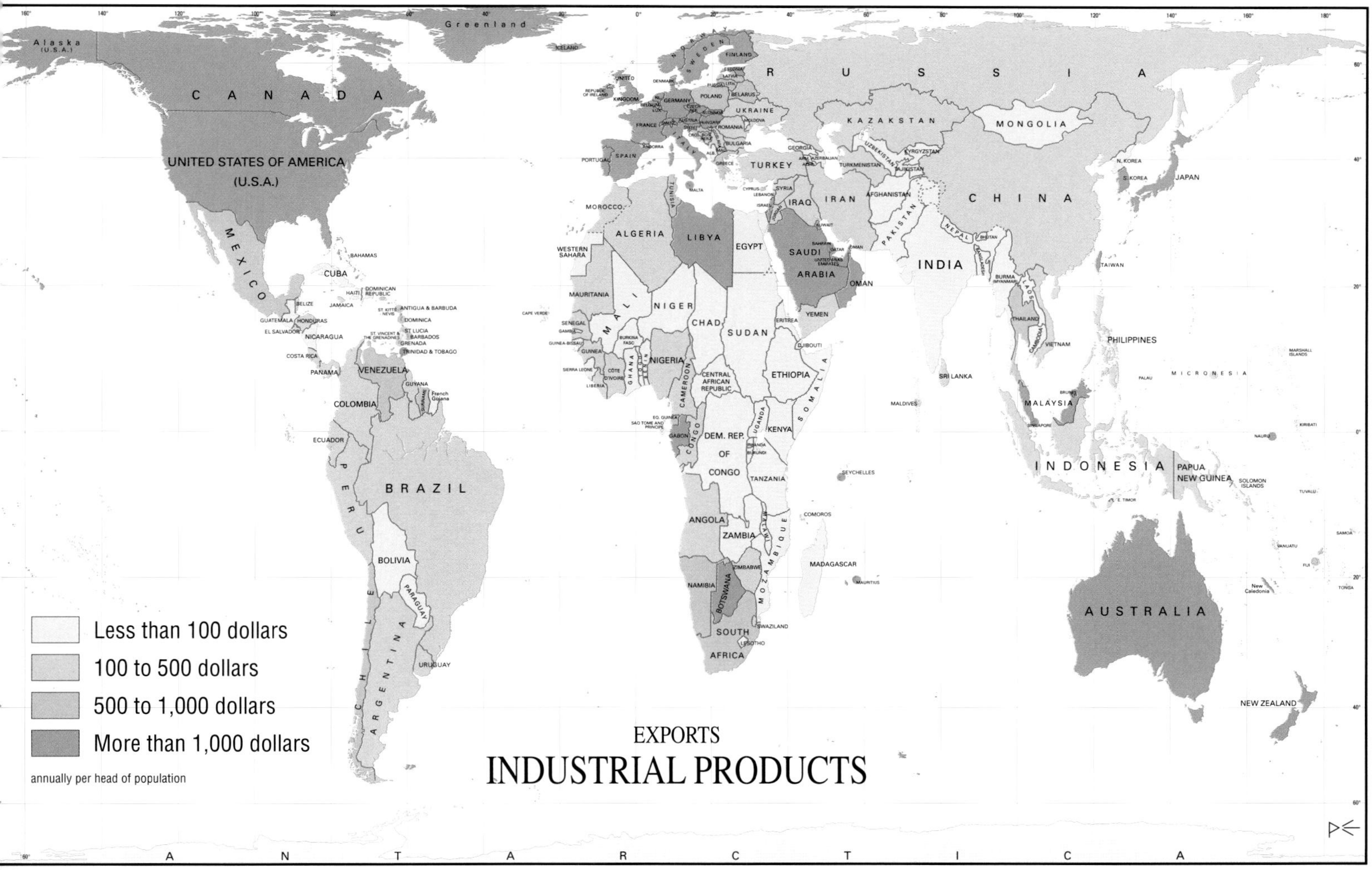

EXPORTS
INDUSTRIAL PRODUCTS

Less than 100 dollars
100 to 500 dollars
500 to 1,000 dollars
More than 1,000 dollars

annually per head of population

TRADE

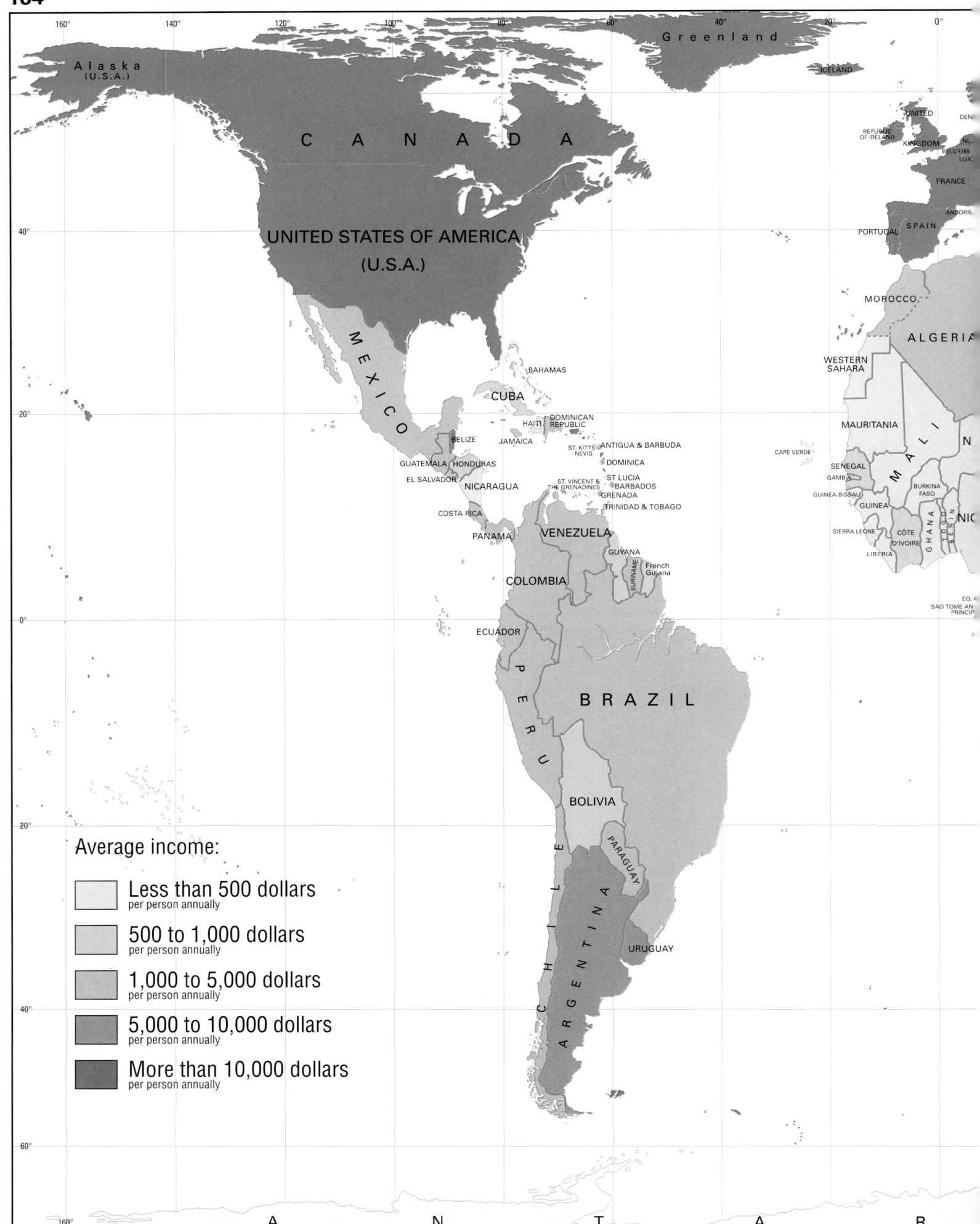

Average income:

Less than 500 dollars
per person annually

500 to 1,000 dollars
per person annually

1,000 to 5,000 dollars
per person annually

5,000 to 10,000 dollars
per person annually

More than 10,000 dollars
per person annually

POOR NATIONS

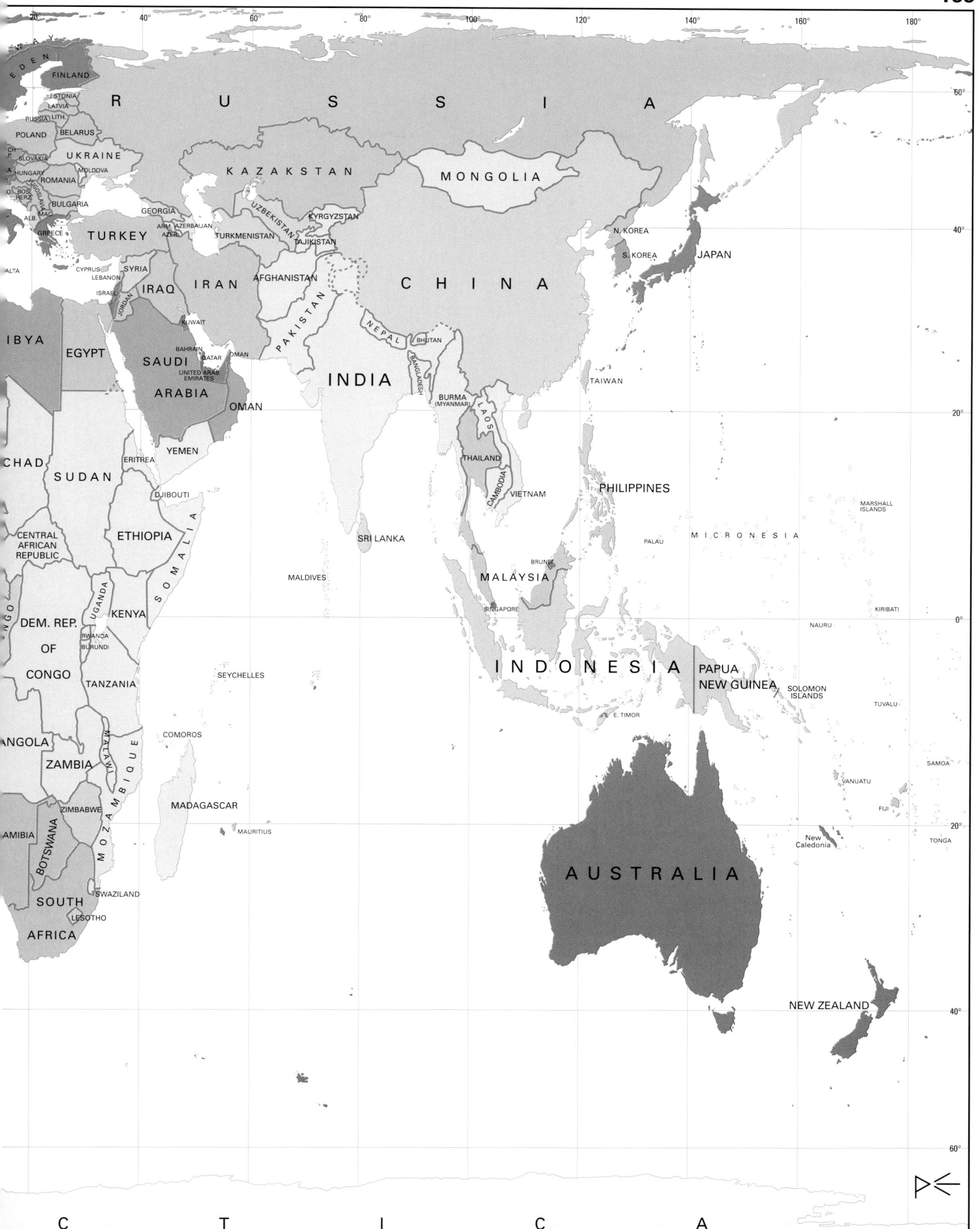

RICH NATIONS

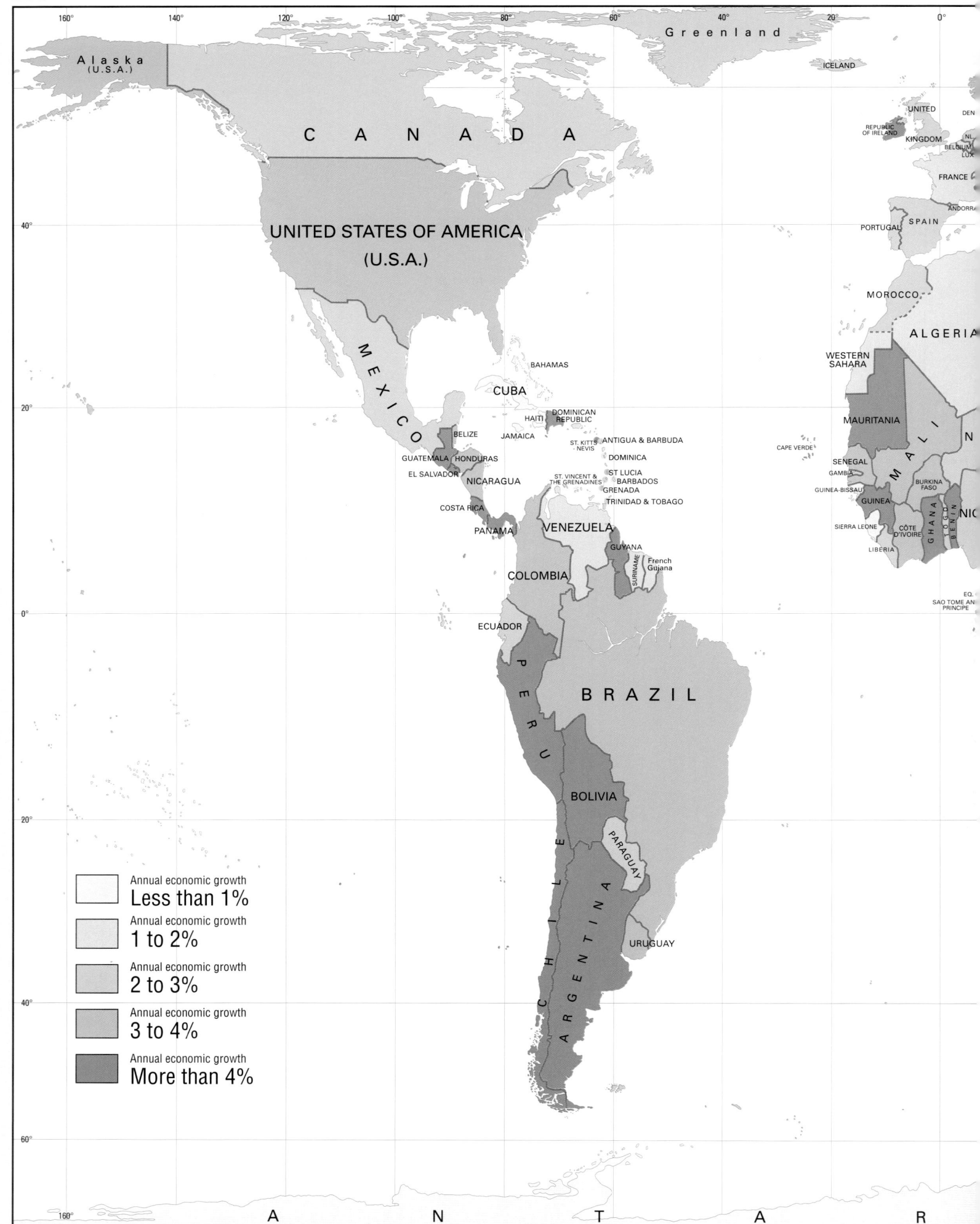

160°　140°　120°　100°　80°　60°　40°　20°　0°

Greenland

ICELAND

Alaska
(U.S.A.)

UNITED
KINGDOM

DEN

NL
BELGIUM
LUX

C A N A D A

FRANCE

ANDORRA

REPUBLIC
OF IRELAND

40°

UNITED STATES OF AMERICA

SPAIN

(U.S.A.)

PORTUGAL

MOROCCO

ALGERIA

WESTERN
SAHARA

BAHAMAS

M
E
X
I
C
O

20°

CUBA

MAURITANIA

HAITI

DOMINICAN
REPUBLIC

CAPE VERDE

M
A
L
I

N

BELIZE

JAMAICA

ST. KITTS
NEVIS

ANTIGUA & BARBUDA

SENEGAL

GUATEMALA

HONDURAS

DOMINICA

GAMBIA

BURKINA
FASO

EL SALVADOR

NICARAGUA

ST LUCIA

GUINEA-BISSAU

ST. VINCENT &
THE GRENADINES

BARBADOS

GRENADA

GUINEA

NIC

COSTA RICA

TRINIDAD & TOBAGO

SIERRA LEONE

CÔTE
D'IVOIRE

G
H
A
N
A

T
O
G
O

B
E
N
I

PANAMA

VENEZUELA

LIBERIA

0°

GUYANA

COLOMBIA

S
U
R
I
N
A
M
E

French
Guiana

EQ.
SAO TOME AN
PRINCIPE

ECUADOR

P
E
R
U

B R A Z I L

20°

BOLIVIA

C
H
I
L
E

P
A
R
A
G
U
A
Y

A
R
G
E
N
T
I
N
A

URUGUAY

Annual economic growth
Less than 1%

Annual economic growth
1 to 2%

40°

Annual economic growth
2 to 3%

Annual economic growth
3 to 4%

Annual economic growth
More than 4%

60°

160°

A　N　T　A　R

ECONOMI

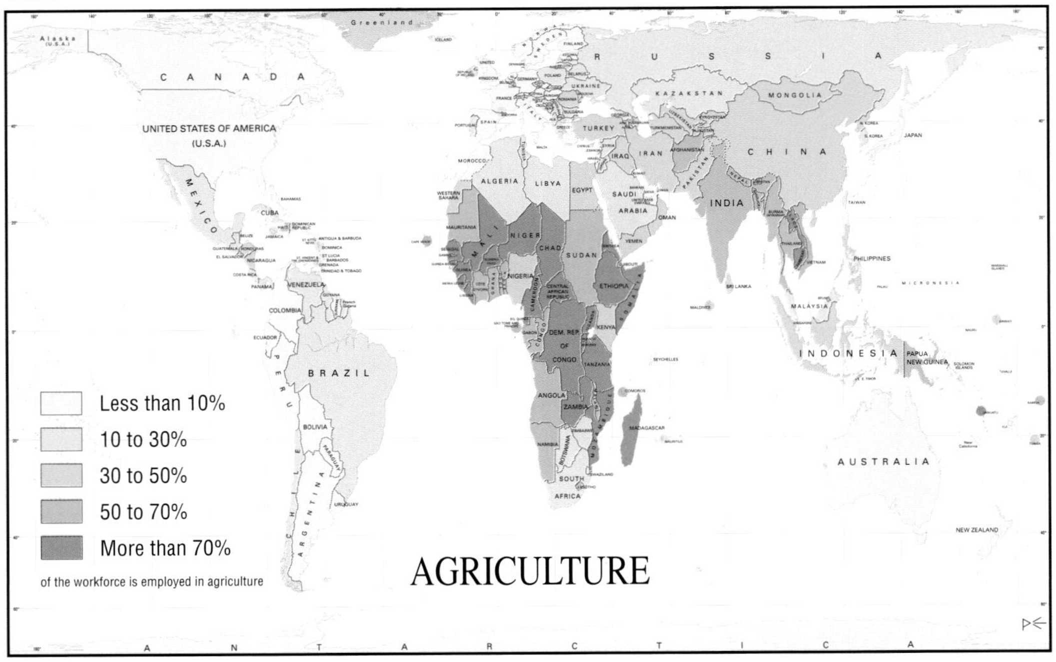

AGRICULTURE

	Less than 10%
	10 to 30%
	30 to 50%
	50 to 70%
	More than 70%

of the workforce is employed in agriculture

TRA

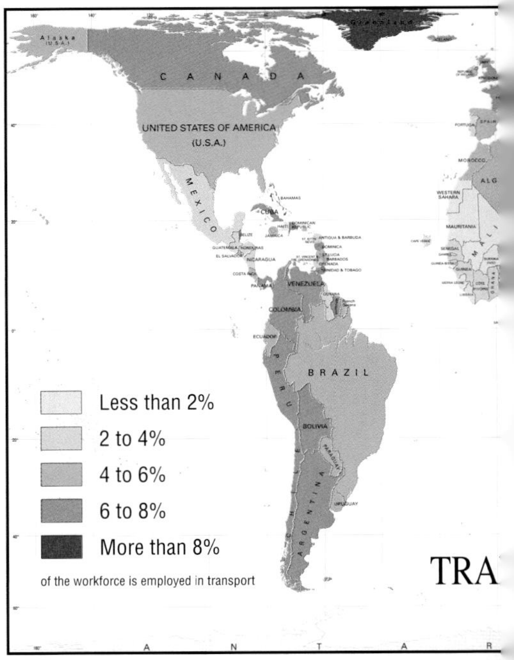

	Less than 2%
	2 to 4%
	4 to 6%
	6 to 8%
	More than 8%

of the workforce is employed in transport

MINING

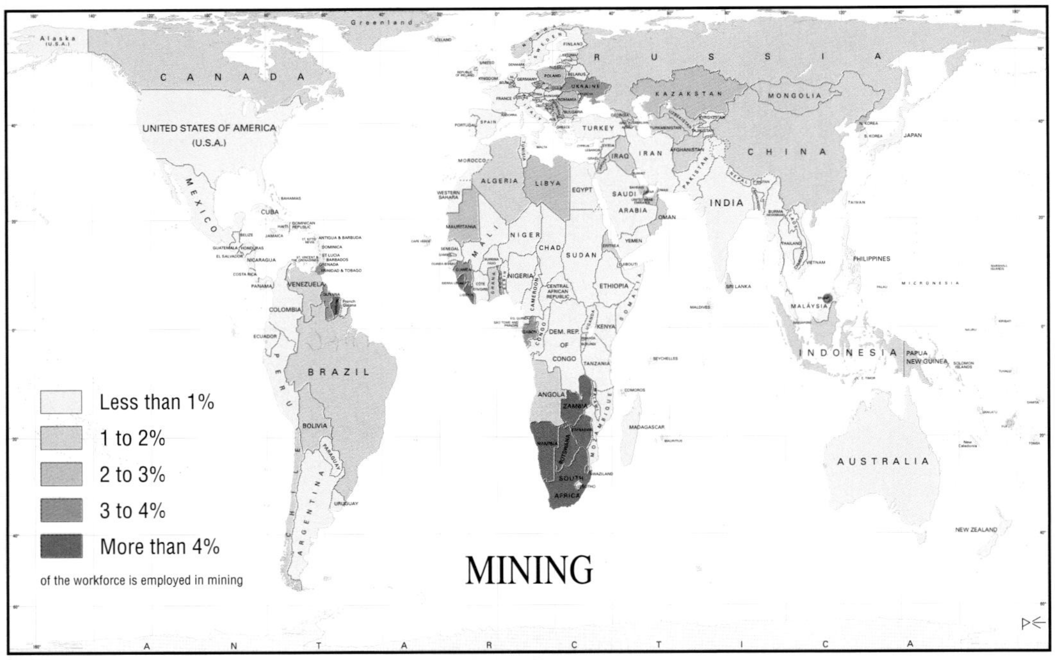

	Less than 1%
	1 to 2%
	2 to 3%
	3 to 4%
	More than 4%

of the workforce is employed in mining

BU

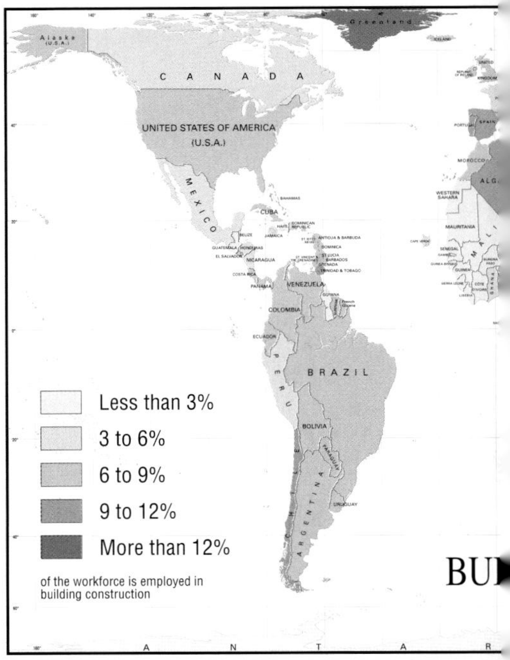

	Less than 3%
	3 to 6%
	6 to 9%
	9 to 12%
	More than 12%

of the workforce is employed in
building construction

ENERGY

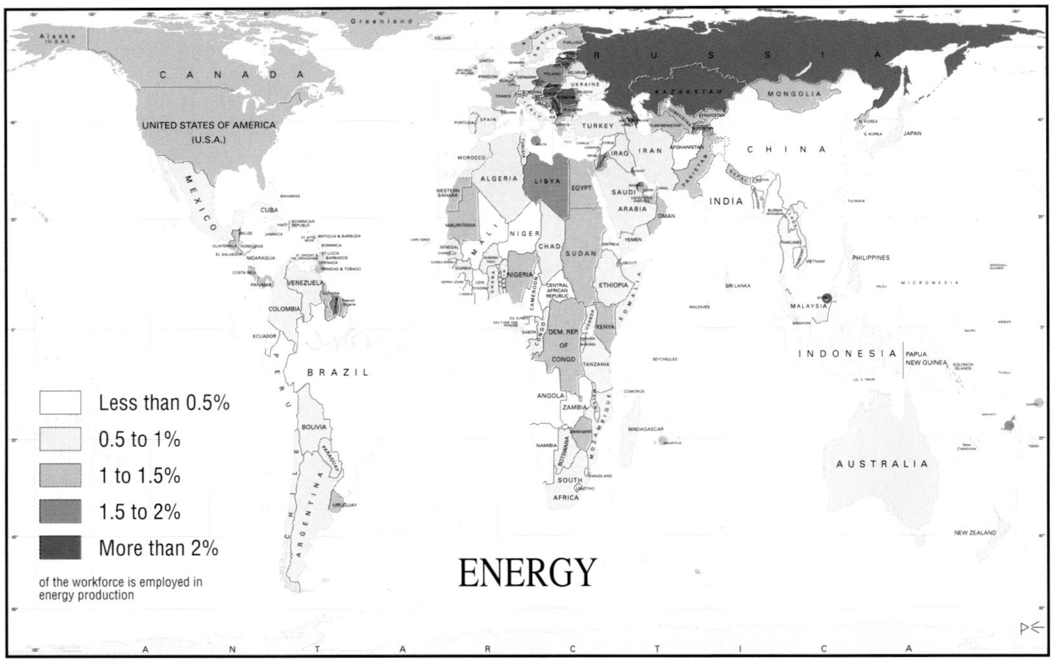

	Less than 0.5%
	0.5 to 1%
	1 to 1.5%
	1.5 to 2%
	More than 2%

of the workforce is employed in
energy production

SOCIAL P

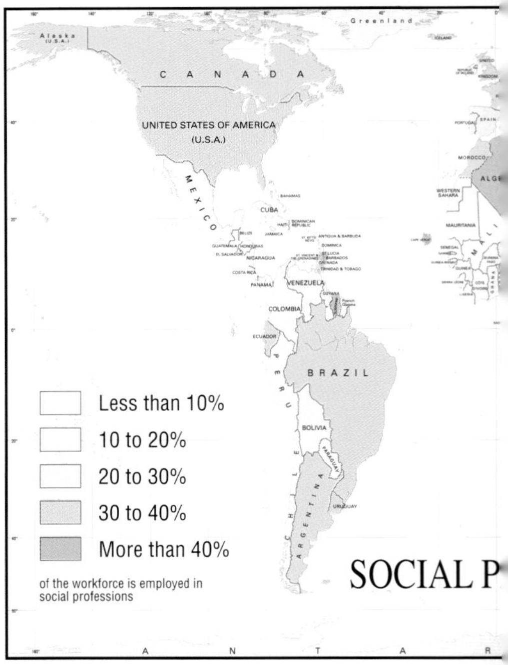

	Less than 10%
	10 to 20%
	20 to 30%
	30 to 40%
	More than 40%

of the workforce is employed in
social professions

EMPLOYMEN

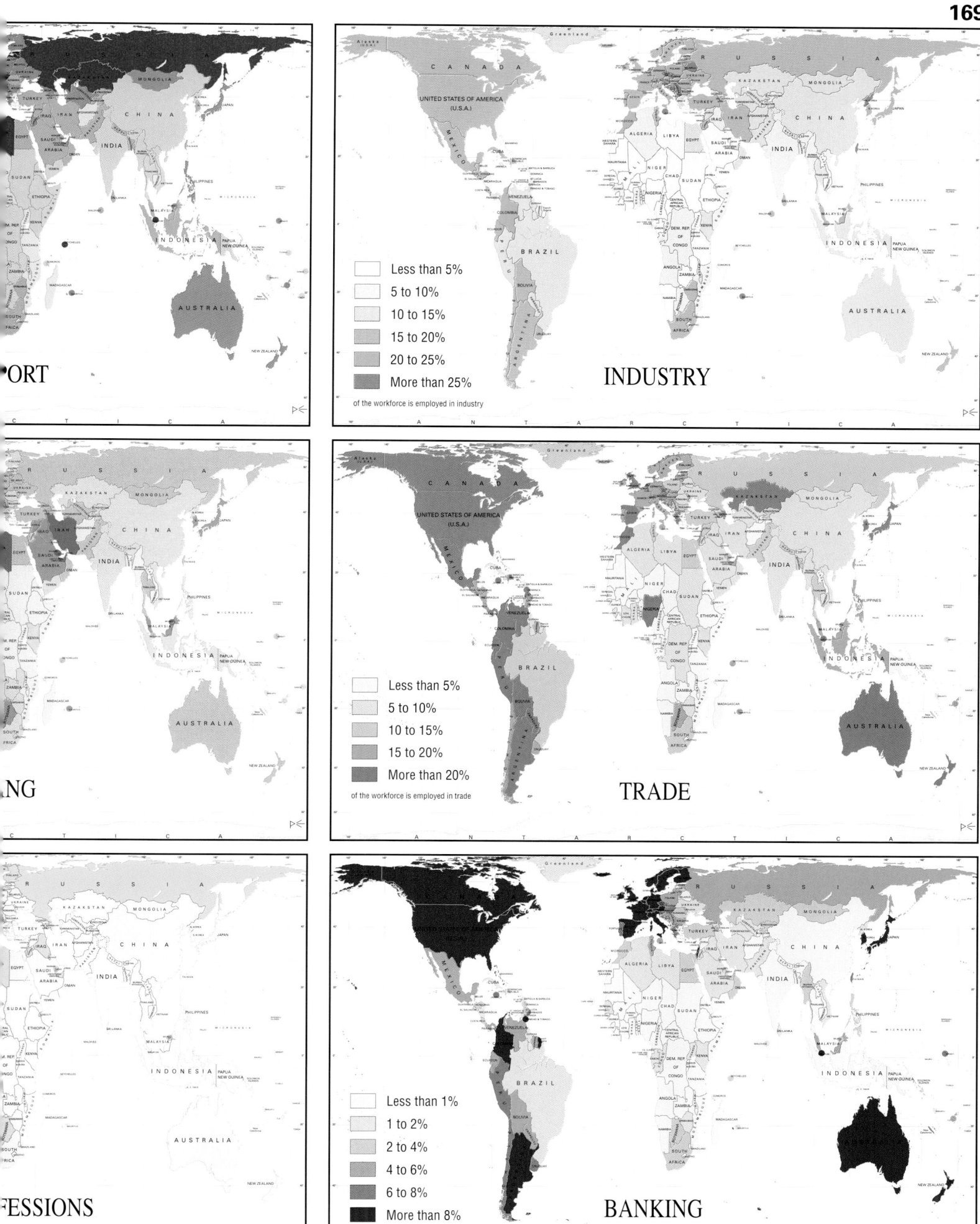

ORT

INDUSTRY

of the workforce is employed in industry

Less than 5%
5 to 10%
10 to 15%
15 to 20%
20 to 25%
More than 25%

NG

TRADE

of the workforce is employed in trade

Less than 5%
5 to 10%
10 to 15%
15 to 20%
More than 20%

FESSIONS

BANKING

of the workforce is employed in banking

Less than 1%
1 to 2%
2 to 4%
4 to 6%
6 to 8%
More than 8%

STRUCTURE

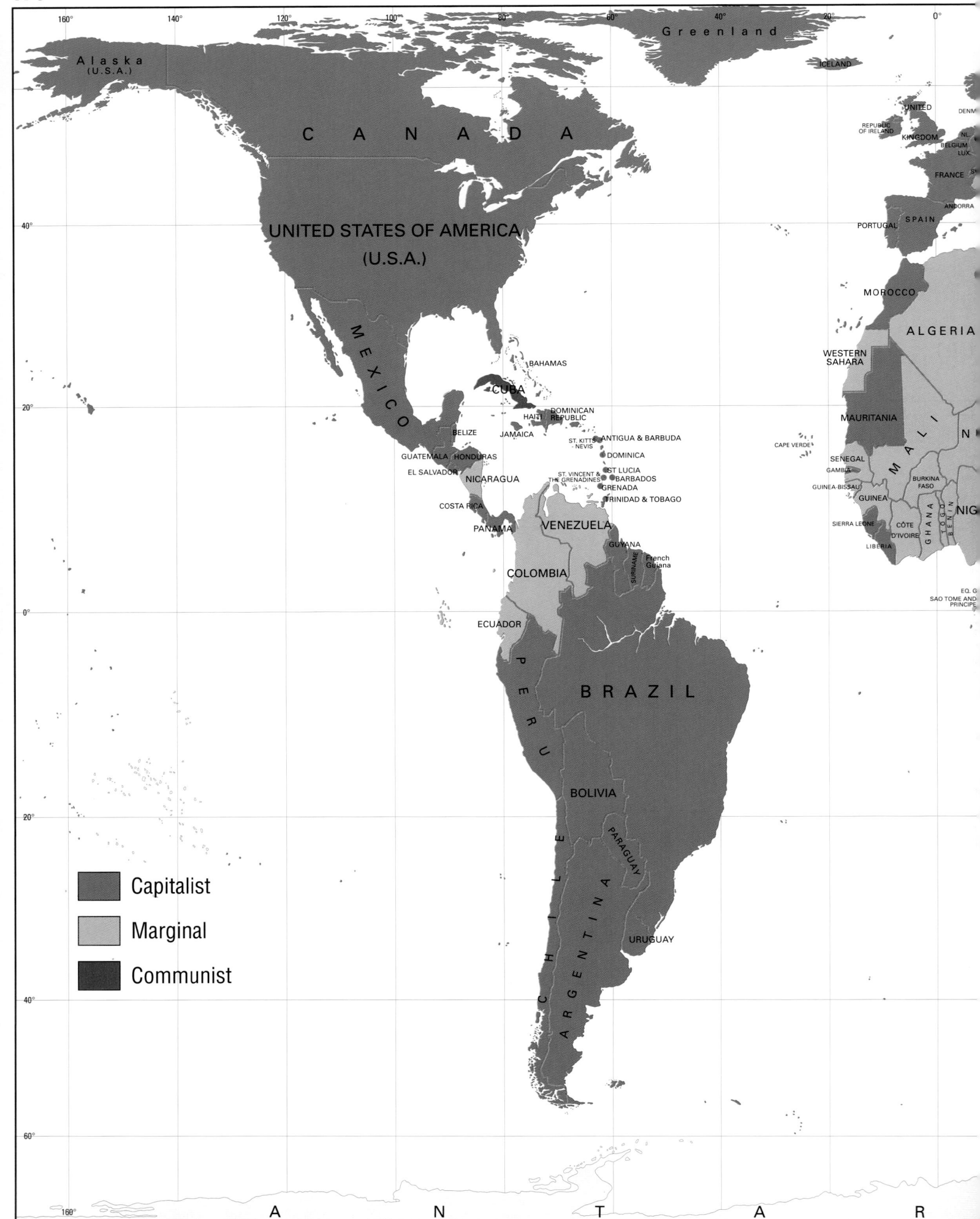

Capitalist

Marginal

Communist

ECONOM

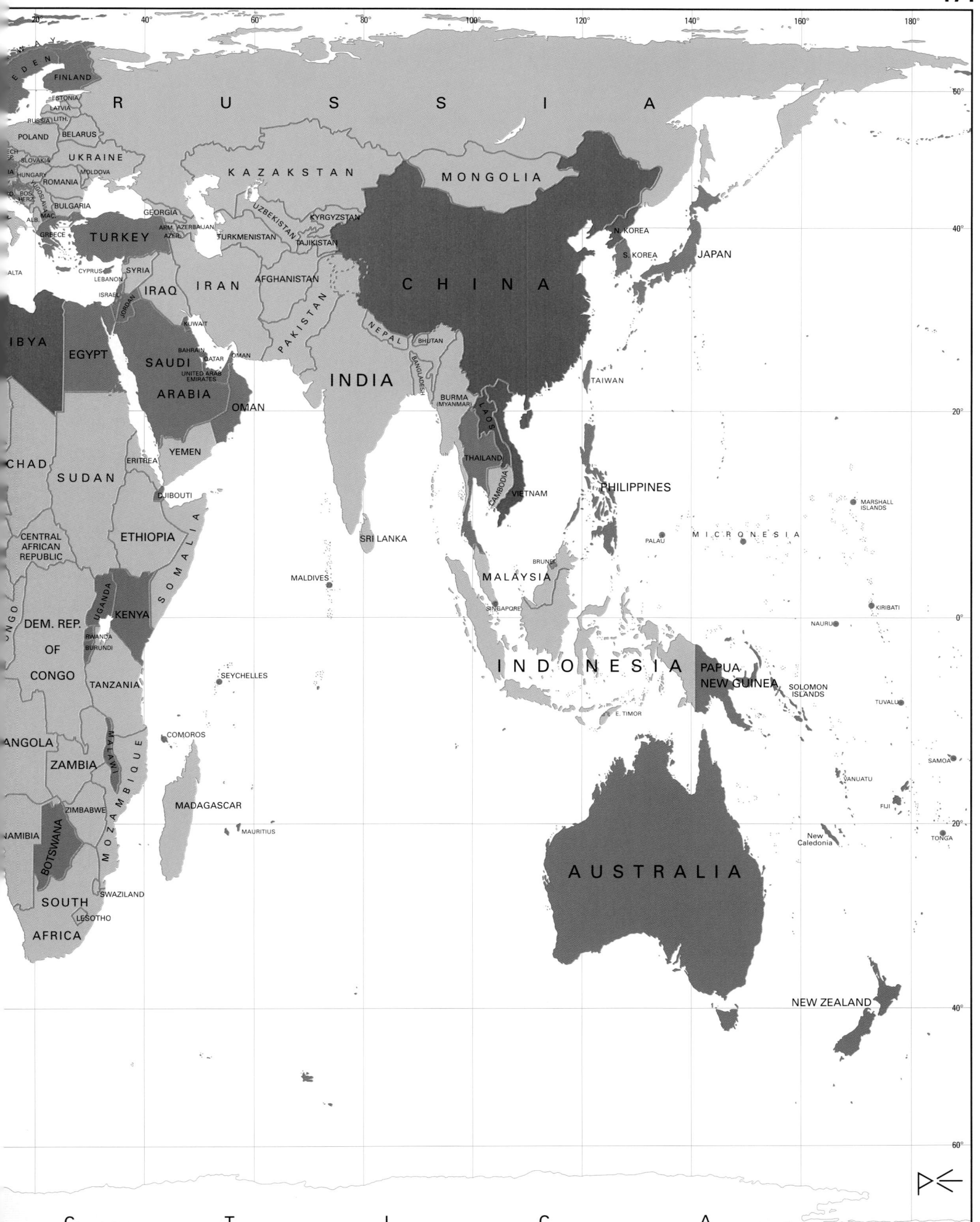

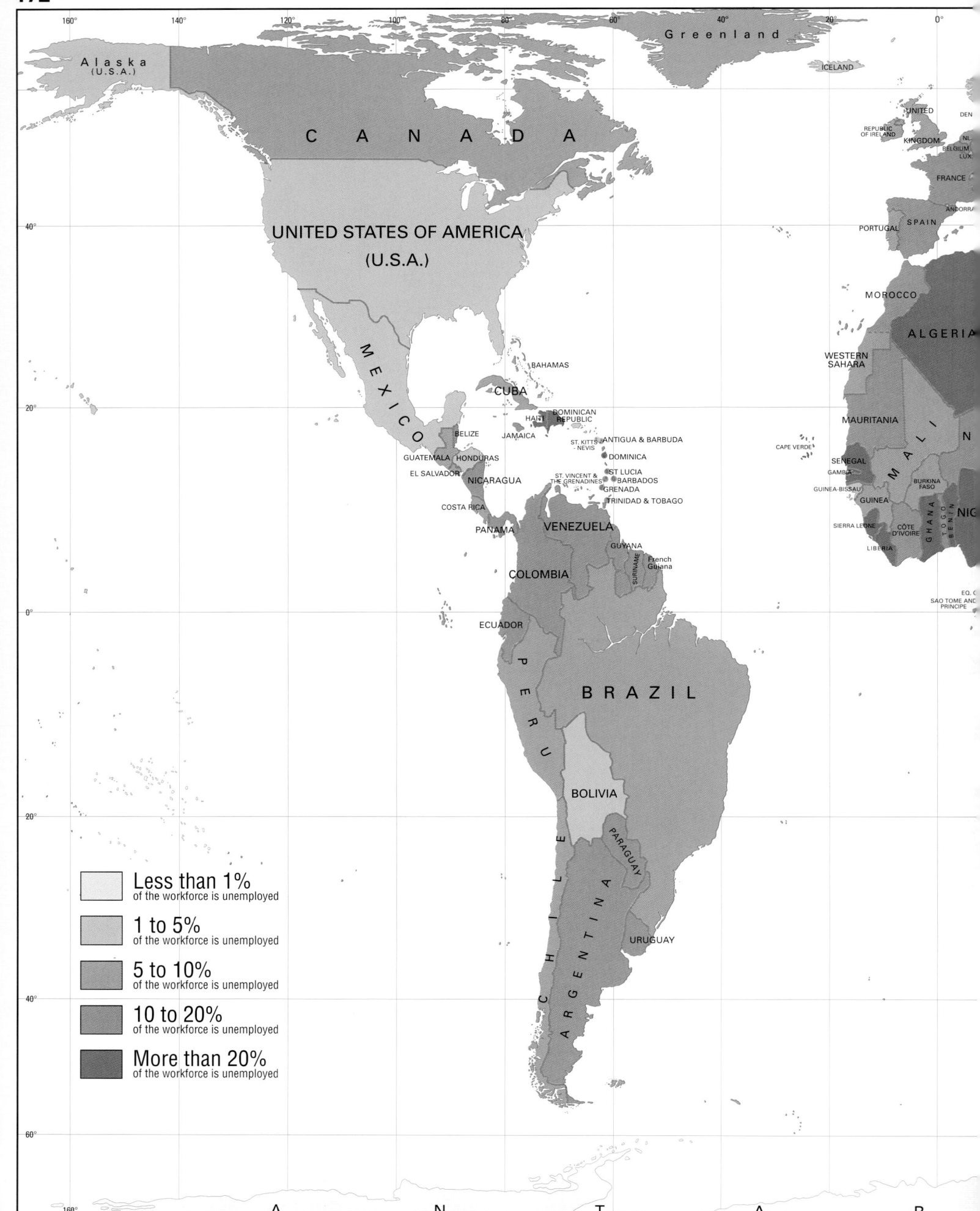

Less than 1%
of the workforce is unemployed

1 to 5%
of the workforce is unemployed

5 to 10%
of the workforce is unemployed

10 to 20%
of the workforce is unemployed

More than 20%
of the workforce is unemployed

UNEMPL

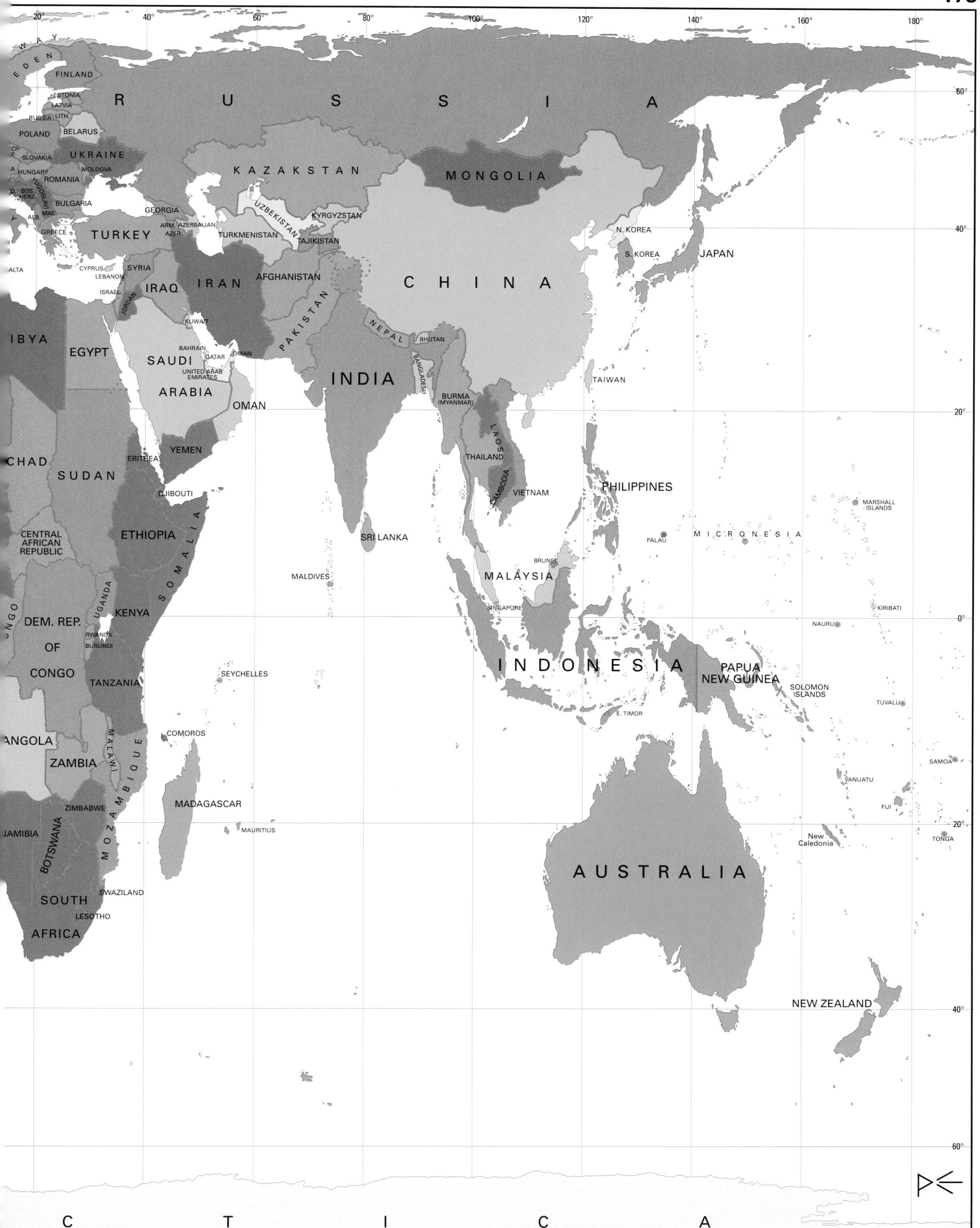

OYMENT

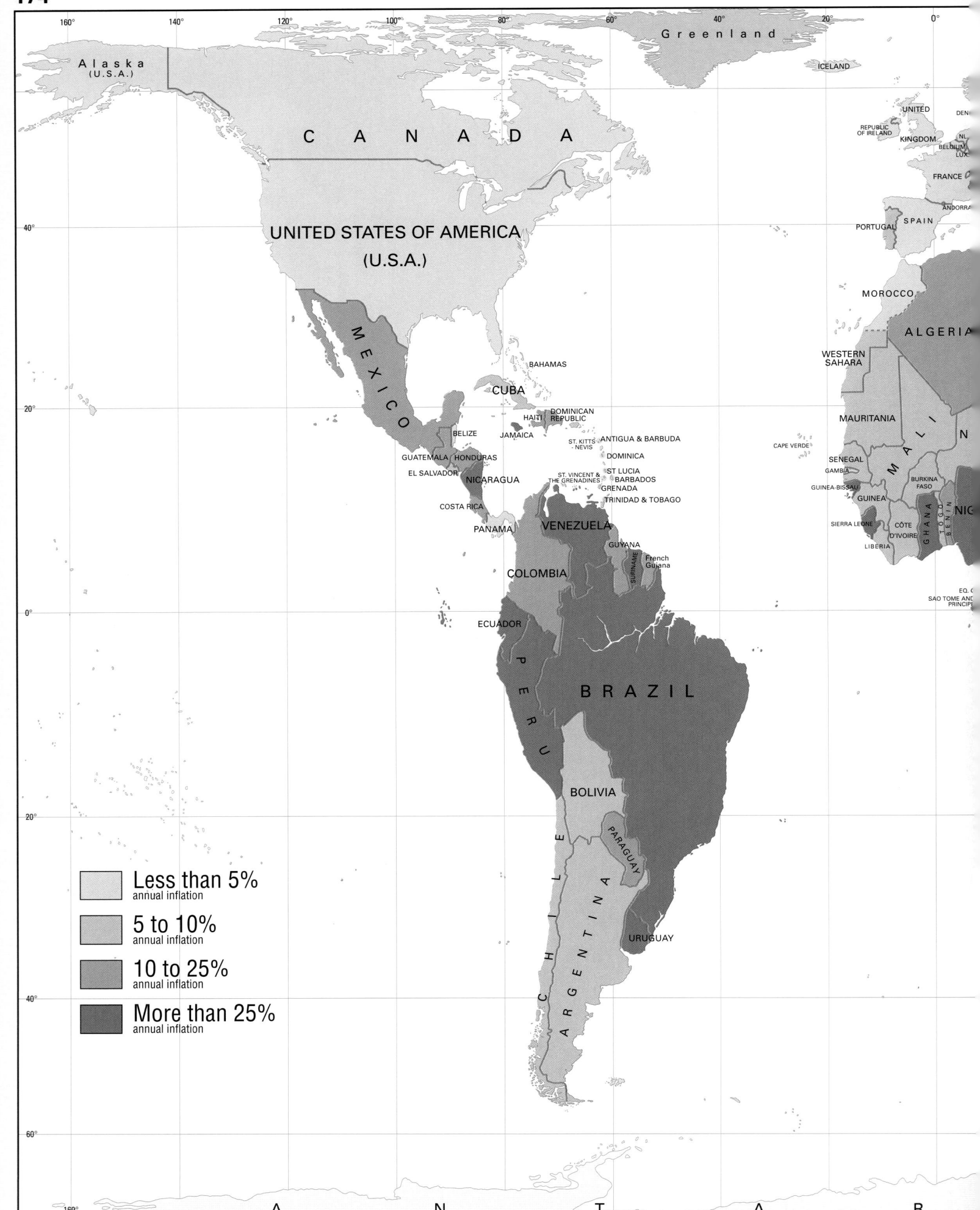

Less than 5%
annual inflation

5 to 10%
annual inflation

10 to 25%
annual inflation

More than 25%
annual inflation

INFLA

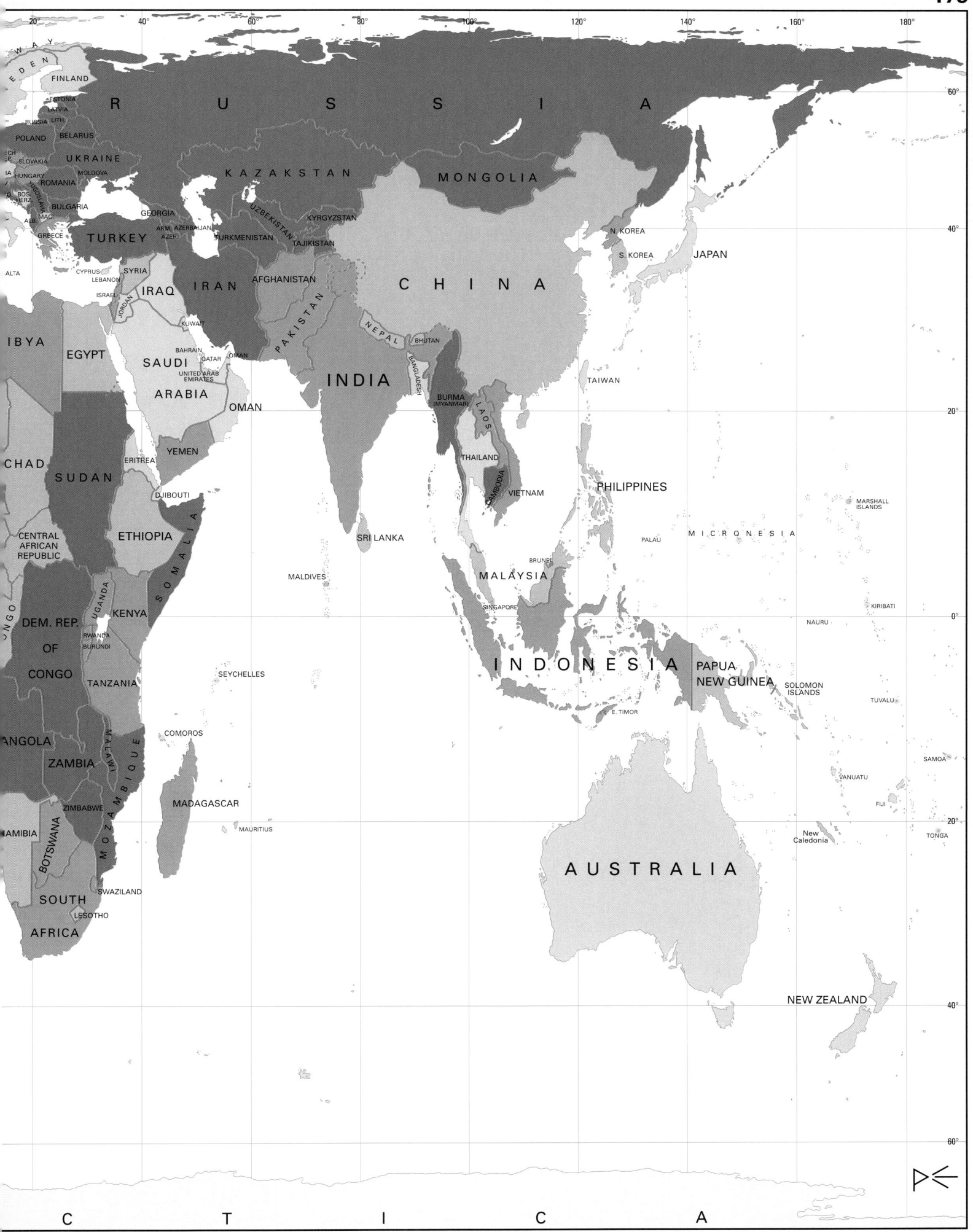

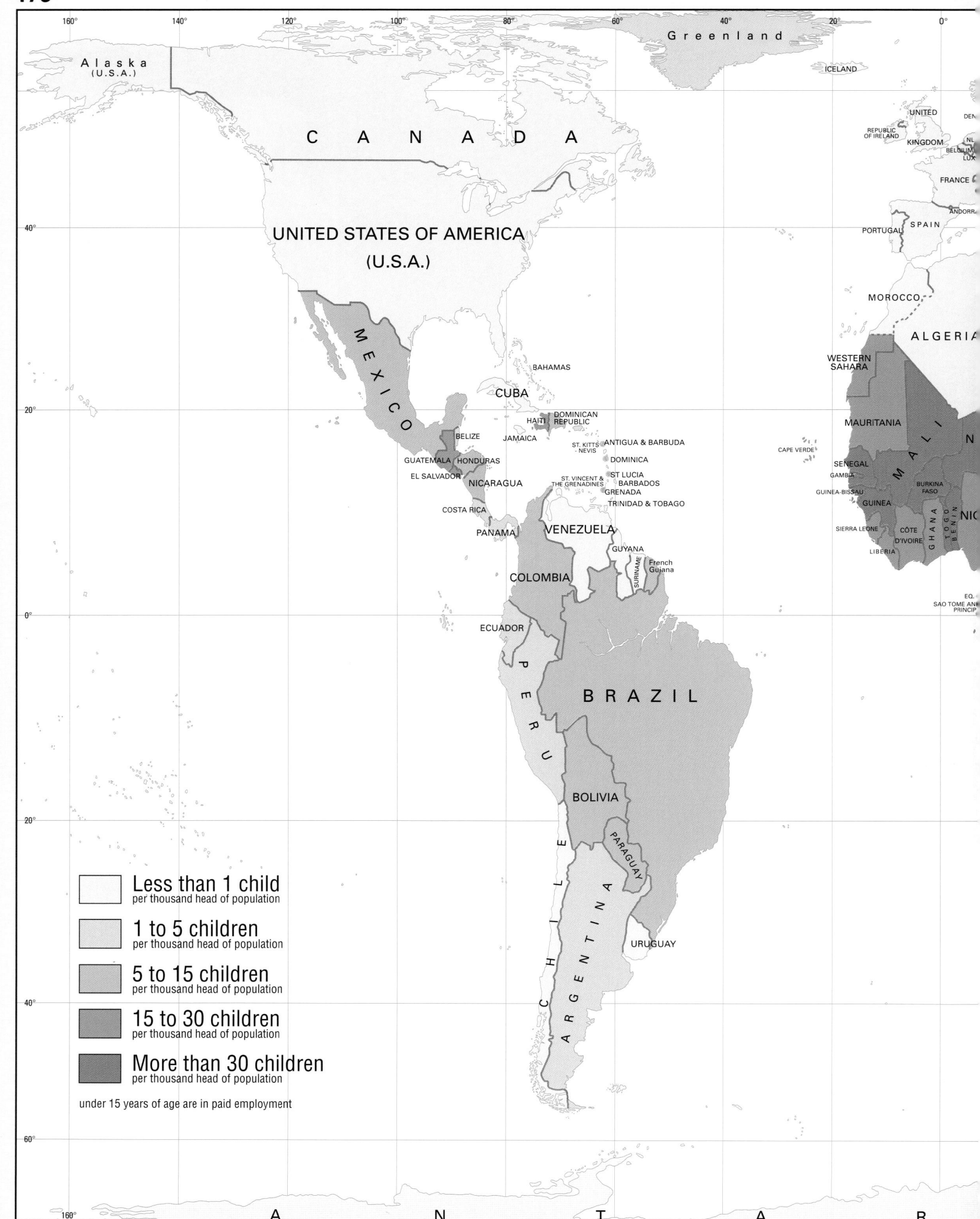

Alaska
(U.S.A.)

C A N A D A

Greenland

ICELAND

UNITED
KINGDOM

REPUBLIC
OF IRELAND

NL
BELGIUM
LUX

FRANCE

UNITED STATES OF AMERICA
(U.S.A.)

ANDORRA

SPAIN

PORTUGAL

MOROCCO

M E X I C O

ALGERIA

BAHAMAS

WESTERN
SAHARA

CUBA

MAURITANIA

MALI

N

DOMINICAN
REPUBLIC
HAITI

CAPE VERDE

JAMAICA

BELIZE

ST. KITTS -
NEVIS

ANTIGUA & BARBUDA

SENEGAL

GUATEMALA HONDURAS

DOMINICA

GAMBIA

BURKINA
FASO

EL SALVADOR

ST LUCIA
BARBADOS
GRENADA

ST. VINCENT &
THE GRENADINES

GUINEA-BISSAU

GUINEA

NICARAGUA

GHANA
TOGO
BENIN

NIC

COSTA RICA

TRINIDAD & TOBAGO

SIERRA LEONE

CÔTE
D'IVOIRE

PANAMA

VENEZUELA

LIBERIA

GUYANA

EQ.
SAO TOME AND
PRINCIP

COLOMBIA

SURINAME

French
Guiana

ECUADOR

P
E
R
U

B R A Z I L

BOLIVIA

C
H
I
L
E

PARAGUAY

A
R
G
E
N
T
I
N
A

URUGUAY

Less than 1 child
per thousand head of population

1 to 5 children
per thousand head of population

5 to 15 children
per thousand head of population

15 to 30 children
per thousand head of population

More than 30 children
per thousand head of population

under 15 years of age are in paid employment

A N T A R

CHILD

Greenland

ICELAND

UNITED

DENM

REPUBLIC
OF IRELAND

KINGDOM

NL

BELGIUM

LUX.

FRANCE

ANDORRA

A L a s k a
(U.S.A.)

C A N A D A

PORTUGAL

SPAIN

MOROCCO

ALGERIA

UNITED STATES OF AMERICA
(U.S.A.)

WESTERN
SAHARA

MAURITANIA

CAPE VERDE

M E X I C O

BAHAMAS

CUBA

BELIZE

DOMINICAN
REPUBLIC

JAMAICA

HAITI

SENEGAL

M

A

L

I

N

GAMBIA

ST. KITTS
- NEVIS

ANTIGUA & BARBUDA

GUATEMALA

HONDURAS

DOMINICA

GUINEA-BISSAU

BURKINA
FASO

NIG

EL SALVADOR

NICARAGUA

ST VINCENT &
THE GRENADINES

ST LUCIA

BARBADOS

GUINEA

SIERRA LEONE

CÔTE
D'IVOIRE

GHANA

TOGO

BENIN

COSTA RICA

GRENADA

TRINIDAD & TOBAGO

LIBERIA

PANAMA

VENEZUELA

GUYANA

COLOMBIA

SURINAME

French
Guiana

EQ. G

SAO TOME AND
PRINCIPE

ECUADOR

P
E
R
U

B R A Z I L

BOLIVIA

C
H
I
L
E

PARAGUAY

A
R
G
E
N
T
I
N
A

URUGUAY

Approaching equality:
Total income of the richest 10% = total income of the poorest 20%

Moderate inequality:
Total income of the richest 10% = total income of the poorest 40%

Severe inequality:
Total income of the richest 10% = total income of the poorest 60%

Gross inequality:
Total income of the richest 10% = total income of the poorest 80%

(The percentage figures for the poorest refer to average values,
which can vary in the individual countries by up to 10%)

A N C A N T A R

160°

INEQU

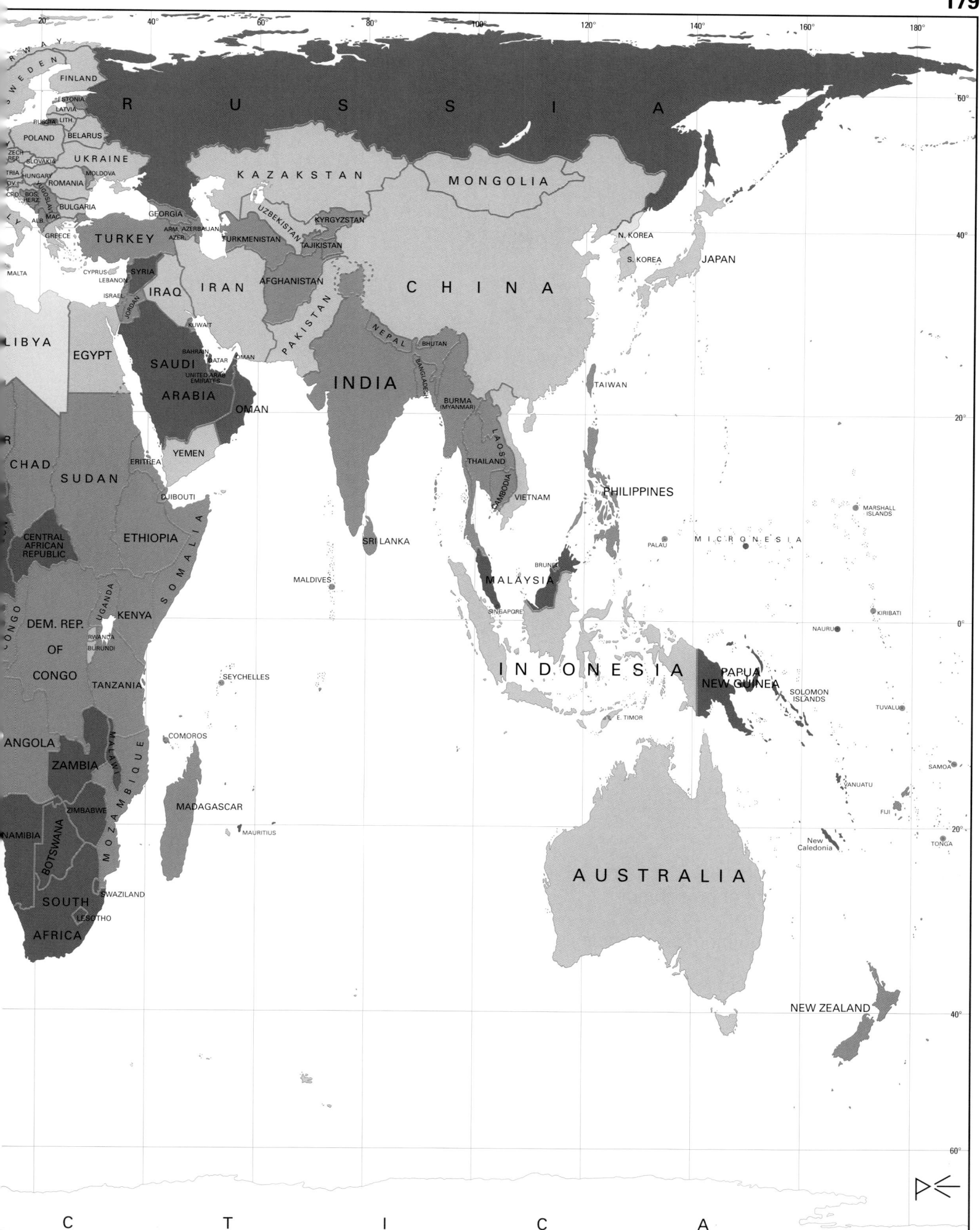

ALITY

Low amount of prostitution

Medium amount of prostitution

High amount of prostitution

PROSTI

RUSSIA
FINLAND
SWEDEN
ESTONIA
LATVIA
LITH.
BELARUS
POLAND
UKRAINE
CZECH REP.
SLOVAKIA
HUNGARY
MOLDOVA
ROMANIA
YUGOSLAVIA
BOS. HERZ.
BULGARIA
MAC.
ALB.
GREECE
TURKEY
GEORGIA
ARM.
AZERBAIJAN
AZER.
KAZAKSTAN
UZBEKISTAN
KYRGYZSTAN
TURKMENISTAN
TAJIKISTAN
MONGOLIA
CHINA
N. KOREA
S. KOREA
JAPAN
MALTA
CYPRUS
LEBANON
SYRIA
ISRAEL
JORDAN
IRAQ
IRAN
AFGHANISTAN
PAKISTAN
NEPAL
BHUTAN
KUWAIT
BAHRAIN
QATAR
UNITED ARAB EMIRATES
OMAN
SAUDI ARABIA
INDIA
BANGLADESH
BURMA (MYANMAR)
LAOS
TAIWAN
LIBYA
EGYPT
CHAD
SUDAN
ERITREA
YEMEN
DJIBOUTI
THAILAND
CAMBODIA
VIETNAM
PHILIPPINES
MARSHALL ISLANDS
CENTRAL AFRICAN REPUBLIC
ETHIOPIA
SOMALIA
SRI LANKA
PALAU
MICRONESIA
BRUNEI
MALAYSIA
MALDIVES
SINGAPORE
KIRIBATI
NAURU
UGANDA
KENYA
CONGO
DEM. REP. OF CONGO
RWANDA
BURUNDI
TANZANIA
SEYCHELLES
INDONESIA
PAPUA NEW GUINEA
SOLOMON ISLANDS
TUVALU
E. TIMOR
COMOROS
ANGOLA
ZAMBIA
MALAWI
MOZAMBIQUE
SAMOA
VANUATU
FIJI
MADAGASCAR
ZIMBABWE
NAMIBIA
BOTSWANA
MAURITIUS
New Caledonia
TONGA
AUSTRALIA
SWAZILAND
SOUTH AFRICA
LESOTHO
NEW ZEALAND
ANTARCTICA
20°
40°
60°
80°
100°
120°
140°
160°
180°
0°

TUTION

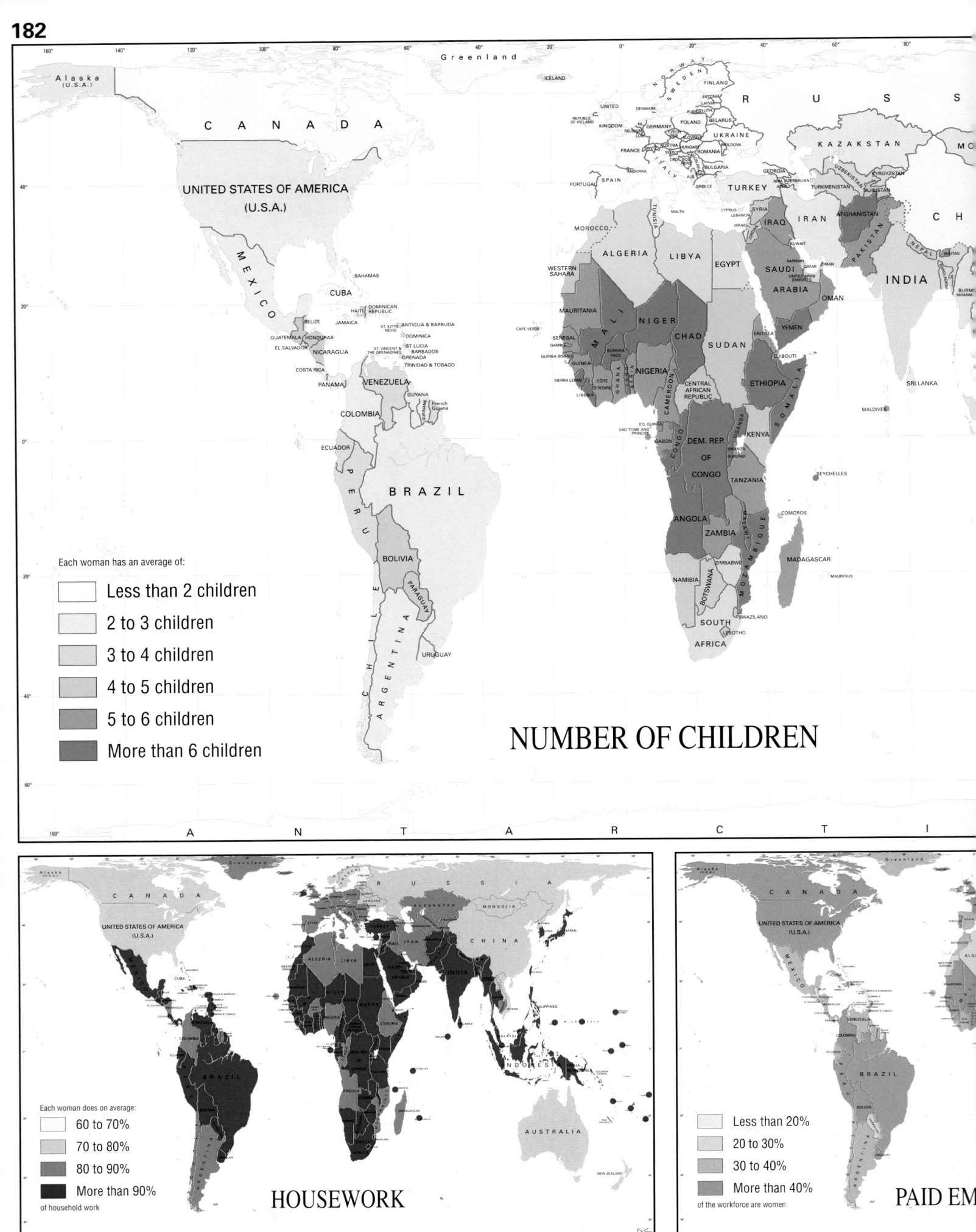

Each woman has an average of:

- Less than 2 children
- 2 to 3 children
- 3 to 4 children
- 4 to 5 children
- 5 to 6 children
- More than 6 children

NUMBER OF CHILDREN

Each woman does on average:

- 60 to 70%
- 70 to 80%
- 80 to 90%
- More than 90%

of household work

HOUSEWORK

- Less than 20%
- 20 to 30%
- 30 to 40%
- More than 40%

of the workforce are women

PAID EM

THE STATUS

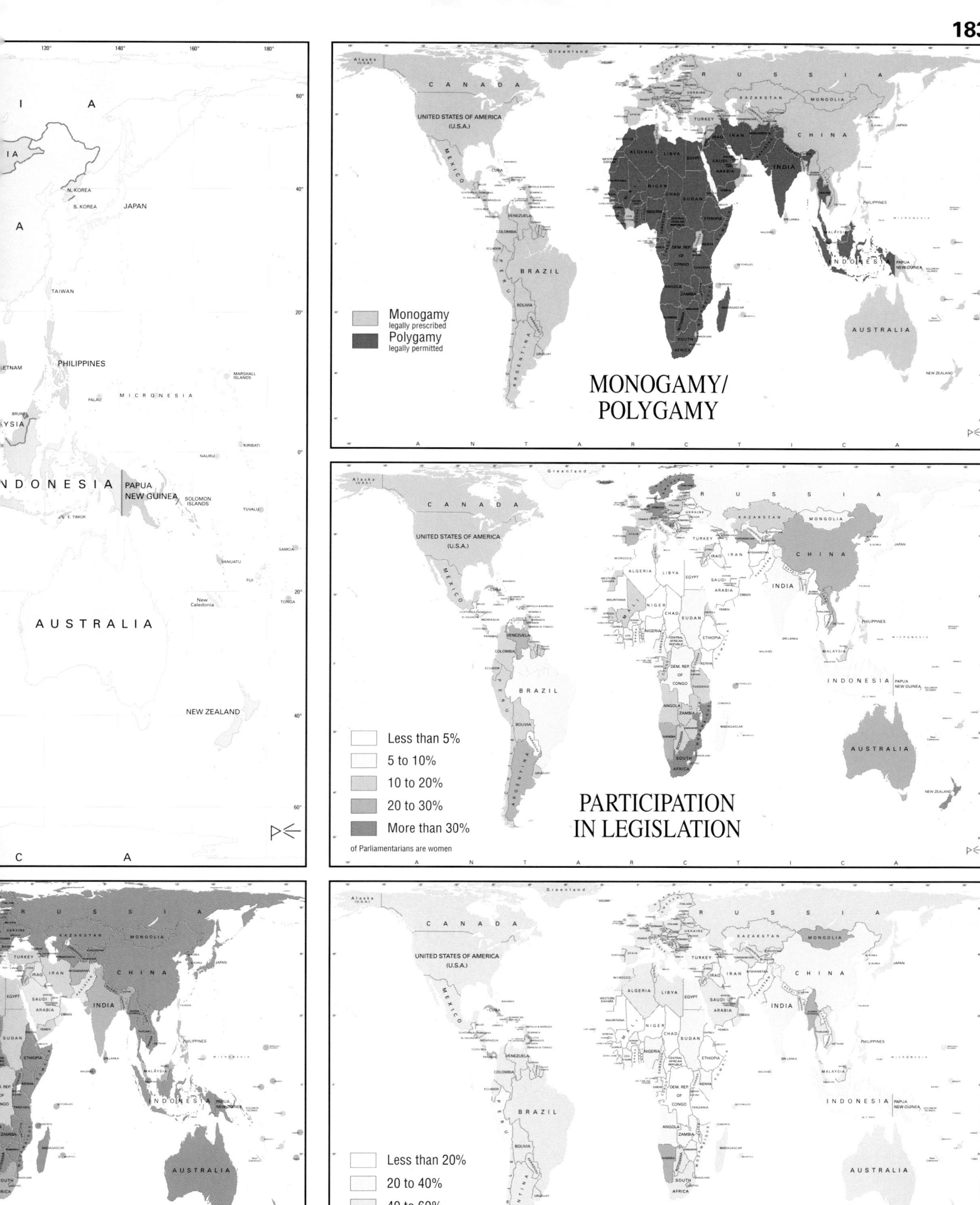

MONOGAMY/ POLYGAMY

Monogamy
legally prescribed

Polygamy
legally permitted

PARTICIPATION IN LEGISLATION

Less than 5%

5 to 10%

10 to 20%

20 to 30%

More than 30%

of Parliamentarians are women

...OYMENT

HIGHER EDUCATION

Less than 20%

20 to 40%

40 to 60%

More than 60%

of enrolled students are women

OF WOMEN

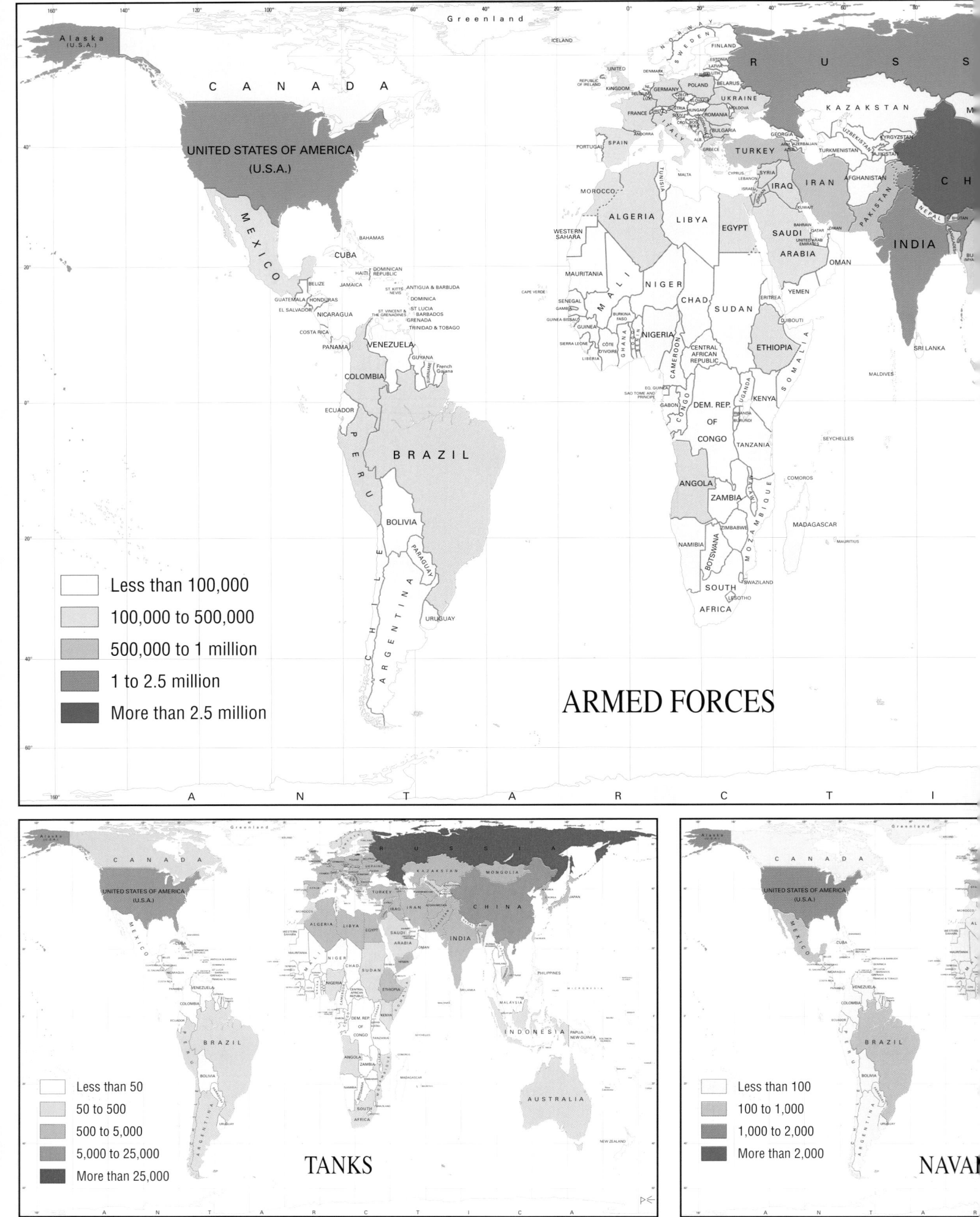

ARMED FORCES

Less than 100,000
100,000 to 500,000
500,000 to 1 million
1 to 2.5 million
More than 2.5 million

Less than 50
50 to 500
500 to 5,000
5,000 to 25,000
More than 25,000

TANKS

Less than 100
100 to 1,000
1,000 to 2,000
More than 2,000

NAVAL

RELATIVE MILIT

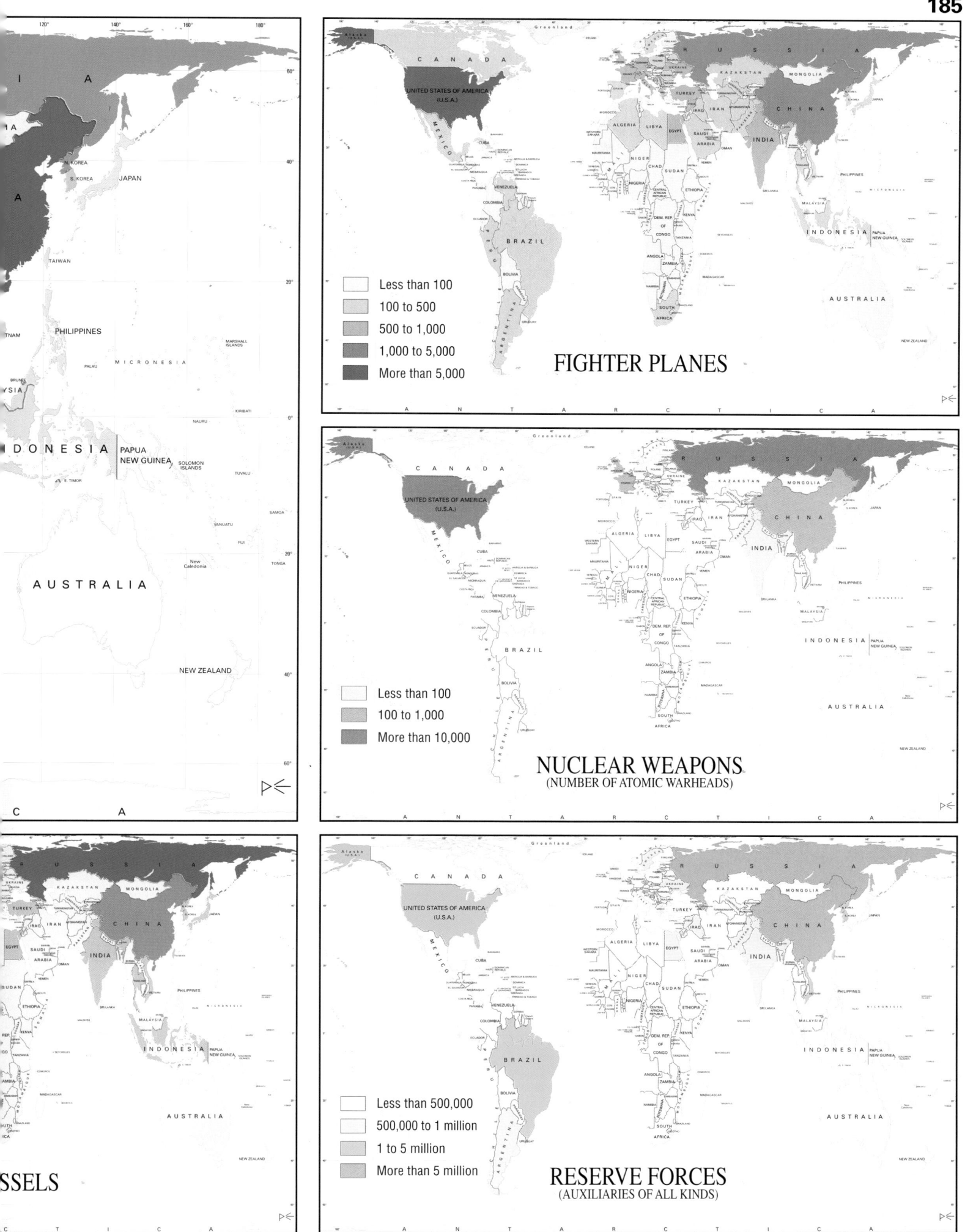

FIGHTER PLANES

Less than 100
100 to 500
500 to 1,000
1,000 to 5,000
More than 5,000

NUCLEAR WEAPONS
(NUMBER OF ATOMIC WARHEADS)

Less than 100
100 to 1,000
More than 10,000

RESERVE FORCES
(AUXILIARIES OF ALL KINDS)

Less than 500,000
500,000 to 1 million
1 to 5 million
More than 5 million

SSELS

ARY STRENGTH

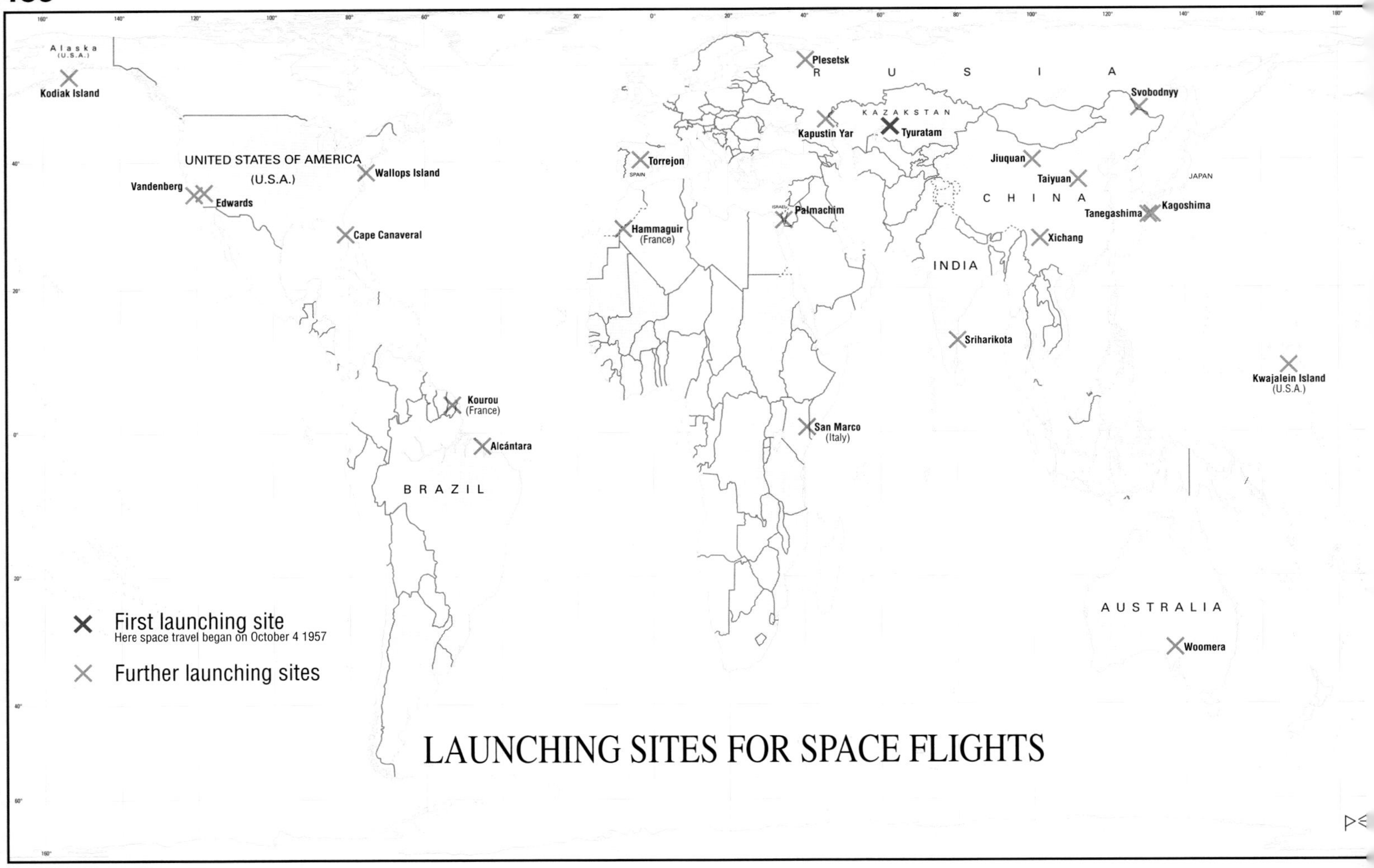

Map 1: Launching Sites for Space Flights

Alaska
(U.S.A.)

Kodiak Island

RUSSIA

Plesetsk

Svobodnyy

KAZAKSTAN

Kapustin Yar

Tyuratam

Jiuquan

UNITED STATES OF AMERICA
(U.S.A.)

Wallops Island

Taiyuan

JAPAN

Vandenberg

Torrejon
SPAIN

CHINA

Edwards

Tanegashima

Kagoshima

Cape Canaveral

Hammaguir
(France)

Palmachim

Xichang

INDIA

Sriharikota

Kwajalein Island
(U.S.A.)

Kourou
(France)

San Marco
(Italy)

Alcántara

BRAZIL

AUSTRALIA

✕ **First launching site**
Here space travel began on October 4 1957

✕ Further launching sites

Woomera

LAUNCHING SITES FOR SPACE FLIGHTS

Map 2: Manned Space Flights

Alaska
(U.S.A.)

Greenland

ICELAND

CANADA

RUSSIA

UNITED STATES OF AMERICA
(U.S.A.)

KAZAKSTAN

MONGOLIA

TURKEY

CHINA

N. KOREA
S. KOREA
JAPAN

MEXICO

IRAN

CUBA

MOROCCO

ALGERIA

LIBYA

EGYPT

SAUDI
ARABIA

OMAN

INDIA

TAIWAN

BAHAMAS

GUATEMALA
HONDURAS
EL SALVADOR
NICARAGUA
COSTA RICA
PANAMA

WESTERN
SAHARA

MAURITANIA

MALI

NIGER

CHAD

SUDAN

YEMEN

THAILAND

VIETNAM

PHILIPPINES

MICRONESIA

VENEZUELA

GUYANA

COLOMBIA

French
Guiana

SENEGAL

NIGERIA

CENTRAL
AFRICAN
REPUBLIC

ETHIOPIA

SRI LANKA

MALDIVES

MALAYSIA

NAURU

KIRIBATI

ECUADOR

DEM. REP.
OF
CONGO

KENYA

INDONESIA

PAPUA
NEW GUINEA

SOLOMON
ISLANDS

TUVALU

BRAZIL

ANGOLA

ZAMBIA

TANZANIA

SEYCHELLES

MADAGASCAR

MAURITIUS

AUSTRALIA

New
Caledonia

VANUATU

FIJI

SAMOA

TONGA

BOLIVIA

NAMIBIA

BOTSWANA

MOZAMBIQUE

ZIMBABWE

PARAGUAY

CHILE

ARGENTINA

SOUTH
AFRICA

SWAZILAND
LESOTHO

URUGUAY

NEW ZEALAND

Countries with manned
spaceships

ANTARCTICA

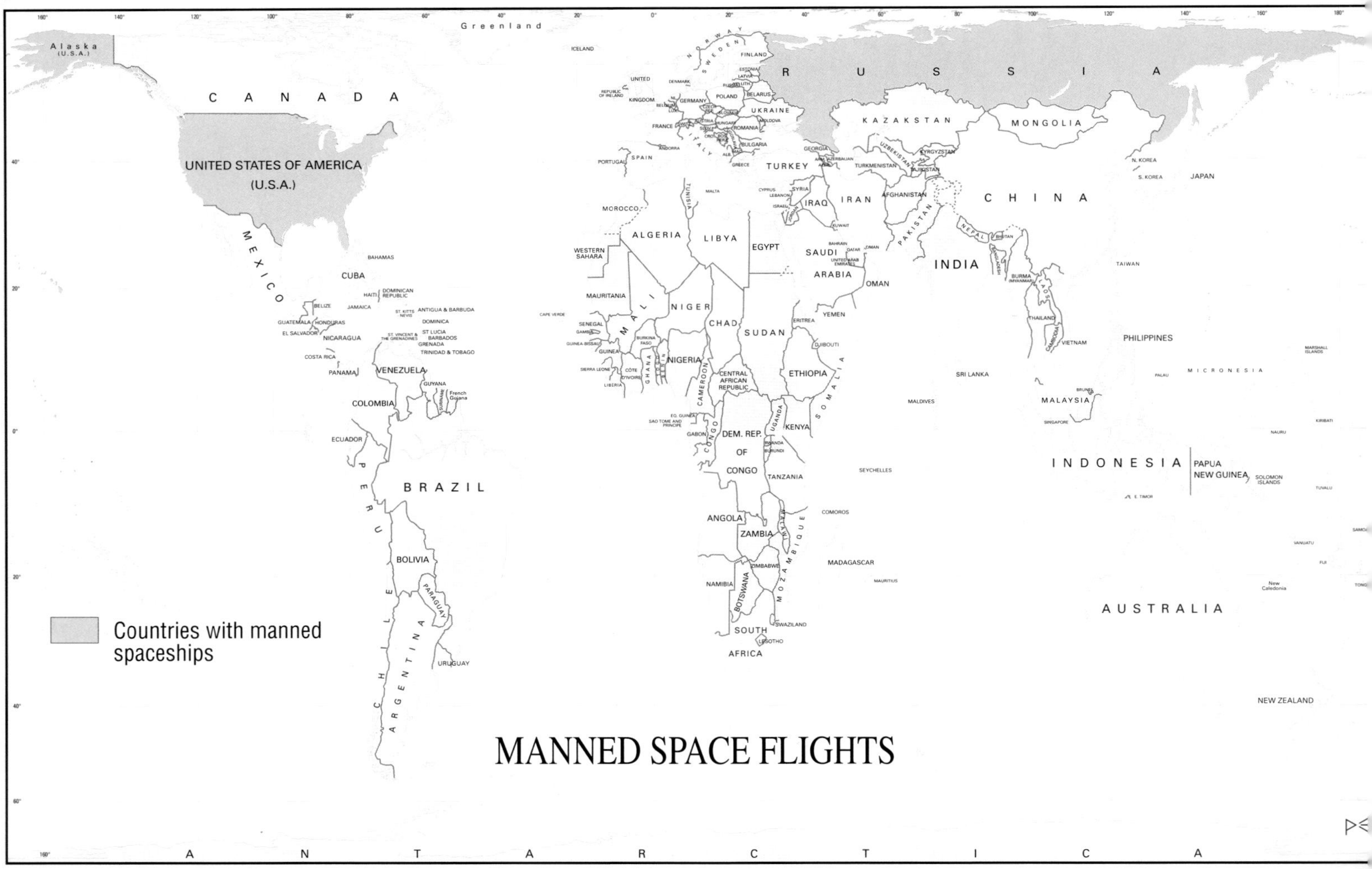

MANNED SPACE FLIGHTS

THE CONQU

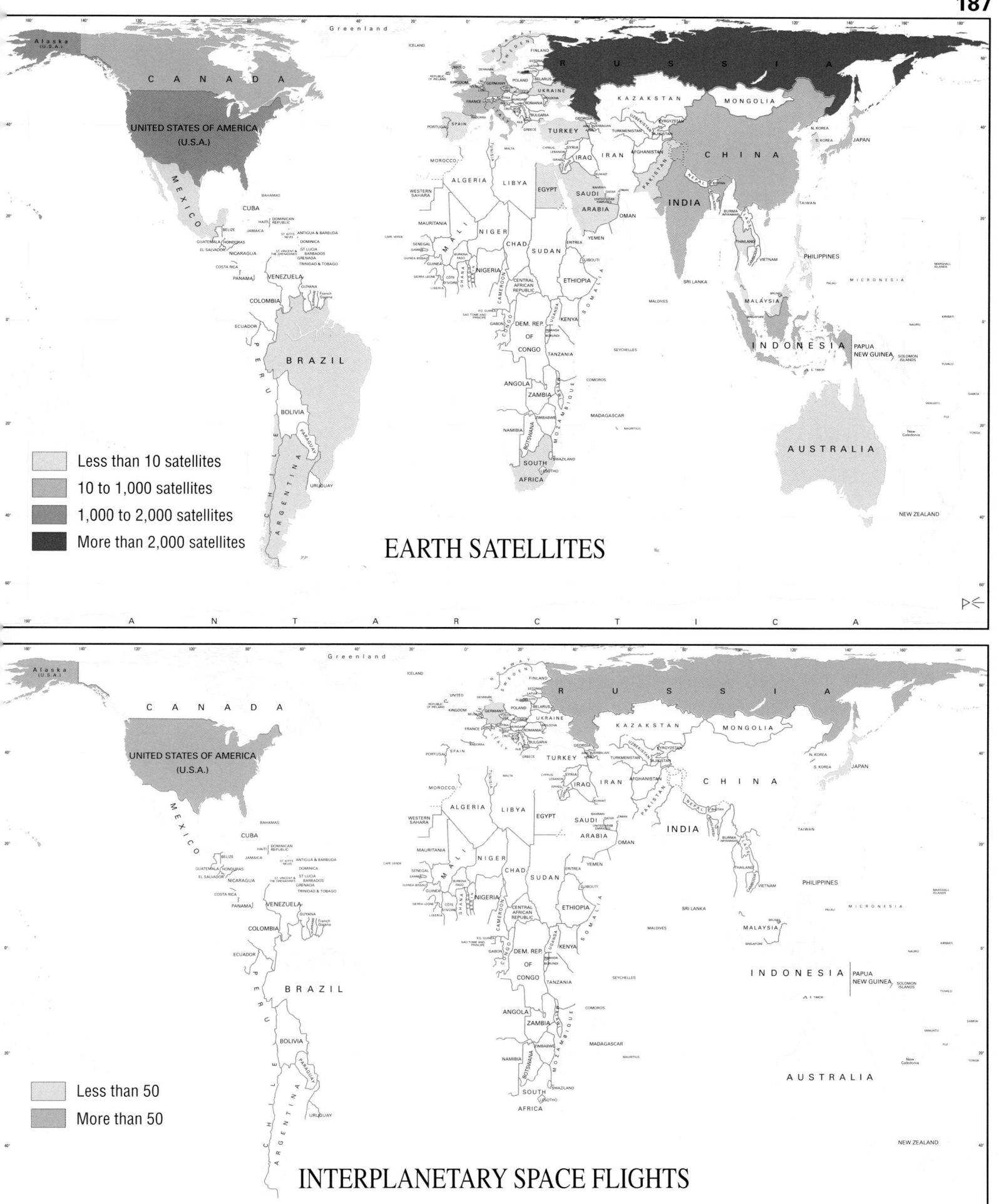

EARTH SATELLITES

Less than 10 satellites
10 to 1,000 satellites
1,000 to 2,000 satellites
More than 2,000 satellites

INTERPLANETARY SPACE FLIGHTS

Less than 50
More than 50

ST OF SPACE

INDEX

Each name in the index is followed by a page number and a letter. On the page referred to, the letter can be found either at the top or at the bottom of the map frame. In the first case, the place is in the upper half of the map vertically below the letter; otherwise it is on the lower half of the map vertically above the letter. If a name extends over several letters, the given letter indicates its beginning.

Names such as countries or oceans which cover a large area on the map are listed with their page number only. However, if they extend over two pages, two page numbers are shown – the left-hand and right-hand page numbers being linked with a dash. Names of countries, oceans, rivers and mountains that extend over more than a double page are listed under each separate page. A dash between two nonconsecutive page numbers means that the place appears on all maps between and including those two pages.

The headwords are in alphabetical order. Names with prefixes like "Saint" or "Bad" can be looked up under the initial letter of the prefix. Place names appear on the maps in their widely-used Anglicised form, or in their local spelling or a standard transliteration of that local spelling. The index also includes local forms of names where the Anglicised form has been used on the map. In these cases the local name is followed by the Anglicised name in brackets. This indicates that the place name appears on the map, at the reference given, in the form shown in brackets, not in its local form.

Aachen ......33 n	Achsu ......54 w	Agnibilekrou ......40 x	Akrerèb ......41 g	Alejandro Sekirk ......30 c
Aaro ......25 v	Acklins ......21 q	Agoare ......41 c	Akritas, Cape ......35 r	Alejsk ......56 d
Aargub ......36 o	Acomayo ......25 n	Agra ......61 c	Aksakovo ......54 m	Aleksandrovskoye ......51 q
Aba (China) ......62 h	Aconcagua ......28 p	Ağri ......54 t	Aksaray ......35 y	Aleksandrovsko-
Aba (Nigeria) ......41 s	Aconguija, Nev. de ......28 s	Agrigento ......37 h	Aksay ......54 m	Sakhalinskiy ......53 r
Aba (Dem. Rep. Congo) ...42 w	Acre ......25 p	Agrínion ......35 r	Akşehir ......35 w	Alekseyevka (Kazakstan) .55 j
Abadan ......39 g	Açu ......27 u	Agryz ......54 m	Aksu ......55 j	Alekseyevka (Ukraine) ....54 d
Abadeh ......39 j	Açu (River) ......27 u	Aguadas ......22 z	Aksuat ......55 f	Alekseyevo ......53 h
Abadla ......36 k	Acude Araras ......27 s	Agua de Chale ......18 e	Aksum ......43 c	Além Paraiba ......29 j
Abaeté ......29 g	Acude Orós ......27 t	Aguapei, Serra ......25 w	Aksumbe ......55 u	Alençon ......34 f
Abaetetuba ......26 l	Ada ......15 v	Agua Prieta ......18 i	Aktag ......56 r	Alenquer ......26 h
Abag Qi ......57 v	Adafer ......36 s	Aguarico ......22 y	Aktau (Kazakstan) ......54 y	Aleppo ......54 q
Abakan ......56 i	Adak ......10 v	Aguas Belas ......27 u	Aktau (Kazakstan) ......55 k	Alert ......91 q
Abakan (River) ......56 h	Adale ......43 v	Aguascalientes ......18 z	Aktaz ......56 s	Alert, Cape ......89 t
Abakan Mountains ......56 h	Adam ......60 o	Aguas Calientes,	Aktogaj (Kyrgyzstan) ......56 n	Alerta ......25 n
Abala ......41 c	Adam's Br. ......64 u	Sierra de ......28 r	Aktogaj (Kazakstan) ......56 c	Alessandria ......34 k
Abalessa ......37 o	Adamaoua, Highlands .....41 u	Aguaytía ......24 x	Aktyubinsk ......55 a	Ålesund ......33 a
Aban ......56 l	Adan ......66 c	Aguaytia (River) ......24 x	Akulivik ......13 s	Aleutian Islands ......10 u
Abancay ......24 z	Adana ......35 z	Aguelock ......36 z	Akure ......41 q	Alevina, Cape ......53 v
Abarqu ......39 k	Adanac ......15 b	Aguelt el Melah ......36 s	Akureyri ......32 c	Alexander Archipelago ....11 x
Abay ......55 j	Adapazari ......35 j	Agueraktem ......36 u	Akwanga ......41 f	Alexander Bay ......48 u
Abay (River) ......43 b	Adarama ......38 x	Aguilas ......36 l	Alabama (River) ......19 j	Alexander Island ......82 w
Abaya, Lake ......43 e	Adare, Cape ......86 s	Agulhas ......48 x	Alabama (State) ......19 k	Alexandra ......79 r
Abbabis ......48 h	Adavale ......74 o	Agulhas, Cape ......48 x	Al Abyar ......35 r	Alexandra, Lake ......77 l
Abbe, Lake ......43 o	Ad Da'ain ......42 e	Aha, Mount ......48 l	Al Adam ......35 s	Alexandra, Land ......50 f
Abbeville ......32 y	Ad Darb ......39 p	Ahaggar ......37 p	Alagoinhas ......27 u	Alexandria (Australia) .....73 s
Abbotabad ......60 m	Ad Dawadimi ......39 r	Ahar ......54 v	Al Ain ......39 y	Alexandria (Egypt) ......38 g
Abbot Ice Shelf ......80 m	Ad Dibdibah ......39 f	Ahmadi ......39 g	Alajuela ......22 g	Alexandria (Louisiana) .....19 g
Abd al Kuri ......43 m	Addis Ababa ......43 c	Ahmadnagar ......61 n	Alakanuk ......10 m	Alexandria (Minnesota) ....15 j
Abdulino ......54 m	Addis Zemen ......43 b	Ahmar Mountains ......43 e	Alakol', Lake ......56 d	Alexandria (Virginia) ......16 y
Abéché ......42 c	Ad Diwaniyah ......39 e	Ahmedabad ......60 y	Al Alamein ......38 g	Al Faiyûm ......38 h
Abengourou ......40 x	Ad Dueim ......42 k	Ahnet ......37 n	Al Amarah ......39 g	Al Farcia ......36 f
Abeokuta ......41 p	Ad Duwaid ......39 c	Ahome ......18 h	Alamogordo ......18 k	Al Faw ......39 g
Aberdeen Lake ......12 y	Adelaide ......77 g	Ahoskie ......16 y	Alamos ......18 i	al Fûla ......42 i
Aberdeen (South Africa) ...49 n	Adelaide Island ......82 u	Ahuachapan ......22 c	Aland Islands ......33 h	Alga ......55 a
Aberdeen (South Dakota).15 h	Adelaide Peninsula ......12 m	Ahwar ......43 i	Alanya ......35 x	Algarroho del Aguila ......30 j
Aberdeen (UK) ......32 x	Adelaide River ......73 c	Ahwaz ......39 g	Al Aqaylah ......37 m	Algarve ......34 n
Aberdeen (Washington) ...14 g	Adélieland ......87 o	Aibak ......60 i	Al Artawiyah ......39 e	Algatart ......55 w
Aberfoyle ......74 o	Aden ......43 h	Aileron ......73 r	Alaşehir ......35 v	Al Gaydah ......43 m
Aberystwyth ......32 w	Aden, Gulf of ......43 h	Ailigandi ......22 k	Alashan Desert ......57 p	Algeciras ......34 p
Abez' ......50 l	Aderbissinat ......41 g	Aim ......53 o	Al Ashkhirah ......60 q	Alger (Algiers) ......34 u
Abha ......39 p	Adi Arkay ......43 b	Aim (River) ......53 n	Alaska 11	Algeria 34/36-37
Abidjan ......40 x	Adigrat ......43 d	Aimorés ......29 k	Alaska, Gulf of 11	Al Ghaydah ......39 w
Abilene ......19 b	Adi Keyih ......43 d	Aïn Beïda ......34 x	Alaska Peninsula ......11 o	Algiers ......34 u
Abingdon Downs ......73 l	Adilabad ......61 q	Ain Benimathar ......36 k	Alaska Range ......11 e	al Hadd, Ras ......60 q
Abitibi ......16 i	Adi Quala ......43 c	Aïn ben Tili ......36 s	Al Aswaa, Ras ......39 n	Al Hadithah (Iraq) ......39 c
Abitibi Lake ......16 j	Adirondack Mountains ......16 z	Ain Oussera ......34 u	Alat ......55 r	Al Hadithah (Saudi Arabia)38 m
Abiyata, Lake ......43 c	Admiralty Inlet ......13 d	Ain Sefra ......34 s	Ala Tau ......55 z	Al Hajar al Gharbi ......39 z
Abkit ......53 k	Admiralty Islands ......71 n	Ain Sukhna ......38 i	Alatyr ......54 i	Al Hajar ash Sharqi ......60 p
Abminga ......77 d	Ado ......41 q	Aioun Abd el Malek ......36 u	Alausí ......22 x	Al Hammâm ......38 h
Abomey ......41 o	Adoni ......64 f	Aiquile ......28 f	Al Awaynat ......37 t	Al Hanakiyah ......39 o
Abong Mbang ......41 w	Adour ......34 f	Aïr ......37 r	Al Aziziyah (Iraq) ......39 e	Al Hasakah ......54 r
Abou Deïa ......42 b	Adrar ......36 l	Airo ......25 n	Al Aziziyah (Libya) ......34 z	Al Hazm ......39 r
Abqaiq ......39 h	Adrar of the Iforas ......36 z	Airy, Mount ......16 w	Albacete ......34 r	Al Hijaz ......38 m
Abra Pampa ......28 f	Adré ......42 d	Aitape ......70 y	Al Bad ......38 k	Al Hillah ......39 s
Abrolhos Archipelago dos.29 m	Adriatic Sea ......35 a	Aiwasedapur ......51 r	al Baida ......43 h	Al Hoceima ......34 q
Abu al Abyad ......39 x	Adwa ......43 c	Aix-en-Provence ......34 j	Al Balyana ......38 i	Aliabad ......39 l
Abu Dara, Ras ......38 z	Adycha ......53 c	Āizawl ......62 o	Albanel Lake ......17 a	Aliança ......25 f
Abu Dhabi ......39 x	Adygalakh ......53 f	Ajaccio ......34 k	Albania ......35 d	Ali-Bagata ......53 a
Abu Habi ......42 k	Adzhima ......59 b	Ajaguz ......56 c	Albany (Australia) ......76 e	Alicante ......34 s
Abu Hadriyah ......39 h	Adzva ......50 k	Ajaguz (River) ......56 b	Albany (Georgia) ......20 j	Alice Springs ......73 r
Abu Hamed ......38 w	Aegean Sea ......35 t	Ajdabiyah ......38 a	Albany (New York) ......16 z	Aligarh ......61 c
Abuja ......41 f	Affolé, Montagnes de l'....40 g	Ajmer ......61 a	Albany (Oregon) ......14 g	Alijos, Rocas ......18 d
Abu Kamal ......39 b	Afghanistan 55/60	Ajni ......55 u	Albany (River) ......16 h	Alindao ......42 q
Abu Madd, Ras ......38 z	Afgoi ......43 t	Ajryk ......55 n	Albany Downs ......74 q	Alipxa ......51 u
Abumonbazi ......42 r	Afif ......39 p	Akabli ......37 n	Al Bardi ......35 t	Ali-Sabieh ......43 e
Abun ......25 r	Afikpo ......41 s	Akchar ......36 o	Al Batinah ......39 z	Al Isawiyah ......38 m
Abun (River) ......25 q	Aflou ......34 t	Ak-Dovurak ......56 i	Al Bayda ......35 r	Aliwal North ......49 o
Abune Yosef ......43 c	Afmadu ......43 s	Akelamo ......69 m	Alberga ......77 d	Al Jabal al Akhdar ......35 r
Abu Shagara, Ras ......38 z	Aftout ......36 w	Akespe ......55 c	Albert, Lake ......42 w	Al Jaghbub ......38 d
Abu Simbel ......38 v	Afuá ......26 l	Aketi ......42 r	Albert Lea ......16 o	Al Jalamid ......39 b
Abu Tig ......38 i	Afyon ......35 w	Akhisar ......35 v	Albert Nile ......42 x	Al Jawf (Libya) ......38 d
Abuye Meda ......43 d	Agadem ......41 j	Akhmîn ......38 i	Alberta ......14 l	Al Jawf (Saudi Arabia) .....39 a
Abuyog ......67 j	Agadèz ......37 r	Akhtyrka ......35 l	Alberton ......17 e	Al Jubayl ......39 h
Abu Zabad ......42 i	Agadir ......36 f	Akimiki Island ......16 i	Al Bir ......38 l	al Junayna ......42 e
Acailandia ......27 n	Agadyr' ......55 k	Akita ......59 o	Ålborg ......33 g	Aljustrel ......36 g
Acámbaro ......19 n	Agailas ......36 p	Akjoujt Faye ......36 p	Albuquerque ......15 p	Al Kamil ......60 p
Acampamento ......26 i	Agamor ......41 a	Akkabak ......55 d	Albury ......78 o	Al Karak ......38 l
Acampamento de Indios .25 w	Agan ......51 q	Akkani ......10 k	Al Busaiyah ......39 e	Al Khaburah ......60 o
Acaponeta ......18 x	Agapa ......51 i	Akkarga ......55 d	Alcantara ......27 b	Al Khamasin ......39 q
Acapulco ......19 n	Agaro ......43 a	Aklavik ......11 k	Alcova ......15 p	Al Khandaq ......38 u
Acarai, Serra ......25 l	Agartalā ......61 z	Aknoul ......34 q	Alcudia ......34 u	Al Khârga ......38 u
Acaraú ......27 f	Agassiz, Cape ......82 w	Akobo ......42 l	Aldabra Island ......47 d	Al Kharja Oasis ......38 u
Acarigua ......23 d	Agassiz Ice Cap ......13 h	Akola ......61 o	Aldama ......18 k	Al Khartum ......42 k
Acatlán ......19 p	Agata ......51 j	Akordat ......43 b	Aldan ......52 x	Al Khaznah ......39 y
Acayucan ......19 r	Agboville ......40 x	Akoupé ......40 x	Aldan (River) ......53 a	Al Kut ......39 l
Accra ......40 z	Agdam ......54 v	Akpatok Island ......13 x	Aldar ......56 l	al Kú, Wadi ......42 g
Achacachi ......25 p	Agdz ......36 h	Akqi ......56 o	Aleg ......40 d	Allahabad ......61 r
Achénoumma ......37 v	Agen ......34 f	Akranes ......32 b	Alej. ......56 d	Allakh-Yun' ......53 c
Achinsk ......56 i	Agnew ......76 g	Akreïjit ......36 s	Alej ......56 d	Allegheny ......16 w

Allegheny Mountains ....16 w
Allende.....................19 a
Allentown..................16 y
Alleppey....................64 e
Alliance....................15 r
Allier......................34 h
Al Lith.....................39 n
Alma........................17 a
Almaden.....................74 b
al Mado.....................43 j
al Mahdad...................43 g
Al Maiyah...................39 d
Al Majm'ah..................39 e
Al Mansura..................38 i
Al Marj.....................35 r
Almaty......................55 z
Almaznyy....................52 f
Almeirim....................26 j
Al Mekhily..................38 c
Almenara....................29 k
Almería.....................34 r
Al'metyevsk.................54 m
al Milk.....................38 u
Al Minyâ....................38 h
Almirante...................22 h
Almora......................61 d
Al Mudauwara................38 l
Al Mughairah................38 m
Al Muglad...................42 i
al Mukalla..................43 k
al Mukha....................43 j
Alor........................69 w
Alor Setar..................65 w
Alota.......................28 e
Alotau......................74 f
al Ouaday...................42 a
Alpena......................16 h
Alpercatas, Serra das.......27 p
Alpha.......................74 q
Alpine......................18 l
Alps........................34 j
Al Qahirah..................38 l
Al Qaisumah.................39 e
Al Qalibah..................38 m
Al Qariyat..................37 i
Al Qunfudhah................39 o
Al Qurain...................39 q
Al Qurnah...................39 f
Alroy Downs.................73 t
Alta........................33 i
Alta Gracia.................28 t
Altah.......................56 h
Altai (Mountains)...........56 e
Altaj.......................56 l
Altaj (High Altai)..........56 y
Altamaha....................20 l
Altamira (Brazil)...........26 j
Altamira (Mexico)...........20 t
Altamonte Springs...........20 l
Altar Desert................18 f
Altares.....................18 m
Altat.......................51 w
Altay.......................56 h
Altejskij...................56 f
Altiplano...................28 d
Alto do Araguaia............29 a
Alto Hama...................44 t
Alto Molócuè................49 k
Alton.......................16 q
Alton Downs.................77 f
Altoona.....................16 x
Alto Paraiso de Goiás ......29 f
Alto Parnaíba...............27 n
Alto Purús..................25 n
Altun Shan..................56 u
Alturas.....................14 v
Altus.......................15 u
Alu.........................71 u
Al Udailiyah................39 t
al Udaiya...................42 i
Al Ulaya....................39 o
Al Uruq al Mutaridah........39 x
Alva........................15 u
Alvarado....................19 r
Alvares.....................25 e
Alvorada....................26 y
Al Wafra....................39 g
Al Wajh.....................38 l
Alwar.......................61 b
Alxa Zuoqi..................57 q

Alyaskitovyy................53 d
Alygdzer....................56 m
Amadeus, Lake...............73 p
Amadjuak Lake...............13 j
Amakinskiy..................52 f
Amapá.......................26 k
Amara.......................43 b
Amarante....................27 a
Amarillo....................15 s
Amasin......................36 p
Amata.......................77 a
Amatenango..................19 t
Amazar......................52 v
Amazon....................25-26
Amazon (Solimões)...........25 b
Ambala......................61 b
Ambalavao...................47 q
Ambam.......................41 v
Ambar.......................51 i
Ambarchik...................10 a
Ambardakh...................53 c
Ambato......................22 z
Ambikapur...................61 t
Ambilobe....................47 e
Ambo........................24 x
Ambohitralanana ....47 g
Ambon.......................69 z
Ambositra...................47 q
Ambovombe...................47 q
Ambriz......................44 e
Amchitka....................10 u
Amderma.....................50 l
Amdo........................61 l
Ameca.......................18 y
Americana...................29 f
American Highlands..........84 z
American Samoa.............230 v
Amery Basin.................85 p
Amery Ice Shelf.............84 n
Ames........................16 o
Amga........................53 a
Amga (River)................53 a
Amguid......................37 p
Amherst.....................17 f
Amiens......................34 h
Amindivi Islands ....64 b
Amistad Reservoir...........19 a
Amizmiz.....................36 g
Amka........................53 q
Amman.......................38 l
Ammassalik..................90 y
Amo.........................52 b
Amol........................54 v
Amolar......................28 l
Amourj......................40 h
Amoy........................63 s
Ampanihy....................47 o
Ampato......................25 n
Amravati....................61 p
Am Raya.....................41 m
Amsel.......................37 p
Amsterdam...................33 n
Amsterdam Island...........231 r
Amudarja....................55 q
Amudat......................42 z
Amund Ringnes Island.......12 m
Amundsen Bay................84 m
Amundsen Gulf...............12 d
Amundsen Scott..............83 z
Amundsen Sea................81 n
Amur (River)................58 k
Amur (Sudan)................38 x
Amursk......................58 m
Amysakh.....................52 h
Anabar......................52 f
Anaco.......................23 h
Anaconda....................14 w
Anadyr'.....................10 g
Anadyr, Gulf of.............10 h
Anadyr Mountains............10 f
Anadyr' (River).............10 f
Anah........................39 c
Anaheim.....................18 x
Anai........................37 t
Anai Mudi...................64 f
Anajás......................26 l
Anaka.......................42 y
Anaktuvuk Pass..............11 e
Anama.......................25 l

Anama, Lake.................51 k
Anambas Islands.............68 i
Anamur......................35 x
Anamur, Cape................35 x
Ananjevo....................55 z
Anantapur...................64 f
Anantnag....................61 a
Anápolis....................29 e
Anar........................39 l
Anarak......................39 k
Anatolia....................54 p
Añatuya.....................28 v
Anauá.......................26 d
Ancha.......................53 d
Anchorage...................11 e
Ancohuma....................25 p
Ancona......................35 a
Ancud.......................30 g
Anda........................58 f
Andahuaylas.................24 z
Andalgalá...................28 s
Åndalsnes...................33 b
Andalusia...................19 k
Andaman Sea.................65 f
Andaman Islands.............65 d
Andapa......................47 f
Anderson (Canada)...........89 b
Anderson (Indiana)..........16 t
Anderson (South Carolina)20 l
Andes................22-25/28/30
Andirlangar.................56 r
Andižan.....................55 w
Andkhoy.....................55 s
Andoas......................24 k
Andong......................58 v
Andoom......................73 j
Andorra.....................34 g
Andöya......................33 f
Andradina...................29 c
Andranovory.................47 o
Andreanof Islands...........10 v
Andreas, Cape...............35 x
Andrées Land................91 r
Andreyevka..................54 k
Andreyevskiy................52 t
Andriamena..................47 q
Andros......................35 l
Andros Island...............21 n
Andulo......................44 u
Andyngda....................52 g
Anéfis......................36 z
Aney........................37 v
Angara......................51 x
Angarsk.....................57 c
Angas Downs.................73 q
Angel de la Guarda ....18 f
Angeleri....................42 w
Angeles.....................67 f
Angel Falls.................23 v
Ångerman....................33 g
Angers......................34 f
Angkor......................66 g
Anglesey....................32 w
Ango........................42 t
Angoche.....................46 l
Angola......................44
Angostura Reservoir.........19 t
Angoulême...................34 g
Angra Dos Reis ....29 i
Angren......................55 v
Angu........................42 s
Anguilla....................21 y
Angurugu....................73 f
Angwa.......................45 r
Anhua.......................63 a
Aniak.......................11 b
Anjouan.....................47 b
Anju........................58 t
Anka........................41 e
Ankacho.....................52 d
Ankang......................62 m
Ankara......................35 x
Ankazoabo...................47 o
Ankazobe....................47 o
Anking......................63 e
Anlong......................62 x
Annaba......................34 x
An'Nahûd....................42 i
Anna Plains.................72 w
Annapolis...................16 y

Annapurna...................61 g
Ann Arbor...................16 u
An Nashash..................39 y
An Nasiriyah................39 e
Annecy......................34 j
An Nimas....................39 p
Anning......................62 u
Annitowa....................73 t
An Nukhaib..................39 b
Anou Mellene................36 z
Ansab.......................39 d
Anschan.....................58 e
Anschluss...................48 h
Anse d'Hainault.............21 q
Anshun......................62 x
Anson Bay...................73 b
Ansongo.....................41 a
Antakya.....................35 x
Antalaha....................47 f
Antalya.....................35 w
Antalya, Gulf of............38 h
Antananarivo................47 q
Antanimora..................47 p
Antarctica..................84
Antarctic Peninsula.........82 u
Antelope Mine...............49 d
Antequera...................34 p
Anthonys Lagoon ....73 s
Anti Atlas..................36 g
Anticosti Island............17 f
Antigua and Barbuda.........21 z
Antipayuta..................51 d
Antipinskiy.................52 m
Antipodes Islands..........223 z
Antofagasta.................28 s
Antofagasta de la Sierra...28 r
Antofalla...................28 q
Antong (Dandong)............58 r
Antonovo....................54 l
Antonovo....................54 l
Antsalova...................47 o
Antsirabe...................47 q
Antsiranana.................47 f
Antsohihy...................47 d
An Tuc......................66 k
Antuerpia...................25 t
Antwerp.....................33 n
Antwerpen (Antwerp).........33 n
Anuradhapura................64 u
Anvers Island...............82 s
Anxi........................56 y
Anxious Bay.................77 c
Anyang......................63 z
Anzhero-Sudzhensk...........56 f
Aomori......................59 c
Aoraki (Mt. Cook)...........79 r
Aosta.......................34 k
Aouderas....................37 r
Aouk........................42 c
Aoukr.......................40 g
Aoukar......................36 w
Aouker......................36 s
Aoulef el Arab..............36 m
Aozi........................37 y
Apalachee Bay...............20 j
Apan........................19 p
Apaporis....................25 a
Aparri......................67 g
Apatou......................26 i
Apatzingán..................18 z
Apennines...................34 m
Apere.......................25 r
Api.........................42 t
Api (River).................42 t
Apiacás, Serra dos ....25 x
Apiaú, Serrado ....23 v
Apizaco.....................19 p
Aplao.......................24 z
Apo.........................69 k
Apodi.......................27 u
Apoera......................26 g
Apollo Bay..................77 w
Apolo.......................25 p
Aporema.....................26 l
Apostle Islands.............16 d
Apóstoles...................28 z
Apoteri.....................23 y
Appalachian Mountains ......16 v
Appleton....................16 r
Apucarana...................29 c
Apuka Chukotskaya ....10 r

Apure.......................23 e
Apurimac....................24 y
Aqaba.......................38 k
Aqaba, Gulf of ....38 k
Aqcha.......................60 h
Aqqikkol, Hu................61 j
Aqua Clara..................29 c
Aquidabán...................28 m
Aquidauana..................28 m
Aquidauana (River)..........28 m
Araara......................43 s
Arabelo.....................23 u
Arabian Desert..............38 c
Arabian Gulf................39 i
Arabian Sea.................60 s
Araca.......................25 g
Aracaju.....................27 u
Aracati.....................27 u
Araçatuba...................29 d
Aracena.....................34 p
Aracui......................29 j
Arad........................35 e
Arafat......................39 o
Arafura Sea.................73 c
Aragarças...................29 c
Araguacema..................26 y
Araguaçu....................26 y
Araguaia....................26 z
Araguaína...................26 z
Araguari....................26 j
Arak........................39 h
Arakan Mountains ....62 o
Arak Bordj..................37 n
Araks.......................54 v
Aral........................56 q
Aral Sea....................55
Aral'sk.....................55 d
Aralsor, Lake...............54 j
Aramac......................74 p
Aramberri...................19 o
Aranos......................48 x
Arapari.....................25 y
Arapey......................28 v
Arapiraca...................27 u
Ar'ar.......................39 b
Araracuara..................24 m
Araranguá...................29 r
Araraquara..................29 r
Araras......................26 v
Araras, Serra das ....29 o
Ararat......................77 v
Ararat, Mount...............54 v
Arari.......................27 b
Ar Arish....................38 j
Arauca......................23 c
Arauca (River)..............23 f
Aravalli Range..............60 z
Araxá.......................29 f
Arba Minch..................43 o
Arbil.......................39 d
Arcas.......................19 u
Archangel...................50 q
Archei......................38 z
Archer's Post...............43 p
Arčman......................55 n
Arco........................14 z
Arcoverde...................27 u
Arctic Bay..................13 d
Arctic Circle...............53 l
Arctic Ocean.10-11/32-33/89
Arctic Red River............11 m
Arctic Village..............11 h
Arctowski...................82 s
Ar Dăg......................54 q
Ardahan.....................54 s
Ardakan.....................39 k
Arde........................43 o
Ardebil.....................54 w
Ardencaple Fjord............91 t
Ardestan....................39 k
Ar Dzargala.................57 j
Arenas......................19 u
Arendal.....................33 c
Arequipa....................25 n
Arere.......................26 l
Areyonga....................73 l
Arezzo......................34 m
Arga........................53 l
Argadargada.................73 l
Arga Sala...................52 l

Argentina 28-33
Argentino Lago ....30 u
Arghandab ....60 g
Argun ....58 c
Argungu ....41 d
Argun Youqi ....58 c
Argun Zuoqi ....58 c
Argut ....56 g
Argyle, Lake ....73 a
Århus ....33 p
Ariamsvlei ....48 x
Ariari ....23 n
Arica (Bolivia) ....28 c
Arica (Colombia) ....25 a
Arica (Peru) ....24 k
Arinos ....29 g
Arinos (River) ....25 x
Aripuan ....25 w
Aripuan (River) ....25 w
Ariquemes ....25 t
Arizona ....18 f
Arizpe ....18 h
Arjeplog ....33 g
Arjo ....43 a
Arjona ....22 m
Arka ....53 r
Arkadelphia ....19 f
Arkagala ....53 g
Arkalyk ....55 w
Arkansas ....15 w
Arkansas City ....15 v
Arkansas (River) ....19 g
Arkansas (State) ....19 f
Arkbajtal ....55 x
Arkhangelsk (Archangel) ..50 q
Arkhara ....58 i
Arklow ....32 v
Arkona, Cape ....33 r
Arktichesgo Instituta ....51 f
Arles ....34 i
Arlington (Texas) ....19 c
Arlington (Washington) .....16 x
Arman ....53 v
Armavir ....54 s
Armenia ....22 z
Armenia ....54 u
Armidale ....78 f
Armstrong (British Columbia) ....14 i
Armstrong (Ontario) ....16 e
Arnauti, Cape ....35 x
Arnhem ....33 n
Arnhem, Cape ....73 g
Arnhem Land ....73 d
Aroab ....48 x
Arrah ....61 u
Ar Ramadi ....39 d
Ar Randa ....39 p
Ar Rawda ....43 i
Arrecifal ....23 q
Arrecife ....36 c
Arriaga ....19 s
Ar Rifa ....39 f
Arrilalah ....73 y
Arrowsmith ....79 s
Ar Rutbah ....39 b
Ar Ruwais ....39 i
Arsen'yev ....58 k
Arsk ....50 t
Arta ....43 f
Artém ....58 k
Artemovskiy ....50 y
Artesia ....18 l
Arthur ....77 x
Arthurs Pass ....79 t
Artigas ....28 z
Artillery Lake ....12 u
Art'omosk ....56 k
Arturo Prat ....82 s
Artyk (Russia) ....53 f
Artyk (Turkmenistan) ......55 o
Aru ....42 w
Aru Islands ....70 r
Arua ....42 x
Aruaña ....29 c
Aruba ....23 c
Arum ....25 h
Arun Qi ....58 e
Arusha ....45 i
Aruwimi ....42 s

Arvaj Cheer ....57 c
Arviat (Eskimo Point) .....13 n
Ary ....52 j
Arys' ....55 u
Arys, Lake ....55 g
Arzamas ....54 g
Asab ....48 v
Asadabad ....60 k
Asahi-dake ....59 d
Asahikawa ....59 d
Asanib ....48 j
Asansk ....51 x
Asayta ....43 e
Asbe Tafari ....43 d
Ascensión Bay ....20 v
Ascensión (Bolivia) ....25 t
Ascensión (Mexico) ....18 j
Ascensión Island ....230 y
Ascoli ....35 a
Asedjrad ....37 n
Asela ....43 d
Asha ....55 a
Ashburton ....79 t
Ashburton (River) ....72 t
Ashburton Downs ....72 s
Asheville ....16 u
Ashgabat ....55 o
Ashland (Montana) ....15 c
Ashland (Wisconsin) ....15 l
Ash Sha'am ....39 l
Ash Sharmah ....38 l
Ash Shihr ....43 k
Ash Shubaiyai ....39 d
Ash Shumlul ....39 g
Ash Shwayrif ....37 i
Ashtabula ....16 v
Ashton ....15 a
Asi ....38 l
Asilah ....34 p
Asimba ....43 d
Asino ....51 u
Asir ....39 p
Askale ....54 s
Asmara ....43 c
Asosa ....42 m
Aspiring ....79 q
Assab ....43 f
Assad Reservoir ....39 a
Assale, Lake ....43 d
As Salman ....39 e
Assamakka ....37 q
As Samawah ....39 e
As Sawadah ....39 r
As Sib ....60 o
As Sidr ....39 n
As Sila ....39 v
Assiniboia ....15 c
As Sua ....39 p
As Sulaiyil ....39 r
As Suq ....39 p
As Suwaiq ....60 o
Astakh ....53 c
Astana ....55 j
Astara ....54 w
Astillero ....25 o
Astoria ....14 v
Astrakhan ....54 i
Asuka ....84 d
Asunción ....28 y
Aswân ....38 w
Asyût ....38 h
Atacama Desert ....28 p
Atakh-Yuryakh ....52 i
Atakor ....37 p
Atakpamé ....41 n
Atalanka ....57 b
Atalaya ....24 y
Atambua ....69 w
Atar ....36 p
Atasu ....55 i
Atbara ....38 w
Atbara (River) ....38 x
Atbasar ....55 h
Atchison ....15 w
Atebubu ....40 z
Athabasca ....14 m
Athabasca (River) ....14 l
Athabasca, Lake ....12 v
Athens (Georgia) ....20 k
Athens (Greece) ....35 t

Athens (Ohio) ....16 v
Atherton ....74 c
Athínai (Athens) ....35 t
Athlone ....32 u
Atholl, Cape ....91 b
Ati ....42 b
Atiak ....42 x
Atico ....24 y
Atikokan ....16 c
Atikonak Lake ....17 f
Atkarsk ....54 h
Atka (USA) ....10 w
Atka (Russia) ....53 i
Atlanta ....20 j
Atlantic City ....16 z
Atlantic Ocean 230
Atlas Mountains 36/37
Atlasovo ....53 y
Atlin, Lake ....11 y
Atlixco ....19 p
Atouat ....66 j
Atoyac ....19 o
Atrato ....22 l
Attawapiskat ....16 g
Attawapiskat Lake ....16 e
Attikamagen Lake ....17 d
At Timan ....42 e
Attopeu ....66 j
Attu ....10 r
Atuel ....30 k
Atyrau ....54 l
Auckland ....79 u
Auckland Island ....231 x
Augathella ....74 p
Augrabies Falls ....48 x
Augsburg ....34 l
Augusta (Georgia) ....20 l
Augusta (Maine) ....17 o
Augusta Victoria ....28 d
Augustus ....72 s
Augustus Downs ....73 v
Augustus, Mount ....72 t
Auld, Lake ....72 x
Aurangabad ....61 n
Aurillac ....34 g
Aurora (Suriname) ....26 h
Aurora (USA) ....15 x
Aurukun ....73 j
Aus ....48 u
Aust. Capital Territory ......78 d
Austin, Lake ....76 e
Austin (Minnesota) ....16 x
Austin (Nevada) ....14 x
Austin (Texas) ....19 d
Austral Downs ....73 t
Australia 72-74/76-78
Austria 33-35
Autlán ....18 y
Auxerre ....34 h
aux Feuilles ....13 v
Auzangate ....25 n
Auzu ....37 x
Avaré ....29 e
Aveiro ....34 a
Avenal ....14 v
Avezzano ....35 a
Avignon ....34 i
Avila ....34 c
Avispas ....18 g
Avon ....76 e
Avon Downs ....73 t
Avon Park ....20 l
Awaran ....60 h
Awasa ....43 p
Awash ....43 p
Awash (River) ....43 p
Awaso ....40 y
Awat ....56 p
Awaynat Wanin ....37 h
Aweil ....42 h
Awetu ....43 r
Awjilah ....38 b
Axel Heiberg Island ....13 b
Ayacucho (Argentina) ....31 c
Ayacucho (Peru) ....24 y
Ayakkum Hu ....56 u
Ayan ....53 p
Ayan (Ilimpeya) ....52 j
Ayan (Nepa) ....52 o
Ayan (River) ....51 k

Ayangba ....41 s
Ayaviri ....25 o
Ayaya ....53 o
Aydabu ....55 h
Aydin ....35 v
Ayers Rock ....73 p
Aykhal ....52 e
Aylmer Lake ....12 v
Ayoûn el Atroûs ....40 g
Ayr (Australia) ....74 q
Ayr (UK) ....32 w
Ayshirak ....55 i
Ayu Islands ....70 c
Ayvalik ....35 u
Azamgarh ....61 s
Azángara ....25 n
Azaouad ....36 x
Azaouak ....41 d
Azaouak (River) ....37 o
Azaouak, Vallée de l' ....41 c
Azefal ....36 o
Azemmour ....36 g
Azerbaijan ....54 v
Azhbulat, Lake ....55 m
Azna ....39 h
Azogues ....24 i
Azopol'ye ....50 s
Azores ....230 k
Azoum ....42 d
Azov, Sea of ....54 c
Azrou ....36 i
Azuero Peninsula ....22 i
Azúl ....31 b
Azum ....42 e
Azurduy ....28 g
Az Zaydiyah ....43 f
Az Zilfi ....39 e
Az Zuqar ....43 f

B

Baacagaan ....57 n
Baalbek ....38 l
Babaçulândia ....26 z
Babahoyo ....22 w
Bab al Mandab ....43 f
Babanusa ....42 i
Babar ....70 o
Babati ....45 i
Babel Thuap ....70 f
Babile ....43 f
Babo ....70 r
Baboua ....41 y
Babuyan Islands ....67 l
Bababal ....27 o
Bacajá ....26 j
Bacan Islands ....69 l
Bacău ....35 h
Bachardok ....55 p
Bachinivas ....18 j
Bachu Liuchang ....56 o
Back ....12 m
Bac Ninh ....62 x
Baco ....67 g
Bacolod ....67 i
Badain Jaran ....57 o
Badajós ....25 g
Badajós, Lago ....25 g
Badajoz ....34 o
Badgastein ....35 a
Bad Hersfeld ....33 p
Badillo ....23 a
Badin ....60 m
Badr Hunain ....39 n
Badu ....70 x
Badu (Island) ....73 j
Baduen ....43 w
Badulla ....64 v
Baeza ....22 y
Bafang ....41 u
Bafang (River) ....40 f
Bafatá ....40 c
Baffin Bay ....13 g
Baffin Island ....13 g
Bafia ....41 u
Bafoulabé ....40 f
Bafoussam ....41 l
Bafq ....39 l
Baft ....60 b

Bafwabalinga ....42 u
Baga ....41 j
Bagadzha ....52 i
Bagamoyo ....45 k
Bagan ....62 e
Bagata ....44 i
Bagazán ....24 m
Bagdarin ....52 s
Bagé ....29 n
Baghdad ....39 e
Baghin ....60 a
Baghlan ....60 b
Bago ....67 h
Bagua ....24 i
Baguinéda ....40 i
Baguio ....67 g
Bagzane ....37 s
Bahamas ....21 b
Bahariya, Oasis ....38 g
Baharu ....66 s
Bahawalpur ....60 l
Baheh ....39 e
Bahia Negra ....28 k
Bahir Dar ....43 b
Bahla ....39 m
Bahrain ....39 i
Bahrain, Gulf of ....39 i
Bahr al Arab ....42 g
Bahr al Ghazel ....42 i
Bahr al Milh ....39 d
Bahu Kalat ....60 l
Baia Mare ....35 f
Baio ....26 l
Baïbokoum ....41 y
Baicheng ....58 e
Baidarata Bay ....50 m
Baidoba ....43 t
Baie Comeau ....17 c
Baie-St.-Paul ....17 a
Baihe ....63 a
Bailundo ....44 u
Baima ....62 g
Baingoin ....61 k
Baiquan ....58 f
Baird Mountains ....11 a
Bairin Youqi ....57 y
Bairin Zouqi ....57 x
Bairnsdale ....78 p
Bais ....67 h
Bait al Faqih ....43 f
Baixingt ....57 t
Baiyanghe ....56 i
Baiyuda ....38 v
Bajan ....57 e
Bajan Baraat ....57 d
Bajanchongor ....57 a
Bajan-Dalaj ....57 p
Bajanleg ....57 n
Bajan-Öndör ....56 z
Bajan Ovoo ....57 h
Bajan-Uul ....56 l
Bajan-Uul (Uldz Gol) ....57 h
Bajeador, Cape ....63 u
Bajo Caracoles ....30 u
Bajram Ali ....55 r
Bajsint ....57 u
Bakchar ....51 s
Baker (California) ....14 x
Baker (Montana) ....15 e
Baker (Oregon) ....14 j
Baker, Lake ....12 z
Baker Lake ....12 z
Bakersfield ....14 x
Bakhta ....51 v
Bakhta (River) ....51 w
Bakhtaran ....39 f
Bakhynay ....52 j
Bako ....40 h
Bakrakondre ....26 g
Baku ....54 x
Balabac ....67 q
Balabac Strait ....67 q
Bala, Cerros de ....25 p
Baladek ....53 n
Balagannakh ....53 c
Balagannakh ....53 k
Balagannoye ....53 u
Balagansk ....57 c
Balaghat ....61 r
Balaipungut ....66 s

Balaka.............46 i
Balakovo..........54 j
Bala Murghab......60 f
Balancán..........19 u
Balāngīr..........61 t
Balashikha........54 d
Balashov..........54 g
Balasore..........61 v
Balaton, Lake.....35 c
Balbi.............71 u
Balboa............22 j
Bald Cape.........76 e
Balearic Islands..34 t
Baley.............57 j
Balgazya..........56 l
Balgo.............73 n
Bali..............69 p
Bali Sea..........69 q
Balikesir.........35 v
Balikpapan........69 e
Balkans...........35 g
Balkhab...........60 i
Balkhash..........55 l
Balkhash, Lake....55 k
Balladonia........76 j
Ballarat..........77 w
Ballé.............40 h
Ballenas Bay......18 f
Balleny Islands...86 w
Balombo...........44 t
Balonne...........78 d
Balotra...........60 z
Balrampur.........61 f
Balranald.........77 j
Balsas (Brazil)...27 n
Balsas (Mexico)...19 u
Balsas (Peru).....24 i
Balta.............25 n
Bălti.............35 i
Baltic Sea........33 t
Baltîm............38 i
Baltimore.........16 y
Baluchistan.......60 e
Bam (Iran)........60 c
Bam (Russia)......52 w
Bama..............41 k
Bamaga............73 k
Bamako............40 h
Bamba (Mali)......40 m
Bamba (Senegal)...40 e
Bambama...........44 f
Bambamarca........24 i
Bambari...........42 p
Bamberg...........33 q
Bambesa...........42 t
Bambesi...........42 m
Bambili...........42 t
Bamboi............40 m
Bamboo Creek......72 v
Bambui............29 g
Bambuyka..........52 t
Bamenda...........41 u
Bamian............60 i
Bamingui..........42 b
Bampur............60 d
Bampur (River)....60 d
Bamyili...........73 d
Banados del Atuel.30 k
Banados del Izozog.28 i
Banagi............45 h
Banalia...........42 t
Banamba...........40 i
Banana............74 s
Banas.............61 o
Banas, Ras........38 y
Ban Ban...........65 m
Banbar............62 c
Bancroft..........16 k
Banda (India).....61 r
Banda
(Demp. Rep. Congo).44 j
Banda Aceh........65 s
Banda Sea.........69 x
Bandama...........40 w
Bandar Abbas......60 a
Bandar Anzeli.....54 x
Bandar-e-Khomeini.39 h
Bandar-e-Lengeh...39 l
Bandar-e-Margam...39 j
Bandar-e-Rig......39 h

Bandarlampung
(Telukbetung).....68 v
Bandar Seri Begawan.69 b
Bandar Sri Aman...68 m
Bandeirante.......26 x
Bandera...........28 v
Banderas Bay......18 x
Bandiagara........40 k
Bandirma..........35 i
Bandundu..........44 i
Bandung...........68 x
Baneh.............54 v
Banes.............21 p
Banff.............14 l
Banfora...........40 k
Bangalore.........64 f
Banganapalle......64 g
Bangassou.........42 r
Bangeta...........71 n
Banggai Islands...69 i
Banggi............67 q
Bangka............68 w
Bangkalan.........69 n
Bangkok (Krung Thep).66 q
Bangladesh........61
Bangor............17 c
Bangoran..........42 c
Bangued...........67 f
Bangui............42 n
Bangweulu, Lake...45 q
Bani..............40 j
Bani Sar..........39 p
Bania.............41 y
Baniara...........74 f
Banja Luka........35 b
Banjarmasin.......69 o
Banjul............40 a
Banket............46 r
Banks Island (Canada).12 d
Banks Islands
(Micronesia)......75 e
Banks Peninsula...79 u
Banks Strait......78 p
Bankura...........61 v
Ban Me Thuot......66 k
Ban Na San........66 q
Bannu.............60 k
Ban Pong..........66 d
Ban Pu Kroy.......66 j
Banswara..........61 n
Ban Thateng.......66 i
Banvalot..........61 i
Banya Fort........43 n
Banyo.............41 v
Banyuwangi........69 p
Banzare Coast.....87 d
Banzart (Bizerte).34 y
Baoji.............62 l
Bao Loc...........66 j
Baoshan...........62 s
Baouna............40 l
Bap...............60 m
Baqên.............62 c
Ba'qubah..........39 e
Bara (Nigeria)....41 n
Bara (Sudan)......42 j
Barabinsk.........56 b
Baracoa...........21 q
Baragoi...........43 o
Barahona..........21 s
Baralaba..........74 r
Baram.............69 b
Baran.............61 o
Baranga...........42 u
Baranoa...........22 m
Baranof Island....11 x
Baranovichi.......33 x
Barat Daya Islands.69 y
Barbacena.........29 h
Barbados..........23 k
Barbas, Cap.......36 n
Barbuda...........21 z
Barcaldine........74 r
Barcelona (Spain).34 h
Barcelona (Venezuela).23 g
Barcelos..........23 u
Barcoo............74 o
Bardai............37 x
Barddhaman........61 v
Bardera...........43 s

Bardeskan.........60 b
Bareilly..........61 d
Barentsburg.......92 o
Barents Island....92 p
Barents Sea.......50 d
Barga.............61 e
Barguzin..........52 q
Bari..............35 c
Barinas...........23 c
Baring, Cape......12 e
Baringo Lodge.....43 n
Baripada..........61 v
Bâris.............38 u
Barisal...........61 x
Barisan Mountains.68 s
Barito............69 c
Barka.............38 z
Barkal............61 z
Barkam............62 i
Barkly East.......49 p
Barkly Tableland..73 s
Barkly West.......49 n
Barkol Hu.........56 w
Barkol Kazak......56 w
Barlee, Lake......76 g
Barlow............11 j
Barmer............60 y
Barnaul...........56 e
Barnes Ice Cap....13 i
Baro..............41 e
Barquisimeto......23 c
Barra.............27 p
Barraca da Boca...26 j
Barra de Navidad..18 x
Barra do Corda....27 o
Barra do So Manuel.25 k
Barranca..........24 j
Barrancabermeja...23 a
Barrancas (Argentina).30 j
Barrancas (Venezuela).23 h
Barranquilla......22 m
Barre.............17 n
Barreira do Campo.26 y
Barreiras.........27 o
Barreiros.........27 w
Barretos..........29 e
Barrhead..........14 l
Barrie............16 w
Barrier Range.....77 h
Barrington Tops...78 f
Barrow............11 c
Barrow, Cape......11 c
Barrow Creek......73 r
Barrow Island.....72 r
Barrow Strait.....13 a
Barsa Kel'mes.....55 c
Barsi.............61 o
Barstow...........14 x
Bartica...........23 y
Bartle Frere......74 c
Bartlesville......15 v
Barumun...........68 e
Baruun Turuun.....56 k
Baruun-Urt........57 i
Barwani...........61 n
Barysh............54 i
Basac.............66 h
Basankusu.........42 p
Bascuñan, Cabo....28 o
Bashi Channel.....63 u
Basilan...........67 t
Basilan (Island)..67 u
Bas-Kouilou.......44 d
Basle (Basel).....34 k
Basoko............42 r
Basotho...........49 b
Basra.............39 g
Bassein...........65 f
Basse Santa Su....40 d
Basseterre........21 y
Bassett...........15 t
Bassikounou.......40 i
Bassila...........41 b
Bass Strait.......77 x
Bastak............39 k
Bastia............34 k
Bata..............41 u

Batagay...........53 a
Batakan...........69 o
Batama............42 u
Batamay...........52 m
Batang............62 f
Batangafo.........42 n
Batangas..........67 g
Batan Islands.....63 v
Batatais..........29 f
Bataysk...........54 e
Batchelor.........73 b
Batha.............42 b
Bathurst (Australia).78 e
Bathurst (Canada).17 e
Bathurst, Cape....12 a
Bathurst Inlet....12 i
Bathurst Island (Canada).12 i
Bathurst Island (Australia).73 b
Bati..............43 d
Batna.............34 w
Batomga...........53 p
Baton Rouge.......20 z
Batouri...........41 x
Batovi............29 b
Batsireet.........57 g
Battambang........66 f
Batterbee Range...82 x
Batticaloa........64 w
Battle Creek......16 t
Battle Mountain...14 x
Batui.............69 h
Batumi............54 s
Baturino..........56 f
Baubau............69 v
Bauchi............41 h
Baunt.............52 s
Baures............25 s
Baurú.............29 d
Bavispe...........18 i
Bawean............69 n
Bawîti............38 g
Bawku.............40 m
Ba Xian...........62 l
Baxoi.............62 e
Bay Islands.......20 v
Bayamo............21 o
Bayamón...........21 v
Bayanga...........41 z
Bayan Har Shan....62 f
Bayan Mod.........57 p
Bayan Obo.........57 s
Bayawan...........67 h
Bay City..........16 u
Bayir.............38 l
Baykal, Lake......52 p
Baykalovo.........51 n
Baykal'skiy Mountains.52 q
Baykal'skoye......52 q
Baykit............51 y
Baykonyr..........55 g
Baymak............55 b
Bayneu............54 m
Bayombong.........67 g
Bayonne...........34 f
Bayóvar...........24 g
Baytown...........19 e
Baza..............36 k
Bazaruto..........46 v
Bazman............60 d
Beagle Bay........72 k
Beagle Gulf.......73 b
Beardmore Glacier.86 c
Beardstown........16 q
Bear Island.......92 p
Bearskin Lake.....15 l
Beatrice..........15 v
Beatty............14 x
Beaufort..........69 d
Beaufort Sea......11/89
Beaufort West.....48 z
Beaumont..........19 e
Beaver (River, Canada).15 b
Beaver (River, USA).15 t
Beaver Creek......11 i
Beavermouth.......14 j
Beawar............61 n
Bébéoura..........41 z
Beckley...........16 v

Bedajós...........26 b
Bedajós, Lago.....26 b
Bedele............43 a
Bedford...........16 s
Bedopa............51 y
Bedourie..........73 u
Beed..............61 o
Beer Sheba........38 k
Beethoven Peninsula.82 x
Befale............42 p
Befandriana Av....47 e
Befori............42 r
Beger.............56 z
Begichev..........52 f
Behbahan..........39 i
Behring Point.....21 o
Behsud............60 i
Bei'an............58 z
Beihai (Pakhoi)...62 z
Beijing (Peking)..57 w
Beira.............46 v
Beirut............38 k
Bei Shan..........56 w
Beitbridge........49 e
Beitun............56 g
Bejaia............34 v
Beja (Portugal)...34 o
Beja (Tunisia)....34 x
Béka..............41 w
Bekabad...........55 v
Bekdas............54 y
Békéscsaba........35 d
Bela..............60 v
Bel'agas..........56 c
Belaja Šhola......56 c
Belarus...........33 x
Bela Vista........49 t
Belaya Tserkov....33 z
Belcher Channel...13 a
Belcher Islands...13 s
Bélel.............41 x
Belém.............26 m
Belem de So Francisco.27 t
Belen (USA).......15 p
Belén (Argentina).28 r
Belen'kaya........52 w
Beles.............43 a
Belesc Cogani.....43 r
Belet Huen........43 t
Beleutty..........55 g
Belev.............54 c
Beleya............43 a
Belfast...........32 v
Belfield..........15 e
Belgaum...........64 d
Belgium...........32-33/34
Belgorod..........35 j
Belgrade..........35 v
Beli..............41 v
Belitung..........68 y
Belize (City).....19 w
Belize (State)....19/20
Bel'kachi.........53 n
Bel'kovskiy.......53 b
Bell..............49 p
Bellary...........64 f
Bella Unión.......28 y
Bella Vista (Argentina).28 x
Bella Vista (Brazil).28 m
Belle Isle, Strait of.17 z
Belleville........16 x
Bellingham........14 h
Bellingshausen....82 x
Bellingshausen Sea.80 l
Bello.............22 m
Bell Peninsula....13 r
Bellyk............56 l
Belmopan..........19 w
Belogorsk.........58 h
Beloit............16 r
Belo Monte........26 k
Belomorsk.........50 n
Beloretsk.........55 b
Belterra..........26 z
Belyuen...........73 b
Belyy Yar.........51 t
Bembe.............44 g
Bembéréké.........41 c
Bemidji...........15 j

Name	Page	Grid
Bena Dibele	44	l
Benadir	43	t
Bena-Tshadi	44	l
Bend	14	h
Benda Range	77	g
Bender Beila	43	l
Bendigo	77	x
Bene	46	v
Benevento	35	a
Bengal, Bay of	64	m
Bengamisa	42	t
Benghazi	35	q
Bengkolan Bay	66	x
Bengkulu	68	s
Benguela	44	r
Ben Guerdane	34	y
Benguerir	36	g
Beni	42	v
Beni Abbès	36	k
Beni Cunif	36	l
Beni Mazâr	38	h
Beni Mellal	36	i
Benin	41	b
Benin City	41	r
Beni (River)	25	q
Beni Saf	34	r
Beni Suef	38	i
Benito Juárez	31	b
Beni Walid	35	n
Benjamin Acéval	28	y
Benjamin Constant	25	b
Benmara	73	g
Bennetta	53	h
Benoni	49	q
Bentinck Island	73	i
Bentiu	42	j
Bentong	66	s
Benue	41	f
Beograd (Belgrade)	35	d
Berber	38	x
Berbera	43	h
Berberati	41	y
Berdale	43	w
Berdyansk	54	c
Berea	16	t
Bereda	43	l
Berekum	40	y
Berenice	38	x
Berens River	15	i
Berezniki	50	w
Berezovka	52	t
Berezovka (River)	53	k
Berezovo	50	z
Berezovo (Koryak Mountains)	10	e
Berezovskaya	52	u
Berga, Cape	51	m
Bergamo	34	l
Bergen	33	a
Berhala Strait	68	h
Berhampore	61	w
Berhampur	61	t
Beringovskiy	10	h
Bering Sea	10	
Bering Strait	10	k
Berkakit	52	x
Berkner Island	83	s
Berlin (Germany)	33	r
Berlin (USA)	17	a
Bermejillo	18	l
Bermejo	28	g
Bermejo (River)	28	h
Bermejo (River)	28	r
Berne	34	j
Bernier Bay	13	b
Bernina	34	l
Bernstorff's Isfjörd	90	w
Beroubouay	41	c
Berrechio	36	h
Berriane	37	a
Bertes	53	f
Bertoua	41	w
Berwick upon Tweed	32	x
Besançon	34	j
Besar	69	q
Besham Qila	60	l
Besikama	69	x
Besima	60	h
Bessemer	20	h
Bestamak	56	b
Bestobe	55	k
Betafo	47	q
Bétaré-Oya	41	x
Betehor	43	c
Bethal	49	r
Bethanie	48	v
Bethany	15	w
Bethel	11	a
Bethlehem	49	p
Betioky	47	o
Betoota	77	h
Bet-Pak-Dala	55	i
Betpak-Dala Steppe	55	h
Betroka	47	q
Betsiboka	47	q
Bettiah	61	h
Betul	61	p
Betwa	61	q
Beverley Springs	72	l
Beyla	40	h
Beysehir, Lake	35	x
Bhadrachalam	64	i
Bhadrakh	61	v
Bhadra Reservoir	64	e
Bhadrathalam	61	r
Bhadravati	64	e
Bhagalpur	61	w
Bhaktapur	61	i
Bhamo	62	r
Bhandara	61	q
Bhanjanager	61	l
Bharatpur	61	b
Bharuch	60	z
Bhatinda	61	a
Bhavnagar	60	y
Bhawanipatna	61	s
Bheri	61	f
Bhilwara	61	n
Bhima	64	e
Bhojpur	61	i
Bhopal	61	p
Bhor	60	z
Bhubaneswar	61	u
Bhuj	60	x
Bhutan	61	k
Bia	62	v
Biak	70	t
Bialystok	33	v
Biankbuma	40	v
Biaza	51	r
Bickle Knob	16	w
Bida	41	e
Bidar	61	p
Bidokht	60	c
Bielsko-Biala	35	d
Bien Hoa	66	j
Bienville, Lake	17	a
Big Bell	76	e
Big Delta	11	g
Biggar	15	b
Big Island	90	e
Bignona	40	b
Big Sandy	15	a
Big Sioux	15	v
Big Spring	19	a
Big Trout Lake	16	d
Bihać	35	b
Bihar	61	u
Bija	56	g
Bijapur	64	e
Bijar	39	g
Bijiang	62	s
Bijie	62	k
Bijsk	56	f
Bikaner	60	m
Bikin	58	l
Bikin (River)	58	m
Bikoro	44	i
Bilaspur	61	s
Bilbao	34	d
Bilecik	35	w
Bili	42	t
Bili (River)	42	s
Bilir	53	q
Biliran	67	i
Billabalon	76	d
Billabong	77	y
Billiluna	73	n
Billings	15	b
Bilma	37	v
Bilma, Grand Erg de	37	v
Biloela	74	s
Biloku	23	x
Biloxi	20	g
Biltine	42	d
Bimbo	42	n
Binalbagan	67	h
Binatang	69	a
Bindura	49	f
Binga	46	p
Bing Bong	73	f
Binghampton	16	y
Bingöl	54	r
Binhai	63	g
Bintuhan	68	t
Bintulu	69	b
Binzert	37	f
Bio Bio	30	h
Bioko Island	41	t
Bir al Hasa	38	y
Birao	42	e
Biratnagar	61	j
Birdsville	77	g
Bir el Khzaim	36	t
Bir Enzarah	36	p
Bireuen	68	b
Bir Gandus	36	n
Birganj	61	h
Birikčul	56	i
Birilyussy	51	w
Birjand	60	d
Birmingham (UK)	32	x
Birmingham (USA)	19	j
Birnin Gwari	41	e
Bernin-Kebbi	41	d
Birobidzhan	58	k
Birou	40	f
Bir Oum Greine	36	r
Bir Shari	39	d
Biru	62	b
Bir Zar	34	y
Biscay, Bay of	34	d
Biscoe Island	82	t
Bishkek	55	x
Bishop	14	w
Biskra	34	w
Bismarck	15	g
Bismarck Archipelago	71	p
Bismarck Range	70	z
Bismarck Sea	71	
Bison	15	f
Bissagos Islands	40	a
Bissau	40	b
Bitam	41	v
Bitkine	42	b
Bitola	35	e
Bitterfontein	48	w
Bitterroot Mountains	14	l
Biu	41	j
Biwa, Lake	58	z
Bjorne Peninsula	13	c
Bla	40	j
Blackall	74	p
Blackburn, Mount	11	h
Black Hills	15	r
Blackpool (UK)	32	w
Blackpool (USA)	14	i
Black Sea	35	
Blackstone Camp	76	m
Black Volta	40	l
Blackwood	76	d
Blagoevgrad	35	f
Blagoveshchensk	58	h
Blagovščenka	56	c
Blair Athol	74	q
Blanca, Bahía	31	a
Blanca, Laguna	30	v
Blanche, Lake	72	x
Blanc, Mont	34	j
Blanco, R.	25	t
Blanding	15	o
Blanquilla	23	g
Blantyre	46	h
Blenheim	79	u
Blida	34	u
Blind River	16	h
Blitta	41	a
Bloemfontein	49	o
Bloemhof	49	o
Bloemhof Reservoir	49	o
Bloomington (Illinois)	16	r
Bloomington (Indiana)	16	s
Bluefield	16	v
Bluefields	22	g
Blue Mountains	14	k
Blue Nile	42	m
Bluenose Lake	12	c
Blue Ridge	16	u
Blue River	14	i
Bluff Knoll	76	f
Blumenau	29	r
Blumut	66	t
Blythe	18	e
Blytheville	16	x
Bo	40	e
Boac	67	g
Boa Esperanca Reservoir	27	o
Boa Esperança	29	g
Boa Fé	24	m
Boatasyn	53	s
Boa Vista	23	w
Bobo-Dioulasso	40	k
Bobruysk	33	y
Boca del Pao	23	g
Boca do Acará	25	g
Boca do Acre	25	g
Boca do Curequeté	25	r
Boca do Jari	26	j
Boca do Moaco	25	c
Boca do Mutúm	25	c
Boca Grande	23	j
Bocaranga	41	y
Boco Mavaca	23	t
Boconó	23	c
Bodala	42	q
Bodaybo	52	s
Bodélé	42	a
Bodö	33	e
Boende	44	k
Boffa	40	c
Boganida	51	l
Bogangolo	42	o
Bogantungan	74	q
Bogda Feng	56	u
Bogdanovich	50	y
Bognes	33	f
Bogo	67	i
Bogor	68	w
Bogorodskoye	53	r
Bogotá	23	n
Bogotol	51	v
Bogra	61	x
Boguchany	51	y
Bogué	40	d
Bohemia Downs	72	z
Bohodou	40	g
Bohol	67	i
Boise	14	x
Boise City	15	s
Bojador	36	o
Bojador, Cap	36	o
Bojeador, Cape	67	f
Bojnurd	55	o
Boké	40	d
Boknfjörd	33	a
Boko	44	g
Bokol Mayo	43	r
Boktor	58	m
Bolaños	18	y
Bole (China)	56	q
Bole (Ghana)	40	l
Bolgatanga	40	m
Bolgrad	35	i
Bolia	44	i
Bolvar (Peru)	24	i
Bolivar (USA)	15	x
Bolivia	25/26/28	
Bollon	74	q
Bolodzhak	53	n
Bologna	34	m
Bolognesi	24	y
Bolomba	42	o
Bolon	58	m
Bolonchén de Rejón	19	u
Bol'senarymskoje	56	f
Bolsevik	55	o
Bol'shaya Balakhnya	52	b
Bol'shaya Glushitsa	54	k
Bol'shaya Kheta	51	g
Bol'sherech'ye	51	q
Bol'shezemel'skaya Tundra	50	j
Bol'shiye Khatymy	52	x
Bol'shoy Lyakhovskiy	53	e
Bol'shoy Onguren	57	e
Bol'shoy Patom	52	t
Bol'shoy Shantar	95	j
Bol'shoy Yenisey	56	m
Bol'shoye Vlasévo	53	r
Bol'shoye Zimovye	53	g
Bolson de Mapimi	18	l
Bolu	35	k
Boluntay	62	b
Bolzano	34	l
Boma	44	e
Bomassa	41	z
Bombale	41	z
Bombay	60	z
Bomberai	70	r
Bömbögör	57	a
Bom Despacho	29	g
Bomi	62	d
Bomi Hills	40	s
Bomili	42	u
Bom Jardim	25	r
Bom Jesus da Lapa	27	u
Bom Jesus de Itabapoana	29	k
Bonaire	23	e
Bonaparte Archipelago	72	l
Bon, Cap	34	z
Bonda	44	e
Bondo	42	s
Bondoukou	40	k
Bone, Gulf of	69	t
Bonete	28	q
Bong	40	t
Bonga	43	n
Bongadanga	42	q
Bongor	41	l
Bongos, Massif des	42	d
Bonifacio	34	k
Bonifacio, Str. of	34	k
Booué	44	e
Booylgoo Springs	76	x
Boqueiro	27	g
Boquilla Reservoir	18	k
Bor	42	x
Bora	42	g
Borah Peak	14	m
Borås	33	g
Borazjah	39	i
Borba	25	j
Borborema, Planalto da	27	u
Bordeaux	34	e
Borden Island	12	g
Borden Peninsula	13	c
Bordj-Bou-Arreridj	34	v
Bordj Bourguiba	34	y
Bordj Flye Sainte Marie	36	k
Bordj Messouda	37	e
Bordj-Moktar	36	z
Bordj Omar Driss	37	e
Borisoglebsk	54	f
Borisov	33	y
Borja	24	j
Borkou	37	y
Borlänge	33	g
Borneo	69	
Bornholm	33	s
Borodino	56	l
Borohoro Shan	56	p
Borolgustakh	52	i
Borovskoye	55	o
Borroloola	73	f
Borshchovochnyy Mountains	52	u
Boru	53	e
Borujerd	39	g
Bor-Yuryakh	52	h
Borzya	57	j

Bosaso...............................43 k
Bose...................................62 y
Bosing...............................63 f
Bosnia-Herzegovina ....35 c
Bosobolo...........................42 p
Bosporus ....35 i
Bossangoa.........................41 z
Bossembélé ....41 z
Bosso................................41 j
Bostan..............................56 r
Bosten Hu.........................56 t
Boston ....17 o
Bothnia, Gulf of................33 h
Botoşani...........................35 h
Botswana........44/46/48-49
Bouaflé.............................40 w
Bou Akba..........................36 g
Bouaké..............................40 w
Bouanga ....44 q
Bouar................................41 y
Bou Arfa...........................36 k
Bouca................................42 o
Boufarik ....37 b
Bougainville, Cape ....72 l
Bougainville (Island) ....71 t
Bougouni...........................40 i
Bougtob.............................34 t
Bou Izakarene ....36 e
Boukombé..........................41 b
Boulder ....15 u
Boulder City......................14 y
Boulia...............................73 v
Boulsa...............................40 m
Boumango..........................44 e
Boumba ....41 x
Boûmdeid..........................40 e
Boundary Peak..................14 w
Boundiali..........................40 i
Boundji..............................44 g
Boungo ....42 q
Bountiful...........................14 z
Bounty Islands ....79 y
Bourail ....75 p
Bourem ....40 m
Bouressa ....37 n
Bourke..............................77 k
Bournemouth.....................32 x
Bou Saada ....34 u
Bousso ....41 m
Boutilimit ....40 c
Bouvet Island...................230 z
Bova Marina ....37 j
Bowen...............................74 r
Bowling Green...................16 s
Bowman............................15 e
Bo Xian.............................63 d
Boxing..............................58 o
Boyabo ....42 o
Boyarka ....51 l
Boyoma Falls.....................42 t
Bozeman............................15 a
Bozoum ....41 y
Brac..................................35 b
Braco Menor do Araguaia 26 y
Bradenton ....20 k
Braeburn ....11 k
Braga ....34 b
Bragança ....27 a
Brahmaputra.....................61 y
Brainerd ....15 j
Brak ....37 i
Brali.................................55 f
Branco ....25 h
Brandberg ....48 g
Brandon (Canada).............15 g
Brandon (USA)..................20 l
Brandvlei..........................48 z
Branson ....15 x
Brasilandia........................29 g
Brasileia ....25 p
Brasilia.............................29 f
Brasilia Legal....................26 g
Brasov ....35 h
Brass................................41 r
Bratislava ....35 c
Bratsk...............................57 a
Bratskoye Reservoir ....57 b
Brattleboro ....17 n
Braunschweig (Brunswick)33 p
Brava................................43 t

Bravo del Norte ....18 l
Bray.................................49 a
Brazil 23-29
Brazilian Plateau ....29 h
Brazos ....19 d
Brazzaville ....44 f
Breadalbane ....73 u
Breda ....33 n
Bredy ....55 c
Breeza Plains ....74 b
Breidhi Fjord ....32 a
Bremen ....33 p
Bremerhaven ....33 p
Bremerton ....14 z
Brescia ....34 l
Brest (France) ....34 c
Brest (Belarus) ....33 w
Bretaña ....24 l
Breves ....26 l
Brewarrina ....78 c
Brewster, Cape ....91 q
Brézina ....34 t
Bria ....42 q
Bridgeport ....16 z
Bridgetown ....23 k
Bridgewater ....17 r
Brig ....34 k
Brighton ....32 y
Brikama ....40 a
Brindisi ....35 c
Brinkley ....15 y
Brisbane ....78 g
Bristol ....32 x
Bristol Bay ....11 o
Bristol Channel ....32 w
British Columbia 11/14
Britstown ....48 z
Brive ....34 g
Brno ....33 s
Broadus ....15 d
Brockville ....16 l
Brod ....35 c
Brodeur Peninsula ....13 c
Broken Hill ....77 h
Brokopondo ....26 h
Brookhaven ....20 f
Brookings ....15 l
Brooks ....14 m
Brooks Range ....11 c
Broome ....72 w
Broome (Mount) ....72 l
Broughton Island ....13 l
Browning ....14 m
Brownsville ....19 d
Brownwood ....19 c
Brumado ....29 j
Brunei ....69 c
Brunei Bay ....69 o
Brunette Downs ....73 s
Brunswick (Georgia) ....20 m
Brunswick (Germany) ....33 p
Brunswick
(New Hampshire) ....17 o
Brunswick Peninsula ....30 u
Brunt Ice Shelf ....83 p
Brussels ....33 n
Bruxelles (Brussels) ....33 n
Bruzual ....23 d
Bryan ....19 d
Bryanka ....51 w
Bryansk ....54 a
Bubiyan............................39 g
Bubye ....49 f
Buçaco ....44 w
Bucaramanga ....23 a
Buchanan ....40 s
Buchanan, Lake ....74 p
Buchan Gulf ....13 h
Buchans ....17 j
Buchara ....55 r
Bucharest ....35 h
Buckingham ....16 l
Bucklin.............................15 l
Bucureşti (Bucharest).......35 h
Budapest ....35 c
Budaun ....61 d
Budd Coast ....87 e
Budjala ....42 p
Buea ....41 t
Buena Esperanza ....30 l

Buenaventura (Mexico) ....18 j
Buenaventura (Colombia) 22 x
Buenos Aires (Argentina).31 c
Buenos Aires (Colombia)..23 n
Buenos Aires, Lago ....30 u
Buerát el Hsun ....35 o
Buffalo (New York)...........16 x
Buffalo (South Dakota).....15 e
Buffalo (Wyoming)............15 c
Buffalo Narrows ....12 v
Bug ....33 v
Bugarikta ....51 v
Bugat ....56 x
Bugorkan ....52 c
Bugsuk ....67 q
Bugul'ma ....54 l
Bugun ....55 d
Bugunda ....52 s
Buguruslan ....54 l
Bu Hasa ....39 w
Bui ....50 q
Buitepos ....48 k
Bujant ....56 m
Bujant-Ovoo ....57 q
Bujba ....56 k
Bujedžul' ....56 j
Bujumbura ....45 d
Bukačača ....57 j
Bukavu.............................45 c
Bukittingti ....68 e
Bukoba ....45 f
Bula ....70 p
Bulag Sum ....57 w
Bulan ....67 i
Bulanavo ....54 m
Bulawayo ....46 p
Buldana ....61 n
Bulgan ....57 p
Bulgan (High Altai)...........56 w
Bulgan (Selenga)...............57 b
Bulgar ....57 i
Bulgaria 35
Bulguntay ....56 t
Buller ....78 o
Bulloo ....77 j
Bulloo Downs
(W.Australia) ....72 v
Bulloo Downs
(Queensland) ....74 n
Bulo Burti ....43 u
Bultfontein ....49 o
Bulun ....53 s
Bulun (River) ....53 k
Bulungu ....44 j
Bulukol ....55 y
Bumba ....42 q
Buna ....43 q
Bunbury ....76 d
Bundaberg ....74 t
Bu Ndjem ....37 j
Bungo Channel.................58 x
Bunguran (Natuna)...........66 x
Buni ....41 i
Bunia ....42 w
Bunkeya ....45 o
Buntok ....69 c
Buol ....69 h
Bourkhaya Bay ....52 m
Bourkhaya, Cape ....53 a
Bur ....52 p
Bur Acaba ....43 s
Buraidah ....39 d
Buramo ....43 g
Buran ....56 f
Burandzha ....53 o
Burang ....61 e
Bur Anod ....43 i
Burao ....43 h
Burdekin ....74 p
Burden, Mount ....12 p
Bure ....43 b
Bureya ....58 i
Bureya (River) ....58 j
Burgakhchan ....53 f
Burgas ....35 i
Burgersdorp ....49 o
Burgon ....56 k
Burgos ....34 d
Bürhanpur ....61 o
Burias ....67 h

Buri Ram ....66 f
Burke Island ....81 a
Burketown.........................73 v
Burkhala ....53 h
Burkina Faso 40-41
Burlington (Colorado) ....15 s
Burlington (Iowa)..............15 y
Burlington (Vermont) ....16 z
Burma 61/62/65/66
Burney ....14 u
Burnie ....77 x
Burni-Nkonni ....41 d
Burns ....14 w
Burns Junction ....14 w
Burqin ....56 g
Burra ....77 g
Burro, Sierra ....19 a
Burrundie ....73 c
Bursa ....35 j
Buru ....69 y
Burundi ....45 d
Burwash Landing ....11 i
Burylbaytal ....55 x
Busanga ....44 l
Busanga (Congo River)....45 n
Bushehr ....39 i
Bushenyi ....42 w
Businga ....42 p
Busira ....44 j
Busselton ....76 c
Busseri ....42 u
Busu-Djanoa ....42 q
Buta ....42 s
Butembo ....42 v
Butiá ....29 p
Butte, Mount ....14 m
Butterworth ....66 r
Butuan ....67 j
Butung ....69 v
Buturlinovka ....54 f
Butwal ....61 g
Buwatah ....39 n
Buyr-Nur ....58 b
Buzuluk ....54 l
Byam Martin Channel......89 p
Bychez ....52 b
Bydgoszcz ....33 t
Bylot Island ....13 f
Byrd ....81 g
Byro ....76 d
Byrranga Mountains ....51 k
Byssa ....52 z
Bystryy ....51 p
Bysyttakh ....53 a
Bytantay...........................53 a
Byuchennyakh ....53 f
Byyangnyr........................53 g

C

Caala ....44 t
Cáatingas ....27 r
Caazapá ....28 z
Caballococha ....25 a
Cabanatuan ....67 g
Cabezas ....28 h
Cabimas ....23 c
Cabinda ....44 d
Cabonga Reservoir ....16 l
Cabool ....16 p
Caboolture ....74 u
Cabo Pantoja ....24 k
Cabora Bassa Reservoir ...46 f
Caborca ....18 f
Cabot Strait ....17 h
Cabrobó ....27 s
Caçador ....29 p
Cáceres (Brazil).................25 x
Cáceres (Spain) ....34 o
Cache Creek ....14 h
Cachi ....28 s
Cachi, Mount ....28 s
Cachimbo ....26 u
Cachimbo, Serra do ....25 z
Cachingues ....44 u
Cachoeira ....27 s
Cachoeira do Arari ....26 l
Cachoeira do Sul ....29 o
Cachoeiro de Itapemirim ..29 k

Cacolo ....44 w
Caconda ....44 t
Cacula ....44 s
Cadan ....56 j
Cadelga ....77 h
Cadillac ....16 t
Cadiz (Philippines)...........67 i
Cádiz (Spain).....................34 o
Cádiz, Gulf of...................34 o
Čadobec ....51 z
Caen ....34 f
Caetité ....27 q
Cafayate ....28 s
Cagaan Bogd Uul ....56 z
Cagaan Gol ....56 h
Cagaan Nuur ....56 h
Cagaan-Olom ....56 l
Cagaan-Uul ....56 m
Cagayan de Oro ....67 w
Cagayan Sulu ....67 r
Cágliari ....34 y
Caguán ....24 l
Caguas ....21 w
Čagyl ....55 n
Caia ....46 v
Caiabis, Serra dos............25 y
Caiaponia ....29 c
Caicara de Orinoco ....23 f
Caicó ....27 u
Caima ....26 l
Caird Coast ....83 f
Cairns ....74 c
Cairo (Al Qahirah) (Egypt)38 i
Cairo (Illinois) ....16 r
Caiundo ....44 u
Cajabamba ....24 i
Cajamarca ....24 i
Cajatamboo ....24 w
Cajázeiras ....27 t
Čajek ....55 x
Cajueiro ....26 v
Calabar ....41 s
Calabozo ....23 e
Calacoto ....25 o
Calais...............................32 z
Calalaste, Cord. de...........28 r
Calama (Brazil).................25 g
Calama (Peru)...................28 d
Calamar (Colombia)..........23 n
Calamar (Venezuela)........22 m
Calamian Group ....67 f
Calanaque ....25 r
Calang ....65 s
Calapan ....67 g
Calatayud ....34 f
Calbayog ....67 j
Calca ....25 n
Calçoene ....26 k
Calcutta ....61 w
Caldera ....28 o
Caldwell ....14 x
Caledon ....48 x
Caleta el Cobre ....28 o
Caleta Olivia ....30 x
Calexico ....18 d
Calgary ....14 l
Cali ....22 y
Calicut ....64 d
Calie Corar ....43 t
Caliente ....14 y
California ....14 v
California, Gulf of.............18 f
Calkini ....20 s
Callao ....24 w
Caloocan ....67 g
Calpulalpan ....19 p
Caltanissetta ....34 t
Calulo ....44 t
Calvert Hills ....73 g
Calverton ....17 n
Calvinia ....48 x
Camabatela ....44 g
Camaçari ....27 t
Camacho ....18 m
Camacupa ....44 u
Camagüey ....21 n
Camaná ....24 z
Camaná (River)................24 z
Čamaqu ....29 p
Camaqu (River)................29 o

Camarones ....30 y
Camaxilo ....44 j
Camballin ....72 y
Cambell River ....14 f
Cambay, Gulf of
(Gulf of Khambhat) .....60 y
Cambodia 66
Cambridge (Delaware) .....16 y
Cambridge (Ohio) .....16 v
Cambridge (UK) ....32 y
Cambridge Bay ....12 j
Camburinga ....73 f
Camden ....20 m
Cameroon 41
Cameroon, Mount ......41 t
Cametá ....26 l
Camiguin ....67 j
Camiri ....28 h
Camisea ....24 z
Camocim ....27 e
Camooweal ....73 u
Camopi ....26 j
Campana ....30 s
Campbell Island ....231 y
Campbell, Mount ....11 l
Campbelltown ....17 d
Campeche ....19 u
Campeche, Bay of ....19 s
Campiègne ....34 h
Campina Grande ....27 v
Campinas ....29 f
Campina Verde ....29 e
Camp Alegre ....26 x
Campobasso ....35 a
Campo de Diauarum ....26 w
Campo dos Parecis .....25 w
Campo Grande ....29 a
Campo Largo ....29 q
Campo Major ....27 q
Campo Mouro ....29 b
Campos ....29 k
Campos Belos ....27 n
Campos (Region) ....27 o
Campos Sales ....27 s
Cam Ranh ....66 k
Canada 11-17/88-90
Cañada de Gómez ....28 v
Canadian ....15 t
Canadian (River) ....15 r
Canairiktok ....17 g
Canakkale ....35 u
Canal do Norte (Brazil) .....26 k
Canal do Sul ....26 l
Canamaria ....25 o
Cananea ....18 h
Canary Islands ....36 a
Canastra, Serra de ....29 g
Canatlán ....18 l
Canaveral, Cape ....20 m
Canavierias ....29 l
Canberra ....78 d
Cancun ....19 x
Candeias ....27 t
Canelones ....31 d
Cangchou ....57 x
Cangkuang, Cape ....68 v
Canguaretama ....27 w
Canguçu ....29 o
Caniapiscau ....17 b
Caniapiscau Reservoir .....17 b
Canicado ....49 g
Canindé ....27 t
Canindé (Jurua) ....25 a
Canindé (River) ....27 r
Canipole ....18 g
Cannanore ....64 d
Cannanore Islands ....64 b
Canoas ....29 q
Canobie ....73 w
Canon City ....15 q
Cantabrian Mountains ......34 c
Cantaura ....23 g
Canterbury Bight ....79 t
Canterbury Plains ....79 s
Can-Tho ....66 i
Canto do Buriti ....27 q
Canton (USA) ....16 v
Canton (China) ....63 p
Cantwell ....11 f
Canudos ....27 s

Canum ....25 i
Canum (River) ....25 j
Canyon ....15 a
Canyushikino ....54 k
Cao Bang ....62 x
Caojian ....62 s
Capanaparo ....23 e
Capanema ....27 a
Capo Bonito ....29 f
Cap-de-la-Madeleine ....17 a
Cap-Haïtien ....21 r
Cape Coast ....40 z
Cape Cora ....20 l
Cape Cuvier ....72 q
Cape Dorset ....13 t
Cape Flattery ....74 c
Cape Girardeau ....16 q
Cape May ....16 z
Cape Parry ....12 c
Cape Town ....48 w
Cape Verde ....230 k
Cape York Peninsula ....73 k
Capella ....74 r
Capelongo ....44 t
Capim ....26 m
Capim Verde ....29 a
Capivara, Serra de ....29 g
Caponga ....27 t
Caprivi Strip ....44 x
Caquetá ....25 a
Carabaya, Cord. de ....25 n
Caracarai ....23 v
Caracas ....23 f
Caracol ....27 p
Carajás ....26 y
Carajás, Serra dos ....26 x
Carandotta ....73 u
Caráquez, Baia de ....22 v
Caratianas ....25 t
Caratinga ....29 j
Carauari ....25 d
Caravelas ....29 l
Caravelí ....24 y
Caraz ....24 w
Carazinho ....29 o
Carbó ....18 g
Carcaraña ....28 v
Carcar Mountains ....43 j
Carcassonne ....34 g
Carcross ....11 k
Cardara ....55 s
Cardarinskoje Reservoir ...55 t
Cardenas ....19 o
Cardiel, Lago ....30 u
Cardiff ....32 w
Cardona ....31 d
Čardžou ....55 r
Carey, Lake ....76 i
Carhue ....30 m
Cariamanga ....24 h
Caribbean Sea 20-21
Caribou ....12 z
Caribou Mountains ....12 s
Caripito ....23 h
Carleton, Mount ....17 d
Carlisle ....32 w
Carlsbad ....18 l
Carmacks ....11 j
Carmelo ....31 s
Carmem ....25 z
Carmen ....22 m
Carmen (Island) ....18 h
Carmen Alto ....28 d
Carmen de Patagones .....30 m
Carmen, Sierra 18-19
Carmila ....74 r
Carnarvon (Australia) .....72 q
Carnarvon (South Africa) ..48 y
Carnarvon Range
(Western Australia) ......72 v
Carnarvon Range
(Queensland) ....74 r
Carnegie ....76 i
Carnegie, Lake ....76 h
Carney Island ....81 p
Carnicobar ....65 q
Carnot ....41 y
Carolina (Brazil) ....27 n
Carolina (Puerto Rico,
USA) ....21 w

Carolina (South Africa) .....49 r
Caroline Islands ....70 m
Caroni ....23 u
Carora ....23 c
Carpathians ....35 f
Carpentaria, Gulf of ....73 h
Carrington ....15 y
Carrizal Bajo ....28 o
Čarsk ....56 c
Carson City ....14 v
Cartagena (Spain) ....34 s
Cartagena (Venezuela) ...22 m
Cartago ....22 y
Cartier Island ....72 k
Cartwright ....17 j
Caruarú ....27 v
Carúpano ....23 h
Čarysskoje ....56 e
Casablanca ....36 q
Casa Grande ....18 f
Casamance ....40 b
Casanare ....23 o
Casa Nova ....27 r
Casa Verde ....29 b
Cascade ....14 k
Cascade Range ....14 u
Cascavel ....29 n
Caserta ....35 a
Casey ....87 f
Casey Bay ....84 l
Casigna ....23 b
Casino ....78 g
Casiquiare ....23 s
Casma ....24 v
Casper ....15 p
Caspian Depression ....54 j
Caspian Sea ....54 x
Cassai ....44 x
Cassamba ....44 w
Cassiar ....11 z
Cassilandia ....29 c
Cassinga ....44 t
Castanhal (Brazil) ....26 m
Castanhal (Brazil) ....26 p
Castelli ....28 w
Castellón ....34 s
Castilla ....28 o
Castries ....23 i
Castro (Brazil) ....29 q
Castro (Chile) ....30 g
Castrovirreyna ....24 x
Cat ....21 p
Catalo ....29 f
Catamarca ....28 s
Catandica ....46 u
Catanduanes ....67 j
Catania ....35 o
Catanzaro ....35 o
Cataract, 1st ....38 w
Cataract, 2nd ....38 u
Cataract, 3rd ....38 u
Cataract, 4th ....38 v
Cataract, 5th ....38 x
Cataract, 6th ....38 w
Cataraman ....67 j
Catatumbo ....23 b
Catbalogan ....67 j
Catende ....27 v
Catengue ....44 s
Catete ....44 s
Catió ....40 c
Catisimiña ....23 u
Cat Lake ....16 c
Catoche, Cape ....20 v
Cato Island ....74 w
Catriel ....30 k
Catrimani ....26 c
Catrimani (River) ....26 b
Catskill Mountains ....16 z
Catua ....28 e
Catuane ....49 t
Catyrk'ol, Lake ....55 x
Čatyrtås ....55 y
Cauca ....22 m
Caucasia ....22 m
Caucasus ....54 t
Caungula ....44 i
Caura ....26 a
Cauvery ....64 g
Cavally ....40 u

Cavanayen ....23 v
Caviana ....26 l
Cavinas ....25 q
Caxias ....25 a
Caxias do Sul ....29 q
Caxito ....44 f
Cayambe ....22 x
Cayenne ....26 j
Cayman Brac ....20 z
Cayman Islands ....20 z
Cayos Miskitos ....22 h
Cazombo ....44 z
Ceará-Mirim ....27 v
Cebu ....67 i
Cebu (Island) ....67 i
Cecerleg ....57 a
Cedar City ....14 z
Cedar Lake ....15 g
Cedar Rapids ....15 y
Cedros ....18 d
Ceduna ....77 c
Ceilândia ....29 e
Celaya ....19 o
Celébes (Sulawesi) ....69 t
Celébes Sea ....69 g
Celeken ....54 z
Cel'us ....56 g
Čemolgan ....55 y
Cencher Mandal ....57 f
Cenderawasih ....70 q
Cenderawasih, Gulf of ....70 s
Central African
Republic 41-42
Central Butte ....15 c
Central City ....16 s
Central Cordillera (Boliva) 28 f
Central Cordillera
(Colombia) ....22 z
Central Cordillera (Peru) ..24 j
Centralia ....14 g
Central Makran Range .....60 g
Central Plateau ....29 f
Central Siberian Uplands .52 b
Central Ural Mountains ...50 x
Cephalonia ....35 a
Ceram ....69 z
Ceram Sea ....69 z
Čeremchovo ....57 b
Čerepovec ....50 o
Ceres (Argentina) ....28 v
Ceres (Brazil) ....29 d
Čerkessk ....54 s
Černogorsk ....56 i
Černyševsk ....52 t
Cerritos ....19 n
Cerro de Pasco ....24 w
Cerro Pinacate ....18 e
Cerros Colorados
Reservoir ....30 j
Cerro Sombrero ....30 w
Cervantes Island ....76 c
Česa Bay ....50 f
Cesar ....23 a
České Budějovice ....35 a
Cess ....40 t
Ceuta ....34 p
Cevennes ....34 i
Ceyhan ....54 p
Chabahar ....60 r
Chacabuco ....31 b
Chachani ....25 n
Chachapoyas ....24 i
Chacharramendi ....30 k
Chaco Austral ....28 v
Chaco Boreal ....28 j
Chaco Central ....28 i
Chad 37/38/41/42
Chad, Lake ....41 k
Chadron ....15 r
Chagai ....60 h
Chagai Hills ....60 g
Chagda ....52 z
Chaghcharan ....60 g
Chagos Archipelago ......231 r
Chaibāsa ....61 v
Chai Si ....66 d
Chaim ....52 o
Chaiten ....30 h

Chaiyaphum ....66 f
Chajari ....28 y
Chakwal ....60 m
Chala ....24 y
Chalaxung ....62 f
Chalbi Desert ....43 o
Chalchaqui ....28 w
Chalhuanca ....24 z
Chalinze ....45 k
Chalkidike ....35 f
Chalkis ....35 s
Challapata ....28 f
Chalons-sur-Saône ....34 l
Chama ....45 s
Chamah ....65 x
Chaman ....60 i
Chamba (India) ....61 b
Chamba (Tanzania) ....45 w
Chambal ....61 o
Chamberlain ....15 t
Chamberlin, Mount ....11 h
Chambeshi ....45 r
Chamcha ....52 f
Chamical ....28 s
Chamo, Lake ....43 o
Champaign ....16 r
Champassak ....66 i
Champlain, Lake ....17 a
Champotón ....20 s
Chañaral ....28 o
Chan Bogd ....57 f
Chancay ....24 w
Chanch ....57 a
Chanchiang ....63 n
Chandigarh ....61 c
Chandler ....17 e
Chandpur ....61 y
Chandrapur ....61 q
Chang ....66 f
Changada ....51 m
Changara ....46 u
Changchih ....63 b
Changchow ....63 n
Changchun ....58 f
Changhua ....63 t
Changji ....56 t
Chang Jiang (Yangtze) .63 a
Changkiakow ....57 w
Changma ....56 z
Chang Mai ....62 s
Changpai Shan ....58 h
Changsha ....63 c
Changshu ....63 n
Changteh ....63 b
Changwu ....62 l
Chani ....28 f
Channel Cape ....76 f
Channel Islands (UK) .....34 d
Channel Islands (USA) ...18 b
Channel-Port-aux-
Basques ....17 i
Chantaburi ....66 f
Chany, Lake ....56 b
Chao'an ....63 r
Chao Phraya ....66 c
Chaoyang ....63 r
Chapa ....52 z
Chapada das
Mangabeiras ....27 n
Chapada Diamantina ....27 r
Chapada do Araripe ....27 s
Chapado dos Gauchos ...29 c
Chapadinha ....27 s
Chapais ....16 m
Chapala, Lake ....18 y
Chaparral ....22 z
Chapayevo ....54 k
Chapayevsk ....54 k
Chapceranga ....57 g
Chapeco ....29 o
Chapleau ....16 h
Chaplino ....54 c
Chara ....52 u
Chara (River) ....52 u
Charaa ....57 d
Charagua ....28 h
Charaña ....25 o
Charata ....28 v
Charcas ....19 n
Charcot Island ....82 w

Chari....41 l
Charikar....60 j
Charleroi....33 n
Charleston (South Carolina)....20 m
Charleston (Virginia)....16 v
Charleville....74 p
Charlotte....20 m
Charlottesville....16 x
Charlottetown....17 f
Char Nuur....56 k
Charouïne....36 m
Charters Towers....74 q
Chartres....32 z
Char Us Nuur....56 j
Chasaat....57 b
Chascomús....31 c
Chasel'ka....51 r
Chasovnya-Vchurskaya....53 d
Chăsuri....54 t
Châteauroux....34 h
Chatgal....57 a
Chatrapur....61 q
Chatsworth (Australia)....73 v
Chatsworth (Zimbabwe)....49 e
Chattahoochee....20 j
Chattanooga....20 j
Chauk....62 p
Chaumont....33 n
Chau Phu....66 h
Chavantina....29 c
Chaves....26 l
Chavirga....57 j
Chaya....52 r
Chay-Povarnaya....53 d
Chebka du Mzab....34 u
Cheboksary....54 i
Chechaouen....34 q
Chech Erg....36 w
Cheduba....65 e
Cheepie....74 o
Cheetham, Cape....86 v
Cheffadene....37 t
Chegdomyn....58 k
Chegga....36 u
Chegutu....49 e
Cheju....58 t
Chekalio....54 c
Chekunda....58 k
Chekurovka....52 l
Chelago....43 q
Chelforó....30 k
Cheliff....34 t
Chelkar....55 c
Chellala....34 t
Chelyabinsk....55 d
Chembe....45 q
Chemdal'sk....52 o
Chemnitz....33 n
Chemult....14 u
Chenab....60 l
Chenachane....36 w
Chen Barag Qi....58 c
Chengchow....63 c
Chengdu (Chengtu)....62 j
Chengshan, Cape....58 r
Chengteh....57 x
Chengtu....62 j
Chennai (Madras)....64 h
Chenxi....63 a
Chen Xian....63 c
Chepes....28 r
Cherbourg....32 x
Cherchell....37 a
Cherdyn....50 w
Cherendey....52 u
Cherepanovo....56 e
Cherkashina....52 e
Cherkassy....35 k
Cherlak....55 l
Cherlen Gol....57 h
Chernaya....51 h
Chernaya (Pechora Sea)....50 j
Chernigov....33 v
Chernikovsk....55 a
Chernovtsy....35 g
Chernyshevskiy....52 e
Chernyy Mys....53 l
Chernyy-Yar....54 h
Cherpiya....51 n

Cherskiy....10 a
Cherskogo Mountains....53 d
Chertovo-Ulovo....53 p
Chesapeake Bay....16 y
Chester....15 a
Chesterfield Islands....74 y
Chesterfield Inlet....13 o
Chesterton Range....74 q
Chetumal....20 u
Chetwynd....12 p
Cheulik....53 c
Chevak....10 m
Chew Bahir, Lake....43 o
Cheyenne....15 r
Cheyenne (River)....15 r
Chhatarpur....61 q
Chhatrapur....61 u
Chhindwara....61 p
Chiai....63 d
Chiang Mai....66 h
Chianje....44 s
Chiapa de Corzo....19 t
Chiba....59 o
Chibagalakh....53 d
Chibagalakh (River)....53 d
Chibaranda....44 x
Chibembe....45 r
Chibia....44 s
Chibougamau....16 m
Chicago....16 s
Chicala....44 w
Chicama....24 i
Chicapa....44 k
Chichaoua....36 g
Chichas, Cordillera de....28 f
Chichón....19 t
Chickasha....15 u
Chiclayo....24 h
Chico (River)....30 w
Chico (USA)....14 u
Chicoutimi-Jonquière....17 a
Chicualacuala....49 i
Chidley, Cape....13 y
Chiefland....20 k
Chiengi....45 d
Chifeng....57 x
Chifwefwe....45 q
Chignik....11 p
Chigorodó....22 m
Chigubo....49 h
Chigul'bach....53 p
Chihuahua....18 j
Chik Ballapur....64 f
Chikhacheva....53 g
Chikmagalur....64 d
Chikwa....46 g
Chilapa....19 o
Chilas....60 m
Childers....74 t
Chile....28/30
Chile Chico....30 u
Chilecito....28 r
Chililabombwe....46 c
Chillagoe....74 b
Chillán....30 h
Chilli....55 t
Chillicothe (Iowa)....15 x
Chillicothe (Ohio)....16 u
Chilliwack....14 h
Chiloe....30 f
Chilok....57 g
Chilok (River)....57 e
Chilonga....46 f
Chilpancingo....19 o
Chilumba....46 h
Chilung....63 v
Chilwa, Lake....45 v
Chimala....45 g
Chimanimani....49 g
Chimbay....55 p
Chimborazo....24 h
Chimbote....24 v
Chimoio....49 g
China (Mexico)....19 b
China (State)....52/55-58/61-63
Chinandega....22 e
Chincha Alta....24 w
Chincha Islands....24 w
Chincheros....24 y
Chinchilla....74 t

Chinchow....58 d
Chincolco....28 o
Chinde....49 j
Chindu....62 d
Chindwin....62 p
Chingola....46 c
Chinguetti....36 q
Chinju....58 t
Chinko....42 s
Chinle....15 o
Chinnamp....58 s
Chinsali....46 f
Chinsi....58 c
Chintalnar....61 r
Chíos....35 t
Chipata....46 f
Chipinge....49 g
Chiplun....60 z
Chippewa Falls....16 c
Chiquían....24 w
Chiquilá....19 x
Chiquita, Laguna....28 u
Chiredzi....49 f
Chirgis Nuur....56 j
Chirinda....51 m
Chiriqui, Gulf of....22 h
Chirripó....22 h
Chisasa....45 n
Chisasibi....16 j
Chisig-Ondör....57 b
Chisinău....35 i
Chiskovo....51 x
Chisoso....45 s
Chistoozernoye....55 l
Chistopol....54 k
Chita....57 h
Chitembo....44 u
Chitina....11 h
Chitradurga....64 f
Chitrāl....60 l
Chittagong....61 y
Chittoor....64 h
Chitunde....46 g
Chiume....44 x
Chiúta....46 g
Chivay....25 n
Chivhu....49 f
Chivilcoy....31 b
Chodzeili....55 p
Choele Choel....30 l
Choiseul....71 v
Choke Mountains....43 b
Chokudakh....53 h
Choma....46 p
Chon Buri....65 k
Ch'öngjin....58 i
Ch'öngju....58 u
Chongqing (Chungking)....62 l
Chönju....58 u
Chonos, Archipelago....30 s
Chorinsk....57 f
Chorracho....27 t
Chorregon....74 n
Chōshi....59 p
Chos Malal....30 i
Choteau....14 m
Chotla, Cerro de....19 n
Chott Djerid....34 x
Chott ech Chergui....36 m
Chott Melrhir....34 w
Chotts ech Chergui....34 t
Choûm....36 q
Choushuidan....56 z
Chovd....57 o
Chovd Gold....56 i
Chövsgöl....57 s
Chövsgöl Nuur....57 a
Christchurch....79 t
Christensen Mountains....84 l
Christiana....49 o
Christian X Land....91 q
Christmas Creek....72 y
Christmas Island....68 u
Chubut....30 l
Chuchow....63 c
Chudinovo....55 e
Chudovo....33 m
Chugwater....15 q
Chuhoi....63 p

Chukchi Sea....10
Chukehagirskoye, Lake....53 p
Chuken....58 m
Chukochye....53 l
Chukot Peninsula....10 j
Chulucanas....24 h
Chulugli....52 t
Chuluman....25 q
Chulym....56 d
Chumakovo....56 d
Chumar....61 d
Chumbicha....28 s
Chumikan....53 o
Chum Phae....65 k
Chumphon....65 i
Chuna....51 y
Ch'unch'ön....58 u
Ch'ungju....58 u
Chungking....62 l
Chunguj Gol....56 k
Chunhuhub....20 t
Chunskiyo....57 a
Chunya....45 g
Chuquibamba....24 z
Chuquicamata....28 d
Chur....34 l
Churapcha....53 a
Churchill....13 n
Churchill, Cape....13 n
Churchill Lake....12 v
Churchill Peak....12 o
Churchill (River, Quebec).17 f
Churchill (River, Saskatchewan)....12 w
Churu....61 a
Churunguara....23 c
Chushakyl'....55 b
Chushul....61 c
Chutag....57 b
Chuūronjang....58 i
Chu Xian....63 f
Chuxiong....62 x
Chuya....52 r
Chuya (River)....52 r
Chuyengo....52 b
Chyul'be....52 z
Cibitoke....45 d
Ciego de Avila....21 n
Ciénaga....23 a
Cienfuegos....20 z
Cilacap....68 y
Čilik....56 o
Cimarron....15 t
Čimkent....55 v
Cincinatti....16 t
Cintra, G. de....36 n
Cipó....27 t
Cirčik....55 u
Circle....11 h
Cirebon....68 y
Cisneros....22 m
Citlaltépetl....19 p
Citrusdal....48 x
Ciudad Acuña....19 a
Ciudad Altamirano....19 n
Ciudad Bolivar....23 h
Ciudad Camargo....18 l
Ciudad del Carmen....19 t
Ciudad Guayana....23 i
Cuidad Guzman....18 y
Ciudad Ixtepec....19 r
Ciudad Juárez....18 j
Ciudad Madero....19 p
Ciudad Mante....19 o
Ciudad Mier....19 b
Ciudad Obregón....18 h
Ciudad Ojeda....32 g
Ciudad Real....34 q
Ciudad Valles....19 o
Ciudad Victoria....19 p
Civitavecchia....34 m
Clanwilliam....48 x
Claraville....73 w
Clarence, Cape....13 c
Clarence Island....82 f
Clarión....18 r
Clarksburg....16 w
Clarksdale....20 f
Clarksville (Arkansas)....16 o
Clarksville (Kentucky)....16 s

Clavering Island....91 s
Clayton....15 r
Clear, Cape....32 t
Clearfield....16 x
Cleopatra Needle....67 e
Clermont....74 q
Clermont-Ferrand....34 h
Cleveland (North Carolina)16 t
Cleveland (Ohio)....16 v
Clifton....78 f
Clifton Hills....77 g
Clingmans Dome....16 u
Clinton (Missouri)....15 x
Clinton (Oklahoma)....15 x
Clinton (South Carolina)....20 l
Clinton Colden Lake....12 v
Clinton Creek....11 i
Clipperton....230 e
Clocolan....49 p
Cloncurry....73 w
Cloquet....15 k
Clorinda....28 y
Cloud Peak....15 c
Clovis....18 m
Cluj Napoca....35 r
Clutha....79 f
Clyde....13 j
Coari....25 g
Coari (River)....25 f
Coast Range....14 t
Coast Mountains....14 g
Coats Island....13 r
Coats Land....83 g
Coatzacoalcos....20 q
Cobar....78 b
Cobija....25 p
Coca....22 y
Cocalzinho....27 b
Cochabamba....28 f
Cochin....64 e
Cochrane (Canada)....16 i
Cochrane (Chile)....30 t
Cockburn....77 n
Cockburn (Mount)....73 o
Coco....22 g
Cocobeach....41 t
Cocoparra Range....78 b
Cocos Islands....65 c
Cocula....18 y
Codajás....25 h
Cod, Cape....17 o
Codera, Cabo....23 f
Codó....27 p
Codrington....21 y
Čodro....56 r
Cody....15 b
Coen....73 k
Coeur d'Alene....14 k
Coffee Bay....49 f
Cogt-Ovoo....57 g
Coiba....22 i
Coihaique....30 u
Coimbatore....64 e
Coimbra....34 o
Coipasa, Lago de....28 e
Coixtlahuaca....19 q
Cojbalsan....57 i
Cojedes....23 e
Colatina....29 k
Colbeck, Cape....81 x
Cold Bay....11 n
Coles Bay....78 q
Colesberg....49 n
Colhué Huapi, Lago....30 w
Colima....18 y
Colima, Nevada de....18 y
Colinas....27 o
Collahuasi....28 d
College Park....20 j
Collie....76 d
Collier Bay....72 k
Collingwood....79 t
Collinsville....74 q
Colnett....18 d
Cologne....33 o
Colomb Bechar....36 k
Colombia....22-25
Colombo....64 u
Colón (Cuba)....20 z
Colón (Panama)....22 j

Colorado ...15 q
Colorado (River, Texas) ...19 d
Colorado (River, Arizona) .14 y
Colorado (River, Argentina)30 m
Colorado Plateau ...14 z
Colorado Springs ...15 q
Colorados ...28 q
Columbia (Missouri) ...15 x
Columbia (South Carolina)20 l
Columbia (Tennessee) ...16 s
Columbia (River) ...14 j
Columbia Plateau ...14 w
Columbus (Georgia) ...19 l
Columbus (Mississippi) ...19 j
Columbus (Nebraska) ...15 u
Columbus (Ohio) ...16 u
Colville ...11 e
Colville Lake ...12 b
Comai ...61 m
Comalcalco ...20 q
Comarapa ...28 g
Combarbala ...28 o
Comilla ...61 y
Comitán ...19 t
Commandante Ferraz ...82 r
Committee Bay ...13 c
Communism, Mount ...55 v
Como (China) ...61 h
Como (Italy) ...34 k
Comodoro Rivadavia ...30 w
Comores Islands ...47 a
Comorin, Cape ...64 s
Comoros ...47 b
Compiègne ...32 z
Compostela ...18 x
Cona ...61 m
Conakry ...40 d
Conceiço do Araguaia ...26 y
Concepción (Argentina)...28 s
Concepción (Bolivia) ...28 i
Concepción (Chile) ...30 q
Concepción (Paraguay)...28 l
Concepción del Oro ...19 a
Concepción del Uruguay ..28 x
Concepción, Laguna ...25 v
Conchi ...28 d
Conchos ...18 k
Concord ...17 n
Concordia (Argentina) ...28 x
Concórdia (Brazil) ...25 e
Concordia (Peru) ...24 k
Concordia (USA) ...15 u
Conde ...27 u
Condobolin ...78 b
Congo ...41-42/44
Congo, Democratic
Republic of ...42/44-45
Congo (River) ...44-45
Conjuboy ...73 z
Connecticut (River) ...17 n
Connecticut (State) ...17 n
Connemara ...73 w
Conrad ...14 m
Conselheiro Lafaiete ...29 i
Constance, Lake ...33 p
Constanţa ...35 i
Constantine ...34 w
Constitución ...30 g
Consuelo Peak ...74 q
Contact ...14 y
Contamaná ...24 l
Contas ...27 r
Contendas do Sincorá...27 r
Contwoyto Lake ...12 h
Conway ...20 e
Coober Pedy ...77 q
Cook ...77 a
Cook, Mount ...79 r
Cook Islands ...230 o
Cook Strait ...79 u
Cooktown ...74 c
Coolah ...78 e
Coolgardie ...76 g
Cooma ...78 g
Coonabarabran ...78 d
Coonamble ...78 c
Coonapoor ...64 d
Coongoola ...77 k
Cooper ...77 h
Cooperation Sea ...85 e

Coorabulka ...73 v
Coorong, The ...77 t
Coorow ...76 d
Coos Bay ...14 t
Cootamundra ...78 d
Cooya Pooya ...72 s
Copenhagen ...33 p
Copiapo ...28 p
Copiapo, Mount ...28 p
Copiapo (River) ...28 p
Copper Center ...11 h
Copper Harbor ...16 e
Coppermine ...12 f
Copperton ...48 z
Coqên ...61 h
Coquimbo ...28 o
Coracora ...24 z
Coral Harbour ...13 r
Coral Sea ...74 f
Corcovado, Gulf of ...30 g
Cordillera Central ...67 g
Cordillo Downs ...77 h
Córdoba (Argentina)...28 u
Córdoba (Mexico) ...19 d
Córdoba (Spain) ...36 j
Cordoba, Sierra de ...28 t
Cordova ...11 g
Corfield ...73 x
Corfu ...35 q
Corfu (Island) ...35 q
Coricudgy ...78 e
Corigliano ...35 o
Corinda ...73 h
Corinda (Lake Galilee) ...73 y
Corinth ...20 g
Corinth, Gulf of ...35 s
Corinto ...29 h
Coriolei ...43 t
Cork ...32 u
Corleone ...37 i
Corner Brook ...17 i
Corno, Monte ...35 a
Cornwall ...16 l
Cornwall Island ...12 m
Cornwallis Island ...12 m
Coro ...23 d
Coroatá ...27 p
Corocoro ...25 p
Coroico ...25 q
Coromandel Coast ...64 h
Coronation Gulf ...12 g
Coronation Island ...82 f
Coronel Murta ...29 j
Coronel Oviedo ...28 z
Coronel Pringles ...31 a
Coronel Suárez ...31 a
Coropuna ...24 z
Corowa ...78 b
Corpus Christi ...19 d
Corque ...28 e
Corrente ...27 o
Corrente (River) ...27 p
Correntina ...27 o
Corrientes ...28 y
Corrientes, Cabo ...22 x
Corrientes (River,
Argentina) ...28 x
Corrientes (River, Peru)...24 k
Corsica ...34 k
Cortina ...34 m
Corubal ...40 c
Corum ...54 o
Corumba ...28 l
Corumbá (River) ...29 e
Corunna ...34 a
Cosalá ...18 k
Coscomatepec ...19 q
Cosenza ...35 o
Cosmonaut Sea ...84 j
Costa Blanca ...34 s
Costa Brava ...34 h
Costa del Sol ...34 q
Costa Marques ...25 s
Costa Rica ...22 g
Cotabato ...67 v
Cotagaita ...28 f
Cotahuasi ...24 z
Côte d'Ivoire ...40
Cotonou ...41 o
Cotopaxi ...22 x

Cottbus ...33 r
Cottonwood ...14 z
Coulman Island ...86 s
Coulomb Point ...72 j
Council Bluffs ...15 v
Courantyne ...23 y
Coventry ...32 x
Cowan, Lake ...76 h
Cowargarzê ...62 e
Cowarie ...77 f
Cowell ...77 e
Cowra ...78 d
Cox's Bzr ...61 y
Cozumel ...20 v
Cradock ...49 o
Craig ...15 p
Craiova ...35 f
Cranbrook ...14 k
Crateús ...27 s
Cravo Norté ...23 p
Cree Lake ...12 v
Creporizinho ...25 l
Cres ...35 a
Crescent City ...14 t
Creston ...15 w
Crestview ...20 h
Creswell Downs ...73 f
Crete (Island) ...35 s
Crete, Sea of ...35 t
Criciúma ...29 r
Crimea ...35 l
Cristalandia ...26 y
Cristalina ...29 f
Cristino Castro ...27 p
Cristóbal Colón ...23 a
Croker, Cape ...73 d
Crooked Island ...21 q
Crookston ...15 i
Cross ...41 s
Crowl ...77 k
Crown Prince Christian
Land ...91 i
Crown Prince Olaf Coast..84 j
Crown Princess Martha
Coast ...83 h
Croatia ...35 b
Croydon ...73 w
Crozet Island ...231 p
Cruz Alta ...29 n
Cruz das Almas ...27 s
Cruz del Eje ...28 t
Cruzeiro do Oeste ...29 b
Cruzeiro do Sul ...24 m
Crystal River ...20 k
Ču ...55 x
Ču (River) ...55 i
Cuamba ...45 v
Cuando ...44 y
Cuangar ...44 w
Cuango ...44 v
Cuanza ...44 t
Cuatrociénegas ...18 m
Cuauhtémoc ...18 j
Cuba ...20-21
Cubango ...44 v
Cuchi ...44 u
Cucuí ...23 r
Cucúi ...25 d
Cúcuta ...23 a
Cuddalore ...64 h
Cuddapah ...64 g
Cue ...76 e
Cuemba ...44 v
Cuenca ...24 h
Cuernavaca ...19 o
Cuiabá ...25 y
Cuiabá (River) ...25 y
Cuito ...44 w
Cuito Cuanavale ...44 w
Cuiuni ...25 f
Cuixi ...63 e
Culbertson ...15 d
Culiacán ...18 j
Cullman ...20 h
Culpeper ...16 x
Culuene ...26 w
Čuluut ...57 a
Culver, Cape ...76 j
Čulym ...56 h
Cumaná ...23 g

Cumberland ...16 x
Cumberland, Lake ...16 t
Cumberland Peninsula ...13 k
Cumberland Plateau ...16 t
Cumberland (River) ...16 t
Cumberland Sound ...13 k
Cunani ...26 k
Cuñaré ...23 n
Cundza ...56 p
Cunene ...48 g
Čunja ...51 y
Cunnamulla ...77 l
Cupica ...22 l
Curaçao ...23 d
Curacautin ...30 h
Curacó ...30 l
Curaray ...24 j
Curbur ...76 d
Curico ...30 i
Curimatá ...27 p
Curitiba ...29 r
Curitibanos ...29 q
Currais Novos ...17 v
Currant ...14 y
Currie ...77 w
Curtin Springs ...73 p
Curtis Island ...79 m
Curua ...26 u
Curua-Uná ...26 i
Curupira, Serra ...25 f
Curuzú Cuatiá ...28 x
Curvelo ...29 h
Cutral-Có ...30 j
Cuttack ...61 v
Cuvelai ...44 u
Cuya ...28 c
Cuyuni ...23 j
Cuzco ...25 n
Cyaring Hu ...62 e
Cyclades ...35 t
Cyprus ...35/38
Cyrenaica ...38 b
Czech Republic ...33-35
Czestochowa ...33 t

D

Da ...62 w
Dabar Tichitt ...36 s
Dabola ...40 f
Dabou ...40 x
Dabsan Hu ...62 c
Dachechang ...57 o
Dachstein ...35 a
Dadanawa ...23 x
Daet ...67 h
Dagana ...40 c
Dagandely ...55 m
Dagupan ...67 g
Dahab ...38 k
Dahar Oualata ...36 t
Daheba ...62 f
Dahlak, Islands ...43 d
Dahna ...39 f
Dāhod ...61 n
Dahongliutan ...61 d
Dai Hai ...57 u
Dailehk ...61 f
Dainkog ...62 e
Daintree ...74 c
Dairen (Dalian) ...58 q
Dairût ...38 h
Dairy Creek ...76 d
Dajarra ...73 j
Dakar ...40 a
Dakhla ...36 n
Dakhla, Oasis ...38 t
Dakshin Gangotri ...84 b
Dal ...33 f
Dala ...44 x
Dalaba ...40 e
Dalandzadgad ...57 o
Dalandžargalan ...57 s
Dalaoba ...56 r
Da Lat ...66 k
Dalbandin ...60 g
Dalby ...78 f
Dalgonally ...73 w
Dalgoye ...52 l

Dalhart ...15 s
Dalhousie, Cape ...11 m
Dalian ...58 q
Dallas ...19 d
Dal'nerechensk ...58 l
Daloa ...40 v
Dalou Shan ...62 k
Dalrymple ...74 r
Dal'stroy ...53 c
Dalton ...20 j
Dalton, Cape ...91 q
Dalou ...62 t
Daly ...73 c
Daly River ...73 b
Daly Waters ...73 d
Damakar ...41 j
Daman ...60 z
Damanhûr ...38 h
Damar ...70 n
Damara ...42 o
Damascus ...38 l
Damaturu ...41 i
Damavand ...39 j
Damavand (Mount) ...39 j
Damba ...44 g
Dambulla ...64 u
Dam Gamad ...42 i
Damghan ...54 z
Dammam ...39 j
Damon ...61 q
Dampier ...72 s
Dampier Downs ...72 w
Dampier Land ...72 j
Dampier Strait ...70 p
Dam Qu ...62 b
Damxung ...61 l
Dana ...10 a
Danakil ...43 e
Danané ...40 u
Da Nang ...66 k
Danba ...62 h
Danbury ...16 z
Dan, Cape ...90 y
Dandelehura ...61 d
Danells Fjord ...90 t
Dang ...56 y
Dangla ...43 b
Dango ...42 f
Daniel ...15 n
Daniëlskuil ...48 z
Dankhar ...61 c
Dankowa, Pik ...55 z
Danmark Fjord ...91 i
Dannebrog Island ...90 x
Dansville ...16 x
Danube, Mouths of the ...35 j
Danube ...33 r
Danville (Illinois) ...16 s
Danville (Virginia) ...16 w
Danzig (Gdansk) ...33 t
Danzig, Gulf of ...33 t
Daora ...36 d
Dao Timni ...37 v
Dapango ...41 a
Dapchi ...41 i
Dapitan ...67 o
Da Qaidam ...56 y
Daqing ...58 f
Daquan ...56 y
Dar'a ...38 l
Daran ...39 h
Darasun ...52 s
Daraut-Kurgan ...55 w
Darband ...60 d
Darbhanga ...61 v
Darchan ...57 d
Dar-el-Beida (Casablanca)36 g
Dar-es-Salaam ...45 k
Dargaville ...79 h
Darién, Gulf of ...22 l
Daringskiy ...55 j
Darj ...37 g
Darjeeling ...61 j
Darlag ...62 g
Darling ...77 i
Darling Range ...76 d
Darnah ...35 s
Darnley, Cape ...85 c
Dartmouth ...17 f
Daru ...70 y

Darvaza 55 o
Darvel Bay 67 r
Darwin 73 c
Darwin (Island) 22 n
Darwin River 73 b
Daryacheh-ye-Bakhtegan 39 l
Daryacheh-ye-Namak 39 i
Daryacheh-ye-Tashk 39 k
Darzin 60 c
Dashizhai 58 d
Dasht 55 n
Dasht (River) 60 r
Dasht-e-Kavir 39 k
Dasht-e-Lut 39 m
Dashuiqiao 62 f
Datong 57 v
Datu, Cape 68 l
Datuk Bay 68 m
Daugav'pils 33 x
Daulat Yar 60 h
Daule 22 w
Daund 61 n
Dauphin 15 g
Davangere 64 e
Davao 67 w
Davao Gulf 67 w
Davenport 16 q
Davenport Downs 73 v
Davenport Range 73 r
David 22 h
Davidson 15 d
Davidson Mount 73 p
Davies 76 m
Davis 85 q
Davis Sea 85 t
Davis Strait 13 m
Davlekanovo 54 m
Dawa 43 p
Dawson (Canada) 11 i
Dawson (USA) 19 m
Dawson Creek 12 q
Dawson Landing 12 t
Dawu 62 h
Daxian 62 l
Dayangshu 58 f
Dayong 63 a
Dayr az Zawr 39 a
Dayton 16 t
Daytona Beach 20 m
Dazhu 62 l
De Aar 49 n
Deacon, Cape 82 z
Deadhorse 11 f
Dead Sea 38 l
Deakin 76 m
Deán Funes 28 t
Dease Lake 11 z
Dease Strait 12 i
Death Valley 14 x
Debba 38 u
Debdou 36 k
Debin 53 i
Débo Lake 40 k
Deborah, Lake 76 f
Debre Birhan 43 d
Debrecen 33 u
Debre-Markos 43 b
Debre Tabor 43 c
Debre Zeit 43 c
Decatur (Alabama) 20 h
Decatur (Illinois) 16 r
Deccan 61 o
Dechang 62 i
Decorah 16 p
Dédougou 40 l
Dedza 46 h
Deep Well 73 r
Deer 15 a
Dêgê 62 f
Degeh Bur 43 g
Degtyarsk Sysert' 55 c
Dehak 60 d
Dehbid 39 k
Dehloran 39 g
Dehra Dun 61 c
Dehui 58 f
Deihuk 60 b
Dej 35 g
Dejen 43 c
De Juh 62 c
De Kalb 16 r
Dekar 48 l
De Kastruskoye 53 r
Dekemehare 43 c
Dekese 44 l
Dékoa 42 o
Delamere 73 c
Delano 14 w
Delareyville 49 n
Delaware 16 y
Delgado, Cape 45 y
Delger 56 m
Delgerdhaan 57 c
Delgo 38 u
Delhi 61 b
Delicias 18 l
Déline (Fort Franklin) 12 c
Delingha 56 z
Dell 14 m
Dellys 34 v
Deloge, Monts 16 k
Delphi 35 s
Del Rio 19 a
Delta 14 z
Delta Downs 73 j
Delta Junction 11 g
Demba 44 l
Dembia 42 s
Dembidolo 42 m
Deming 18 j
Demini 23 u
Demnate 36 h
Dempo 68 t
Demyanka 51 o
Dem'yanovka 55 f
Demyanskoye 51 n
Denau 55 t
Deneżkin Kamen 50 x
Dengkou 57 q
Dengqên 62 d
Denham 76 b
Deniliquin 77 x
Denison 15 w
Denizli 35 w
Denman Glacier 85 s
Denmark 33
Denmark Strait 32 a
Denpasar 69 p
D'Entrecasteaux Islands 71 r
D'Entrecastleaux, Cape 76 c
Denver 15 q
Deogarh 61 u
Depósito 23 w
Deputatskiy 53 d
Dêgên 62 f
Dera Bugti 60 k
Dera Ghazi Khan 60 k
Dera Ismail Khan 60 k
Derbent 54 w
Derby (Australia) 72 k
Derby (UK) 32 x
Dergachi 54 j
Derm 48 j
Dêrong 62 g
De Rose Hill 73 r
Derudeb 38 y
Derwent 77 y
Derzhavinsk 55 g
Desaquadero
(River, Argentina) 28 r
Desaquadero
(River, Bolivia) 28 d
Descalvados 25 x
Dese 43 c
Deseado 30 x
Desertas 36 a
Des Moines 16 o
Des Moines (River) 15 w
Desna 54 a
Desolación 30 t
Dessau 33 q
Desterrada Pérez 19 v
Dete 46 p
Detroit 16 u
Det Udom 66 h
Deva 35 f
Devils Lake 15 h
Devon Island 13 c
Devonport 77 x
Dez 39 h
Dezful 39 g
Dezhgan 39 l
Dhahran 39 h
Dhaka 61 y
Dhamar 34 g
Dhanbad 61 v
Dhandhuka 60 z
Dharmapuri 64 g
Dharmsala 61 b
Dharwar 64 d
Dhaulāgiri 61 g
Dhofar 39 x
Dhuburi 61 y
Dhule 61 n
Diaca 45 x
Dialafara 40 f
Dialakoto 40 d
Diamaa 34 w
Diamante 28 w
Diamante (River) 28 r
Diamantina 26 q
Diamantina
(Minas Gerais) 29 i
Diamantina (River) 73 w
Diamantina Lakes 73 w
Diamantino 25 y
Diamou 40 e
Dian-Chi 62 v
Dianópolis 27 n
Diapaga 41 b
Dibba 60 n
Dibella 41 j
Dibrügarh 62 c
Dickinson 15 e
Didesa 43 a
Diéni 40 h
Didwana 61 a
Diego de Almargro 28 p
Diéma 40 g
Digne 34 j
Digos 67 w
Digul 70 w
Dijon 34 i
Dikhil 43 e
Dikimdya 52 w
Dikson 51 f
Dikwa 41 j
Dila 43 p
Dilaram 60 g
Dili 69 x
Di Linh 66 k
Dilling 42 j
Dillingham 11 p
Dillon 14 m
Dilolo 44 y
Dimas 18 w
Dimbelenge 44 m
Dimbokro 40 w
Dinagat 67 j
Dinajpur 61 w
Dinar 39 i
Dinaric Alps 35 b
Dinder 42 m
Dingbian 57 r
Dinggyê 61 j
Dinguiraye 40 f
Dingxi 62 j
Ding Xian 57 v
Dinsor 43 s
Diourbel 40 b
Dipolog 67 u
Dirâng 62 b
Dire Dawa 43 e
Dirkou 37 v
Dirranbandi 78 c
Disappointment, Lake 72 x
Discovery Bay 77 u
Discovery, Cape 91 g
Disko Bay 90 k
Diu 60 y
Divinópolis 29 h
Divisoes, Serra das 29 d
Divnoye 54 g
Divriği 54 q
Dixon Entrance 14 b
Diyala 39 e
Diyarbakir 54 r
Dja 41 x
Djado 37 u
Djado Plateau 37 u
Djamaa 37 c
Djanet 37 s
Djebel Amour 37 a
Djebel Bani 36 g
Djebel Serkout 37 q
Djebel Ouarkziz 36 f
Djebel Tahat Telertheba 37 q
Djelfa 34 u
Djenné 40 j
Djerba 37 g
Djermaya 41 l
Djibo 40 m
Djibouti (City) 43 f
Djibouti (State) 43 f
Djidjelli 37 c
Djolu 42 r
Djougou 41 b
Djúpivogur 32 f
Dmitrov 50 p
Dneprodzerzhinsk 35 l
Dnepropetrovsk 35 l
Dnieper 35 l
Dniester 35 g
Doab-i Mikhe Zarin 60 i
Doba 41 m
Dobryanka 50 w
Doce 29 j
Docker River 73 o
Doda Betta 64 f
Dodge City 15 t
Dodoma 45 h
Dogai Coring 61 j
Dogondoutchi 41 c
Do'gyaling 61 j
Doha 39 w
Doi Inthanon 62 s
Dois Irmos, Serra do 27 r
Dolak Island 70 u
Dolgany 51 j
Dolo 43 s
Dolomites 34 m
Dolon 56 b
Dolores 31 c
Dolphin and Union Strait 12 f
Domba 62 d
Dombarovskiy 55 c
Dombås 33 b
Dome Fuji 84 f
Domeyko 28 o
Dominica 23
Dominican Republic 21
Don 54 e
Donald 77 w
Dondo (Angola) 44 s
Dondo (Mozambique) 46 v
Dondo Bay 69 g
Dondra, Head 64 v
Donegal Bay 32 u
Donets 54 d
Donetsk 54 d
Dong 57 n
Dongbatu 56 y
Dongfang 62 z
Dongfanghong 58 k
Donggala 69 f
Dong Hoi 66 j
Dong Jian 63 q
Dongjingcheng 58 l
Dongkalang 69 g
Dongle 57 n
Dongliao 58 e
Donglük 56 u
Dongnan Quiling 63 o
Dongola 38 u
Dongou 42 n
Dongqiao 61 l
Dongsheng 57 t
Dong-Ujimqin Qi 57 x
Dongzhen 57 p
Donors Hill 73 v
Doomadgee 73 u
Dora Lake 72 w
Dorbod 58 f
Dordabis 48 j
Dordogne 34 g
Dori 40 m
Doro 40 m
Döröö Nuur 56 k
Dorowa 49 f
Dorrego 31 a
Dortmund 33 o
Doruma 42 u
Dos de Mayo 24 k
Doshi 60 j
Dosso 41 c
Dothan 19 l
Douala 41 u
Doualayel 41 w
Douaouir 36 x
Douentza 40 l
Douglas (UK) 32 w
Douglas (Arizona) 18 h
Douglas (Wyoming) 15 q
Douglas Range 82 w
Dourada, Serra 26 z
Dourados 29 a
Douro 34 b
Dove Bay 91 t
Dover 32 z
Dover, Strait of 34 g
Dover Foxcroft 17 b
Dovsk 33 z
Dowlatabad 60 b
Dracena 29 c
Drakensberg 49 q
Drake Passage 82 c
Drammen 33 c
Drava 35 c
Dreikikir 70 y
Dresden 33 r
Dresvyanka 50 j
Drosh 60 l
Drovyanaya 51 b
Dr. Pedro P. Pen 28 i
Drumheller 14 m
Drummondville 17 a
Druzhina 53 g
Dryden 15 k
Drygalski Island 85 t
Drysdale 72 m
Dschang 41 u
Dua 42 q
Duaringa 74 r
Duba 38 l
Dubai 39 y
Dubawnt Lake 12 x
Dubbo 78 d
Dublin (Ireland) 32 v
Dublin (USA) 20 k
Dubna 50 p
Dubois 14 m
Dubovskoye 54 g
Dubrovnik 35 c
Dubuque 16 q
Duchess 73 v
Duero 34 d
Dudinka 51 h
Dudypta 51 k
Duékoué 40 v
Duero 34 e
Dugiuma 43 s
Dukhan 39 v
Duki 53 o
Dukou 62 u
Dulan 62 e
Dulce 28 v
Dugla-Kyuyel' 52 r
Dulia 42 s
Duluth 15 k
Dumaguete 67 i
Dumai 68 f
Dumka 61 w
Dumont d'Urville Sea 87 o
Dumont d'Urville 87 o
Dumyat 35 x
Duna 35 c
Dunărea 35 g
Dunay 52 k
Dunbar 73 k
Dundalk 32 v
Dundas 91 b
Dundas Harbour 13 e
Dundas Peninsula 12 g
Dundee (South Africa) 49 r
Dundee (UK) 32 x
Dunedin 79 s
Dungas 41 g
Dungu 42 v
Dungun 66 t
Dungunab 38 y

Dunhua ....58 h
Dunhuang ....56 x
Dunkwa ....40 z
Duqm ....60 o
Durack Range ....72 m
Durango (Mexico) ....18 x
Durango (USA) ....15 p
Duranzo ....28 z
Durban ....49 s
Durham ....16 x
Duri ....68 f
Durma ....39 r
Durrës ....35 d
Durrie ....77 x
Dusak ....55 p
Dusa Mareb ....43 v
Dushan ....62 y
Dushanbe ....55 u
Düsseldorf ....33 o
Dusti ....55 u
Dutch Harbor ....10 z
Dutlwe ....49 a
Dvina 33/50
Dvina Bay ....50 p
Dwangwa ....45 t
Dwarka ....60 w
Dwarsberg ....49 c
Dyalinya ....53 b
Dyer, Cape ....13 m
Dyersburg ....16 v
Dzachuj ....56 y
Dzag ....56 m
Džambul ....55 v
Dzaoudzi ....47 c
Dzavchan Gol ....56 k
Dzereg ....56 j
Dzerzhinsk ....50 r
Dzerzhinsky ....54 f
Dzhaksy ....55 g
Dzhalinda ....52 x
Dzhambul ....55 e
Dzhamm ....53 a
Dzhankoy ....35 x
Dzhara ....52 d
Dzhardzhan ....52 k
Dzhelinde ....52 f
Dzhelon ....52 m
Dzhezkazgan ....55 h
Dzhungdzhur Mountains ..53 p
Dzhunkun ....52 e
Dzhusaly ....55 f
Džida ....57 d
Džida (River) ....57 d
Dzilam de Bravo ....19 v
Dzioua ....37 c
Džirgatal ....55 v
Džizak ....55 u
Dznankoy ....54 b
Dznetygara ....55 d

E

Eagle Plain ....11 k
Eagle Summit ....11 g
East Cape ....79 x
East China Sea ....63 k
Easter Group ....76 b
Easter Island ....230 r
Eastern Cordillera
(Bolivia) ....25 s
Eastern Cordillera
(Colombia) 22-23
Eastern Cordillera (Peru) .24 k
Eastern Ghats ....61 s
Eastern Sierra Madre ....19 o
East Falkland ....31 p
East London ....49 q
Eastmain ....16 k
Eastmere ....74 p
East Millinocket ....17 c
Easter Siberian Sea ....53 i
East Timor ....69 x
East Turkestan ....56 o
Eau Claire ....16 c
Eau Claire, Lac à l' ....13 u
Eauripik Atoll ....70 l
Ebe ....52 j
Ebebiyin ....41 u
Ebinur Hu ....56 q

Ebola ....42 q
Ebolowa ....41 u
Ebro ....34 f
Echo Bay (Port Radium) ..12 e
Ecija ....34 p
Eclipse Sound ....88 y
Ecuador 22/24
Ed Damazin ....42 m
Ede ....41 q
Edéa ....41 u
Eden ....15 o
Edessa ....35 e
Edge Island ....92 p
Edinburgh ....32 x
Edirne ....35 h
Edith Ronne Ice Shelf .....83 o
Edith Ronne Land ....83 s
Edjeleh ....37 f
Edmonton ....14 m
Edmundston ....17 c
Edsel Ford Range ....81 u
Edson ....14 k
Eduardo Castex ....30 l
Edward, Lake ....45 c
Edward River ....73 j
Edwards Plateau ....19 a
Edward VII Peninsula ....81 x
Edzo ....12 r
Efate ....75 e
Effingham ....16 r
Egadi ....34 z
Egersund ....33 a
Egijn Gol ....57 b
Egmont ....79 u
Eğridir, Lake ....35 w
Egvekinot ....10 h
Egypt 35/38
Eidfjord ....33 b
Eight Degree Channel ......64 o
Eighty Mile Beach ....72 v
Eil ....43 k
Eilerts-de-Haan-Gebergte 26 g
Einasleigh ....73 y
Eindhoven ....33 n
Eirunepé ....25 b
Eje Volcanico ....19 o
Ejido Insurgentes ....18 f
Ejin Qi ....57 n
Ejutla ....19 o
Ekalaka ....15 d
Ekibastuz ....55 l
Ekimchan ....53 n
Ekiti ....41 q
Ekoli ....44 m
Ekonda ....52 b
El Arco ....18 f
El Aaiún ....36 d
El Aricha ....36 k
Elat ....38 k
Elato Atoll ....71 a
Elaziğ ....54 q
Elba ....34 l
El Banco ....23 a
El Barcat ....37 t
El Baúl ....23 e
El Bayadh ....34 s
Elbe ....33 o
Elbert, Mount ....15 p
Elblag ....33 u
El Bordo ....22 y
Elbrus ....54 x
El Bur ....43 v
Elburz Mountains ....54 x
El Cajon ....18 c
El Calafate ....30 v
El Callao ....23 i
El Canton ....23 c
El Carmen ....25 t
El Carrizalillo ....18 k
El Cerro ....25 u
El Chilicote ....18 l
El Chinero ....18 e
El Dab ....43 i
El Dere ....34 v
El'dikan ....53 b
El Djem ....34 y
El Djouf ....36 t
El Dorado (Arkansas) ....19 g
Eldorado (Brazil) ....29 a
Eldorado (Uruguay) ....29 n

Eldorado (Canada) ....12 c
El Dorado (Kansas) ....15 v
El Dorado (Mexico) ....18 w
El Dorado (Venezuela) .....23 i
Eldoret ....43 n
El Eglab ....36 v
Elektrostal ....54 d
Elemi Triangle ....42 z
El Encanto ....23 o
Elephant Island ....82 e
Eleuthera ....21 c
El Fasher ....42 q
El Fuerte ....18 l
El Fugha ....37 k
El Gal ....43 l
El Gezira ....42 l
Elgin (UK) ....32 k
Elgin (USA) ....16 r
El Goléa ....37 a
Elgon ....42 z
El Hamurre ....43 x
El Hank ....36 t
El Hasheisa ....42 m
Eliseu Martins ....27 p
Elista ....54 h
Elizabeth ....16 z
Elizabeth City ....16 y
Elizabeth Reef ....78 k
Elizabethtown ....16 t
El Jadida ....36 f
El Jebelein ....42 l
Elkedra ....73 s
El Kere ....43 s
El Khenachich ....36 v
Elkins ....16 w
Elko ....14 x
Ellef Ringnes Island ....12 k
Ellensburg ....14 i
Ellesmere Island ....91 f
Elliot (S. Africa) ....49 q
Elliot Bay ....77 x
Elliot, Mount
(Queensland) ....74 q
Elliott (Australia) ....73 e
Elliott, Mount
(W. Australia) ....72 z
Ellisras ....49 c
Ellsworth Land ....81 b
Ellsworth Mountains ....81 d
El Maia ....36 x
El Maitén ....30 i
El Mango ....23 s
El Mansour ....36 l
El Meghaier ....37 c
Elmira ....16 y
El Mreïti ....36 t
El Obeid ....42 j
El Oso ....23 t
El Oued ....34 w
El Paso ....18 k
El Porvenir ....18 k
El Real ....22 k
El Salado ....30 w
El Salto ....18 x
El Salvador (State) 22
El Salvador (Chile) ....28 p
El Sauz ....18 k
Elsey ....73 e
El Sherana ....73 d
El Socorro ....18 f
El Sombrero ....23 e
El Sueco ....18 k
Eltanin Bay ....80 m
El Tigre ....23 h
Elton ....54 i
El Triunfo ....18 u
El Tule ....19 a
El Uach ....43 r
Eluru ....64 i
Elvira ....24 m
El Wak ....43 q
Ely ....14 y
Emba ....55 b
Emba (River) ....55 a
Embarcación ....28 g
Embu ....43 o
Emden ....33 o
Emerald ....74 r
Emi Koussi ....37 y
Emmen ....33 n

Emmet ....74 o
Emory Peak ....18 m
Empalme ....18 h
Emporia (Kansas) ....15 v
Emporia (Virginia) ....16 x
Empredrado ....28 y
Emu ....58 h
Emu (River) ....77 v
Encarnación ....28 z
Encounter Bay ....77 s
Endako ....14 f
Ende ....69 u
Enderby Land ....84 l
Endicott Mountains ....11 d
Endybal ....52 m
Eneabba ....76 d
Engaño, Cape ....67 h
Engel's ....54 l
Engenheiro Dolabela ....29 i
Engerdyakh ....52 h
Enggano ....68 s
England ....32 x
English Channel ....32 x
English River ....16 d
Engoordina ....77 d
Enid ....15 u
Enkan ....53 q
Enna ....37 i
Ennadai Lake ....12 x
Ennedi ....38 p
Ennis ....15 a
Enschede ....33 o
Ensenada ....18 c
Enshi ....62 m
Entebbe ....42 y
Enterprise ....12 r
Entroncamento ....27 n
Enugu ....41 s
Envira ....25 b
Envira (River) ....25 n
Enyélé ....42 n
Equatorial Guinea 41
Erba ....38 y
Erdene ....57 t
Erdene Büren ....56 i
Erdene Cagaan ....57 w
Erdenedalaj ....57 p
Erdenet ....57 c
Erdi ....38 o
Erebus ....86 r
Ereğlí ....35 y
Ereğli (Black Sea) ....35 j
Erenhot ....57 u
Erexim ....29 o
Erfoud ....36 i
Erfurt ....33 p
Ergedzhey ....52 h
Erg el Ahmar ....36 w
Erger Raoui ....36 k
Erguig ....42 a
Ergun ....52 v
Ergun Yuoqi ....52 v
Erie ....16 w
Erie, Lake ....16 v
Erigavo ....43 j
Erimbet ....55 r
Erimo ....59 d
Eritrea ....43 d
Erldunda ....73 q
Ermelo ....49 r
Er Mreyer ....36 t
Ernabella ....77 b
Ernakulam ....64 e
Erode ....64 f
Eromanga ....73 x
Erozionnyy ....53 h
Er Rahad ....42 j
Errego ....46 j
Erromango ....75 s
Ershiyizhan ....52 x
Ertai ....56 u
Ertix He ....56 f
Erzincan ....54 r
Erzurum ....54 s
Esbjerg ....33 o
Escalante ....15 n
Escanaba ....16 f
Escondido ....18 c
Escondido (River) ....22 g
Escoumins ....17 b

Escuinapa ....18 x
Escuintla ....22 c
Ese ....42 u
Eséka ....41 u
Eshowe ....49 s
Esk ....74 t
Eskimo Point ....13 n
Eskişehir ....35 w
Eslamada-e-Gharb ....39 f
Esmeralda ....73 x
Esmeraldas ....22 w
Esmeraldas (River) ....22 w
Espanola ....16 l
Española ....22 p
Esperance ....76 h
Esperanza (Antarctica) .....82 g
Esperanza (Argentina) ......28 v
Esperanza (Argentina) ......30 v
Esperanza (Mexico) ....18 u
Esperanza (Peru) ....25 v
Espinal ....22 z
Espinnaco, Serra do ....29 i
Espiritu Santo ....75 d
Espiritu Santo Bay ....20 u
Espiritu Santo (Island) .....18 k
Espita ....19 w
Espoo ....33 j
Espungabera ....49 g
Esquel ....30 h
Esquina ....28 x
Essaouira ....36 f
Essen ....33 o
Essendon, Mount ....72 v
Essequibo ....23 x
Esso ....53 y
Estación Babicora ....18 l
Estacion Trincheras ....18 k
Estancia ....27 u
Estcourt ....49 r
Estelí ....22 e
Estevan ....15 e
Estherville ....15 w
Estmain ....16 l
Estonia ....33 j
Etah ....61 d
Etap Bajanmönch ....57 t
Etawah ....61 d
Ethiopia 42-43
Ethiopian Highlands ....43 b
Etna ....35 s
Etosha Pan ....48 h
Etykan ....53 g
Etzatlán ....18 y
Eubboea ....35 s
Eucla ....76 m
Eucumbene, Lake ....77 z
Eufaula ....20 i
Eugene ....14 g
Eulo ....74 o
Euphrates ....39 f
Eureka (California) ....14 t
Eureka (Canada) ....13 c
Eureka (Nevada) ....14 x
Eureka (Utah) ....14 z
Eurinilla ....77 h
Europe Island ....46 z
Evans Lake ....16 j
Evans Strait ....13 r
Evanston ....15 n
Evansville ....16 s
Everard, Lake ....77 c
Everard Park ....77 b
Everest ....61 i
Everett ....14 h
Everglades ....20 m
Evinayong ....41 u
Evje ....33 b
Evora ....34 o
Évreux ....32 y
Ewirgol ....56 t
Ewo ....44 g
Exeter ....32 w
Exeter Sound ....13 m
Exmouth ....72 q
Exmouth Gulf ....72 q
Eyakit-Tërdë ....52 f
Eyik ....52 h
Eyre ....76 k
Eyre, Lake ....77 e
Eyre Peninsula ....77 d

Ezequil Ramos Mexia
Reservoir................30 j
Ez Zemoul el Akbar.........37 d

F

Fachi................37 t
Facundo...............30 v
Fada ....38 o
Fada-Ngourma ....41 a
Faeroe Islands..........32 i
Fafen ....43 t
Faggo ....41 h
Fagnano, Lago ....30 w
Faguibine Lake..........40 k
Faidzabad..............55 v
Fairbanks.............11 g
Fairmont (Minnesota)....15 w
Fairmont (W. Virginia)....16 w
Fairweather, Mount........11 x
Faisalabad.............60 m
Faizabad...............61 f
Fakfak.................70 q
Falcon Reservoir........19 b
Falkland Islands/
Islas Malvinas..........31 p
Fallon..................14 w
Falster................33 q
Famagusta..............35 y
Famatina, Sierra de.........28 q
Fana.................40 i
Fandriana..............47 r
Fangshan..............63 t
Fang Xian.............63 a
Fangzheng..............58 r
Fan si Pan............62 v
Faradje................42 w
Farafangana............47 r
Farafra................38 f
Farafra, Oasis..........38 g
Farah..................60 e
Farahrod...............60 f
Farah Rud..............60 f
Faranah ....40 f
Farasen, Island.........39 o
Faraulep Atoll..........70 m
Farewell, Cape ....90 l
Farewell Island.........80 l
Fargo..................15 i
Faribault..............15 k
Faridpur...............61 x
Farim..................40 c
Farkovo................51 h
Farmington ....15 o
Faro (Brazil)..........26 g
Faro (Canada) ....11 l
Faro (Portugal) ....34 o
Farrukhabad............61 d
Farsi..................60 f
Fartak, Ras...........43 m
Fasa..................39 k
Faskari................41 e
Fataki.................42 x
Fatala.................40 d
Fatehpur...............61 r
Fátima.................26 y
Fatsa..................54 p
Fatunda ....44 i
Fatzeh.................54 b
Fauresmith.............49 o
Fauro..................71 u
Faxa Bay..............32 a
Faya...................37 z
Fayetteville (Arkansas).....15 w
Fayetteville (Carolina)..16 x
Fayetteville (Tennessee)..16 s
Fayu..................71 d
Fazilka................60 m
Fdérik.................36 q
Federated States of
Micronesia ....71 c
Fedorovskiy............53 c
Fedulki................50 z
Feijó..................25 o
Feira de Santana........27 s
Felipe Carrillo Puerto......20 u
Fengfeng...............63 c
Fengje.................62 m
Fengning...............57 w

Fengqing...............62 s
Feodosiya..............54 p
Ferdows................60 b
Ferfer.................43 u
Fergana................55 w
Fergus Falls...........15 i
Fériana................34 x
Ferkéssédougou.............40 k
Ferlo..................40 c
Fernandina.............22 o
Fernandina Beach...........20 m
Fernando de Noronha ....27 l
Fernandópolis..........29 d
Ferrara................34 m
Ferreira Gomes ....26 k
Ferreñafe..............24 h
Fès....................36 i
Feshi..................44 i
Festus.................16 q
Fethiye................35 w
Fetisovo...............54 z
Fezzan.................37 u
Fiambalá...............28 r
Fianarantsoa...........47 p
Fiche..................43 c
Ficksburg..............49 q
Figuig.................36 l
Fiji...................75 l
Fik....................43 e
Filadelfia.............28 k
Filchner Ice Shelf..........83 t
Filingué...............41 c
Filtu..................43 r
Fimbul Ice Shelf...........83 j
Finch Hatton ....74 r
Findlay................16 u
Fingoè.................45 r
Finike.................35 w
Finisterre, Cape........34 a
Finke..................77 d
Finke (River)..........77 d
Finland................33
Finland, Gulf of........33 i
Firat..................54 q
Firenze (Florence) ....34 m
Firozpur...............61 a
Firuzabad..............39 j
Fish...................48 x
Fisher Strait..........13 q
Fishguard..............32 w
Fiske, Cape...........83 n
Fitzcarrald............24 z
Fitzroy (Queensland)....74 s
Fitzroy (Western Australia)72 x
Fitzroy Crossing ....72 z
Flagstaff..............15 n
Flathead Lake..........14 m
Flattery, Cape ....14 f
Flensburg..............33 p
Flinders...............73 w
Flinders Bay...........76 c
Flinders Island........78 q
Flinders Range.........77 g
Flin Flon..............15 f
Flint..................16 u
Flint (River)..........20 j
Floraville.............73 v
Florence (Italy).......34 m
Florence (South Carolina) 20 m
Florence (Tennessee).......20 h
Florencia..............22 z
Florentino Ameghino
Reservoir..............30 y
Flores.................20 s
Flores (Island)........72 j
Flores Sea.............69 t
Floriano...............27 p
Florianópolis..........29 s
Florida (Uruguay)......31 d
Florida (USA)..........20
Florida Bay............20 m
Florida, Straits of.........20 m
Flower's Cove..........17 j
Fly....................70 x
Foggia.................35 b
Foley..................13 g
Fomich.................52 c
Fond du Lac ....16 r
Fonseca, Gulf of........22 d
Fontanillas............25 w

Fonte Boa..............25 e
Fontur.................32 e
Foochow................63 t
Forbes.................78 c
Forécariah.............40 d
Forel, Mt. ....90 z
Formosa (Argentina) ....28 x
Formosa (Brazil).......29 f
Formosa do Rio Preto......27 o
Formosa, Serra ....25 z
Formoso................29 g
Forrest River..........73 w
Forsayth...............73 x
Forsyth................15 c
Fort Albany............16 i
Fortaleza (Bolivia) ....25 q
Fortaleza (Brazil).....27 g
Fortaleza (Brazil).....25 s
Fort Beaufort..........49 o
Fort Black.............12 v
Fort Chipewyan.........12 t
Fort Collins...........15 q
Fort-de-France.........23 i
Fort Dodge.............15 w
Forte Carumbo..........44 k
Fortescue..............72 u
Forte Veneza...........26 v
Fort-Foureau...........41 k
Fort Frances...........15 k
Fort Franklin..........12 c
Fort Gardel............37 r
Fort Good Hope.........12 a
Fort Hope..............16 e
Fortin Garrapatal ....28 i
Fortin General Diaz ......28 j
Fortin Gral. Eugenio Garay28 i
Fortin Hernandarias.........28 i
Fortin Juan de Zalazar ....28 k
Fortin Madrejón..........28 k
Fortin Max Parades.........28 k
Fortin Ravelo...........28 j
Fort Lauderdale.........20 m
Fort Laird.............12 p
Fort Macleod ....14 m
Fort McMurray..........12 t
Fort McPherson.........11 k
Fort Morgan............15 r
Fort Myers.............20 l
Fort Nelson
(British Columbia)...........12 p
Fort Nelson (Manitoba).....13 n
Fort Norman............12 o
Fort Peck Reservoir.......15 d
Fort Pierce............20 m
Fort Portal............42 w
Fort Providence ....12 r
Fort Qarain ....38 d
Fort Resolution ....12 t
For Rupert.............16 k
Fort Sandeman..........60 j
Fort Scott.............15 w
Fort-Sevčenko ....54 x
Fort Severn............13 p
Fort Simpson...........12 p
Fort Smith (Canada)........12 u
Fort Smith (USA).......15 w
Fort St. John..........12 q
Fort Stockton..........18 m
Fort Walton Beach..........20 i
Fort Wayne.............16 t
Fort William...........32 v
Fort Worth.............19 c
Fort Yukon.............11 g
Foshan.................63 o
Fossil Bluff...........82 x
Foumban................41 v
Foum El Aassane.........36 g
Fourdou................40 d
Fouta Djalon...........40 d
Foveaux Strait.........79 q
Fowler's Bay...........77 b
Foxe Basin.............13 g
Foxe Channel...........13 s
Foxe Peninsula.........13 t
Fox Harbour............17 j
Fox Islands............10 z
Foz do Cunen...........48 e
Foz do Iguaçú..........29 n
Foz do Mamoriá.........25 d
Foz do Pauini..........25 d

Franca ....29 f
France 32-33/34
Franceville............44 f
Francisco Beltro ....29 o
Francistown............49 c
Frankfort..............49 q
Frankfurt..............33 r
Frankfurt (am Main)........33 p
Frankland..............76 d
Frankland Range........78 o
Franklin Mountains .....12 o
Franklin Strait........12 m
Franz Josef Land.............50 h
Fraserburg.............48 y
Fraserdale.............16 i
Fraser (Newfoundland).....13 y
Fraser (River,
British Columbia) ....14 h
Fraser Island..........74 u
Fraser Range ....76 i
Frazier Downs ....72 w
Frederick..............15 h
Frederick E. Hyde Fjord ...91 j
Fredericksburg.........16 x
Fredericton............17 d
Frederikshavn..........33 c
Fredonia...............16 w
Fredrikstad............33 d
Freeport...............16 q
Freetown...............40 d
Fregon.................77 a
Freiburg...............33 o
Fremantle ....76 d
French Guiana..........26 i
French Polynesia............230 p
Fresco.................26 x
Fresnillo..............18 z
Fresno.................14 v
Frewena................73 r
Fria...................40 d
Frias..................28 s
Frio, Cabo (Brazil)........29 j
Frio, Cape (Namibia)....48 e
Frisian Islands........33 n
Frobisher Bay (Iqaluit)....13 w
Frobisher Lake ....12 v
Frome, Lake ....77 g
Frontera...............19 t
Front Range............15 q
Frutal.................29 e
Frylinckspan...........48 z
Fuding.................63 h
Fuerte.................18 i
Fuerte Olimpo..........28 k
Fuerteventura..........36 c
Fujairah...............39 y
Fujin..................58 k
Fujiyama...............59 n
Fuka...................38 f
Fukui..................58 z
Fukuoka................58 v
Fukushima..............59 o
Fukuyama...............58 x
Funchal................36 a
Fundy, Bay of..........17 e
Fünen..................33 p
Funhalouro.............49 h
Funing.................62 x
Funtua.................41 f
Furmanovka.............55 w
Furmanovo..............54 k
Furnas Reservoir.......29 g
Furneaux Group ....78 p
Fury and Hecla Strait ......13 e
Fushun.................58 f
Fusin..................58 d
Fu Xian................58 q
Fuyang.................63 d
Fuyu...................58 f
Fuyuan.................58 l
Fuyun..................56 h
Fuzhou (Foochow).......63 e

G

Ga.....................40 l
Gabela.................44 t
Gabès..................37 f
Gabès, Gulf of ....34 y

Gabon..................41/44
Gabon (River)..........44 c
Gaborone...............46 o
Gadag..................64 e
Gadsden................19 l
Gaferut................71 a
Gafoua.................41 k
Gafsa..................37 e
Gagarin................54 b
Gagnoa.................40 w
Gagnon.................17 c
Gagyu Hu...............63 g
Gainesville (Florida)...20 k
Gainesville (Georgia)......20 j
Gairdner, Lake.........77 d
Gairo..................45 i
Gai Xian...............58 e
Gaktsynka..............53 p
Gala...................61 k
Galanino...............51 x
Galapagos Islands......22 q
Galati.................35 h
Galbraith..............73 j
Galcaio................43 v
Galdhöpiggen...........33 b
Galena.................11 c
Galesburg..............16 q
Galilee, Lake ....73 z
Galimyy................53 k
Galiwinku..............73 f
Galle..................64 v
Gallegos...............30 v
Gallinas, Cabo.........23 b
Gällivare..............33 h
Gallup.................15 o
Galt...................57 a
Galveston..............19 e
Galway.................32 u
Galway Downs...........77 i
Gama...................29 f
Gambaga................40 m
Gambela................42 m
Gambell................10 k
Gambia.................40
Gambo..................42 q
Gamboma................44 g
Gamboola...............73 l
Gambos.................44 s
Ganda..................44 t
Gandadiwata............69 s
Gandajika..............44 m
Gandak.................61 g
Gander.................17 k
Gandi..................42 f
Gandia.................34 s
Gandsya................54 v
Gandu..................27 s
Gangan.................30 j
Ganganagar.............60 m
Gangapur...............61 b
Gangaw.................62 p
Gangca.................57 n
Ganges.................61 t
Ganges Delta ....61 x
Ganhezi................56 u
Gan Jiang..............63 d
Gannett Peak ....15 o
Ganta..................40 u
Gao....................41 a
Gao'an.................63 d
Gaotai.................57 n
Gaoua..................40 k
Gaoual.................40 d
Garalo.................40 i
Garanhuns..............27 v
Garapu.................26 w
Garba Tula.............43 p
Garberville............14 t
Garda, Lake ....34 m
Garden City ....15 t
Gardez.................60 j
Gardo..................43 j
Garhchiroli............61 q
Garies.................48 x
Garimpo Cumaru.........26 x
Garissa................43 q
Garland................19 d
Garmabe................42 w
Garmenka...............57 b
Garmsar................39 j

Garoe ....43 j
Garonne ....34 g
Garoua ....41 j
Garoua Boulaï ....41 x
Garry Lake ....12 l
Garwa ....61 t
Gary ....16 s
Garyarsa ....61 d
Gar Zangbo ....61 e
Garzê ....62 g
Garzón ....22 z
Gascoyne ....72 s
Gascoyne Junction .72 r
Gas Hu ....56 v
Gashua ....41 i
Gaspar Strait .....68 w
Gaspé ....17 e
Gastre ....30 j
Gatton ....74 t
Gauhati ....61 z
Gavbandi ....39 k
Gavio ....27 s
Gävle ....33 g
Gawan ....59 b
Gawler ....77 w
Gawler Ranges .....77 d
Gaxun Nur ....57 n
Gaya (India) ......61 u
Gaya (Niger) ......41 c
Gayndah ....78 f
Gaza ....38 k
Gaziantep ....54 q
Gbadolite ....42 p
Gbarnga ....40 t
Gdansk ....33 t
Gdynia ....33 t
Gebe ....67 z
Gedaref ....43 a
Geelong ....77 w
Geelvink Channel ..76 c
Gê'gyai ....61 e
Geidam ....41 i
Geita ....45 f
Gejiu (Kokiu) .....62 v
Gela ....35 n
Gelib ....43 s
Gêlo ....25 y
Gemena ....42 p
Gemsa ....38 j
Gemsbok ....48 x
General Acha ......30 l
General Alvear ....30 k
General Belgrano ..83 s
Beneral Belgrano Plateau 83 o
General Bernardo
O'Higgins ....82 s
General Carrera, Lago 30 t
General Conesa ....30 l
General Güemes ....28 t
General Juan Madariaga 31 d
General Pico ......30 m
General Roca ......30 k
General San Martin 82 v
General Santos ....67 w
General Viamonte ..31 x
General Villegas ..30 m
Geneva ....34 i
Geneva, Lake ......34 j
Genève (Geneva) ...34 i
Genoa ....34 k
Genoa, Gulf of ....34 k
Genova (Genoa) ....34 k
Genovesa ....22 p
Geographical Society
Island ....91 r
George ....48 z
George IV Sound ...82 z
George, Lake (USA) 20 l
George, Lake (Uganda) 45 d
George Land ....50 h
Georgetown (Australia) 73 x
Georgetown (Cayman
Islands, UK) ......20 y
Georgetown (Gambia) 40 c
Georgetown (Guyana) 23 l
George Town
(Pinang, Malaysia) 65 w
Georgetown (USA) ..21 a
George V Land .....86 y
Georgia ....20 k

Georgia (State) ...54 t
Georgian Bay ......16 i
Georgia, Strait of 14 g
Georgiievka ....56 d
Georgina ....73 v
Georg von Neumayer 83 g
Gera ....33 q
Geral de Goiás, Serra 29 f
Geral do Parana, Serra 29 f
Geraldton (Australia) 76 c
Geraldton (Canada) 16 f
Gerasmikova ....51 p
Gerede ....35 k
Gerlachovsky ......35 d
Germania Land .....91 t
Germany 33
Germiston ....49 q
Gerona ....34 h
Gêrzê ....61 c
Gettysburg ....15 g
Getz Ice Shelf ....81 q
Geureudong ....65 u
Gewane ....43 d
Geyhan ....35 z
Ghadames ....37 f
Ghadir ....43 g
Ghaem-Shahr ....54 z
Ghaghara ....61 t
Ghana 40-41
Ghandi Sagar Reservoir 61 l
Ghanzi ....48 m
Ghardaia ....34 u
Ghariyan ....34 z
Ghat ....37 s
Ghazaouet ....36 k
Ghaziabad ....61 c
Ghazipur ....61 t
Ghazni ....60 j
Ghelinsor ....43 v
Ghent ....34 h
Ghion ....43 b
Ghorian ....60 e
Ghubeish ....42 h
Ghugri ....61 v
Giahel ....43 k
Giamama ....43 s
Gibb River ....72 m
Gibraltar ....34 p
Gibraltar, Str. of 34 p
Gibson Desert .....72 y
Gidgealpa ....77 g
Gidgee ....76 y
Gidole ....43 o
Gifford ....88 x
Gifu ....58 z
Giganta, Siera de la 18 g
Gijón ....34 c
Gila Desert ....18 f
Gilbert River .....74 a
Gilbués ....27 o
Giles Meteorological
Station ....73 n
Gilf Kebir Plateau 38 r
Gilgil ....43 n
Gilgit ....61 a
Gillam ....13 n
Gillette ....15 d
Gimbi ....43 a
Gingin ....76 d
Gingoog ....67 w
Giohar ....43 u
Giresun ....54 q
Giri ....42 n
Girishk ....60 g
Gironde ....34 f
Gisborne ....79 x
Gisenyi ....45 d
Gitarama ....45 d
Giza ....38 h
Gizhduvan ....55 r
Gizhiga ....53 m
Gjoa Haven ....12 m
Glace Bay ....17 h
Gladmar ....15 d
Gladstone ....74 t
Glasgow (Kentucky) 16 t
Glasgow (Montana) .15 c
Glasgow (UK) ......32 w
Glazov ....50 v
Glenayle ....76 h

Glendive ....15 d
Glenelg ....77 u
Glen Falls ....16 z
Glengyle ....77 g
Glen Helen ....73 q
Glen Innes ....78 f
Glenmorgan ....78 d
Glennallen ....11 g
Glenns Ferry ......14 y
Glenormiston ......73 u
Glenroy ....72 m
Glenwood Springs ..15 p
Globe ....18 h
Glubinnoye ....58 l
Goa ....64 d
Goageb ....48 v
Goalpara ....61 y
Goba ....43 q
Gobabis ....48 k
Gobernador Gregores 30 v
Gobi 56-57
Gochas ....48 j
Godavari ....64 l
Gode ....43 s
Goderich ....16 v
Godhavn ....90 k
Godhra ....60 z
Godinlave ....43 v
Gods Lake ....15 j
Godthâb (Nuuk) ....90 u
Goiána ....27 w
Goianésia ....29 e
Goiânia ....29 d
Goiás ....29 d
Goiatuba ....29 d
Gokwe ....46 q
Gol (Norway) ......33 b
Gol (Russia) ......52 t
Golan Heights .....38 l
Gol'chikha ....51 g
Gold Coast (Australia) 78 z
Gold Coast (Ghana) 40 z
Golden ....14 k
Goldfield ....14 x
Goldsboro ....16 x
Goldworthy ....72 u
Golmud ....62 c
Golyshmanovo ......55 y
Goma ....45 c
Gombari ....42 w
Gombe ....41 i
Gomel ....33 y
Gomera ....36 x
Gómez Palacio .....18 l
Gonaïves ....21 r
Gonam ....52 z
Gonam (River) .....52 z
Gonbad-e-Kavus ....54 z
Gonder ....43 b
Gongbo'gyamda .....62 b
Gonggar ....61 l
Gonghe ....62 g
Gongola ....41 h
Gongpoquan ....56 z
Gongshan ....62 f
Gongxi ....63 e
Gonzales ....19 d
Good Hope, Cape of 48 w
Gooding ....14 y
Goodnews Bay ......11 n
Goondiwindl ....78 e
Gooty ....64 f
Gorakhpur ....61 f
Gordon ....77 x
Gordon Downs .....73 n
Gore (Chad) ....41 m
Gore (Ethiopia) ...43 b
Gore (New Zealand) 79 r
Goreis ....48 h
Gorel'de ....55 q
Gorelova ....53 m
Gorgan ....54 z
Gorgona ....22 x
Gorgora ....43 b
Gor'kiy (Nizhiy Novgorod) 50 r
Gorlovka ....54 d
Gornak ....56 z
Gorno-Chuyskiy ....52 r
Gornyy ....58 m
Gornyy Kazymsk ....51 a

Goroka ....70 z
Gorongosa ....46 u
Gorontalo ....69 i
Gorotiré ....26 x
Gorshechnoye ......54 d
Gorzow-Wikp ....33 s
Gosford ....78 f
Göteborg ....33 d
Gotland ....33 g
Göttingen ....33 p
Goudoumaria ....41 i
Gouin Reservoir ...16 m
Goukou ....58 d
Goulburn ....78 e
Goulmina ....36 i
Goumeré ....40 x
Goundam ....40 k
Goura ....41 g
Gourara ....36 m
Gouré ....41 h
Gouro ....37 z
Gov'Chonin ....56 w
Governador Valadares 29 j
Govorovo ....52 l
Goya ....28 x
Goyder's Lagoon ...77 g
Goyoum ....41 x
Goz Beïda ....42 d
Gozo ....35 n
Graaff-Reinet .....49 n
Grabo ....40 v
Gracias á Dios, Cape 22 h
Gradaús, Serra ....26 x
Grafton (Australia) 78 g
Grafton (USA) .....15 s
Graham Bell Island 50 m
Graham Island .....13 b
Graham Land ....82 u
Grahamstown ....49 o
Grain Coast ....40 t
Grajaú ....27 n
Grajaú (River) ....27 o
Granada (Nicaragua) 22 f
Granada (Spain) ...34 q
Gran Canaria ......36 b
Gran Chaco ....28 h
Grand Bahama Island 21 a
Grand Bank ....17 j
Grand-Bassam ......40 x
Grand Caicos ......21 s
Grand Canal ....57 w
Grand Canyon ......14 z
Grand Cayman ......20 z
Grand Centre ......15 a
Grande (Brazil) ...29 h
Grande (Nicaragua) 22 g
Grande (Venezuela) 23 i
Grande, Bahia .....30 w
Grande Cache ......14 j
Grande Comore .....47 b
Grande de Gurapa ..26 k
Grande de Santiago, Rio 18 y
Grande Prairie ....14 j
Grand Erg de Bilma 37 u
Grande, Rio
(River, Bolivia) ..28 g
Grande, Rio
(River, Campos, Brazil) 27 p
Grande, Rio (River, Brazil) 29 h
Grande, Rio (River, USA) 19 b
Grand Forks ....15 l
Grand Island ......15 u
Grand Junction ....15 o
Grand-Lahou ....40 w
Grand Marais ......16 d
Grand-Mére ....17 z
Grand Pantanal ....28 m
Grand Rapids (Minnesota) 15 k
Grand Rapids (Michigan) 16 t
Grand Santi ....26 i
Grangeville ....14 k
Granite Downs .....77 c
Granite Peak (Australia) 76 k
Granite Peak (USA) 15 a
Gran Laguna Salada 30 x
Gran Sabana ....23 v
Grant Island ......81 r
Grants ....15 p
Grants Pass ....14 t
Granville ....32 x

Gravatá ....27 v
Gray, Cape ....87 o
Grayling ....16 g
Graz ....35 b
Great Abaco Island 21 b
Great Anyuy ....10 x
Great Australian Bight 76 k
Great Bahama Bank .21 n
Great Barrier Reef 74 b
Great Barrier Island 79 i
Great Basin ....14 x
Great Bear Lake ...12 d
Great Bitter Lake .38 j
Great Britain and
Northern Ireland ..32
Great Dividing Range 78
Great Eastern Erg .34 w
Great Exuma Island 21 p
Great Falls ....15 a
Great Fish ....49 o
Great Inagua Island 21 q
Great Karasberg ...48 w
Great Karoo ....48 z
Great Khingan Mountains 58 c
Great Plain ....63 c
Great Salt Lake ...14 z
Great Sandy Desert 72 x
Great Slave Lake ..12 t
Great Smoky Mountains 16 u
Great Tiraz ....48 u
Great Victoria Desert 76 x
Great Wall ....57 u
Great Western Erg .36/37
Great Whale River .16 l
Greater Antilles ..20/21
Greece 35
Greeley ....15 q
Greely Fjord ......91 e
Green Bay ....16 e
Green Head ....76 c
Greenland 90-91
Greenland Sea .....91 w
Greenough ....76 d
Green River ....15 n
Green River (River) 15 o
Greensboro ....16 w
Greensburg ....16 w
Greenvale ....74 b
Greenville (Alabama) 20 i
Greenville (Liberia) 40 t
Greenville (Mississippi) 20 f
Greenville (North Carolina) 16 x
Greenville (South Carolina) 20 k
Gregory Downs .....73 u
Gregory, Lake .....72 z
Gregory Range .....74 c
Greifswald ....33 r
Grenada ....23 j
Grenoble ....34 j
Grey Bull ....15 c
Greymouth ....79 s
Grey Range ....77 i
Greytown ....49 s
Gribingui ....42 b
Griekwastad ....48 z
Griffith ....77 k
Grinell Peninsula .13 a
Grise Fjord ....13 e
Groblersbrug ......46 p
Groblersdal ....46 q
Groblershoop ......48 y
Grodno ....33 v
Grong ....33 d
Groningen (Netherlands) 33 s
Groningen (Suriname) 26 g
Groot ....49 n
Groote Eylandt ....73 g
Grootfontein ......48 j
Groot Winterhoek ..48 x
Grosseto ....34 m
Gross Glockner ....34 m
Groznyi ....54 u
Grudziadz ....33 t
Grünau ....48 w
Grungedal ....33 b
Gryazi ....54 z
Guaçu ....29 a
Guadalajara (Mexico) 18 z
Guadalajara (Spain) 34 x
Guadalcanal ....71 x

Guadalquivir ....34 p
Guadalupe ....18 z
Guadalupe (Island)...........18 c
Guadalupe Peak...............18 l
Guadalupe Victoria...........18 y
Guadalupe-y-Calvo...........18 j
Guadeloupe 21
Guadiana ....34 o
Guadix ....36 k
Guafo, Gulf of...................30 f
Guaicurus ....28 l
Guainia ....23 q
Guaira ....29 n
Guajará Mirim ....25 r
Guajira Peninsula ....23 b
Gualeguay.........................28 x
Gualeguay (River) ....28 x
Gualeguaychu ....28 x
Guallatiri ....28 c
Guam ....231 j
Guamini ....31 a
Guanahacabibes
Peninsula..........................20 w
Guanaja ....20 v
Guanajuato ....19 n
Guanambi ....29 i
Guanare ....23 d
Guandacol ....28 q
Guangnan ....62 x
Guangyuan ....62 k
Guangzhou (Canton).......63 p
Guanipa ....23 h
Guantiánamo ....21 p
Guan Xian ....62 i
Guapi ....22 x
Guaporé ....25 s
Guaqui ....25 o
Guarabira ....27 v
Guarai ....26 z
Guarapuava ....29 p
Guarantinguetá ....29 q
Guarda ....34 b
Guardafui, Cape ....43 l
Guàrico ....23 e
Guarulhos ....29 f
Guasave ....18 i
Guásimas ....18 h
Guatemala 19/22
Guatemala (City) ....22 c
Guaviare ....23 q
Guayabero.........................23 n
Guayaquil ....24 g
Guayaquil, Gulf of............24 g
Guaymas ....18 g
Guazapares ....18 j
Guba ....43 a
Gubakha ....50 w
Gudur ....64 h
Gudvangen ....33 a
Guéckedou ....40 g
Guedi ....42 b
Guelb er Richat ....36 r
Guélengdeng ....41 l
Guelma ....37 d
Guelta Zemmur ....36 q
Guémar ....37 d
Güera ....36 n
Guerara ....34 v
Guercif ....36 j
Guernsey ....34 e
Guga ....53 p
Gugu ....43 d
Guguang ....69 d
Guia ....36 b
Guiana Highlands..............23 s
Guidjiba ....41 k
Guiglo ....40 u
Guijá ....46 t
Guimaras ....67 h
Guinan ....62 g
Guinea 40
Guinea Bissau 40
Guinea, Gulf of ....41 p
Güines ....20 y
Guir ....36 k
Güiria ....23 i
Guiyang (Kweiyang).........62 x
Gujarkhan ....60 m
Gujranwala ....60 m
Gujrat ....60 m

Gulbarga ....61 p
Gul'ča ....55 x
Gulf of Mexico 20
Gulfport ....20 g
Gulian ....52 v
Gulistan ....55 u
Gulkana ....11 h
Gulu ....42 x
Gulya ....52 v
Gumare ....48 l
Gumbiro ....45 v
Gumti ....61 s
Gümüşhane ....54 q
Guna ....61 p
Guna (Mount) ....43 c
Gungu ....44 j
Gunnbjrn Fjeld ....91 n
Gunnedah ....78 e
Gunpowder ....73 v
Gunter ....61 r
Guntur ....64 h
Guoju ....63 i
Gurdaspur ....61 a
Gurgei ....42 f
Gurguéia ....27 p
Gurha ....60 y
Guri, Lago de ....23 i
Guro ....46 u
Gurskoye ....59 a
Gurué ....46 j
Gurun ....54 q
Gurupi ....26 y
Gurupi (River) ....27 a
Gurupizinho ....26 m
Guru Sikhar ....60 z
Gurvan Ozagal ....57 i
Gusau ....41 e
Gushan ....58 r
Gusinoozersk....................57 e
Gutara ....56 m
Guthrie ....15 u
Guyana 23/25/26
Guyang ....57 t
Guymon ....15 s
Guyuan ....62 k
Gvardeyets ....53 g
Gwa ....62 p
Gwai ....49 c
Gwai River ....49 c
Gwalior ....61 p
Gwanda ....49 d
Gweru ....49 e
Gwydir ....78 d
Gyaring Co ....61 j
Gyda ....51 e
Gydan Bay.........................51 d
Gydan Peninsula ....51 d
Gyirong ....61 j
Gyldenlves Fjord ....90 w
Gympie ....78 g
Gynym ....52 z
Győr..................................35 c

H

Haarlem ....48 z
Haast ....79 q
Haast Bluff ....73 p
Hab ....60 v
Habaswein ....43 q
Hab Chauki ....60 v
Habshan ....39 x
Hachioji ....59 n
Ha Coi ....62 y
Hadarba, Ras ....38 z
Haddad ....42 c
Hadejia ....41 h
Hadejia (River) ....41 g
Hadera ....38 k
Hadilik ....56 s
Hadley Bay ....12 i
Hadramaut ....43 j
Haeju ....58 s
Haena ....18 p
Hafun, Ras ....43 l
Hagadera ....43 q
Hagere Hiywot ....43 c
Hagerstown ....16 x
Ha Giang ....62 x

Hague, The........................33 n
Hagunia ....36 d
Haifa ....38 k
Haikow ....63 n
Ha'il ....39 b
Hailar ....58 c
Hailar (River) ....58 b
Hainan ....63 n
Hainan Strait ....63 n
Haines ....11 x
Haines Junction ....11 k
Haiphong ....62 y
Haiti 21
Haiya ....38 y
Haiyan ....62 h
Hajiabad ....39 l
Hajjah ....43 f
Hakkâri ....54 t
Hakodate ....59 c
Halaban ....39 q
Halaib ....38 z
Halawa ....18 r
Halcon ....67 g
Hale ....76 e
Hal Flood Range ....81 t
Halifax...............................17 s
Halil Rud ....60 b
Hall Beach ....13 e
Halle ....33 q
Hallett ....86 s
Halley Bay ....83 f
Hall Island ....50 j
Hall Islands ....71 e
Hall Land ....91 f
Hall Peninsula ....13 x
Halls Creek ....73 n
Halmahera ....69 m
Halmstad ....33 r
Ham ....41 l
Hama ....38 m
Hamada du Guir ....36 j
Hamada du Tinrhert...........37 d
Hamada el Haricha............36 w
Hamada el Homra ....37 g
Hamada of Dra ....36 h
Hamadan ....39 h
Hamada Safia ....36 v
Hamadat Tingharat............37 g
Hamamatsu ....59 n
Hamar ....33 d
Hamarro Hadad ....43 f
Hambantota ....64 v
Hamburg ....33 p
Hämeenlinna ....33 i
Hamelin Pool ....76 c
Hamersley Range..............72 s
Hamhung ....58 u
Hami ....56 x
Hamilton (Alaska) ....11 a
Hamilton (Australia)..........77 v
Hamilton (Canada) ....16 w
Hamilton (Idaho)...............14 l
Hamilton (New Zealand)...79 v
Hamilton Downs ....73 q
Hamilton Inlet ....17 i
Hammami ....36 t
Hammam Lif ....37 g
Hammerfest ....33 j
Hammond ....20 f
Hamoud ....40 e
Hampton (Oregon) ....14 v
Hampton (Virginia) ....16 y
Hampton Tableland ....76 l
Hamrat al Shaikh ....42 h
Hamun-e Jaz Murian.........60 c
Hancheng ....63 a
Handeni ....45 j
Handgai ....57 l
Hangayn Mountains ....57 a
Hangchow ....63 h
Hanggin Houqi ....57 q
Hangzhou (Hangchow)....63 h
Hankö ....33 i
Hann ....72 l
Hanna ....14 m
Hannah Bay ....16 j
Hannibal ....16 p
Hannover ....33 p
Hanoi ....62 x
Hanover (Hannover)..........33 p

Hanover (Island)...............30 s
Hanover (South Africa).....49 n
Hanover (USA)..................17 n
Han Shui............................63 b
Hantan ....57 v
Hanzhong ....62 k
Haouach ....38 l
Happy Valley-Goose Bay .17 g
Hapur ....61 c
Harad ....39 u
Harare ....46 s
Haraza ....42 j
Haraze Mangueigne ....42 c
Harbin ....58 g
Harda ....61 p
Hardangerfjörd..................33 a
Hardec Králove..................33 s
Hardin ....15 c
Harding ....49 r
Hardy ....16 p
Harer ....43 e
Hargeisa ....43 g
Hargele ....43 s
Har Hu ....56 z
Hari ....68 h
Hari Rud ....60 f
Harlingen ....19 c
Harlowtown ....15 a
Harper ....40 u
Harper Island ....13 y
Harqin ....58 c
Harricana ....16 k
Harrington Harbour...........17 h
Harrisburg ....16 y
Harrismith ....49 q
Hartford ....17 n
Harts Range ....73 s
Harudj el Asued ....37 l
Hasa ....39 h
Hasalbag ....56 n
Hassan ....64 e
Hassel Sound ....12 l
Hassi bel Guebbour..........37 d
Hassi Inifel ....37 b
Hassi Maroket ....38 a
Hassi Messaoud ....34 w
Hassi Touareg ....37 c
Hastings (New Zealand)...79 w
Hastings (USA).................15 u
Hatches Creek ....73 s
Ha Tinh ....62 x
Hat Lek ....66 g
Hatteras, Cape ....16 y
Hattiesburg ....20 f
Hat Yai ....66 q
Hauberg ....83 o
Haugesund ....33 a
Hauraki Gulf ....79 v
Haute Kotto ....42 r
Hauts Plateaux ....36 m
Havana ....20 x
Haverhill ....17 o
Havre ....15 a
Havre-St-Pierre ....17 f
Hawaii ....18 r
Hawaiian Islands ....18 o
Hawera ....79 u
Hawi ....18 r
Hawke Bay ....79 w
Hawr al Hammar ....39 f
Hawthorne ....14 w
Hay ....77 j
Hay River...........................12 s
Hay River (River)..............12 r
Hayes ....13 a
Hayes Halv ....91 c
Haynan ....43 j
Hays (USA) ....15 t
Hays (Yemen) ....43 f
Hazard ....16 u
Hazaribagh ....61 u
Hazelton ....14 e
Head of Bight....................77 a
Healesville ....78 o
Heard Island ....231 r
Hearst ....16 h
Hearst Island ....82 x
Hebel ....74 q
Heber City ....15 n
Hebrides ....32 h

Hecate Strait.....................14 c
Hechi ....62 y
Hefei ....63 f
Hefeng ....63 a
Heihe ....58 g
Heilbron ....62 p
Helena, Mount ....14 m
Helen Reef ....70 d
Heligoland Bight ....33 o
Hell-Ville ....47 e
Helmand ....60 f
Helmeringhausen ....48 v
Helsingborg ....33 r
Helsingfors (Helsinki) .....33 j
Helsingör ....33 q
Helsinki ....33 j
Helwân ....38 i
Henbury ....73 q
Hendersonville ....16 u
Hendijan ....39 h
Hendrik Verwoerd
Reservoir ....49 o
Hengchun ....63 u
Hengduan Shan ....62 e
Hengyang ....63 b
Henrietta Maria, Cape ......16 i
Henryetta ....15 v
Henry Kater Peninsula .....13 j
Henties Bay ....48 g
Henzada ....65 f
Heppner ....14 i
Herat ....60 f
Herbert Vale ....73 u
Heredia ....22 g
Hereford ....15 s
Hermosillo ....18 g
Herrick ....78 p
Herschel............................11 j
Hervey Bay ....74 u
Hexigten Qi ....57 x
Heze ....63 d
Hibbing ....15 k
Hibbs, Point ....77 x
Hickory ....16 v
Hidalgo del Parral.............18 k
Hidden Valley ....73 d
High Altai ....56 v
High Atlas ....36 h
High Knob ....16 u
Highlands (Scotland) ....32 w
High Level ....12 s
High Prairie ....12 r
High River ....14 l
Hiiumaa ....33 i
Hilla ....39 e
Hillsboro ....16 u
Hilo ....18 s
Hima' ....16 r
Himalaya 61
Himatnagar ....60 z
Himeji ....58 y
Himeville ....49 r
Hindmarsh, Lake ....77 u
Hindu Kush ....60 j
Hinlopen Strait..................92 o
Hirafok ....37 o
Hirakud Reservoir.............61 t
Hiroshima ....58 x
Hisar ....61 a
Hoa Binh ....62 x
Hoare Bay ....13 l
Hobart (Tasmania) ....77 y
Hobart (USA)....................15 u
Hobbs ....18 m
Hochfeld ....48 j
Hochwan............................62 k
Ho Chi Minh (Saigon)......66 j
Hodal ....61 b
Hodda ....43 k
Hoddur ....43 s
Hodeida ....43 f
Hoeryöng ....58 i
Hohoi ....63 c
Hoh Xil Shan ....61 l
Hoima ....42 x
Hoit Taria ....56 y
Hokang ....58 i
Hokitika ....79 s
Hokkaidö ....59 d
Hola ....43 q

Holbrook .... 15 n
Hold with Hope Peninsula 91 s
Holguín .... 21 p
Hollick Kenyon Plateau .... 81 d
Holman Island .... 12 e
Holstebro .... 33 o
Holt Sum .... 57 x
Holy Cross .... 11 b
Holyhead .... 32 w
Hombori .... 40 l
Home Bay .... 13 k
Homodji .... 41 k
Homs .... 38 m
Honda .... 22 z
Honda Bay .... 67 e
Hondo .... 20 t
Hondo Reservoir ...... 28 t
Hondo (River) .... 19 w
Honduras 19-20/22
Honduras, Gulf of .... 20 v
Hönefoss .... 33 c
Hong Ha .... 62 w
Hong Kong .... 63 q
Hongliuyuan .... 56 y
Hongyuan .... 62 i
Hongze .... 63 g
Honiara .... 71 x
Honolulu .... 18 p
Honshú .... 59 n
Hood Cape .... 76 g
Hooker, Cape ...... 86 t
Hooker Creek ...... 73 p
Hooker Island ...... 50 i
Hooper Bay .... 10 m
Hopa .... 54 s
Hope .... 14 h
Hopedale .... 17 h
Hopes Advance, Cape .. 13 w
Hopetown .... 49 n
Hopin .... 62 q
Hopkins, Lake .... 73 n
Hormuz, Strait of .. 39 m
Horn, Cape (Chile) .. 30 x
Horn, Cape (Iceland) .. 32 b
Horn, Cape (Norway) .. 91 p
Hornavan .... 33 g
Horqin Youyi Qianqi .. 58 d
Horqin Zuoyi Zhongqi .. 58 e
Horsham .... 77 v
Hoseinabad ...... 39 l
Hoshab .... 60 t
Hoshangabad .... 61 p
Hoshiarpur ...... 61 b
Hospet .... 64 e
Hossororo ...... 23 k
Hoste .... 30 w
Hotan .... 56 p
Hotan (River) .. 56 p
Hotazel .... 48 z
Hot Springs .... 15 r
Hottah Lake .... 12 e
Houailu .... 75 p
Houck .... 15 o
Houghton ...... 16 e
Houma (China) .. 63 a
Houma (USA) .... 19 h
Houndé .... 40 l
Houston ...... 19 d
Houtman Abrolhos .. 76 b
Houxia .... 56 t
Howar .... 38 g
Howe, Cape .... 78 r
Howship ...... 73 n
Howship (Mount) .. 73 d
Hoyo .... 42 w
Hradec Králové .. 35 b
Hsinchu ...... 63 u
Hsuchang .... 63 e
Huachinango .. 20 n
Huacho ...... 24 v
Huacrachuco .. 24 w
Huadian ...... 58 g
Huahaizi .... 56 x
Hau Hin ...... 65 j
Huai .... 63 d
Huai'an ...... 57 v
Huaibei ...... 63 e
Huaiji .... 63 o
Huainan (Hwainan) .. 63 e
Huairen ...... 57 u

Huaiyin .... 63 g
Huajuapan de León .. 19 p
Hualien .... 63 v
Huallaga .... 24 k
Huamanrazo .... 24 y
Huancabamba .. 24 h
Huancané ...... 25 o
Huancapi ...... 24 y
Huancavelica .. 24 x
Huancayo ...... 24 y
Huanchaca, Serra de .. 25 v
Huang .... 63 a
Huangchuan .... 63 d
Huan Jiang .... 62 l
Huanren ...... 58 f
Huanta .... 24 y
Huánuco ...... 24 x
Huapanapan .. 19 p
Huaping ...... 62 u
Huara .... 28 c
Huaral .... 24 w
Huaraz .... 24 v
Huarmey ...... 24 v
Huascaran .... 24 w
Huasco .... 28 o
Huasco (River) .. 28 p
Huashixia .... 62 f
Huatabampo .. 18 h
Huauchinango .. 19 p
Hudiksvall .... 33 g
Hudson .... 16 z
Hudson, Cape .. 86 y
Hudson Bay .... 13 q
Hudson Bay (Saskatchewan) .. 15 f
Hudson Land .. 91 s
Hudson Strait .. 13 v
Hue .... 66 j
Huehuetenango .. 19 u
Huelva .... 34 o
Huesca .... 34 f
Huéscar ...... 36 j
Hufuf .... 39 u
Hughenden .... 73 y
Hughes .... 11 d
Hugli .... 61 w
Huhehot ...... 57 u
Hūichŏn ...... 58 t
Huila, Nev. de .. 22 y
Huili .... 62 u
Huinan .... 58 f
Huinca Renancó .. 30 m
Huixtla ...... 19 t
Huize .... 62 v
Huizhou ...... 63 q
Hulaifah ...... 39 a
Hulin .... 58 k
Hull .... 16 l
Hulls Cove .... 17 p
Huluun Nuur .. 57 j
Huma .... 58 g
Humahuaca .... 28 f
Humaitá ...... 26 o
Humansdorp .. 49 n
Humboldt .... 14 w
Humera ...... 43 b
Hume Reservoir .. 78 c
Humphreys Peak .. 15 n
Hun .... 37 j
Húna Bay .... 32 b
Hunchun ...... 58 l
Hungary 33/35
Hungchui .... 62 y
Hungtze, Lake .. 63 f
Hunter Island .. 77 w
Huntington .. 16 u
Hunt, Mount .. 12 n
Huntsville (Canada) .. 16 j
Huntsville (Texas) .. 19 e
Huntsville (Tennessee) .. 19 k
Hunyani ...... 46 e
Huolongmen .. 58 g
Huo Xian .... 63 b
Hurghada .... 38 k
Huron .... 15 h
Huron, Lake .. 16 h
Hutanopan .. 68 d
Hutchinson .. 15 u
Huth .... 43 g
Huxley, Mount .. 72 z

Huyani .... 49 e
Hval Sound .. 91 c
Hvar .... 35 b
Hwainan ...... 63 e
Hwange ...... 46 o
Hwangju ...... 58 t
Hwangshih .... 63 d
Hyderabad (India) .. 61 q
Hyderabad (Pakistan) .. 60 w
Hyesanjin .... 58 h
Hyndman Peak .. 14 y

I

Iaco .... 25 p
Iaşi .... 35 h
Iba .... 67 f
Ibadan ...... 41 q
Ibagué ...... 22 z
Ibarra ...... 24 i
Ibb .... 43 g
Ibba .... 42 v
Ibembo ...... 42 s
Iberia ...... 25 o
Ibi .... 41 h
Ibiapaba, Serra da .. 27 r
Ibicui ...... 28 z
Ibitunane .. 27 q
Ibiza .... 34 t
Ibologero .. 45 g
Ibotirama .. 27 q
Ibra .... 42 f
Ibri .... 39 z
Ica .... 24 x
Içá .... 25 b
Ica (River) .. 24 x
Içana .... 25 d
Iceland 32
Içel (Mersin) .. 35 y
Icha .... 53 x
Ichang ...... 63 a
Ichera ...... 52 q
Ichilo ...... 25 s
Ichinskaya Sopka .. 53 y
Ich'on ...... 58 t
Icó .... 27 t
Icy, Cape .... 11 a
Idaho .... 14 k
Idaho Falls .. 14 z
Idaye .... 41 i
'Idd al Ghanam .. 42 e
Ideles ...... 37 p
Iderijn Gol .. 57 a
Idfu .... 38 w
Idhan Awbari .. 37 g
Idhan Murzuq .. 37 u
Idi .... 65 u
Idiofa ...... 44 j
Idlib .... 38 l
Idri .... 37 i
Idutywa ...... 49 q
Idyum ...... 52 z
Idžim ...... 56 j
Ifakara ...... 45 i
Ifalik Atoll .. 70 l
Ife .... 41 q
Iférouane .. 37 r
Iffley ...... 73 w
Igaluit ...... 90 l
Iganga ...... 42 y
Igarka ...... 51 h
Igbetti ...... 41 c
Ighil .... 36 h
Igli .... 36 k
Igluligaarjuk (Chesterfield Inlet) .. 13 o
Igombe ...... 45 f
Igra .... 50 v
Iguaçú ...... 29 o
Iguala ...... 19 o
Iguatu ...... 27 s
Iguidi Erg .. 36 i
Iharaña ...... 47 f
Ihosy ...... 47 p
Ija .... 57 a
Ijebu Ode .. 41 q
Ika .... 52 p
Ikanbujmal .. 56 u

Ikela .... 42 r
Ikelenge ...... 44 z
Ikerasassuaq .. 90 t
Ikerre .... 41 q
Ikom .... 41 t
Il'a .... 57 h
Ilagan .... 67 h
Ilam .... 39 f
Ilan .... 63 v
Ilaro .... 41 p
Ilbenge ...... 52 k
Ilebo .... 44 k
Ie de France .. 91 u
Ilek .... 54 l
Ilesha ...... 41 g
Ilha do Bananal .. 26 y
Ilhéus ...... 29 l
Ili .... 56 p
Iliamna Lake .. 11 q
Iligan ...... 67 v
Ilimniir .... 53 i
Ilimpeya .... 52 b
Ilimsk ...... 57 c
Ilir .... 57 a
Illampu ...... 28 d
Illapel ...... 28 o
Illéla ...... 41 d
Illela ...... 41 d
Illimani .... 25 q
Illinois .... 16 q
Illizi ...... 37 r
Illmani ...... 28 e
Ilmer, Lake .. 33 m
Ilo .... 25 n
Iloilo ...... 67 h
Ilorin ...... 41 d
Il'pyrskiy .. 10 a
Imataca, Serrania de .. 23 i
Imatra ...... 33 l
Imbros ...... 35 t
im Chapyeva .. 53 i
im Gastello .. 53 g
Imi .... 43 s
Imilili ...... 36 o
Imperatriz .. 27 n
Imperia ...... 34 x
Imperial .... 15 s
Impfondo .... 42 n
Imphāl ...... 62 p
In Abalene .. 37 n
In Afeleh .... 37 s
In Alay ...... 36 x
Inambari .... 25 o
In Amenas .. 37 e
In Amguel .. 37 p
Iñapari ...... 25 o
Inari, Lake .. 33 k
In Azaoua .. 37 r
In Azaraf .... 37 n
Inca de Oro .. 28 p
Ince, Cape .. 35 m
Inch'ŏn ...... 58 t
Independence .. 15 w
Independence Fjord .. 91 i
Inderborskiy .. 54 k
India 60-61/64
Indiana (Australia) .. 73 s
Indiana (USA) .. 16 s
Indianapolis .. 16 s
Indian Head .. 15 e
Indian Ocean .. 231-231
Indiara ...... 29 d
Indigirka .... 53 g
Indonesia 68-70
Indore ...... 61 n
Indragiri .... 68 g
Indravati .... 61 r
Indus 60
Indus Delta .. 60 v
In Ebeggi .... 37 q
In Ekker .... 37 p
Inezgane .... 36 f
Infiernillo Reservoir .. 18 z
Inga .... 44 f
Ingende ...... 44 j
Ingeniero Guillermo Nueva Juárez .. 28 i
Ingeniero Jacobacci .. 30 j
Ingham ...... 74 c

Ingili .... 53 o
Inglefield Land .. 91 d
Inglewood .... 78 e
Ingoda ...... 52 t
Ingolf Fjord .. 91 j
Ingraj Bazar .. 61 w
Ingrid Christensen Coast .. 85 n
In Guezzam .. 37 p
Inhambane .. 46 v
Inhaminga .. 46 v
Inhassoro .. 46 v
Ining .... 56 p
Inirida ...... 23 g
Inja .... 56 g
Injaptuk .... 57 f
Injune ...... 74 r
Inkerman .... 73 j
Inkisi-Kisantu .. 44 g
Inland Sea .. 58 x
Inn .... 33 q
Innamincka .. 77 h
Inner Mongolia .. 57
Innisfail .... 74 c
Innsbruck .. 34 m
Inongo ...... 44 i
Inoni .... 44 g
In Salah .... 37 a
Inscription, Cape .. 76 a
Insein ...... 65 g
Inta .... 50 k
In Talak .... 41 c
Intelewa .... 26 h
International Dateline .. 86 q
International Falls .. 15 k
Inthanon .... 66 c
Inukjuak .... 13 t
Inuvik ...... 11 k
Invercargill .. 79 q
Inverell .... 78 e
Inverness .. 32 j
Inverway .... 73 g
Investigator Strait .. 77 r
Investigator Group .. 77 c
Inya .... 53 s
Inya (River) .. 53 s
Inyanga .... 46 t
Inza .... 54 h
Iolotan ...... 55 r
Iona .... 48 f
Ionian Sea .. 35 p
Iowa .... 16 o
Iowa City .. 16 o
Ipameri .... 29 f
Ipatinga .... 29 j
Ipiales ...... 24 j
Ipiau ...... 29 l
Ipin .... 62 j
Ipixuna .... 25 g
Ipoh .... 66 r
Iporanga .. 29 r
Ipswich (Australia) .. 74 u
Ipswich (UK) .. 32 z
Ipu .... 27 r
Iqaluit (Frobisher Bay) .. 13 w
Iqe .... 56 x
Iquique .... 28 c
Iquitos ...... 24 m
Iracema .... 25 u
Irai .... 29 o
Iráklion .... 35 t
Iramaia .... 27 r
Iran 39/54-55/60
Iranshahr .. 60 e
Irapuato .... 19 n
Iraq 39/54
Irbid .... 38 l
Irebu .... 44 h
Irece .... 27 r
Ireland 32
Irgiz .... 55 d
Irharharene .. 37 d
Irigui ...... 40 j
Iringa ...... 45 h
Iriomote .... 63 w
Iriri .... 26 u
Irish Sea .. 32 w
Irkestam .. 55 x
Irkutsk .... 52 o
Irondro .... 47 e
Iron Knob .. 77 e

Iron Mountain ....16 e
Iron Range......................73 l
Ironwood........................16 d
Irrawaddy...................62-65
Irrawaddy, Mouths of the..65 f
Irta ....50 t
Irtysh ....51 n
Irving ....19 d
Iryupinsk ....54 f
Isabal, Lago de ....20 s
Isabela ....22 o
Isabella ....22 o
Isabella, Cordillera.........22 f
Isačenko ....51 h
Isa Fjord ....92 o
Isafjördur ....32 a
Isalo Mountains ....47 p
Isangi ....42 s
Isangila Falls ....44 f
Isayevskiy ....51 l
Isbil ....43 g
Iseyin ....41 c
Isfahan ....39 j
Ishasha River ....45 d
Isherton.........................23 x
Ishim ....51 n
Ishim (River) ....51 o
Ishinomaki ....59 p
Isil'kul ....55 j
Isinga ....57 g
Isiolo ....43 o
Isiro ....42 v
Isisford ....73 y
Iskenderun ....35 z
Iskine ....54 l
Islamabad ....60 m
Island Falls ....12 x
Island Lagoon ....77 e
Island Lake ....51 j
Islands, Bay of...............79 h
Islay ....32 v
Ismâilîya ....38 j
Isna ....38 v
Isoka ....45 s
Israel......................35/38
Israelite Bay..................76 j
Issyk-Kul ....55 u
Issyk-Kul, Lake ....56 n
Istanbul ....35 i
Istlán ....18 y
Itabaiana ....27 u
Itaberaba ....27 r
Itaboca ....26 o
Itabuna ....29 l
Itacaiúnas ....26 y
Itacajá ....27 n
Itacoatiara ....25 j
Itaituba ....25 l
Itajai ....29 r
Italy 34-35
Itamaraju ....29 l
Itamataré ....27 a
Itanagar ....62 b
Itaobim ....29 j
Itapetinga ....29 k
Itapetininga ....29 e
Itapeva ....29 e
Itapicuru ....27 t
Itapicuru (Serra das
Alpercatas) ....27 p
Itapicuru Mirim ....27 c
Itapicuru, Serra do ....27 o
Itapipoca ....27 f
Itaporanga ....27 t
Ithaca ....16 y
Itigi ....45 g
Itinga ....26 z
Itiquira ....25 y
Itonamas ....25 s
Ittoqqortoormiit...............91 r
Itui ....25 a
Ituiutaba ....29 d
Itumbiara ....29 d
Itungi ....45 t
Ituri ....42 t
Iturup ....59 t
Ituxi ....25 r
Iuaretê ....25 b
Iultin ....10 h
Ivaipor ....29 p

Ivalo ....33 k
Ivangrad........................35 d
Ivanhoe ....78 a
Ivano Frankovsk ....35 g
Ivanovo ....50 q
Ivdel' ....50 y
Ivinhema ....29 b
Ivittuut ....90 t
Ivohibe ....47 q
Ivory Coast ....40 v
Ivujivik ....13 t
Iwaki ....59 p
Iwo ....41 p
Ixiamas ....25 p
Ixopo ....49 r
Ixtlán ....18 y
Izadkhast ....49 j
Izamal ....19 v
Izhevsk ....50 v
Izhma ....50 v
Izimbiri ....42 r
Izki ....60 p
Izmir ....35 u
Iztmil ....35 j
Izúcar de Matamoros........19 p
Izvestkovyy ....58 j
Izyum ....54 c

J

Jabal adh Dhanna ....39 w
Jabal al Qamar................39 w
Jabal al Qara ....39 x
Jabal at Tinef ....39 a
Jabal Nuqay ....37 y
Jabalpur ....61 q
Jabal Tuwaya ....39 s
Jablanica ....35 c
Jaboato ....27 w
Jaburu ....25 f
Jaca ....34 f
Jaçara ....29 c
Jacaré ....27 r
Jacareacanga ....25 k
Jacaretinga ....25 v
Jaciara ....25 z
Jaciparaná ....25 s
Jackson (Alabama)...........19 j
Jackson (Michigan) ....16 t
Jackson (Mississippi) ......19 i
Jackson (Tennessee) ....16 f
Jackson (Wyoming) ....15 n
Jackson Island ....50 j
Jacksonville (Florida).......20 m
Jacksonville (Illinois)........16 q
Jacksonville
(North Carolina)..............21 a
Jacmel ....21 r
Jacobabad ....60 i
Jacobina ....27 r
Jacona ....18 z
Jacques Cartier, Mount ....17 d
Jacui ....29 o
Jacundá ....26 y
Jacundá (River) ....26 l
Jadu ....34 z
Jaen ....24 h
Jaén ....34 q
Jafene ....36 u
Jaffa (Yafo) ....38 k
Jaffna ....64 h
Jafura ....39 v
Jagdalpur ....61 s
Jaggang ....61 d
Jaghbub, Oasis ....38 d
Jaghin ....60 b
Jagtial ....61 q
Jaguaro ....29 o
Jaguaribe ....27 t
Jagüe ....28 q
Jahra ....39 g
Jahrom ....39 k
Jaicós ....27 r
Jailolo ....69 l
Jaipur ....61 b
Jaisalmer ....60 k
Jakarta ....68 w
Jakes Corner ....11 l

Jakobstad (Pietarsaari) ....33 i
Jalaid Qi ....58 e
Jalalabad ....60 k
Jalapa ....19 q
Jalaula ....39 e
Jalda ....54 o
Jalgaon ....61 n
Jalingo ....41 i
Jalna ....61 o
Jalpaiguri ....61 k
Jalu ....38 b
Jalu Oasis ....38 b
Jamaica 21
Jamalpur ....61 y
Jamanxim ....25 l
Jamari ....25 t
Jamarovka ....57 g
Jambi ....68 h
Jambogan ....67 g
James (River, S.Dakota) ...15 h
James (River, Virginia) .....16 x
James Bay ....16 k
James Bay (Bay) ....16 i
Jameson Land ....91 c
James Ross Island ....82 t
Jamestown (North Dakota)15 h
Jamestown (Pennsylvania)16 w
Jammu ....61 a
Jammu and Kashmir ....61 a
Jamnagar ....60 x
Jamshedpur ....61 u
Jamuna ....61 x
Jamysevo ....56 b
Janaúba ....29 i
Janaucú ....26 l
Jane Peak ....79 q
Janesville ....16 r
Jangijul' ....55 u
Jánina ....35 q
Janjira ....60 z
Jan Mayen ....32 h
Janos ....18 j
Januária ....29 h
Janzur ....37 h
Japan.......................58-59
Japan, Sea of ....58 y
Japurá ....25 c
Jaramillo ....30 x
Jardim ....28 m
Jari ....26 j
Jarma ....37 u
Jaroslavl ....50 p
Jartai ....57 q
Jarú ....25 t
Jarud Qi ....58 d
Jaruu ....56 m
Jashpurnagar ....61 t
Jask ....60 o
Jason Pensinsula ....82 u
Jasper (Canada) ....14 j
Jasper (Indiana) ....16 s
Jasper (Texas) ....19 f
Jatai ....29 c
Jati ....60 w
Jatobá ....26 w
Jatobal ....26 y
Jatuarana ....25 i
Jaú ....25 g
Jauaperi ....26 c
Jauja ....24 x
Jaumave ....19 o
Jauperi ....25 h
Java ....68 x
Java Sea ....69 z
Jawand ....60 g
Jawhar ....60 z
Jaya (Mount) ....70 l
Jayapura ....70 w
Jaypur ....61 s
Jebba ....14 d
Jebel Ali ....39 y
Jebel Igdet ....36 g
Jebel Marra ....42 f
Jeberos ....24 j
Jebri ....60 h
Jeddah ....39 n
Jefferson City ....16 p
Jeffreys Bay ....49 n
Jekabpils ....33 w
Jekebpils ....33 w
Jelebri Corner ....11 l
Jeleninskij ....52 s

Jember..........................69 o
Jenda ....45 t
Jens Munk Island ....13 f
Jequié ....27 s
Jequitinhonha ....29 k
Jerbent ....55 p
Jeremoabo......................27 t
Jerez ....18 z
Jerez de la Frontera ....34 p
Jerramungup ....76 p
Jersey ....32 x
Jerusalem ....35 y
Jessore ....61 x
Jesup ....20 l
Jesús Carranza ....20 p
Jevlach ....54 v
Jhang-Maghiana ....60 l
Jhansi ....61 q
Jhang-Maghiana ....60 l
Ji'an ....63 p
Jianchuan ....62 t
Jiangcheng ....62 u
Jiangjumiao ....56 u
Jiangjuntai ....56 z
Jiangmen (Kongmoon) .....63 o
Jiangquanzi ....56 z
Jianping ....57 y
Jianshui ....62 v
Jianyang ....62 j
Jiaohe ....58 h
Jiao Xian ....58 p
Jiaozuo ....63 c
Jiayin ....58 i
Jiayuguan ....56 z
Jibóia ....25 b
Jieyang ....63 q
Jigzhi ....62 h
Jihlava ....33 s
Jijiga ....43 f
Jili Hu ....56 g
Jilin (Kirin) ....58 g
Jima ....43 b
Jiménez ....19 p
Jiménez (Mexican
Plateau) ....18 l
Jinan (Tsinan) ....63 e
Jinchang ....57 o
Jinchuan ....62 h
Jingdong ....62 u
Jinghong ....62 t
Jingning ....62 k
Jing Xian ....62 z
Jingyu ....58 g
Jingyuan ....62 j
Jinhe (Borohoro Shan) .....56 r
Jinhe ....58 d
Jining ....63 e
Jinja ....42 z
Jinka ....43 n
Jinping ....62 v
Jinsha ....62 k
Jinsha Jiang ....62 t
Jiparaná ....25 u
Jipijapa ....24 g
Jirin Gol ....57 x
Jishou ....62 m
Jiuding Shan ....62 j
Jiuquan ....56 z
Jiwani ....60 r
Jizan ....43 f
Joaçaba ....29 p
Joo Monlevade ....29 i
Joo Pessoa ....27 w
Joaquín V. González ....28 u
Jodhpur ....60 z
Joensuu ....33 l
Jofane ....49 h
Johannesburg ....49 p
John Day ....14 j
John Day (River) ....14 i
Johnsons Crossing ....11 l
Johnston, Lakes ....76 g
Johnstown ....16 w
Johor ....68 h
Johor Baharu ....68 h
Joinville ....29 r
Joinville Island ....82 g
Jojoca ....26 v
Jojutla ....19 o
Joliet ....16 r

Jolo ....67 t
Jolo Group ....67 t
Jomda ....62 e
Jonesboro ....16 q
Jones Sound ....13 d
Jönköping ....33 o
Joplin ....15 w
Jordan (USA)..................15 c
Jordan (State).................38
Jorhāt ....62 p
Jorullo ....19 n
Jos ....41 g
José Bonifácio ....25 v
José de San Martin ....30 v
Joseph Bonaparte Gulf.....73 a
Joseph, Lake ....17 e
José Rodrigues ....26 x
Jryupinsk ....54 f
Juan Aldama ....18 z
Juan de Fuca, Strait ....14 g
Juan de Nova (Island) .....47 a
Juan Fernández Islands...30 c
Juanjuí ....24 j
Juan Sola ....28 h
Juarez, Sierra de ....18 d
Juàzeiro ....27 s
Juàzeiro do Norte ....27 s
Juazohn ....40 u
Juba ....42 x
Jubany ....82 x
Juba (River) ....43 s
Jubbah ....39 b
Júcar ....34 s
Juchatengo ....19 q
Juchipila ....18 z
Juchitán ....20 p
Juiz de Fora ....29 i
Juli ....25 o
Juliaca ....25 o
Julia Creek ....73 w
Julian ....62 j
Juliana Top ....23 y
Jullundur ....61 a
Junagadh ....60 x
Junan ....63 g
Junction City ....15 v
Jundah ....77 i
Jundiai ....29 g
Juneau ....11 y
Junee ....78 c
Junggar Pendi ....56 j
Junín ....31 a
Junin de los Andes ....30 h
Juntuliang ....57 s
Jura ....34 j
Juruá ....25 d
Juruena ....25 w
Juruena (River) ....25 w
Justo Daract ....28 s
Jutaí ....25 c
Juatí (River) ....25 c
Juticalpa ....22 e
Jutland ....33 p
Juyom ....39 k
Jwaneng ....49 a
Jyväskylä ....33 k

K

K2 ....55 z
Kaabong ....42 x
Kabaena ....69 u
Kabakly ....55 q
Kabala ....40 f
Kabale ....45 d
Kabalebo Reservoir ....23 z
Kabalo ....45 b
Kabanjahe ....68 c
Kabba ....41 r
Kabinda ....45 a
Kabo ....42 o
Kabompo ....44 z
Kabompo (River) ....44 z
Kabondo Dianda ....45 c
Kabongo ....45 a
Kaboudia, Cape ....34 z
Kabul ....60 j
Kabul (River) ....60 j
Kabului ....18 c

Kabunga	45 c	Kalimantan	69	Kangiqsujuaq	13 v	Karaton	54 m	Katanning	76 e
Kabwe	45 p	Kaliningrad	33 u	Kangmar	61 k	Karaul	51 g	Katchall	65 r
Kabyrga	55 e	Kalininsk	54 g	Kangmar (Zhari Namco)	61 h	Karaulkeldy	55 a	Katesh	45 h
Kachalola	45 r	Kaliro	42 y	Kangnŭng	58 v	Karayulgun	56 p	Katete	45 s
Kachikattsy	52 m	Kalispell	14 l	Kangro	61 h	Karazhingil	55 j	Katgi	61 r
Kachiry	56 a	Kalisz	33 t	Kangto	62 b	Karbala	39 d	Katherina	38 j
K'achta	57 e	Kalkfeld	48 h	Kangxiwar	61 d	Karbi	65 v	Katherine	73 c
Kadali	52 s	Kalkfontein	48 l	Kani	40 i	Karchev	54 b	Kathiawar	60 x
Kadan	65 h	Kalkrand	48 i	Kaniama	44 m	Karet	36 s	Kathmandu	61 h
Kadina	77 f	Kalli	76 e	Kanin Nos, Cape	50 d	Kargasok	51 s	Kati	40 h
Kadiri	64 g	Kalmar	33 s	Kanin Peninsula	50 e	Kargil	61 b	Katima Mulilo	49 a
Kadnoye	54 d	Kalni	61 y	Kankakee	16 r	Kargo	51 l	Katiola	40 j
Kadoma	49 e	Kaloko	45 a	Kankan	40 g	Kargopol	50 p	Katompi	45 a
Kadugli	42 j	Kalole	45 b	Kanker	61 s	Kari	41 h	Katoomba	78 d
Kaduna	41 f	Kalomo	45 n	Kankossa	40 f	Kariba	46 q	Katowice	33 t
Kaduna (River)	41 e	Kalpa	61 c	Kankroli	60 z	Kariba Reservoir	46 q	Katsina	41 f
Kadzherom	50 w	Kaltag	11 b	Kannapolis	16 w	Karima	38 v	Kattakurgan	55 s
Kadzhi	51 s	Kaluga	54 c	Kannauj	61 e	Karimata	68 l	Kattegat	33 q
Kaédi	40 d	Kalumburu	72 m	Kano	41 g	Karimata Strait	68 k	Katun'	56 f
Kaesŏng	58 t	Kalyazin	50 p	Kanona	45 r	Karīmganj	61 z	Katyl'ga	51 l
Kafanchan	41 f	Kama	50 v	Kanpur	61 e	Karimnagar	61 l	Kauai	18 p
Kafue	46 d	Kamanga	52 n	Kansas	15 u	Karisimbi	45 d	Kaula	18 o
Kafue, Lake	49 c	Kamanjab	48 g	Kansas City	16 o	Karkheh	39 f	Kaunas	33 v
Kaga	55 b	Kamba	41 c	Kansk	56 l	Karkinitskiy Bay	35 k	Kaura Namoda	41 f
Kaga Bandoro	42 o	Kambia	40 d	Kantchari	41 a	Karla-Aleksandra	50 k	Kavalerovo	58 l
Kagan	55 s	Kambove	45 n	Kantemirovka	54 e	Karlik Shan	56 x	Kavali	64 h
Kagizman	54 t	Kamchatka	10/53	Kanuku Mts.	23/26	Karlovac	35 b	Kaval'kan	53 p
Kagora	41 g	Kamchatsk	10 n	Kanye	49 a	Karlsbad	33 r	Kaválla	35 f
Kagoschima	58 v	Kamen	51 k	Kanyu	49 a	Karlskrona	33 s	Kavendou	40 e
Kahal Tabelbala	36 k	Kamenets-Podol'skiy	33 x	Kaohsiung	63 t	Karlsruhe	33 p	Kavieng	71 r
Kahama	45 f	Kamenka	54 g	Kaolack	40 b	Karlstad	33 q	Kavkaz	54 p
Kahan	60 j	Kamenka (Angara)	51 x	Kaoma	45 n	Karma	42 c	Kavumu	42 v
Kahemba	44 j	Kamenka (Don)	54 e	Kaoyui Lake	58 o	Karmé	41 l	Kaw	26 j
Kahnuj	60 b	Kamen-na-Obi	56 c	Kapalala	45 q	Karnak	38 j	Kawambwa	45 q
Kahoolawe	18 q	Kamensk	57 e	Kapanga	44 m	Karnal	61 b	Kawasaki	59 n
Kahului	18 r	Kamensk-Shakhinskiy	54 e	Kapatu	46 e	Karnali	61 f	Kawatop	26 h
Kaiama	41 f	Kamensk-Ural'skiy	50 y	Kapčagaj	55 y	Karnaprayag	61 d	Kawio	69 k
Kaidu	56 s	Kamet	61 d	Kapchagayskoye		Karoi	49 e	Kawio Islands	67 w
Kaifeng	63 d	Kamiji	44 m	Reservoir	56 o	Karonga	46 h	Kawlin	62 q
Kai Islands	70 q	Kamileroi	73 v	Kapedo	43 n	Karora	38 z	Kaya	40 m
Kaikoura	79 u	Kamina	45 a	Kapia	44 j	Karoy	55 l	Kayan	69 d
Kaili	62 y	Kamkaly	55 v	Kapingamarangi Atoll	71 g	Kárpathos	35 u	Kayanza	45 d
Kailua	18 r	Kamloops	14 i	Kapiri Mposhi	46 d	Karrats Fjord	90 m	Kaycee	15 c
Kailu He	58 d	Kamo	51 y	Kapka	42 d	Karridale	76 c	Kayes	40 d
Kaimana	70 r	Kamoa Mts.	23/26	Kapoeta	42 z	Kars	54 t	Kayonza	45 e
Kainji Reservoir	41 d	Kampala	42 x	Kapona	45 d	Karshi	54 y	Kaysatskoye	54 i
Kairouan	34 y	Kampar	66 r	Kapsabet	43 n	Karsi	55 t	Kayseri	35 z
Kaiser Franz Josephs		Kampar (River)	66 s	Kapsan	58 h	Karskiye Vorota, Proliv	50 j	Kayunga	42 y
Fjord	91 r	Kampene	45 b	Kapuas	69 a	Kartaly	55 d	Kazabegi	54 u
Kaitaia	79 g	Kamskoje Reservoir	50 v	Kapuskasing	16 h	Karumba	73 i	Kazach	54 u
Kaiyuan	58 f	Kamuli	42 y	Kapustin-Yar	54 i	Karun	39 h	Kazachinskoye	57 f
Kaiyuan	62 v	Kamyshin	54 h	Karaaul	56 b	Karunjie	72 m	Kazach'ye	53 c
Kajaani	33 k	Kan	56 k	Kara-Balta	55 x	Karwar	64 c	Kazakdarya	55 p
Kajabbi	73 v	Kanaaupscow	16 l	Karabas	55 m	Karymskoje	57 i	Kazakstan	55 e
Kajiado	45 i	Kanab	14 z	Kara-Bogaz-Gol	54 z	Kasai	44 j	Kazak Uplands	55 d
Kajnar	56 a	Kananda	52 b	Karabük	35 k	Kasaji	44 z	Kazalinsk	55 d
Kajo-Kaji	42 x	Kananga	44 l	Karabutak	55 c	Kasala	43 a	Kazan'	54 j
Kajrakkumskoje Reservoir	55 v	Kanash	54 i	Karachi	60 v	Kasama	45 r	Kazandžik	55 n
Kaka	43 c	Kanawolo	40 j	Kara Dag	54 q	Kasambule	45 b	Kazerun	39 j
Kakamas	48 y	Kanazawa	58 z	Karaganda	55 k	Kasanga	45 r	Kazhim	50 u
Kakamega	42 z	Kanbe	66 a	Karagayly	55 l	Kasar, Ras	39 n	Kazumba	44 l
Kakenge	44 l	Kanbetlet	62 p	Karaginskiy Island	10 o	Kasba Lake	12 x	Kazungula	49 a
Kakhovskoye Reservoir	54 c	Kanchanaburi	65 i	Karaj	39 i	Kasembe	45 p	Kazym	51 o
Kakinada	64 j	Kanchipuram	64 h	Karakax	61 c	Kasempa	45 n	Kazymskaya	51 n
Kaktovik	11 h	Kanchow	63 p	Karakoram Range	61 a	Kasenga	45 p	Kazyr	56 k
Kakuma	42 z	Kand	60 i	Karakore	43 c	Kasese	42 w	Kearney	15 c
Kalaallit Nunaat		Kandahar	60 h	Karakul, Lake	55 x	Kashan	39 j	Keban Lake	54 q
(Greenland)	90-91	Kandalaksa	50 a	Kara Kum	55 o	Kashgar	55 y	Kebili	37 f
Kalabagh	60 l	Kandalaksa Gulf	50 a	Karakumskiy Canal	55 r	Kashgert	50 z	Kebkabiya	42 f
Kalachinsk	55 l	Kandangan	69 p	Karalon	52 t	Kashing	63 h	Kebnekaise	33 g
Kalach-na-Donu	54 g	Kandi	41 c	Karalundi	76 f	Kashiwazaki	59 n	Kebri Dehar	43 t
Kalahari	48 n	Kandrian	71 p	Karaman	35 y	Kashkanteniz	55 j	Kediri	69 n
Kalakan	52 u	Kandy	64 v	Karamay	56 r	Kashmar	60 c	Kédougou	40 d
Kalamai	35 r	Kandychan	53 v	Karamea Bight	79 s	Kashmir	61 a	Kedrovyy	51 n
Kalamare	49 b	Kane	16 x	Karamysheva	51 z	Kasindi	45 d	Kedva	50 v
Kalamazoo	16 t	Kánea	35 t	Karana	39 v	Kaskalen	55 y	Keele Peak	11 m
Kalamba	42 o	Kane Basin	91 e	Karanambo	23 x	Kasli	55 c	Keeroongooloo	77 i
Kalandula	44 u	Kanem	41 l	Karand	39 e	Kasongo	45 b	Keetmanshoop	48 w
Kalao	69 u	Kaneohe	18 q	Karang	40 b	Kasongo-Lunda	44 h	Keflavík	32 a
Kalaqi	58 d	Kang	48 m	Karaozek	55 o	Kass	42 f	Kegen	56 p
Kalar	52 u	Kangalassay	52 m	Karasaj	55 z	Kassel	33 p	Keibeb	48 j
Kalasin	66 g	Kangan (Australia)	72 u	Karasay	56 r	Kasserine	34 y	Keimoes	48 y
Kalat	60 i	Kangan (Iran)	39 j	Karasayo	61 g	Kastamonu	35 l	Kéita ou Doka	42 b
Kalbarri	76 b	Kangaroo Island	77 v	Karasburg	48 w	Kasulu	45 e	Kekuk	53 y
Kalekol	43 n	Kangavar	39 f	Kara Sea	50 l	Kasungu	45 t	Kel'	52 k
Kalemie	45 d	Kangchenjunga	61 j	Karashoky	55 l	Kasur	61 a	Kelafo	43 t
Kalemyo	62 p	Kangding	62 h	Karasino	51 h	Kata	52 n	Kelang	68 f
Kalevala	33 m	Kangean	69 p	Karasuk	56 b	Kataba	49 a	Kelantan	66 s
Kalgoorlie	76 g	Kangerlussuaq	91 n	Karatal	56 n	Katamobagu	67 w	Kelem	43 n
Kalima	45 b	Kangiqsualujjuaq	13 x	Kara Tau	55 v	Katanda	44 m	Kélibia	34 z

Kéllé..............................44 g
Kellerberrin....................76 e
Kellog............................51 u
Kelo..............................41 l
Kelowna.........................14 i
Keluang..........................68 h
Kembolcha......................43 d
Kemerovo.......................56 f
Kemi..............................33 j
Kemi (River)....................33 k
Kemijärvi........................33 k
Kemkara.........................53 q
Kemmerer.......................15 n
Kemp Land......................85 a
Kempsey.........................78 g
Ken...............................61 r
Kenadsa.........................36 j
Kenai.............................11 e
Kenai Peninsula...............11 e
Kenamuke Swamp............42 z
Kencha...........................53 q
Kendari..........................69 v
Kendégué........................42 b
Kenema..........................40 s
Kenge............................44 h
Kenhardt.........................48 y
Kenitra...........................36 h
Kenmare.........................15 f
Kenmaur.........................49 d
Kennedy.........................62 p
Kenner...........................19 n
Kennya...........................53 c
Keno Hill........................11 k
Kenora...........................15 j
Kenosha..........................16 r
Kentau...........................55 u
Kent Group......................78 p
Kenton...........................16 u
Kentucky.........................16 s
Kenya.........................43/45
Kenya (Mount).................43 o
Kenzou...........................41 x
Keokuk...........................16 p
Kerch'...........................54 c
Kerekyano......................52 k
Kerema..........................71 n
Keren............................43 b
Kerguelen.....................231 r
Kericho..........................43 n
Keirči............................55 s
Kerinci...........................68 f
Keriske..........................53 a
Keriya............................61 f
Kerkenna Islands..............34 z
Kerma............................38 u
Kermadec Islands.............79 l
Kerman...........................60 b
Kérouané........................40 h
Kerrville.........................19 b
Kerzaz...........................36 l
Kesagami Lake.................16 j
Kesen............................59 p
Keshvar..........................39 g
Ket...............................51 s
Keta, Lake.......................51 l
Ketapang........................68 l
Ketchikan........................11 y
Key Afer.........................43 n
Keyano...........................17 a
Keyi..............................56 q
Key Largo.......................20 n
Key West........................20 y
Kez...............................50 v
Khabalakh.......................52 r
Khabarovsk......................58 m
Khabary..........................56 b
Khairpur.........................60 j
Khakhar..........................53 o
Khakhea.........................48 m
Khalesavoy......................51 r
Khal'mer-Yu.....................50 m
Khamasin........................39 r
Khambhat........................60 y
Khamis Mushait................39 q
Kham-Keut......................66 h
Khammam........................64 h
Khampa..........................52 j
Khamra..........................52 s
Khandwa.........................61 o
Khandyga........................53 b

Khangokurt......................50 z
Khanh Hung.....................66 i
Khani.............................52 v
Khanka, Lake...................58 k
Khantau..........................55 x
Khantayka.......................51 h
Khantayskoye, Lake...........51 i
Khantayskoye Reservoir......51 h
Khanty-Mansiysk...............51 n
Khanyangda.....................53 r
Khara-Aldan....................53 a
Kharabalio.......................54 i
Kharagpur.......................61 v
Kharalakh.......................52 k
Kharan...........................60 h
Khara-Tala......................53 j
Khara-Tas.......................53 b
Khargon..........................61 o
Kharkov..........................54 c
Kharstan.........................53 d
Khartoum........................42 k
Khartoum North................42 l
Khasalakh.......................52 k
Khash............................60 e
Khashm al Girba...............43 a
Khash Rud.......................60 f
Khastakh........................53 e
Khatanga........................52 a
Khatanga (River)...............52 a
Khatyngnakh....................53 n
Khatyngnakh
(Chereskogo Mountains)..53 g
Khatyrka.........................10 f
Khay..............................39 o
Khayber..........................39 a
Khemarat........................66 h
Khemis Miliana.................34 t
Khemisset.......................36 h
Khenchela.......................34 w
Kherson..........................35 k
Kheta.............................51 m
Kheta (River)....................51 m
Khiaw............................65 k
Khmel'nitskiy...................35 h
Khobolchan......................53 d
Khochot..........................52 j
Khokiley.........................51 i
Kholmsk..........................59 c
Khomokashevo.................52 p
Khomotovka.....................54 b
Khoms...........................35 n
Khong............................66 i
Khongo..........................53 i
Khongsey........................53 i
Khon Kaen......................65 l
Khonu............................53 f
Khoppuruo......................52 v
Khor (Iran)......................39 l
Khor (Russia)...................58 l
Khordogoy.......................52 g
Khorgo..........................52 f
Khorixas.........................48 g
Khormuj.........................39 i
Khoronkhu......................52 m
Khoronnokh.....................52 j
Khorramabad...................39 g
Khorramshahr..................39 g
Khouribga.......................36 h
Khoy..............................54 u
Khroma..........................53 f
Khrom-Tau......................55 b
Khuff.............................39 q
Khujand..........................55 u
Khulais...........................39 n
Khulm...........................60 i
Khulna...........................61 x
Khurais..........................39 t
Khurasan........................55 o
Khurd............................60 h
Khusf.............................60 c
Khuzdar.........................60 i
Khuzdzhakh....................53 f
Khyber Pass....................60 l
Kiambi...........................45 c
Kiamusze........................58 j
Kibangou........................44 e
Kiberg, Cape....................33 m
Kibiti.............................45 k
Kibombo.........................45 a
Kibondo.........................45 e

Kibre Mengist..................43 q
Kibuye...........................45 d
Kichi Kichi.......................37 x
Kidal.............................37 n
Kidira.............................40 e
Kiel...............................33 p
Kiel Bay..........................33 p
Kielce............................33 u
Kieta.............................71 u
Kiev..............................35 j
Kiev Reservoir..................33 y
Kiewietskuil.....................48 z
Kiffa..............................40 e
Kigali.............................45 d
Kigilyakh.........................53 d
Kigisa............................13 k
Kigoma...........................45 d
Kiik...............................55 j
Kiikkaškan.......................55 m
Kii Strait.........................58 y
Kijabe............................43 n
Kikagati..........................45 e
Kikao.............................49 a
Kikiakki..........................51 s
Kikki..............................60 s
Kikondja.........................45 a
Kikori............................70 z
Kikwit...........................44 i
Kilembe..........................44 k
Kilibo.............................41 o
Kilifi..............................45 l
Kilimanjaro......................45 j
Kilindoni.........................45 k
Kilkoris...........................42 z
Killarney.........................32 u
Killeen...........................19 c
Kil'mez...........................50 u
Kilosa............................45 i
Kimball, Mount.................11 h
Kimberley........................49 n
Kimberley Downs..............72 l
Kimberley Plateau.............72 m
Kimchaek........................58 i
Kimpese..........................44 f
Kimvula..........................44 g
Kinabulu.........................67 p
Kindersley.......................15 b
Kindia............................40 d
Kindu.............................45 a
Kineshma........................54 f
Kinesma.........................50 r
Kingaroy.........................74 t
King Christian IX Land........90 z
King Christian X Land........91 a
King City........................14 u
King Frederick VI Coast.....90 v
King Frederick VIII Land.....90 n
King George Island...........82 e
King Island......................77 w
King Leopold and
Queen Astrid Coast.........85 r
King Leopold Range...........72 l
Kingman.........................14 z
Kingombe.........................45 b
Kingoonya.......................77 o
King Oscars Fjord.............91 r
King Peninsula..................81 a
Kingri............................60 k
King Salmon.....................11 p
King Sound......................72 k
Kingsport.........................16 u
Kingston (Canada)............16 y
Kingston (Jamaica)...........21 o
Kingston (USA)................16 z
Kingston upon Hull...........32 y
Kingstown.......................23 j
Kingsville........................19 c
Kingtehchen....................63 f
King Wilhelm II Land.........85 s
King William Island...........12 m
King Williams Town...........49 p
Kinhwa..........................63 g
Kinkala..........................44 g
Kinoosao........................12 x
Kinshasa.........................44 h
Kintampo........................40 m
Kintus............................51 o
Kinyeti...........................42 y
Kipaka............................45 b
Kipembawe......................45 g

Kipushi...........................45 o
Kirakira..........................75 a
Kirbey............................52 b
Kirbey (Arga-Sala)............52 d
Kirenga..........................52 q
Kirensk..........................52 q
Kirgiz Steppe...................55 a
Kiri...............................44 j
Kiribati.........................231 l
Kirikkale.........................35 y
Kirim.............................42 i
Kirin..............................58 g
Kirinyaga (Kenya).............43 o
Kirit..............................43 h
Kiritimati......................230 b
Kiriwina or Trobriand
Island.........................71 r
Kiriyestyakh....................52 l
Kirkenes.........................33 l
Kirkland Lake...................16 j
Kirkpatrick, Mt.................86 c
Kirksville........................15 x
Kirkuk...........................39 e
Kirkwood.........................49 o
Kirov.............................50 t
Kirovakan........................54 u
Kirovograd.......................35 k
Kirovsk..........................50 a
Kirovskiy.........................58 l
Kirrikkale........................54 o
Kirs...............................50 u
Kirsanov.........................54 g
Kirthar Range...................60 i
Kiruna............................33 h
Kirundu..........................45 a
Kisangani........................42 s
Kisarawe.........................45 k
Kiseleva.........................53 h
Kisel'ovsk.......................56 g
Kishtwar.........................61 a
Kisi...............................58 j
Kisigu............................45 g
Kisii..............................45 h
Kisima............................43 o
Kisimaio.........................43 s
Kiska.............................10 t
Kislovodsk.......................54 s
Kissidougou.....................40 g
Kisumu...........................45 g
Kita...............................40 g
Kita-Kjūshū.....................58 v
Kitale............................43 n
Kitami............................59 d
Kit Carson.......................15 r
Kitchener-Waterloo............16 w
Kitgum...........................42 y
Kithira............................38 c
Kitimat...........................14 d
Kitui..............................45 j
Kitunda..........................45 f
Kitutu............................45 c
Kitwe.............................45 p
Kiukiang.........................63 e
Kivitoo...........................13 l
Kivu, Lake.......................45 c
Kizema...........................50 r
Kizilirmak........................35 l
Kiziltepe.........................54 r
Kiz'lar...........................54 v
Kizyl-Arvat......................55 n
Kizyl Jilga.......................61 o
Klabat............................67 w
Klaeng...........................65 k
Klagenfurt.......................35 a
Klamath Falls...................14 u
Klar...............................33 e
Klerksdorp......................49 e
Kliapeda.........................33 u
Klin...............................57 k
Klin (Moscow)..................50 o
Klintsy...........................54 a
Knob, Cape.....................76 f
Knox Coast......................87 l
Knoxville (Iowa)................15 x
Knoxville (Tennessee).......16 u
Knud Rasmussens Land...91 d
Knysna...........................48 z
Kobbo...........................43 d
Kobdo...........................56 i
Kobe.............................58 y

København (Copenhagen)33 q
Kobenni.........................40 g
Koblenz.........................33 o
Kobuk............................11 c
Kobya............................52 l
Kočečum........................51 m
Koch Bihr.......................60 k
Kochechum......................52 b
Kochi.............................58 y
Kochikha........................51 k
Kochubey........................54 v
Kodarma.........................61 v
Kodiak...........................11 r
Kodiak (Island).................11 r
Koës..............................48 x
Koforidua........................40 z
Kogon............................40 c
Koh-e-Baba.....................60 i
Kohīma..........................52 o
Koidern..........................11 j
Koidu............................40 f
Kokand..........................55 v
Kokaral..........................55 c
Kokchetav.......................55 i
Kokiu............................62 v
Kok-Jangak.....................55 x
Kokkola..........................33 i
Kokoma..........................16 s
Kokonau.........................70 t
Kokpekty........................56 d
Koksoak.........................13 w
Kokstad.........................49 r
Kokuora.........................53 f
Kokwo...........................43 n
Kola..............................50 c
Kolaka...........................69 u
Kolar.............................64 c
Kolari............................33 j
Kolarovgrad.....................35 h
Kolbio............................43 r
Kolda............................40 c
Kolding..........................33 p
Kole..............................42 t
Kolesovo.........................53 i
Kogujev..........................50 g
Kolhapur........................64 c
Kolik'yegan......................51 q
Kolin.............................33 s
Kolkata (Calcutta).............61 w
Kolmya...........................53 j
Köln (Cologne).................33 o
Kolokani.........................40 h
Kolomna.........................54 e
Kolomyya........................35 g
Kolono...........................69 u
Kolpashevo......................51 t
Kolpino..........................33 m
Koltovkinda......................52 u
Kolva.............................50 w
Kolva (Bol'shezemel'skaya
Tundra)........................50 j
Kolwezi..........................46 b
Kolyma..........................53 j
Kolmyskiy Mountains.........53 j
Kolymskiy Plain................53 j
Komadugu......................41 j
Komanda.........................42 w
Komandor Islands.............10 p
Komatipoort.....................49 g
Komelek.........................53 a
Komoé...........................40 x
Kom Ombo......................38 g
Komotini.........................35 g
Kompong Cham................66 i
Kompong Chhnang...........66 h
Kompong Som..................66 h
Komsberg.......................48 j
Komsomolets....................55 e
Komsomolets (Island)........51 k
Komsomol'sk....................51 u
Komsomol'skaya...............85 n
Komsomol'skiy.................50 z
Komsomol'sk-na-Amure....53 p
Konda............................51 n
Kondakovo......................53 j
Kondoa Irangi..................45 i
Kondon..........................58 m
Kong.............................40 k
Kongbo..........................42 g
Kongmoon......................63 g

Kongor...................48 m
Kongor...................42 x
Kongsvinger............33 d
Kongwa..................45 i
Koniakari...............40 f
Konkouré...............40 d
Konongo.................40 z
Konosa..................50 p
Konotop.................54 a
Konqi....................56 t
Konso...................43 o
Kontagora..............41 e
Kontum..................66 j
Konya...................35 y
Konzaboy...............53 l
Kopet Dag..............55 o
Kopiago.................70 y
Korča...................35 e
Korčula.................35 b
Korda...................51 y
Kordofan...............42 j
Korea, North...........58
Korea, South..........58/63
Korea Bay..............58 r
Korea Strait...........58 v
Korennoye..............52 c
Koreyver...............50 k
Korf.....................10 b
Korhogo.................40 j
Kor-i-Hisar............60 h
Korinth..................35 s
Kōriyama...............59 o
Korkodon...............53 j
Korkodon (River).......53 k
Korla....................56 s
Korliki..................51 x
Koro.....................40 i
Korobovskiy............55 l
Korogwe.................45 j
Koronadal..............67 w
Koror....................70 y
Koro Sea...............75 m
Korosten...............35 i
Koro Toro..............42 b
Korsakov...............59 d
Korti....................38 v
Korti Linchang.........56 g
Koryaken Mountains....10 d
Kos-Agač...............56 h
Kosciuszko, Mount......77 z
Kosha...................38 u
Košice...................35 d
Kosrae..................71 m
Kossou Reservoir.......40 v
Kosti....................42 l
Kostino..................51 u
Kostroma...............50 q
Kosyu...................50 x
Kószalin................33 s
Kota.....................61 o
Kota Baharu............66 s
Kotabaru...............69 q
Kotabumi................68 u
Kota-i Ashro...........60 j
Kota Kinabalu..........69 c
Kotamobagu............69 j
Kotel'nich..............50 t
Kotel'nikovo...........54 g
Kotel'nyy..............53 b
Kotel'nyy (Island).....53 d
Kotido..................42 z
Kotikova................58 l
Kotka...................52 k
Kotlas..................50 s
Koto.....................59 b
Kotri....................60 v
Kotto....................42 q
Kotturu.................64 e
Kotui....................51 l
Kotuykan...............52 b
Kotzebue................11 a
Kotzebue Sound........10 m
Kouango................42 p
Koudougou.............40 l
Kougouleu..............41 u
Kouilou.................44 d
Koukdjuak..............13 i
Koulamoutou...........44 d
Koulikoro..............40 i
Koulou..................41 c

Koumpentoum..........40 c
Koumra.................41 m
Kounala.................40 j
Koundara...............40 d
Koundougou............40 k
Kourou..................26 j
Kouroussa..............40 g
Koutouba...............40 k
Kouyou..................44 g
Kova.....................51 z
Kovel'...................33 w
Kovrizhka..............10 a
Kovroy..................54 f
Kowares.................48 g
Kowloon.................63 q
Koxlax..................56 p
Koyma Reservoir.......64 c
Koyuk...................11 a
Kozan...................35 z
Kozáni...................35 r
Kozhevnikovo..........52 e
Kpalimé.................41 n
Kpandu..................41 n
Kpessi...................41 a
Kra, Isthmus of.........66 d
Krakatau................68 v
Krakow..................33 t
Kramatorsk............54 c
Kramfors................33 f
Krasino..................50 i
Krasnaya Yaranga......10 j
Krasnoarmeyesk........55 i
Krasnoarmeyskiy.......10 e
Krasnobrodskij.........56 g
Krasnodar..............54 r
Krasnojarsk............56 j
Krasnokamsk..........50 v
Krasnosel'kup.........51 s
Krasnoslobodsk........54 h
Krasnotur'insk........50 x
Krasnoufimsk..........50 w
Krasnousol'skiy.......55 a
Krasnoyarskiy..........55 i
Krasnoyarskoye Reservoir56 i
Krasnyye-Baki.........50 s
Krasnyy-Yar...........54 i
Kratie...................66 i
Kreb en Naga..........36 u
Kremenchug............35 l
Kremenchugskoye
  Reservoir.............35 l
Kresty..................51 i
Krichev..................33 z
Krishna.................64 g
Krishnagiri.............64 f
Kristianstad...........33 r
Kristiansund...........33 b
Krivoy Rog.............35 k
Krk......................35 a
Kronok..................53 z
Kronprins Frederiks
  Bjaerge...............90 z
Kroonstad..............49 p
Kropotkin...............54 f
Kropotkin
(Patomskoye Plateau)..52 t
Krotovka...............54 l
Kruglikovo..............58 m
Kruis, Cape............48 f
Krung Thep (Bangkok)..66 e
Ksabi....................36 l
Ksabi Talsinnt..........36 j
Ksar el Boukhari.......37 a
Ksar el Kebir..........34 o
Ksar es Souk..........36 j
Ksar Torchane.........36 q
Kuala Belait...........69 b
Kuala Kubu Baharu....68 u
Kuala Lipis............66 s
Kuala Lumpur..........66 r
Kuala Terengganu......66 t
Kuancheng.............57 y
Kuandang...............69 j
Kuandian................58 f
Kuango..................44 h
Kuantan.................66 t
Kuba.....................54 w
Kuban'..................54 d
Kubor....................70 z
Kuching.................68 m

Kudu-Kuyuel'...........52 v
Kudymkar..............50 v
Kufrah Oasis...........38 p
Kugluktuk (Coppermine)..12 f
Kugulta.................54 g
Kuhak....................60 f
Kuh Lab, Ras...........60 u
Kuito....................44 u
Kukan...................58 k
Kul......................39 l
Kul'ab...................55 u
Kulagino................54 k
Kulai....................68 h
Kulakshi................55 a
Kulaly...................54 x
Kulanoy.................55 b
Kular....................53 a
Kule.....................48 k
Kulgera.................77 b
Kulinda.................52 o
Kul'sary................54 m
Kultay...................54 y
Kulu.....................61 c
Kulunda.................56 b
Kulundinskaya Steppe..56 b
Kulundinskoje, Lake....56 b
Kulynigol...............51 s
Kuma....................54 t
Kumari..................54 t
Kumamoto..............58 w
Kumanovo..............35 e
Kumarina...............76 f
Kumasi..................40 z
Kumertau..............55 a
Kumkuduk..............56 w
Kunar...................60 l
Kunašir.................59 f
Kunduz..................60 j
Kungrad................55 o
Kungu...................42 o
Kungur..................50 w
Kungur (Mount)........55 y
Kunlun Shan...........61 h
Kunming................62 v
Kunsan..................58 t
Kuntuk..................53 t
Kununurra..............73 a
Kuogastakh............53 a
Kuopio..................33 k
Kuoyka..................52 i
Kupang..................69 v
Kupino..................56 b
Kuqa....................56 q
Kura.....................54 t
Kuragino................56 j
Kuraj....................56 g
Kurčum..................56 e
Kürdžali................35 g
Kureyka.................51 j
Kureyskaya.............52 r
Kurgal'dzhino.........55 i
Kurgan..................55 f
Kurgan-T'ube..........55 u
Kuria Muria Islands....60 n
Kuri Bay................72 j
Kuril Islands..........59 g
Kurleja..................57 l
Kurmuk..................42 m
Kurnool.................64 f
Kursk...................54 c
Kurtalan................54 s
Kurtamysh.............55 e
Kuruman................48 z
Kurundi.................73 s
Kurunegala.............64 u
Kurun Uryak...........53 o
Kur'ya..................50 w
Kusagan-Olokh.........53 a
Kushiro.................59 e
Kushmurun............55 f
Kuska...................60 e
Kuskokwim.............11 b
Kuskokwim Mountains..11 c
Kustanay...............55 e
Kut......................66 f
Kutacane...............68 d
Kütahya.................35 v
Kutaisi..................54 z
Kutch, Gulf of.........60 w

Kutch, Rann of.........60 x
Kutno...................33 t
Kutu.....................44 i
Kuujjuaq...............13 w
Kuujjuarapik...........16 k
Kuusamo................33 i
Kuwait..................39 g
Kuwait (State).........39
Kuybyschevskoye
  Reservoir............54 j
Kuyygan................55 x
Kuzmov'ka.............51 w
Kuznetsk...............54 i
Kvigtind.................33 e
Kwale...................45 k
Kwanga.................45 a
Kwangju................58 t
Kwango.................44 h
Kweilin..................63 n
Kweiyang...............62 x
Kwe Kwe...............46 r
Kwethluk...............11 a
Kwigillingok...........11 a
Kwiha...................43 d
Kwikila.................74 d
Kwilu....................44 i
Kwoko..................70 q
Kyaikto.................65 h
Kyaka...................45 e
Kyanjojo................42 x
Kyaukme................62 r
Kyaukpyu...............62 o
Kyauktaw..............62 o
Kycham-Kuyuel'.......53 g
Kynuna.................73 x
Kyoga, Lake...........42 y
Kyōto...................58 z
Kyrbana.................53 j
Kyren...................57 b
Kyrgyday...............52 j
Kyrta....................50 w
Kystatyam.............52 j
Kysyl-Suluo............53 c
Kysyl-Yllyk............52 f
Kytyl-Zhura............52 k
Kyuekh-Bulung........52 f
Kyushe..................55 n
Kyūshū.................58 w
Kyusyur................52 l
Kyyiv (Kiev)...........33 z
Kyyjärvi................33 j
Kyzyk...................54 y
Kyzyl....................56 k
Kyzyl-Chaja...........56 h
Kyzyl-Chem...........56 l
Kyzyl-Dzhar...........55 i
Kyzyl Kum.............55 r
Kyzyl-Orda............55 s
Kyzyluy.................55 f
Kzyltu...................55 j

L

La Almarcha...........34 r
La Asunción...........23 h
La Banda...............28 t
La Barca................18 z
Labaz, Lake............51 l
Labé....................40 e
Labe (Elbe)............33 f
Laboulaye..............30 m
Labrador................17 e
Labrador City.........17 c
Labrador Sea..........13 z
Lábrea..................25 e
Labuha.................67 y
Labuk Bay.............67 g
Labytnangi............50 m
La Calera...............28 o
La Campana............18 m
La Carbonera..........19 c
La Carlota..............28 u
La Ceiba................19 x
Lacepede Bay.........77 t
Lachlan.................78 a
La Chorrera...........24 m
Lac la Martre.........12 r
La Concepción........23 b

Laconia.................17 n
La Crosse...............16 q
Ladoga, Lake..........33 m
Lady Frere.............49 p
Lady Grey..............49 p
Ladysmith (South Africa)..49 r
Ladysmith (USA).......16 d
Lae......................71 o
Laem Ngop.............66 v
La Escalera............23 w
La Esmeralda..........23 t
La Esperanza..........25 u
Lafayette (Indiana)....16 s
Lafayette (Lousiana)...19 g
Lafia....................41 p
Laghouat...............34 u
Lagos (Nigeria).......41 p
Lagos (Portugal)......36 g
La Grande..............14 j
La Grande Rivière.....16 m
Lagrange...............72 w
Laguna de Bay.........67 g
Lagunas.................28 c
Lagunillas..............28 g
Lahad Datu............69 e
Lahat...................68 u
Lahej....................43 p
La Higuera.............28 o
Lahore..................61 a
Lahti....................33 j
Lai.......................41 m
Laibin...................62 z
Lai Chau................62 v
Laichou Bay...........58 p
Laingsburg.............48 y
Laisamis................43 p
Laiyang.................58 v
Laiyuan.................57 v
Lajeado.................29 o
Lajes....................29 q
Lajes (Cáatingas).....27 v
Lajinha.................25 k
La Julia.................30 v
La Junta................15 r
La Junta................18 j
Lake Charles..........19 g
Lake City (Florida)....20 l
Lake City (South Carolina)20 m
Lake Harbour..........13 w
Lake Havasu City.....18 e
Lake Jackson..........19 d
Lakeland...............20 l
Lake Nash.............73 u
Lake Ozark............15 x
Lake Providence......20 u
Lake River.............16 h
Lake Seul..............15 k
Lakeview...............14 v
Lakhpat.................60 w
Lakki....................60 l
Lakota..................40 w
Lakselv.................33 j
Lakshadweep.........64 b
Lalara...................44 d
Laleh Zar..............60 b
Lalin....................58 g
Lalitpur.................61 p
Lalyo....................42 x
Lama-Kara.............41 a
La Mancha.............18 m
Lama, Lake............51 i
Lamar...................15 s
La Martre, Lake.......12 r
Lambaréné.............44 c
Lambasa................75 m
Lambayeque...........24 g
Lambert Glacier.......84 y
Lambert Land.........91 l
La Merced..............24 x
Lamia...................35 s
La Misión...............18 c
Lamon Bay.............67 h
La Montaña............24/25
Lamotrek Atoll........71 a
Lampalla................24 y
Lampang................66 d
Lampedusa.............34 z
Lanai....................18 q
Lanbi....................65 h
Lancang.................62 t

Lancang Jiang ....62 t
Lancaster ....14 w
Lancaster (California) ....18 c
Lancaster (Pennsylvania) ..16 y
Lancaster Sound ....13 d
Lanchow ....62 j
Lândana ....44 d
Landeck ....34 l
Lander ....15 o
Landes ....34 f
Landless Corner ....45 p
Land's End ....32 v
La'nga Co ....61 e
Langano, Lake ....43 c
Langdon ....15 h
Langhko ....62 r
Langkawi ....66 q
Langöyo ....33 e
Langsa ....66 p
Lang Son ....62 x
La Noria ....25 v
Lansing ....16 t
Lanus ....31 c
Lanxi ....58 g
Lanzarote ....36 c
Lanzhou (Lanchow) ....62 j
Laoag ....67 f
Laoang ....67 j
La Oroya ....24 x
Laos 62/65-66
La Palma ....22 k
La Paragua ....23 h
La Parilla ....18 y
La Paz (Argentina) ....28 r
La Paz (Bolivia) ....25 p
La Paz (Honduras) ....22 d
La Paz (Mexico) ....18 u
La Paz (Paraná,
 Argentina) ....28 x
La Paz Bay ....18 h
La Pedrera ....25 b
La Pérouse Strait ....59 c
La Piedad ....18 z
La Plata ....31 c
Lappeenranta ....33 k
Lappland ....33 j
Laptev Sea ....52 h
Laptev Strait ....53 e
La Puntilla ....24 g
La Quiaca ....28 f
Lar ....39 k
Larache ....36 h
La Radisson ....16 k
Laramie ....15 q
Laranjal ....25 k
Larba ....52 w
Laredo ....19 b
Largo ....20 k
La Rioja ....28 r
Lárisa ....35 s
Larkana ....60 i
Larnaca ....35 y
La Rochelle ....34 e
La-Roche-sur-Yon ....34 e
La Romana ....21 u
La Ronge, Lake ....15 d
La Rons'yer ....50 l
Laropi ....42 x
Larrimah ....73 e
Larsen Ice Shelf ....82 v
Larvik ....33 c
Lar'yak ....51 z
Las Anod ....43 i
Las Bocas ....18 h
Las Cruces (Mexico) .....18 u
Las Cruces (USA) ....18 j
Las Davé ....43 j
Las Entimias ....18 m
La Serena ....28 o
Las Flores ....31 b
Las Heras ....30 w
Lashio ....62 r
Lashkargah ....60 g
Lasho Joâyin ....60 e
Las Koreh ....43 j
Las Lajas ....30 i
Las Lajitas ....28 t
Las Lomas ....24 h
Las Lomitas ....28 w
Las Palmas ....36 b

La Spezia ....34 l
Las Piedras ....25 n
Las Plumas ....30 x
Lastoursville ....41 w
Las Trincheras ....23 g
Las Vegas (Arizona) ......14 y
Las Vegas (New Mexico) .15 q
Latacunga ....24 h
Latady Island ....82 x
Latady Range ....82 z
La Tagua ....24 k
Latakia ....35 z
Latina ....34 m
La Tuque ....17 a
Latur ....61 o
Latvia ....33 w
Launceston ....77 y
La Unión ....24 w
Laura ....73 l
La Urbana ....23 f
Laurel ....19 i
Laurie Island ....82 g
Lausanne ....34 j
Laut ....69 q
Lavapié, Punta ....30 g
La Vega ....21 s
La Venturosa ....23 q
La Vibora ....18 m
La Victoria ....23 f
Lavumisa ....49 s
Lawa ....62 r
Lawdar ....43 h
Lawn Hill ....73 u
Lawra ....40 l
Lawrenceburg ....16 s
Lawton ....19 c
Layla ....39 s
Lazarev Sea ....83 j
Learmonth ....72 q
Leavenworth ....15 w
Lebanon (State) 38
Lebanon (USA) ....16 p
Lebap ....55 p
Lebú ....30 g
Lecce ....35 c
Leduc ....14 m
Leeds ....32 x
Leesburg ....20 l
Leeton ....78 b
Leeuwarden ....33 n
Leeward Islands ....21 x
Legazpi ....67 i
Leghorn (Livorno) ....34 l
Legnica ....33 s
Leh ....61 c
Le Havre ....34 f
Leiah ....60 k
Leicester ....32 y
Leigh Creek ....77 f
Leipzig ....33 q
Leiria ....34 n
Leiyang ....63 o
Le Kef ....34 x
Lekki ....41 p
Le Mans ....34 g
Lema Shilindi ....43 s
Lemmon ....15 f
Lemsid ....36 p
Lena ....52 l
Leng Hu ....56 w
Lenina ....55 w
Leningradskaya ....86 w
Leninsk ....55 e
Len'ki ....56 c
Lensk ....52 s
Léo ....40 l
Leoben ....35 b
Leonardville ....48 j
León (Mexico) ....19 u
León (Nicaragua) ....22 e
León (Spain) ....34 c
Leonora ....76 h
Lepsy ....56 b
Le Puy ....34 h
Lerdo ....18 l
Lerida ....73 y
Lérida (Colombia) ....25 b
Lérida (Spain) ....34 g
Lerwick ....32 k
Lesbos ....35 t

Les Cayes ....21 q
Leschenault, Cape ....76 c
Leskovac ....35 e
Lesnaya ....53 z
Lesosibirsk ....51 w
Lesotho ....49 p
Lesozavodsk ....58 l
Lesser Antilles ....23 e
Lesser Slave Lake ....12 s
Lesser Sunda Islands .....69 r
Lesser Zab ....39 d
Leszno ....33 s
Lethbridge ....14 m
Lethem ....23 x
Leticia ....25 b
Leti Islands ....69 z
Letlhakane ....49 b
Letlhakeng ....49 c
Letsok-Aw ....66 c
Leuser ....65 u
Levelland ....18 m
Levêque, Cape ....72 j
Levkas ....35 q
Lewis ....32 i
Lewis Hill ....17 i
Lewiston (Idaho) ....14 k
Lewiston (Maine) ....17 o
Lewiston (Montana) ......15 b
Lexington ....16 t
Lexington Park ....16 y
Leyte ....67 j
Lhari ....62 b
Lhasa ....61 l
Lhazê ....61 j
Lhazhong ....61 i
Lhokseumawe ....65 u
Lhoksukon ....65 u
Lhorong ....62 d
Lhozhag ....61 l
Lhünzë ....62 b
Liadong Wan ....57 z
Liangcheng ....63 g
Liangpran ....69 c
Lianjiang ....63 n
Lian Xian ....63 o
Lianyuan ....63 b
Liao ....58 e
Liaodun ....56 w
Liaotong Bay ....58 e
Liaoyang ....58 e
Liaoyuan ....58 f
Liard ....12 o
Libby ....14 k
Libenge ....42 o
Liberal ....15 t
Liberdade ....25 e
Liberia (State) 40
Liberia (Costa Rica) ......22 f
Libertador General
San Martin ....28 g
Liboi ....43 q
Libreville ....41 t
Libya 37/38
Libyan Desert ....38 d
Libyan Plateau ....38 e
Licancabur ....28 e
Licata ....37 i
Lichinga ....46 i
Lichtenburg ....46 o
Lichuan ....62 m
Lida ....33 w
Lidköping ....33 q
Liebig, Mount ....73 p
Liechtenstein 34
Liège ....34 i
Lienyunkang ....63 g
Liepāja ....33 u
Ligurian Sea ....34 k
Lihue ....18 p
Lijiang ....62 g
Likasi ....45 o
Likati ....42 r
Likoto ....45 a
Likouala ....41 x
Likouala-aux-Herbes .....41 z
Lille ....32 z
Lillehammer ....33 d
Lilongwe ....45 t
Lima (Paraguay) ....28 m
Lima (Peru) ....24 w

Lima (USA) ....16 t
Limassol ....35 y
Limay ....30 j
Limbe (Cameroon) ....41 t
Limbe (Malawi) ....46 i
Limerick ....32 u
Lime Village ....11 d
Limmen Bight ....73 f
Limnos ....35 t
Limoeiro ....27 v
Limoges ....34 g
Limon ....15 r
Limón ....22 h
Limpopo ....49 g
Linah ....39 d
Linares ....19 b
Lincang ....62 t
Lincoln (Argentina) ....31 a
Lincoln (USA) ....15 v
Lincoln Sea ....91 h
Linda Downs ....73 u
Linde ....52 k
Linden ....23 y
Lindi ....45 x
Lindi (River) ....42 t
Lindo ....28 l
Line Islands ....230 a
Linganamakki Reservoir ...64 d
Lingayen ....67 f
Lingayen Gulf ....67 f
Lingbao ....63 a
Lingga Islands ....68 i
Lingomo ....42 q
Lingshan ....62 z
Lingsugur ....64 f
Linguère ....40 c
Linhai ....58 f
Linhares ....29 l
Linhe ....57 r
Linkiang ....58 g
Linköping ....33 f
Linkou ....58 i
Linosa ....34 z
Linqing ....63 d
Lins ....29 d
Linsia ....62 i
Lintao ....62 i
Linton ....15 g
Linxi ....57 x
Linz ....35 a
Linze ....57 n
Lion, Gulf of ....34 i
Liouesso ....41 y
Lipa ....67 g
Lipari Islands ....35 n
Lipetsk ....54 e
Lipez, Cord. de ....28 e
Lira ....42 y
Lisala ....42 p
Lisboa (Lisbon) ....34 n
Lisbon ....34 n
Lisburne, Cape ....10 m
Lishui ....63 g
Lismore ....78 g
Listowel Downs ....77 k
Listv'anka ....57 c
Litang ....62 z
Litang ....62 g
Litchfield ....16 q
Lithgow ....78 e
Lithuania ....33 v
Litke ....53 g
Litke (Novaya Zemlya) ...50 j
Litovko ....58 m
Little Andaman ....65 d
Little Anyuy ....10 a
Little Cayman ....20 z
Little Current ....16 i
Little Diomede ....10 l
Little Falls ....15 j
Little Karoo ....48 y
Little Khinggan Mountains 58 h
Little Rock ....15 x
Little Salmon ....11 d
Little Scarcies ....40 e
Little Swartberg ....48 y
Litunde ....45 v
Liuba ....62 l
Liuchou ....62 z
Liuhe ....58 g

Liupo ....45 y
Liushuquan ....56 w
Live Oak ....20 k
Liverpool ....32 w
Liverpool Land ....91 r
Livingston ....15 a
Livingstone ....46 o
Livingstone Mountains ...45 u
Livingstonia ....46 h
Livingston Island ....82 s
Livny ....54 d
Livorno ....34 l
Liwa Oasis ....39 x
Li Xian ....63 a
Li Yuba ....42 u
Lizarda ....27 n
Ljamin ....51 o
Ljubljana ....35 a
Ljungan ....33 f
Ljusnan ....33 f
Llanos ....23 b
Llanos de Chiquitos ....28 i
Llanos de los Caballos
Mestenos ....18 l
Llanos de Mojos ....25 s
Llanquihue, Lago ....30 g
Llata ....24 w
Llera ....19 o
Lloydminster ....15 a
Llullaillaco ....28 c
Loa ....28 c
Lobatse ....46 o
Lobaye ....42 n
Loberia ....31 b
Lobito ....44 r
Lobos ....31 b
Lobos, Cape ....18 f
Lobos Island ....24 g
Lobva ....50 x
Lockhart River ....73 l
Loddon ....77 w
Lodja ....44 m
Lodwar ....43 n
Łódź ....33 t
Loeriesfontein ....48 x
Loffa ....40 s
Lofoten Islands ....33 d
Log ....54 g
Logan ....15 n
Logan, Mount ....11 i
Logone ....41 l
Logroño ....34 e
Loikaw ....65 n
Loi-lem ....62 r
Loire ....34 f
Loiyangalani ....43 o
Loja ....24 h
Lokandu ....45 a
Lokichar ....43 n
Lokichokio ....42 z
Lokitaung ....43 n
Lokoja ....41 r
Lokomo ....41 x
Lokori ....43 n
Lokshak ....52 z
Lolland ....33 q
Lolworth ....74 p
Lomami ....45 a
Loma Mts. ....40 f
Lombarda, Serra ....26 j
Lombardina ....72 j
Lombok ....69 g
Lomé ....41 o
Lomela ....44 m
Lomela (River) ....44 k
Lomza ....33 u
Londonderry ....32 v
Londonderry, Cape ....72 x
London (Canada) ....16 v
London (UK) ....32 y
Londrina ....29 d
Longa ....44 w
Long Beach ....18 b
Longchuan ....63 g
Longhua ....57 g
Long Island (Bahamas) ...21 p
Long Island (USA) ....17 n
Longjiang ....58 e
Longlac ....16 f
Long Range ....17 l

Longreach......................73 y
Long Strait....................10 g
Longview (Texas) ....19 e
Longview (Washington)...14 g
Longxi..........................62 j
Long Xuyen..................66 h
Longyan.......................63 r
Longyearbyen...............92 o
Longzhen......................58 g
Lonkin.........................62 q
Lönsdal.......................33 e
Lontra.........................26 x
Lookout Mountain..........17 f
Loongana.....................76 l
Lop Buri......................65 j
Lopcha........................52 w
Lopez..........................67 h
Lop Nur.......................56 v
Lopori.........................42 q
Loptyuga......................50 t
Lora............................60 h
Loralai........................60 j
Lorca..........................34 r
Lord Howe Island ....78 k
Lordsburg....................18 i
Lorenço.......................26 j
Loreto (Bolivia) ....25 s
Loreto (Mexico) ....18 g
Lorica.........................22 m
Lorient........................34 d
Loruk..........................45 i
Lorukumu.....................43 n
Los Alamos..................15 p
Los Angeles (Chile) ....30 h
Los Angeles (Mexico) ....18 f
Los Angeles (USA) ....18 f
Losap Atoll...................71 f
Los Blancos ....28 i
Los Burros ....18 g
Los Menucos ....30 j
Los Mochis ....18 i
Los Vientos ....28 p
Lot..............................34 y
Lotta...........................33 l
Louangphrabang ....62 v
Loubomo......................44 e
Louchuan......................62 b
Louga..........................40 b
Lougheed Island ....12 j
Louisiade Archipelago .....74 g
Louisiana ....20 d
Louis Trichardt ....49 e
Louisville.....................16 t
Louis XIV, Point ....16 j
Lovat..........................33 m
Lovelock ....14 w
Løvenørn, Kap..............90 x
Lowa..........................45 b
Lower California ....18 f
Lower Egypt ....38 h
Lower Hutt ....79 v
Lower Red Lake ....15 j
Loxton........................48 z
Loyalty Islands.............75 r
Loyang........................63 b
Loyoro........................42 z
Luachimo.....................44 k
Lua Dekere..................42 p
Luambo.......................45 o
Luan...........................57 w
Luanda........................44 e
Luang.........................66 q
Luang Prabang..............65 l
Luang, Thale ....66 r
Luangua......................45 r
Luangwa......................45 s
Luanhaizi.....................62 b
Luanshya....................45 p
Luapula.......................45 p
Luau...........................44 y
Luba...........................41 t
Lubang........................67 f
Lubango.......................44 s
Lubao.........................45 a
Lubbock.......................19 a
Lübeck........................33 p
Lübeck Bay..................33 p
Lubefu........................44 m
Lubero.......................45 c
Lubilanji......................44 m

Lublin.........................33 v
Lubny.........................35 l
Lubuklinggau................68 t
Lubuksikaping...............68 e
Lubumbashi..................45 p
Lubungu......................45 n
Lubutu........................45 b
Lucala.........................44 t
Lucapa........................44 k
Lucas..........................25 z
Lucena (Philippines).......67 g
Lucena (Spain) ....36 j
Lucerne.......................34 k
Luchegorsk..................58 l
Luchou........................62 k
Lüchun........................62 v
Lucira.........................44 r
Luckhoff......................49 n
Lucknow......................61 e
Lucusse.......................44 x
Lucy Creek ....73 t
Lüda (Dalian) ....58 q
Luddington...................16 s
Lüderitz.......................48 t
Ludhiana......................61 b
Ludlow........................18 d
Luebo.........................44 k
Luena (Angola) ....44 w
Luena (River) ....44 y
Luena (Zaïre) ....45 n
Luengué......................44 x
Lüeyang.......................62 k
Lufeng........................63 q
Lufkin.........................19 e
Luga...........................33 l
Lugansk.......................54 e
Lugenda......................45 v
Lugh Ganana................43 s
Lugovatka....................51 u
Lugovoi.......................55 w
Lugu...........................61 g
Luhombero...................45 w
Luiana........................44 y
Luidzhi........................50 i
Luiza..........................44 l
Luján..........................31 b
Lujlang........................63 e
Lukacheck ....53 n
Lukenie.......................44 k
Lukolela.......................44 i
Lukuga........................45 b
Lukula........................44 e
Lukulu.........................44 z
Lukumburu...................45 u
Lukunskiy.....................52 b
Lule............................33 h
Luleå..........................33 i
Luleburgaz...................35 i
Lulong.........................57 y
Lulonga.......................42 o
Lulonga (River).............42 o
Lumbala......................44 y
Lumbala N'Guimbo.........44 x
Lumberton ....21 a
Lumbo.........................45 y
Lumding......................62 o
Lumi...........................70 x
Lumsden......................79 q
Lumu..........................69 f
Lün............................57 d
Lundazi.......................45 s
Lunga.........................45 o
Lunggar.......................61 g
Lungue-Bungu...............44 y
Luni............................60 y
Luobei.........................58 j
Luobuzhuang................56 t
Luocuan......................62 m
Luoding.......................63 n
Luoguhe......................57 m
Luohe.........................63 c
Luoshan......................63 c
Luozi..........................44 f
Lupar..........................68 m
Luputa........................44 m
Luqu..........................62 h
Luremo.......................44 i
Lúrio..........................45 w
Lusaka........................46 c
Lusambo......................44 m

Lushoto.......................45 k
Lusk...........................15 q
Lutembo......................44 x
Luton..........................32 y
Lutselk'e (Snowdrift)......12 u
Lutsk..........................35 g
Lützow Holm Bight ....84 h
Luvua.........................45 b
Luvuei.........................44 x
Luwingu.......................45 r
Luxembourg (City) ....33 n
Luxembourg (State) 33-34
Luxi............................62 s
Luxor..........................38 j
Luzi............................44 x
Luzon..........................67 f
Luzon Strait ....63 u
L'viv...........................35 g
L'vovka.......................51 g
Lyckseie......................33 g
Lydenburg....................49 e
Lynchburg....................16 w
Lyndhurst.....................74 o
Lyndon........................72 r
Lynn Lake ....12 x
Lynwood......................74 x
Lyon (Lyons)................34 i
Lyon Inlet ....13 e
Lyons (France) ....34 i
Lyons (River) ....72 r
Lyubinskiy....................55 j

M

Ma'an.........................38 l
Maas (Netherlands).........33 n
Maas (Somalia) ....43 v
Maasin........................67 j
Maatsuyker Island ....77 x
Maba..........................42 d
Mabote.......................49 h
Mabrouk......................36 y
Macaé.........................29 j
McAlester.....................15 v
McAllen.......................19 c
MacAlpine Lake.............12 k
McArthur......................73 f
Macane.......................49 g
Macao.........................63 p
Macapá.......................26 k
Macas.........................24 i
Macau.........................27 u
Macauley Island ....79 h
McClintock...................13 n
McClintock Channel ....12 k
McClintock Island ....50 j
McClure Strait...............12 d
McComb......................20 f
McCook.......................15 t
McDermitt ....14 w
Macdonald, Lake ....73 n
Macdonell Ranges..........73 q
Macedonia (F. Y. R.)......35 e
Maceió........................27 v
Macenta......................40 g
McGrath......................11 d
Mach..........................60 i
Machachi.....................24 h
Machačkala..................54 w
Machaila......................49 g
Machakos....................45 j
Machala......................24 h
Macharetí....................28 h
Machettie, Lake ....73 v
Macheng......................63 d
Machilipatnam...............64 i
Machiques....................23 b
Machuan......................61 g
Macia.........................49 g
Macina........................40 j
Mack..........................15 o
Mackay.......................74 r
Mackay, Lake ....73 o
Mackenzie....................12 p
Mackenzie (River) 11-12
Mackenzie Bay ....11 j
Mackenzie King Island .....12 g
Mackenzie Mountains......12 o
Mackinaw City ....16 g

McKinlay ....73 w
McKinley, Mount ....11 e
Maclear.......................49 q
McLennan.....................12 s
McLeod Lake ....14 g
McLeod, Lake ....72 q
Macmillan.....................11 l
McMurdo......................86 r
Macomia......................45 y
Mâcon.........................34 i
Macon (Georgia) ....20 k
Macon (Missouri) ....16 p
Macquarie....................78 d
Macquarie Harbour........77 w
Macquarie Island ....231 x
MacRobertson Land.......85 b
Macuarichic..................18 j
Macuje........................24 m
Macusani.....................28 c
Macuspana...................19 t
Madagascar..................47
Mada'in Salih ....38 m
Madama.......................37 u
Madang.......................71 n
Madaoua......................41 e
Madeira (Island) ....36 a
Madeira (River) ....25 j
Madenijet....................56 b
Madera ....18 j
Madidi.........................25 p
Madikeri......................64 e
Madimba......................44 g
Madingou.....................44 f
Madison.......................16 r
Madiun........................69 n
Mado Gashi ....43 q
Madoi.........................62 f
Madrakah.....................39 o
Madrakah, Ras ....60 p
Madras (India) ....64 h
Madras (USA)...............14 h
Madre de Dios ....25 q
Madre, Laguna ....19 d
Madre, Sierra ....67 g
Madre del Sur, Sierra .....19 p
Madre Occidental, Sierra..18 k
Madre Oriental, Sierra.....19 o
Madrid.........................34 d
Madula........................42 t
Madura........................69 o
Madura Strait ....69 o
Madurai.......................64 f
Madziwadzido................49 d
Maebashi.....................59 o
Mae Sot ....66 d
Maevatanana.................47 q
Mafeteng......................49 p
Mafia Island ....45 l
Mafra..........................29 c
Mafraq........................38 l
Magadan......................53 v
Magadi........................45 i
Magdagachi..................52 y
Magdalen Islands ....17 g
Magdalena (Argentina)....31 c
Magdalena (Bolivia) ....25 s
Magdalena (Island).........30 t
Magdalena (Mexico) ....18 h
Magdalena (River)..........22 z
Magdalena (USA)...........18 j
Magdeburg...................33 q
Magelang.....................68 z
Magellan Straits ....30 v
Maggieville...................73 j
Maghama.....................40 e
Magnetic North Pole......89 r
Magnitogorsk................55 c
Magrur........................42 q
Maguarinho, Cabo..........26 m
Magude.......................49 g
Magwe........................62 q
Mahabad......................54 v
Mahabo.......................47 p
Mahaddei Uen...............43 u
Mahagi........................42 x
Mahajan......................60 m
Mahajanga....................47 q
Mahakam.....................69 d
Mahalapye...................49 c
Mahalevona..................47 f

Mahallat......................39 h
Mahânadi.....................61 s
Mahanoro.....................47 r
Maha Sarakham............65 l
Mahavavy.....................47 p
Mahbubnagar ....64 f
Mahd adh Dhahab.........39 o
Mahdia........................37 g
Mahenge......................45 i
Mahesana....................60 y
Maicao........................23 b
Maiduguri.....................41 k
Maigudo......................43 o
Maihar........................61 r
Maiko.........................42 t
Maimana......................60 h
Maimeča......................51 m
Main...........................34 l
Mai-Ndombe, Lake ....44 i
Maine..........................17 b
Mainé-Soroa ....41 i
Mainling......................62 b
Mainoru......................73 e
Maiodao Islands ....57 z
Maiquetía.....................23 e
Mait...........................43 i
Maitencillo....................28 o
Maitri..........................83 m
Maizhokunggar..............61 m
Majene........................69 s
Maji...........................43 n
Makjadikgadi Pans ....46 n
Makalu........................61 i
Makambako..................45 h
Makanza......................42 o
Makarikha....................50 j
Makarov.......................59 d
Makarova.....................51 g
Makassar Strait ....69 e
Makat..........................54 m
Makaw........................62 r
Makeni........................40 e
Makeyevka...................54 d
Makgadikgadi Pans ....49 b
Makinsk.......................55 i
Makkovik.....................17 h
Makokou......................41 w
Makongolosi ....45 g
Makopong.....................48 m
Makoua.......................44 g
Makrah........................43 l
Makri..........................61 s
Maksimicha..................57 f
Maksimovka..................59 a
Makteir.......................36 r
Maku..........................54 u
Makurdi.......................41 t
Makushino....................55 g
Makuyuni.....................45 i
Mâl............................40 d
Mal. Lyakhovskiy ....53 e
Malabar Coast ....64 d
Malabo........................41 t
Malacca.......................68 f
Malacca, Strait of..........68 e
Malad City ....14 z
Málaga (Colombia) ....23 b
Málaga (Spain) ....34 q
Malagarasi...................45 e
Malaita........................71 y
Malakal........................42 k
Malang........................69 n
Malanga.......................45 v
Malange.......................44 u
Mälar, Lake ....33 f
Malargue......................30 i
Malaripó......................26 h
Malaspina....................30 x
Malatya.......................54 q
Malawi.....................45-46/49
Malawi, Lake ....46 i
Malaya (Malaysia) ....66 s
Malaya (Russia) ....53 i
Malaya Baranikha..........10 z
Malayan Peninsula ....66 v
Malayan Sea ....67 o
Malaybalay Bislig...........67 w
Malayer.......................39 h
Malaysia....................65-69
Malčin.........................56 j

Maldives 64
Maldonado ....31 e
Male ....64 p
Maléa, Cape ....35 s
Malegaon ....61 n
Malekula ....75 d
M. Aléman Reservoir ....19 q
Malemba Nkulu ....45 b
Malème-Hodar ....40 c
Malhada ....29 i
Malheur Lake ....14 w
Mali 36-37/40-41
Malik ....69 l
Malindi ....45 l
Malka ....53 x
Malkachan ....53 x
Mallapunyah ....73 f
Mallorca ....34 u
Malmesbury ....48 w
Malmö ....33 r
Malmyzh ....50 u
Maloca ....26 h
Maloca Velha ....26 h
Malonga ....44 z
Måløy ....33 a
Malozemelskaja Tundra ...50 h
Malpelo ....22 v
Malta (State) 35/37
Malta (USA) ....15 b
Maltahöhe ....48 i
Maluwe ....40 l
Malykay ....52 z
Malyutka ....52 z
Malyy Lyakhovskiy ....53 e
Mama ....52 s
Mama (Cherskogo
Mountains) ....53 f
Mamadysh ....54 k
Mamanguape ....27 w
Mamantel ....19 u
Mamazair ....55 x
Mambasa ....42 v
Mamberamo ....70 v
Mamfe ....41 t
Mamoré ....25 r
Mamoriá ....25 d
Mamou ....40 e
Mampikony ....47 e
Mampong ....40 z
Man ....40 u
Man, Isle of ....32 w
Mana (French Guiana) .....26 i
Mana (Hawaiian Islands) ..18 o
Mana (River) ....56 j
Mana Elena ....28 c
Manacapuru ....25 h
Manado ....69 j
Managua ....22 f
Managua, Lake ....22 e
Manakara ....47 q
Manama ....39 i
Manambolo ....47 o
Manamo ....23 i
Mananara ....47 f
Mananara (River) ....47 q
Mananjary ....47 r
Manankoro ....40 i
Manar ....43 g
Manas ....56 t
Manas Hu ....56 s
Manaus ....25 j
Manchan ....56 i
Manchester (UK) ....32 x
Manchester (USA) ....17 n
Manchouli ....57 j
Manchuria ....58 f
Máncora ....24 g
Mand ....39 j
Mandabe ....47 p
Mandach ....57 r
Mandal ....57 e
Mandal (Hangayn
Mountains) ....57 a
Mandala ....70 w
Mandalay ....62 q
Mandalgov' ....57 r
Mandal-Ovoo ....57 p
Mandasor ....61 n
Mandaue ....67 i
Mandera ....43 r

Mandimba ....46 i
Mandla ....61 r
Mandoto ....47 p
Mandritsara ....47 e
Mandurah ....76 d
Mandvi ....60 w
Mandya ....64 e
Mangalmé ....42 e
Mangalore ....64 d
Mangnai ....56 w
Mangochi ....46 i
Mangoky ....47 o
Mangole ....69 k
Mangueni Plateau ....37 u
Mangui ....52 w
Manhattan ....15 v
Manhuaçu ....29 j
Mani ....40 t
Maniamba ....46 i
Manicoré ....25 i
Manicouagan ....17 c
Manicouagan Reservoir ...17 c
Maniitsoq ....90 v
Manila ....67 f
Manila Bay ....67 f
Manily ....10 b
Maningrida ....73 e
Manipa, Strait of ....69 y
Manisa ....35 v
Manitoba ....15 g
Manitoba, Lake ....15 h
Manitoulin Island ....16 i
Manitouwadge ....16 g
Manitowoc ....16 s
Maniwaki ....16 l
Manizales ....22 z
Manjacaze ....49 h
Manjimup ....76 d
Manjra ....61 p
Manjuri ....25 e
Man Kabat ....62 e
Mankato ....15 j
Manlaj ....57 r
Manley Hot Springs ....11 f
Mannar ....64 u
Mannar, Gulf of ....64 t
Mannheim ....33 p
Manning ....12 r
Manoa ....25 r
Manokwari ....70 r
Manombo ....47 n
Manonga ....45 g
Manono ....45 b
Mano River ....40 s
Manpojin ....58 g
Mansa ....45 q
Mansel Island ....13 e
Mansfield (Ohio) ....16 u
Mansfield (Pennsylvania) .16 y
Mansi ....62 y
Manso ....29 b
Mansôa ....40 b
Manta ....24 g
Mantalingajan ....67 r
Mantaro ....24 x
Mantecal ....23 g
Mantena ....29 k
Mantiqueira, Serra da ......29 h
Manú ....25 n
Manuel ....19 p
Manuel Urbano ....25 o
Manuelzinho ....25 m
Manyami ....45 k
Manyapa ....69 d
Manych Gudilo Lake ....54 g
Manyoni ....45 g
Manyuan ....57 q
Manzanillo ....21 o
Manzini ....49 s
Manzurka ....57 d
Mao (Chad) ....41 l
Mao (Dominican Republic)21 s
Maoke (Mountains) ....70 t
Mapaga ....69 f
Mapai ....49 g
Mapam Yumco ....61 f
Mapati ....44 f
Mapia Islands ....70 f
Mapinhane ....49 i

Maple Creek ....15 a
Mappi ....70 v
Mapuera ....25 k
Maputo ....49 t
Maqên ....62 g
Maqên Gangri ....62 f
Maquela do Zombo ....44 g
Maquinchao ....30 j
Mar, Serra do ....29 r
Mara ....45 g
Mara ....25 e
Marabá ....26 y
Maracá ....26 l
Maracaçumé ....27 b
Maracaibo ....23 b
Maracaibo, Lake ....23 b
Maracaju ....29 a
Maracaju, Serra de ....29 a
Maracay ....23 e
Maradah ....37 l
Maradi ....41 f
Maragheh ....54 v
Marajó ....26 l
Marajó Bay ....26 m
Maralal ....43 r
Marambio ....82 t
Marand ....54 v
Maranguape ....27 t
Maranoa ....78 c
Marañón ....24 k
Marape ....25 y
Maraş ....54 p
Marathon ....16 f
Maravatio ....19 o
Maraveh-Tappeh ....55 n
Marawah ....39 w
Marawi ....67 v
Marble Bar ....72 u
Marcelino ....25 d
Marchena ....36 i
Marchena (Island) ....22 p
Marcy, Mount ....16 z
Mardan ....60 m
Mar del Plata ....31 c
Mareeba ....74 b
Margai Caka ....61 i
Margaret River ....72 z
Margarita ....23 g
Margaritovo ....58 m
Margherita Peak ....42 w
Margilan ....55 w
Marhoum ....34 s
Maria Cleofas ....18 x
Maria Madre ....18 w
Marea Magdalena ....18 w
Mariana Islands, Northern231 j
Marianna ....20 j
Maribor ....35 a
Maridi ....42 w
Maridi (River) ....42 w
Marie Byrd Land ....81 d
Mariehamn ....33 h
Mariental ....48 j
Marietta (Georgia) ....20 j
Marietta (Ohio) ....16 v
Mariinsk ....56 q
Mariinskoye ....53 q
Marilia ....29 d
Marinduque ....67 g
Marinette ....16 f
Maringa (Dem. Rep.
Congo) ....42 q
Maringá (Brazil) ....29 b
Marioka ....59 p
Marion ....16 v
Marion Downs ....73 v
Maripa ....23 g
Mariscal Estigarribia ....28 j
Maritime Alps ....34 j
Mariupol ....54 d
Markakol', Lake ....56 f
Markam ....62 g
Markapur ....64 g
Marken ....49 g
Markha ....52 g
Markit ....56 o
Markoka ....52 f
Markovo ....10 d
Marlborough (Australia) ....74 s
Marlborough (Guyana) .....23 k

Marmara, Sea of ....35 i
Marmarica ....35 s
Marneuli ....54 u
Maro ....42 b
Maroantsetra ....47 e
Maroochydore ....74 u
Maroua ....41 k
Marovoay ....47 c
Marowijne ....26 h
Marqua ....73 t
Marquesas Islands ....230 p
Marquette ....16 f
Marrakech ....36 g
Marree ....77 f
Marresale ....51 a
Marrupa ....45 w
Marsa Alam ....38 x
Marsabit ....43 p
Marsala ....34 z
Marsa Matruh ....35 u
Marseilles ....34 i
Marsella ....24 k
Marshall (Arkansas) ....15 x
Marshall (Minnesota) ....15 i
Marshall (Missouri) ....15 x
Marshall (Texas) ....20 c
Marshall Islands ....231 l
Marshal'skiy ....53 d
Marshfield ....16 z
Martaban, Gulf of ....65 g
Martinez ....31 b
Martinez de la Torre ....19 q
Martinique ....23 j
Martinique Passage ....23 i
Martinsville ....16 w
Martuk ....55 a
Marungu Mountains ....45 d
Mary ....55 q
Maryborough
(Queensland) ....74 u
Maryborough (Victoria) .....77 v
Marydale ....48 y
Maryevka ....54 j
Mar'yevka ....55 h
Mary Kathleen ....73 v
Maryland ....16 y
Maryvale ....73 y
Masai Steppe ....45 i
Masaka ....42 x
Masalembo ....69 p
Masamba ....69 t
Masan ....58 u
Masasi ....45 x
Masawa ....43 d
Masbate ....67 i
Masbate (Island) ....67 i
Mascara ....36 m
Maseru ....49 p
Mashhad ....55 p
Masia-Mbio ....44 h
Masi-Manimba ....44 i
Masindi ....42 x
Masinloc ....67 f
Masirah ....60 p
Masisea ....24 y
Masisi ....45 c
Masjed-e-Soleiman ....39 h
Maskana ....38 m
Mason City ....15 x
Massachusetts ....17 n
Massaguet ....41 l
Massakori ....41 l
Massangena ....49 g
Massangulo ....45 u
Massenya ....41 l
Massif Central ....34 h
Massinga ....49 i
Massingir ....49 g
Mastabah ....39 n
Mastakh ....52 j
Masteksay ....54 k
Masterton ....79 v
Mastuj ....60 m
Masturah ....39 n
Masuda ....58 w
Masuguru ....45 x
Masvingo ....49 f
Matadi ....44 f
Matagalpa ....22 f
Matagami ....16 k

Mataj ....56 o
Matam ....40 d
Matamoros ....19 d
Matamoros
(Mexican Plateau) ....18 m
Matane ....17 d
Matankari ....41 c
Matanzas ....20 y
Matapan, Cape ....35 r
Mataram ....72 f
Mataranka ....73 d
Mategua ....25 t
Matehuala ....19 n
Mateur ....37 f
Mathura ....61 b
Matías Romero ....20 p
Mato Grosso ....25 w
Mato Grosso Plateau ...26/29
Mato, Sierra de ....23 t
Matruh ....38 f
Matsue ....58 x
Matsumoto ....59 n
Matsusaka ....58 z
Matsuyama ....58 x
Matucana ....24 w
Matun ....60 k
Matundu ....42 s
Maturín ....23 h
Maturuca ....23 w
Matyl'ka ....51 t
Mau, Cape ....66 u
Maúa ....45 w
Maués ....25 k
Maués (River) ....25 k
Maui ....18 r
Maule ....30 h
Maulvī Bazār ....61 y
Maumere ....69 v
Maun ....48 m
Mauna Kea ....18 r
Mauna Loa ....18 r
Maunaloa ....18 q
Maurice, Lake ....77 a
Mauritania 36/40
Mauritius ....47 y
Mavinga ....44 x
Mawson ....85 z
Maxcanú ....19 u
Maxwelton ....73 x
May, Cape ....16 z
Maya ....68 l
Maya (River) ....53 s
Maya (River) ....53 p
Mayaguana Island ....21 r
Mayagüez ....21 v
Mayamba ....44 h
Mayamey ....55 n
Maychew ....43 d
Mayer ....18 g
Maykain ....55 l
Maykop ....54 r
Maymakan ....53 o
Maynopil'gyn ....10 g
Mayo ....11 k
Mayo (River) ....24 j
Mayoko ....44 e
Mayon ....67 i
Mayor-Krest ....53 f
Mayotte ....47 c
May Pen ....21 n
Maysville ....16 u
Mayumba ....44 c
Mayupa ....23 v
Mayuram ....64 h
Mayya ....52 m
Mazabuka ....49 c
Mazalet ....41 g
Mazán ....24 m
Mazanillo ....18 y
Mazar ....56 n
Mazar-i Sharif ....60 i
Mazaruni ....23 w
Mazatenango ....22 a
Mazatlán ....18 w
Mazo Cruz ....25 o
Mazunga ....49 e
Mazunzut ....62 e
Mbabane ....49 s
Mbaïki ....42 n
Mbaké ....40 c

Mbala....46 f
Mbale....42 z
Mbalmayo....41 v
Mbandaka....44 i
M'Banza-Congo....44 g
Mbanza-Ngungu....44 g
Mbarara....42 x
Mbari....42 r
Mbé....41 k
Mbesuma....45 s
Mbeya....45 f
Mbini....41 t
Mbini (River)....41 u
Mbomou....42 s
Mbour....40 a
Mbout....40 e
Mbrés....42 p
Mbuji Mayi....44 m
Mbulu....45 h
Mbuyuni....45 i
Mcherrah....36 i
Mchinji....46 g
Mdrak....66 k
Mead Lake....14 y
Meadow Lake....15 b
Meadville....16 w
Mearim....27 n
Mecejana....27 g
Mecca....39 n
Méchéria....34 s
Medan....68 d
Medea....37 a
Medellín....22 z
Médenine....34 y
Mederdra....40 c
Medford....14 t
Medi....42 x
Medicine Hat....15 a
Medina....39 n
Mediterranean Sea....34-35
Medje....42 u
Mednogorsk....55 a
Mednyy, Cape....51 j
Medvežjegors....50 o
Meekatharra....72 u
Meerut....61 c
Mega....43 p
Megalo....43 r
Meghna....61 y
Meharry, Mount....72 u
Mehdia....36 h
Mehran....39 f
Mehriz....39 k
Meiganga....41 x
Meighen Island....12 l
Meigu....62 i
Meiktla....62 q
Meishan....62 i
Mei Xian....63 r
Mejicana....28 q
Mejillones....28 b
Mékambo....41 w
Mekele....43 c
Meknès....36 i
Mekong....66 g
Mekong Delta....66 i
Mekongga....69 u
Melambes....35 t
Melanesia....74 i
Melbourne (Australia)....77 x
Melbourne (USA)....20 m
Meletsk....51 v
Melfi....42 a
Melfort....15 d
Melilla....34 r
Melitopol....35 m
Melo....29 n
Melville....15 e
Melville Bay....91 b
Melville Island (Canada)....12 g
Melville Island (Australia)....73 c
Melville Lake....17 h
Melville Peninsula....13 d
Memmingen....33 p
Memphis (Egypt)....38 h
Memphis (USA)....16 z
Ménaka....41 b
Menawashei....42 z
Mendebo Mountains....43 q

Menderes....35 v
Mendi (Ethiopia)....42 m
Mendi (Papua New Guinea)....70 y
Mendocino, Cape....14 s
Mendoza....28 q
Mengoub....36 k
Menkere....52 j
Menominee....16 f
Menongue....44 v
Menorca....34 v
Menyapa....67 p
Menyuan....62 h
Menza....57 f
Menzies....76 g
Meoqui....18 k
Meraia....36 u
Merak....68 w
Merauke....70 w
Merca....43 t
Merced....14 v
Mercedario....28 p
Mercedes (Argentina)....30 l
Mercedes (Buenos Aires, Argentina)....31 b
Mercedes (Corrientes, Argentina)....28 y
Mercedes (Uruguay)....31 c
Mergenevo....54 l
Mergol....56 x
Mergui....65 i
Mergui Archipelago....65 h
Mérida (Mexico)....19 v
Mérida (Spain)....34 p
Mérida (Venezuela)....23 b
Mérida, Cordillera de....23 b
Meridian....20 q
Merir....70 d
Meriruma....26 h
Merowe....38 v
Merrill....16 d
Mersa Metruh....38 f
Mersa Teklay....39 n
Mersín....35 y
Mértola....36 g
Mertz Glacire....87 n
Meru....45 j
Meru (Mount)....45 i
Mesa....18 g
Mesa del Nayar....18 y
Mesa de Yambi....25 a
Meseta del Cerro Jáua....23 t
Meseta de Somuncurá....30 k
Mesfinto....43 b
Messaad....34 u
Messalo....46 j
Messina (Italy)....35 n
Messina (Zimbabwe)....49 e
Messoyakha....51 e
Meta....23 r
Meta Incognita Peninsula....13 w
Metán....28 t
Metema....43 a
Metlaoui....37 e
Metlili Chaamba....34 u
Metoro....45 y
Metsiamonong....49 a
Metu....43 a
Metz....33 n
Meulaboh....65 t
Mexiana....26 l
Mexicali....18 d
Mexican Plateau....18-19
Mexican Water....15 o
Mexico....18-19/20
Mexico City....19 o
Meymeh....39 i
Mezcalapa....20 q
Mežđurečensk....56 g
Mezen'....50 e
Mezen' Gulf....50 e
Mezen' (River)....50 e
Mezquital....18 y
M'guiden....37 a
Mhangura....49 e
M. Hidalgo Reservoir....18 i
Mhow....61 n
Miahuatlán....19 q
Miami (Florida)....20 m
Miami (Oklahoma)....15 w

Mianeh....54 w
Miang....65 j
Mianwali....60 l
Mianyang....62 j
Mianyang....63 c
Miaodao Qundao....58 q
Miarinarivo....47 r
Michigan....16 t
Michigan, Lake....16 s
Michurinsk....54 f
Micronesia....71 a
Midar....36 j
Middelburg....49 n
Middelburg....49 r
Middle Andaman....65 e
Middle Atlas....36 i
Middleboro....15 j
Middlesbrough....32 y
Middleton (Australia)....73 w
Middleton (Canada)....17 f
Middleton Reef....78 k
Midelt....36 i
Midi....39 p
Midland (Canada)....16 w
Midland (Michigan)....16 u
Midland (Texas)....18 m
Midway Island....223 m
Mieso....43 d
Miguel Auza....18 l
Mikhaylova....54 i
Mikhaylova (Taimyr Peninsula)....51 g
Mikhaylovka....54 g
Mikumi....45 j
Mikun....50 t
Milan....34 k
Milang....62 u
Milano (Milan)....34 k
Mildura....77 i
Mile....62 v
Miles....78 e
Miles City....15 d
Milestone....15 d
Mileura....76 e
Milford....14 z
Milford Sound....79 p
Milgun....76 f
Milingimbi....73 e
Milk....15 b
Mil'kovo....53 y
Milk River....14 m
Mille, Lake....15 k
Millerovo....54 e
Millicent....77 u
Millstream....72 t
Millungera....73 x
Milne Land....91 p
Milos....35 t
Milparinka....77 i
Milwaukee....16 r
Mimongo....44 d
Mina....56 k
Minab....39 m
Minas....31 e
Mina Saud....39 g
Minas Gerais....29 n
Minatitlán....19 s
Minch....32 i
Mindanao....67 x
Minden....19 f
Mindoro....67 f
Mindoro Strait....67 f
Mineiros....29 b
Minfeng....56 q
Minga....45 p
Mingecaurskoje Reservoir....54 v
Mingenew....76 d
Mingoyo....45 x
Mingshui....56 y
Minhe....62 i
Minicoy....64 p
Min Jiang....63 r
Min Jiang (Wuyi Shan)....62 i
Minle....57 n
Minna....41 f
Minneapolis-St. Paul....16 b
Minnedosa....15 c
Minnesota (State)....15 j
Minnesota (River)....15-16
Minnie Creek....72 s

Miño....34 a
Minot....15 f
Minqing....63 s
Minto Atoll....71 h
Minto Inlet....12 e
Minto, Lake....13 u
Minusinsk....56 j
Min Xian....62 j
Minya Konka....62 h
Min'yar....55 b
Mirabad....60 e
Miracema do Norte....26 z
Miraflores....24 m
Miramar....31 c
Miran....56 u
Miranda....28 m
Miranda Downs....73 k
Mirbat....39 y
Mirbat, Ras....39 y
Miri....69 b
Miriam Vale....74 t
Mirim, Lagoa....29 o
Mirjaveh....60 e
Mirny....85 j
Mirnyy....52 f
Mirpur Khas....60 w
Kirsale....43 w
Mirzapur....61 t
Miscou, Point....17 e
Misgar....61 a
Misheguk Mountain....11 a
Misión San Fernando....18 e
Miskolc....35 d
Misool....70 o
Missinaibi....16 h
Mississippi (State)....20 f
Mississippi (River)....16 z
Mississippi Delta....20 g
Missoula....14 l
Missour....36 j
Missouri (River)....15 w
Missouri (State)....15 x
Mistassini....17 a
Mistassini, Lake....16 m
Misurata....35 o
Mitatib....43 a
Mitchell (Australia)....78 c
Mitchell (USA)....15 u
Mitchell (River)....73-77
Mitchell River....73 j
Mitla....19 q
Mito....59 o
Mitrovica....35 d
Mitú....25 b
Mitumbar Mountains....45 b
Mitwaba....45 b
Mitzic....41 v
Miyako....63 x
Miyazaki....58 w
Miyun....57 x
Mizan Teferi....43 n
Mizda....34 z
Mjösa, Lake....33 c
Mkomazi....45 j
Mkumbura....46 f
Mkuze....49 t
Mmabatho....49 n
Moab....15 o
Moa (Island)....73 k
Moa (River)....40 s
Moanda....44 e
Mobaye....42 p
Mobayi-Mbongo....42 q
Mobeka....42 q
Mobile....20 h
Mobridge....15 g
Mocajuba....26 m
Moçambique....45 y
Mocimboa da Praia....45 y
Mocoa....24 j
Moctezuma....18 h
Moctezuma (River)....19 o
Mocuba....45 v
Modena....34 l
Modesto....14 u
Modjamboli....42 q
Moe....77 x
Moengo....26 h

Moenkopi....15 n
Mogadishu....43 u
Mogdy....58 l
Mogilev....33 z
Mogilev Podol'skiy....35 i
Mogoča....52 u
Mogochin....51 s
Mogojto....52 r
Mogok....62 r
Mohammadia....34 s
Moheli....47 a
Mohoro....45 k
Moincêr....61 e
Mointy....55 k
Mo-i-Rana....33 e
Mojave....14 w
Mojo....28 f
Mojones....28 r
Moju....26 m
Mokambo....45 p
Mokil Atoll....71 l
Mokolo....41 k
Mokowe....45 l
Mokp'o....58 t
Molde....33 b
Moldova....35 i
Molepolole....49 b
Molgary....56 b
Moline....16 q
Mollendo....24 z
Molócuè....46 k
Molodetschno....33 x
Molodezhnaya....84 l
Molodo....52 j
Molokai....18 q
Molopo....49 n
Moloundou....41 y
Moluccas....69 l
Molucca Sea....69 k
Moma....46 y
Mombasa....45 k
Momboyo....44 j
Mompós....23 a
Monaco....34 k
Monapo....46 l
Mona-Quimbundo....44 x
Mončegorsk....50 a
Mönch Chajrchan....56 j
Monclova....19 a
Moncton....17 e
Mondo....41 l
Mondy....57 a
Monga....42 r
Mongalla....42 y
Monghyr....61 v
Möng Küng....62 r
Mongo....42 b
Mongola....42 p
Mongolia,....56-57
Mongolo....52 d
Möng Ton....62 r
Mongu....44 y
Monguno....41 j
Möng Yai....62 r
Monkira....77 h
Monkoto....44 k
Mono....71 u
Mon'obut....52 z
Monroe....19 g
Monrovia....40 s
Montalvo....24 j
Montana....15 a
Mont aux Sources....49 o
Monte Alegre....26 i
Monte Alto....29 e
Monte Dourado....26 j
Montego Bay....21 n
Montemorelos....19 b
Montepuez....45 x
Monte Quemado....28 u
Monterey....14 u
Montería....22 l
Montero....25 t
Monteros....28 s
Monterrey....19 b
Montes Claros....29 i
Montevideo (Uruguay)....31 d
Montevideo (USA)....15 i
Montgomery....20 i
Monticello....15 o

Mont-Joli ...... 17 c	Mostaganem ...... 34 s	Muddy Gap ...... 15 p	Muskegon ...... 16 s	Nagqu ...... 61 l
Mont Laurier ...... 16 m	Mosting, Cape ...... 90 w	Mudgee ...... 78 e	Muskogee ...... 15 w	Nagykanizsa ...... 35 c
Montmagny ...... 17 b	Mosul ...... 54 t	Mudginbarry ...... 73 d	Muslimbagh ...... 60 j	Naha ...... 63 z
Monto ...... 74 s	Mota ...... 43 b	Mueda ...... 45 x	Musmar ...... 38 y	Nahanni Butte ...... 12 p
Montpelier ...... 15 n	Motagua ...... 22 c	Muerto Meer ...... 20 p	Musoma ...... 45 g	Nahuel Huapi, Lago ...... 30 h
Montpellier ...... 34 h	Motihari ...... 61 h	Mufulira ...... 45 p	Mussende ...... 44 u	Naiband ...... 60 b
Montréal ...... 16 m	Motorchuna ...... 52 l	Muğla ...... 35 v	Mussera ...... 44 f	Naij Tal ...... 62 c
Montrose ...... 15 o	Motril ...... 36 j	Mugrab ...... 55 r	Mustahil ...... 43 t	Naiman Qi ...... 58 d
Monts des Ouled Nail ...... 37 b	Motul ...... 20 t	Muhairiqah ...... 39 r	Mustang ...... 61 g	Nain (Canada) ...... 13 z
Montserrat ...... 21 y	Motykleyka ...... 53 u	Muhammad Qol ...... 38 z	Musters, Lago ...... 30 w	Nain (Iran) ...... 39 k
Montsinery ...... 26 j	Moudjéria ...... 40 e	Muhammad, Ras ...... 38 k	Muswellbrook ...... 78 f	Nairobi ...... 45 j
Monywa ...... 62 p	Mouila ...... 44 d	Mühling Hoffman	Mût ...... 38 t	Naivasha ...... 45 i
Moomou ...... 42 s	Moul ...... 41 j	Mountains ...... 83 j	Mutankiang ...... 58 h	Najaf ...... 39 d
Moonie ...... 78 e	Mould Bay ...... 12 e	Muinak ...... 55 p	Mutare ...... 49 g	Najafabad ...... 39 i
Moora ...... 76 d	Moulins ...... 34 h	Muji ...... 56 o	Mutoko ...... 49 g	Najd ...... 39 c
Moore, Lake ...... 76 e	Moulmein ...... 65 h	Mukachevo ...... 33 v	Mutomo ...... 45 k	Najin ...... 58 j
Moorhead ...... 15 i	Moulouya ...... 36 j	Mukana ...... 45 o	Mutoray ...... 51 z	Najran ...... 39 q
Moose Jaw ...... 15 d	Moundou ...... 41 l	Mukden (Shenyang) ...... 58 c	Muttaburra ...... 74 o	Nakamura ...... 58 x
Moose Lake ...... 15 g	Mount Coolon ...... 74 q	Mukuku ...... 45 q	Mutuali ...... 45 w	Nakasongola ...... 42 x
Moosonee ...... 16 i	Mount Dalrymple ...... 74 r	Mukumbura ...... 49 f	Muxima ...... 44 s	Nakfa ...... 38 z
Mopeia ...... 46 v	Mount Darwin ...... 49 f	Mulanje ...... 46 i	Muzaffarabad ...... 60 m	Nakhl ...... 38 k
Mopti ...... 40 k	Mount Douglas ...... 74 q	Mulata ...... 26 i	Muzaffarnagar ...... 61 c	Nakhodka ...... 51 e
Moquegua ...... 25 n	Mount Dutton ...... 77 d	Mulga Park ...... 77 a	Muzaffarpur ...... 61 u	Nakhon Pathom ...... 65 j
Moradabad ...... 61 c	Mount Elliot ...... 74 q	Mulgrave ...... 17 g	Muztag ...... 61 j	Nakhon Ratchasima ...... 65 k
Morafenobe ...... 47 p	Mount Fletcher ...... 49 o	Mulhouse ...... 34 j	Muztag (Yurungkax He)...61 e	Nakhon Sawan ...... 65 j
Moran ...... 15 n	Mount Florence ...... 72 t	Muligort ...... 50 z	Muz Tau ...... 56 f	Nakhon Si Thammarat ....65 w
Morava (River, Slovakia) ..35 b	Mount Frere ...... 49 r	Muling ...... 58 j	Mvolo ...... 42 w	Nakina ...... 16 f
Morava (River, Yugoslavia)35 e	Mount Gambier ...... 77 u	Mull ...... 32 v	Mvomero ...... 45 j	Naknek ...... 11 p
Moray Firth ...... 32 j	Mount Hagen ...... 70 z	Mullaittivu ...... 64 v	Mvurwi ...... 46 s	Nakonde ...... 45 s
Mordaga ...... 57 l	Mount House ...... 72 m	Mullewa ...... 76 d	Mwanza ...... 45 l	Nakuru ...... 45 j
Morden ...... 15 h	Mount Isa ...... 73 v	Mulongo ...... 45 b	Mwatate ...... 45 k	Nal'čik ...... 54 t
Mordovo ...... 54 f	Mount Magnet ...... 76 f	Multan ...... 60 l	Mweka ...... 44 k	Nalgonda ...... 61 q
Moree ...... 78 e	Mount Minnie ...... 72 s	Mulu ...... 67 o	Mwene Ditu ...... 44 m	Nalut ...... 34 z
Morehead ...... 16 u	Mount Morgan ...... 74 s	Mulundo ...... 44 t	Mwenezi ...... 49 e	Nalychevo ...... 53 y
Morehead City ...... 21 b	Mount Seabrook ...... 76 e	Mulym'ya ...... 50 z	Mwenga ...... 45 c	Nama ...... 28 c
Morelia ...... 19 n	Mount Sturgeon ...... 74 n	Mumbai (Bombay) ...... 60 z	Mweru, Lake ...... 45 c	Namaacha ...... 49 t
Morella ...... 74 o	Mount Surprise ...... 74 b	Mumbué ...... 44 v	Mwingi ...... 45 j	Namacurra ...... 46 w
Morelos ...... 19 s	Mount Vernon (Australia)..72 t	Mumbwa ...... 45 o	Mwinilunga ...... 44 z	Namakzar-e Shadad ...... 60 c
Moreton Island ...... 78 g	Mount Vernon (Illinois)......16 r	Mumra ...... 54 j	Myajlar ...... 60 x	Namanga ...... 45 i
Morgan ...... 77 g	Mount Vernon	Muna (Island) ...... 69 v	Myakit ...... 53 i	Namangan ...... 55 v
Morichal ...... 23 p	(Washington) ...... 14 h	Muna (River) ...... 52 h	Myanaung ...... 65 a	Namanyere ...... 45 e
Morin Dawa ...... 58 f	Mount Wedge ...... 73 q	München (Munich) ...... 34 l	Myanmar (Burma) ..62/65/66	Namapa ...... 46 l
Morley River ...... 11 m	Mountain Village ...... 11 a	Muncie ...... 16 t	Myingyan ...... 62 q	Nambour ...... 78 g
Mornington ...... 73 h	Moura ...... 25 h	Mundo Novo ...... 27 s	Myitkyina ...... 62 r	Nambuangongo ...... 44 f
Mornington (Island) ...... 73 h	Mourdi Depression ...... 38 o	Mundri ...... 42 x	Mymensingh ...... 61 x	Nam Can ...... 66 u
Moro ...... 60 j	Moussoro ...... 41 m	Mundubbera ...... 74 s	Mynaral ...... 55 x	Nam Co ...... 61 k
Morobe ...... 71 o	Moutong ...... 69 u	Mundybas ...... 56 g	Mynbulak ...... 55 u	Namco ...... 61 l
Morocco 36	Moutouroua ...... 41 k	Mungindi ...... 78 d	Myroodah ...... 72 x	Nam Dinh ...... 62 x
Morogoro ...... 45 j	Moven ...... 77 l	Munich ...... 34 l	Myrtle Beach ...... 21 a	Nametil ...... 46 l
Moro Gulf ...... 67 u	Mowming ...... 63 y	Münster ...... 33 o	Mys ...... 53 m	Namialo ...... 45 x
Morokovo ...... 10 e	Moxico ...... 44 x	Muntok ...... 68 i	Mysore ...... 64 f	Namib ...... 48 g
Morokweng ...... 49 n	Moyale ...... 43 p	Munugudzhak ...... 53 l	Mys Shmidta ...... 10 h	Namibe ...... 48 e
Moroleón ...... 19 n	Moyeni ...... 49 q	Mununga ...... 45 q	Mys Zelaniya ...... 51 a	Namibia 44/48
Morombe ...... 47 n	Moyero ...... 52 l	Muonio ...... 33 j	My Tho ...... 66 i	Namies ...... 48 x
Morón ...... 21 n	Moyobamba ...... 24 j	Muqdisho (Mogadishu) ...... 43 u	Mytisci ...... 54 d	Namjagbarwa Feng ...... 62 c
Mörön ...... 57 a	Moyu ...... 61 d	Muraé ...... 29 j	Myylybulak ...... 55 l	Nam Kaub ...... 48 k
Morona ...... 24 j	Mozambique 45-46/49	Murallón ...... 30 t	Mzimba ...... 45 t	Namlea ...... 69 y
Morondava ...... 47 o	Mozambique Channel ...... 46 z	Murashi ...... 50 l	Mzuzu ...... 45 t	Namoi ...... 78 e
Morondo ...... 40 l	Mozhaysk ...... 54 c	Murat Nehri ...... 54 r		Namolok ...... 71 f
Moroni ...... 47 a	Mozyr ...... 33 y	Muratus Mountains ...... 69 p		Namonuito Atoll ...... 71 c
Moron Us He ...... 61 m	Mpaathutlwa Pan ...... 48 l	Murchison ...... 76 d	**N**	Nampala ...... 40 j
Morotai ...... 69 m	M'Pala ...... 44 f	Murchisson ...... 41 g		Nampula ...... 46 k
Moroto ...... 42 z	Mpanda ...... 45 e	Murcia ...... 34 r	Naalehu ...... 18 r	Namutoni ...... 44 u
Morozovsk ...... 54 g	Mpata ...... 44 j	Murdochville ...... 17 e	Naba ...... 62 q	Namwala ...... 45 n
Morrinhos ...... 29 d	Mpessoba ...... 40 l	Mures ...... 35 e	Nababeep ...... 48 v	Nan ...... 65 j
Morris ...... 16 r	Mpika ...... 45 s	Murfreesboro ...... 16 s	Nabberu, Lake ...... 76 s	Nanaimo ...... 14 g
Morro Grande ...... 26 h	Mporokoso ...... 45 r	Murgab (River,	Naberezhnyje Celny ...... 54 l	Nanbu ...... 62 k
Morshansk ...... 54 f	Mpulungu ...... 46 e	Afghanistan) ...... 60 h	Nabk ...... 38 l	Nancha ...... 58 i
Morteros ...... 28 v	Mpwapwa ...... 45 i	Murgab (River, Tajikistan) 55 w	Nabk Abu Qasr ...... 39 a	Nanchang ...... 63 e
Mortes ...... 26 x	Msaken ...... 37 g	Murgenella ...... 73 d	Nabukjuak ...... 13 g	Nanchung ...... 62 k
Mortlock Islands ...... 71 k	Msata ...... 45 j	Murgon ...... 74 t	Nacala ...... 45 y	Nancy ...... 34 i
Morven ...... 74 q	Mtito Andei ...... 45 j	Murgoo ...... 76 d	Nacaome ...... 22 v	Nanda Devi ...... 61 d
Morvi ...... 60 y	Mtubatuba ...... 49 t	Muriege ...... 44 x	Nacaroa ...... 45 y	Nanded ...... 61 p
Moryakovskiy Zaton ...... 51 s	Mtwara ...... 45 y	Murillo Atoll ...... 71 f	Nachičevan ...... 54 u	Nandi ...... 75 k
Moscow (Russia) ...... 54 c	Muanda ...... 44 d	Murmansk ...... 50 a	Nachingwea ...... 45 w	Nanfeng ...... 63 e
Moscow (USA) ...... 14 k	Muang Chiang Rai ...... 65 i	Murom ...... 54 f	Nachodka ...... 58 k	Nanga Eboko ...... 41 w
Mosegda ...... 52 u	Muang Khoa ...... 62 u	Muroran ...... 59 c	Nacogdoches ...... 19 c	Nanga Parbat ...... 61 a
Moses Lake ...... 14 i	Muar ...... 68 u	Murray ...... 77 g	Nadiad ...... 60 z	Nanga Pinoh ...... 69 a
Mosetse ...... 49 b	Muarabadak ...... 69 e	Murray Bridge ...... 77 g	Nador ...... 36 j	Nanga Sokan ...... 68 m
Moshi ...... 45 j	Muarabungo ...... 68 g	Murray Lake ...... 70 x	Nadym ...... 51 p	Nangdoi ...... 62 h
Mösjöen ...... 33 d	Mubarek ...... 55 s	Murrumbidgee ...... 77 j	Nafud ...... 39 h	Nangomba ...... 45 w
Moskva (Moscow) ...... 54 c	Mubende ...... 42 x	Murukta ...... 52 a	Naga ...... 67 i	Nangqên ...... 62 e
Mosomane ...... 49 b	Mubi ...... 41 j	Mururoa ...... 230 q	Nagano ...... 59 n	Nangsin Sum ...... 57 r
Mosquitos Coast ...... 22 g	Mucajá ...... 25 k	Murwillumbah ...... 78 e	Nagarjuna Reservoir ...... 64 s	Nangtud ...... 67 h
Mosquitos, Gulf of ...... 22 i	Muchinga Mountains ...... 45 r	Murzuq ...... 37 v	Nagasaki ...... 58 v	Nangurukuru ...... 45 k
Mossaka ...... 44 h	Muconda ...... 44 x	Musa Ali ...... 43 f	Nagaur ...... 60 m	Nan Xian ...... 62 b
Mosselbaai ...... 48 z	Mucubela ...... 46 x	Musala ...... 35 f	Nagercoil ...... 64 s	Nan Hulsan Hu ...... 62 d
Mossendjo ...... 44 e	Mucuim ...... 25 f	Musandam, Ras ...... 60 n	Nagornyy ...... 52 x	Nanjing (Nanking) ...... 63 g
Mossman ...... 74 b	Mucuri ...... 29 k	Muscat ...... 60 p	Nagoya ...... 58 z	Nanking ...... 63 g
Mossoró ...... 27 u	Mucusso ...... 48 l	Musgrave Ranges ...... 77 a	Nagpur ...... 61 p	Nanning ...... 62 z

Nanortilak ....90 s
Nanpang Jiang ....62 w
Nanping ....63 s
Nansen Land ....91 i
Nansen Sound ....89 s
Nanshan Islands............67 a
Nansio ....45 g
Nantes ....34 f
Nantulo ....45 x
Nantung ....63 h
Nanuque ....29 k
Nanxiong ....63 p
Nanyang ....63 b
Nanyuki ....43 o
Nanzhang ....63 a
Nanzhao ....63 b
Nao, Cabo de la ....34 s
Napalkovo ....51 c
Nape ....62 w
Napier ....79 w
Naples (Florida)..............20 l
Naples (Italy)..................35 a
Napo ....24 k
Napoleon ....16 t
Napoli (Naples)...............35 a
Nara ....40 i
Naracoorte ....77 u
Narasun ....57 h
Narat ....56 r
Narathiwat ....65 x
Narbonne ....34 h
Nares Strait ....91 d
Naribis ....48 h
Narijnteel ....57 n
Narmada ....60 z
Narodnaja ....50 k
Narodnaya ....50 x
Narok ....45 h
Narrabri ....78 e
Narrandera ....78 b
Narrogin ....76 e
Narromine ....78 c
Narsarsuaq ....90 t
Narsimhapur ....61 q
Narsinghgarh ....61 p
Narubis ....48 w
Narva ....33 k
Narvik ....33 f
Nar'yan Mar ....50 i
Naryn ....56 m
Naryn (Naryn Taragay) .....55 y
Narynkol ....56 p
Naryn Taragay ....56 n
Nashville ....16 s
Näsi, Lake ....33 j
Nasik ....60 z
Nasir ....42 l
Naskaupi ....17 g
Nassau ....21 b
Nasser, Lake ....38 v
Nata ....49 b
Natal ....27 w
Natanz ....39 i
Natashquan ....17 g
Natashquan (River) ....17 g
Natchitoches ....20 d
Nathan River ....73 f
Natitingou ....41 b
Natividade ....26 z
Natron, Lake ....45 i
Natuna ....66 x
Natuna Islands ....66 x
Naulila ....44 t
Nauru ....231 y
Naurzum ....55 f
Nauta ....24 l
Nauzad ....60 g
Navadwip ....61 w
Navarin, Cape ....10 h
Navio, Serra do ....26 j
Navirai ....29 a
Navlya ....54 b
Navoi ....55 s
Navojoa ....18 h
Navolato ....18 i
Navrongo ....40 m
Navsari ....60 z
Nayakhan ....53 l
Naykhin ....58 m

Nazaré ....27 t
Nazarovka ....54 f
Nazarovo ....56 i
Nazas ....18 l
Nazca ....24 y
Nazimovo ....51 w
Nazina ....51 r
Nazret ....43 d
Nazwa ....60 o
Nazym ....51 n
Nazyyayevsk ....55 i
Nchelenge ....45 q
N'Dalatando ....44 t
Ndareda ....45 h
Ndélé ....42 c
Ndendé ....44 d
N'Djamena ....41 l
Ndji ....42 e
Ndjolé (Cameroon) ....41 v
Ndjolé (Gabon) ....41 v
Ndola ....46 d
Neagh, Lough ....32 v
Neale, Lake ....73 o
Near Islands ....10 r
Nebit-Dag ....54 z
Nebo ....74 r
Nebraska ....15 s
Nebraska City ....15 v
Nechako Reservoir ....14 e
Nechi ....22 m
Necochea ....31 c
Necoclí ....22 l
Nêdong ....61 m
Neds Creek ....76 f
Neepawa ....15 g
Neftekamsk ....54 m
Negage ....44 q
Negele ....43 q
Negoiu ....35 g
Negola ....44 t
Negotka ....51 s
Negro Reservoir ....28 z
Negro (River, Argentina)...30 m
Negro (River, Brazil) ....25 e
Negro (River, Uruguay) .....29 n
Negros ....67 h
Nehbandan ....60 d
Nehe ....58 f
Nehri ....54 s
Neijiang (Neikiang) ....62 k
Neiriz ....39 k
Neishabur ....55 o
Neiva ....22 z
Nekempt ....43 b
Neleger ....52 m
Nel'gese ....53 b
Nelidovo ....50 n
Nel'kan ....53 p
Nellore ....64 h
Nelson (Canada) ....14 k
Nelson (New Zealand)......79 t
Nelson (River) ....13 n
Nelson Forks ....12 p
Nelson Strait ....30 s
Nelspruit ....49 s
Néma ....40 i
Nembudziya ....46 r
Nemen ....33 v
Nemuro ....59 e
Nemuy ....53 p
Nenana ....11 f
Nenjiang ....58 f
Nen Jiang (River) ....58 f
Neosho ....15 w
Nepa ....52 q
Nepal 61
Nepalganj ....61 f
Nepa (River) ....52 p
Nephi ....14 z
Nepoko ....42 v
Nera ....53 f
Nerča ....52 t
Nerchinskiy Zavod ....52 u
Nerpich'ye, Lake ....53 m
Nerrima ....72 x
Neryungri ....52 w
Ness, Loch ....32 j
Neter ....53 r
Netherlands 33
Netherlands Antilles..21 x/23 e

Netta ....37 e
Nettilling Lake ....13 j
Neubrandenburg..............33 r
Neuquén ....30 k
Neuquén (River) ....30 i
Neuruppin ....33 r
Neuva Alejandría ....24 l
Nevada (Missouri) ....15 w
Nevada (State) ....14 w
Nevada, Mount ....28 q
Nevada, Sierra ....36 k
Nevado, Sierra del...........30 j
Nevanka ....56 m
Nevel'..............................33 y
New ....23 y
Newala ....45 x
New Amsterdam ....23 y
Newark (New York)..........16 z
Newark (Ohio) ....16 u
New Bedford ....17 o
New Bern ....16 y
New Braunfels ....19 c
New Britain ....71 q
New Brunswick ....17 d
Newburgh ....16 z
New Caledonia ....75 o
Newcastle (Australia) ....78 f
Newcastle (Canada).........17 d
Newcastle (South Africa)..49 r
Newcastle (USA) ....15 q
Newcastle upon Tyne ....32 x
Newcastle Waters ....73 h
New Crown ....77 d
New Delhi ....61 b
Newfoundland ....17 g
New Georgia ....71 w
New Georgia Islands........71 v
New Glasgow ....17 f
New Guinea 70
New Hampshire ....17 n
New Haven ....17 n
New Hebrides ....75 f
New Iberia ....19 g
New Ireland ....71 s
New Jersey ....16 z
New Kandla ....60 x
New Liskeard ....16 j
Newman ....72 v
Newman, Mount ....72 u
New Meadows ....14 k
New Mexico ....15 p
New Norfolk ....77 y
New Orleans ....20 f
New Plymouth ....79 u
Newport (Arkansas) ....16 s
Newport (Tennessee) ....16 u
Newport News ....16 y
New Providence Island.....21 o
New Richmond ....17 d
New Siberian Islands........53 d
New South Wales ....78 c
Newton ....15 x
New Ulm ....15 j
New York (City) ....16 z
New York (State) ....16 y
New Zealand 79
Neyto, Lake ....51 a
Nezhin ....33 z
Ngabang ....68 m
Ngamring ....61 i
Ngangala ....42 y
Ngangla Ringco ....61 g
Ngaoundéré ....41 x
Ngatik Atoll ....71 j
Ngauruhoe ....79 v
Ngidinga ....44 g
N'Giva ....48 h
Ngo ....44 g
Ngoring ....62 e
Ngoura ....41 m
Ngouri ....41 l
Ngourti ....41 j
Ngudu ....45 g
Nguigmi ....41 j
Ngukurr ....73 f
Ngulu Atoll ....70 h
Nguru ....41 h
Nhamunda ....25 k
Nha Trang ....66 l
Nhill ....77 u

Nhulunbuy ....73 g
Niafounké ....40 k
Niagara Falls ....16 w
Niak ....61 h
Niamey ....41 b
Niangara ....42 u
Nia Nia ....42 u
Nias ....68 c
Nicaragua 22
Nicaragua, Lake ....22 f
Nice ....34 j
Nichatka, Lake ....52 u
Nicholls Town ....21 a
Nicholson ....73 n
Nička ....55 r
Nicobar ....65 q
Nicobar, Great ....65 r
Nicobar, Little ....65 r
Nicosia ....35 y
Nicoya, Gulf of ....22 f
Nicoya Peninsula ....22 f
Nidym ....51 z
Niefang ....41 u
Niemba ....45 c
Niénokoué ....40 v
Nieuw Nickerie ....23 z
Nieuwoudtville ....48 x
Niğde ....35 z
Niger 37/41
Niger (River) ....41 e
Nigeria 41
Nihau ....18 o
Niigata ....59 o
Nikolayev ....35 k
Nikolayevsk ....54 h
Nikolayevsk-na-Amure .....53 r
Nikol'sk ....50 s
Nikol'skiy ....55 v
Nikopol ....35 l
Nikshahr ....60 q
Nilang ....61 d
Nile ....38 u
Nile Delta ....35 w
Nilka ....56 q
Niman ....53 n
Nîmes ....34 h
Nimule ....42 y
Ninbing ....73 a
Nindigully ....74 r
Nine Degree Channel.......64 p
Ninety Mile Beach
(Australia) ....77 z
Ninety Mile Beach
(New Zealand) ....79 g
Ning'an ....58 i
Ningde ....63 t
Ningdu ....63 q
Ningjin Shan ....62 d
Ningming ....62 y
Ningpo ....63 h
Ningshan ....62 m
Ningyuan ....63 o
Ninnis Glacier ....86 z
Niobrara ....15 s
Nioki ....44 h
Niokolo Koba ....40 d
Nioro du Sahel ....40 g
Nipigon ....16 e
Nipigon Lake ....16 d
Niquero ....21 o
Nis ....35 e
Nishinoyima ....58 y
Nitchequon ....17 b
Niterói ....29 i
Niubiziliang ....56 v
Nizamabad ....64 f
Nizhinevartovsk ....51 g
Nizhneangarsk.................57 r
Nizhneimbatskoye ....51 v
Nizhniy Novgorod ....50 r
Nizhniy Tagil ....50 x
Nizhniy Yenangsk ....50 s
Niznaya Tunguska ....52 a
Nižneudinsk ....56 m
Niž Taimyra ....51 n
Njombe ....45 u
Nkambe ....41 u
Nkawkaw ....40 z
Nkayi ....49 b
Nkhata Bay ....45 u

Nkhotakota ....45 t
Nkolabona ....41 v
Nkongsamba ....41 u
Noatak ....11 a
Noatak River ....11 a
Nochixtlán ....20 o
Nockatunga ....77 i
Nogales ....18 h
Noginsk ....54 d
Noginskiy ....51 v
Nohar ....61 a
Nok Kundi ....60 f
Kokou ....41 l
Nola ....41 y
Nolinsk ....50 u
Nom ....56 x
Nome ....10 m
Nomgon ....57 q
Nomhon ....62 e
Nonacho Lake ....12 v
Nonburg ....50 h
Nong Khai ....65 l
Noonamah ....73 c
Noorvik ....11 b
Noranda ....16 j
Nordenshel'da Arch. ....51 k
Nordostrundingen ....91 k
Nordvik ....52 e
Nordvik, Cape ....52 f
Norfolk (Nebraska) ....15 u
Norfolk (Virginia) ....16 y
Norfolk Island ....79 d
Noril'sk ....51 h
Normanby (Island)............74 g
Normanton ....73 j
Norman Wells ....12 b
Norovtin ....57 h
Norrköping ....33 f
Norrtälje ....33 g
Norseman ....76 h
Norte, Cabo ....26 l
Norte, Punta ....30 m
Norte, Punta
(Samboronbón Bay) ....31 d
Norte, Serra do ....25 w
Northam ....76 e
Northampton ....76 x
North Andaman ....65 e
North Anyuskiy Mountains10 b
North Battleford ....15 b
North Bay ....16 j
North Baykal Plateau........52 r
North, Cape (Canada) ....17 h
North Cape (New Zealand)79 g
North Cape (Norway) ....33 k
North Caribou Lake ....16 c
North Carolina ....16 v
North Channel (UK) ....32 v
North Dakota ....15 f
North Dvina ....50 r
North East Land ....92 c
Northern Ireland ....32 v
Northern Mariana Islands231 j
Northern Sporades ....35 t
Northern Territory ....73 q
Northern Ural Mountains ..50 x
Northern Uvaly ....50 s
North Fork ....14 x
North Horr ....43 o
North Island ....79 u
North Lincoln Land ....13 f
North Natuna ....68 x
North Pagai ....68 u
North Platte ....15 t
North Pole ....92 a
North Saskatchewan ....15 a
North Sea ....32 z
North Sosva ....50 y
Northumberland Strait ....17 f
Northway Junction ....11 h
North West Cape ....72 x
North-West River ....17 g
Northwest Territories ...11-12
Norton ....15 t
Norton Sound ....11 a
Norvegia, Cape ....83 g
Norway 33
Norway House ....15 h
Norwegian Bay ....13 b
Norwegian Sea 33

Norwich.............................32 z
Noshul'.............................50 t
Nosratabad.......................60 c
Nossob.............................48 y
Nosy-Bé...........................47 e
Nosy Boraha......................47 s
Noto................................37 j
Nôtre Dame Bay................17 k
Nottingham.......................32 y
Nottingham Island ....13 s
Nouâdhibou ....36 n
Nouâdhibou, Cape ....36 n
Nouakchott.......................36 n
Nouamrhar........................36 o
Nouméa............................75 q
Nouna..............................40 k
Nova Alvorada..................29 a
Novabad...........................55 v
Nova Crixas......................29 d
Nova Gaia........................44 u
Nova Goleg ....46 u
Nova Olinda do Norte.......25 j
Novara.............................34 k
Nova Russas.....................27 r
Nova Scotia......................17 f
Novay..............................51 m
Novaya Kakhova ....54 b
Novaya Kakhovka ....35 l
Novaya Sibir'....................53 h
Novaya Zemlya ....50 j
Novgorod..........................33 l
Novillo Reservoir ....18 h
Novisad............................35 d
Novo Aripuan....................25 i
Novocherkassk..................54 e
Novodolinka......................55 k
Novo Friburgo...................29 j
Novograd Volynskiy...........33 x
Novo Hamburgo.................29 q
Novoilinovka.....................59 a
Novoishimskiy....................55 h
Novokiyevskiy Uval ....58 i
Novokuzneck.....................56 g
Novolazarevskaya..............83 m
Novomoskovsk (Russia)...54 e
Novomoskovsk (Ukraine) .54 c
Novorossiyka.....................52 z
Novorossiysk.....................54 q
Novoryonye ....52 b
Novoshakhtinsk.................54 e
Novosibirsk.......................56 e
Novo Uzensk.....................54 j
Novo-Vyatsk......................50 u
Novoyerundinskiy...............51 x
Novyy..............................52 c
Novyy (Vilyuy)...................52 f
Novyy Port........................51 b
Nowgong..........................62 o
Nowra..............................78 e
Noyabr'sk.........................51 q
Nsah................................44 y
Nsanje.............................46 v
Ntadembele......................44 h
Ntam...............................41 w
Ntoroko...........................42 w
Nuanetsi...........................49 g
Nuatja..............................41 n
Nuba Mountains ....42 j
Nubian Desert...................38 x
Nueltin Lake ....12 y
Nueva Rosita.....................19 a
Nueve de Julio..................31 a
Nuevitas...........................21 o
Nuevo..............................20 r
Nuevo Casas Grandes.....18 j
Nuevo Gulf ....30 m
Nuevo Laredo ....19 a
Nu Jiang...........................62 e
Nukiki..............................71 w
Nullagine..........................72 v
Nullarbor..........................77 a
Nullarbor Plain..................76 l
Numan..............................41 i
Numkaub..........................48 k
Numto..............................51 p
Nunap Isua
(Cape Farewell).............90 t
Nunatak ....13 k
Nunavut........................12-13
Nungnain Sun...................57 y

Nungo..............................45 w
Nunivak............................10 m
Nunligran..........................10 j
Nuoro..............................34 k
Nura................................55 i
Nurabad...........................39 i
Nuremberg........................34 m
Nuri................................18 i
Nürnberg (Nuremberg) .....34 m
Nur Turu...........................56 w
Nuru................................55 k
Nusaybin..........................54 s
Nushki.............................60 h
Nutak...............................13 z
Nutwood Downs ....73 e
Nuuk...............................90 u
Nuussuaq Halv..................90 l
Nuweiba...........................38 k
Nuyts Archipelago ....77 c
Nuyts, Cape......................76 d
Nyahururu.........................43 o
Nyainqentangla Shan.......62 c
Nyainrong.........................61 m
Nyakanazi.........................45 e
Nyaksimvol........................50 y
Nyala...............................42 f
Nyalam.............................61 i
Nyamapanda......................49 g
Nyamboyoto......................51 e
Nyanga.............................49 g
Nyanyadzi.........................49 f
Nyasa, Lake
(Lake Malawi)................45 u
Nyazepetrovsk...................55 b
Nyda...............................51 c
Nyeboe Land ....91 g
Nyêmo.............................61 l
Nyima..............................61 j
Nyimba.............................45 r
Nyingchi...........................62 c
Nyíregyháza......................35 e
Nyiri Desert......................45 j
Nyiru...............................43 n
Nylstroom.........................49 d
Nyngan............................78 c
Nyong..............................41 u
Nysh................................53 r
Nyunzu.............................45 c
Nyurba.............................52 h
Nyurchan..........................53 v
Nyuya..............................52 t
Nyuya (River)....................52 r
Nyvrovo...........................53 r
Nzega..............................45 f
Nzérékoré........................40 u
N'Zeto.............................44 e

O

Oahe, Lake ....15 g
Oahu...............................18 p
Oajazeiras........................27 t
Oakes..............................15 h
Oakland...........................14 u
Oaklands..........................78 o
Oakley.............................15 t
Oak Ridge ....16 t
Oala Panja........................55 w
Oamaru............................79 s
Oates Land ....86 w
Oatlands...........................77 y
Oaxaca............................20 o
Ob' (River)........................56 e
Ob', Gulf of ....51 c
Obbia..............................43 w
Oberá..............................29 n
Obi.................................69 l
Obidos.............................25 m
Obihiro.............................59 d
Oblukovino........................53 x
Obninsk............................54 c
Obo................................42 u
Obo Liang ....56 w
Obombo............................48 g
Oboyan'............................54 c
Obrique............................36 i
Obsči Syrt........................54 l
Obuasi.............................40 z
Ocala...............................20 l

Ocaña.............................23 a
Ocean Falls ....14 d
Oceanside.........................18 c
Ocha...............................53 r
Ocoña.............................24 z
Ocoña (River)....................24 z
Ocotlán............................18 z
Oda (Ghana)......................40 z
Oda (Mountain)..................38 y
Odemira...........................36 f
Odense.............................33 p
Oder................................33 r
Odessa (USA)....................18 m
Odessa (Ukraine)...............35 l
Odienné...........................40 i
Odintsovo.........................54 c
Oeiras..............................27 q
Oenpelli...........................73 d
Ofira...............................38 k
Ogaden............................43 t
Ogbomosho.......................41 c
Ogden..............................14 z
Ogeechee.........................20 l
Ogilvie Mountains ....11 i
Ogoamas..........................69 g
Ogoja..............................41 t
Ogoki..............................16 f
Ogooué............................44 c
Ogoron.............................52 z
Ogun...............................41 p
Ogurčinskij........................54 y
Ohanet.............................37 c
O' Higgins, Lago................30 t
Ohio (State)......................16 u
Ohio (River)......................16 u
Ohrid Lake ....35 d
Oiapoque..........................26 k
Ōita................................58 w
Ojgun Nuur ....56 l
Ojinaga............................18 l
Ojo Caliente......................18 z
Ojo de Liebre, Lac..............18 e
Ojos del Salado..................28 q
Oka................................54 f
Oka (Vostochny
Mountains).....................57 a
Okahandja.........................48 i
Okakarara..........................48 j
Okara..............................60 m
Okaukuejo.........................48 h
Okavango..........................48 m
Okavango Delta.................48 m
Okayama...........................58 x
Okeechobee, Lake ....20 l
Okene..............................41 r
Okha...............................53 s
Okhotsk............................53 s
Okhotsk, Sea of.................59 g
Okhotskiy-Perevoz.............53 b
Oki.................................58 x
Okinawa............................63 z
Oklahoma..........................15 t
Oklahoma City...................15 u
Okondja............................44 e
Okoyo..............................44 g
Oktyabr'isk........................51 y
Oktyabrskiy.......................52 z
Oktyabr'skiy......................54 m
Oktyabr'skiy (Kamchatka) 53 x
Oktyabr'skoy Revolutsii.....51 k
Öland...............................33 s
Olavarría..........................31 a
Olbia...............................34 l
Old Crow..........................11 j
Oldéani............................45 h
Olds................................14 l
Olean...............................16 x
Olekma............................52 v
Olekminsk.........................52 v
Olenëk.............................52 e
Olenëk (River)...................52 g
Olëng-Sala........................52 h
Oleni...............................51 d
Ölgij...............................56 j
Olinda..............................27 w
Oliva...............................28 u
Oliva, Cord. de ....28 p
Olivares...........................28 p
Oliveira............................29 h
Ollague............................28 p

Ollita, Cord. de ....28 p
Olmos..............................24 h
Oloitokitok........................45 i
Ol'okama..........................52 v
Olomouc...........................33 s
Olongapo..........................67 f
Olov'annaja.......................57 i
Oloyskiy Mountains ....10 a
Olsztyr.............................33 u
Olympia............................14 g
Olympus...........................35 y
Olyutorskiy.......................10 d
Olyutorskiy, Cape..............10 q
Ōma................................59 c
Omaha.............................15 v
Omak...............................14 i
Oman..........................39/60
Oman, Gulf of ....60 p
Omaruru...........................48 h
Omboué............................44 b
Ombu...............................61 i
Omchali............................54 z
Omdurman.........................42 k
Omeo...............................78 p
Omnya.............................53 n
Omo................................43 n
Omolon............................53 l
Omoloy............................53 a
Omsk...............................55 k
Omsukchan........................53 k
Onangué, Lake ....41 q
Oncócua...........................48 f
Ondangwa.........................48 h
Ondo...............................41 q
Öndör..............................57 j
Öndör Chaan ....57 x
Ondor Sum ....57 u
Onega..............................50 p
Onega Bay ....50 o
Onega, Lake ....50 o
Onega (River)....................50 p
Onegva Yar.......................51 q
O'Neill.............................15 u
Onekotan..........................59 k
Ongjin..............................58 s
Ongniud Qi ....57 x
Ongole.............................64 h
Onitsha............................41 s
Onkuchakh.........................52 f
Onon Gol ....57 g
Onseepkans.......................48 w
Onslow.............................72 r
Ontario.............................14 k
Ontario (Province)..............16 c
Ontario, Lake ....16 x
Oobagooma........................72 k
Oodnadatta........................77 d
Ooldea.............................77 b
Oologah Lake ....15 w
Ooratippra.........................73 t
Ootacamund ....64 e
Opal...............................55 y
Opala..............................42 s
Opelika............................20 i
Ophir...............................68 e
Opienge............................42 u
Opochka............................33 y
Opornyy............................54 m
Oporto.............................34 a
Oppdal.............................33 c
Opuwa.............................48 f
Oradea.............................35 e
Orai................................61 q
Oran (Algeria)....................34 s
Orange.............................78 d
Orange (River)...................48 y
Orange, Cabo ....26 k
Orangegebirgte..................26 h
Orbost.............................78 u
Orcadas............................82 g
Orchontuul.......................57 d
Ord (Mount)......................72 l
Ord (River)........................73 a
Ord River ....73 a
Ordos..............................57 s
Ordynskoye.......................56 d
Örebro.............................33 e
Orechovo-Zujevo................54 e
Oregon.............................14 w
Orel................................54 c

Orel', Lake ....53 q
Orellana...........................24 i
Orellana (Ucayali)..............24 k
Orenburg..........................54 m
Orense.............................34 a
Orgejev............................35 i
Orgon Tal ....57 u
Orillia..............................16 j
Orinoco............................23 h
Orinoco Delta.....................23 i
Oristano...........................34 x
Oriximiná..........................25 m
Orizaba............................19 z
Orkney Islands ....32 k
Orlando............................20 m
Orléans............................32 z
Orleans, Isle d'..................17 b
Orlik...............................57 a
Orlinga............................57 a
Ormara.............................60 t
Ormoc.............................67 j
Ornsköldsvik......................33 g
Orocué.............................23 o
Orog Nuur ....57 n
Orög Nuur ....56 i
Oroluk Atoll ....71 i
Oron (Russia).....................57 h
Oron (Russia).....................52 t
Oronoque..........................23 y
Oroqen Zizhiqi...................58 e
Oroquieta..........................67 v
Orotukan..........................53 i
Oroumieh..........................54 u
Orovada............................14 w
Oroville (California)............14 u
Oroville (Washington).........14 i
Oroyek.............................53 j
Orsha..............................33 y
Orsk...............................55 b
Orto-Ayan.........................52 m
Orto-Kyuyel'.....................52 m
Ortonville.........................15 i
Orupembe.........................48 f
Oruro..............................28 e
Os.................................55 w
Ōsaka..............................58 z
Oscrovnoy.........................94 i
Oshakati...........................48 h
Oshawa.............................16 w
Oshkosh............................16 r
Oshmarino.........................51 f
Oshogbo...........................41 d
Oshtoran..........................39 f
Oshwe..............................44 j
Osijek..............................35 c
Osinovo............................51 v
Oskaloosa.........................15 x
Oskara, Cape ....51 l
Oslo................................33 d
Oslofjord...........................33 c
Osnabrück.........................33 o
Osóriô.............................29 q
Osorno.............................30 g
Ossa...............................77 x
Ossora.............................10 c
Ostashkov.........................50 n
Ostend.............................32 z
Östersund.........................33 e
Ostrava............................35 c
Ostrov.............................33 l
Ostrovnoy.........................10 b
Ōsumi Channel ....58 v
Osvaldo Cruz.....................29 d
Otaru..............................59 b
Otavalo............................24 i
Otavi...............................48 i
O.T.Downs ....73 e
Otish Mountains ....17 b
Otjiwarongo ....48 h
Otog Qi ....57 r
Ot-Siyen..........................52 i
Ottawa (Canada)................16 m
Ottawa (USA)....................15 w
Ottawa (River)...................16 x
Ottawa Islands ....13 s
Ottuk...............................55 y
Ottumwa...........................15 x
Oturkpo............................41 t
Otuzco.............................24 i
Otway, Cape ....77 v

Ouadane........................36 r
Ouadda..........................42 e
Ouagadougou................40 m
Ouagat..........................42 d
Ouahigouya...................40 l
Ouahila...........................36 i
Ouake............................42 p
Oualata.........................36 u
Oualidia.........................36 f
Ouallam.........................41 b
Ouandago.....................42 o
Ouandja.........................42 d
Ouangolodougou..........40 i
Ouaqui...........................26 i
Ouara............................42 s
Ouarane.......................36 s
Ouargla..........................34 v
Oubangui......................42 p
Oudeïka.........................36 y
Oudtshoorn....................48 y
Oued Zem.....................36 h
Ouémé..........................41 b
Ouerrha........................36 j
Ouesso..........................41 y
Ouezzane.....................36 i
Ouham...........................42 a
Ouidah...........................41 o
Oujda.............................34 r
Oujeft............................36 q
Ouled Djellal...................34 v
Oulou............................42 d
Oulu...............................33 j
Oulu, Lake.....................33 k
Oum..............................36 g
Oum Hadjer..................42 b
Ounianga Kebir.............38 n
Ouricuri.........................27 s
Ourinhos......................29 d
Ourique.........................36 g
Outat-el-Hadj................36 j
Outjo..............................48 h
Ouyen...........................77 v
Ouyu Bezze Denga.......41 j
Ovalle...........................28 u
Ovamboland..................48 i
Oviedo..........................34 c
Ovoot............................56 k
Ovoot Chural................57 o
Övre Årdal.....................33 b
Owando........................44 h
Owensboro...................16 s
Owen Sound.................16 i
Owen Stanley Range.....71 o
Owo...............................41 r
Owyhee.........................14 x
Oxapampa....................24 x
Oxford............................32 x
Oyapock........................26 j
Oyem.............................41 v
Oyero Arys....................55 g
Oymyakon.....................53 e
Oyo................................41 p
Oysurdakh.....................53 j
Oyun-Kyyuel'.................53 c
Oyun-Yurege.................53 a
Ożalilabad.....................54 w
Ozamiz..........................67 v
Ozark Plateau...............15 x
Ozhogina (River)...........53 x
Ozhogino, Lake.............53 g
Ozhogino.......................53 h

P

Paamiut.........................90 t
Pabna............................61 x
Pacáas Novos, Serra dos 25 s
Pacajá...........................26 k
Pacaraima, Serra..........23 v
Pacasmayo...................24 h
Pacaya..........................24 k
Pachino........................37 j
Pachitea.......................24 y
Pachuca........................19 o
Pacific Ocean.........230-231
Pacoval.........................26 i
Padang..........................68 e
Padangpanjang.............68 f
Padangsidempuan.........68 d

Padauiri.........................25 f
Padre Bernardo.............29 e
Padre Paraiso................29 k
Padua...........................34 m
Paducah........................16 r
Padunskoje, More..........33 m
Paektu-san....................58 h
Pafuri............................49 f
Pag................................35 a
Paga-Conta...................26 u
Pagadian.......................67 u
Pagalu...........................41 r
Page..............................15 n
Pahokee........................20 m
Päijänne, Lake..............33 j
Paita..............................24 g
Pajule............................42 y
Pakanbaru.....................68 g
Pakaraima Mountains....26
Pakhoi...........................62 z
Pakistan........................60
Pakkoku........................62 p
Pak Sane......................66 g
Pakse............................66 i
Pala...............................41 k
Palana...........................53 z
Palangkaraya................69 b
Palanpur........................60 z
Palapye.........................49 c
Palata............................20 l
Palatka..........................53 v
Palau.............................70 e
Palawan.........................67 d
Paleleh..........................69 h
Palembang.....................68 u
Palenque.......................20 r
Palermo (Colombia).......24 m
Palermo (Italy)...............35 c
Palghat..........................64 f
Palgrave........................72 s
Palgrave, Mount............72 s
Pali................................60 z
Palk Strait......................64 h
Palliser, Cape................79 v
Palma............................34 u
Palmares......................27 w
Palma Soriano...............21 p
Palmeirais.....................27 p
Palmeira los Indlos........27 v
Palmeiras......................27 n
Palmer (Alaska).............11 f
Palmer (Graham Land)...82 t
Palmer Land..................82 x
Palmerston North...........79 v
Palmira..........................22 y
Palm Springs.................18 d
Palmyra.........................38 m
Palmyra Island............230 a
Palmyras Point..............61 w
Paloich..........................42 l
Palomani.......................25 p
Palopo...........................69 t
Palo Santo....................28 x
Palpa.............................24 x
Palparara.......................73 w
Palu...............................69 g
Pamangkat....................68 k
Pambarra......................49 h
Pamir.............................55 x
Pamlico Sound..............16 y
Pampa de las Salinas....28 r
Pampa de los Guanacos..28 v
Pampas.........................24 y
Pampas (River)..............24 y
Pamplona (Colombia).....23 b
Pamplona (Spain)..........34 f
Pamyat..........................56 j
Pamzal..........................61 c
Panaji............................64 c
Panamá (City)...............22 j
Panama..........................22
Panamá Canal...............21 j
Panamá, Gulf of............22 j
Panay............................67 g
Panda............................49 h
Pandamatenga...............49 a
Pandharpur....................61 n
Pandie Pandie...............77 g
Panevėžhys...................33 w
Panfilov..........................56 o

Pangi.............................45 b
Pangin...........................62 c
Pangi Range..................61 a
Pangkalanbrandan.........68 d
Pangkalanbuun..............69 n
Pangkal Kalong..............66 s
Pangkalpinang...............68 j
Pangnirtung...................13 l
Pangody.........................51 c
Pangong Tso.................61 d
Panipat..........................61 b
Panjgur..........................60 g
Pankshin........................41 h
Panna............................61 r
Pannawonica.................72 s
Panovo..........................51 o
Panova (Angara)............51 z
Pantelleria.....................34 z
Panter Downs................72 l
Pánuco.........................19 p
Pan Xian.......................62 w
Panyabungan................68 e
Paoting..........................57 v
Paotow..........................57 t
Papai.............................23 z
Papantla........................19 c
Paphos..........................35 x
Paposo..........................28 o
Papua, Gulf of.........70 z
Papua New Guinea 70-71/73/74
Pará...............................26 z
Parabel..........................51 r
Paraburdoo....................72 t
Paracatu........................29 f
Paracatu (River)............29 g
Paracel Islands..............66 m
Paragominas.................27 a
Paraguá (Brazil).............25 u
Paragua (Venezuela).....23 u
Paraguacu.....................27 s
Paraguai........................25 x
Paraguaná Peninsula.....23 d
Paraguari.......................27 z
Paraguay.....................28-29
Paraiba..........................27 v
Paraiba do Sul...............29 j
Paraíso..........................29 b
Paraíso do Norte de Goiás 26 y
Parakou.........................41 c
Paramaribo....................26 h
Paramirim......................27 q
Paramušir......................59 l
Paraná (Argentina)........28 w
Paraná (Brazil)..............26 z
Paraná (River, Argentina) 28-29
Paraná (River, Brazil).....26
Paranaguá.....................29 s
Paranaiba......................29 d
Paranam........................26 h
Paranapanema...............29 c
Paranapiacaba, Serra....29 r
Paranavai......................29 c
Paraparaumu.................79 u
Parapeti.........................28 i
Paratunka......................53 y
Parbhani........................61 o
Parbig............................51 s
Parding..........................61 j
Pardo.............................29 b
Pardo (Brazilian Plateau) 29 l
Parepare........................69 s
Parecis, Serra dos.........25 u
Pariaguán......................23 y
Paria, Gulf of.................23 i
Parima, Serra................23 u
Pariñas, Cabo................24 f
Parintins........................25 l
Paris (France)................34 h
Paris (USA)....................19 e
Parkano.........................33 i
Parker Range.................76 f
Parkersburg...................16 v
Parkes............................78 c
Parma............................34 l
Parnaíba........................27 e
Parnaíba (River)............27 d
Parnamirim....................27 s
Parnu.............................33 j
Paromay........................53 z
Paroo.............................77 k

Parras............................18 m
Parry Islands..................12 h
Parry Sound...................16 j
Parsons..........................16 n
Partida, Roca.................18 s
Paru...............................26 i
Paru de Oeste...............25 l
Parvatipuram.................61 t
Paryang.........................61 j
Parys.............................49 p
Pasadena.......................19 e
Pasangkayu...................69 f
Pascagoula....................20 g
Pasig.............................67 g
Pasni.............................60 t
Paso de los Indios.........30 w
Paso de los Toros..........28 z
Paso Limay....................30 i
Paso Real......................20 p
Passau...........................35 a
Passmore......................77 c
Passo Fundo..................29 o
Passos..........................29 g
Pastakh..........................53 i
Pastaza..........................24 j
Pasto.............................24 j
Pastos Bons..................27 p
Patagonia.......................30 u
Patandar........................60 g
Paterson........................16 z
Pathankot......................61 a
Patia..............................24 i
Patiala...........................61 b
Patience.........................26 i
Pativilca.........................24 v
Patkai Mountains...........62 p
Patna.............................61 o
Patnos...........................54 t
Pato Branco...................29 o
Patom............................52 u
Patomskoye Plateau......52 s
Patos.............................27 u
Patos de Minas..............29 f
Patos, Lagoa dos...........29 p
Patquía..........................28 r
Pátrai (Patras)...............35 r
Patras............................35 r
Patrasuy........................50 x
Patrocinio......................29 f
Patta Island...................43 r
Pattani...........................68 f
Pattullo, Mount..............11 z
Patuca...........................22 g
Patzcuaro......................19 n
Pau................................34 f
Pau de Ferros................27 u
Pauini............................25 c
Paulatuk........................12 c
Paulistana......................27 r
Paulo Alfonso................27 t
Pauri..............................61 g
Pausa............................27 p
Pavlodar.........................55 m
Pavlogard.......................54 c
Pavlovsk........................54 e
Pavlovsk........................56 d
Pavon............................23 o
Paxson...........................11 g
Payakumbuh..................68 f
Pay-Khoy.......................50 l
Paynes Find...................76 e
Paysandú.......................28 y
Payturma........................51 k
Pay-yer..........................50 m
Peace River...................12 s
Peace (River).................12 t
Peak Charles.................76 g
Peak Downs...................74 r
Peak Hill........................76 f
Pearl City.......................18 p
Pearsall.........................19 b
Pearson Island..............77 c
Peary Channel...............89 r
Peary Land....................91 i
Pebane..........................46 x
Pebas............................25 a
Pečenga........................33 m
Pechora..........................50 w
Pechora (River)..............50 w
Pechora Sea..................50 i

Pecked..........................77 m
Pecos............................18 m
Pecos (River).................18 m
Pecs..............................35 c
Pedasi............................22 j
Pedirka..........................77 d
Pedra Azul.....................29 k
Pedreiras.......................27 o
Pedro Alfonso................26 z
Pedro Gomes.................25 z
Pedro Luro....................30 m
Peel Bay........................76 c
Peel Sound....................12 m
Peg Ariak.......................70 r
Pegu..............................65 g
Pehuajó..........................31 a
Peipus, Lake (Lake Chud) 33 l
Peixe.............................26 z
Pekalongan....................68 z
Peking............................57 w
Pelagie Islands..............34 z
Peleng............................69 i
Peljesac.........................35 c
Pelly..............................11 l
Pelly Bay.......................13 b
Pelly (Bay).....................13 b
Pelly Crossing................11 j
Pelotas...........................29 p
Pelsart Group................76 b
Pelvoux.........................34 j
Pematangsiantar...........66 q
Pemba...........................45 y
Pemba Island................45 l
Pembroke.......................16 k
Penas Gulf.....................30 s
Pendembu......................40 f
Pendleton......................14 j
Penedo..........................27 v
Pene-Tungu....................42 t
Penganga.......................61 p
Penge............................45 a
Penglai...........................58 q
Pengpu..........................63 e
Penitente, Serra do.......27 n
Penki..............................58 e
Penner...........................64 h
Pennsylvania.................16 w
Penny Ice Cap...............13 k
Penong..........................77 c
Penonomé......................22 i
Pensacola......................20 h
Pensacola Mountains....83 u
Penticton.......................14 i
Pentland........................74 p
Pentland Firth................32 i
Penukonda.....................64 f
Penza.............................54 h
Penzance.......................34 c
Penzhino........................10 c
Penzhinskaya, Gulf of....10 a
Penzhinskiy Mountains...10 a
Peoria............................16 q
Perabumulih...................68 v
Perak.............................66 r
Perambalur.....................64 g
Percival Lakes...............72 y
Pereira...........................22 x
Pereshchepino...............35 m
Pérez.............................20 t
Pergamino......................31 a
Péribonca......................17 a
Pericos..........................18 j
Perija, Sierra de............23 b
Periquitos.......................29 c
Perito Moreno................30 v
Perlas Archipelago.........22 j
Perm'.............................50 w
Perote............................19 p
Perpignan......................34 h
Perry..............................20 k
Perry Island...................12 k
Perryton.........................15 t
Perryville.......................16 z
Persepolis......................39 j
Perseverancia................25 t
Perth (Australia).............76 z
Perth (Canada)..............16 l
Perth (UK)......................32 w
Peru...........................24-25
Perugia..........................34 m

Pervomaysk................33 z
Pervoural'sk..............50 x
Pesagi....................68 u
Pescara...................35 a
Peschanyy, Cape...........92 j
Peshawar..................60 l
Peski.....................55 g
Pesqueira.................27 v
Petaling Jaya.............68 f
Petatlán..................19 n
Petauke...................45 r
Peterborough (Australia)..77 g
Peterborough (Canada).....16 x
Peter Island..............80 j
Petermann Range...........76 m
Peter Pond Lake...........12 u
Petersburg................16 x
Peters Mine...............23 x
Petitsikapau Lake.........17 d
Peto......................19 v
Petoskey..................16 y
Petra.....................38 k
Petrel....................82 g
Petrolina.................27 r
Petropavlovka.............52 y
Petropavlovsk.............55 i
Petropavlovsk-
Kamchatskiy...............53 y
Petrópolis................29 i
Petrovka..................55 h
Petrovsk-Zabajkal'skij....57 f
Petrozavodsk..............50 n
Petukhovo.................55 g
Petushkova................10 e
Peureulak.................65 u
Pevek.....................10 d
Phalaborwa................49 f
Phalsund..................60 y
Phangan...................65 j
Phatthalung...............68 e
Phayao....................65 j
Phenix City...............20 i
Phetchabun................65 k
Phetchaburi...............65 i
Phiafay...................66 i
Philadelphia..............16 z
Philippines...............67
Philippine Sea...........231 i
Philipsburg...............21 y
Phitsanulok...............65 j
Phnom Penh................66 h
Phoenix...................18 g
Phoenix Island...........231 z
Phongsali.................62 u
Phrae.....................65 j
Phu Chong.................66 i
Phuket....................65 u
Phulabāni.................61 t
Phu Quoc..................66 g
Piacenza..................34 l
Pianguan..................57 t
Piauí.....................27 q
Piauí, Serra de...........27 q
Pibor Post................42 z
Pico da Neblina...........25 e
Pico de Aneto.............34 g
Picos.....................27 r
Pico Truncado.............30 w
Picton....................79 u
Pic Toussidé..............37 w
Picuún Leufú..............30 i
Pidi......................45 a
Pidurutalagala............64 v
Piedrabuena...............30 w
Piedras Negras............19 a
Pielis, Lake..............33 l
Pierce....................14 k
Pierre....................15 g
Pietarsaari (Jakobstad)...33 i
Pietermaritzburg..........49 s
Pietersburg...............49 d
Piet Retief...............49 r
Pietrosu..................35 g
Pigu......................40 m
Pigüe.....................31 a
Pijijiapan................19 t
Pik-Aborigen..............53 i
Pikelot...................71 b
Pikes Peak................15 g
Pikeville.................16 x

Pik Grandioznyi...........56 l
Pikhtovka.................56 d
Pikounda..................41 y
Pik Pobedy................56 p
Pilo Arcada...............27 q
Pilar.....................28 y
Pilaya....................28 g
Pilcomayo.................28 g
Pilibhit..................61 d
Pilsen (Plzen)............35 a
Pim.......................51 o
Pimenta Bueno.............26 q
Pimenteiras...............25 v
Pinacate Desert...........18 c
Pinang (Indonesia)........68 l
Pinang (George Town,
Malaysia).................65 w
Pinang (Island)...........65 w
Pinar del Río.............20 w
Pinawa....................15 i
Pindobal..................26 m
Pindus....................35 r
Pine Bluff................19 g
Pine City.................15 k
Pine Creek................73 c
Pinega....................50 r
Pinega (River)............50 r
Pine Island Bay...........81 b
Pingelap Atoll............71 l
Pingguo...................62 y
Pingle....................63 n
Pingliang.................62 l
Pingnan...................63 n
Pingsiang.................63 c
Pingtingshan..............63 b
Pingtung..................63 u
Pingxiang.................62 x
Pinheiro..................27 b
Pini......................65 v
Pinnaroo..................77 u
Pinos.....................19 n
Pinos, Isla de............20 y
Pinotepa Nacional.........19 p
Pinsk.....................33 w
Pinta.....................22 p
Pintados..................28 c
Pinto.....................28 u
Pioner....................51 j
Pionerskaya...............85 r
Pionerskiy................50 y
Piorini...................25 f
Piorini, Lago.............25 g
Piotrków..................33 u
Pipangikum Lake...........15 k
Pipmuacan Reservoir.......17 b
Piquiri...................29 o
Piracuruca................27 d
Piraeus...................35 s
Pirajiba..................27 p
Piraju....................29 e
Pirané....................28 x
Piranhas..................25 g
Pirapetinga...............25 g
Pirapora..................29 h
Pires do Rio..............29 e
Piripiri..................27 q
Piritu....................23 g
Pirot.....................35 f
Pisa......................34 l
Pisagua...................28 c
Pisco.....................24 x
Pishin....................60 r
Pissis....................28 q
Pita......................40 e
Pitcairn Island..........230 q
Pite......................33 h
Piteşti...................35 g
Pithara...................76 e
Pittsburgh................16 w
Pittsfield................16 z
Piura.....................24 g
Piura (River).............24 g
Pixa......................61 d
Pizhma....................50 s
Pjasina...................51 h
Pjasina, Lake.............51 h
Pjatigorsk................54 t
P.K.le Roux Reservoir.....49 n
Placa.....................29 b
Placetas..................21 n

Plainview.................19 a
Plamennyy.................10 f
Plara-Açu.................26 v
Plast.....................55 d
Platbakkies...............48 w
Plate, River..............31 d
Plato.....................22 m
Platte....................15 u
Plauen....................34 m
Plavsk....................54 c
Playa Azul................18 z
Plaza Huincul.............30 j
Pleiku....................66 j
Plenty, Bay of............79 w
Plétipi, Lake.............17 b
Pleven....................35 g
Plibo.....................40 u
Ploieşti..................35 h
Plovdiv...................35 g
Plumtree..................49 c
Plymouth..................32 w
Plymouth (Island).........21 z
Plzen.....................35 a
Po........................40 m
Po (River)................34 m
Pocatello.................14 z
Poconé....................25 y
Pocos de Caldas...........29 g
Podgorica.................35 c
Podkamennaya Tunguska.....51 w
Podkamennaya Tunguska
(River)...................51 x
Podolsk...................54 d
Podporoze.................50 o
Podukkottai...............64 g
Podutesnaya...............10 p
Pofadder..................48 x
Pogo......................40 j
Po Hai....................57 y
Poinsett, Cape............87 g
Pointe-à-Pitre............21 z
Pointe-Noire..............44 d
Point Hope................10 m
Poitiers..................34 y
Pokacheva.................51 p
Pokaran...................60 l
Pokhara...................61 g
Poko......................42 u
Pokrovka..................56 a
Pokrovsk..................52 l
Pokrovsk (Vostochny
Mountains)................56 m
Poland....................33
Poli......................41 j
Poligus...................51 x
Polillo Islands...........67 h
Politovo..................50 t
Polkan....................51 w
Pol'kyko..................51 m
Polotsk...................33 y
Polovinka.................53 n
Polovinka (Patomskoye
Plateau)..................52 t
Polson....................14 l
Poltava...................35 m
Polui.....................51 a
Polunochnoye..............50 y
Polur.....................64 h
Pol'yanovo................50 z
Pomeranian Bay............33 r
Pomona....................48 u
Pon.......................33 h
Ponape....................71 h
Ponca City................15 v
Ponce.....................21 v
Pondicherry...............64 h
Pond Inlet................13 g
Pongo.....................42 u
Pongola...................49 q
Ponta Branca..............29 b
Ponta da Pedra............25 x
Ponta Grossa..............29 q
Ponta Pora................28 m
Pontdrif..................49 d
Ponterrada................34 b
Pontianak.................68 l
Pontine Mountains.........54 o
Ponton....................76 i
Poopó, Lake...............28 e
Popayán...................22 y

Popigay...................52 d
Popigay (River)...........52 e
Poplar Bluff..............16 q
Popocatépetl..............19 o
Popokabaka................44 h
Popomanaseu...............71 y
Popondetta................71 p
Porangatu.................26 y
Porbandar.................60 w
Porcupine.................11 i
Porog.....................50 w
Poronaysk.................59 d
Porpoise Bay..............87 q
Portachuelo...............25 s
Portadown.................32 v
Portage...................16 q
Portage la Prairie........15 h
Port Albert...............78 p
Portales..................18 l
Port Alfred...............49 p
Port Alsworth.............11 d
Port Angeles..............14 g
Port Arthur...............78 p
Port Augusta..............77 f
Port-au-Prince............21 r
Port-Bergé-Vaovao.........47 d
Port Burwell..............13 x
Port-Cartier..............17 d
Port Charlotte............20 k
Port Davey................77 x
Port-de-Paix..............21 q
Port Edward...............49 r
Portel....................26 k
Port Elgin................16 v
Port Elizabeth............49 o
Port-Gentil...............41 t
Port Harcourt.............41 r
Port Hardy................14 g
Port Hedland..............72 t
Portimo...................36 f
Port Keats................73 b
Portland (Australia)......77 u
Portland (Maine, USA).....17 o
Portland (Oregon, USA)....14 g
Port Lincoln..............77 d
Port Louis................47 x
Port Macquarie............78 g
Port Menier...............17 e
Port Moresby..............71 n
Port Nolloth..............48 v
Porto (Oporto)............34 a
Pôrto Alegre..............29 p
Pôrto Alegre (Purus)......25 q
Pôrto Alegre (Serra do
Roncador).................26 x
Pôrto Alegre (Xingu)......26 w
Porto Alexandre (Tômbua)..48 d
Porto Amboim..............44 r
Pôrto Artur...............26 u
Pôrto Atlántico...........25 y
Pôrto de Moz..............26 z
Pôrto do Cajueiro.........25 z
Pôrto dos Gauchos.........25 x
Pôrto dos Meinacos........26 w
Pôrto Esperança...........28 l
Pôrto Esperidio...........25 w
Pôrto Franco..............27 n
Port of Spain.............23 i
Pôrto Grande..............26 k
Pôrto Jofre...............25 y
Pôrto Murtinho............28 k
Pôrto Naçional............26 z
Porto Novo................41 o
Pôrto Poet................26 i
Pôrto Santana.............26 k
Pôrto So José.............29 b
Porto Seguro..............29 l
Pôrto Velho...............25 s
Portoviejo................24 g
Port Philip Bay...........77 x
Port Pirie................77 f
Port Radium...............12 g
Port Safaga...............38 k
Port Said.................35 x
Port Shepstone............49 s
Portsmouth
(New Hampshire)...........17 o
Portsmouth (Ohio).........16 u
Portsmouth (Virginia).....16 y
Port St. Johns............49 r

Port Sudan................38 z
Portugal..................34
Porva.....................54 m
Porvenir (Bolivia)........25 p
Porvenir (Chile)..........30 v
Posadas...................28 z
Poso......................69 g
Pospelicha................56 c
Posse.....................29 g
Postavy...................33 x
Postmasburg...............48 z
Posto Alto Manissaua......26 u
Posto Cocraimore..........26 w
Posto Curuá...............25 m
Potapovo..................51 h
Potchefstroom.............49 p
Poteau....................20 c
Potenza...................35 b
Potgietersrus.............49 e
Poti (Brazil).............27 q
Poti (Georgia)............54 s
Potiskum..................41 h
Potosí....................28 f
Potrero del Llano.........20 n
Potsdam...................33 q
Pottuvil..................64 w
Pouso Alegre..............29 g
Povungnituk...............13 t
Powder....................15 d
Powell Basin..............82 g
Powell, Lake..............15 n
Powell River..............14 f
Poyang, Lake..............63 e
Poza Rica.................19 q
Poznan....................33 t
Pozo Colorado Monte.......28 k
Pozo del Tigre............28 w
Prachin Buri..............65 k
Prachuap Khiri Khan.......65 j
Prague....................35 a
Praha (Prague)............35 a
Prainha...................26 i
Prainha Nova..............25 i
Pratt.....................15 u
Precordillera.............28 q
Predivinsk................51 x
Preparis..................65 e
Prescott..................18 f
Presidencia de la Plaza...28 w
Presidencia Roque
Sâenz Peña................28 w
Presidente Dutra..........27 o
Presidente Hermes.........25 u
Presidente Prudente.......29 c
Presnogor'kovka...........55 g
Presnovka.................55 g
Prešov....................35 e
Prespa Lake...............35 e
Presque Isle..............17 c
Prestea...................40 y
Prêto do Igapó-Acu........25 i
Pretoria..................49 p
Priargunsk................57 k
Pribilof Islands..........10 y
Price.....................15 n
Prieska...................48 z
Priluki...................35 x
Primavera.................82 s
Primorsk..................54 h
Primorsko-Akhtarsk........54 d
Prince Albert.............15 d
Prince Albert Peninsula...12 f
Prince Albert Road........48 y
Prince Albert Sound.......12 f
Prince Albert, Cape.......12 b
Prince Charles Island.....13 g
Prince Charles Mountains..84 m
Prince Edward Island
(Canada)..................17 f
Prince Edward Island
(S. Africa)..............231 o
Prince George.............14 g
Prince Gustav Adolf Sea...12 i
Prince Harald Coast.......84 g
Prince Karls Forland......91 z
Prince of Wales Strait....12 c
Prince of Wales Island
(Canada)..................12 l
Prince of Wales Island
(USA).....................11 y

Prince of Wales Island
(Australia) ......73 j
Prince Patrick Island ....12 d
Prince Regent Inlet ....13 b
Prince Rupert ....14 c
Princess Astrid Coast ......83 l
Princess Charlotte Bay ....73 l
Princess Elizabeth Land ...85 q
Princess Ragnhild Land ...84 c
Princess Ragnhild Coast ..84 d
Princeton ....16 r
Principe ....41 s
Prinzapolca ....22 h
Pripet ....33 y
Pripet marshes ....33 x
Pristina ....35 d
Prizren ....35 e
Probolinggo ....69 o
Prochladnyj ....54 t
Prof. van Bloomenstein
Lake ....26 h
Progreso ....20 s
Prokopjevsk ....56 f
Prome ....65 f
Propriá ....27 u
Proserpine ....74 r
Providence ....17 o
Providencia ....25 n
Providencia (Island) ....22 i
Provideniya ....10 k
Provo ....15 n
Prudhoe Bay ....11 f
Prudhoe Land ....91 c
Prut ....35 h
Przemyśl ....33 v
Przeval'sk ....55 z
Pskov ....33 l
Pskov, Lake ....33 l
Pucallpa ....24 y
Pucheng ....63 f
Pudukkottai ....64 g
Puebla ....19 p
Pueblo ....15 q
Puelches ....30 l
Pu'er ....62 t
Puerto Acosta ....28 d
Puerto Aisén ....30 t
Puerto Alegre ....25 u
Puerto Angel ....19 q
Puerto Armuelles ....22 h
Puerto Asis ....24 k
Puerto Ayacucho ....23 r
Puerto Barrios ....19 v
Puerto Berrio ....23 a
Puerto Boyaca ....23 n
Puerto Cabello ....23 e
Puerto Cabezas ....22 h
Puerto Carreño ....23 r
Puerto Cisnes ....30 t
Puerto Cortés (Honduras) .19 w
Puerto Cortés
(Costa Rica) ....22 g
Puerto Cumarebo ....23 d
Puerto del Rosario ....36 c
Puerto Deseado ....30 y
Puerto Escondido ....19 p
Puerto Heath ....25 p
Puerto Huitoto ....24 l
Puerto Inca ....24 y
Puerto Juárez ....19 x
Puerto La Cruz ....23 f
Puerto Leguizamo ....24 l
Puerto Lempira ....22 g
Puerto Limón ....23 n
Puertollano ....34 q
Puerto Lobos ....30 l
Puerto Lopez ....23 o
Puerto Madryn ....30 l
Puerto Maldonado ....25 o
Puerto Marquez ....25 r
Puerto Miraña ....25 a
Puerto Montt ....30 g
Puerto Morelos ....19 x
Puerto Natales ....30 t
Puerto Nuevo ....23 q
Puerto Pardo ....24 k
Puerto Peñasco ....18 e
Puerto Piñasco ....28 l
Puerto Plata ....21 t
Puerto Portillo ....24 z

Puerto Presidente
Stroessner ....29 n
Puerto Princesa ....67 e
Puerto Rico (Bolivia) ....25 q
Puerto Rico (Peru) ....24 y
Puerto Rico (USA) ....21 v
Puerto San Augustín ....25 a
Puerto San Julián ....30 w
Puerto Sastre ....28 k
Puerto Suárez ....28 l
Puerto Vallarta ....18 y
Puerto Villamil ....22 o
Puerto Villarroel ....25 s
Puesta Varadero ....24 z
Pugal ....60 m
Pujehun ....40 r
Pukaki, Lake ....79 s
Pukch'ong ....58 h
Pula ....35 a
Pular ....28 d
Pullman ....14 k
Pulo Anna ....70 d
Pulog ....67 g
Pulu ....61 e
Pumasillo ....24 z
Puná ....24 h
Pune ....60 z
Punia ....42 u
Puno ....25 o
Punta Aguja ....24 f
Punta Alta ....31 a
Punta Arenas ....30 u
Punta Chirambirá ....22 x
Punta Delgada (Chile) ......30 w
Punta Delgada (Argentina)30 m
Punta Galera ....22 v
Punta Manzanillo ....22 k
Punta Norte ....30 m
Punta Prieta ....18 e
Puntarenas ....22 f
Punto Fijo ....23 c
Puquio ....24 y
Pur ....52 j
Pur (Siben'an Uvaly) ....51 e
Pura ....51 h
Puri ....61 v
Puricama ....23 u
Purnia ....61 v
Purros ....48 f
Pursat ....66 g
Purtuniq ....13 u
Puruliya ....61 v
Purus ....25 h
Purwokerto ....68 y
Pusan ....58 v
Pushchino ....53 y
Pushkino ....54 i
Pusur ....61 x
Putao ....62 e
Putian ....63 s
Putorana Mountains ....51 j
Putrajaya ....68 f
Putre ....28 c
Puttalam ....64 u
Putumayo ....24 l
Puzla ....50 v
Pweto ....45 c
Pyaozero, Lake ....33 m
Pyapon ....65 g
Pyasina Bay ....51 f
Pyatigory ....50 v
Pyinmana ....62 q
Pymta ....53 x
Pyŏngyang ....58 s
Pyramid Lake ....14 v
Pyramids ....38 h
Pyrenees ....34 f
Pyrgos ....35 r
Pyu ....62 r

Q

Qaanaaq (Thule) ....91 c
Qaen ....60 c
Qagan ....57 k
Qagan Nur ....57 v
Qagcaka ....61 f
Qahan Qulut ....57 k
Qaisar ....60 g

Qala Panja ....60 l
Qal'at Bishah ....39 p
Qalat-i Chilzai ....60 h
Qamar, Bay ....39 w
Qamdo ....62 e
Qaminis ....35 q
Qânâq (Thule) ....91 c
Qapqal ....56 p
Qaqortoq ....90 t
Qara ....38 e
Qarah Tarai ....60 h
Qareh Su ....39 h
Qarhan ....56 y
Qarqan ....56 t
Qarqi ....56 s
Qaryat al 'Ulya ....39 f
Qasr ....38 g
Qatar ....39 v
Qatrun ....37 v
Qattara Depression ....38 f
Qazvin ....54 x
Qen ....57 n
Qena ....38 j
Qeqertarsuaq (Godhavn) .90 k
Qeqertarsuaq (Island) ......90 l
Qeshm ....60 a
Qeshm (Island) ....60 a
Qeys ....39 k
Qian Gorlos ....58 f
Qianjiang ....62 m
Qianning ....62 g
Qiansuo ....62 t
Qianwei ....62 j
Qian Xian ....62 l
Qianyang ....63 a
Qiaowan ....56 z
Qiemo ....56 s
Qijiang ....62 k
Qijiaojing ....56 w
Qila Ladgasht ....60 f
Qila Saifullah ....60 j
Qilian Shan ....56 y
Qing'an ....58 h
Qingchuan ....62 j
Qingdao (Tsingtao) ....58 p
Qinghai Hu ....57 n
Qingyang ....62 l
Qingyuan ....58 f
Qing Zang Gaoyuan ....62 a
Qinhuangdao ....57 y
Qinling Shan ....62 l
Qinzhou ....62 z
Qionglai ....62 i
Qiqian ....52 v
Qiqihar (Tsitsihar) ....58 f
Qiquanhu ....56 u
Qira ....61 e
Qitai ....56 u
Qitaihe ....58 j
Qi Xian ....63 c
Qlom ....53 a
Qma ....61 g
Qojur ....54 w
Qom ....39 i
Qomsheh ....39 i
Qotbabad ....60 a
Quala-I Nau ....60 f
Quanzhou ....63 n
Quarai ....28 z
Quchan ....55 o
Queanbeyan ....78 d
Québec ....17 a
Quebec (Province) ....13 u
Queen Astrid and
King Leopold Coast ....85 r
Queen Charlotte Strait ......14 e
Queen Charlotte Islands ...14 b
Queen Elizabeth Islands ..12 d
Queen Louise Land ....91 s
Queen Mary Land ....85 s
Queen Maud Gulf ....12 k
Queen Maud Land ....84 c
Queen Maud Range ....81 k
Queensland ....74 r
Queenstown (Australia) ....77 x
Queenstown
(New Zealand) ....79 r
Queenstown
(South Africa) ....49 p
Queimada ....26 k

Queimadas ....27 s
Quéléssebougou ....40 i
Quelimane ....46 w
Quelpart Island (Cheju) ....58 t
Querétaro ....19 o
Querrha ....34 p
Quesnel ....14 h
Quetta ....60 i
Quezaltenango ....22 b
Quezon ....67 g
Quibala ....44 t
Quibaxe ....44 g
Quibdo ....22 y
Quilán, Cabo ....30 f
Quillabamba ....24 z
Quillacollo ....28 f
Quillagua ....28 c
Quilon ....64 r
Quilpie ....77 j
Quimbele ....44 h
Quince Mil ....25 n
Quincy ....16 p
Quines ....28 s
Quinghai Hu ....62 g
Quinhon ....66 l
Quiñones ....18 t
Quirinópolis ....29 d
Quissico ....49 i
Quitapa ....44 v
Quiteve ....44 t
Quitexe ....44 g
Quito ....24 h
Quixadá ....27 s
Qujing ....62 w
Qumar Heyan ....62 b
Qumarlêb ....62 g
Qunaitra ....38 l
Qungtag ....61 j
Quorn ....77 f
Quraiyat ....60 p
Qus ....38 j
Qusair ....38 k
Quseima ....38 k
Quynh Luu ....62 x
Quzhou ....63 g

R

Raahe ....33 j
Raas Caseyr
(Cape Guardafui) ....43 l
Raba ....72 h
Rabableh ....43 j
Rabak ....42 l
Rabang ....61 e
Rabat ....36 h
Rabaul ....71 r
Rabbit Lake ....12 x
Rabyanah ....38 o
Race, Cape ....17 l
Rach Gia ....66 h
Racine ....16 r
Radhanpur ....60 x
Radom ....33 u
Rae ....12 s
Rae Isthmus ....13 c
Rae Lakes ....12 r
Raeside, Lake ....76 h
Rafaela ....28 v
Rafaii ....42 r
Rafha ....39 d
Rafsanjan ....39 l
Raga ....42 g
Ragusa ....35 n
Raha ....69 v
Rahad ....43 a
Rahad al Berdi ....42 f
Rahimyar-Khan ....60 l
Raichur ....64 f
Rainier, Mount ....14 h
Rainy Lake ....15 k
Raipur ....61 s
Raisut ....39 x
Rajada ....27 s
Rajahmundry ....64 i
Rajang ....69 a
Rajanpur ....60 k
Rajasthan Canal ....60 m
Rajgarh ....61 o

Rajkot ....60 x
Raj Nandgaon ....61 r
Rakaposhi ....61 a
Raka Zangbo ....61 i
Raleigh ....16 x
Rama ....22 g
Ramah ....13 y
Ramanathapuram ....64 t
Ramdurg ....64 d
Rameswaram ....64 u
Ramhormoz ....39 h
Ramlat al Wahiba ....60 p
Ramlat Rabyana ....37 x
Ramlu ....43 e
Ramos ....26 i
Rampur ....61 d
Rampur (Rann of Kutch) ..60 w
Rampura ....61 n
Ramree ....65 e
Ramsar ....54 x
Ramshir ....39 h
Ramu ....43 r
Ramu (River) ....70 z
Rancagua ....30 i
Ranchi ....61 u
Ranco, Lago de ....30 h
Randa ....43 f
Randers ....33 p
Randolph ....15 v
Rangoon ....65 g
Rangpur ....61 x
Raniganj ....61 w
Rankin Inlet ....13 n
Ranong ....65 i
Rantauprapat ....68 e
Rantekombola ....69 s
Rantoul ....16 h
Rao Go ....66 h
Rapak ....69 s
Rapel ....30 h
Rapid City ....15 e
Rapti ....61 g
Rapulo ....25 r
Raqqah ....39 a
Ras al Khaimah ....39 l
Ras-al-Ma ....36 l
Ras Dashén ....43 c
Ras Ghârib ....38 j
Ras Halileh ....39 l
Rasht ....54 x
Ras Koh ....60 h
Raskoh ....60 g
Ras Nuh ....60 s
Rason, Lake ....76 j
Rassokha ....53 h
Ras Tannurah ....39 i
Ratangarh ....61 a
Rat Islands ....10 t
Ratlam ....61 n
Ratnagiri ....64 c
Raton ....15 v
Ratta ....51 t
Ratz, Mount ....11 y
Raub ....65 x
Raub Kuala Kubu ....66 s
Rauch ....31 b
Ravansar ....39 e
Ravenna ....34 m
Ravensthorpe ....76 g
Ravor ....60 b
Rawalpindi ....60 m
Rawlinna ....76 x
Rawlins ....15 p
Rawson ....30 l
Raya ....69 u
Raychikhinsk ....58 h
Rayones ....19 a
Rayong ....65 g
Razan ....39 h
Razdolnoye ....53 n
Razmak ....60 k
Reading (USA) ....16 y
Reading (UK) ....32 x
Read Island ....12 g
Reboly ....33 h
Rebricha ....56 k
Recherche Archipelago ....76 i
Recife ....27 w
Reconquista ....28 w
Recovery Glacier ....83 v

Recreio ....25 w
Recreo ....28 s
Red Bluff ....14 u
Red Deer ....14 m
Redding ....14 u
Redenço ....26 y
Redeyef ....37 d
Red Lake ....15 k
Red Pass ....14 j
Red River (Canada) ....15 i
Red River (USA) ....20 d
Red Sea ....38 y
Red Wing ....15 k
Regensburg ....34 m
Reggane ....36 y
Reggio ....35 o
Regina ....15 d
Régina ....26 j
Registan ....60 g
Registro ....29 s
Rehoboth ....48 i
Reims ....34 i
Reindeer Lake ....12 x
Reitz ....49 q
Reivilo ....49 n
Reliance ....12 v
Relizane ....34 t
Remada ....34 y
Remanso ....27 q
Remarkable, Mount .....73 a
Remeshk ....60 c
Renascença ....25 d
Rengat ....68 g
Renk ....42 l
Renland ....91 q
Renmark ....77 h
Rennell Island ....74 m
Renner Springs ....73 r
Rennes ....34 e
Rennick Glacier ....86 u
Reno ....14 v
Repetek ....55 r
Republican ....15 u
Repulse Bay ....13 c
Requena ....24 l
Resistencia ....28 x
Resolute ....12 m
Resolution Island ......13 y
Retkucha ....10 d
Retreat ....77 j
Réunion ....47 w
Revelstoke ....14 j
Revilla Gigedo Islands ....18 t
Rewa ....61 r
Rewari ....61 b
Rey ....22 k
Reyes ....25 q
Reykjanes ....32 a
Reykjavik ....32 b
Reynosa ....19 b
Rhallamane ....36 s
Rhine ....34 k
Rhinelander ....16 e
Rhode Island ....17 o
Rhodes ....35 v
Rhodes (Island) ....35 v
Rhodope ....35 g
Rhône ....34 i
Riau Islands ....68 h
Ribas do Rio Pardo ...29 a
Ribat ....60 n
Ribauè ....46 k
Ribeiro Preto ....29 f
Riberalta ....25 r
Riboiro Gonçalves .....27 o
Rice Lake ....15 l
Rich ....36 j
Richards Bay ....49 t
Richardson ....11 g
Richfield ....14 z
Richland ....14 i
Richmond (Australia) ...74 n
Richmond (Indiana) ...16 t
Richmond (Virginia) ...16 x
Richmond Range ....79 t
Richwood ....16 v
Riddle ....14 x
Ridgecrest ....14 w
Rif ....36 i
Rifle ....15 p

Rift Valley 42/45
Riga (Latvia) ....33 w
Riga (Russia) ....52 p
Riga, Gulf of ....33 i
Riggins ....14 k
Rigolet ....17 i
Rig-Rig ....41 k
Rihand Reservoir ....61 s
Riiser Larsen Peninsula ...84 h
Riiser Larsen Sea .....84 d
Riiser Larsen Ice Shelf ....83 g
Rijeka ....35 a
Rime ....42 b
Rimini ....34 m
Rimouski ....17 c
Rinčin Lchumbe ....57 a
Ringwood ....73 s
Riobamba ....24 h
Rio Branco ....25 p
Rio Claro ....29 f
Río Colorado ....30 m
Rio Cuarto ....30 m
Rio de Janeiro ....29 i
Rio de Oro ....36 n
Río Gallegos ....30 w
Rio Grande (Argentina) ...30 x
Rio Grande (Brazil) ....29 p
Rio Grande (Mexico) ...18 z
Riohacha ....23 a
Rioja ....24 j
Rio Largo ....27 v
Río Mayo ....30 v
Rio Mulatos ....28 e
Riosucio ....22 l
Río Tercero ....28 t
Río Turbio ....30 u
Río Verde (Mexico) ....19 n
Rio Verde (Brazil) ......29 c
Rio Verde de Mato Grosso ...29 a
Riposto ....37 j
Rissani ....36 i
Rito ....44 w
Ritscher Highland ......83 i
Rivadavia ....30 m
Rivas ....22 f
Rivera ....28 z
River Falls ....15 k
Riversleigh ....73 u
Riverton (Canada) .....15 i
Riverton (USA) ....15 o
Rivière du Loup ....17 b
Rivungo ....44 y
Riwoqê ....62 d
Riyadh ....39 s
Riyan ....43 k
Rjazan ....54 e
Roanoke ....16 w
Roanoke (River) ....16 y
Roanoke Rapids ....16 x
Roatán ....20 v
Robe ....77 h
Roberval ....17 a
Robinhood ....73 y
Robinson, Cape ....82 v
Robinson Crusoe ....30 d
Robinson River
(Papua New Guinea) ...74 e
Robinson River (Australia) 73 g
Roboré ....28 k
Roçadas ....44 s
Roca, General ....30 x
Rocas, Atol das ....27 w
Rocha ....31 e
Rochelle ....16 r
Rochester (Maine) .....17 o
Rochester (Minnesota) 16 p
Rochester (New York) ...16 x
Rockefeller Plateau ....81 x
Rockford ....16 r
Rockhampton ....74 t
Rock Hill ....20 l
Rockingham ....20 m
Rock Springs ....15 o
Rockstone ....23 x
Rockwood ....16 t
Rocky Harbour ....17 i
Rocky Mount ....16 x
Rocky Mountains 12/14
Rocky Mountain House ...14 g

Roda Velha ....27 o
Rodeo ....18 l
Rodina ....51 x
Rodino ....56 c
Rodrigues ....24 m
Roebuck Plains ....72 x
Roes Welcome Sound ...13 p
Rogachevka ....54 e
Rogaguado, Lago ......25 r
Rogagua, Lago ....25 r
Rogers, Mount ....16 v
Rohtak ....61 b
Roi Et ....66 g
Rokel ....40 e
Rolla ....16 p
Rolleston ....74 q
Roma ....74 r
Roma (Rome) ....34 m
Romaine ....17 f
Romania 33/35
Romano, Cape ....20 l
Romanova ....57 b
Romanovka ....57 h
Rome ....34 m
Rommani ....36 h
Roncador, Serra do ...26 w
Ronda (Pakistan) ....61 a
Ronda (Spain) ....36 i
Rondônia ....25 u
Rondonópolis ....29 a
Rong'an ....62 z
Rongjiang ....62 z
Ronne Entrance ....82 y
Roodepoort ....49 p
Roosevelt Island ....81 z
Roper ....73 f
Roper Bar ....73 e
Roques, Islas los ....23 f
Roraima ....26 d
Roraima, Mount ....23 w
Rosa, Monte ....34 k
Rosário ....27 c
Rosario ....28 f
Rosario (Paraná) ....28 w
Rosario de Arriba ....18 d
Rosario de la Frontera ....28 t
Rosário do Sul ....29 n
Rosario Oeste ....25 y
Rosarito ....18 c
Rosarito
(Sabastían Vizcaino Bay) .18 e
Rosa Zárate ....24 h
Roscrea ....32 u
Roseau (Dominica) ....23 j
Roseburg ....14 t
Roseires, Lake ....42 m
Rose River ....73 f
Rosetown ....15 b
Rosetta ....38 h
Rosiori ....35 g
Roslavl ....54 a
Ross Barrier ....86 o
Ross Ice Shelf ....81 l
Ross Island ....86 r
Rosso ....40 b
Ross River ....11 m
Ross Sea ....81 v
Rossville ....73 m
Rostock ....33 q
Rostov ....54 e
Roswell ....18 l
Rothera ....82 v
Roti ....69 v
Rotorua ....79 w
Rotterdam ....33 n
Rouen ....34 g
Round ....78 f
Roundup ....15 b
Rourkela ....61 r
Rovno ....35 h
Rovnoye ....54 i
Rowley ....90 k
Rowley Island ....13 g
Roxas ....67 n
Rosborough Downs ...73 u
Roydale Isle ....16 e
Rtishchevo ....54 h
Ruacana ....48 g
Ruahine Range ....79 v
Ruapehu ....79 v

Rubačje ....56 n
Rub'al Khali ....39 f
Rubcovsk ....56 d
Ruby ....11 d
Rudbar ....60 f
Rudnaya Pristan ....58 m
Rudnya ....54 g
Rudolf ....50 k
Rufiji ....45 j
Rufino ....31 a
Rufunsa ....46 e
Rugby ....15 g
Rügen ....33 r
Ruhengeri ....45 d
Rui Barbosa ....27 r
Ruijin ....63 r
Ruki ....44 i
Rukwa, Lake ....45 f
Rumbek ....42 w
Rum Cay ....21 q
Rumford ....17 b
Rumphi ....45 t
Rundu ....48 k
Rungu ....42 v
Rungwa ....45 g
Rungwa (River) ....45 f
Rungwe ....45 t
Ruoqiang ....56 u
Rupat ....68 f
Rupert ....16 l
Rupisi ....49 f
Rupununi ....26 e
Rurópolis ....26 u
Rusape ....46 t
Ruse ....35 h
Russas ....27 c
Russell Range ....76 i
Russia 10/33/50-59
Russkaya ....81 s
Russkaya (River) ....51 f
Russkaya Gavan ....50 l
Russkiy ....51 l
Rustavi ....54 u
Rustenburg ....49 p
Ruteng ....69 t
Rutenga ....46 s
Rutland ....17 n
Rutshuru ....42 v
Ruvuma ....46 j
Ruzayevka ....55 g
Rwanda 42/45
Rybinsk ....50 p
Rybinsker Reservoir ...50 p
Rycroft ....12 r
Ryūkyū Islands ....63 x
Rzeszów ....35 e
Ržev ....54 b

S

Saadatabad ....39 k
Saarbrücken ....34 j
Saaremaa ....33 h
Sab'Abar ....38 m
Sabah ....69 d
Sabana de Cardona ...23 s
Sabaya ....28 d
Sabha ....37 i
Sabie ....49 e
Sabinas ....19 a
Sabinas Hidalgo ....19 a
Sabkhat Matti ....39 w
Sable, Cape (Canada) ...17 r
Sable, Cape (USA) ....20 l
Sabrina Coast ....87 e
Sabun ....51 s
Sabyndy ....55 i
Sabzevar ....55 n
Sabzevaran ....60 c
Šachrisabz ....55 t
Sachs Harbour ....12 c
Saco Uen ....43 s
Sacramento ....14 u
Sacramento (River) ...14 u
Sacramento, C. del ...31 c
Sa'dah ....43 g
Sado ....59 n
Safaniyah ....39 g
Safar ....60 g

Safford ....18 h
Safi ....36 f
Saga (China) ....61 h
Saga (USSR) ....55 e
Šagan ....56 b
Sagar ....61 q
Sagastyr ....52 l
Sagastyr ....52 l
Saginaw ....16 u
Sagiz ....54 m
Šagonar ....56 k
Sagres ....36 f
Sagua la Grande ....20 z
Sagyr ....52 a
Sahara 36/37
Saharan Atlas 36/37
Saharanpur ....61 c
Sahel ....40 i
Sahil al Jazir ....60 o
Sahiwal ....60 n
Sahuaripa ....18 i
Sahuayo ....18 z
Sai Buri ....65 x
Saigon (Ho Chi Minh) ...66 j
Saihan Toroi ....57 n
Saikhoa Ght ....62 f
Saimaa, Lake ....33 k
Ste-Agathe-des-Monts ...16 m
St. Alban's ....17 j
Sto. André ....29 g
Ste-Anne-des-Monts ...17 d
St. Anthony ....17 k
St.-Augustin ....17 i
St.-Augustin (River) ...17 i
St. Augustine ....20 m
St. Brieuc ....34 d
St. Catharines ....16 w
St. Christopher and Nevis 21 x
St. Cloud ....15 j
St. Croix ....21 w
Saint-Denis ....47 w
St. Eleanors ....17 f
St. Elias Mountains ...11 j
St. Étienne ....34 h
Ste-Foy ....17 a
St. George (Australia) ...74 q
St. George (USA) ......14 z
Saint George's ....23 i
St.-Georges (Canada) ...17 b
St. Georges
(French Guiana) ....26 j
St. George's Channel ...32 v
St. Helena ....230 z
St.-Hyacinthe ....17 a
St. Jean, Lac ....17 a
St.-Jérôme ....16 m
Saint John ....17 d
St. John's (Antigua and
Barbuda) ....21 z
St. John's (Canada) ...17 l
St. Joseph ....15 w
St. Joseph, Lake ......15 l
St. Kitts/Nevis ....21 x
St. Laurent ....26 i
St. Lawrence ....74 r
St. Lawrence, Gulf of ...17 g
Saint Lawrence Island ...10 l
St. Lawrence (River) ...17 c
St. Louis (Senegal) ...40 b
St. Louis (USA) ....16 q
Saint Lucia ....23 j
St. Lucia (USA) ....49 l
St. Lucia Passage .....23 j
St. Malo, Gulf of ....32 x
St.-Marc ....21 r
Ste.-Marguerite ....17 d
Sta. Maria de Nieva ...24 j
St. Martin ....21 y
St. Marys ....78 h
Saint Matthew ....10 k
St. Matthew's ....66 c
St. Nazaire ....34 d
St. Paul (Liberia) ....40 t
St. Paul (River) ....17 i
St. Paul Island ....231 i
St. Paul-Minneapolis ...16 b
St. Petersburg (Russia) ...33 l
St. Petersburg (USA) ...20 k
St. Pierre and Miquelon ...17 j
St. Quentin ....34 k

St. Roch Basin..............12 m
St.-Siméon....................17 b
St. Stephen...................17 c
St. Thomas ....16 v
Saint Vincent and
Grenadines.................23 j
St. Vincent, Cape ....34 n
St. Vincent Gulf...........77 f
St. Vincent Passage........23 j
Saintes.........................34 f
Sajak...........................56 b
Sajama ....25 p
Sajanogorsk.................56 j
Sajnsand......................57 s
Sak...............................48 y
Saka ....43 q
Sakai............................58 z
Sakakah........................39 b
Sakakawea Reservoir .....15 f
Sakami.........................16 m
Sakata ....59 o
Sakhalin...................53/59
Sakhandzha................52 l
Sakhon Nakhon...........66 h
Sakir............................60 i
Salaberry-De-Valleyfield....16 m
Salada Laguna ....18 d
Saladillo.......................31 a
Salado ....30 k
Salado (Bahia
Samboronbón)...........31 c
Salado (Chaco Austral) ....28 u
Salaga ....40 m
Salajar.........................69 t
Salal............................42 a
Salalah........................39 x
Salamanca (Chile).......28 o
Salamanca (Mexico).........19 n
Salamanca (Spain).......34 c
Salamat ....42 b
Salar de Antofalle ....28 q
Salar de Arizaro...........28 r
Salar de Atacama.........28 d
Salar de Pipanaco.......28 s
Salar de Pocitos ....28 r
Salar de Uyuni.............28 d
Salar Punta Negra........28 p
Saldanha ....48 v
Sale ....77 y
Salé ....36 h
Salekard.......................50 m
Salem (India) ....64 f
Salem (USA) ....14 g
Salerno........................35 a
Salgueiro.....................27 t
Sali..............................36 z
Salima..........................45 u
Salina (Kansas) ....15 u
Salina (Utah) ....14 z
Salina Cruz..................20 p
Salinas (Brazil) ....25 w
Salinas (Ecuador)........24 g
Salinas (Mexico)..........19 n
Salinas (USA)...............14 u
Salinas Grande............28 t
Salinas Grandes............28 f
Salinópolis..................27 a
Salisbury......................16 z
Salisbury Island (Canada)13 t
Salisbury Island (Russia)..50 i
Saljany........................54 w
Salluit..........................13 u
Sallûm.........................35 t
Sal'um..........................50 k
Salmon.........................14 l
Salmon (River) ....14 l
Salmon River Mountains ..14 l
Salsacate.....................28 s
Sal'sk..........................54 f
Salta ....28 t
Saltillo.........................19 a
Salt Lake City ....14 z
Salt Lakes...................76 g
Salto ....28 y
Salton Sea ....18 d
Salvador......................27 t
Salvatierra...................19 n
Salwa..........................39 v
Salween.......................65 h
Salzburg......................35 a

Samagaltaj....................56 l
Samar...........................67 j
Samara.........................54 k
Samarga ....59 a
Samarinda.....................69 d
Samarkand....................55 t
Samatiguila...................40 i
Samaumá ....25 j
Samba...........................45 a
Samba (Maringa)..........44 l
Samba Caju..................44 g
Sambalpur....................61 u
Sambas ....68 l
Sambava ....47 f
Sambhar.......................61 a
Samborombón Bay..........31 d
Same ....45 j
Samfya ....45 q
Samirah........................39 c
Samoa.........................231 z
Sámos..........................35 u
Sampit..........................69 o
Samrong.......................66 g
Samsang.......................61 g
Samsun.........................35 m
Samui ....65 j
San'a.............................43 q
San................................40 j
Sanae...........................83 i
Sanaga ....41 v
San Agustín de Valle
Fértil..........................28 r
Sanandaj.......................39 f
San Andrés ....22 i
San Andrés Tuxtla ....19 r
San Angelo ....19 b
San Antonio (Chile) ....30 h
San Antonio (USA).........19 c
San Antonio de los Cobres28 r
San Antonio Oeste ....30 l
Sanaw ....39 v
San Benedicto ....18 u
San Bernardino ....18 c
San Bernardo ....30 i
San Blas ....18 i
San Blas, Cape ....20 i
San Borja......................25 q
San Buenaventura.........19 a
San Carlos (Colombia).....23 r
San Carlos (Luxon,
Philippines)................67 f
San Carlos (Mexico).........18 g
San Carlos (Negros,
Philippines)................67 i
San Carlos (Nicaragua)....22 g
San Carlos de Bolivar .....31 a
San Carlos de Bariloche ..30 i
San Carlos del Zulia........23 b
Sanch ....57 b
Sanchakou....................56 o
San Clemente ....18 b
San Cristobal.................75 a
San Cristóbal (Argentina).28 v
San Cristóbal (Columbia) .24 m
San Cristóbal (Ecuador)...22 q
San Cristóbal (Venezuela)23 b
San Cristóbal las Casas...21 n
Sancti Spiritus ....21 n
Sandakan......................69 e
Sanderson ....18 m
Sandia ....25 o
San Diego ....18 c
San Diego, Cabo ....30 y
Sandoa ....44 y
Sandoway ....62 p
Sandpoint ....14 k
Sandstone ....76 f
Sandusky......................16 u
Sandy Bay ....76 i
Sandy Cape ....77 w
Sandy Lake ....15 k
San Estanislao ....28 z
San Felipe (Chile)...........28 o
San Felipe (Lower California,
Mexico).....................18 e
San Felipe (Mexico).......19 n
San Felipe (Venezuela)...23 d
San Fernando (Chile).......30 i
San Fernando
(Philippines)..............67 g

San Fernando (Venezuela)23 j
San Fernando de Atabapo 23 r
San Fernando de Apure...23 c
San Francisco (Argentina).28 u
San Francisco (USA).......14 t
San Francisco de Macoris.21 t
San Francisco de Rincón.18 z
San Francisco del Oro .....18 k
San Gabriel ....22 y
Sangan..........................60 g
Sangareddi ....61 p
Sange ....45 c
Sanggau........................68 m
Sangha ....41 z
Sanghar ....60 w
Sangihe.........................69 k
Sangihe Islands..............69 k
Sangijn Dalaj Nuur ....56 m
Sangli............................61 n
Sangmelima...................44 w
Sangre de Cristo Range...15 q
Sangruma ....62 f
Sangyyakhtakh...............52 x
San Guillermo...............18 k
San Ignacio (Apere,
Bolivia).....................25 r
San Ignacio (Argentina)...28 y
San Ignacio (Bolivia) ....25 v
San Ignacio (Peru) ....24 i
San Ignacio, Laguna ......18 f
San Ildefonso Peninsula..67 h
San Javier ....25 u
San Joaquin ....25 s
San Jorge ....22 m
San Jorge, Gulf of ....30 x
San Jose (USA)...............14 u
San José (Mexico)..........18 h
San José (Costa Rica) .....22 d
San Jose (Philippines)......67 g
San José (Venezuela) ......23 r
San José de Amacuro......23 j
San Jose de Buenavista ..67 g
San José de Chiquitos .....25 v
San José de Jáchal ....28 q
San José del Guaviare......23 o
San Jose de Mayo ....31 d
San José de Ocune..........23 p
San Juan (Argentina) ......28 q
San Juán (Chile)..............24 x
San Juan (Dominican
Republic) ....21 s
San Juan (Puerto Rico)....21 w
San Juan (Venezuela)......23 s
San Juan (River,
Columbia) ....22 y
San Juan (River, USA).....15 n
San Juan (River,
Argentina).................28 r
San Juan (River,
Costa Rica)...............22 g
San Juan Bautista ....28 z
San Juan del Norte ....22 g
San Juan de los Lagos.....18 z
San Juan do los Morros ...23 e
San Juan Mountains.......15 p
San Juanico...................18 f
San Julián ....30 w
San Justo ....28 w
Sankuru.........................44 m
San Lázaro, Cape ....18 f
San Lorenzo (Ecuador) ....24 h
San Lorenzo (USA) ....18 j
San Lorenzo (Mount).......30 u
San Lucas......................18 u
San Lucas, Cape ....18 u
San Luis ....28 s
San Luis de la Paz ....19 o
San Luis de Tapajós ....25 l
San Luis, Lago de ....25 s
San Luis Obispo..............14 v
San Luis Potosi ....19 n
San Luis-Rio Colorado ....18 e
San Malo, Golfe de ....34 e
San Marcos ....19 o
San Marino....................34 m
San Martin (Argentina)....28 q
San Martin (Bolivia) ....25 t
San Martín de los Andes..30 i
San Martin (River) 25/28
San Matías ....25 w

San Matias Gulf.............30 m
Sanmenhsia..................63 a
San Miguel (Bolivia) ....25 t
San Miguel (El Salvador) .22 d
San Miguel del Monte .....31 c
San Miguel de Tucumán ..28 t
Sanming ....63 s
San Nicolas (Argentina) ..31 a
San Nicolas (USA) ....18 a
Sanniquellie..................40 u
Sanouyah ....40 f
San Pablo (Bolivia).........28 e
San Pablo (River, Bolivia) 25 u
San Pablo (Philippines)...67 g
San Pédro ....40 v
San Pedro (Argentina)....28 t
San Pedro (Paraguay)......28 y
San Pedro (Paraná,
Argentina)................28 w
San Pedro de Atacama ...28 d
San Pedro de las Colonias18 m
San Pedro de Lloc ....24 h
San Pedro Sula..............19 w
San Rafael (Argentina).....30 j
San Rafael (Venezuela) ...23 b
San Ramón de la
Nueva Orán ....28 g
San Salvador.................22 d
San Salvador (Island,
Bahamas) ....21 q
San Salvador (Island,
Ecuador) ....22 p
San Salvador de Jujuy .....28 s
Sansanné-Mango ....41 a
San Sebastián ....34 e
Santa ....24 v
Santa Ana (Beni, Bolivia).28 e
Santa Ana (Bolivia).........25 r
Santa Ana (Serra de Santiago,
Bolivia).....................28 k
Santa Ana (El Salvador)...22 c
Santa Ana (Mexico)..........18 h
Santa Ana (USA)............18 c
Santa Barbara (Mexico) ...18 k
Santa Barbara (USA) .....14 v
Santa Barbara
(Venezuela) ....23 s
Santa Catalina (Chile) .....28 p
Santa Catalina
(Island, USA) ....18 c
Santa Catalina
(Island, Mexico).........18 h
Santa Clara (Colombia)....25 b
Santa Clara (Cuba) ....20 z
Santa Clotilde ....24 l
Santa Corazón ....25 w
Santa Cruz (Bolivia) ....28 h
Santa Cruz (Brazil).........24 m
Santa Cruz (Chile)..........28 o
Santa Cruz (Peru) ....24 h
Santa Cruz (Spain).........36 b
Santa Cruz (USA)...........14 u
Santa Cruz (Island,
California) ....18 a
Santa Cruz (Island,
Eduador)...................22 p
Santa Cruz (River,
Argentina).................30 v
Santa Cruz Island...........75 d
Santa Elena, Cabo ....22 f
Santa Elena de Uairen.....23 v
Santa Fé (Argentina) ......28 w
Santa Fe (USA)..............15 q
Santa Filomena ....27 o
Santa Helena ....25 l
Santai ....62 k
Santa Inés (Brazil)...........27 o
Santa Inés (Chile)...........30 l
Santa Isabel (Argentina)..30 k
Santa Isabél (Brazil)........25 v
Santa Isabel (Ecuador)....24 h
Santa Isabel (Peru) ....24 l
Santa Isabel
(Solomon Islands) .....71 x
Santa Lucia ....24 m
Santa Maria (Amazon,
Brazil).......................25 j
Santa María (Argentina) ..28 r
Santa Maria (Brazil).........29 o
Santa Maria (Ecuador).....22 o

Santa Maria (Mexico) ......18 k
Santa Maria (Peru) ....24 l
Santa Maria (Venezuela)..23 e
Santa Maria da Vitória ....27 p
Santa Maria di Leuca,
Capo ....35 p
Santa Marta ....23 a
Santana ....27 p
Santana do Araguaia......26 x
Santana do Ipanema ......27 u
Santana do Livramento ...29 n
Santander (Colombia) .....22 y
Santander (Spain) ....34 d
Santanghu ....56 x
Santarém (Brazil) ....25 m
Santarém (Portugal) ....34 o
Santa Rosa (Argentina)...30 l
Santa Rosa (Brazil) ....25 n
Santa Rosa (California) ....14 t
Santa Rosa (Colombia)....23 p
Santa Rosa (Honduras)....22 d
Santa Rosa (New Mexico)15 q
Santa Rosa (Island)........18 a
Santa Rosa del Conlara ...28 s
Santa Rosalia ....18 g
Santa Teresa ....73 r
Santa Teresinha ....26 x
Santiago (Argentina) ....29 n
Santiago (Chile)..............28 o
Santiago (Dominican
Republic) ....21 t
Santiago (Panama) ....22 l
Santiago (River) (Mexico)18 y
Santiago (River) (Peru) ..24 i
Santiago de Chuco..........24 v
Santiago de Compostela ..34 b
Santiago de Cuba............21 p
Santiago del Estero ....28 t
Santiago Ixcuintla ....18 x
Santiago Papasquiaro ......18 k
Santiago, Serra de ....28 k
San Tiburcio ....19 n
Santo Amaro ....27 t
Santo Angelo ....29 n
Santo Antônio ....25 t
Santo Antônio (Negro)......25 i
Santo Antônio de Içá.......25 d
Santo Antônio de Jesus ...27 s
Santo Corazón ....28 k
Santo Domingo..............21 t
Santos ....29 g
Santos Dumont..............25 c
Santo Tomás ....24 z
Santo Tomé ....28 z
San Valentin ....30 t
San Vincente ....18 c
San Vicente de Cañete ...24 w
San Yanaro ....23 q
Sanyati ....45 q
Sanyuan ....62 m
Sanza Pombo ....44 h
São Borja......................28 z
São Carlos....................29 e
São Félix ....26 z
São Félix (Illha do
Bananal) ....26 x
São Félix do Xingu ....26 x
São Francisco (Island) ....29 s
São Francisco (River)......29 i
São Francisco, Serra.......27 r
São Gabriel ....29 n
Sao Hill ....45 h
São Joo de Araguaia ......26 z
São Joo do Piauí ....27 q
São José ....29 r
São José (Negro) ....25 d
São José do Anauá ....25 h
São José do Egito ....27 u
São José do Rio Preto .....29 d
São José do Ribamar ......27 c
São José dos Campos .....29 g
São José do Xingu ....26 w
Saolat ....69 m
São Lourenço ....25 z
São Luis ....27 b
São Luis de Montes Belos 29 c
São Marcos Bay ....27 c
São Mateus ....29 l
São Miguel de Gyamá.....27 a
São Miguel do Araguaia ..26 x

São Miguel dos Campos	27 v	Sauqira, Bay	39 z	Sem-Tripa	26 v
São Paulo	29 g	Sauré	25 k	Sena	45 u
São Paulo de Olivença	25 c	Saurimo	44 x	Senador Pompeu	27 s
São Pedro do Piauí	27 q	Sava	35 c	Sena Madureira	25 o
São Raimundo das Mangabeiras	27 n	Savalou	41 o	Senanga	44 z
São Raimundo Nonato	27 q	Savannah Downs	73 x	Sencha	52 l
São Romo	29 g	Savannah (Georgia)	20 m	Sendai	59 p
São Roque, Cabo	27 w	Savannah (Tennessee)	20 g	Seneca, Lake	16 x
São Sebastião	26 v	Savannakhet	66 h	Senegal	40
São Sebastio (São Paulo)	29 h	Savanur	64 d	Senegal (River)	40 c
São Tomé	41 s	Savate	44 u	Senekal	49 p
São Tomé (Island)	41 r	Saveh	39 h	Seney	16 f
São Tomé and Principe	41/44	Savé (Benin)	41 o	Senhor do Bonfim	27 s
Sapele	41 r	Save (Mozambique)	49 h	Senja	33 f
Saposoa	24 j	Sawla	40 l	Senjavin Group	71 k
Sapporo	59 c	Sawu	69 u	Sennar	42 m
Sapri	35 o	Sawu Sea	69 u	Senneterre	16 k
Sapt Kosi	61 i	Say	41 b	Seoni	61 q
Saqqez	54 v	Sayaboury	62 u	Seoul	58 u
Saquenay	17 b	Sayan Mountains	56 i	Sepik	70 y
Sarajevo	35 d	Saydy	53 b	Sepone	66 j
Sarakhs	55 q	Sayhut	43 l	Sepopa	48 l
Saraktash	55 a	Sayram Hu	56 q	Sept-les	17 d
Saran	55 j	Sayula	18 y	Serebr'ansk	56 d
Sarangani Islands	67 w	Sayun	43 k	Sere Kunda	40 a
Sarangarh	61 q	Say-Utes	54 z	Seremban	68 f
Saranpaul	50 y	Sayylyk	53 z	Serengeti	45 h
Saransk	54 h	Sbaa	36 m	Serenje	45 q
Sarapul	54 m	Scarborough	23 j	Sergach	54 h
Sarapulskoye	58 l	Ščerbakty	56 b	Sergino	50 z
Sarar	39 d	Schefferville	17 c	Sergiyev Posad	50 p
Sarasota	20 k	Schenectady	16 z	Sermata	70 o
Saratov	54 i	Schizuoka	59 n	Serowe	49 b
Saravan	60 e	Schmidta	51 i	Serpent's Mouth	23 i
Sarawak	69 b	Schreiber	16 f	Serpuchovo	54 d
Saraya	40 e	Schuangliao	58 e	Sérrai	35 f
Saraysu	55 g	Schwabenland	83 k	Serra Acarai	25 l
Sarbaz	60 e	Schwangyashan	58 j	Serra Aguapei	25 w
Sarbisheh	60 d	Schweizer-Reneke	49 o	Serra Curupira	25 f
Sarbulak	56 h	Schwerin	33 q	Serra da Batista	27 r
Sardinia	34 l	Sciacca	34 z	Serra da Canastra	29 g
Sarek	33 g	Scoresby Land	91 q	Serra da Capivara	29 g
Sarempaka	69 d	Scoresby Sound	91 q	Serra da Ibiapaba	27 r
Sargasso Sea	21 c	Scorpion Bay	76 m	Serra da Mantiqueira	29 h
Sargento Lores	24 i	Scotia Sea	82 d	Serra das Alpercatas	27 p
Sargodha	60 l	Scotland	32 w	Serra das Araras	29 o
Sarh	42 b	Scott Base	86 r	Serra das Divisoes	29 c
Sari Bulak	56 h	Scottsbluff	15 r	Serra da Tabatinga	27 p
Sari-i Pul	60 h	Scranton	16 y	Serra de Huanchaca	25 v
Sarikei	68 m	Sea of Crete	38 e	Serra de Maracaju	29 a
Sarina	74 r	Seabra	27 q	Serra de Pianí	27 q
Sarkand	56 p	Searchlight	14 y	Serra de Santiago	28 k
Šarlauk	55 n	Seattle	14 h	Serra do Apiaú	23 v
Sarmi	70 v	Sebastian Vizcaino Bay	18 e	Serra do Cachimbo	25 z
Sarmiento	30 w	Sebuku Bay	69 e	Serra do Dois Irmos	27 r
Sarmiento Peninsula	30 w	Sedalia	16 o	Serra do Espinnaso	29 i
Särna	33 e	Sedan	34 i	Serra do Itapicuru	27 o
Sarnia	16 v	Seddon, Kap	91 b	Serra do Mar	29 r
Sarolangun	68 t	Sededema	53 i	Serra do Navio	26 j
Sarychik	54 l	Sedova	50 i	Serra do Norte	25 w
Saryg-Sop	56 l	Sefid	54 x	Serra do Penitente	27 r
Sarykamysskoje, Lake	55 n	Sefrou	36 i	Serra do Roncador	26 w
Saryozek	55 z	Segamat	65 y	Serra dos Apiacás	25 x
Sásabe	18 g	Segera	45 k	Serra dos Caiabis	25 y
Sasaram	61 t	Ségou	40 j	Serra dos Carajás	26 x
Sasebo	58 v	Segovia	34 d	Serra dos Pacáas Novos	25 s
Saser	61 c	Seguedine	37 v	Serra dos Parecis	25 u
Saskatchewan (Province)	12/15	Séguéla	40 i	Serra do Tiracambu	27 a
Saskatchewan (River)	15 e	Segura	34 r	Serra do Tombador	25 x
Saskatoon	15 c	Sehwan	60 i	Serra Dourada	26 z
Saskylakh	52 f	Seine	34 g	Serra do Urucui	27 o
Sassandra	40 w	Seke Banza	44 f	Serra do Valentim	27 p
Sassandra (River)	40 z	Sekoma	49 a	Serra Formosa	25 z
Sassari	34 k	Sekondi-Takoradi	40 z	Serra Geral de Goiás	27 n
Sasykkol', Lake	56 c	Selaru	70 p	Serra Geral do Parana	29 f
Satadougou	40 f	Selatan, Cape	69 p	Serra Gradaús	26 x
Satara (India)	64 d	Selby	15 g	Serra Lombarda	26 j
Satara (South Africa)	49 f	Selebi-Phikwe	49 d	Serra Pacaraima	23 u
Satawal	71 b	Selenga	57 e	Serra Paranapiacaba	29 r
Satawan Atoll	71 g	Selety-Tengiz Lake	55 j	Serra Parima	23 u
Satipo	24 y	Sélibabi	40 e	Serra So Francisco	27 r
Satu Mare	33 v	Šelichov	57 c	Serra Talhada	27 t
Satun	65 w	Selma	20 h	Serra Tapirapecó	23 t
Saucillo	18 l	Semarang	68 z	Serra Tumucumaque	26 i
Saudi Arabia	38-39	Sembé	41 x	Serrania de Imataca	23 l
Saul	26 i	Semeru	69 n	Serrinha	27 t
Sault Ste. Marie	16 g	Semipalatinsk	56 c	Sêrtar	62 g
		Seman	39 k	Serule	49 c
		Semnu	37 j	Sêrxu	62 e
		Semonaicha	56 d	Sesayap	69 d

Sese Islands	42 y	Shelby	14 m
Sesheke	44 z	Shelekhova, Gulf of	53 x
Sesriem	48 h	Shenandoah	16 x
Sessa	44 x	Shenber	55 f
Sete Lagoas	29 i	Shendi	38 w
Setif	34 v	Shenmu	57 t
Settat	36 h	Sheno	43 d
Setúbal	34 n	Shepparton	77 x
Seul, Lac	16 c	Sherbro Island	40 f
Sevan, Lake	54 u	Sherbrooke	17 a
Sevastopol	35 k	Sherda	37 x
Severn	16 e	Sheridan	15 c
Severnaja	51 i	Sherman	19 d
Severnaya Zemlya	51 i	Sherman Basin	12 m
Severnoye	54 l	Sherman Island	80 m
Severodvinsk	50 q	Shestakova	53 g
Severomuysk	52 u	Shetland Islands	32 k
Sevi	56 k	Shetpe	54 y
Sevilla	34 p	Shevli	53 x
Seville (Sevilla)	34 p	Sheya	52 h
Sewa	40 f	Shibeli	43 e
Seward	11 f	Shibing	62 l
Seward Peninsula	10 m	Shiguaigou	57 t
Seychelles	231 p	Shihezi	56 s
Seym	54 b	Shihkiachwang	57 u
Seymchan	53 j	Shihtsuishan	57 u
Seymour	77 x	Shikar Pur	60 i
Sfax	34 y	Shikoku	58 x
Shache	55 z	Shilabo	43 t
Shackleton Ice Shelf	85 t	Shiliguri	61 k
Shackleton Range	83 u	Shilkan	53 l
Shadrinsk	55 e	Shillong	62 n
Shahdol	61 r	Shimanovsk	52 y
Shahgarh	60 k	Shimonoseki	58 v
Shahjahanpur	61 p	Shinas	39 z
Shahjui	60 i	Shindand	60 e
Shahr-e-Kord	39 i	Shingwedzi	49 f
Shajapur	61 o	Shintuya	25 n
Shakamku	48 k	Shinyanga	45 g
Shakawe	48 l	Shiping	62 l
Shakhty (Russia)	54 e	Shiquanhe	61 d
Shakhty (Kazakstan)	55 b	Shir	39 k
Shala, Lake	43 b	Shirane-san	59 n
Shaliangzi	56 x	Shiraz	39 j
Shamattawa	13 o	Shisanzhan	58 g
Shamrock	15 t	Shishinda	43 n
Shandan	57 o	Shishmaref	10 l
Shanghai	63 i	Shivera	51 w
Shangjao	63 f	Shivpuri	61 o
Shangkiu	63 d	Shiyan	63 a
Shangnan	63 a	Shkodër	35 d
Shangshui	63 d	Shokal'skogo Str.	51 m
Shang Xian	62 m	Sholapur	61 o
Shangyi	57 v	Shomvukva	50 u
Shangzhi	58 h	Shorobe	49 a
Shannon (Island)	91 t	Shoshong	46 o
Shannon (River)	32 u	Shostka	54 a
Shanshan	56 v	Showak	43 a
Shantar	53 p	Show Low	18 h
Shantung	58 p	Shreveport	19 f
Shaohing	63 h	Shuangcheng	58 g
Shaokwan	63 p	Shuangjiang	62 s
Shaowu	63 f	Shuangliao	58 g
Shaoyang	63 b	Shubra al Kheima	38 h
Shaqra	39 r	Shuga	55 l
Sharbithat	39 y	Shuga (Gulf of Ob')	51 p
Sharbithat, Ras	60 o	Shule	56 x
Sharjah	39 y	Shumikha	55 e
Shark Bay	76 b	Shumougou	57 l
Sharlyk	54 m	Shunte	63 p
Sharqat	39 d	Shuo Xian	57 t
Shashe	46 o	Shurgaz	60 d
Shashemene	43 p	Shush	39 g
Shashi	49 d	Shwangliao	58 g
Shasi	63 b	Shwebo	62 g
Shasta, Mount	14 u	Shyok	61 c
Shatsk	54 f	Si	63 o
Shaunavon	15 b	Siakwan	62 l
Shawinigan	17 a	Sialkot	61 a
Shawnee	15 v	Sian	62 m
Shay Gap	72 v	Siangfan	63 b
Shazaoyuan	56 x	Siangtan	63 b
Shcherbakovo	53 m	Siargao	67 k
Shchuch'ye	51 a	Siauliai	33 v
Sheberghan	60 h	Šibenik	35 h
Sheboygan	16 r	Siberia	51 o
Sheffield	32 x	Siberian Uvaly	51 a
Shelayevo	56 m	Siberut	68 c
Shelburne	17 r	Sibi	60 j
		Sibirjakov	51 e

Sibiti....................44 e	Singkawang.................68 l	Słupsk......................33 s	Sorong.......................70 p	Srinagar....................61 a
Sibiu......................35 g	Singkep.......................68 l	Slutsk......................33 x	Soroti........................42 y	Stafonovo..................50 f
Sibolga..................68 d	Singkilbaru...............66 p	Smallwood Reservoir....17 f	Söröya.......................33 i	Stakhanov..................54 d
Sibu......................69 a	Singtai......................63 c	Smara.......................36 r	Sorsk........................56 i	Stampriet..................48 j
Sibut......................42 o	Sining........................57 o	Smederevo.................35 e	Sorsogon...................67 i	Standerton.................49 r
Sibuyan..................67 h	Sinjai.........................69 t	Smidovich..................50 j	Sortavala...................33 m	Stanford....................15 a
Sicasica..................28 e	Sinjar........................54 s	Smith......................14 l	Sosna.......................52 b	Stanley (Falkland Is.)....31 p
Sichuan Pendi.........62 j	Sinkat........................38 y	Smith Bay..................13 g	Sosnovka...................57 f	Stanley (N. Dakota)......15 f
Sicilian Channel........34 z	Sinn..........................58 m	Smithfield..................49 o	Sos'va.......................50 y	Stannakh-Khocho.........52 l
Sicily.....................35 n	Sinnamary..................26 j	Smith's Falls...............16 l	Sosyko......................54 e	Stanovoy Mountains.....52 y
Sicuani..................25 n	Sinop.........................35 m	Smithton..................77 w	Souanké.....................41 x	Stanthorpe.................78 l
Sidatun..................58 l	Sintang......................68 m	Smolensk...................33 z	Soubré.......................40 v	Staraja Russa.............33 m
Sîdi Barrâni.............38 e	Sinú...........................22 m	Smyley Island............82 z	Souk-Ahras.................34 w	Stara Zagora..............35 h
Sidi-bel-Abbes.........34 s	Sinugif.......................43 j	Snag.......................11 l	Sôul (Seoul)................58 u	Star.Dom....................53 d
Sidi Bennour...........36 e	Sinūiju.......................58 s	Snake......................14 j	Sounda......................44 v	Stargard....................33 s
Sidi Ifni.................36 e	Sinyaya......................52 k	Snake River (USA)........15 a	Souré........................26 m	Staritsa.....................51 s
Sidi Kacem.............36 i	Sinyuga......................52 s	Snare River................12 s	Sousse.......................34 y	Staritsa (Moscow).........50 n
Sidley, Mount..........81 f	Sioux City...................15 v	Snares Islands............79 p	South Africa.........46/48-49	Star. Kayakhnyy..........52 b
Sidney (Montana).......15 e	Sioux Falls..................15 v	Snowdrift..................12 u	Southampton Island.....13 q	Star. Kheydzhan..........53 s
Sidney (Nebraska)......15 r	Sioux Lookout..............16 c	Snowy......................78 o	Southampton (UK)........34 f	Staryy Nadym..............51 p
Sidorovoko..............51 f	Siple (Mountain)...........81 b	Snowy Mountains.........78 q	Southampton (USA)......17 n	Staryy Oskol...............54 d
Siedlce..................33 v	Siple (Research Sta.).....81 q	Soai Dao...................65 k	South Andaman...........65 e	Staten Island..............30 z
Siegen-Kyugel.........52 m	Siple Island................81 q	Sobat......................42 k	South Anyuskiy Mountains 10 b	Statesboro.................20 l
Siena.....................34 l	Sipora........................68 e	Sobradinho Reservoir....27 r	South Australia...........77 b	Stavanger..................33 a
Sierra Blanca Peak.....18 k	Siquijor......................67 i	Sobral.......................27 f	South Bend.................16 s	Stavropol'..................54 t
Sierra Burro............19 a	Sira...........................56 i	Soči.........................54 r	South Bug...................35 k	Stavropolka................55 f
Sierra Carmen.......18/19	Siracha......................65 j	Socompa...................28 c	South Carolina............20 m	Steamboat.................12 p
Sierra Colorada.........30 j	Siracusa (Syracuse).......35 o	Socorro (Colombia)........23 n	South China Sea......66-67	Steamboat Springs.......15 p
Sierra de Aguas Calientes 28 r	Siraj...........................60 b	Socorro (USA).............18 j	South Dakota...............15 g	Steelpoort..................49 e
Sierra de Cordoba......28 t	Sir Edward Pellew Group .73 g	Socorro (Island)...........18 u	South East Cape..........77 y	Steenkool...................70 q
Sierra de Famatina.....28 c	Siret..........................35 h	Socotra....................231 c	Southend...................12 w	Steenstrup Glacier........91 b
Sierra de Juarez........18 d	Sirha.........................61 i	Soda Springs..............15 n	Southend-on-Sea..........32 y	Stefansson Island.........12 j
Sierra de la Giganta....18 g	Sir James McBrien, Mount 12 o	Söderhamn.................33 f	Southern Alps..............79 r	Steinhausen................48 i
Sierra del Nevado.......30 j	Sirjan........................60 a	Södertälje..................33 f	Southern Cross............76 f	Steinkier....................33 d
Sierra de Mato..........23 t	Sir Joseph Banks Group ..77 e	Sodiri.......................42 j	Southern Indian Lake......12 z	Steinkopf...................48 w
Sierra de Perija.........23 b	Sirohi........................60 z	Sodo........................43 o	Southern Ocean...........87 t	Stephenville................17 h
Sierra de Velasco.......28 r	Sironcha....................64 h	Sofala Bay.................46 v	Southern Sierra Madre....19 p	Stepnyak....................55 i
Sierra Leone............40	Sirpur........................64 g	Sofia........................35 f	Southern Sporades........35 u	Sterling.....................15 r
Sierra Madre............67 g	Sirsa.........................61 a	Sofiya (Sofia)..............35 f	South Georgia Islands.....31 y	Sterlitamak.................55 a
Sierra Morena...........34 p	Sirte.........................35 o	Sofiysk......................53 o	South Horr..................43 o	Stettin (Szczecin).........33 r
Sierra Nevada (Spain)...34 q	Sirte Desert................37 k	Sofiysk (Amur).............59 b	South Island................79 r	Stevens Point..............16 d
Sierra Nevada (USA).....14 v	Sirte, Gulf of...........35/38	Sogamoso..................23 o	South Magnetic Pole......87 q	Stewart
Sierra Vista............18 h	Sirwa........................43 h	Sogeri.......................71 o	South Natuna Islands.....68 l	(British Colombia).........11 z
Sigil......................65 t	Si Sa Ket...................66 g	Sognefjörd.................33 a	South Orkney Islands.....82 g	Stewart
Signy......................82 g	Sishen.......................48 z	Sogo Nur...................57 o	South Pagai.................68 r	(Yukon Territory)..........11 i
Siguiri.....................40 g	Sisimiut.....................90 i	Sohâg.......................38 i	South Platte.................15 s	Stewart Crossing..........11 k
Sihabuhabu.............65 v	Sisophon....................66 g	Sohar.......................39 z	South Pole..................81 m	Stewart Island.............79 p
Sihochac.................19 u	Sisseton.....................15 i	Soje.........................49 b	South Saskatchewan......15 a	Stewart, Mount............74 l
Sikar......................61 a	Sitapur......................61 a	Šokalsky....................51 c	South Scotia Ridge........82 f	Stewart (River)............11 k
Sikasso...................40 i	Sitka.........................11 x	Sokcho......................58 v	South Shetland Islands....82 r	Steynsburg.................49 o
Sikhote-Alin.............58 m	Sittang.......................65 g	Sokodé......................41 a	Southwest Cape...........79 p	Steytlerville.................49 n
Sikonge...................45 g	Sittwe........................62 o	Sokolo.......................40 i	Sovetsk......................33 v	Stikine......................11 z
Siktyakh..................52 k	Siuri..........................61 w	Sokoto.......................41 d	Sovetskaya..................84 w	Stilbaai.....................48 y
Silao......................19 n	Sivas.........................54 p	Sokoto (River)..............41 c	Sovetskiy....................50 z	Stirling......................32 w
Silay......................67 h	Siverek......................54 r	Sokyrbulak.................55 b	Soyapa......................18 i	Stockholm..................33 g
Silchar....................62 o	Sivuch.......................53 v	Soledade...................25 b	Soyo........................44 e	Stockton....................14 u
Silet......................37 o	Siwa.........................38 e	Solikamsk..................50 w	Spaatz Island..............82 z	Stoke-on-Trent............32 w
Silifke.....................35 y	Siwa, Oasis................38 e	Sol Iletsk...................54 m	Spain...................34/36	Stolbovoy...................50 i
Siligir.....................52 f	Sixtymile....................11 i	Solimões...................23 s	Spanish Town..............21 o	Stolbovoy (Island).........53 c
Siling Co..................61 k	Siziman......................59 b	Solodniki...................54 n	Spartanburg.................20 l	Stonehenge.................77 l
Siljan, Lake.............33 e	Skagen, Cape..............33 c	Solok........................68 f	Spassk Dal'niy.............58 k	Stony Rapids...............12 v
Šilka......................57 j	Skagerrak...................33 b	Sololo.......................43 p	Spearfish...................15 e	Stony River.................11 c
Silkwood.................73 m	Skagway.....................11 x	Solomon Islands.......71/74	Spence Bay.................13 a	Store Koldewey............91 u
Sillanjnuay..............28 d	Skardu......................61 a	Solomon Sea..............74 k	Spencer.....................15 w	Storkerson Peninsula......12 i
Silver City...............18 i	Skeena......................14 d	Solor Islands...............69 v	Spencer, Cape.............77 r	Storm Bay..................77 z
Simao....................62 t	Skellefte....................33 g	Solovjevsk..................57 i	Spencer Gulf................77 e	Storm Lake.................16 n
Simcoe, Lake...........16 j	Skellefteå...................33 h	Solwezi......................45 n	Spitsbergen.................92 o	Stors, Lake................33 e
Simenga..................52 d	Skibotn......................33 h	Somalia....................43	Split.........................35 b	Storuman....................33 f
Simeulue..................68 b	Skikda.......................34 w	Somerset...................16 t	Spokane.....................14 j	Strahan......................77 x
Simferopol'..............54 o	Sklad........................52 j	Somerset East.............49 n	Spratly Islands.............66 z	Stralsund....................33 q
Simikot...................61 f	Skoer Fjord.................91 u	Somerset Island............13 a	Springbok...................48 w	Strand......................48 w
Simla.....................61 c	Skopin.......................54 e	Son.........................61 t	Springdale..................17 j	Strasbourg.................34 j
Simpson Desert.........73 l	Skopje.......................35 e	Sonaly......................55 l	Springfield (Colorado).....15 s	Strathleven.................73 k
Simpson Peninsula.....13 b	Skovorodino................52 x	Songea.....................45 u	Springfield (Illinois).......16 q	Strathmay..................73 k
Simušir...................59 i	Skukuza.....................49 f	Songkhla...................65 w	Springfield	Streaky Bay................77 c
Sinadogo.................43 u	Skye.........................32 v	Songo.......................45 s	(Massachusetts)...........17 n	Strelka......................53 i
Sinai Peninsula........38 j	Slamet.......................68 y	Sonhat......................61 s	Springfield (Missouri).....15 x	Strelka (Yenisey).........51 w
Sinawan..................37 g	Slana........................11 h	Sonoyta.....................18 f	Springfield (Ohio).........16 u	Strelka-čunja..............52 a
Sincelejo.................22 m	Slave Coast................41 o	Sonsonate..................22 c	Springs.....................46 q	Strezhevoy.................51 q
Sinclair Mills............14 h	Slave Lake..................14 l	Sonsorol....................70 d	Springsure...................74 r	Strickland...................70 x
Sind.......................61 p	Slave River..................12 u	Sopo.......................42 g	Spruce Knov................16 w	Strömsund..................33 f
Sindi......................42 f	Slessor Glacier.............83 u	Sorabai....................60 k	Squaw Habor..............11 n	Stryy........................35 f
Šinedžinst...............57 n	Slidell........................19 i	Sordongnokh (Russia)....53 l	Sredinnyy Mountains......53 y	Stung Treng................66 i
Sines......................34 n	Sligo.........................32 u	Sordongnokh (Russia)....53 p	Srednekolymsk.............53 j	Sturge Island...............86 v
Sinewit...................71 v	Slippers Bay................48 w	Soria........................34 e	Sredniy.....................53 w	Sturgeon Bay..............16 f
Singa......................42 m	Sloven.......................33 w	Sorocaba...................29 f	Sredniy Kalar...............52 t	Sturgeon Falls.............16 j
Singapore................66 t	Sliven.......................35 h	Sorochinsk..................54 m	Sretensk.....................57 k	Sturt Creek.................73 n
Singatoka.................75 k	Slovakia.....................35 c	Sorochinsk..................54 m	Srikakulam..................64 k	Sturt Desert................77 h
Sing Buri.................65 j	Slovenia.....................35 a	Soria........................34 e	Sri Lanka...................64	Stutterheim.................49 p
Singida.....................45 h	Sl'ud'anka...................52 l	Sorol Atoll..................70 j	Sri Mohangarh.............60 k	Stuttgart....................34 l

Styr ....33 w
Suakin ....38 z
Suanhwa ....57 w
Suata ....23 g
Subotica ....35 d
Suceava ....35 h
Süchbaatar ....57 d
Suchow (Xuzhou) ....63 f
Suchow (Suzhou) ....63 h
Suchumi ....54 r
Suckling, Mount ....74 e
Sucre ....28 f
Sucuaro ....23 q
Sucunduri ....25 j
Sucuriu ....29 b
Sucurundi ....25 j
Sudan 38/42-43
Sudbury ....16 i
Sudd ....42 j
Suddie ....23 k
Sudety 35
Sudocje, Lake ....55 o
Sudr ....38 j
Sue ....42 u
Suez ....38 j
Suez Canal ....38 j
Suez, Gulf of ....38 j
Sugdža ....57 e
Suglan ....53 a
Sugoy ....53 k
Sugun ....55 y
Suhai Hu ....56 x
Suhait ....57 q
Suhsien ....63 e
Suide ....57 t
Suifenhe ....58 j
Suihua ....58 g
Suileng ....58 g
Suining ....62 k
Sui Zian ....63 c
Suj ....57 r
Sukabumi ....68 w
Sukhana ....52 h
Sukhinichi ....54 b
Sukhona ....50 r
Sukkur ....60 j
Suknah ....37 j
Sulaiman ....60 k
Sulaimaniyah (Iraq) ....39 e
Sulaimaniyah
(Saudi Arabia) ....39 t
Sulaiman Range ....60 k
Sula Islands ....69 k
Sulan Cheer ....57 s
Sulawesi (Celébes) ....69 t
Suleya ....55 b
Suli Hu ....56 x
Sullana ....24 g
Sullivan ....16 p
Sulphur Springs ....19 e
Sultan ....60 f
Sultanpur ....61 s
Sulu Archipelago ....67 s
Sulu Sea ....67 s
Sulzberger Ice Shelf ....81 v
Sum ....56 l
Sumaih ....42 v
Sumail ....60 o
Sumarokovo ....51 v
Sumatra ....68 f
Sumba ....69 s
Sumbawa ....69 r
Sumbawa Besar ....69 r
Sumbawanga ....45 v
Sumbe ....44 s
Sümber ....57 e
Sumbu ....45 e
Sumgait ....54 x
Sumprabum ....62 r
Sumy ....35 l
Sunan ....57 n
Suncho Corral ....28 u
Sundance ....15 d
Sundargarh ....61 t
Sunda Strait ....68 v
Sunderland ....32 y
Sundsvall ....33 g
Sungaigerung ....68 v
Sungai Ko-lok ....65 x
Sungaipenuh ....68 f

Sungai Petani ....66 q
Sungai Siput Utara ....65 x
Sungari ....58 j
Sun Kosi ....61 i
Suntar ....52 g
Sunwu ....58 g
Sunyani ....40 y
Suolama ....52 e
Suon-Tit ....52 x
Suordakh ....53 c
Superior ....15 k
Superior, Lake ....15 m
Suphan Buri ....66 d
Sur (Oman) ....60 q
Sur (Lebanon) ....60 q
Surab ....60 h
Surabaya ....69 o
Surakarta ....68 z
Surat (Australia) ....74 r
Surat (India) ....60 z
Suratgarh ....60 m
Surat Thani ....65 w
Surgat ....51 p
Surigao ....67 j
Surin ....65 m
Suriname 23/26
Susanville ....14 v
Šusenskoje ....56 j
Susquehanna ....16 y
Sutam ....52 y
Sutherland ....48 x
Sutlej ....60 m
Suttor ....74 p
Sutun'ya ....52 m
Suva ....75 l
Suvorka ....57 c
Suwâlki ....33 v
Suwar ....39 b
Suyevatpaul ....50 y
Suzun ....56 d
Svalbard ....92 o
Svartenhuk ....90 m
Svartisen ....33 e
Sveg ....33 e
Svendborg ....33 q
Sverdlovsk
(Yekaterinburg) ....50 y
Sverdrup Channel ....89 r
Sverdrup Islands ....12 k
Svetlaya ....59 a
Svetlovodnaya ....58 m
Svetozarevo ....35 e
Svobodny ....58 h
Swakopmund ....48 g
Swan ....76 d
Swan Hill ....77 v
Swan Island ....19 z
Swan River ....15 f
Swansea (Australia) ....77 z
Swansea (UK) ....32 w
Swat ....60 m
Swatow ....63 r
Swaziland 46/49
Sweden 33
Sweeney Range ....83 n
Sweetwater ....19 a
Sweetwater (River) ....15 o
Swellendam ....48 y
Swift Current ....15 b
Switzerland 33/34
Syagannakh ....53 f
Sydney (Australia) ....78 t
Sydney (Canada) ....17 h
Sydney Ice Cap ....13 d
Syktyvkar ....50 y
Sylhet ....61 y
Sym ....51 u
Sym (River) ....51 v
Symya ....50 m
Syowa ....84 i
Syracuse (USA) ....16 y
Syracuse (Sicily) ....35 o
Syrdarja (River) ....55 s
Syria 38-39/54
Syrian Desert ....38 m
Syzran ....54 j
Szczecin ....33 r
Szczecinek ....33 s
Szeged ....35 d
Szeping ....58 f

T

Tabah ....39 c
Tabajara ....25 u
Tabarka ....34 x
Tabas ....39 m
Tabatinga, Serra da ....27 p
Tabelbala ....36 j
Tablas ....67 h
Table Island ....13 a
Tableland ....72 m
Tabletop ....72 x
Tabor ....53 i
Tabora ....45 f
Tabou ....40 v
Tabriz ....54 v
Tabuk ....38 l
Tacámbaro ....19 n
Tachakou ....56 r
Tacheng ....56 e
Tacloban ....67 j
Tacna ....25 n
Tacoma ....14 h
Tacora ....25 o
Tacuarembó ....28 z
Tacutu ....23 w
Tademait, Hama da ....36 m
Tadjourah ....43 f
Tadmur ....38 m
Taegu ....58 v
Taejon ....58 u
Tafassâsset, Ténéré du ....37 s
Taftan ....60 e
Taganrog ....54 d
Tagant ....36 r
Tagap Ga ....62 d
Tagbilaran ....67 i
Taghit ....36 k
Tagounite ....36 h
Taguatinga ....27 n
Tagum ....67 x
T'agun ....56 f
Tagus ....34 o
Tahifet ....37 q
Tahiti ....230 o
Tahlequah ....16 n
Tahoua ....41 e
Tahrud ....60 c
Tai ....40 v
Tai'an ....63 e
Taibus Qi ....57 w
Taichow ....58 p
Taichung ....63 t
Ta'if ....39 o
Taigu ....57 u
Tailai ....58 e
Tai, Lake ....63 e
Taima ....38 m
Taimba ....51 y
Taimura ....51 z
Taimyr ....51 l
Taimyr, Lake ....51 m
Taimyr Peninsula ....51 i
Tainan ....63 u
Taiobeiras ....29 j
Taipei ....63 v
Taiping ....65 w
Taitao Peninsula ....30 s
Taiwan 63
Taiwan Strait ....63 t
Taiyuan ....57 u
Ta'izz ....43 g
Tajarhi ....37 v
Tajikistan ....55 v
Tajito ....18 z
Tajo ....34 q
Tajsara, Cord. de ....28 g
Tajura ....37 i
Tak ....65 i
Takamatsu ....58 y
Takatshwaane ....48 m
Ta-Kaw ....62 s
Takestan ....39 h
Takhta Bazar ....55 r
Takijuak Lake ....12 g
Takla Makan Desert ....56 r
Takpa Shiri ....62 b
Takua Pa ....65 u
Takum ....41 u
Talak ....37 p

Talandzha ....58 j
Talara ....24 g
Talata Mafara ....41 e
Talaud Islands ....69 l
Talavera de la Reina ....34 p
Talawana ....72 v
Talbot ....76 k
Talca ....30 h
Talcahuano ....30 g
Talcher ....61 u
Taldy-Kurgan ....56 n
Taliabu ....69 j
Taliqan ....60 k
Talitsa ....50 z
Talkeetna ....11 f
Tall'Afar ....39 c
Tallahassee ....20 j
Tall Kalakh ....38 l
Tal'menka ....56 e
Talodi ....42 j
Talon ....53 u
Taloyoak (Spence Bay) ....13 a
Taloye ....52 y
Taltal ....28 o
Taluma ....52 w
Talwood ....78 e
Tamala ....76 c
Tamale ....40 m
Tamanrasset ....37 p
Tamassoumit ....36 p
Tamazula ....18 z
Tamazunchale ....19 p
Tambacounda ....40 d
Tambara ....49 h
Tambelan Islands ....68 j
Tambey ....51 b
Tambo (Australia) ....74 b
Tambo (Peru) ....24 y
Tambo (Peru) ....25 n
Tambor ....48 f
Tambov ....54 f
Tambura ....42 u
Tamč ....56 k
Tamchaket ....36 r
Tamentit ....36 l
Tamiahua Lagune ....19 q
Tamitatoala ....26 v
Tampa ....20 k
Tampere ....33 j
Tampico ....19 p
Tamsagbulag ....57 k
Tamshiyaco ....24 m
Tamu ....62 p
Tamworth ....78 e
Tanabe ....58 z
Tanacross ....11 h
Tanahbala ....68 d
Tanahjampea ....69 u
Tanahmerah ....70 v
Tana (Kenya) ....43 g
Tana (Norway) ....33 l
Tana (River, Norway) ....33 k
Tana, Lake ....43 b
Tanama ....51 e
Tanami Desert ....73 p
Tanana ....11 e
Tanbar ....77 h
Tanchoj ....57 d
Tandil ....31 b
Tanega ....58 w
Tanezrouft ....36 y
Tanezrouft-n-Ahenet 36/37
Tanga (Tanzania) ....45 v
Tanga (Russia) ....57 g
Tanganyika, Lake ....45 d
Tanggula Shan ....61 k
Tanghe ....63 c
Tangier ....34 p
Tangorin ....74 o
Tangra Yumco ....61 i
Tangshan ....57 y
Tangub ....67 u
Tanguiéta ....41 b
Tanimbar Islands ....70 o
Tanjung ....69 c
Tanjungbalai ....65 w
Tanjungkarang ....68 v
Tanjungpandan ....68 x
Tanjungpura ....65 v

Tanjungredeb ....69 e
Tannu Mountains ....56 j
Tano ....40 y
Tanot ....60 k
Tanout ....41 g
Tanque El Revés ....18 m
Tanta ....38 h
Tantan ....36 e
Tanzania 42/45/46
Tao'an ....58 d
Taolañaro ....47 q
Taoudenit ....36 w
Taourirt ....36 k
Taouz ....36 j
Taoyüan ....63 u
Tapachula ....19 t
Tapajós ....25 l
Tapaktuan ....65 t
Tapanahoni ....26 h
Tapauá ....25 f
Tapauá (River) ....25 e
Tapeta ....40 t
Tapirapecó, Serra ....23 t
Tapirapua ....25 x
Tapis ....68 z
Tapsui ....50 y
Tapti ....60 z
Tapurucuara ....25 f
Taquaras ....25 s
Taquari ....28 m
Tara ....55 y
Tara (River) ....55 m
Tarabuco ....28 g
Taracuá ....25 c
Taragay ....55 y
Tarakan ....69 e
Taran ....51 c
Taranto ....35 c
Taranto, Gulf of ....35 p
Tarapoto ....24 j
Taraq ....39 x
Tararua Range ....79 v
Tarat ....37 s
Tarata ....25 o
Tarauacá ....25 n
Tarauacá (River) ....25 a
Tarbagatay Mountains ......56 d
Tarbaj ....43 q
Tarbes ....34 f
Tarcoola ....77 c
Taree ....78 g
Tareya ....51 j
Tarfaya ....36 d
Tarhuna ....35 n
Tarialan ....57 b
Tariat ....57 c
Tariat (Hangayn
Mountains) ....57 a
Tarif ....39 x
Tarija ....28 g
Tarim ....56 q
Tarim (River) ....56 r
Tarim Basin ....56 q
Tarim Liuchang ....56 t
Tarime ....45 g
Tarim Kot ....60 h
Tarka La ....61 k
Tarkwa ....40 z
Tarlac ....67 f
Tarnak ....60 i
Taroom ....74 r
Taroudannt ....36 g
Tarragona ....34 g
Tarso Ahon ....37 y
Tartagal ....28 h
Tartary, Gulf of ....59 b
Tartu ....33 k
Tartus ....35 z
Tarutung ....68 d
Tasauz ....55 p
Tashigang ....61 l
Tachkent ....55 v
Tasik Malaya ....68 x
Task ....41 h
Taskesken ....56 c
Tas-Kumsa ....53 a
Tas-Kumyr ....55 w
Tasman Bay ....79 t
Tasmania ....77 w
Tasman Sea ....78 d

Tassili-n-Ajjer ...37 r
Tassili Oua-n-Hoggar ...37 p
Tasso Fragoso ...27 o
Tastagol ...56 g
Tas-Tumus ...52 m
Tastyp ...56 h
Tas-Yuryakh ...52 f
Tata ...36 g
Tatarsk ...55 l
Tataurovo ...57 e
Tathlina Lake ...12 r
Tathlith ...39 q
Tatty ...55 x
Tatung ...57 o
Tatvan ...54 s
Tauá ...27 s
Taubaté ...29 g
Taumarunui ...79 v
Taumaturgo ...24 z
Taunggyi ...62 r
Taupo ...79 w
Taupo, Lake ...79 w
Tauranga ...79 w
Taurus ...35 x
Tavda ...50 z
Tavda (River) ...50 z
Tavira ...36 g
Tavoy ...65 h
Tavua ...75 l
Tawau ...69 e
Tawitawi ...67 s
Tawitawi Group ...67 s
Taxco ...19 o
Tayabamba ...24 w
Tayebad ...60 d
Taygonos, Cape ...53 z
Taymylyr ...52 j
Tayshet ...56 m
Taz ...51 f
Taz (River) ...51 f
Taz Bay ...51 d
Taza ...36 j
Tazenakht ...36 h
Tazirbu ...38 a
Tazovskiy ...51 e
Tazzarine ...36 i
Tbilisi ...54 u
Tchibanga ...44 c
Tchien ...40 u
Tchin-Tabaradene ...41 e
Tcholliré ...41 k
Te Anau ...79 p
Te Araroa ...79 x
Tea Tree ...73 r
Tebessa ...34 x
Tebicuary ...28 y
Teboursouk ...34 y
Techiman ...40 z
Tecka ...30 i
Tecomán ...18 y
Tecpan ...19 n
Tecuala ...18 x
Tedžen ...55 p
Teelin ...56 m
Tefé ...25 f
Tefé (River) ...25 e
Tegal ...68 y
Tegguidda-n-Tessoum ...41 e
Tegina ...41 e
Tegucigalpa ...22 e
Teguldet ...51 v
Tegyulte-Terde ...52 z
Tehchow ...57 w
Tehran ...39 j
Tehuacan ...19 q
Tehuantepec ...19 r
Tehuantepec, Gulf of ...19 r
Tehuantepec, Isthmus of ...19 s
Teide, Pico de ...36 a
Tekax ...19 v
Tekes ...56 q
Tekes (River) ...56 q
Tekeze ...43 c
Tekiliktag ...61 e
Tekirdağ ...35 h
Teku ...69 i
Tela ...19 w
Tel-Aviv-Yaffa ...38 k
Tele ...42 s
Teleckoje, Lake ...56 g

Telefomin ...70 x
Telegraph Creek ...11 y
Telemaco Borba ...29 q
Telemba ...57 h
Telémélé ...40 e
Teles Pires ...25 x
Tell Atlas ...34 t
Teller ...10 m
Telmen Nuur ...56 l
Telsen ...30 k
Telukbetung (Bandarlampung) ...68 v
Tema ...41 n
Temacine ...37 d
Tembenchi ...51 y
Tembenchi (River) ...51 k
Tembo ...41 v
Temir ...55 b
Temirtau ...55 j
Témiscaming ...16 j
Temnikov ...54 g
Temosachic ...18 j
Temple ...19 d
Temuco ...30 g
Tena ...24 j
Tenacatita ...18 x
Tenali ...64 i
Tenalr ...53 h
Tenasserim (River) ...65 i
Tenasserim Coast ...65 h
Tendaho ...43 d
Ten Degree Channel ...65 d
Tendelti ...42 k
Tendrara ...36 k
Ténéré ...37 s
Ténéré, Erg du ...37 t
Tenerife ...36 a
Tenerife (Island) ...36 b
Ténès ...34 t
Tenchong ...62 s
Tengiz, Lake ...55 h
Tenkasi ...64 s
Tenke ...52 g
Tenkeli ...53 e
Tenkodogo ...40 m
Tennant Creek ...73 r
Tennessee (State) ...16 r
Tennessee (River) ...16 r
Tenosique ...19 t
Tensift ...36 f
Tenterfield ...78 f
Teófilo Otoni ...29 j
Tepatitlán ...18 z
Tepeji ...19 o
Tepi ...42 z
Tepic ...18 x
Téra ...41 a
Terbu ...37 w
Terek ...54 u
Terensay ...55 c
Teresina ...27 q
Terezinha ...26 j
Termes de Rio Hondo ...28 t
Termez ...55 t
Termination Island ...76 h
Terminos, Laguna de ...19 u
Termit, Massif de ...41 i
Termit N. ...41 h
Ternate ...69 l
Terney ...58 m
Terni ...34 m
Ternopol' ...35 g
Terrace ...14 d
Terrace Bay ...48 f
Terra Firma ...48 z
Terra Preta ...25 j
Terra Haute ...16 s
Terror ...86 r
Teruel ...34 f
Terutao ...66 q
Tesig ...57 c
Teslin ...11 l
Tessalit ...36 z
Tessaoua ...41 f
Tete ...46 q
Tété ...42 d
Tetere ...52 o
Tetuan ...34 p
Tetyushi ...54 j
Teuco ...28 w

Teulada, Cape ...34 x
Tevriz ...51 o
Têwo ...62 i
Texarkana ...19 e
Texas ...19 a
Texas City ...19 e
Texcoco ...19 p
Teya ...51 w
Tezejet ...55 p
Tezew ...33 t
Teziutlán ...19 p
Tezpur ...62 n
Thabazimbi ...49 c
Thailand ...62/65/66
Thailand, Gulf of ...66 e
Thakhek ...66 h
Thallon ...78 d
Thamarit ...39 x
Thames ...32 x
Thamud ...39 u
Thane ...60 z
Thanh Hoa ...62 x
Thanjavur ...64 h
Thap Put ...65 u
Tharad ...60 y
Thar Desert ...60 k
Thargomindah ...77 j
Tharthar, Lake ...39 c
Thasos ...35 g
Thaton ...65 h
Thatta ...60 v
Thayetmyo ...65 f
Thebes ...38 i
Theda ...72 m
Thedford ...15 t
Thelon ...12 w
Theodore ...74 s
Theodore Roosevelt ...26 q
The Pas ...15 f
Thermai, Gulf of ...35 s
The Sound ...33 q
Thessalonika ...35 f
Thessaloniki (Thessalonika) ...35 f
Thief River Falls ...15 i
Thiès ...40 b
Thika ...45 j
Thimphu ...61 k
Thingangyun ...65 g
Thionville ...34 i
Thiruvananthapurum (Trivandrum) ...64 r
Thistle I. ...77 z
Thlewiaza ...12 z
Thollon ...77 m
Thomasville ...20 j
Thompson ...12 y
Thompson Falls ...14 l
Thomson ...74 n
Thon Buri ...65 j
Thorntonia ...73 v
Three Hummock Island ...77 x
Three Kings Island ...79 g
Three Rivers (Australia) ...76 f
Three Rivers (USA) ...19 c
Thule ...91 c
Thunder Bay ...16 e
Thurso ...32 k
Thurston Island ...80 m
Thylungra ...77 j
Tiancang ...57 n
Tiancheng ...57 n
Tianguá ...27 e
Tianjin (Tientsin) ...57 x
Tianjun ...56 z
Tianlin ...62 x
Tiaret ...36 m
Tibati ...41 q
Tibé ...40 h
Tibesti ...37 y
Tibet ...61 g
Tiburon ...18 f
Tichitt ...36 s
Tichla ...36 o
Tichvin ...50 r
Ticul ...19 v
Tidikelt ...37 n
Tidjikja ...36 q
Tidra ...36 l

Tielongtan ...61 d
Tien Shan ...56
Tienshui ...62 k
Tientsin ...57 x
Tierra Blanca ...19 q
Tierra Colorada ...19 o
Tierra del Fuego ...30 w
Tiete ...29 d
Tieyon ...77 c
Tifariti ...36 r
Tifton ...20 k
Tigieglo ...43 t
Tigil' ...53 y
Tigre (Peru) ...24 x
Tigre (Venezuela) ...23 h
Tigris ...39 d
Tiguentourine ...37 e
Tijuana ...18 c
Tikhoretsk ...54 e
Tikrit ...39 d
Tiksi ...52 m
Tilamuta ...69 i
Tilemsés ...41 d
Tilemsi ...36 z
Tillabéri ...41 b
Tillamook ...14 g
Tillia ...41 d
Tilrhemt ...34 u
Timané ...28 k
Timan Ridge ...50 h
Timaru ...79 s
Timbaúba ...27 v
Timbedgha ...40 g
Timber Creek ...73 b
Timbouctou (Timbuktu) ...40 l
Timbuktu ...40 l
Timeiaouine ...37 o
Timétrine ...36 y
Timia ...37 r
Timimoun ...36 m
Timiris, Cap ...36 n
Timişoara ...35 e
Timmins ...16 i
Timón ...27 q
Timor ...69 x
Timor Sea ...69 x
Timpton ...52 y
Timsah ...37 w
Tindouf ...36 g
Tiné ...42 e
Tinerhir ...36 i
Tinfouchy ...36 i
Tingo María ...24 x
Tingri ...61 i
Tinogasta ...28 r
Tinos ...35 t
Tinrhert Hamada ...37 e
Tinsukiā ...62 d
Tintina ...28 u
Tinyay ...53 a
Tin Zaouatene ...37 o
Tioman ...68 h
Tipperary ...73 c
Tiracambu, Serra do ...27 a
Tirana ...35 d
Tiranë (Tirana) ...35 d
Tiraspol ...35 j
Tirekh ...52 m
Tirekhtyakh ...53 c
Tirgelir ...53 e
Tirgu Mureş ...35 g
Tirich Mir ...60 l
Tiroungoulou ...42 e
Tiruchchirappalli ...64 f
Tirunelveli ...64 t
Tiruntán ...24 l
Tirupati ...64 h
Tisdale ...15 c
Tisisat Falls ...43 b
Tisza ...35 d
Tit ...37 p
Titaf ...36 m
Tit-Ary ...52 l
Titicaca, Lake ...25 o
Titule ...42 t
Titusville ...20 m
Tizimín ...19 w
Tizi Ouzou ...34 v
Tiznit ...36 f
Tlacotalpan ...19 r

Tlalamabele ...49 b
Tlaltenango ...18 z
Tlapacoyan ...19 q
Tlaxiaco ...19 p
Tlemcen ...34 s
Tlisen ...37 l
Tmed Bu Haschlscha ...37 y
Toamasina ...47 n
Toba & Kakar Ranges ...60 j
Tobago ...23 j
Toba, Lake ...68 d
Tobelo ...67 y
Tobermorey ...73 t
Tobermorey (Australia) ...73 x
Tobermorey (Canada) ...16 l
Tobi ...70 c
Tobo ...70 o
Tobol' ...55 e
Tobol' (River) ...55 d
Tobol'sk ...51 l
Tobruk ...38 e
Tocache Nuevo ...24 w
Tocantínia ...26 z
Tocantinópolis ...26 z
Tocantins ...26 z
Tocopilla ...28 c
Tocorpuri ...28 e
Tocuyo ...23 d
Todertang ...43 n
Todos Santos (Bolivia) ...25 r
Todos Santos (Mexico) ...18 u
Toéssé ...40 m
Togiak ...11 n
Togliatti ...54 k
Togo ...41
Togtoh ...57 t
Togyz ...55 d
Tok ...11 n
Tokar ...38 z
Tokko ...52 u
Tokko (River) ...52 v
Tokoroa ...79 w
Toktogul ...55 x
Toktogul Reservoir ...55 w
Tokuma ...53 a
Tokushima ...58 y
Tōkyō ...59 o
Tolbo Nuur ...56 i
Toledo (Brazil) ...29 o
Toledo (Philippines) ...67 i
Toledo (Spain) ...34 q
Toledo (USA) ...16 u
Toledo Bend Reservoir ...20 d
Tolga ...37 c
Toli ...56 r
Toliara ...47 n
Tolka ...51 s
Tolka (River) ...51 r
Tolo, Gulf of ...69 h
Tolon ...52 r
Tolstoy, Cape ...53 x
Toluca ...19 o
Tolybay ...55 d
Tom' ...56 g
Tomah ...16 q
Tomar ...55 l
Tomatlán ...18 y
Tombador, Serra do ...25 x
Tombigbee ...20 h
Tombôco ...44 f
Tômbua (Porto Alexandre) ...48 e
Tomé-Açu ...26 m
Tomi ...42 o
Tomini, Gulf of ...69 g
Tommot ...52 y
Tomo ...23 g
Tompo ...53 b
Tom Price ...72 t
Tom Price, Mount ...72 t
Tomra ...61 i
Tomsk ...51 t
Tomtor ...53 a
Tomtor (Cherskogo Mountains) ...53 a
Tonalá ...19 s
Tonatins ...23 r
Tondano ...67 w
Tonga ...42 k
Tonga (State) ...231 z

Tongguzbasti ....56 q
Tonghae.................58 v
Tonghai ....62 u
Tongian Islands ....67 u
Tongjiang ....58 k
Tongliao ....58 e
Tongren.................62 h
Tongren (Wu Jiang) ....62 m
Tongsa Dzong ....61 l
Tongshan ....63 d
Tongtian ....62 e
Tongtianheyan ....62 b
Tongulakh ....52 j
Tongxin ....57 q
Tongyu ....58 e
Tongzi ....62 l
Toni ....42 v
Tonk ....61 o
Tonking ....62 w
Tonking, Gulf of ....62 y
Tonkling ....63 f
Tonle Sap ....65 m
Tonnel'nyy ....57 h
Tonopah ....14 x
Tonsina ....11 g
Tontantins ....25 c
Tonzang ....62 v
Toolebuc ....73 v
Toompine ....77 j
Toora-Chem ....56 l
Toowoomba ....78 f
Topeka ....15 v
Topia ....18 k
Topko ....53 p
Top Springs ....73 c
Torbat-e-Heidariye ....60 d
Torbat-e-Jam ....60 d
Torbert, Mount ....11 d
Torgo ....52 u
Torim ....18 h
Torino (Turin) ....34 k
Torit ....42 y
Torne ....33 i
Torngat Mountains ......13 y
Tornio ....33 i
Toro ....28 p
Torodi ....41 b
Toro Doum ....41 m
Toro, Lago del.........30 t
Toronto ....16 w
Tororo ....42 z
Torrabai ....48 f
Torrens Creek ....74 o
Torrens, Lake ....77 e
Torreón ....18 l
Torres Strait ....73 k
Tortkuduk ....55 k
Tortolas ....28 p
Tortosa ....34 g
Tortuga ....23 f
Torud ....39 l
Torun ....33 t
Torzhok ....50 n
Toson Cengal ....56 m
Tostado ....28 v
Toteng ....48 m
Totma ....50 l
Totness ....23 z
Totora ....28 f
Tottori ....58 y
Touba ....40 i
Toubkal ....36 g
Touboro ....41 k
Touggourt.............34 w
Tougué ....40 e
Toukoto ....40 g
Toulépleu.............40 u
Toulon ....34 j
Toulouse ....34 g
Toungoo ....62 r
Tours ....34 g
Toussoro ....42 e
Touws River ....48 x
Townsend ....15 a
Townsville ....74 u
Toxkan ....56 o
Toyama ....58 z
Toyon-Tirekh ....52 m
Tozeur ....34 x
Trabzon ....54 r

Trail...................14 j
Traill Island ....91 r
Trang ....65 v
Transantarctic
Mountains ....83 v
Trans Canada Highway....16 c
Transhimalaya ....61 g
Trapani ....34 z
Traralgon ....77 y
Trarza ....40 c
Travers ....79 t
Treinta-y-Tres ....31 f
Trelew ....30 l
Trenque Lauquen ....31 a
Trenton ....16 z
Tres Arroyos ....31 b
Três Bocas ....25 a
Tres Coraçoes ....29 h
Tres Isletas ....28 w
Tres Lagos ....30 u
Tres Marias ....29 s
Tres Marias Islands .....18 w
Tres Marias Reservoir ...29 g
Tres Puntas, Cabo ......30 y
Tres Rios ....29 i
Triangulos ....19 t
Trichur ....64 e
Trier ....34 j
Trieste ....35 a
Tríkala ....35 r
Trincomalee ....64 v
Trinidad and Tobago .....23 j
Trinidad (Bolivia) ......25 s
Trinidad (Colombia) .....23 o
Trinidad (Cuba)........20 z
Trinidad (USA) ....15 q
Trinity Peninsula ......82 t
Tripolis (Greece).......35 u
Tripoli (Lebanon) ......38 l
Tripoli (Libya) ....37 i
Tripolitania ....37 h
Tristan da Canha ....222 y
Trivandrum ....64 r
Trobriand or
Kiriwina Island ....71 r
Trofimovsk ....52 l
Troickoje ....56 f
Trois Rivières ....17 a
Troitsk ....55 d
Troitsko-Pechorsk .....50 w
Troitskoye ....55 a
Trombetas ....25 l
Trompsburg ....49 n
Tromsö ....33 g
Trondheim ....33 c
Trondheimsfjord ......33 c
Trosh ....50 j
Troy ....35 u
Troyekurovo ....54 e
Troyes ....34 i
Troynoy ....51 f
Trujillo (Honduras) .....20 v
Trujillo (Peru) ....24 u
Trujillo (Spain) ....34 p
Truk Islands ....71 e
Truro ....17 f
Tsaidam Basin ....56 w
Tsaochuang ....63 f
Tsaratanana Mountains ....47 e
Tsau ....48 m
Tsavo ....45 j
Tsavo National Park .....45 k
Tschita ....52 r
Tsentral'nyy ....56 j
Tsévié ....41 n
Tshabong ....48 z
Tshane ....48 l
Tshele ....44 e
Tshikapa ....44 k
Tshimbalanga ....44 z
Tshofa ....45 a
Tsholotsho ....49 c
Tshuapa ....44 l
Tsihombe ....47 p
Tsimafana ....47 o
Tsimlyanskoye
Reservoir ....54 g
Tsinan ....63 e
Tsingtao ....57 z
Tsining ....57 u

Tsinling Shan ....56 z
Tsiribihina.............47 p
Tsiroanomandidy ....47 p
Tsitsihar ....58 f
Tsoe ....49 a
Tsugaru Channel ....59 b
Tsumeb ....48 j
Tsumkwe ....48 k
Tsunyi ....62 l
Tsuruga ....58 z
Tsushima ....58 v
Tswiza ....49 f
Tuamotu Archipelago.....230 p
Tuan Giao ....62 v
Tuangku ....65 u
Tuapse ....54 r
Tuareg ....40 m
Tubaro ....29 r
Tubuai Islands ....230 o
Tubutama ....18 g
Tuckanarra ....76 f
Tucson ....18 g
Tucumá ....26 x
Tucumcari ....15 r
Tucupita ....23 i
Tucuruí ....26 l
Tuekta ....56 f
Tueré ....26 k
Tugela ....49 r
Tugolukovo ....54 f
Tuguegarao ....67 g
Tugur ....53 p
Tugur (River) ....53 o
Tukalan ....52 a
Tukangbesi Islands.....69 v
Tuktoyaktuk ....11 l
Tula (Mexico) ....19 o
Tula (Russia) ....54 r
Tula Mountains ....84 m
Tulancingo ....19 p
Tulcán ....24 i
Tulcea ....35 i
Tuli ....49 d
Tuli (River) ....49 d
Tulia ....15 s
Tulihe ....57 m
Tulit'a (Fort Norman) ....12 b
Tully ....74 c
Tulsa ....15 v
Tulua ....22 y
Tulum ....19 w
Tulun ....57 a
Tumaco ....24 h
Tumanskiy ....10 v
Tumany ....53 k
Tumat ....53 d
Tumatumari ....23 x
Tumba, Lake ....44 i
Tumbangsamba ....69 b
Tumbes ....24 g
Tumen ....58 i
Tumkur ....64 f
Tumu (Ghana) ....40 l
Tumu (Libya) ....37 v
Tumucumaque, Serra....26 i
Tunduma ....45 t
Tunduru ....45 v
Tungabhadra Reservoir....64 e
Tungabhadra (River) ....64 f
Tungaru ....42 k
Tungchuan ....62 m
Tungchwan ....62 v
Tunghwa ....58 f
Tungtin, Lake ....63 b
Tungus-Khaya ....52 k
Tunguskoye Mountains ....51 w
Tuni ....61 s
Tunis ....34 y
Tunis, Gulf of ....34 y
Tunisia 34/37
Tunja ....23 n
Tunor ....52 c
Tunuyán ....28 q
Tunuyán (River) ....28 r
Tunxi ....63 f
Tuolba ....52 w
Tuostakh ....53 c
Tuostakh (River) ....53 c
Tupanacca ....25 h
Tupelo ....19 l

Tupik ....52 v
Tupinambarama, Ilha ....25 z
Tupiza ....28 f
Tupper ....12 q
Tupungato ....30 i
Tuquan ....58 d
Túquerres ....24 i
Turabah ....39 o
Turan ....43 g
Turbat ....60 s
Turee Creek ....72 u
Turgattal ....55 e
Turgay ....55 e
Turgayskaya Valley ....55 e
Turgen ....56 i
Türgen (High Altai) .....56 x
Turhal ....35 m
Turiaçu ....27 b
Turin ....34 k
Turinsk ....50 z
Turkana, Lake ....43 n
Turkannakh ....52 j
Turkestan ....55 u
Turkey 35/54
Turkey Creek ....73 a
Turkmenbashi ....54 z
Turkmenistan ....55 o
Turks and Caicos
Islands ....21 s
Turku ....33 h
Turneffe Islands ......19 w
Túrnovo ....35 h
Turnu-Severin ....35 f
Turočak ....56 g
Turpan ....56 u
Turrialba ....22 h
Turtkul' ....55 q
Turtkhan ....51 h
Turukhansk ....51 h
Turum ....42 k
Tuscaloosa ....20 h
Tuticorin ....64 t
Tutóia ....27 d
Tutonchany ....51 x
Tutonchany (River) .....51 j
Tuul Gol ....57 d
Tuvalu ....231 y
Tüvsinsiree ....57 g
Tuxpan ....18 x
Tuxpan (Bay of
Campeche) ....19 q
Tuxtepec ....20 o
Tuxtla Gutiérrez ......19 s
Tuyen Quang ....62 x
Tuyun ....62 y
Tuz, Lake ....35 y
Tuz Khurmatu ....39 e
Tuzla ....35 d
Tvayan ....53 x
Tver ....50 o
Twee Rivier ....48 k
Twee Rivieren ....48 y
Twilight Cove ....76 k
Twin Falls (Canada) ....17 e
Twin Falls (USA).........14 y
Twin Rocks ....76 h
Twizel ....79 s
Tyler ....19 e
Tym ....51 s
Tymovskoye ....59 d
Tynda ....52 w
Tynset ....33 d
Tyre (Sour) ....38 k
Tyrma ....58 k
Tyrrhenian Sea ....34 z
Tyry ....53 c
Tyubelyakh ....53 e
Tyugene ....52 l
Tyugyuren ....53 e
Tyukalinsk ....55 l
Tyukyan ....52 h
Tyumen ....50 z
Tyung ....52 h
Tyungulyu ....52 m
Tzaneen ....49 e

Tzekung..............62 j
Tzepo................57 x

U

Uainambi ....25 b
Uanle Uen ....43 u
Uaroo ....72 r
Uatum ....25 j
Uaupés ....25 d
Uaupés (River) ....25 c
Ubari ....37 u
Ube ....58 w
Ubeda ....34 q
Uberaba ....29 e
Uberaba, Lagoa ....28 l
Uberlandia ....29 e
Ubon Ratchathani ......66 h
Ubundu ....45 a
Ucayali ....24 l
Uch ....60 l
Uchami ....51 y
Uchami (River) ....51 x
Uchiura Bay ....59 c
Uchkuduk ....55 r
Uchur ....53 n
Uda ....53 n
Uda (Vostochny
Mountains) ....56 m
Uda (Yablon Mountains) ....57 g
Udachnyy ....52 e
Udaipur ....60 z
Udanna ....53 f
Uddevaua ....33 d
Udd, Lake ....33 f
Udine ....34 m
Udokan ....52 u
Udon Thani ....65 l
Udskoye ....53 n
Uebonti ....69 h
Uele (Russia) ....52 z
Uele
(Dem. Rep. Congo) ....42 r
Uelen ....10 l
Uel'kal ....10 h
Uengan, Cape ....50 m
Ufa ....55 a
Ufa (River) ....55 a
Ugagli ....52 y
Ugalla ....45 e
Uganda 42/45
Ugashik ....11 o
Ughelli ....41 r
Ugoyan ....52 x
Ugulan ....53 x
Ugun ....52 z
Uige ....44 g
Uil ....54 m
Uil (River) ....55 a
Uinta Mountains ......15 c
Uis Mine ....48 g
Uitenhage ....49 n
Ujjain ....61 o
Ujung Pandang.......69 s
Ukerewe, Islands .....45 f
Ukhta ....50 v
Ukiah ....14 t
Ukraine ....35 j
Ukta ....53 g
Ukukit ....52 y
Ukwi ....48 l
Ulaan Uul ....56 m
Ulaanbaatar
(Ulan Bator) ....57 e
Ulaga ....53 a
Ulakhan Botuobuya ....52 e
Ulan ....56 z
Ulan Bator ....57 e
Ulan-Khol ....54 v
Ulansuhai Nur........57 s
Ulan-Ude ....57 e
Uldz Gol ....57 s
Ulety ....57 h
Ulgij ....56 h
Ulgumdzha ....52 h
Ulgumun ....52 h
Uliastaj ....56 m
Ulindi ....45 d
Ul'kan ....57 e

Ul'kenkaroy, Lake ....55 j
Ullawarra ....72 r
Ulovo ....53 j
Ulsan ....58 v
Ulua ....22 d
Ulukuut ....53 o
Ulundi ....49 s
Ulungur ....56 h
Ulungur Hu ....56 h
Uluru (Ayers Rock) ....77 a
Ulu Tau ....55 g
Ul'ya ....53 r
Ul'yanovsk ....54 i
Ul'yanovskoye ....55 k
Umala ....25 j
Uman' ....35 j
Umbakumba ....73 g
Ume ....33 g
Umeå ....33 h
Umm as Samim ....39 y
Umm as Sawin ....60 n
Umm el Abid ....37 j
Umm Inderaba ....42 j
Umm Keddada ....42 h
Umm Luj ....38 z
Umm Mirdi ....38 w
Umm Qasr ....39 f
Umm Ruwaba ....42 k
Umm Saggat ....42 e
Umm Sa'id ....39 w
Umm Saiyala ....42 k
Umnak ....10 y
Umtata ....49 q
Umzinto ....49 s
Unaí ....29 f
Unaizah ....39 d
Unalakleet ....11 b
Unalaska ....10 y
Unare ....23 g
Uncia ....28 f
Ungava Bay ....13 x
Ungava Peninsula ....13 u
Unio ....27 q
Unio da Vitória ....29 d
Unio dos Palmares ....27 v
Unimak ....10 z
Unimak Pass ....10 z
Unini ....23 v
Unión ....30 l
United Arab Emirates 39
United States
of America 11/14-20
United States Range ....91 g
Unža ....50 r
Uoyan ....57 n
Upata ....23 i
Upemba, Lake ....45 b
Upernavik ....90 m
Upington ....48 y
Upper Egypt ....38 v
Upper Red Lake ....15 j
Uppsala ....33 f
Uqlat al Suqur ....39 b
Urad Qianqi ....57 s
Ura J'ube ....55 u
Urak ....53 r
Ural ....54 l
Ural'sk ....54 k
Urals, South ....55 b
Urandangi ....73 u
Uranium City ....12 u
Uraricoera ....23 w
Uraricoera (River) ....23 v
Urbano Santos ....27 c
Urcos ....25 n
Urdakh ....53 h
Urdžar ....56 d
Uren ....50 s
Urengoy ....51 e
Urfa ....54 r
Urga ....55 o
Urgal ....58 k
Urgenč ....55 p
Urho ....56 f
Uriariti ....25 x
Uritskiy ....55 f
Uritskoye ....52 w
Urluk ....57 e
Urmia, Lake ....54 u
Urru Co ....61 j

Uruaçu ....29 e
Uruapan ....18 z
Urubamba ....24 z
Urubamba (River) ....24 z
Urucará ....25 k
Urucu ....25 f
Uruçui ....27 p
Uruçui, Serra do ....27 o
Uruguaiana ....28 z
Uruguay 28-29/31
Uruguay (River) ....28 x
Urumchi ....56 t
Urup ....59 h
Urusha ....52 w
Uruzgan ....60 i
Uryung-Khaya ....52 f
Usa ....50 j
Usakos ....48 h
Usal'gin ....53 p
Us'-Bel'dir ....56 m
Useless Loop ....72 p
Ushiarah ....39 f
Ushakova ....51 e
Ushuaia ....30 w
Ushumun ....52 y
Usino ....71 n
Üsküdar ....35 j
Usman ....52 x
Usolje Sibirskoje ....57 b
Uspenskiy ....55 k
Ussuri ....58 l
Ussuriysk ....58 k
Ust'-Avam ....51 j
Ust'-Belaya ....10 f
Ust'-Belogolovoye ....53 x
Ust'-Charky ....53 c
Ust'-Chayka ....52 p
Ust'-Džilinda ....57 h
Ust'-Ilimpeya ....52 b
Ust'-Kada ....57 b
Ust'-Kamengorsk ....56 e
Ust'Kamo ....51 y
Ust'-Kara ....50 m
Ust'-Karenga ....52 t
Ust'-Karsk ....57 k
Ust'-Kata ....55 b
Ust'Kolik'yegan ....51 q
Ust'Kulom ....50 u
Ust'-Kureyka ....51 h
Ust'-Kut ....52 o
Ust'-Kuyga ....53 b
Ust'Ilimsk ....52 n
Ust'-Maya ....53 n
Ust'-Mil ....53 n
Ust'-Muya ....52 t
Ust'-Nera ....53 e
Ust'Niman ....53 n
Ust'Nyukzha ....52 v
Ustobe ....56 e
Ust-Olenёk ....52 h
Ust'Omchug ....53 h
Ust'-Ordynskij ....52 o
Ust'Ozernoye ....51 u
Ust'-Ozilinda ....52 s
Ust'Pit ....51 w
Ust'-Port ....51 g
Ust'-Sopochnoye ....53 w
Ust'-Sugoy ....53 j
Ust'-Tigil' ....53 y
Ust'-Timpton ....52 y
Ust'Tsil'ma ....50 u
Ust'Tym ....51 s
Ust'Tyrma ....58 j
Ust'-Un'ya ....52 z
Ust-Urt Plateau ....54 z
Ust'-Uyskoye ....55 e
Ustya ....50 r
Usu ....56 r
Usumacinta ....19 u
Utah ....14 z
Utah Lake ....15 n
Utica ....16 z
Utila ....20 v
Utkholok ....53 x
Utopia ....73 x
Utrecht (Netherlands) ....33 n
Utrecht (South Africa) ....49 r
Utsunomiya ....59 o
Utta ....54 i
Utubulak ....56 g

Uummannaq ....90 m
Uvalde ....19 b
Uvinza ....45 q
Uvs Nuur ....56 j
Uweinat ....38 r
Uyandi ....53 d
Uyandina ....53 e
Uyar ....56 k
Uyёdey ....53 c
Uyole ....45 q
Uyuk ....55 v
Uyuni ....28 e
Uzbekistan ....55 r
Užgorod ....35 f
Uzhur ....56 h
Užice ....35 d
Uzynkair ....55 q

V

Vaal ....49 q
Vaal Reservoir ....49 p
Vaalwater ....49 c
Vaasa ....33 i
Vác ....35 d
Vacaria ....29 q
Vach ....51 r
Vachs ....55 u
Vadodara ....60 z
Vaduz ....34 k
Vaga ....50 r
Vaigač ....50 k
Valcheta ....30 l
Valdés Peninsula ....30 m
Valdez ....11 g
Valdivia ....30 q
Val-d'Or ....16 k
Valdosta ....20 k
Vale de Sonho ....29 b
Valenç ....27 t
Valença do Piauí ....27 q
Valence ....34 i
Valencia (Spain) ....34 s
Valencia (Venezuela) ....23 e
Valenciennes ....34 h
Valentim, Serra do ....27 p
Valentine ....15 t
Valera ....23 c
Valga ....33 k
Valki ....35 m
Valladolid (Mexico) ....19 w
Valladolid (Spain) ....34 d
Valle de la Pascua ....23 f
Valle de Santiago ....19 n
Valledupar ....23 a
Valle Grande ....25 s
Vallejo ....14 u
Vallenar ....28 o
Valletta ....35 n
Valley City ....15 h
Valleyview ....14 k
Valparaíso ....28 o
Valsad ....60 z
Vals, Cape ....70 u
Valuyki ....54 d
Vanado Tuerto ....28 v
Vanavara ....52 n
Van Buren ....17 d
Vancouver ....14 g
Vancouver Island ....14 e
Vandalia ....16 r
Van Diemen, Cape ....73 b
Van Diemen Gulf ....73 c
Vänern, Lake ....33 e
Vangaindrano ....47 r
Van Gölu ....54 t
Vangou ....58 l
Vangunu ....71 w
Vang Vieng ....62 v
Van Horn ....18 l
Vanimo ....70 x
Van, Lake ....54 t
Van Rees Mountains ....70 u
Vanrhynsdorp ....48 x
Vanrook ....73 k
Vansittart Island ....13 x
Vantaa ....33 j
Vanua Levu ....75 m
Vnuatu ....75 d

Van Wyksvlei ....48 y
Vanzevat ....50 z
Vanzhil'kynak ....51 s
Varanasi ....61 s
Varaždin ....35 b
Vargas Guerra ....24 j
Varillas ....28 c
Varna (Russia) ....55 d
Varna (Bulgaria) ....35 i
Várzea Grande ....25 y
Vasa Barris ....27 t
Vasjugan ....51 r
Västerås ....33 f
Västervik ....33 f
Vasyuganye ....51 p
Vatican City ....34 m
Vatnajökull ....32 d
Vättern, Lake ....33 e
Vatyna ....10 j
Vaughn ....15 q
Vaughn (Montana) ....15 a
Vaughn (New Mexico) ....18 l
Vaupés ....25 a
Växjö ....33 s
Vayalpad ....64 g
Vayvida ....51 x
Vegreville ....14 m
Vel ....50 q
Velasco, Sierra de ....28 r
Veles ....35 e
Velhas ....29 i
Velichayevskoye ....54 u
Velikaya ....10 f
Velikaya Kema ....58 m
Velikije Luki ....33 z
Velikiy Ustyug ....50 s
Velikovisochnoye ....50 i
Vella Lavella ....71 u
Vellore ....64 g
Velmo 1-oye ....51 w
Velsk ....50 r
Venada ....49 e
Venado Tuerto ....31 a
Vendenga ....50 t
Venezia (Venice) ....34 m
Venezuela 23/26
Venezuela, Gulf of ....23 c
Veniaminof, Mount ....11 p
Venice ....34 m
Venice, Gulf of ....34 m
Ventuari ....23 s
Ventura ....14 w
Vera ....28 w
Veracruz ....19 q
Vera, Laguna ....28 y
Veraval ....60 x
Verde, Cape ....40 a
Verde Grande ....29 i
Verde (River) (Brazil) ....29 b
Verde (River) (Mexico) ....19 o
Verde (River)
(Paraguay) ....28 j
Verdigris ....15 w
Vereeniging ....46 q
Vergemont ....73 x
Verissimo-Sarmento ....44 x
Verkhneimbatskoye ....51 v
Verkhneural'sk ....55 c
Verkhnevilyuysk ....52 i
Verkhniy Tura ....50 x
Verkhnyaya Amga ....52 y
Verkhnyaya Taimyra ....51 l
Verkhnyaya Toyma ....50 s
Verkhoyansk ....53 a
Verkhoyanskiy
Mountains ....52 k
Vermelha, Lagoa ....29 p
Vermont ....17 n
Vernadsky ....82 t
Vernal ....15 o
Verona ....34 l
Versino-Darasunskij ....57 j
Veshenskaya ....54 f
Vest Fjord ....33 e
Véstia ....29 c
Veszprém ....35 c
Vetekhtina ....52 k
Vetluga ....50 j
Vetluzhskiy ....50 j
Vetrenyy ....53 h

Vey Vozh ....50 v
Vezdekhodnaya ....52 d
Viacha ....25 p
Vicenza ....34 m
Vichada ....23 q
Vichadero ....29 n
Vicksburg ....19 h
Victor Harbor ....77 s
Victoria (Argentina) ....28 w
Victoria (Brazil) ....26 j
Victoria
(British Columbia) ....14 g
Victoria (Chile) ....30 h
Victoria (Hong Kong) ....63 q
Victoria (Texas) ....19 c
Victoria de las Tunas ....21 o
Victoria Falls ....49 b
Victoria Island ....12 h
Victoria, Lake ....45 f
Victoria Land ....86 l
Victoria (Mount, Burma) ...62 o
Victoria, Mount (Fiji) ....75 l
Victoria (Mount,
Papua New Guinea) ....71 o
Victoria Range ....76 c
Victoria River Downs ....73 b
Victoria (River) ....73 b
Victoria (State) ....77 w
Victoria Strait ....12 l
Victoria West ....48 z
Victorica ....30 l
Victorino ....23 r
Vicuña Mackenna ....30 m
Vidim ....57 c
Vidin ....35 f
Viedma ....30 m
Viedma, Lago ....30 u
Vienna ....35 b
Vien Pou Kha ....62 u
Vientiane ....62 v
Vietnam 62/66
Vigan ....67 f
Vigia ....26 m
Vigo ....34 a
Vijayawada ....64 i
Vikna ....33 c
Vila ....75 e
Vila Bittencourt ....25 b
Vila de Sena ....46 u
Vila Velha ....29 k
Vila Velha (Serra
Lombarda) ....26 k
Vilhena ....25 v
Viliga-Kushka ....53 l
Viljujskoje Reservoir ....52 k
Vilkitskogo ....92 k
Vilkicky ....51 d
Villa Ahumada ....18 k
Villa Angela ....28 v
Villa Bella ....25 r
Villa Delores ....28 s
Villaguay ....28 x
Villa Guillermina ....28 w
Villa Hayes ....28 y
Villahermosa ....19 t
Villa Iris ....30 m
Villa Maria ....28 u
Villa Media Agua ....28 q
Villa Montes ....28 h
Villa Ocampo ....18 k
Villa Ojo de Aqua ....28 u
Villarica ....30 h
Villa San Martín ....28 t
Villa Unión (Argentina) ....28 q
Villa Unión (Mexico) ....18 x
Villavicencio ....23 n
Villazón ....28 f
Vilnius ....33 w
Vilyuy ....52 j
Vilyuy Mountains ....52 j
Vilyuysk ....52 j
Vindhya Range ....61 n
Vineland ....16 z
Vinh ....62 x
Vinita ....16 n
Vinnitsa ....35 l
Vinson Massif ....81 d
Vioolsdrif ....48 v
Virac ....67 i
Virawah ....60 x

Virden ....15 f
Virginia (Minnesota) ....15 k
Virginia (State) ....16 x
Virginia Range ....76 i
Virgin Islands ....21 x
Virú ....24 x
Virundunagar ....64 g
Visalia ....14 v
Visby ....33 g
Vischarv ....55 w
Viscount Melville Sound ...12 g
Viseu ....27 a
Vishakhapatnam ....61 t
Vista Alegre ....25 c
Vistula ....35 e
Vitebsk ....33 z
Viterbo ....34 m
Vitichi ....28 f
Viti Levu ....75 k
Vitim ....52 r
Vitim (River) ....52 s
Vitim Plateau ....52 s
Vitimskiy ....52 s
Vitória ....34 d
Vitória ....29 k
Vitória da Conquista ....29 j
Vivi ....51 y
Vivi (River) ....51 k
Vivi, Lake ....51 k
Vize ....51 d
Vizeaino Desert ....18 e
Vizianagaram ....61 t
Vizinga ....50 t
Vladikavkaz ....54 u
Vladimir ....54 f
Vladivostok ....58 k
Vlorë ....35 d
Vltava ....35 a
Vohidiala ....47 r
Volcán Tres Virgenes ....18 f
Volga ....54 h
Volga Heights ....54 h
Volgograd ....54 h
Volksrust ....49 r
Volochanka ....51 j
Volochsk ....53 m
Volodarskoye ....55 h
Vologda ....50 q
Volokolamsk ....50 o
Volokon ....52 o
Volonga ....50 g
Vólos ....35 u
Vol'sk ....54 i
Volta Lake ....41 n
Volta Redonda ....29 i
Vorkuta ....50 l
Vorob'yeva ....52 s
Voronezh ....54 e
Vorontsovka ....52 s
Vorozheyka ....56 h
Vosburg ....48 z
Vostochny Mountains ....56 l
Vostok I ....85 o
Votkinsk ....50 v
Vovodo ....42 s
Voyeykov Ice Shelf ....87 e
Voyvozh ....50 w
Vozrozhdeniya ....55 p
Vraca ....35 f
Vrendenburg ....48 w
Vrsac ....35 e
Vryburg ....49 n
Vryheid ....49 s
Vung Tau ....66 j
Vyaz'ma ....54 b
Vyborg ....33 l
Vyčegda ....50 v
Vydrino ....56 m
Vym' ....50 u
Vyngapur ....51 q
Vysni Volocek ....50 o
Vyzakova ....54 i

W

Wa ....40 l
Wabag ....70 z
Wabash ....16 s
Wabowden ....15 h

Wabush ....17 d
Waco ....19 d
Waco-Kungo ....44 t
Wad ....60 l
Wad Banda ....42 i
Waddan ....37 k
Waddington, Mount ......14 f
Wadi ad Dawasir ....39 q
Wadi al Akhdar ....38 m
Wadi al Arish ....38 j
Wadi al Batin ....39 f
Wadi al Ghadaf ....39 c
Wadi al Hamd ....38 m
Wadi al Hamim ....38 c
Wadi al Hayl ....39 a
Wadi al Jarin ....39 p
Wadi al Jawf ....39 r
Wadi al Jiz ....39 v
Wadi Allaqi ....38 w
Wadi Araba ....38 k
Wadi Ar'ar ....39 b
Wadi ar Rimah ....39 d
Wadi as Sirhan ....38 m
Wadi Aswad ....39 z
Wadi ath Thartar ....39 c
Wadi bin Khawtar ....39 x
Wadi Bishah ....39 p
Wadi Gabgaba ....38 w
Wadi Garara ....38 w
Wadi Hadain ....38 x
Wadi Halfa ....38 v
Wadi Hawran ....39 b
Wadi Ibib ....38 y
Wadi Masilah ....39 u
Wadi Oitbit ....39 y
Wadi Oko ....38 y
Wadi Qena ....38 j
Wadi Seidna ....38 v
Wadi Shihan ....39 w
Wadi Tathlith ....39 q
Wadi Tibal ....39 b
Wad Medani ....42 m
Wager Bay ....13 b
Wagga Wagga ....77 y
Wagin ....76 e
Wagon Mound ....15 q
Wagontire ....14 v
Waigeo ....70 c
Waikabubak ....69 s
Waikato ....79 v
Wailuku ....18 q
Waingapu ....69 t
Wainwright (Canada) ......15 a
Wainwright (USA) ....11 b
Waipahu ....18 p
Waipara ....79 t
Wairoa ....79 x
Waitaki ....79 s
Wajir ....43 q
Waka ....42 p
Wakatipu, Lake ....79 q
Wakayama ....58 z
Wake Island ....231 l
Wakkanai ....59 c
Walagan ....52 x
Wałbrzych ....35 b
Walcott ....14 e
Waldburg Range ....76 e
Walden ....15 p
Wales (UK) ....32 w
Wales (USA) ....10 m
Wales Island ....13 c
Walewale ....40 m
Walgett ....78 c
Walgreen Coast ....81 c
Walikale ....45 c
Walinga ....71 o
Wallabi Group ....76 b
Wallace ....14 k
Wallal Downs ....72 v
Walleroo ....77 f
Walla Walla ....14 j
Walsenburg ....15 q
Walsh ....74 b
Walterboro ....20 m
Walvis Bay ....48 g
Wamba (Nigeria) ....41 g
Wamba (River) ....44 i
Wamba
(Dem. Rep. Congo) ......42 v

Wamena ....70 v
Wanaaring ....78 a
Wandels Sea ....91 j
Wandingzhen ....62 s
Wandoan ....78 e
Wanganui ....79 u
Wanganui (River) ....79 v
Wangaratta ....78 o
Wangmo ....62 v
Wangqing ....58 i
Wang Saphung ....65 k
Wanhsien ....62 l
Wanning ....63 n
Wannoo ....76 c
Wanyuan ....62 l
Warangal ....64 h
Waratah Bay ....77 x
Warburton ....72 z
Warburton (River) ....77 f
Warburton Lake ....12 t
Warder ....43 u
Wardha ....61 v
Warin Chamrap ....66 h
Warmbad ....46 q
Warner Robins ....20 k
Waroona ....76 d
Warrabri ....73 r
Warrawagine ....72 v
Warrego ....74 p
Warrenton ....49 n
Warri ....41 r
Warrnambool ....77 v
Warsaw ....33 u
Warta ....33 t
Warwick ....74 t
Warzawa (Warsaw) ....33 u
Washington DC ....16 y
Washington (State) ....14 h
Washington, Cape ....86 s
Washington Court
House ....16 u
Washington Land ....91 f
Washington, Mount ....17 o
Washita ....15 v
Watampone ....69 t
Waterbury ....17 n
Waterford ....32 y
Waterloo ....16 p
Waterton ....16 y
Watertown ....15 i
Waterval Boven ....49 r
Waterville ....17 b
Watsa ....42 v
Watsi ....44 k
Watsi Kengo ....44 k
Watson Lake ....12 h
Wau ....42 h
Wauchope ....73 r
Wau el Kebir ....37 x
Wau en Namus ....37 y
Wausau
(Massachusetts) ....17 n
Wausau (Wisconsin) ......16 d
Wave Hill ....73 c
Wawa (Canada) ....16 g
Wawa (Nigeria) ....41 c
Waxxari ....56 l
Waycross ....20 k
Webster City ....15 x
Weda ....69 m
Weda Bay ....69 m
Weda, Tulek ....69 m
Weddell Sea ....82 y
Wei ....62 k
Weichang ....57 x
Weifang ....58 o
Weimar ....33 q
Weinan ....62 m
Weining ....62 j
Weipa ....73 k
Weiser ....14 k
Weisse ....51 b
Weiya ....56 x
Welbourn Hill ....77 c
Weldiya ....43 d
Welkite ....43 c
Welkom ....49 o
Wellesley Islands ....73 i
Wellington (Australia) .....78 d
Wellington (Chile) ....30 s

Wellington
(New Zealand) ....79 v
Wellington
(South Africa) ....48 x
Wells ....14 y
Wema ....44 l
Wenatchee ....14 i
Wenchhow ....63 h
Wendo ....43 p
Wendover ....14 y
Wenlock ....74 a
Wenquan ....56 q
Wenquan
(Tanggula Shan) ....61 m
Wenshan ....62 w
Wentworth ....77 i
Wepener ....49 p
Wernecke Mountains ......11 k
Weser ....33 p
Wessel Islands ....73 g
West Bank ....38 l
West Cape ....79 p
West Cape Howe ....76 r
Western Australia ....76 f
Western
Cordillera 24-25/28
Western Cordillera
(Colombia) ....22 y
Western Ghats 60/64
Western Sahara 36
Western Sierra Madre .....18 k
West Falkland ....31 o
West Fayu ....71 a
West Frankfort ....16 r
Westgate ....77 l
West Group ....76 h
Westhope ....15 f
West Ice Shelf ....85 y
Westlock ....14 m
Westmar ....74 s
West Memphis ....16 q
Westmoreland ....73 h
West Palm Beach ....20 m
West Papua ....70 u
Westport (Ireland) ....32 t
Westport
(New Zealand) ....79 s
West Siberian Sea ....51 g
West Virginia ....16 v
West Wyalong ....78 b
Wetar ....69 x
Wetaskiwin ....14 m
Wewak ....70 z
Wexford ....32 v
Weyburn ....15 e
Whakatane ....79 w
Whale Cove ....13 n
Whangarei ....79 h
Wheeler Peak (Nevada) ...14 y
Wheeler Peak
(New Mexico) ....15 q
Wheeling ....16 w
Whidby Point ....77 d
Whim Creek ....72 t
White ....15 y
White Cliffs ....77 i
Whitecourt ....14 k
Whitefish Lake ....12 v
Whitehorse ....11 l
White Island ....92 d
White, Lake ....73 o
White Nile 38/42
White River (Canada) ......16 g
White River (USA) ....15 t
White Sea ....50 b
White Volta ....40 m
Whitewood ....73 y
Whitney, Mount ....14 w
Whittle, Cape ....17 n
Wholdaia Lake ....12 w
Whyalla ....77 e
Wichita ....15 v
Wichita Falls ....19 b
Wien (Vienna) ....35 b
Wiesbaden ....34 j
Wight, Isle of. ....32 v
Wilcannia ....77 i
Wilczek Island ....50 l
Wilhelmshaven ....33 o
Wilkes Land ....87 a

Wilkins Sound ....82 w
Wilemstad ....23 d
Willeroo ....73 c
Williamsburg ....16 y
Williams Lake ....14 h
Williamson ....16 v
Williamsport ....16 x
Willis Islands ....74 f
Williston (S.Africa) ....48 y
Williston (USA) ....15 e
Williston Lake ....12 p
Willmar ....15 j
Willow ....11 f
Willowmore ....48 z
Willowra ....73 q
Wills, Lake ....73 n
Wilmington (Carolina) .....21 a
Wilmington (Delaware) ....16 y
Wilpena ....77 g
Wilson Bluff ....76 m
Wilson's Promontory ......77 y
Wiluna ....76 g
Winburg ....49 p
Windau ....33 h
Windhoek ....48 i
Windorah ....77 i
Windsor (Canada) ....17 j
Windsor (USA) ....16 u
Winisk ....16 g
Winisk (River) ....16 f
Winisk Lake ....16 f
Winnemucca ....14 w
Winning ....72 r
Winnipeg ....15 i
Winnipeg, Lake ....15 i
Winnipeg (River) ....15 j
Winnipeg Beach ....15 i
Winnipegosis ....15 g
Winnipegosis, Lake ....15 g
Winona (Mississippi) ......19 i
Winona (Wisconsin) ....16 p
Winslow ....15 n
Winston Salem ....16 w
Winter Garden ....20 l
Winterhoek, Groot ....48 x
Winton ....73 x
Wisconsin ....16 g
Wiseman ....11 f
Wismar ....33 q
Witbank ....49 r
Witherspoon, Mount ....11 g
Witpütz ....48 v
Witrivier ....49 f
Witsand ....48 x
Wittenberge ....33 q
Wittenoom ....72 u
Witvlei ....48 j
Włocławek ....33 t
Woleai Atoll ....70 l
Wolf ....22 o
Wolf Creek ....14 m
Wolf Point ....15 d
Wollaston Foreland ....91 t
Wollaston Lake ....12 w
Wollaston Peninsula ....12 f
Wollogorang ....73 h
Wollongong ....78 f
Wolmaransstad ....49 o
Wonarah ....73 s
Wondoola ....73 w
Wonganoo ....76 g
Wŏnju ....58 u
Wŏnsan ....58 u
Wonthaggi ....77 x
Woodgreen ....73 r
Woodlark ....71 r
Woods, Lake of the ....15 k
Woodstock ....17 d
Woodward ....15 t
Woomera ....77 e
Worcester
(South Africa) ....48 x
Worcester (USA) ....17 n
Worland ....15 o
Worthington ....15 v
Wotu ....69 u
Wowan ....74 s
Wrangel Island ....10 h
Wrangell ....11 l
Wrangell Mountains ....11 h

Wrath, Cape ....32 j
Wright Peak ....80 m
Wrigley ....12 p
Wrocław ....33 t
Wuchow ....63 o
Wuda ....57 q
Wudao ....57 z
Wudil ....41 q
Wudinna ....77 d
Wudu ....62 j
Wuhan ....63 d
Wuhsi ....63 h
Wuhu ....63 f
Wüjang ....61 e
Wu Jiang ....62 l
Wukari ....41 u
Wular, Lake ....61 a
Wuliang Shan ....62 t
Wunnummin Lake ....16 e
Wuqi ....57 r
Würzburg ....34 k
Wutunghliao ....62 i
Wuwe ....62 i
Wuwei ....57 p
Wuyiling ....58 i
Wuying ....58 i
Wuyi Shan ....63 r
Wuyo ....41 i
Wuyuan ....57 s
Wuzhong ....57 r
Wyandra ....77 k
Wyloo ....72 s
Wyndham ....73 a
Wynyard ....15 d
Wyoming ....15 o
Wytheville ....16 v

X

Xainza ....61 k
Xai-Xai ....49 h
Xamavera ....48 k
Xambioá ....26 z
Xam Nua ....62 w
X-Muteba ....44 v
Xapuri ....25 p
Xar Burd ....57 p
Xar Hudak ....57 v
Xar Moron ....57 z
Xar Moron (Inner
Mongolia).......................57 t
Xhumo ....49 a
Xi ....58 c
Xiachengzi ....58 i
Xiamen (Amoy)...............63 s
Xiangcheng ....62 g
Xiang Jiang ....63 o
Xiangquan ....61 e
Xiangride ....62 e
Xi'an (Sian) ....62 m
Xianyang ....62 l
Xiao'ergou ....58 e
Xide ....62 i
Xieng Khouang ....62 v
Xifeng ....62 l
Xi Jiang (Si) ....63 o
Xikou ....57 m
Xilin Hot ....57 w
Xilin Qagan Obo ....57 u
Ximiao ....57 n
Xin'anjiang ....63 g
Xin Barag Youqi ....57 k
Xin Barag Zouqi ....57 l
Xincai ....63 c
Xinge ....44 w
Xingsagoinba ....62 g
Xingu ....26 v
Xingu (River) ....26 w
Xinguara ....26 y
Xingxingxia ....56 y
Xingyi ....62 w
Xingzi ....63 d
Xinhe ....56 q
Xinhuang ....62 m
Xinkai ....58 d
Xinmin ....58 e
Xin Xian ....57 u
Xinyang ....63 c
Xinyu ....63 d

Xinyuan ....56 q
Xique-Xique ....27 v
Xitieshan ....56 y
Xi Ujimqin Qi ....57 x
Xiushui ....63 d
Xixabangma Feng ....61 i
Xixiang ....62 l
Xorkol ....56 v
Xuancheng ....63 e
Xuanwei ....62 w
Xueweng ....63 u
Xungba ....61 f
Xunke ....58 h
Xuwen ....63 n
Xuyong ....62 k

Y

Ya'an ....62 i
Yabassi ....41 u
Yabelo ....43 o
Yablonovy Mountains .....57 g
Yabrai Yanchang ....57 p
Yacimiento ....30 u
Yacuiba ....28 h
Yada ....51 b
Yadrin ....54 h
Yafo ....38 k
Yagra ....61 f
Yahuma ....42 r
Yakeshi ....57 l
Yakima ....14 i
Yako ....40 l
Yakoma ....42 r
Yakovlevka ....51 g
Yakrik ....56 q
Yaku ....58 w
Yakutat ....11 w
Yakutsk ....52 m
Yala (Ghana) ....40 m
Yala (Thailand) ....65 x
Yalata ....77 b
Yali ....44 k
Yalifafu ....44 l
Yalinga ....42 r
Yallalong ....76 d
Yalleroi ....74 p
Yalong Jiang ....62 h
Yalu ....58 f
Yalutorovsk ....50 z
Yama ....53 w
Yamagata ....59 o
Yamaguchi ....58 w
Yamal Peninsula ....51 a
Yambio ....42 v
Yamburg ....51 d
Yambuya ....42 s
Yamma Yamma, Lake .....77 h
Yamussoukro ....40 w
Yamsk ....53 w
Yamuna ....61 r
Yamzho Yumco ....61 l
Yana ....53 b
Yan'an ....57 s
Yanbu al Bahr.................38 z
Yanchang ....63 a
Yandja ....44 h
Yandun ....56 x
Yangambi ....42 s
Yangarey ....50 l
Yangbajain ....61 k
Yangchow ....63 f
Yangchuan ....57 v
Yangd Sum ....57 w
Yangjiang ....63 o
Yangoda ....51 h
Yangon (Rangoon) ....65 g
Yangtze ....63 a
Yanhuqu ....61 f
Yankton ....15 u
Yanov Stan ....51 g
Yanqi Huizu Zizhixian .....56 t
Yanrey ....72 r
Yanshan ....57 x
Yantai ....63 h
Yany-Kurgan ....55 t
Yanzhou ....63 e
Yaoundé ....41 v
Yapen ....70 z

Yapeyú ....28 z
Yap Islands ....70 h
Yaptiksale ....51 k
Yaqui ....18 h
Yaraka ....77 j
Yaransk ....50 t
Yaransu ....54 j
Yarda ....37 z
Yarkant ....56 o
Yarkino ....51 y
Yarlung Zangbo Jiang .....61 k
Yarmouth ....17 q
Yarongo ....51 a
Yarraloola ....72 s
Yarraman ....78 f
Yarrie ....72 v
Yarroto, Lake ....51 b
Yartsevo ....51 v
Yarumal ....22 m
Yashikera ....41 c
Yashkino ....53 o
Yashkul' ....54 h
Yasin ....55 x
Yasnaya Polyana ....58 m
Yasothon ....66 h
Yata (Bolivia) ....25 r
Yata
(Central African. Rep.).....42 e
Yathkyed Lake ....12 y
Yatolema ....42 s
Yatsushiro ....58 w
Yauri ....25 n
Yauyos ....24 w
Yavari ....24 m
Yavatmal ....61 p
Yaxian ....62 z
Yazd ....39 k
Yazdan ....60 d
Ye ....65 h
Yebbi Bou ....37 y
Yecheng ....55 z
Yécora ....18 i
Yeggueba ....37 v
Yei ....42 w
Yekana ....42 r
Yekaterinburg ....50 y
Yelets ....54 d
Yeletskiy ....50 m
Yelizavety, Cape ....53 r
Yelkhovka ....54 k
Yellowknife ....12 t
Yellow River
(Huang He).....................63 f
Yellow Sea ....58 r
Yellowstone ....15 c
Yelma ....76 w
Yeloguy ....51 u
Yeloguy (River) ....51 t
Yelvertoft ....73 u
Yelwa ....41 d
Yemen 39/43
Yenakiyevo ....54 d
Yendi ....41 a
Yengisar ....56 r
Yengisu ....56 t
Yenisey ....51 u
Yenisey Bay ....51 f
Yenisey Mountains ....51 w
Yeniseysk ....51 w
Yenki ....58 i
Yenyuka ....52 w
Yeo, Lake ....76 j
Yepachic ....18 i
Yepoko ....51 d
Yeppoon ....74 t
Yerbogachen ....52 c
Yerema ....52 q
Yerevan ....54 t
Yermak ....55 l
Yermaki ....57 f
Yermakovo ....51 p
Yermakovo (Yenisey).......51 g
Yermentau ....55 k
Yermo ....18 l
Yeropol ....10 c
Yerupaja ....24 w
Yesil' ....55 f
Yessey ....52 a
Yet ....43 s
Yet-Kyuyel' ....52 i

Yetti ....36 t
Yeva-Liv ....50 m
Yeyka ....52 c
Yeysk ....54 d
Yguazú ....29 n
Ygyatta ....52 g
Yi'an ....58 f
Yichun ....58 i
Yidin ....62 g
Yidu ....63 a
Yimuhe ....57 l
Yinchuan ....57 q
Yingde ....63 o
Yingkow ....57 z
Yipinglang ....62 u
Yirrkala ....73 g
Yirshi ....57 l
Yishan ....62 y
Yi Xian ....57 z
Yiyang ....63 b
Ylas-Yuryakh ....52 c
Ynykchanskiy ....53 q
Yogyakarta ....68 z
Yokadouma ....41 x
Yoko ....41 w
Yokohama ....59 o
Yokosuka ....59 o
Yola ....41 j
Yolin Mod ....58 d
Yolombo ....44 m
Yondeng ....57 p
Yong'an ....63 s
Yongchuan ....62 k
Yongden ....62 i
Yongding ....57 w
Yongren ....62 u
Yopal ....23 o
Yopurga ....55 z
York ....32 y
York, Cape (Australia) .....73 k
York, Cape (Greenland) ...91 b
York Factory ....13 o
Yorke Peninsula ....77 f
Yorkton ....15 f
Yoshkar Ola ....54 j
Yōsu ....58 u
Youngstown ....16 v
Youshashan ....56 v
Youyang ....62 m
Yozgat ....35 z
Ypé Jhú ....28 m
Yreka ....14 u
Ystad ....33 r
Ytyk-Kyuyel' ....53 a
Yuan Jiang ....63 a
Yuanjiang ....62 u
Yuanlin ....57 m
Yuanshanzi ....57 n
Yuba City ....14 u
Yubi, Cap ....36 c
Yucatán Peninsula...........20 t
Yucatán, Straits of ....20 v
Yuci ....63 b
Yudoma ....53 q
Yudoma-Krestovskaya......53 q
Yuendumu ....73 q
Yueyang ....63 c
Yugorenok ....53 p
Yugoslavia 35
Yugo-Tala ....53 i
Yu Jiang ....62 y
Yukhta ....57 e
Yukon ....11 b
Yukon Territory ....11 c
Yukta ....52 c
Yule ....72 t
Yuli ....56 t
Yulin ....63 n
Yulin (Great Wall) ....57 s
Yulongxue Shan ....62 y
Yuma ....18 e
Yun ....63 e
Yunhe ....63 g
Yunmeng ....63 c
Yurga ....51 l
Yuribey ....51 d
Yurimaguas ....24 j
Yurungkax ....61 e
Yushu ....62 d

Yushu (Manchuria) ....58 g
Yuti ....28 i
Yutian ....61 e
Yutze ....57 u
Yu Xian ....57 v
Yuzhno-Sakhalinsk..........59 d

Z

Zabad ....43 f
Zabol ....60 e
Zabré ....40 m
Zacatecas ....18 z
Zacatecoluca ....22 c
Zacualtipan ....19 p
Zadar ....35 b
Zadoi ....62 d
Zagazig ....38 i
Zaghouan ....34 y
Zagora ....36 i
Zagreb ....35 b
Zagros Mountains ....39 i
Zahedan ....60 d
Zahksykan ....55 h
Zahlé ....38 l
Zahran ....39 q
Zajsan ....56 e
Zajsan, Lake ....56 e
Zakamensk ....57 c
Zakopane ....35 d
Zakouma ....42 b
Zalanga ....41 h
Zalantun ....58 e
Zalari ....57 b
Zalim ....39 p
Zalingei ....42 f
Zambeke ....42 l
Zambezi ....44 y
Zambia 44-45/46/49
Zamboanga ....67 u
Zamko ....41 h
Zamora (Ecuador) ....24 h
Zamora (Mexico) ....18 z
Zamora (Spain) ....34 c
Zamość ....33 v
Zamzor ....56 m
Zanda ....61 d
Zangguy ....56 o
Zangla ....61 b
Zanjan ....54 w
Zanjón ....28 q
Zante ....35 q
Zanzibar ....45 k
Zanzibar Island ....45 k
Zapala ....30 i
Zaporozh'ye ....35 m
Za Qu ....62 d
Zarafshan ....55 s
Zaragoza ....22 m
Zarand ....39 m
Zarand (Tehran)..............39 i
Zaranj ....60 e
Zárate ....31 b
Zaraza ....23 g
Zard ....39 h
Zarghunshar ....60 j
Zargun ....60 l
Zaria ....41 f
Zaris ....48 h
Žarma ....56 c
Zarqa ....38 l
Žursuat ....56 c
Zarumilla ....24 g
Zarzis ....34 z
Zaskar ....61 c
Zastron ....49 p
Zatish'ye ....53 l
Zavitinsk ....58 i
Zawa ....56 o
Zayü ....62 e
Zealand ....33 q
Zebak ....55 v
Zedness ....36 r
Zeerust ....49 b
Zêkog ....62 u
Zelenga ....54 j
Zella ....37 l
Zel'onoje Ozero ....52 u
Zémio ....42 s

Zemmour ....36 r
Zenica ....35 c
Zeya ....52 y
Zeya (River) ....52 z
Zeydan ....39 i
Zeyski ....52 z
Zhagaly ....54 k
Zhag'yab ....62 e
Zhaltyr ....55 i
Zhamshi ....55 l
Zhanay ....55 q
Zhangjiaquan ....56 x
Zhangpu ....63 r
Zhaosu ....56 p
Zhaotong ....62 j
Zhaoyuan ....58 f
Zhari Namco ....61 i
Zharkamys ....55 a
Zhaxi Co ....61 h

Zhecheng ....63 d
Zhelezinka ....55 l
Zheleznodorozhnyy ....50 u
Zhenghe ....63 g
Zhenghuang Qi ....57 v
Zhenglan Qi ....57 w
Zhengzhou
(Chengchow) ....63 c
Zhenning ....62 x
Zhenping ....63 a
Zhenyuan ....62 u
Zhidoi ....62 d
Zhigansk ....52 j
Zhirkova ....53 k
Zhitomir ....35 i
Zholymbet ....55 j
Zhongba ....61 g
Zhongdian ....62 g

Zhongshan ....85 p
Zhongwei ....57 p
Zhongye Islands ....67 b
Zhoushan Islands ....63 i
Zhoushan Qundao ....58 r
Zhungqu ....62 j
Zhupanovskiy ....53 y
Zichang ....62 m
Žigalovo ....57 c
Zigazê ....61 j
Zighan ....38 o
Ziguinchor ....40 b
Zihuatenejo ....19 n
Zilinan ....35 c
Zima ....57 b
Zimbabwe ....49 s
Zimbabwe (State) ...45/46/49
Zinapécuaro ....19 n
Zinder ....41 g

Zinga ....42 n
Zintan ....37 h
Žioj ....54 x
Zipaquirá ....23 n
Zirō ....62 c
Zitácuaro ....19 n
Ziway, Lake ....43 c
Ziya ....57 w
Zlatoust ....55 c
Zliten ....37 j
Zmiyevka ....54 c
Znamenka ....35 k
Znojmo ....33 s
Zogang ....62 e
Zoigê ....62 i
Zolotoy ....53 c
Zomba ....45 u
Zongo ....42 o
Zoo Baba ....37 v

Zorritos ....24 g
Zorzor ....40 t
Zouar ....37 x
Zouerate ....36 q
Zq'gya-Zangbo ....61 l
Zrenjanin ....35 d
Zubova-Polyana ....54 g
Zug ....36 p
Zugspitze ....34 m
Zumbo ....45 r
Zürich ....34 k
Zuru ....41 e
Zuwarah ....34 z
Zuwaylah ....37 w
Zvishavane ....49 e
Zvolen ....35 c
Zyryanka ....53 i
Zyryanka (Yenisey Bay) ...51 f